AMERICAN CULTURAL HERITAGE SERIES 1
Jack Salzman, *General Editor*

Vachel Lindsay, *circa* 1925

LETTERS OF VACHEL LINDSAY

Edited by
MARC CHÉNETIER

Burt Franklin & Co.

Published by Burt Franklin & Co.
235 East Forty-fourth Street
New York, New York 10017

© 1979 by Burt Franklin & Co., Inc.
All rights reserved

Library of Congress Cataloging in Publication Data

Lindsay, Nicholas Vachel, 1879–1931.
Letters of Vachel Lindsay.

(American cultural heritage;)
Includes index.
1. Lindsay, Nicholas Vachel, 1879–1931—
Correspondence. 2. Poets, American—20th century—
Correspondence. I. Chénetier, Marc, 1946–   II. Series.
PS3523.I58Z48 1978   811'.5'2 [B]   79-21437
ISBN 0-89102-173-6

O^K √

Designed by Bernard Schleifer

Manufactured in the United States of America

Contents

Foreword

by NICHOLAS CAVE LINDSAY

Marc, Dear Friend,

You have here done a large work, collecting and selecting my father's letters in a way which shows the line of his concerns for the first quarter of the twentieth century. It will be a permanent resource for scholars who concern themselves with these years as it is already a gift to us, his descendants, who live under the shadow of his often grotesque image when we must appear in public.

A group of letters of this sort is a picture; the printing of it in a book is the hanging of the picture on exhibition. Three things count here: the frame, the title, and the light in which it is viewed. In each case, when we select one out of the several possibilities, we risk changing the naked intent of the picture. It's a risk, but isn't it necessary? Since the picture is worth hanging. A frame, a light, a title.

A Homeric boast suggests itself as title: "The son of Vachel Thomas the Doctor, father of Nicholas Cave, the Carpenter," a fine, male title. Yes, and it would also be possible to follow the female line. Yet, let me say a better one, the one suggested by the subject himself: "The Soul of the U.S.A., 1900–1930." If this hints that the U.S.A. was left soul-less after 1931, may we not take the painter's vision with a grain of salt?

As to light, a picture can be hung and lighted in such a way that the surface reflections make portions of it invisible or only visible if the viewer lies on the floor, or stands on a chair, or involves himself in some other gymnastics, and in this case it is usual for other parts of the picture to become hid in glare as the first area finally comes into clarity. We'll try to avoid this. Here are two lights ready at hand. On the right is the one named "See the noble soul driven to earth," which indeed harmonizes well with the frame and title. But here, look at this: there is such a lot of sentimental apparatus required to support it that it gets in the way when a person's trying to see. Perhaps we should use the one on the left, the simpler light: "He did his thing."

For frame, now, let's go to the professional framers, the U.S. Information Agency. They have their films of Robert Frost's last public performance, Sarah Lawrence College, 1962, which he dedicates to Vachel Lindsay. Frost cracking jokes at the expense of the U.S. Government, the camera crews, the official academic institution where he is speaking. He courts with love words and praises his audience. He tells of the times when he and Vachel Lindsay would walk together, talk together, of the time (*ca.* 1917) when Lindsay proposed a poets' contest to the gang of American poets who were together then. It was to be a poem on John L. Sullivan, the Strong Boy of Boston, on the occasion of his death. Indeed, several of them wrote poems, but most were parodies. They didn't take the aged Strong Boy seriously, and only Lindsay wrote a substantial poem. Amongst his reminiscences, Frost leaves us four sides of his brother poet's character with which to make our frame.

"Well, some of these young people as they are nowadays, they think it's necessary to be crazy to be an artist or a poet, it's a requirement and they know they don't have it, so they go off in some corner and try to pretend to be crazy. There was no pretense to *that* boy: he was the real thing." This is one side of our frame: "No fake, but really crazy."

The show goes on. Frost speaks of Lindsay's (ridiculous) generosity both in spirit and in material things: "I'm a peasant, but *him*? He was noble." This gives a second side to the frame.

Later, after the performance, as the group of kinfolk, publicity agents, photographers, college presidents, professors, deans and one thing and another are gathered in the Sarah Lawrence President's house for cocktails, and Frost is eating his scrambled eggs, there begins that mixture of aggression and rhapsody for the ages that passes for private conversation with old poets.

N.L.: In the inauguration of President Kennedy, you said, "This is a victory for the cause I represent." What cause is that?

Frost (in a large voice): God. [It's a dirty word in 1962. People spill drinks, mop up.]

N.L.: That Word of God, it's a danger, isn't it? How? Risky. An acid to eat, fire to burn up all that's precious to a man.

Frost: Risk? Danger? You'll have to get that idea out of your head. No danger to it. It's just a matter of life and death, that's all.

[God's Word which is not dangerous. Let this be a third side of our frame.]

Frost: What are you doing in New York? I thought you were carpentering in the south?

N.L.: I am here to get a college degree.

Frost: See here. Don't join the certified. Give'em hell. The bastards.

Let this command, then, complete our frame.

To sum up: we have, in these letters a picture entitled "The Soul of the U.S.A." It is lit from the left by the light "He did his thing." The two sides of the picture's frame are these:

"He was no fake, but *really* crazy."

"He was noble."

At the top is "Don't join the certified," and at the bottom is "God's word which is not dangerous."

So, Marc,
May God be with you
and with the readers of this book you have made
and with me too,

Nick.

NICHOLAS C. LINDSAY

Acknowledgments

Through the years a great number of individuals and libraries have helped me collect the letters of Vachel Lindsay. Special gratitude and affection go, of course, to Nicholas Cave Lindsay, without whom this project would never have seen the light of day, and to Jack Salzman, whose trust and efforts have allowed this enterprise to find a much needed outlet.

For special research, help, and information my thanks go to Gérald Antoine, Françoise Balibar, Jean-Marie Bonnet, Régis Durand, Claude Richard, and André Le Vot, whose various contributions made much material available. Without Paul Le Moal, I would not have been allowed to begin work on Vachel Lindsay.

Thanks to Jean-Pierre Dupuy and Bernard Vincent a number of material tasks were made easier.

Laurette Véza has been directing my work on Vachel Lindsay these past nine years. Her insights and suggestions are largely responsible for the completion of this supplementary project.

Elizabeth Graham has repeatedly and cordially opened to me the archives of the Vachel Lindsay Home in Springfield, Illinois. Her courtesy and hospitality are deeply appreciated. Owen Hawley has provided helpful bibliographical information. the late Norman Holmes Pearson gave me special access to the Vachel Lindsay–Sara Teasdale correspondence in 1975 and offered help and support as well as special encouragement. Margaret H. Carpenter's assistance has also been a great value.

A special grant in 1975 from the American Council of Learned Societies made possible a great deal of research. Richard Downar's patience and courtesy will not be forgotten.

Among the many individuals who gave me information on Vachel Lindsay along the way, Conrad Aiken, Dennis Camp, Pierre Dussert, Elizabeth T. Fowler, Benjamin Kizer, C. P. Lee, Myron Lounsbury, Ann Massa, T. M. Pearce, Ron Primeau and Dennis Schafer, Louis Untermeyer and Blair Whitney are especially remembered.

The welcome I received from the staff of all the libraries and collections to which I was granted access and which I visited was most gratifying. Nothing could have been accomplished without the many people who take daily care of these collections. To all those I do not know personally but who helped with such regularity and conscience go my sincerest thanks.

Many libraries extended their courtesy over the years and made available letters that have not been reproduced here. I would like to thank, for the insights they have allowed, the Spokane Historical Society, the Bodleian Library, M. K. C. Murray, the University of Iowa Library, Hiram College, Vassar College, the Chicago Historical Society, the University of Minnesota, the University of West Virginia, Notre Dame University, the University of Southern Illinois at Carbondale, Washington State University, Northwestern University, the State Historical Society of Wisconsin, the Library of Congress, and the University of Michigan at Ann Arbor.

The letters that found their way into this volume were graciously made available by the following institutions and people to whom I express my debt:

The Bancroft Library, Berkeley, California, with special thanks to James D. Hart, Estelle Rebec and Marie Byrne; the Brown University Library, with special thanks to

Professor Sherman and M. Clifton Jones; the Humanities Research Center of the University of Texas, Austin, with special thanks to Ellen S. Dunlap for biographical information on Idella Purnell Stone and John Weatherwax; the Armstrong Browning Library, Baylor University, Waco, Texas, with gratitude to Jack W. Herring for his time and support; the Enoch Pratt Free Library of Baltimore; the Lincoln Library, Springfield, Illinois, for letters in the Sangamon Valley Collection made available through Edward J. Russo; Margaret Sandburg, for hospitality, help, and warm encouragement as well as permission to use letters from Vachel Lindsay to her father; the Dartmouth College Library and Walter W. Wright; the Houghton Library, Harvard University; the Henry E. Huntington Library, San Marino, California, and Daniel H. Woodward; the Lilly Library, Indiana University, with special thanks to Cecil K. Byrd for collaboration over the years and Saundra Taylor, curator of manuscripts; Random House Inc., Alfred A. Knopf, Inc., and Harold Ober Associates for their courtesy in letting me reproduce passages from The Big Sea *by Langston Hughes; the Abernethy Library of Middlebury College and E. Rosenfeld and Robert Buckeye of Special Collections; the Archives of the Memorial Library of Marquette University and R. N. Hamilton, S.J.; the Newberry Library, Chicago, and Diana Haskell; the New York Public Library for permission to reproduce six letters in the Macmillan Company Records, four letters in the R. W. Gilder Papers, two letters in the H. L. Mencken Papers and the Spingarn Collection, all being a part of the Manuscripts and Archives Division of the New York Public Library, Astor, Lenox, and Tilden Foundations, with special thanks for help to Faye Simkin; the Rare Books and Special Collections of the Princeton University Library, with thanks to Wanda M. Randall, who first helped, and Jean F. Preston, who later did; the Swarthmore College Peace Collection; the Poetry Collection of the Lockwood Memorial Library in the State University of New York at Buffalo for letters in the Untermeyer Papers (Louis Untermeyer had been kind enough to grant me permission to use the letters of Vachel Lindsay in his possession in 1971); the Vachel Lindsay Collection, George Arents Research Library for Special Collections at Syracuse University, with special thanks to Dianne Melnychuk and Carolyn A. Davis; the Department of Special Collections, the University of Chicago Library, with thanks to Mary E. Jansen for care and professional thoroughness, and to Mr. Allison and Ms. McFadden; the Special Collections of the University of Oregon Library and Martin Schmitt; the American Literature Collection, University of Southern California Library and Glenn W. Bunday; Elizabeth Graham and Dennis Camp, curators of the Vachel Lindsay Home, and the Vachel Lindsay Association for continued support and care. Nothing could have been accomplished without the outstanding help of the staff of the University of Virginia: My very special thanks to the Clifton Waller Barrett Vachel Lindsay Collection of the Alderman Library at the University of Virginia, and especially to Edmund Berkeley, Jr., Curator of Manuscripts; to Michael Plunkett, Assistant Curator of Manuscripts; and to Joan St. Crane, Curator of American Literature. Their enthusiastic support equaled the cordiality of their welcome. In the Alderman Library are also many people whose names, although I do not know them, belong here.*

My thanks go also to the Collection of American Literature, Beinecke Rare Book and Manuscript Library, Yale University, and its curator, Donald Gallup, with respectful memories of the few precious days spent in the company of Professor Norman Holmes Pearson.

Nick Lindsay has managed to transform our acquaintance into a much cherished friendship. This book is inscribed to him and his wife, DuBose, as a token of affection.

And, in these last lines, I extend my gratitude to three ladies who have endured the bulk of my efforts, have allowed me prolonged isolation from them in my study, and, for years, have gone on vacation without me. I understand they miraculously love me still. Odile, Marion, and Chloé Chénetier made this book with me.

Chronology

1842	Nicholas Lindsay, of Scottish origins, marries Martha Ann Cave, a presumed descendant of Pocahontas, in Kentucky. She gives birth on August 31, 1843, to Vachel Thomas Lindsay, father of the poet.
1846	Ephraïm Samuel Frazee, descended from the Spanish family of Don Alphonso Iphan and born in Kentucky, marries Frances Austen. They live on a prosperous farm in Rush County, Indiana. She gives birth on February 20, 1848, to Esther Catherine Frazee, mother of the poet.
1865	The Lindsay plantation turns into a poor farm when the federal government confiscates the cattle and frees the slaves because of the Lindsay's sympathies for the Southern cause during the Civil War.
1866	Vachel Thomas Lindsay begins medical practice in Cotton Hill, Illinois, southeast of Springfield.
1869–75	Catherine Frazee teaches mathematics in Glendale, Ohio, and painting at Hocker College, Kentucky.
1871	Vachel Thomas Lindsay marries a childhood friend, Olive, who dies two and a half months later.
1875	Vachel Thomas Lindsay sails for Europe in the company of his sister, Eudora Lindsay, who teaches at Hocker College, and a friend of the latter's, Catherine Frazee.
1875–76	Vachel Thomas Lindsay spends the winter in Vienna, studying medicine, and joins his two companions in Italy the following spring.
1876	Back from Europe, Vachel Thomas Lindsay settles in Springfield, Illinois, in July. On November 30, he marries Catherine Frazee.
1878	Birth of Olive Lindsay, sister of the poet.
1879	November 10: birth of Nicholas Vachel Lindsay (henceforth called VL here). Three daughters will be born later. All three will die within three weeks of scarlet fever.

1889   Birth of Joy Lindsay, sister of the poet.

1893   VL enters Springfield High School; one of his teachers there is
            Susan Wilcox.

1896   William Jennings Bryan campaigns for the presidency. VL hears
            him speak in Springfield.

1897   In June, VL graduates from Springfield High School. In September,
            he and his sister Olive enter Hiram College, Hiram, Ohio, an in-
            stitution founded by the Disciples of Christ (Campbellites) in
            1850. VL studies medicine there. He takes part in the production
            of the college annual, *The Spider Web*, and in that of the college
            paper. He reads extensively and writes "The Last Song of Lucifer"
            and "The Battle."

1899   November 27: VL abandons his medical studies.

1900   In June, VL leaves Hiram College and returns to Springfield.

1901   January 2: VL arrives in Chicago to attend the Art Institute. He
            lives on South Paulina Street. In April he moves to Jackson Avenue.
            In September he is in Springfield for a brief visit. He works from
            September to December in the toy department of Marshall Field's
            department store in Chicago. In December he writes "Star of My
            Heart."

1902   VL attends the Art Institute again. Until 1903 he is totally absorbed
            in his studies, and he reads and writes a great deal.

1903   VL spends the summer alone in Springfield. There he draws and
            writes. In September he becomes engaged to Ruth Wheeler in
            Akron, on his way to New York City, where he is going to register
            at the New York School of Art, directed by William Chase. Robert
            Henri is his principal teacher there. He attends the Disciples
            Church, St. Paul's, and the Metropolitan Museum of Art with equal
            fervor. He tries in vain to get several of his drawings and poems
            published.

1904   *The Critic* publishes "The Queen of Bubbles." In June Olive marries
            Paul Wakefield after the latter has finished his medical training at
            Rush Medical College. VL spends the following summer at home.
            His first visions come to him. A period of intense activity follows.
            That same summer he writes "A Prayer in the Jungles of Heaven,"
            draws his "Map of the Universe," and writes a book that he later
            destroys all but completely: *Where Is Aladdin's Lamp?*

1905   Back in New York, VL tries to get his work published but meets
            with no success. He rents an apartment with friends, including
            G. M. Richards. He recites "The Tree of Laughing Bells" at Robert
            Henri's. Henri advises him to give up painting and to devote all
            his energies to poetry. In March, having had copies of an illustrated
            poem—"We Who Are Playing Tonight"—printed, VL tries to sell
            them in the streets of New York. He tries again, this time with
            "A Cup of Paint." Another attempt takes place in April. VL breaks
            his engagement to Ruth Wheeler. In October he is a hired hand
            at the Nicholls Gas Tubing Company. At night he teaches art his-
            tory at the YMCA on a voluntary basis. His success is such that
            soon the YMCA pays him for his lectures. He then relinquishes
            his job at the Nicholls Company. Paul and Olive leave for China.
            Throughout the year, VL has visions, particularly on
            December 23.

1906   March 3: VL sails for Florida with his friend Edward Broderick.
            Their trip takes them to Jacksonville via Charleston. They walk
            together until March 11, then VL goes on alone from Orlando to
            Tampa. He rejoins Broderick, and they reach Jacksonville by
            train. Broderick then leaves for New York. March 19: VL begins
            a two months' tramp, during which he walks 600 miles from Jack-
            sonville to Grass Springs, Kentucky. Throughout May he stays
            with his aunt Eudora Lindsay South. In June he is back in Spring-
            field, and on June 23 the Lindsay family sails for Europe. They see
            England, Holland, Germany, Belgium, and France before leaving
            via England. VL visits many museums, including the Louvre and
            the British Museum. On September 4, on the way back, VL has
            a particularly clear vision of Christ. Between November 10 and
            Christmas, he composes in New York "I Heard Immanuel Sing-
            ing." During the fall and winter he is a guide in the Metropolitan
            Museum of Art and lectures at the YMCA.

1907   In January VL begins a series of lectures on Sidney Lanier's poetry.

1908   April 28: VL leaves New York for Springfield, on foot. He travels
            through New Jersey, Pennsylvania, and Ohio. May 18: He reaches
            Hiram and rides a train back to Springfield. In August VL is a
            witness to the race riots in Springfield. He lectures for the YMCA
            in Springfield and Sangamon County. He writes "On the Building
            of Springfield."

1909   VL campaigns for the Anti-Saloon League, which pays him for it.
            In February he speaks for the centennial of Lincoln's birth. He
            lectures to miners of Ridgely, near Springfield. In July he pub-
            lishes at his own expense, the first of his *War Bulletins.* The second
            comes out in August, the third on August 30. A fourth follows in

September (*The Tramp's Excuse*) and a fifth and last in November. *The War Bulletins* are replaced in December by the *Sangamon County Peace Advocate* and later in the winter by the *Spring Harbinger*. VL sends all these publications to a number of people, including Witter Bynner, Ezra Pound, William Marion Reedy, Anna Hempstead Branch, Jessie B. Rittenhouse, F. S. Davis, and Arthur Davison Ficke.

1909–12   VL writes at home, stopping only for debates and lectures.

1910   VL publishes seven hundred copies of *The Village Magazine*. In the summer he meets Octavia Roberts. In November and December he organizes a "Ruskin Revival" for the YMCA based on his five lectures on the subject.

1911   VL becomes a construction worker for two months. He writes "The Eagle That Is Forgotten," published in the *Illinois State Register*. In March *Current Literature* reviews *The Village Magazine*. Hamlin Garland orders a copy from VL and invites him to come and address the Cliff Dwellers' Club in Chicago. VL becomes a member of the club. In April Hamlin Garland visits VL's parents.

1912   May 29: VL leaves on foot for California, planning to walk up the Pacific Coast from Los Angeles to Seattle and back to Springfield. He takes with him copies of *Rhymes to Be Traded for Bread*, *The Gospel of Beauty*, and a book of illustrations he has assembled himself. In July he harvests in Kansas. August 5: He camps out with his parents in Colorado. After leaving them on August 22, he gives up his walk on September 12, in New Mexico, and rides the train to Los Angeles, where he spends a month and writes "General William Booth Enters into Heaven." In Oakland he stays several weeks with Olan E. James. In October he returns to Springfield. Several of his poems come out in various magazines.

1913   *Poetry* publishes "General Booth" in January. In April VL meets Harriet Monroe. In July *Poetry* publishes some "Moon-Poems." In the fall *General William Booth Enters into Heaven and Other Poems* is published by Mitchell Kennerley, and in November VL is awarded a $100 prize by *Poetry*.

1914   VL recites "The Congo" at the Lincoln Banquet in Springfield in February, and then on March 1 at the *Poetry* Banquet in Chicago, attended by William Butler Yeats. In February, after a few weeks of intensive correspondence, VL goes to see Sara Teasdale in St. Louis. In April Joy Lindsay marries Ben Blair. In May VL's parents leave for China, where they are going to visit Paul and Olive Wakefield. VL begins work on "The Chinese Nightingale." In July

"The Santa Fé Trail" and "The Fireman's Ball" appear in *Poetry*. VL meets Harriet Vaughn Moody in Chicago. He goes to New York with Sara Teasdale. They meet Edwin Markham, the Benét brothers, Floyd Dell, Joyce Kilmer, and Louis Untermeyer, and plan to marry. In August VL is back in Springfield working on "The Chinese Nightingale," "The Ghosts of the Buffaloes," and six poems on the war, including "Abraham Lincoln Walks at Midnight." In September *The Congo and Other Poems* is published by Macmillan and *Adventures While Preaching the Gospel of Beauty* by Kennerley. In November Dr. and Mrs. Lindsay return from China. In December Sara Teasdale marries a businessman, Ernst Filsinger.

1915   Lindsay recites for President Wilson's cabinet in February. "The Chinese Nightingale" is published in *Poetry*. VL tours Eastern universities reciting. *The Art of the Moving Picture* is published by Macmillan. In November Lindsay is awarded the Levinson Prize for "The Chinese Nightingale."

1916   In January VL meets John Masefield. *A Handy Guide for Beggars* is published by Macmillan. In November VL stages, with Eleanor Dougherty, a series of "Poem-Games," first at Maurice Browne's Little Theatre, then in Mandel Hall at the University of Chicago.

1916–18   VL recites all over the United States.

1917   In May VL begins *The Golden Book of Springfield*. He falls in love with Isadora Bennett. *The Chinese Nightingale and Other Poems* comes out in September. VL registers for the draft.

1918   September 20: VL's father dies.

1919   January–April: VL recites. Summer: VL writes "Bryan, Bryan, Bryan, Bryan." Isadora Bennett gets married.

1920   In January *The Golden Whales of California and Other Rhymes in the American Language* is published. March–June: The first of VL's recital tours under the aegis of A. J. Armstrong is undertaken. August: VL travels to England with his mother. September 20: Bell publishes *The Daniel Jazz and Other Poems* in London. October 15: VL recites at Oxford University. He is introduced to Robert Bridges, Robert Nichols, and Robert Graves and sees John Masefield again. He recites at Cambridge and in Westminster Central Hall. November 20: *The Golden Book of Springfield* is published. It meets with critical disaster in spite of favorable comments by William Rose Benét in the December 18 *New York Post*.

1921   Spring: VL has a reciting tour in the East. Summer: He goes on a hiking trip in the Rockies with Stephen Graham. In November, after returning from Glacier National Park with Graham to Springfield, he has another reciting tour in the West.

1922   February 1: VL's mother dies. VL comes back to Springfield but resumes his tour after eight days.

1923   In January, while in Gulfport, Mississippi, Lindsay collapses and cancels the rest of his tour. He undergoes a sinus operation in April. *Going-to-the-Sun* and the *Collected Poems* are published.

1923–24   VL teaches contemporary poetry in Gulf Park Junior College for Girls, Gulfport, Mississippi, headed by an old Hiram friend, Richard "Zim" Cox. He falls in love with one of his students, Elizabeth Mann Wills.

1924   In July VL goes to Spokane, where, until 1925, he will live in the Hotel Davenport, then, until 1929, in several rented houses. He visits Glacier National Park several times.

1925   In February VL meets Elizabeth Conner. The third edition of the *Village Magazine* is printed at VL's expense. May 19: VL marries Elizabeth Conner. She is twenty-three; he, forty-five. The same day, the second edition of VL's *Collected Poems* is published. The fourth edition of the *Village Magazine* is printed. In October VL visits New York with Elizabeth. At Christmas, passing through Springfield, VL vituperates against the women who have "spoiled" him of his house, rented off to a club by his family.

1926   March 9: VL begins a new reciting tour. He is in great financial difficulties. May 28: The poet's daughter, Susan Doniphan Lindsay, is born. *Going-to-the-Stars* comes out the same day. In July *The Candle in the Cabin* is published. August 26: The Lindsays leave for Glacier National Park.

1926–27   VL's financial situation deteriorates.

1927   September 16: VL's son, Nicholas Cave Lindsay, is born.

1928   March 3: VL publicly and violently attacks the Spokane businessmen.

1928–29   October–March: At the cost of inhuman efforts, VL, in one long tour of the East and Middle West, wipes out all of his debts. His health declines. In November a special $500 prize is awarded him by *Poetry* for his entire corpus.

1929   VL returns to Spokane in March. *The Litany of Washington Street* is
          published. April: The Lindsays go back to Springfield for good.
          May 10: VL recites "The Virginians Are Coming Again" at a
          Chicago banquet organized by *Poetry* in his honor. August: VL
          teaches in State College, Pennsylvania. October: He tours Texas
          and California. *Every Soul is a Circus* comes out. November: VL
          recites in the First Christian Church in Springfield. Then he takes
          to the road again, returning home only for a short while around
          Christmas.

1930   VL is made Doctor Honoris Causa by Hiram College.

1930–31   VL is constantly on tour, except for brief periods in Springfield.

1931   In January VL records some of his poems in New York City. In
          August he stays briefly in Minocqua, Wisconsin, for a solitary
          vacation. November 10: VL turns fifty-two. He is touring. No-
          vember 29: VL is back in Springfield. The next day his recital in
          Springfield's First Christian Church is an enormous success.
          December 5: VL commits suicide by swallowing a bottle of Lysol.
          His death is officially attributed to heart failure.

Introduction

MOST AMERICANS and Europeans who specialize in American cultural
studies will respond to Vachel Lindsay's name with the same associations: "The Congo," "General William Booth Enters into Heaven," the
Midwest, Edgar Lee Masters, Carl Sandburg, "an evangelist in rhyme,"
"a poet who jazzed poetry," and so forth. This traditional image is as
limited as it is inaccurate.

Lindsay always wanted to be a painter; he studied for years in the
Chicago Art Institute and was a student of William Chase and Robert
Henri at the New York School of Art. He never renounced that preoccupation. His very vocabulary when speaking of his poetic achievements
often partakes of the graphic artist's terminology. Practices and directions that seemingly contradict themselves in his life and works are
united on aesthetic grounds. Some have considered him a belated fun-
damentalist; others, a dangerous radical; others again, a naive clown, a
half-boiled uncouth militant of nostalgic Midwestern and populist
causes, or, as Amy Lowell would have it, a "middle westerner of the
middle class." Still others have thought him great only in what they
liked, while they were miserable—or "impossible," to use T. S. Eliot's
word—about elements they could not accept. What appeared dispersed,
heterogeneous, and incoherent is, however, the active transcription of
one unified vision of the world, in homothetic terms, on various fields.
Lindsay, the world's first film critic, wrote *The Art of the Moving Picture* in
1915. D. W. Griffith was just beginning then; Sergei Eisenstein was ten
years away. While Isadora Duncan revolutionized dancing and Pablo
Picasso began—as John Dos Passos once wrote—"to rebuild the eye,"
Vachel Lindsay took up "Les Jeux Floraux" and invited people to dance
his works in the frame of what he called "The Poem Games." The architects and landscapers of the turn of the century found in him a more
than willing ear. Everything plastic fascinated Lindsay—a visionary
who said in his notebooks, "My eyes are Imperial," who thought that
"men see first."

For Lindsay, the different systems of signs were, at the same time, parallel and identical. Mostly they had the same origins and were, therefore, equal expressions of the world of ideas that his Platonist conscience envisaged. Thoughts were pictures in the air; pictures were given, sent by something above; the Logos found multiple channels to manifest itself, but it did not vary: The world was a message, and all systems of signification were attempts to re-create that world, to stem its flow toward the original Word. A keen eye, furthermore, enabled him to discern the similarities in shapes, and his formal approach confirmed his conviction that all signs were equal. His interest in calligraphy was based on its being placed at a philosophic crossroads. Ideas could be found again through forms created by gestures of the body; personality went to meet the truth of the universe by mere physical action. "Make the free flowing line the basis of your work and build upon it gradually all the other elements of composition you so little understand." To him, as to the Symbolists, every line or form was "the verb of an idea." Channeling ideas into forms found similar expression and explanation for Lindsay and, say, Alfred Kubin, Jan Toorop, or Maurice Denis. His intense study of forms, however, led him away from the strictly symbolistic apprehension of reality toward what, to some, are the distinctive marks of all truly modern art, a consciousness and an avowal of the semiotic character of all pictorial and poetic production.

If, with the Symbolists, Lindsay first thought artistic production consisted in "clothing the Idea with a sensible form," he soon became convinced that the interplay of forms themselves was significant enough. His research from then on oscillated between, on the one hand, the construction of a semiotic system that could fit and express both his personal reality and thought and the reality and culture of the land in which he lived and, on the other, a fascinated struggle with spontaneous forms, lines, and shapes that came to his mind. Guillaume Apollinaire, in 1907, wrote that "all plastic writings: the hieratic Egyptians, the refined Greeks, the voluptuous Cambodians, the productions of ancient Peruvians, the small statues of African Negroes proportioned to fit the passions that inspired them [can] interest an artist and help him develop his personality." That a poet should have taken such plastic examples tells of the accentuated convergence and mutual influence of the various arts of the period: Painting turned to a reflection on signs; poetry, to a study of plastic representation and spatial ordering of the linquistic message. Lindsay's own development of written signs into drawings that turned into the creative, inspirational source of his poems lay in the same ideological swath that was being cut all through Europe: somewhere between Wilhelm von Humboldt and René de Saussure, on the one hand, and Charles Blanc (whose "grammar of the drawing arts" came out in 1867) and Henri Matisse, on the other. Between the Impressionists, Malevitch, and Mondrian had begun the thaw of iconic signs that was to revolutionize the approach to signification. Vachel Lindsay was part of that movement, however far removed from it in space and culture and conscience. Codes began to be disrobed, the corporeal and sensual expressivity of forms irrupted onto the scene, gestures became recognized as constituents of systems, black and white struggled on canvases while form and content contracted a definitive wedding. Vachel Lindsay's interest in Paul Klee and Vasili Kandinski, his unintentionally acting in accordance with Giovanni Boldini's wild strokes, his own blend of what Charles Olson was to define in 1959 as "topos, typos and tropos" found a summary in his saying that "out of rhythm came words and form," in his fascination with patterns and movement, in his desire to prove that at the same time, rhythm can be rendered by words and the shapes of letters and forms can organize thought. The emergence of the visual as a new language and of language itself as texture, of canvases and poems as systems, found in Lindsay a somewhat untutored but enthusiastic supporter.

"We are sweeping into new times, in which the eye is invading the province of the ear and in which pictures are crowding all literature to the wall," Lindsay wrote in an unpublished manuscript on the cinema. Such a sentence gives an idea of the importance of Vachel Lindsay's theoretical and practical breakthrough, one that was on the direct line from Symbolism to modern art, one that may well be the missing link between artists of the late nineteenth century and such moderns as Jackson Pollock and Mark, Tobey, between Imagism and today's research on the relations of illustrations to poetic texts, between the logocentric rule of nineteenth-century civilization and the media theories of Marshall McLuhan, nearly all of whose basic ideas Lindsay explored and expressed as early as 1915. "Edison is the new Gutenberg," he wrote. "He has invented the new printing."

A prophet in many important areas, Lindsay foresaw the use and power of the electronic media as "a real part of the community life" — of radio, of course, but also of television, and even the use of movies in such fields as advertising.

His study of Egyptian hieroglyphs began in earnest with his writing of *The Art of the Moving Picture,* one of the chapters of which is devoted to Egypt. The film as text and as writing is not divided from the film as pictures: Hieroglyphics organize pictures into a language, and so can the movies. Images dominate the modern psyche, and literacy is replaced by an all-out attack of pictures on the mind. Lest the mind become an "overgrown forest of unorganized pictures," some order must be found and people must learn to read images as they did letters. Light and forms prevail over oral and written language, and signs are the privileged way of access to national unity: "More and more hieroglyphics; more and more speed are making one nation of all the tribes and tongues under this government and really makes them a separate tribe."

His research was always aimed at reunifying a language gone wrong, at harmonizing expressive forms with the needs of the time. His poetry, derived from his art and film studies, consisted mainly in his attempt to elaborate, in his own verse, a system of "American Hieroglyphics." The main idea was to unify expression so that the country could take hold of itself once more, renew its mythology, revivify it, and reorganize the national unconscious. Such was the shamanic dimension of Lindsay's enterprise. His search was for a democratic art founded on the common recognition of signs capable of defining the national identity. The cultural nature of perception he clearly understood, and he tried to homogenize the people's references. American civilization had to ground itself in the education of the eye—in the storing of, and work on, a limited but expansible set of fundamental pictures that might sum up the American experience, fertilize reflection, allow new combinations, and reveal new vistas. Democracy could only progress through the acquisition of the new language of images and signs, the mastering of the new visual tide flooding the country. Films, billboards, cartoons, advertisements, magazines, postcards, stills, illustrated books, photographs—all added to the more traditional units of visual expression: paintings, frescoes, architecture, gardening and landscaping, dance, pageants. The poet's task became largely to be the educator and mentor of the masses' visual and visionary abilities and tastes: "From the development of the average eye, cities akin to the beginning of Florence will be born among us as surely as Chaucer came, upon the first ripening of the English tongue, after Caedmon and Beowulf."

Poetry, art, the movies, American Hieroglyphics will have the same part to play; all will have to show the American people to the American people, using the most suitable means because, as Lindsay notes, "there is many a babe in the proletariat, not over four years old, that has had more picture enter its eye than it has had words enter its ear." In the last analysis, all of Lindsay's experience and reflections on his own art and that of others will have served but one great purpose: to help America define herself and thereby to improve democracy, "to bring the nobler side of the equality idea to the people who are so crassly equal. . . . Then the people's message will reach the people at last."

Vachel Lindsay's obsession with the various modes of signification shines through the 199 letters I have selected out of the thousands available. I have not chosen these letters on the basis of the quantity of grist

they could bring to my theoretical mill or the help they could give in
destroying for good the hackneyed image of the jingleman and corn-fed
pious howler; on the contrary, many of the letters that were apt to support my arguments most clearly are not here, simply because the haste
in which they were written reduced their literary value. I hope, however, that the wide variety of my selections will prove my point even
more forcefully by drawing attention away from the too well-known images and poems of Vachel Lindsay to his less well-known preoccupations: to his single-minded devotion to the task of providing a verbal
transcription of his graphic and poetic egg, "The Map of the Universe";
to his struggle toward the Book of Books that *The Golden Book of
Springfield* should have been but could not possibly be; to his exploration
of the various semiotic realms that could best account for his vision.

His was indeed a syncretic mind, and the violence of his desire to
"break like a wave on the rock of the United States"—one thinks irresis-
tibly of Vladimir Mayakovski and of Charles Péguy—gave him the
power to unify into a coherent whole his formal preoccupations, an imagination out of the ordinary, and a rare gift for innovative expression.
The slightly irresponsible buoyancy that Ezra Pound discerned in
Lindsay, which made Pound condemn a talented poet for sheer refusal
to adapt to the poetic demands and problems of the hour, does not hold
for a moment once one starts leafing through these pages of doubt, un-
rest, and relentless questioning of the poetic form. True, Vachel Lindsay
was no intellectual, if by this term one means a person able to discern at
all times the implications of what he is doing, or someone who lives by
conceptions and theories and can account for them in abstract terms.
Lindsay lived his craft and would not distance himself from his material.
He would not become an expatriate even though he stood out as a de-
nouncer of Babbittry in an age when the term did not yet exist. (His *War
Bulletins* of 1906 are far more aggressive toward the philistines and
middle-class complacence than Lewis's books ever explicitly become.)
He would not take refuge in any sort of ivory tower and give up his
exhausting contacts with the American land and its people. A man in
love with life, a man of reflection and enthusiasm, eager to be of service
to the national community, a reformer at heart, mixed up and eclectic in
his thought but dominated and unified by an all-encompassing visionary imagination that accounts for the single-mindedness of his
praxis—Lindsay was all this and more. I hope these letters will serve as
samples of a true poet's life and reflections and will give the true measure of the maimed artificial image generated by the period of the
"Higher Vaudeville," however interesting a period in itself.

We are dealing here with a man's life and death. These pages poi-
gnantly illustrate the despair born of incomprehension that gradually

pervaded a man of trust and hope, the constant hammering of a warped image that reduces a face to a mere mask and a rich and many-colored personality to a paranoid and a repetitious entertainer, increasingly bitter and betrayed, capable still, in the midst of what critics called his personal creative desert, of the most powerful creations of his poetic life. Can anyone in good faith plead for a definitive judgment of sterility to be cast on the post-1920 Lindsay, whose "Billboards and Galleons," "How to Write a Poem," "The Virginians Are Coming Again," and other texts of great beauty appeared during those last years of his life? These letters show how a man of insight is fashioned into a freak and ultimately destroyed, how the star system allows a poet to be bullied out of shape, how the public image shaped by the media and their thirst for exoticism at all cost distorts the quiet voice of true contemplators.

Many of Lindsay's letters are missing from this collection. The reader aware of the details of this poet's life will notice conspicuous absences: Only a few of the letters to A. J. Armstrong (previously published by Baylor University but unfortunately out of print) have been included; the letters to Nellie Vieira (already available in dissertation form) have been omitted; so have those to Sara Teasdale (except one), which will, I hope, appear as a separate publication in the course of time. Before Norman Holmes Pearson's untimely death, a joint project was under way that will have to be resumed by other scholars under new circumstances. The letters Lindsay wrote to his many more or less fleeeting loves have generally not been included, either because they were not available (Isadora Bennett, Octavia Roberts, Ruth Wheeler, and others) or because they were of uneven or merely anecdotal value (E. M. Wills and others). But some have found their way into this volume because I did not want to leave entirely aside any aspect of Lindsay's personality. My general approach has consisted of including those letters that seemed most appropriate both for an in-depth grasp of Vachel Lindsay's poetic explorations and imagination and for a clear, practical overall view of his life. The stylistic quality of the letters has also been taken into account, for effects of variety and coherence. The letters vary extremely in length from the short notes Lindsay wrote when he had no time for what he called a real letter, usually containing a promise of a longer letter as soon as time permitted, to the enormous 16- to 32-page letters he sent at different periods of his life. Letter writing was something special for Lindsay. Besides the constant and obsessive desire for personal acquaintance and the keeping up of friendships at their highest level of intensity, there is something more magical in his letters: the sheer physical pleasure he felt at filling pages of blank paper with words in an increasingly sprawling hand. He would say, "I will draw you a letter" as easily as he would propose to "write a drawing." The gusto with which he felt his arm and hand gliding across the page, "armed," as it were, with a pen filled with drawing ink, was more often than not sustained through the entire length of his longest missives. Lindsay "sculpted," so to speak, the letters that formed his words. Curlicues and other flourishes testify to his calligraphic desires. "Viewed as a book, this letter is short," he wrote at the end of an exceptionally long letter. Late in his life, Lindsay publicly deplored the fact that his addictive propensity for letter writing should have eaten up so much of his natural time. Had he, he explained, written one good page of poetry or prose for every letter of greater magnitude, he might have had the time to write all he wanted when the going was good. But letter writing is writing too, as Carl Sandburg once judiciously observed, and letter writing was a part of Lindsay's vision of life. The image of a message carrying ambiguous signs across the country to a friend must have appealed to a poet whose conception of poetry always included communication and whose thirst for ubiquity and dissolution presided over all of his ethereal, Uranian imagery.

In these letters, I have corrected inadvertent misspellings. But I have retained the original spelling where it was unmistakably altered by Lindsay on purpose and it is conducive to insights into the humor and ideas of the poet ("McMillion" for "MacMillan," "expatriot" for "expatriate," and the like). Some words that are constantly or occasionally misspelled in the correspondence give indications of his pronunciation—the most frequent being "privilige," "brillian," "appitite," "tenative," "pardner," "troubador," "tward," "amature," "religon," and "religous." The reader may also perversely appreciate "synonomous" or a few "yukalalys." These have all been corrected in this volume.

While working with these letters, I have had the good fortune to gain the trust and friendship of Lindsay's family, particularly Nicholas Cave Lindsay; his wife, Du Bose Lindsay; and their children. Without their encouragement and affection, I would probably not have undertaken the publication of these letters. They have transformed rather dry and exacting work into a labor of love. All of these pages, naturally, are for them.

MARC CHENETIER

Paris, August 1979

1

TO SUSAN WILCOX

New York
57 West 57th Street
January 4, 1903

My Dear Miss Wilcox:[1]
The "Knights That Ride"[2] was based on a dream. I woke up suddenly one Sunday afternoon with a vivid impression that—"'Good Luck' cried the knights that Ride" was the last line of a poem by Browning. But I could not remember the poem and had to write what the lines implied. They carried with them an impetuous current of air and black riding figures, and a curious minglement of disaster and goodwill. Before I was awake enough to see the paper in the twilight I had ground out this that I humbly send. The other stuff explains itself, "The Soul of Lincoln"[3] is too long a poem for a picture. But I cut it down from thirty, then twenty stanzas. None of this is exactly my best, though I think you will find some new things in the "Soul of Lincoln" as well as some reprehensibly old ones. Someday I am going to foreswear angels, chains, hearts, Harps, dreams, etc and be good. I begin to find myself enwrapped in Mannerisms that to so old a victim of my work as you are, may be annoying. But I plead the picture as my excuse—and you haven't seen the picture. Nevertheless, scold me, my dear friend. As to reform—let me insist that I have just made a decided step in advance in the "Wings of the Morning" which I shall send you shortly. I think our little talks of last summer will show themselves here in a way I hope will please you. "The Wings of the Morning"[4] is a direct descendant of "The Last Song of Lucifer"—the first heir I think. There is no pretense at symbolism or allegory, no dream of anything sermonic, all my sinful energies are directed to produce music, swift motion, and the sense of laughter and happiness, with entirely new costumes and scenery and a new "Star".

Very Sincerely Yours

NICHOLAS VACHEL LINDSAY

Why don't you write?

1

Notes

1. Susan Wilcox had been VL's English teacher in Springfield High School. He referred all his work to her for correction and advice. She was to remain his most treasured confidante.
2. The source for "The Knights That Ride," which VL did not include in the *Collected Poems*, may have been a faint reminiscence of Robert Browning's "Childe Roland to the Dark Tower Came," with which he was thoroughly familiar.
3. Traces of "The Soul of Lincoln" may have provided the basis for his other poems based on Lincoln, among which, besides the never finished "The Land of Lincoln," the twenty-third stanza of "The Litany of Heroes" (*Collected Poems*, p. 192) and "Abraham Lincoln Walks at Midnight" (*Collected Poems*, p. 53) stand out.
4. "The Wings of the Morning" became, in the *Collected Poems*, the subtitle for "The Tree of Laughing Bells" (*Collected Poems*, p. 213). "The Last Song of Lucifer" was written at Hiram College in 1897 on the basis of VL's drawing *The Shield of Lucifer*.

2

TO E. S. AMES

New York, May 18, 1904

My Dear Brother Ames:
As soon as I can I will call upon Mr. Reynolds.[1] It will be an honor to know him. I thank you very sincerely for your letter of cheer. I rejoice that your church is standing by you. I am still a member of your church in spirit. In New York I have been attending St Patrick's and the Church of the Paulist Fathers. I have on my table here the manual of Prayer for the Catholic services, and about one thousand pages of Catholic tract in the form of two books for converts. I am determined to sooner or later understand this church as it sees itself, that is, in as great a degree as I have time and leisure of Sundays. I am willing to be rather considered a backslider for a while, if it must be, for the sake of this new knowledge. Your sermon "Living in all good Conscience" was a great strength, and calming balm to me this morning. In several of the personal relations of my life I have come to an important decision and I was much in need of what you have written. You are my priest in this matter, at least you have given strength. Accept my gratitude.

But there are more important things than my private soul conflicts, which I have wanted to set before you, I feel by the tone of your last letter, you are in a mood to give me a hearing. When I have talked to you I have often been stupid and confused. I give my main strength to my cause, and you must forgive the poor appearance I make out of working hours. You may find me as unconvincing as of old, when we meet in conversation, more worthy of kindness than of disciples.

I want a following, yet have done nothing yet to inspire one. Still I feel I shall have one in the end. I will win it by my work not by my conversation.

When I came to Chicago I sat down to write such a letter to Dr. Willett[2] as I now write to you, stating my cause as I might best. I am afraid he marked me down for a colossal egotist. I believed implicitly those YMCA and College axioms—*that one determined and consecrated man could butt into the world and paint it all white in a generation.* I cheerfully undertook the task, with Art for my principal weapon. As for the world—I have learned, that even so powerfully centered a mind as Spencer's can only "bend the current" of thought for a while, and that in his own province. Even the greatest of us write in water and are gone. So I shall trim down my ambition by bending some small current a little bit, and in choosing my task I shall not choose what would be most beautiful to do, but as you say in your sermon I shall "choose a few good things and live by them rather than to claim belief in still nobler and more numerous good things that always lie upon the shelf."

I have discovered how little even the biggest can do, though I was of a different opinion on Hiram Hill.[3] I also feel disposed to mark out a task more in harmony with my *abilities* than my ideals. The things I am most able to do, the things I will do, are not the highest, except in the eyes of a few, I would like to live such a life as Abraham Lincoln, as Burns or Wordsworth or some other friend of the people. Yet the more I push my education the more I develop those exclusive attenuated virtues in art that please the few. And in letters likewise I am more apt to please the specialists than my closest friends. An art like this and a verse like this will never do the task of Wordsworth however I set my will and pray.

But I am not prepared to say my mission is to the few. I am prepared by now to set myself to the task of building up my special abilities, trusting that they are my best revelation and into whatever paths they shall lead me I shall follow them. If I merely win a triumph as an artist in verse and line, I shall accept the judgement of Jehova and live in good conscience.

Now I must tell you where they will probably lead me, as you are a man I am anxious should follow my progress with understanding. I can deny myself the discipleship of many, if in the matter of Art and letters I can find a few followers like you, not blind advocates, but those who are willing to feel my soul rules in one or two tiny rooms in the universe, and when you step into them, I have done a work for your entertainment that is worth while.

My ancestors were all men of action, statesmen, rulers of men. It is hard for me to respect my army, for it is an assembly of ornamental shadows and dreams, when I thought to have commanded men. And my sermons I must preach only to myself, to exhort myself to be true to my art and writing.

Some of my *second rate* work is of a didactic kind of writing. And there is a certain remote touch with human character in my drawing, but if my work wins a high place I fear it will be the decorative qualities that are most potent in winning that place. I *may* go into the market place yet and sketch my impressions. I may even excel at character drawing, and the depicting of throbbing human life. I rather hope to do this in my drawing. But this is neither serving the devils nor the angels. It merely states the problem, at best, to put character studies on paper. It is probably the farthest thing I can reasonably hope for in drawing. I had thought of making my designing into cartooning. But it becomes more designing and less cartooning every day. Be sure I shall follow out my abilities, along the line of best and readiest development, rather than torture them to fit any preconcieved ideal [sic], however precious. I hope to make the drawing the principal task of my life, rather than writing. I congratulate myself on every poem I can refrain from writing as heartily as I congratulate myself when I get a picture made. A house divided against itself cannot stand, and in my life, drawing shall be paramount over writing. I have in the main succeeded in suppressing my insatiable writing proclivity. What I write these days is better because it is occasional, and irresistible when it comes. I write only those things it is impossible to choke. I haven't written verses now for three months, and on the whole I have devoted this entire year to drawing.

My ideal for my religious life is that of a religious tramp, a wanderer from Church to Church, following the leading of "the Gleam", seeking new impressions and vivid insights into the religious life of all men. I have had many of these in the past, yet have left few on record. The most I can hope for my verse is that it will some day become the record of my best impressions in these Churches. I shall not force it, I can scarcely promise. I merely hope. When you see signs of it in my writing, I ask your congratulations, though it may be a while before they are due.

These two things then are the largest I can *hope* for as the result of my great programme laid down three years ago. I *may* draw character sketches with sympathy. I *may* write about the Church universal with insight.

The things I am *sure* to do are not so lofty, a certain delicate kind of designing, a certain decorative sort of verse—these I am sure to produce till I die. They shall occupy the main strength of my life. I can only *hope* I may be led into those higher hopes I have indicated. I *may* succeed in living for Humanity and the Church. I shall certainly be faithful to Art.

I do not know whether you are one of those who think art is justified when it is unmoral but not immoral, wholesome but not consecrated. Sometimes I am. Especially in the midst of my work. Then I have faith in art as a mission. But in the colder hours of thought such as this, I hope and dream it may even become consecrated to a task. Still I shall not trouble myself too much about it. It is a satisfaction to speak of these things occasionally to such a man as you are. I have faith in *your* fight, and the task you have set yourself. In a sense you are my proxy, fighting battles I wish I had the strength to undertake. But I must humbly keep to my little task. I may be somewhat of a wanderer, as I follow the leadings of the Art Spirit, the Comforter of Art. I trust you, and you will likewise trust me, though I seem to wander far among the churches. I hope to bring you back some good thing at last.

Very Sincerely

NICHOLAS VACHEL LINDSAY

Notes

1. "Mr. Reynolds" must have been a friend of Dr. Edward Scribner Ames, who led the Church of the Disciples of Christ (Campbellites) in Chicago and was a spiritual mentor to VL for a number of years.
2. Dr. Herbert Lockwood Willett, a colleague of Dr. Ames's and a Chicago clergyman, also was editor of *The Christian Century*.
3. Hiram Hill refers to Hiram College, the Campbellite educational institution at Hiram, Ohio, headed, when VL was a student there (1897—1900), by the Reverend Eli Vaughn Zollars, ex-pastor of Springfield's Christian Church, a close friend of VL's father, Vachel Thomas Lindsay, and future president of the Texas Christian University, Waco, Texas.

3

TO SUSAN WILCOX

New York
May 1, 1905

My Dear Miss Wilcox:
I think of you many times, and wonder why you do not write. A letter from you would be exceedingly welcome. I presume you are having the same beautiful Spring Weather there as we have here. New York never looked so well. I have had two long walks today, and feel like another, tonight, and may take it.

I have forwarded several copies of "We Who Are Playing"[1] to Mama, and if you feel that you would like to give one to any of your friends, ask her for it. They are for any one who really likes them. I am going to have another edition struck off pretty soon.

The picture may not be an ideal illustration, but it is the best grotesque I ever did, and illustrates the first verse in a fashion. I am going to get out more of this sort of thing, from time to time.

I wish we could have a good evening talk. It would be a great treat. New York has not yet surrendered, but there is still a great deal of hope. Whenever I look at my book[2] I remember our evenings together, and my debt to you. Whatever the fate of the volume as it stands, the whole experience was of tremendous value, it was inevitable, it had to be done, whatever came later. It has been the means of winning the good opinion of many people not publishers, and the principal stories always take when I tell them, with the assistance of the book. I think though that when they are published, it will be in verse. The story of the crucified angels—and several others, are going into verse sometime. I have been surprised at the success of the Wings of the Morning.[3] Fred Richardson and Robert Henri had fits over it, and both read it to their wives a second time. And lesser lights have taken a flattering interest in it. I have written and drawn nothing of importance since I have been here, addressing myself to the question of finding a place for myself. They are lavish with praise and short on positions. That is the summary. I have met open doors of appreciation everywhere, but when it comes to results they say "Go to the next neighbor, it isn't our line". Well, something will happen yet. I never was more hopeful or clearer in conscience and ambition. My immediate plans however are not so clear, depending upon the chance approval of this man or that.

My mind is not bent toward discussing my immediate plans tonight, but I would like to have some words with you on the state of poetry in America. It is an interesting situation.

Books of poems that have been reviewed with flaming endorsement by every principal critic in America, that have been given ample space in critical columns, and have in one way or another been worthy of the praise—have been passed by the public. No amount of advertisement can force the public to buy more than the most limited edition. The whole fashion of the times is against it. No amount of argument can prevent the publishers from classifying my book as poetry. So they figure immediately on the most limited of editions, and when they look at the extra plates, and the illustrations, the things look too expensive. I have about reconciled myself to this view of the case, and use the book as a bid for work, and it has already opened certain doors for me. And its usefulness in talking over my work is very great. It is my diploma, as it were, and will continue so for some time, and whenever I have the chance of an hour with a man, I clinch him every time, with the book. The stories take well when told, and the thing is to me a mine of suggestions for new work and new plans, as I judge the effect of the various pictures and stories upon all my friends. Among the pictures, the soul of the Butterfly and the soul of the Spider[4] take most of all. No one whose opinion I really value has failed to remember these. And the same might be said of The Tree of Laughing Bells. One might say that is even popular. I can simply say I am surprised, and vastly more hopeful that that phase of my work will take. My figures only excite passing interest. The Soul of the Spider beats them all, so far as staying qualities are concerned.

Well, I have wandered off the subject—which was the state of Poetry in America. The question is—what method will break the spell? I have invented a formula—but I don't write that kind of verse. The formula—two thirds Kipling, one third W. J. Bryan. It might not be poetry?

The state of American Civilization becomes a surprisingly personal matter, since I am forced to reason about these things. My own selfish interests are at stake, and I am amazed to realize for the first time what Europeans mean by American Hurry, American restlessness, brashness, lack of tradition, omnivorous industrialism. Things go at a hotter clip every minute. Of course there is poetry in this. But can I respond to it? And ought I? Can I stride the steam engine and go puffing over the prairies?

There is a whole lot that Whitman did not put in. It is the Metallic roar, the terrible overhead railroads, the harshness of it all, that dulls every fine sensibility for the greater part of every day. What little time is left for the soul to live is so little a man cannot read a poem twice.

He can scarcely read a novel. He leaves them to his wife, and crams short stories in a quick-lunch sort of way. The only way to make him read a poem twice is to contruct a jingle haunting as a popular tune, a jingle that can almost be whistled. And that is a forlorn hope. I am going to think it over. Please write to me.

Very Sincerely

NICHOLAS VACHEL LINDSAY

Notes

1. "We Who Are Playing Tonight" was a privately printed pamphlet containing the poem and the picture that VL tried to peddle in the streets of New York in March 1905. He tried again to peddle poetry in public places in March and April of the same year, the last time with another pamphlet entitled "A Cup of Paint." As usual, he first tried to sell his production but soon enough gave it away. The same thing later happened with *The Village Magazine,* the first *War Bulletins*—he did not even try to sell the following ones—and all the pamphlets and broadsides he privately printed in later years. Numerous reprints of "The Map of the Universe" (1904) and of later broadsides were given away at great expense to their author.
2. "The book" here mentioned is *Where Is Aladdin's Lamp?*, written, illustrated, and bound by hand with decorations in 1904, the same year "The Map of the Universe" was drawn, in the wake of the composition and drawing of "The Queen of Bubbles." "The Queen of Bubbles" had been accepted by *The Critic* the same year and was VL's first publication. *Where Is Aladdin's Lamp?* remains his seminal work; even though only fragments of the destroyed book remain, many elements went into the composition of a great variety of poems and the first seed of *The Golden Book of Springfield* (1920) is also found there. It lays out VL's highly idiosyncratic cosmogony. Made up of pictures, verses, and prose narratives, "the book" never was published.
3. "The Tree of Laughing Bells, or The Wings of the Morning" had impressed Robert Henri. When VL read his poem to Henri and Henri's wife, the artist encouraged him to devote himself entirely to poetry instead of pursuing his artistic schemes.
4. "The Soul of the Butterfly" and "The Soul of the Spider" were prominent on "The Map of the Universe." Lindsay used them again in his book, then in *The Village Magazine.* They eventually appeared in the *Collected Poems* (pp.366—67), along with the quatrains they had generated.

4

TO THE MACMILLAN COMPANY

New York, May 17, 1905

Dear Sirs:

I send you about thirty poems, selected from eight years work.[1] I hope it is enough for a volume. If the manuscript is accepted, I would like to discuss plans for decorating it, and inserting one or more illustrations. I have had four years training at Life work, in Chicago Art Institute, and here under Chase and Henri. If you so desire, I can call with the illustrations. Pen and ink designing is my specialty.

Very sincerely

NICHOLAS VACHEL LINDSAY
304 West 56th Street

Note

1. Among the poems VL mentions for this projected first collection must have been most of his output going back to 1897 ("eight years work"), among which "The Battle" and "The Last Song of Lucifer." "Star of my Heart" (1901), "The Triumph of Friendship" (1898), and "A Midnight Pantheism" (1901) may have been included, as well as "The Cup of Paint" and "We Who Are Playing Tonight." A certain number of texts excerpted from *Where Is Aladdin's Lamp?* were probably in the collection, particularly "The Queen of Bubbles," "A Prayer in the Jungles of Heaven," and "The Tree of Laughing Bells." The night before, VL had jotted in his notebook: "God Help us all to be Brave," but it is doubtful that this should have developed so soon into the future "Litany of Heroes" (*Collected Poems*, pp. 185—94).

5

TO SUSAN WILCOX

New York
August 16, 1905

My Dear Miss Wilcox:

I do not think the world would be monotonous if there were a few more in it like you. I wish there were two or three of you in New York. Really, it would be such a pleasure to talk things over. You help me so much to sustain a mood that I myself desire to keep. What I am with you, is what I consider it my business to be all the time. The plane on which we thought and talked is one in which I am so very much more comfortable than most any other.

I am feeling the hunger for our old friendship today, because, it may be, of the season, and the wonderful things we began to plan this time last year. I owe you an inestimable debt for the mere kindness of your heart and the readiness of your mind in that enterprise. It was plainly as good a time to you as to me, which is the best part of the memory, and therefore I do not have to thank you too much.

It was a lovely spree and I have no regrets, just for the pleasure of the doing, it was worth while. And I look on my dog-eared yellow books, with the same pleased pride and the same self-complacency as ever. I know the experience was invaluable, and it will afford me a standard of comparison, a system and a starting point ever after.

I have a friend who has half promised to find a publisher about Christmas for the Lucifer episode, in its prose setting, omitting mention of the lamp.

But I am too full of new projects to spend too much time on the old. For the sake of preserving them, I would like to have my best poems privately printed, and probably will do it, when I can afford it.

My critics, when they are willing to express themselves say these things—That the book has too much in it, that one tenth would be more effective, and that at first glance it looks very expensive, though closer scrutiny shows it is not so expensive after all. I have had that list of opinions from several.

Letters are no satisfaction. It is much easier to talk for an evening, than write for an hour. Nevertheless there are some things I must place before you, I know you want to know my plans. I suppose most people would not call them plans at all. Aside from the question of fussing around for some money,[2] which nearly drives me crazy sometimes, and for which I have no really sensible plans, I have a rather clear cut notion of how I intend to develop.

I feel I was on the right track for ultimate results in Aladdin's lamp, it indicates several things I will ripen and carry further. In poetry, the system of the Universe[3] set down in it, after ripening, (the Jungles of Heaven and all that), shall some day see their place in rhyme. It is quite an undertaking, but I have already ripened the system of things, the cosmogony there laid down. The meaning changes with experience, but the elements of the spectacle remain the same. I may some day be able to state those elements with power, and with simplicity, and they can serve other men as they have served me. In short, in poetry I anticipate carrying farther the promise of the Tree of Laughing Bells and Lucifer. My note books are full of the plot, I really see myself much readier to put these vast things into rhyme than last year, and by a proper pruning and simplicity, make the pictures plain. I have arrived at a point where the overwhelming gloom of the conception is mended, without impairing the pictorial value. With leisure and a free conscience, I feel I could embark on the enterprise. With money on my conscience, I cannot steal the time to write poetry. I feel confident however, that I will please you with this thing when it is written. It begins to assume more simplicity, and the passion for luxuriance has departed from me, in this dream at least, I am eager to be at it. I feel strong enough to do it. A bold statement? I will admit there are other things I do not feel so prepared to undertake which Fate will probably thrust upon me. It is pleasanter to be bold with the Universe than with men. It seems I am doomed to go out snatching money from men who do not want me to have it. I have got to make faces, and stand on my head, then pass the hat.

But I have plans in the matter of Art. I have had a great struggle with myself in this matter, unimportant to other folks, for it has no outward showing—the question of which one had the best right to my heart of hearts devotion—Art or letters. For a time at least I see the thing now settled, and I frankly conceive that I have more to say in poetry than art. And it took all the art courage out of me for a while. But now my fingers begin to tingle again to be doing, and I have some rather definite plans of some little picture books I shall make, possibly by hand, with wood-blocks, using little bits of color, and printing in editions of ten or twenty. In my present state of finances it will save printers bills, it will sufficiently multiply my work to put it in the hands of my friends and keep it from loss, it will be a form of art expression, and above all, it will be a step along lines already taken. I will bind the books with hand made covers, after the manner of Aladdin's Lamp, only on leather rather than paste board. I have made two already, the only difficulty being there is no method of duplication, they are made by hand straight through. I am willing to design separate covers, it is such a joy, but by the wood block method, I can make as many duplicates of the interiors as there is a demand for. I have made quite a study of Japanese work—which was done on this principle.

I am going to develop this sooner or later, my books shall not be half baked forever.

I may have a chance for an art lectureship in Zollars' college in Waco Texas which goes by the name of Texas Christian University.[4] Three lectures are complete, which I hope to read you sometime. It has been a pleasure to write them, an unexpected pleasure, since I took them up merely as a possible piece of practical wisdom. I may give them somewhere yet. I find I am full of the subject and can produce indefinitely, if there is a demand. But it is our duty I presume, never to do what we can, and rather absurd to suppose any one would ask me to do anything I am prepared to do.

I am certainly hungry for another period of creation. I would make most any sacrifice to obtain it. I am not anxious for anything so much as the leisure and the free conscience to work out these plans for books and poetry. I am fairly bursting with six months of pent up energy in these matters. Business is with me, like Latin and anatomy were. I have the sand to *let my own plans alone* for the sake of business, but never the nerve to attack business with a whole heart. I have not written a poem or made a picture for six months, I have conscientiously abstained from doing what I have been hungering and thirsting to do. I have been up and down the city begging, begging and peddling for work, I have tried every possible line, yet lots of the time with the same indifference and paralysis of the mind with which I used to look my old Latin books in the face, hour after hour. I have done a little drawing and writing, but not with my whole soul, merely as an opiate when the world became a jangle.

There is only one plan I have, however I may seem to twist and turn to superficial observers. I want to earn leisure and solitude, that I may do the highest honor possible to the dreams that beset me. *I have only one duty—to give them form and setting, putting my whole strength into them.*

Sometimes I think of doing it at home—but that is a terrible imposition. It is sordid to take shelter and money from those that will consider your success failure, and your failure success. I hate myself for that. I am my father's curse.

Yet the sharp shame has been gone for the little while I am preparing these lectures. I feel I am doing my best, and I have a right to ask the old folks to be patient. My mother seems to think Zollars will give me the place. I am not too hopeful, but till it is decided, I can at least have a respite at entirely congenial work. And I am getting in some good licks. I am happy and busy as a bumble bee. It is curious how easily we are pleased sometimes. I feel I have written unexpectedly well, with ease, with order and with a little experience. At the worst I can put these lectures in the drawer, where with Aladdin, they can be in royal company.

Wishing you as happy a summer as I have now, I remain,

NICHOLAS V. LINDSAY

Notes

1. "My dog-eared yellow book" is *Where Is Aladdin's Lamp?*, bound in yellow pasteboard and richly decorated.
2. Money problems were besieging VL then as ever. They are mentioned further on in reference to potential job openings. Dr. Lindsay kept sending money to his son as often as he could. But VL felt awkward about the situation; all the more so because he knew his father did not favor his artistic plans and somewhat resented VL's dropping out of his medical courses at Hiram in 1900.
3. VL's speculations on "the system of the Universe" were then in full swing. Poems were inspired by "The Map of the Universe" at a great rate, and the commentaries on the meaning of the "map" grew more and more sophisticated.
4. The lectures "intended" for Zollars's institution were eventually delivered at the New York YMCA during the last months of 1905.

6

TO SUSAN WILCOX

New York
The Rutledge
One, West Eighty Second
December the third,
Nineteen hundred and five.

My Dear Miss Wilcox:

For several reasons I have thought of you at special times this summer and fall. I was thinking of it in Church this morning—of my debt to you and of my need. I really didn't stop to notice last January, that I was in need, or in debt. In the first place, preoccupied with breaking into the city. And in the second place every evening I dedicated to a long

letter to my fair lost lady of Ohio.[1] And about May, at last having it
made plain to me that a man cannot make a living for two and live the
life absolutely essential to me, I broke the engagement. Now dame
rumor being very kind, has probably prepared your mind on this point.
Possibly I wrote you of it at the time. I pray you, judge me not. It was
hard. I thought as much of her as I ever will of living mortal.

I hardly had time to discover I was lonely till late this summer. Since
then I have made friends with several very fine women. I believe it was
earlier in the year I broke the engagement, I don't remember, possibly
March. Well—anyway I have had time to get lonely, and against my
will, against principles and resolves, in hours of weariness I have sought
out other women for help, for comfort, for assistance. Selfishly of course,
I anticipate the occasion. So be it.

And I am in the end awfully dissatisfied with myself. I find I ask too
much of some very smart and unselfish people—and I have wondered
why, several times; and I have at last seen plainly, you have spoiled me.
Of course that is worth it all, the art life is the search for excellence, and
you are the one so excellent in unselfishness and resource of mind, that
you completely satisfied my desire for help. I have had several offer to
help and they really want to help and give me full sympathy, yet the
fact remains that they do *not* help.

Miss Moss and Miss Squire[2] do not quite come under this category,
for if I was in art alone, no help could be better than theirs; in the matter
of art companionship, they completely filled my hearts need. (A frank
confession is a satisfaction to me, it cleans the air, and I can go on). But
I am in the midst of new questions now—and I would like to have some
good Saturday night talks with *you*, in which you would make me feel
you understood everything I said, completely. Most gracious and rare
is your gift, and though my sense of debt comes late, be sure it is sincere.
And I lay hold upon this sensation of indebtedness while it is present
with me, and spread it at your feet. Make the most of it, lets both make
the most of it today.

What then, is my present manner of life?

I lecture Tuesday night at the 57th Street YMCA,[3] second largest in
America. Also Wednesday. But in a small room. I sit at the head of a
table, around which are seated fifteen to twenty men, some of them my
most loyal personal friends. On Tuesday I lecture on art. Wednesday
on Poetry. Friday I take practically the same crowd to the Metropolitan
Museum and to some one collection, prepared for on Tuesday. Every
other Thursday I lecture for the 23 st YMCA, to a bunch about the same
size. Saturday I carry advertisements for the 57th street association all
day. That is, the only way to be allowed to lecture on my chosen themes,
is to do enough chores to pay for my salary anyway, which is $12 1/2

This unexpected gift of the generous friendship of splendid young men, most of them two or three years younger, gentlemen in every sense, is a thing I do not by any means deserve, and I do thank the good Lord for them. Here is a great good gift that seems to bring no distress, no aftermath, though I suppose in this happiness there is the germ of a tragedy as in every other. I shall take it without surprise I hope when it comes.

I feel that if I cannot in the end win leisure to write by lecturing, I can work with my hands and

Letter to Susan Wilcox, December 3, 1905

10 I never expect to be happier than now, and ~~so~~ though my cup does not run over it is comfortabbly full. There is always some cause for discontent, our lives are blest indeed when we are not facing ~~tragedy~~ in our own personal ~~fortunes~~. And I am rich in opportunity, rich in friends, more especially men friends. I have ~~some~~ half dozen who mean as much to me as I ever expected any
to me
one to mean ~~to mean~~. If I should lose them I should need to write six in memoriams, if I had the soul of Tennyson. But that is in every sense pure speculation. In the first place they are all very healthy.

a week. My total income, when all things are running, is about $30 for every two weeks, including both associations. So I have about all to do I can handle, to keep studied up on my lectures, and in personal touch with the members. Half of them come and go like flies, all sorts of tanglefoot tactics are necessary to keep that fifteen or twenty, to justify the use of the room.

Yet there are rays of hope. Several art students who are *good painters* are loyal. My personal friends here in this eating club spread my prestige a bit. And they are touchingly loyal, and it puts me on my mettle when they come to my lectures. I want them to come first because they are my friends, but secondly because they feel their brains and their temperaments are undergoing a delightful change. The problem of creating the real atmosphere of art and Poetry in that little room is with me day and night, and the question of giving the fellows the *real thing*, of really carrying the artists forward is warm in my head all the time. Meanwhile, I am classified as the YMCA Religious Department, because the only man I could interest in me happened to be Powlinson, the religious director 57th st. He himself is a very broad man, but it keeps him pretty busy explaining how Art and Poetry are part of his Evangelism, especially since they are uttered by a person not markedly religious. Hence the necessity that I make myself busy carrying tickets and printing oceans of signs. He has to put on the check he gives me "Bible Study" which is a fine point in conscience. He explains that is merely a technicality, but it looks to me like tainted money.

The ticket distribution, which occurs on Friday and Saturday is in itself well on the way to making a YMCA man of me, it is so interesting in itself. Powlinson has decided to broaden his policy, and by his direction I took the tickets into every saloon on the route, and after asking the bartenders permission, placed a little pile on them by the cigar lighter, where men might pick them up as they went out. My route is over the most interesting part of New York, and the theatre section of Broadway runs across it, and the experience is rich, absolutely great. I am going to endeavor to carry out all the tickets I can, and dodge the sign-painting, which wears out my soul. They want it in a hurry, and they want it inartistic and mechanical, this sign painting.

My life has certainly been rich in experience this fall. This summer I swore softly to myself I would either get some kind of work by October first, or go into the river. And I most decidedly meant it. I was near crazy and Nicholls, one of those with whom I had been rooming all summer has a father who runs a gastubing factory. I had no special notions of what that might be and it was not till about September 20 that I tacketed [*sic*] him on the subject. Up to that time President Zollars of Texas Christian University had more or less promised me a place lecturing. But not hearing from the President by the Twentieth, I tack-eted [*sic*] Nicholls, and when he found me willing to do simple stupid manual labor, in fact, preferring it, he took me up at once, and for October and most of November I worked in his factory ten hours a day and never enjoyed anything like it in my life. I loved the men and the work, I got a tremendous physical stirring up, I learned to lift barrels full of gas-tubing into a wagon by myself, it was the old Marshall Field episode over again. And I feared it would end the same way, I would get tired or indifferent and go back to be dependent on people again. Therefore I lectured at night, and fought every inch of the way and the YMCA allowed me to do it as a *favor*, seeing so few came. Finally by a desperate wrestle I succeeded in persuading the religious department that I could do better and . . . get daytime to study in. Therefore I was offered twenty five dollars for two weeks of lectures, at the end of that time I was to be dropped, if I did not make good. I increased the attendance on each of the classes from eight and ten to fifteen and twenty. The two weeks are ended, and it's up to them. They may put me permanently on the force, or they may not. I feel serene in either event. It's too much work to covet, and it isn't my destiny, merely a chunk of raw experience, which is valuable only as it refines my fibre as an artist. I consider all this not in the main path, unless it be con-sidered *experience* as we do air and sunshine, an essential element in every life, in every real personality. I much doubt whether any of the things I am now doing will be even indirectly worked over into my writing or drawing. The only hope is that as a result souls will be born beneath the raiment of my dreams, that there will be more blood in the veins of my prophets, more witchcraft in the fingers of Balrudador, more order, and reason and serene health and simple massiveness in the Jungles of Heaven and on the three thrones.[4] I find I have some rather unexpected resources as a leader of men, I am nearer my mother than I knew, when it comes to playing the oracle, and bullying the minds of those who listen, and I have more of her powers as a speaker, in my best lectures, than I ever bargained for. But when you hear reports on these matters, be not deceived, I do not mistake my calling. With the help of the good Jehova I shall some day begin the search of Aladdin's lamp again, and set those dreams in order. I *know* they are my best self, and everything else is preparation.

But to return to the beginning of this letter, I am dissatisfied with myself in the matter of woman. Everything else is beautiful.

What I ask of my women friends you have supplied in the past, when we could see each other. If the YMCA fails me, I have my mind serenely ready to go back to gas tubing, where a job is waiting for me. But with woman it is not so. I can find no rest. I want a woman near me where I could talk out a thousand phases of my present experience while it is hot within me. Letters are no satisfaction. There seems to be no interchange without the personal presence.

Now I am human enough to often desire the thing for which woman stands in the best romance and I know the lack of romance adds to the discontent. But it is a thing I have foregone, and can for the most part forego, if I had this other.

I write this letter with pleasure, not with wailing. I have pointed out my only discontent. Otherwise I wish you to rejoice with me in the fullness and the many unexpected happinesses of my life. I never expect to be happier than now, and though my cup does not run over it is comfortably full. There is always some cause for discontent, our lives are blest indeed when we are not facing tragedy in our own personal fortunes. And I am rich in opportunity, rich in friends, more especially men friends.[5] I have some half dozen who mean as much to me as I ever expected any *one* to mean to me. If I should lose them I should need to write six In Memoriams, if I had the soul of Tennyson. But that is in every sense pure speculation. In the first place they are all very healthy. This unexpected gift of the generous friendship of splendid young men, most of them two or three years younger, gentlemen in every sense, is a thing I do not by any means deserve, and I do thank the good Lord for them. Here is a great good gift that seems to bring no distress, no aftermath, though I suppose in this happiness there is the germ of a tragedy as in every other. I shall take it without surprise I hope, when it comes.

I feel that if I cannot in the end win leisure to write by lecturing, I can work with my hands and have the evenings. If I can work ten hours, every day, and give three lectures a week of nights, there is a chance for me yet.

As to the *tragedy of missions,*[6] which no doubt looks larger on your Horizon than these small matters of mine, I have my moments of suspense and wonder and apprehension, but I *must* be a fatalist in the matter. To choose the absolute right—to say they were right or wrong, is impossible. Their lives are not in my world, we can only shout across the seas; I trust them, I hope for them they have enlisted, they are part of the far flung battle line of missions. If they live their lives and think them out honestly, they have a chance to become very wise before they die. Living or dead they are essentially true to themselves, they stand pure before my eyes, however foolish, and I am in no place to set my wisdom over theirs, and they can trust me to think kindly, and do my best to sympathize. They are essentially romantic-religious, and I envy them the *romance*. If they are killed in a week after landing, as the old folks seem to anticipate, I can only hope it is without torture. Mere death is no matter to be apprehensive about, so far as I can see. Of course I have never died, and may be mistaken. It often looks most seasonable. There is the martyr's crown for some, and for even the worst of us a sweet epitaph. I suppose after I have lost many, that are really dear, the question of immortality will seem more worth while.

The boys up stairs are singing love songs with all their full young hearts. I suppose every one has a vision of some fair lady. Thank the Lord for their songs, and for the good faces they see, and for all His many bounties.

Isn't it amusing, that I am put down in the hand bill as of Columbia University? The committee made some mistake in that matter. I feel that the New York School of Art is a more memorable institution. There are many Universities in this land, But there is only one Chase School. Goodby. Write to me a line.

Very sincerely

NICHOLAS VACHEL LINDSAY

Notes

1. "My fair lost lady in Ohio" was Ruth Wheeler, to whom VL had become engaged in the fall of 1903; on his way to New York and Chase's "School of Art," he had stopped off in Akron, Ohio. In the early months of 1905 VL broke off the relationship; a letter sent at the end of March and another written to his parents in April made it plain that he did not wish to continue a frustrating relationship that distance, both social and geographical, made increasingly intolerable.
2. Miss Moss and Miss Squire were probably among his New York acquaintances. They could not be further identified.
3. VL's YMCA lectures first began in the evenings after his day's work in the Nicholls Gas Tubing Company, where his friend Nicholls had found him a job to alleviate his financial troubles and smooth over difficulties with his parents. The lectures gradually met with such success that daily attendance made it possible for the YMCA to pay the lecturer. VL then left the Nicholls Company. VL had tried to finance his way through the Chicago Art Institute in 1901 by working in the toy department of Marshall Field's. He began work in September and quit on December 5, overwhelmed by the hardships confronting a simple laborer during the holiday-season toy rush.
4. "The three thrones" are the central designs in "The Map of the Universe." They stand for the Trinity but are empty because their occupants are at present at work redeeming the world.
5. Among VL's men friends in New York were George Mather Richards, a designer and a lifelong friend, Gutzon Borglum the sculptor, MacClain, a Scot in whose company VL had visions in the streets of New York in 1905, and Edward Broderick, with whom he took his first tramp in the South the following year.
6. "The tragedy of missions" was something VL often confronted through his mother's missionary preoccupations. Traces of his reflections on the subject will be found in "Foreign Missions in Battle Array" (*Collected Poems*, p. 338).

7

TO SUSAN WILCOX

Nahego Club
1 West 82nd St
New York
February 28, 1906

My Dear Miss Wilcox:
Our correspondence does not flourish. I wish I could see you; nobody knows when I will though. No one has taken your place, always remember that.

I am going to hunt Aladdin's lamp day after tomorrow. We have no old magician in our company, only Broderick, a literary man of my age. We two take a boat to Jacksonville Florida, then start across the country afoot, west and north.[1] I shall devote till June 23 to walking. Broderick will keep with me for a month, then return to work here, in Presby's Advertising agency, of which he is a leading literary man. My people do not know of this expedition. I shall write to them after I am well on the road. I meet them in Philadelphia, June 23, to start to Europe (I take up my work with the West Side YMCA next fall. They are entirely in sympathy with my expedition, and I may lecture on it next winter).[2]

We will probably have a great many adventures of a disagreeable or sordid kind, but we have made up our minds to stand the racket. We will have no money when we reach Florida. We will be armed with several letters of introduction[3] and carry one clean shirt and collar, for use in emergencies. Otherwise the open road and the hand-out for ours.

My dear lady, will you write to me here when you feel so constrained. I will have my mail forwarded from week to week.

All the members of the club are prospering. I only wish I had a bit more time this morning, or rather I wish you were here to talk to me, and I would take the time. Maybe I will write you letters of adventure on the road. We will see. They may not give us postage stamps.

Broderick is a man with the highest literary standards, especially in Prose, who is forced to advertising and hack-work for a living. He will enter into the expedition with just the right spirit. He wants to do the orange groves, and the Tennessee mountains this month. I don't know what I will do then, maybe work into Kentucky and into Indiana, and visit my kin.

With love,

VACHEL

Notes

1. See the Chronology for a more precise account of VL's and Broderick's southern tramp.
2. It has been conjectured that his aunt Eudora Lindsay South's influence was instrumental in convincing VL's parents to take him along to Europe: She was supposed to have been so touched by his appearance at the end of his 1906 southern tramp that she had written to tell the good that might be expected from such a change. It is made clear here that the European trip had in fact been arranged, including VL, before he started on his southern journey.
3. One letter of introduction was written by M. Powlinson, head of the YMCA where VL lectured.

8

TO SUSAN WILCOX

Griffin, Georgia
April 2, 1906

My Dear Miss Wilcox:

Your letter has been a good companion for me on my journey. I have sent word to the friends in New York who have the copies of my official report of my wanderings to forward them to you. Select what you please. I hope they will come in time. When you are through with them, please hand to Joy.[1] I will instruct my family as to their further disposal. There are about three of my verses that fit the present situation in any measure. I presume you have them. "Woe to the Weary Fireflies" and "The Breast of the Earth" and "I want to be Wandering".[2] I do not consider these especially marked utterances along the tramp-line however. Richard Hovey and Bliss Carman's "Songs from Vagabondia",[3] William Vaughn Moody's "Road Hymn for the Start";[4] Anna Hempstead Branch's[5] "The Heart of the Road" and "The Keeper of the Half-Way House"; Kipling's "For to Enjoy" and many another by the excellent Rudyard—expound the wanderlove better than I.[6] I will venture however, few of these people have done as much walking as your servant, and this time I may be able to outwrite them on the theme.

And of course there is the redoubtable Whitman[7]—whom I neither love nor hate. No man can equal him in voicing the sentiment of the open-road; the reason he does not hold me is because my mind is over-decorative in its appetites at present. Sinbad and Aladdin for mine.

I find however a new beauty in life, and in my heart, that goes beyond decoration. A new element entered my life, aside and apart from its usual formulas, in the friendship of the splendid men I have known in New York this year, and in the realization of the splendid heart strength of some of my oldest friends, like Miss Wilcox. This is an experience that comes without pictures or words, it is too new to me to have an Art form. And it has been enhanced for me walking along the road, with letters from all these in my pocket, and I feel that life can have other methods of happiness besides the search for Beauty, or mere pictorial and picturesque adventure, or intellectual adventure. Of course all these things are preached, and the preacher can blandly remind us that he said so, and His master said so, long ago. It is easy to be unctuous and orthodox. All this comes straight from my note-book. Almost every day I find myself in a glow of wonder over the tenderness of the Southern Hospitality. I do not stay in any one place long enough for the people to lose the glamor of Romance. They are actors in intense little dramas—from the hour I knock on the door to the hour I go.[8]

NICHOLAS VACHEL LINDSAY

Notes

1. Joy is VL's sister, who later married Ben Blair (see letter 158).
2. "Woe to the Weary Fireflies" and "The Breast of the Earth" were not included in the *Collected Poems*. "I Want to Be Wandering," long taken to be a typical poem of the tramping days, was in fact part of *Where Is Aladdin's Lamp?* and concerned more spiritual matters. It was included in the *Collected Poems* under the title "I Want to Go Wandering" (p. 293).
3. Carman, a Canadian (1861—1929), and Hovey, an American, met at Harvard in 1885 and were close until Hovey's death in 1900. Their *Songs from Vagabondia* came out in 1894, *More Songs from Vagabondia* in 1896. Carman remains one of the more important Canadian poets.
4. William Vaughn Moody (1869—1910), a famous playwright and poet, married Harriet Converse Brainerd the year before he died, and she was to become VL's friend. W. V. Moody's plays *The Great Divide* (1906) and *The Faith Healer* (1909) met with great success. His *Selected Poems* came out in 1931, the year VL died.
5. Anna Hempstead Branch (1865—1935) is best known for her collections of poems, among which *The Heart of the Road and Other Poems* (1901) was favored by VL. *The Shoes That Danced and Other Poems* had come out the preceding year (1905).
6. For further judgments on Kipling, see letters 3 and 11.
7. VL's lifelong debate on the nature and worth of Whitman's art is illustrated in several letters (see in particular letter 132).
8. *A Handy Guide for Beggars*, published in 1916 by Macmillan, contains quite a few sketches of VL's southern walk. "The Flower of Mending" (*Collected Poems*, p. 329) was written at the end of that trip and recited at Excelsior Institute, established near Frankfort, Kentucky, by VL's aunt Eudora Lindsay South (see letter 162).

9

TO R. W. GILDER

Springfield, Illinois
July 16, 1908

Mr. Richard Watson Gilder
Editor of The Century Magazine

My Dear Mr. Gilder:[1]
In the winter of 1903 and 1904 I called at the Critic office with a bundle of verses under one arm and pictures under the other. Mr. Torrence received me, and gave me such appreciation on the verses I had never yet had from mortal man. And as far as the pictures I had drawn, he desired to submit them to a better authority. A month or so later I received an enthusiastic note from him, saying Miss Gilder had decided to print some of the poems and pictures. At the Critic office, in her name, he accepted eight of the poems, and several of the drawings. And here comes the point. I was informed that Miss Gilder had taken drawings and pictures home to you—you were sick at the time—and that you had said that I was nothing less than a genius in both departments. And Mr. Torrence informed me that the Century Office was waiting to welcome me with open arms. Also that you seldom committed yourself on a youth, but had staked your reputation as a prophet in my case. Now all this was uncalled for, and it made me drunk. There was a cruel morning after. Mr. Torrence requested that I write a 300 word account of my life, from my own standpoint, to be published in the February Critic. He took a magazine in his hand and showed me how there was to be a picture on one page, a poem on the next, a picture on the next, etc, till half a score of pages or so were covered, and as he expressed it, the public be taken by storm, bit hard.

Nothing contented with this, he introduced me to Miss Zona Gale,[2] at the San Remo Hotel, who confirmed all these reports. I was laurelled, petted, and informed in every language that the great Gilder had decided to make me great, that I had no reason to doubt it. I called at the Century office, and found you were at home sick, and they told me to take my drawings around to the Sunday Newspapers. Nothing appeared in the February Critic. In the March Critic appeared The Queen of Bubbles, but the illustration was omitted, and the poem was incomprehensible without it. My grand 300 word life of myself was cut down to a paragraph on page 211. But I was young, and drunk and patient, and afraid of the grand literary Gods. Nothing further appeared till April 1905, when one of my poorer drawings and slighter poems was reproduced.[3] Meanwhile, remembering the approval of the Great Gilder was not to be taken lightly I went home and from June to December wrote my best book with my best illustrations, in which all my poems were given a sort of fairy tale setting. I did all this assuming not that you were a busy editor, but a great searcher who had at last found the genius for whom he had been looking, who was willing to be patient with me a little, and learn my ways. I know now that only a person with imagination white hot could get anything out of the book whatever its merit.

Well, I think it was early that winter, about January or February, a year or so after you had hailed me as the grand discovery of the age, that I left *Aladdin's Lamp* with you, and after two weeks you returned it with a chilly note. Then I awoke from my year's trance. I realized that either Mr. Torrence and Miss Gale brought their imagination to play in every relation of life, or that you had a mighty good forgetter, for the pictures in that book were better than any you had seen before, and the poems were the same you had once praised.

The tale is not ended. I waited through 1906 and 1907 and into 1908 for the rest of my grand array of verses to appear in the Critic—now Putnam's. Last fall as a sort of stimulant I illustrated the six still in their possession, since my drawings had been returned to me. I am confident these pictures were superior to anything I had before done. If my poor little scratches were worthy of praise then, so were these now. These last drawings were returned to me, and about last March or so, the poems, with a letter to the effect that the longer they were kept, the harder they were to print.

So, it seems, I am through with that house, to which your word gave me entrance.

I feel that I still have a claim upon you till you have explained these mysteries. I know an editor's job must be thankless at best, and I can comprehend the score of ways in which you might have been misquoted, and misunderstood. But if I have a claim, I want to know it, and do it justice.

The printed matter I send[4] gives you some notion of what I have been about these last years, at the New York West Side Y.M.C.A. in the Winter months. If you telephone to the *Religious Department* you will be informed as to my ability to interest pious young men in Art, Poetry and the Metropolitan Museum.

I and a bunch of young Art students have given successful picture-shows there, and we have also decorated our rendezvous near by—the Pig and the Goose Restaurant, 355 West 58th Street.[5] If you are at all interested in my progress as a decorator, and an influence among other decorators, you might send a trusty deputy to look the place over. If you are interested in my one other appearance in magazine print, read The Man Under the Yoke in the Outlook, June 1, 1907.[6] If you are interested in my capacity to make musical verse, read the Last Song of Lucifer which I send. If you are interested in my ability to condense the Encyclopaedia Britannica into twenty-eight stanzas, for the benefit of my Y.M.C.A. class in History, read *"God Help us All to be Brave,"*[7] which I send. The poem was very much used in the Religious Department of the West Side Y.M.C.A. this spring, and by telephoning Mr. Hills, Mr. Fisher or Mr. Powlinson, they will give you the details. Also they will tell you what use has been made of my decorative designs in connection with the History Class. If you will telephone to Allen McCurdy, assistant pastor of the Rutgers Presbyterian Church or Dr. Robert McKenzie, pastor, they will inform you that I preached a sermon the Sunday evening a week before Easter, on the *Holiness of Beauty,* in their pulpit.[8]

I propose that you assist me to publish a volume of poems, with my own decorations and embellishments, leading off with the historical poem I send, and using it for the title poem. *The Heroes of Time* might be a better title for it. I have already a design for every stanza. The Y.M.C.A. will certify to the popular quality of the designs.

I will probably be in New York again soon—January the first—that is, to resume my Y.M.C.A. work. Meanwhile, if you are interested, and you really liked my work long ago—you will send me a word of friendship. If you are not—I may not be vexed very much after all, for sometimes I am not interested in Nicholas Vachel Lindsay myself.

Hoping for a glad answer, I remain,

Very Sincerely,

NICHOLAS VACHEL LINDSAY.

Notes

1. Richard Watson Gilder (1844–1909) had edited *Scribner's Monthly* from 1870 to 1881. He took over the editorship of *The Century Magazine* in 1881 and retained it to the day of his death. His books of poetry include *The New Day* (1876) and *Five Books of Song* (1900).
2. Jeannette Gilder (1849–1916), Richard's sister, was in charge of *The Critic,* where (Frederic) Ridgely Torrence, poet and playwright in his own right, then worked. Torrence later became poetry editor of *The New Republic* (1920–33). A friend of William Vaughn Moody and Edwin Arlington Robinson, he was best known for his plays, which were distinctly "Negro" in inspiration. In 1914, at age thirty-nine, he married Olivia H. Dunbar, after sharing a part of his life with Zona Gale when both were involved in the "Villa Laura" community in New York. Zona Gale

(1874—1938) wrote her first novel, *Romance Island,* in 1906. A belated Transcendentalist, she was also a reporter and shared with VL common Midwestern origins and preoccupations.
3. The poem that appeared in the April 1905 *Critic* was "At Noon on Easter Day."
4. "The printed matter" VL was enclosing comprised copies of his YMCA lectures on art.
5. The decoration of the Pig and Goose restaurant had been undertaken along with G. M. Richards, among others, and free meals were obtained for the duration of the project.
6. "The Man Under the Yoke" was reprinted as an episode of *The Handy Guide for Beggars* (pp. 5—13).
7. "God Help Us All to Be Brave," begun in 1905, became "The Heroes of Time" and was eventually printed in the *Collected Poems* under the definitive title "Litany of the Heroes" (pp. 185—94).
8. VL's sermons on "The Holiness of Beauty" illustrate a much cherished theme in his work and thoughts. "The Gospel of Beauty," derived from those sermons, gave its title to *Adventures While Preaching the Gospel of Beauty,* published in 1914, and before that to one of the collections of essays and poems VL took along with him on his 1912 tramp to California. It had been privately printed, as had *Rhymes to Be Traded for Bread,* its companion collection (reprinted in R.F. Sayre's *Vachel Lindsay: Earth Man and Star-Thrower,* Eakins, New York, 1968).

10

TO R. W. GILDER

Springfield, Illinois
October 4, 1908

Mr. Richard Watson Gilder
Editorial Department, Century Magazine
New York City

My Dear Sir:

Your subtle note, offering hearty personal friendship as a balm for official neglect has been gratefully received. I am just old and battered enough to know that your friendship is worth more than a magazine opening, and young and eager enough to take you at your word. I shall consider you my friend out of your office hours and not talk shop.

Of late I find a sort of glory easy to get, easier to get than money, and have not the bitterness of some of the obscure. Therefore a lost chance for eminence does not stab me as once it did.

The friendship of an older man is a peculiar thing. The young man is asked to make good, by the older man, and to report on it from time to time. The older man will take a deep interest, if he is still building up a following, since he is wise enough to know that is the only way to build up enthusiasm of a personal sort for his own work. If he has arrived at a secure position, like the editor of the Century, or several captains of finance I call my friends, his attitude is more that of an uncle, or a grandfather. He wants to see the youngster get there, but he don't want to be disappointed. And having a wide circle of youngsters, he is apt to have a hurried impersonal word of affection for each one, unless some enterprising grandson camps on his doorstep with a letter like this I am writing.

Young as I am, dear sir, I have written letters like this one of yours to me, several different winters to the fifty members of my Y.M.C.A. class in New York. I have made each letter different, though I forgot half the faces and two thirds of the names. I knew, as you do, the value of a personal hold, and the value of spiritual heirs.

So—with this preliminary, be assured I consider your note an open door, but not a letter of adoption. I probably am through with New York for many a day, but if I return I hope to get as well acquainted as you will find comfortable. I consider every veteran's friendship an acquisition to be duly treasured.

I might as well be frank now, and say that while you have liked some of my verses, I have never liked any of yours. That clears the air on that score. But I have the profoundest respect for the magazine you have fostered, as the thunderer, the Times among magazines, the type for them all—the point of departure and return for them all. Also for the type of citizen-life you have led I have the profoundest respect, and wish there were many more of your sort. There are probably other things about you deserving of praise—but these have come directly in my way.

I know that as a rule, the genuine communion of souls is between disciples only a day or so younger, and their teacher who is disguised as a comrade. I learned long ago to look for the sure thing of friendship from men of ability a little younger, and young disciples and comrades are the only necessities. The older man is merely a recorder of things done, a recognizer of the accomplished fact. The old men that value me, do it because of the young men I bind to me, the young men who seem to understand me. They—the old men—do not expect to understand. They examine credentials, and take the rest for granted. All these things are set forth in better style in a paragraph of F. W. H. Myers sketch of Wordsworth[1]—where first I learned them. But I have found them true one hundred times in New York.

So sir, I have qualified my zeal for your friendship with many words, but I hope I have not abated your interest in my blatant ego. Shameless and sinful honesty shall be our beginning, however we end.

I send you a booklet,[2] which demonstrates that I am setting forth on the joyous task of building up a little following here, similar to that I have in New York. I assure you there is no drunkenness like that which comes to the soul when you have stirred a young man's ideals and made him talk about his philosophy of life till twelve o'clock over a cup of cocoa—or as the Y.M.C.A. puts it—a "social hour".

My greatest follies will come about because these boys have flattered me, and made me think myself an infallible oracle, my greatest sacrifices will be to win the drink of their praise. Incidentally, I hope to build up a new generation of "leading citizens in embryo" in this Y.M.C.A. Springfield needs a new civic ideal, nearer that of Florence or Athens, and the Y.M.C.A. is the natural place to preach it. We have a big new booming Association, and in ten years, if I am here every fall, I may build up a saving remnant who will love civic beauty as well as civic righteousness, and legitimate civic revelry, as well as puritanic reform.

Rehab and Mammon have ruled this town a long time, and its only hope is to make itself unique. Reformers cannot be always screeching, and young men cannot be always fleeing from temptation. Almost all of the fellows who graduated from High School with me here twelve years ago[3] have gone, with disgust. There was only commonplace success for the sober-minded and ambitious, there was only commonplace vice for the gilded youth. They left the town to the fools, the villains and the weak. The Y.M.C.A. crumbled and blew away. Politics fostered and broke a dozen times. Therefore riot and scandal. We have had three or four murders—two suicides since the riots that had nothing to do with them.

These people need a vision of a possible Springfield. We need better music, theatres, carnivals, customs, we need to make it a matter of peculiar distinction to be the honorable Lord Mayor of this town, even if we have to dress the poor man up in a ruff and knee britches—excuse me breeches.

In New York—though I always drink soft drinks, I buy poison liquor for my friends, and we have many noble conversations in beer-gardens. But here I find myself the rabidest kind of a local option man,[4] hating the two brewery [organs], though one is well written, and loving the two local option papers, though both are indifferent-smart. And I would as soon step into a fire as a saloon. Local Option will win, then we will have a sad time of it, a clean and deadly town. The election comes in two years. If we haven't the dream of a lovelier Springfield, we will be no better off.

Very sincerely,

NICHOLAS VACHEL LINDSAY

Notes

1. The "sketch of Wordsworth" by F. W. H. Myers was written in 1881 for the "English Men of Letters Series." VL had read it at Hiram College.
2. VL had left New York April 28, 1908, and walked back to Hiram, Ohio. In August he had witnessed the Springfield race riots. He had lectured a great deal for the YMCA in Sangamon County. The booklet mentioned here must have been a small collection of lectures, drawings, and short epigrammatic texts on ethnic diversity and its importance in building America, as illustrated by "On the Building of Springfield," the title of a poem written that year.
3. VL had actually graduated from Springfield High School in June 1897, eleven not "twelve years ago."
4. VL's lectures for the Anti-Saloon League began officially in 1909. He talked every Sunday in the mining towns of Sangamon County surrounding Springfield. Though a "dry," VL was not so out of strict principle. Always tolerant of "wets," he later held the amendment on prohibition to be inadequate. See his letters to his wife and to H. L. Mencken. His fight against the saloon and the "bartender" found its way into his poetry in such poems as "The Drunkard's Funeral" (*Collected Poems*, p. 147) and "The Drunkards in the Street" (*Collected Poems*, p. 289), "On Reading Omar Khayyam" (*Collected Poems*, p. 337), and "Drink for Sale" (*Collected Poems*, p. 336).

11

TO R. W. GILDER

Springfield Illinois
November 6, 1908

Mr. Richard Watson Gilder
The Century Magazine—

My Dear Sir:
You ask me how Lincoln's name counts in this town. He is of course a convenient climax for sermons on civic righteousness, but none of them have been much heeded. The negro is as heartedly [sic] hated here as anywhere by the general populace. As far as the sober can see, we are as likely to have ten riots as one. But I can tell you more in a future letter. I am going to give the matter a special probing this week. Next Wednesday we have a special discussion on the negro, for which I must prepare, and if possible I may turn the material into an article for the Outlook.

I hate the necessary probing into the tenderloin where the whole business began and ended, and the interviews with the self-avowed political sinners who run the town, and who have the information.

Lincoln stands with those of us who have him in our hearts, as the great example of a ruler risen from the ranks, rather than as a friend of the negro. He satisfies so well the dream of a straight road from the log cabin to the white house. So I was taught in the Springfield ward schools, and the Lincoln patriotism triumphed over the political opinions of a Southern-feeling household. If there were ever two things my father wanted me to do they were to hate Lincoln and the Republican Party. My school training was enough to counteract this, though it was well through High School before the prejudice was all gone. There is a bank here called the Lincoln Bank—owned by a Lincoln-collector, one of the miniature skyscrapers of the town. It has a dignity justifying its name.

There are twenty five thousand visitors a year to the Lincoln home.

Of course, Springfield people know the Negro's debt to Lincoln, but as the theme grows more perplexing, they do not like to think on it, and not through any disrespect, they think of him in the matter he surely accomplished—the restoration of the union, and the furnishing of a great example of Americanism. We know too well he did not completely solve the race question.

You ask of me the list of my preferences in verse. I have been lecturing on poets these three or four years, and have grown mighty orthodox—it gives a new value to folks I had long taken for granted, like Tennyson, Kipling, Lanier[1]—to explain them to a Y.M.C.A. audience one is forced to exaggerate the commonplace in them, and find it not so commonplace after all. So my poetical authors are the regulation list, beginning with Shakespeare, Milton and coming forward to Yeats, and not leaving out any one mentioned in big type in the Literature primers. I have become so inveterate an interpreter in styles of architecture and painting and sculpture that I am still less conscious of preferences there and feel a discomfort over the omission of *any* of the leading spectacles along the corridors of time, from Edfu to Madison Square.

I remember when I struck the Art Institute Chicago—the only collections I enjoyed were the Japanese and the Egyptian. That was in 1900. My first love among the Poets was Edgar Poe—when I first entered High School. I could have been called a Poe-crank for my whole High School period. Thinking it all over now, without the book of poems in my hand, in a most matter-of-fact mood—I can say that Ulalume is one of the great works of art to me, and no other work of his has the same staying power—I know of nothing in the catalogue of beautiful things for which I have more respect. At the same time I cannot make others see it, and as a Y.M.C.A. spellbinder Kipling's Galley-slave far excels it. Even when I add the devotion of my heart to Ulalume, the audience is indifferent. I went through all phases with Poe—from the Griswold point of view to the Ingram; then Woodberry, Stedman and Woodberry at last.[2] Long ago I gave him up as a man—he was a pretty small potato after all. But if I wrote a story—I would like to write Ligeia, Elenora, The Masque of the Red Death, The Fall of the House of Usher, The Manuscript Found in a Bottle. Of them all—I have reread Ligeia, and the Red Death till I spend years trying to forget them, that I may read them afresh. I have a pretty good forgetter, but these two I have reread to an extent that was really outrageous. I have made whole parlorfulls of boarding-house folks listen to them against their will, when they were impatient to play charades. Still Poe was a folly of me youth. Swinburne was the folly of seven years later. From 1900 till I began to lecture—he was an obsession. I began with a second-hand copy of Ballads and Sonnets. A school teacher had owned the book once and had satisfied her conscience by writing "Dreadful" "Horrible but beautiful" "Artistic but scandalous" "A loftier strain" etc all through. With my gentle female guide, I did a deal of slumming, grinning all the while, but after all I tore out most that she condemned and felt like a gentleman. And I memorized the rest—the "Loftier Strain" in our Lady of Pain, and all the choruses of Atalanta, and the Hymn to Proserpina, which was almost a religious revelation to me, and the Deserted Garden, and others I memorized later. The only thing that moderated my pace was the fact that one cannot lecture on Swinburne twice a week. I believe I would have gone clear daft over the man's music, if I had not been compelled to study the other men, to prepare lectures. Yet I cannot respect the man. His picture betrays him. He is a bigger personality than Poe, but there is something weak, uncanny and perverted in his face. I would strenuously defend him to a Y.M.C.A. audience, as having a right to his liberty, and to live out the twisted personality God gave him, but I doubt if I would like to meet him. And I might add that his range of subject matter betrays him. His Hebraic note is splendid and sincere, his "Ode to Athens" point of view is the same, his blast for freedom is affected fanatical, pedantic and artificial in the impression it makes, whatever the heart behind it. His vice is likewise affected, fanatical, pedantic, artificial.

Poe at the beginning and Swinburne at the end of what I might call the Hot House period of my life, are my two great passions. I do not remember any passions in my private life to compare with them, and in a public way nothing so vast has entered my blood, except the hunger for praise. That is, nothing in the domain of unreason. I love History, but that is reasonable and Comparative Religion, but that is reasonable. At one time or another I have read most all of the poets with enthusiasm. I have had months when I talked little else but Milton. And there are few that like him, as I discovered. Of late I have been re-reading Byron, with a great admiration for what may be called his European significance, his place in the history of the times. Here was a rhymer who made them bow down—a rhymer whom even the newspapers had to respect, whose stanzas were more sincere than the proclamations of Napoleon and as much a part of the life of the time.

So many of my dearest friends don't see a place for the rhymer in the world—here is one they would have been compelled to bow down to. When I loved Poe I could not love this rhetorician—this bombastic half-educated rake, this affected Byron—but I have lived just long enough to feel that Don Juan is pretty wholesome plain speaking, and Art be hanged.

Any editor who can produce such a combination of bitter preachment and pregnant political shouting is entitled to my admiration, and my envy, even if he does it in makeshift rhyme. Brother Byron impresses me as a misbehaving but wholesome kind of a person, pretty near to a full sized man, though not a great brain, not a great artist, of course. I read him just a little, and admire him a great deal.

What are your literary adventures of late? Or any other adventures! I am sure the Singer building[3] is one of the most beautiful things in the world, in some lights and aspects, but possibly I may not return to walk under its shadow, being very fond of old Sangamon County Illinois. So tell me all about the new wonders in the old town.

Very sincerely,

NICHOLAS VACHEL LINDSAY

Notes

1. VL had given a series of lectures on Lanier in January 1907 at the New York YMCA.
2. Rufus Wilmot Griswold, John Henry Ingram, Edmund Clarence Stedman, (1833–1908), and George Edward Woodberry were all noted Poe critics. Woodberry (1855—1930) was a poet in his own right and VL's contemporary. Ingram, a clerk in the London General Post Office, wrote *Edgar Allan Poe, His Life, Letters and Opinions* (London, 1886: J. Hogg, 2 vols.). Woodberry's biography, *Edgar Allan Poe* (1885; rep. 2 vols. 1909), VL had read early. Griswold (1815—57) worked with Poe on *Graham's Magazine* and was probably the most unreliable source upon which VL could have drawn: Horace Greeley once branded Griswold "the worst liar and least likable man in American literature" and "the most expert and judicious thief who ever handled scissors." Ingram's biography of Poe was the first to denounce and correct Griswold's "errors." VL's lifelong insistence on Poe's "magic" represents a view easily acquired by reading the works of critics who had not done much to remove the coat of the "jingleman" from Poe's shoulders. VL later suffered an identical predicament at the hands of other critics. For further comments on Poe, see, in particular, letters 21 and 94.
3. The Singer Building had just been completed in New York. Forty-seven stories

high, it remained the highest in the city until the Metropolitan Life Insurance Building and the Woolworth Building topped it a few years later. VL's passion for skyscrapers was transcribed in parts of *The Art of the Moving Picture* (1916) and many later poems and articles.

12

TO R. W. GILDER

Springfield Illinois
November 29, 1908

My Dear Mr. Gilder:

It gives me the greatest pleasure to acknowledge the arrival of your book of verses. When I have read more of it I will say more about the inside. But the mere act means a deal. I am glad that any one living in our town is so much worth your while. I wish we knew just how to rehabilitate Springfield in the eyes of the world.[1] We cannot get juries that will do anything to the rioters. Yet the rioters did not represent public opinion, do not represent it. It's so hard to get law and order people on the jury.

I think every middle sized town faces the same issue—the lack of a medieval wall,[2] to keep her talent at home. The really able people have their interest centered elsewhere, the network of civilization makes them almost as interested in the remotest part of the land, as their own city. They look to centers of culture or finance in the big cities. They contribute to eastern magazines. They are in National politics. Their money is in statewide corporations. Every really able household is more sensitive to college circles, religious circles, etc, than to civic. Only those ill-educated or wicked, whose sole reading is the local paper, whose sole politics is ward politics, who have travelled little, and whom our able people never influence, take a first hand interest in the town.

The only way out is to build a medieval wall around our city culture, till the musicians, writers, artists, architects have a direct influence upon the history of the town.[3] I am going to see what can be done toward getting them together at the Y.M.C.A., or here in my room. Also I want to try what can be done with the boys of 12 to 16 in the matter of Civic Patriotism, especially along the line of the City Beautiful. I want them to feel what a glory it is to build a town. None of them have ever realized what a real Florence would be like. It is a beautiful opportunity. I take up my work with the Y.M.C.A. Juniors in a week.

I know I will find in your verses the kind of a man who cares for these things. You helped to make New York a place worthy of the pilgrimage of a great many of my fellow students there. I have seen your name on all sorts of committees. I remember your verse on the City Club printed matter—"Our city *must be noble, must be pure*".

I have found plenty of "Lincoln Collectors" in the town. You ask for some man whose life was formed on Lincoln's. There are plenty of politicians who collect relics, and old families proud of personal reminiscences. In this house where I write he often visited, in the parlor down stairs he has attended receptions.[4] But I do not know any man with sufficient intimacy to say that Lincoln formed his soul, or has made him any greater than he was naturally. J. McCarm Davis, a local politician advertises himself as "A Republican of the Stalwart Lincoln Type". There you are.

The sort of people who do not riot have certainly invoked Lincoln's name in season and out, since the riot. He has certainly helped to form the public opinion that exists among them. They keenly feel that his ashes and his home are a sacred trust—but men have been ruled off our juries who have confessed to reading sermons of this character. The defense will not have them. It is hard to know which is Springfield. I never meet a friend but speaks of Lincoln with honor, of the Riot with shame. But when I go down town Saturday night I do not see one face I know—people by the thousands pouring by. What they want on the square Saturday night is a mystery to me. Our parks are beautiful and well lit then, but absolutely deserted. That Saturday night bunch furnishes our jurors and our rioters as well. I do not see them at the Y.M.C.A., the Church, nor on the street in the daytime. They are workmen from the suburbs, farmers in town for a good time, hired girls and their beaus, and all that and all that. There were forty thousand people in Springfield when I left about '97. Now that I return there are sixty thousand and men prophesy one hundred thousand. The twenty thousand new people are all on our streets Saturday night. All the newspapers preach law and order, and all the business associations. And we will not have new riots, because it "hurts business" and taxes for riot damages will come heavily for two years: But how much the name of Lincoln is revered by our Saturday night crowd I do not know. They hate the negro because he is a rival in manual labor. I think it is a calumny that they tried to burn the home of Lincoln. I do not find any one in the town who believes it, but I shall ask the keeper of the home.

There are 4000 negroes in town, 300 were driven out.[5]

I am not such a "pretending workman" as you may think. I thoroughly enjoy unskilled, unthinking labor for three months at a time. I worked in Marshall Field's wholesale building, Chicago, from September to Christmas, pushing a big truck, about 1900, and in New York about three years ago or four—I spent about the same period in the Nicholls tubing works, rolling cotton bales up out of the cellar to be woven into tubes—the kind that are used on drop-lights—and carrying tubes in bunches of twenty five across the factory on my shoulders, and packing them in barrels and boxes. I enjoy that sort of a thing immensely. Also I turned tramp twice in my life, once through Florida, Georgia, North Carolina, Tennessee and Kentucky, once through New Jersey and Pennsylvania, into Ohio. I have perfect confidence in the Generosity of North and South, and could start out tonight at seven o'clock and make for San Francisco afoot, without a cent—in the rain—and get there with more pleasure than pain. Being a miner is more respectable than this I suppose, and I welcome the excuse, for the side of life it brings will be allied to the Tramp life, yet will have a Y.M.C.A. excuse. They are blowing the poor fellows up at a terrible rate these days—it is certainly a live issue.

Unless I mistake my destiny, I shall go deeper and deeper into this side of life as I grow older, it is my goal—I have cut every cord that could hold me back from any sort of industrial experiment. I am under financial social personal obligation to not a mortal in the world—at least under no obligation that will keep me from this sort of a thing. Only gradually and at considerable cost have I cut my spiritual and social cords. I am under obligations to work at speaking and mining for the Y.M.C.A. here for one year—but that serves my purpose, and is not rigidly binding.

Now I will tell you something fantastic. I would like to start a new order of Franciscans—of the strict observance—with the vows of chastity and absolute poverty, (not humility, alas!). I would like them to be art students of the highest culture, and Sir Galahads, every one. I would like to put them on the high roads of America to preach the hatred of money, and the gospel of poverty, and beauty, and the free gifts of the sun and rain, to every hamlet in the land. But alas, the most talented friends I have are either money lovers or Launcelots of some sort, or married and committed to the present social system. I must wait a long time I am afraid, to set up my orders.

I thank you for permission to paste your long and generous letter into my copy of your work. I feel sure I will get a good many insights into Richard Watson Gilder, in the next few weeks. It will be as though you had been writing to me all your days. I have two friends in this town who have spoken to me about your verses. One, a school teacher,[6] a veteran inspirer of the young in our High School, spoke of your work last summer with the greatest loyalty and admiration and my best young lady friend at present—who is reading your book with me had already developed the same loyalty.

Tonight at ten I go out to inspect a mine all night. I shall remember your letter in the black lungs of the earth.

Brook-farm—tut-tut—my father was raised in a Kentucky log cabin, though it ruled a big farm. He taught me something about real work.

Very sincerely

NICHOLAS VACHEL LINDSAY

Notes

1. The opening reference is to the August 1908 Springfield race riots.
2. "The medieval wall" of which he dreams he will find in the works of Ralph Adams Cram (1863—1942)—*Walled Towns*—and in the "Rim Rock" of Spokane in 1924.
3. For VL's ideas on city planning and architecture, see *The Golden Book of Springfield, The Village Magazine, The Art of the Moving Picture,* and the series of articles he wrote for the Spokane papers entitled "Lumberjack Philosophy" (*Spokane Chronicle*, August 1, 1928, to January 30, 1929).
4. The house where VL lived (603 South Fifth, Springfield) had once seen a reception by Mrs. O. M. Smith, who was related to Lincoln, which Lincoln had attended.
5. Elsewhere (*Collected Poems*, p. 23), VL says the black population represented 20 percent of the total population of Springfield. The correct figure, as examplified here, is closer to 6 percent (*Source*: Statistics of the U.S. Bureau of the Census).
6. The schoolteacher mentioned here is Susan Wilcox.

13

TO FLOYD DELL—*The Chicago Evening Post*

Springfield, Illinois
September 6, 1909

Dear Sir:[1]

It will give me great pleasure to have you repeat my offer in regard to the Tramp's Excuse[2] in the Literary Review. The Last Song of Lucifer may be had on the same terms, if you think it worth mentioning. The Tree of Laughing Bells is out of print, but I will be glad to know your opinion of it, in a private way, just the same. It has been praised excessively by Robert Henri, the master who meant most to me in New York, in Art, and Fred Richardson, whose Composition Classes meant most in Chicago. But most folks pass it by, even when they like my stuff—most civilized folks. Around the firesides in the south, where they couldn't read or write, it was treated with hospitality, when I recited it.

If you will take the Preface to my book, The Tramp's Excuse, The Explanation of the Map of the Universe,[3] in conjunction with the enclosed printed matter, you will grasp me according to my usual methods of advertising, and also understand the central springs of that advertising. I have often tried in one way or another to spring on my small public the stuff that is organized in *The Map of the Universe*, but since I have only given it in bits and threads, in between the routine of work and study, they have set me down as one likely to become irresponsible at a certain point—that is when I talk about what really concerns me.

In War Bulletin Number Three and The Tramp's Excuse, they get the whole system at one fell swoop. Or rather it emerges cautiously in the Hymn to the Sun,[4] and in *Heaven*, and *The Little Yellow Bird*, and *The Sorceress*, and *Aladdin's Lamp*, and then the fell swoop at the end of the book. If you can assure the dear public that I *have* a system, that I am *not* disorganized or irresponsible, that all I require is patience and a second reading—well—I will be deeply grateful.

Very Sincerely

Nicholas Vachel Lindsay
223 South 6th

I may add—that *patience* is the one quality the American Person of Talent does not possess—however talented he may be. And as to the Average citizen—you are a newspaper man—you know.

Notes

1. Floyd Dell (1887–1969), a reporter since 1905 on a Davenport, Iowa, paper, became assistant literary editor of the *Chicago Evening Post* (in 1909) and succeeded Francis Hackett as its editor in 1911. He became associate editor of *The Masses* (1914—17) and of *The Liberator* (1918—24), having left Chicago for New York in 1913.
2. *The Tramp's Excuse* was the title of *War Bulletin* Number 4, published in September 1909. *War Bulletin* Number 1 had been issued by VL on July 19, Number 2 on August 4, and Number 3 on August 30. Number 5 came out around Thanksgiving Day that same year.
3. "The Explanation of the Map of the Universe" was reprinted in *The Village Magazine* in all its successive editions.
4. "The Hymn to the Sun" reappears in the *Collected Poems* (p. lii) under the title "Johnny Appleseed's Hymn to the Sun." It first appeared in *The Tramp's Excuse* along with "In Heaven," "The Little Yellow Bird of Weariness," "Aladdin's Lamp and the Cities of the Wise."

14

TO E. S. AMES

Quincy, Illinois
September 26 1909

My Dear Dr. Ames:
Under separate cover I have sent you The Tramps Excuse—a collection of my best shorter verses, and The Creed of a Beggar[1]—a summary of my pet religious ideas. Any one who will certify that he is a habitual reader of poetry is welcome to a copy of the book, as long as they last.

I feel that the beggar's Creed will appeal to you more than to Dr. Willett[2] or Editor Morrison.[3] I feel they will consider it in the light of the poems and take it for the poem's sake, though I may be wrong.

My best and most interested friends say that the War Bulletin number three is wild, illogical, inconsistent, anarchistic and obscure. It must be all there, for they all say so. Nevertheless, though it be a poor thing, it is my naked soul, an honest and tolerably well proportioned confession, a photograph of the ideas to which I hold most tenaciously. It does me this service at least. People cannot overestimate me or mistake me any more. They know where I stand, though it be on most dubious ground. Through the very composite character of my creed, one friend grasped one part, one another—before it was printed—now they have it all. You fellows get after Billy Sunday. I owe to him the line—"The Personal Savior from Sin"—. I cannot altogether reject one who gave me that.

I signed his card with all my heart. Also I chose between two masters—Buddha and Christ—and thenceforth Buddha was only my brother.

One difficulty with the creed is its extreme condensation. I could write a whole Bulletin on each phrase. Some phrases, such as "Christ the Singing Immanuel" condense years of search and discovery, which you will realize if you read the last poem in my book and the lines of Explanation in the preface.

Bulletin Number three was written with reference to my home town. I was active in so many kinds of work, and I could not bear to be misunderstood by my fellow-workers. They must know how I stand, even if it costs me their confidence. And then I wanted a sort of commentary to send along with the Tramp's Excuse, as I send it to you.

The Story of the Boats of the Prophets[4] was written long ago. It represents a self that is only asleep, not dead. Yet to many of my friends it is my first big declaration on the Mystical point of view, and they cannot stomach it, and they assume it is a sudden aberration on my part. As a matter of fact I published it in justice to one whole phase of my past life, and my present mood is more in the poem on The Building of Springfield, or Why I voted the Socialist Ticket.[5] Still, the very printing of the Bulletin brought back some of the old self, and it is only because of the rude joggles of this practical world that I let the mysteries alone today. I feel way underneath a hundred stories like the Boats of the Prophets—but no one wants to hear them. So I lecture for the Anti-Saloon League.

Mr. Hallinan Editor of the Evening Post[6] has spoken of you with a great deal of loyalty in a recent letter. He says he swears by you. I am glad to hear it. I have just written in regard to the Bulletin and the poems to Morrison and Dr. Willett. I will be glad to send the book to any list of your friends who will truly truly [*sic*] care for it. And I can spare a lot of War Bulletins—(Number Three)

Very Sincerely

NICHOLAS VACHEL LINDSAY
603 South Sixth
Springfield Illinois

(In Quincy only today)

Notes

1. "The Creed of a Beggar" opened *War Bulletin* Number Three.
2. For information on Dr. Willett, see note 2 to letter 2.
3. Charles Clayton Morrison headed the Disciples Publication Society.
4. "The Story of the Boats of the Prophets" was a part of *Where Is Aladdin's Lamp?* and a metaphor for VL's views on redemption. "The Empty Boats" (*Collected Poems*, p. 350) relays part of its contents. "I Heard Immanuel Singing" (*Collected Poems*, p. 369) was composed after a vision VL had on board ship returning from Europe in the early fall of 1906. It brought together his notion of an Apollo-like Christ figure linking his own aesthetic and mystic views.
5. "Why I Voted the Socialist Ticket" is on p. 301 of the *Collected Poems*.
6. The editor of the *Chicago Evening Post* was T. J. Hallinan.

15

TO E. S. AMES

Springfield, Illinois
October 21, 1909

My Dear Doctor Ames:
Will your friends care, if I write to them? The letter I enclose appears to be to you exclusively, but with your permission, I will keep the rest. I am just beginning to hear from the book from strangers not yet in my circle, and it braces me up wonderfully. There was such a consuming silence about War Bulletin Number Three that I was about to lose my nerve. But your friends have taken it as well as I could ask—they have met me half-way, so I begin to feel it is not below my standard. T. J. Hallinan of the Evening Post is the only person who has taken it for just exactly what it is worth—and a bit more. He took it as a unit. Its contradictions are a part of the plot as it were. They were no more my own devising than is my own skeleton, with one shoulder lighter than the other. Every line in War Bulletin Number Three records deep grooves in my soul, wrought by Time and *inveterate habit,* and hardly a point in it but has been a matter of daily speculation and conversation sometime within the last few years.

People who absolutely reject it are absolutely rejecting me, and it is plain such people want me to be utterly and entirely different from myself. Of course I can expect to be met no more than half-way by the best people—a half-way meeting, such as your friends have given me is all *I* can give to any man. I am vastly pleased with both letters. I am rather amused at the list of my "Literary Influences". My knowledge

Whitman, Browning, Oscar Wilde,
Maeterlink and the Vedas

 . . .   of the poets mentioned, even the "Vedas" is most perfunctory or *non-devotional* at least. The Mahavagga is Pali from Ceylon. Most of my Buddhist enthusiasm was born from the study of *Architectural Remains* in the South Kensington Museum and the British Museum, especially the marvellous gates and rails and reliquaries from the Sanchi and Amaraviti Topes. You will do well to assume with my ideas of History and Religion that it all came in through the eye first, and any distortion came later. My eye is orthodox sir. I have not lectured these years in a well balanced museum for nothing.[1]

As for my ideas of *art form* in poetry—and pen and ink drawing—they
are formed definitely by four men: Poe, Coleridge (in his two or three
magical poems) Blake and Beardsley. Then again—Poe, Coleridge Blake
and Beardsley. Then again—Poe, Coleridge, Blake and Beardsley. These
are the *necromancers*, the *Wizards*, the *Magi* in English—and Beardsley
is the solitary magician in pen and ink. I read other poets more—now,
I think I have a most orthodox and well-balanced list of enthusiasms,
from Shakespeare to Keats, and I do not set the men I have named
above the rest. But they are *my* masters, they have done *my* special kind
of a thing, and I will consider I have made myself understood the more
my work is compared with theirs, artistically, and its shortcomings noted
from that standpoint. None of these were full Shakespeare-sized men,
though supreme in their own way. But Rembrandt who ranks with
Shakespeare, was a wizard with the brush, and it is a comfort to me to
think of him as a supreme world-conquering artist, who was almost
exclusively a wizard. It is as though Shakespeare had expanded Macbeth
and the Tempest into twenty cosmic plays. And it is as definite and
individual an art-feeling as is the Greek temperance and serenity, as the
Gothic Savagery and Aspiration. The Egyptian Priesthood for thousands
of years struck this one note, for thousands of years their pylons, Pyr-
amids, Mummies and obelisks overwhelmed the people by their vast
suggestion of *Magic*. It is as though one vast man had designed it all.
So not only Rembrandt the Supreme but Egypt the Eternal found room
in this point of view for supreme attainment.

Maeterlinck and the folks of the Celtic revival owe a deal to the
writers I have named, and acknowledge it.[2] I have never settled down
to give them the attention they deserve, and cannot acknowledge them
as influences, however glad I would be to do so.

Wizards and prophets have always fought for supremacy in my soul,
their work does not always run parallel. Wizardry is the Art of the
Unseen, while by comparison Religion is the Morals of the Unseen. The
Map of the Universe is *Wizardry*, it has no morals, or logic, to speak of.

Well—well—your friends [*sic*] letters have cheered me immensely.

Very sincerely

Nicholas Vachel Lindsay

Miss Conger's poem on the Sun of Faith is *The Goods*. Tell her I want
more.[3]

Notes

1. VL had visited the British Museum during his 1906 European tour, as well as the Louvre in Paris and many other museums in Belgium and Germany,
2. Maurice Maeterlinck's "The Blue Bird" had come out in 1909.
3. Mary Josephine Conger was editor and publisher of *Progressive Woman*, a feminist paper, from 1907 to 1914. She wrote and published poems in local Chicago papers early in life and became editor of *Home Life Magazine* (1915—18) and *The Mother's Magazine*. She may be the person referred to here.

16

TO WITTER BYNNER

Springfield Illinois
November 10, 1909

My Dear Mr. Bynner:[1]
It gives me a deal of pleasure to send you the printed matter under separate cover. I have read your verse with pleasure and edification, and, as you say to me, would be glad to read more. If you have any of your volumes about you, please send to my house—603 South 5th.

I send you the printed matter[2] in duplicate, hoping you will hand the extra copy to the smartest man you know. If you know any one of our sort in England, send it there. I have a fancy I would like to know a few rhymers in England, since I have a bit of a circle of friends in both Chicago and New York. I want to feel the rhyming pulse of the world. I want to walk through England some day and call on a poet or so. Think it over.

The War Bulletin had two purposes—at least. First—I was tired of trying to peddle manuscripts. I wanted a place where I could print a thing as soon as I wrote it, and hand it to my growing circle of friends. Secondly I was so advertised and boosted by the Y.M.C.A. here that the whole town seemed to see those mystic syllables written on my forehead with all their sugary sanctity, conservatism and officialdom. Everything I said was listened to and everything applauded and *ignored*.

So I started the War Bulletin and told them all to Go to Hell in so many words on the first page. Since then I have had the fixed wrathful *attention* of my betrayed community. The Creed of a Beggar caused more cases of Spiritual Indigestion and Sea Sickness than anything since the

Whale swallowed Jonah by mistake. Since the Chicago Papers have taken me up my neighbors have given up the really painful hypothesis that I have gone mad—(which hypothesis I can never laugh about—somehow), and have decided I am merely a cuss with a touch of intellect, and I am fairly happy watching them squirm under credentials brought in from out of town. I am solid with all four newspapers here, and everything in the way of a newspaper clipping gets re-printed locally. I'll educate old Springfield yet. No man however, so far, from the Presbyterian Minister to the Swedenborgian leader of the Single Tax group, can understand the Creed of a Beggar. If the editor of the Chicago Evening Post had not written me a long, perfectly comprehending and sympathetic letter, I would have decided I had worms in my skull, for I have used that creed a long time.

I want to be judged when I die by Poe, Beardsley, Blake and Coleridge. I want to be considered a small imitator of those large men, in all matters of Art Form and Art Motive. I feel that the estimate in the Friday Literary Review is just, well balanced and merciful, as to the *soul* part of my work.

If your letter had come at night, my answer would have been short. It comes in the morning, and I am all too wordy about my poor self.

If you ever see the Greatest Man in the United States—the Villon who does not lie—the Prince in Disguise, the Blear Reincarnation of God-knows-who, the Seventh Son of a Seventh Son, the long lost Dauphin, that rare reprint of the Anatomy of Melancholy, the happy and vine crowned child of an Ink Bottle and a Waste Basket, Brother of Wilkins Micawber though lean, Brother of James McNeill Whistler though amiable, brother of Christopher Marlowe though Virtuous, Brother of St. Francis though a Pagan, in short—if you ever see W. S. Dunbar[3] print collector, Stogy Smoker and Universal Statesman—give him my love. He is the only man in the world *I* know, that *you* know. I presume I owe the honor of your letter to him. Peace to his ashes—his stogy ashes.

Having many more things to write without the necessary presumption to write them

I remain
Very Sincerely Yours

NICHOLAS VACHEL LINDSAY

Notes

1. Witter "Hal" Bynner (1881—1968) was associate editor of *McClure's*, then worked with the firm of Small, Maynard and Company. Very much influenced by Chinese and American Indian poetry, he was a close friend of Arthur Davison Ficke, with whom he put together in 1916 the "Spectrist" hoax. "Spectra" was supposed to be the work of two new adherents of the Imagist school, "Emmanuel Morgan and Anne Knish." Bynner published *Pins for Wings* in 1920 under the name of Emmanuel Morgan, and *Caravan* in 1925 under his own name. Also associated with the hoax was Marjorie Allen Seifert, under the name of "Elijah Hay."
2. The printed matter enclosed by VL was copies of the *War Bulletins*.
3. On W. S. Dunbar, see letter 21.

17

TO LUCY BATES

Springfield Ill
Thursday evening
May 26, 1910

My Dear Lucy:[1]
Tonight I saw you dance, and that is all I remember of the play. I feel that I understand for the first time what a free spirit is, delivered from mortal mind. Your name is Ariel. Your soul is sister to Shelley and Adonais. Your artistry and inspiration are from on high and there is no touch of the earth on your sandals. I quoted Scripture to myself: "That which is perfect is come". I wish I could write the Greek of the age of Sophocles and praise you in the name of Apollo. Well done, little sister, well done. I have seen thousands of dancers, but have never seen dancing before.

Very sincerely

NICHOLAS VACHEL LINDSAY

Note

1. Lucy Bates (no relation to Katharine Lee Bates) was a Springfield friend of VL's. The poem "How a Little Girl Danced" was probably written in the wake of that performance. It was originally published in March 1914 in Margaret Anderson's *Little Review* (pp. 18—19) and is reproduced on p. 64 of the *Collected Poems*, inscribed to Lucy Bates. It was first subtitled "Being a Reminiscence of Certain Private Theatricals."

18

TO WITTER BYNNER

Springfield Ill.
July 6, 1910.

My Dear Mr. Bynner:
The list of approved verses that got me under the fifth rib is about half the book.[1] *Hill Songs*, The Robin, Clover, The Hypocrite, *The Pretty Ladies*, the Chaplet, Marcello Marco, *Now O My Mother*, The Interval, *Bacchanalian*, Two Songs, *The Lantern*, Mari Spiridonava.

Those underlined [italics as typeset] contain the most adhesive properties, so far as my mortal mind is concerned. I have not read your work for ten days, and going over your table of contents these remain dewy fresh in the memory. Your book travels in my suit-case when I go out to speak for the Anti-Saloon League, and affords me consolation on the long train rides. Thus sir, you indirectly enhance and make effective the work of the Church Militant. I shall see to it that Gabriel puts it down to your credit whenever his moving finger writes.

You ought to hear me roar on Sundays.[2] And I wear a Black tailed coat. In fact I am completely disguised as a country preacher.

Tell me something about yourself. I like the style of your correspondence, only it isn't steady enough. By some slight hints you have dropped, you are in the condition of the man who has been saved without being sanctified. A man in that peculiarly romantic condition is always a good correspondent, especially for us fellows who can't sin, and who have to depend upon men of the world to know what is really going on. Its like compounding a felony, isn't it? We let the other fellows pull the chestnuts of experience out of the fire, while we supply the Philosophy and the Sermons.

Well, each man is gloriously called to his station in life, and Hypocrisy has always attracted me as a calling. Its just as the Bartender says—if *I* don't sell the stuff, the other man will. So if I don't put on the black coat and white tie—the other fellow will. There's *got* to be a certain number of Hypocrites to guard the doors of respectability, and see that everybody but Walt Whitman keeps his shirt on. I like the pious air. It becomes me. Now call me St. Nick all you please to do so.

I wish I was man enough to write a memorial of O. Henry.[3] Please write an In Memoriam of him that will show what the Real folks think.

In his last book are two masterpieces—A Municipal Report and Past One at Rooneys. The Volume is entitled Strictly Business. Our friend

Brand Whitlock[4] seems to have stirred up all the animals by his pamphlet on The Enforcement of Law in Cities. There is one reformer who writes like a gentleman.

The Turn of the Balance is a great book.

The Village Magazine[5] which I am illustrating and writing at present is intended for two sorts of folks. (1) The preachers and farmers I encounter in the small towns in Illinois on my Anti-Saloon Expeditions. I meet *wonderful people* every Sunday, and find the loveliest kind of *dry villages*. My message in the book is in brief—that in these small towns there is the best raw material for a truly artistic and spontaneous life in our state, that will produce the *Beauty-Making citizen*. And I take it for granted that the true purpose of our Civilization is to make the *Beauty Creator* supreme in life. And we want as many of him as possible. The Illinois Village is now Beautiful, and should become ideal.

It is the discovery of my life, the Illinois Village. I had had so much of Broadway I had forgotten there were wheatfields still.

So the Preacher shall receive in each village, one copy of the Magazine, and be urged to peruse it. There will be only one number issued.

(2) The other people who shall have the Magazine are my fellow Art Students in New York and Chicago, and a few Eminent Writers with whom I have the honor of a personal acquaintance. To these, and to my personal friends I have sent an announcement that the book is coming, and is for all who are truly worthy. Not many will cry for it. I am safe. I hope that you will send me, in return for your copy or copies, a volume of your verses printed since The Ode to Harvard Volume, I have been so pleased with work I have seen of late. "Luck" for instance.

Write to me sir. I am lonely as Hell and Brimstone.

Very Sincerely

NICHOLAS VACHEL LINDSAY

The Village Magazine will be out about September 15th.

Notes

1. The only collection of poems put out by Bynner in 1910 was *Young Harvard*, published in 1907. Bynner was then living and writing in Cornish, New Hampshire.
2. VL "roared on Sundays" for the Anti-Saloon League.
3. O. Henry (William Sidney Porter) had died on June 5 of tuberculosis, at the age of forty-eight. His last book of short stories, *Strictly Business*, came out in 1910.
4. Brand Whitlock (1869—1934), a novelist and diplomat, was an admirer of VL's idol, John Peter Altgeld. As clerk in the office of the secretary of state in Springfield,

Whitlock made out in secret the governor's pardons for the Haymarket rioters. From 1905 to 1913 he was mayor of Toledo, Ohio, and he was later given a diplomatic appointment by President Woodrow Wilson.

5. VL had printed seven hundred copies of the first issue of *The Village Magazine* in 1910. During VL's lifetime, *The Village Magazine* was reprinted three times and was modified and enriched each time.

19

TO WITTER BYNNER

Springfield, Illinois
Oct. 1, 1910

My Dear Mr. Bynner:

Thank you so much for the list, especially Ezra Pound. God made *him*, and I have just written to tell him so. The book on the Village will be out in about two weeks.

I am deeply appreciative of your willingness to introduce my work to Small, Maynard and Company. I have been introduced a good many times in my life to publishers and the like, to no special avail, and expect to continue a rather private citizen for some time, more because I am a philosopher, than because I just want to. If you think you can drag my name into the limelight and nail it there so it won't fade away, all I have to say is "Barkis is Willin' ", but mighty skeptical; grateful most of all, for one more loyal friend.

But *wait* till you see the Village Book! I feel more confident every day that it will edify God's chosen people—you and I and yours. It is me *last* plunge, my *last* tract; hereafter I surrender to the age. Tis Childe Roland's last blast upon the Ram's horn, and on the whole it is a good deal of a toot. Hereafter I shall save money, and buy real estate, and get married and raise babies and all that. Do you know any real nice girls who do the cooking and washing at home, yet are always neat, and can converse about the Upanishads?

I shall *save money* for three years, then go courting, somewhere.

And for a good "old gentlemanly
vice"
I think I shall take up with
avarice.

Meanwhile the Angels be with you and Alnasax guard you from the evil eye.

Very Sincerely

NICHOLAS VACHEL LINDSAY

20

TO MISS VAN DERVEER

Springfield Ill.
October 4, 1910.

My Dear Miss Van Derveer:

By this time, I suppose, you are so choked with presents, my little tribute will not get all the attention it would a month back. Nevertheless I hope you will pause in the gay while a moment and reflect solemnly upon the fact that Harold has a bald headed bachelor friend out here in Illinois, who wishes you every good thing in the world. If there are any dryads in the trees in your part of Elizabeth New Jersey, I hope you may get acquainted with them. If there are any fairies dancing in the grass, I hope you may have the fortune to behold them. If you meet Mister Moon at twilight, I hope you will have the leisure and the disposition to eat the bread of idleness with him, if you meet the Wizard Wind at Sunrise I hope he will tell you many fine poems. This will be indeed fitting for Harold is a Poet, as you no doubt understand, and the Wizard Wind will not blow you where he cannot follow. May you spend many days in Windland together. If you get blown as high as the Seventh Heaven, I hope you will take the time, before you descend, to look up the Shield of Lucifer, which is one of the real curiosities of that place. And all your life long I pray you may be able to return to the Castle of Love and its deep domestic Peace, however the storm flowers may roar without.

All of which noble sentiments will possibly be more plain to you if you investigate a package of drawings[1] which I have sent under separate cover.

Wishing you and Harold every noble splendor and Christian happiness that life can hold I remain

Yours with love

NICHOLAS VACHEL LINDSAY

Note

1. The package of drawings evidently included "The Map of the Universe," from which several metaphors in the letters derive. Other drawings ("Mister Moon," "The Wizard Wind," "The Shield of Lucifer") were part of the *Village Magazine* that came out two weeks later.

21

TO WITTER BYNNER

Springfield Ill
Feb. 18, 1912

My Dear Mr. Bynner:
It is Sunday morning and I feel the presence of leisure in an extra sense though I am never in much of a hurry. So I sit down for a romantic enterprise—the writing of a letter to Mr. Witter Bynner—which shall for the most part have no objective point but the airing of myself on this pleasant Sabbath Spring morning. For it looks more like Spring than any day since last Spring. The birds make little noises—and there is a lot of sunshine in the Governor's yard. I live next to Governor Deneen.

Before I proceed to the main business of inconsequential discourse—let me introduce friend Franz Rickaby.[1] The enclosed book looks awfully important to him—being his first baby. He is just out of High School. He has been a printer for six months—that is running a press for another man—and now that man has quit business and Rickaby goes out on a farm—to be a hand awhile. His employer in this case is an old chum just married. I think you will concede that my after-word is in accord with the Village Magazine Philosophy. I wish I could write it in the back of every such booklet printed in the state. We have too much Lorimer[2] and near-Lorimerism because we have too little Poetry and New Poetry.

If you will write Rickaby—Springfield Illinois—the best verses that you very much admire and the verses you much condemn it will do him good.

He is a friend of mine.

I am busy writing "Vignettes by a Mendicant"[3] these being prose sketches of begging experiences I have had—only shorter and more condensed than any heretofore. When my article in the American Magazine comes out "A Handy Guide for beggars" containing the eight rules of the road—I want to then issue a Book—under the same title—using the "Handy Guide" for the preface and following up with road Sketches that have mainly appeared in the Outlook—viz: American—Handy Guide for Beggars.

Sketches in the Outlook: The Man Under the Yoke
                          The Man with the Apple-Green Eyes
                          The Gnome
                          The House of the Loom
                          The City of Collars
                          Lady Iron-Heels

Sketches Unpublished yet: A Shrine Made with Hands.
                           Near Shickshinny
                           Death The Devil and Stupidity
                           The Old Gentleman with the Lantern

Vignettes Unpublished: The Old Lady at the Top of the Hill
                        Crossing Clinch River
                        Mist Rain and Thunder
                        and others.

If Small Maynard Publishes "Rhymes that Were Traded for Bread" would they like to publish this "Handy Guide" as a companion volume?

Or would they Like to Print it later?

Or do you advise me to Submit the book proposition to the Outlook—who have printed most of my stuff? I understand they publish books.

I have just submitted the 4 sketches Unpublished yet to Zulblin of the 20th Century Magazine.[4] I would like to have him publish them and play them up strong. They make a sort of Series of themselves—called "Adventures of a Religious Mendicant".

Seth Mayle is trying to peddle a bunch of my new poems—which—if your firm takes my book I would like to have you sort over and put the best into the book. I doubt if Seth will sell any.

Here is a list of the Titles of my new verses. Some of them Mayle has—some he hasn't.

The Flight of Mona Lisa—:

(Showing how Leonardo took her away to Heaven with him.)

The Rose and the Lotus.[5]

(A poem on the opening of the Panama Canal. Showing how the Genius of the West—the Rose—and the Genius of the East—the Lo-

tus—shall henceforth be wedded.)
    The Grave of the Proud Farmer.
    (Being an elegy on an aristocratic and Religious pioneer.)
    The Battle Line of Missions.
    (A Church Poem.)
    Galahad—Knight Who Perished.
    (A White Slave Poem.)
    Songs that Perish.
    The Missionary Misgiving.
    The Knight in Disguise.
    (A Memorial of O. Henry.)
    Lazarus and Dives
    (Sociological)
    The Rose and The Lotus is undoubtedly the most important in the set.

    I wish you could interest the Panama Exposition people in it. Seth is still trying to sell it—so whatever the commercial ethics of the matter may be please bear in mind. But I venture to copy it here for you.
    I hope you can read my writing.

           The Rose and the Lotus

           The Wide Pacific Waters
           And the Atlantic meet.
           With cries of joy they mingle.
           In tides of Love they greet.
           Above the drowned ages
           A wind of wooing blows.
           The red rose woos the Lotus—
           The Lotus woos the rose.

           The Lotus conquered Egypt.
           The Rose was Loved in Rome.
           Great India crowned the Lotus:
           France was the rose's home.
           Old China crowned the lotus:
           They crowned it in Japan.
           But Christendom espoused the rose
           Ere Christendom began.

           The lotus speaks of slumber.
           The rose is as a dart.
           The Lotus is Nirvana.
           The Rose is Mary's heart.

The Rose is deathless—restless.
The Splendor of our pain—
The calm of bitter labor
That builds—not all in vain.

The Genius of the Lotus
Shall heal earth's too-much fret.
The Rose in blinding glory
Shall waken Asia yet.
Hail to their loves, ye peoples!
Behold—a world-wind blows
That aids the ivory lotus
To wed the red red rose!

It seems to me that this poem, deftly handled—has publicity possibilities. As soon as I hear you people have definitely taken my book—I
shall call in my new rhyme stuff from Seth—and submit it all to you—the
best to go into the volume.

I did not intend to air my literary plans to you this morning—but
here you have them. If you want to give me an opinion on Mayle—I
will be glad to get it.

It isn't money I want, but an audience:

Mr. Garland[6] has been boosting me strong with Mayle—or rather
with his pardner who signs his name so I can't read it.

I am reading Ruskin[7] and Tolstoï of late. I think I shall specialize on
those gentlemen. I would like to lay hold on the immortal essence of
those gentlemen—by some sort of transfusion of blood. I know the
limitations of both pretty well—nevertheless they are in a particular way
my masters: I should say—that if I chose three literary masters
today—they would be the incongruous seeming three—Ruskin—Tolstoï
and Edgar Poe. Ruskin—because he helps me to feel it is worth while
to dream of future America—the Aesthetic Commonwealth—the Ripe
Civilization—full of Happy Healthy Beauty Producing human Beings.
I would write, if I could, a different Utopia than any ever written and
it should be much Ruskinized[8]—in the broadest sense—that is— Art is
a Public matter—a Religious matter—a Socialistic matter if you please.
But after all Ruskin is Unhuman—and Tolstoï sees men plain. I would
like to be as clear-visioned as Tolstoï in looking at the individual man
or woman and his spiritual estate. I would like to understand as he
understood the heart-break of religion and the dream of brotherhood.
I envy him his world-strength—the terrible grip with which he laid hold
on bleeding life. And Tolstoï symbolizes to me one more thing—he was
almost an avowed Buddhist in his "great going forth from home", his
perpetual struggle toward renunciation and spiritual peace and self-

mastery. I think I know a great deal more about Nirvana than Tolstoï still Tolstoï is nearer to Buddha than any great international 19th century character—and to Christ as Well. If I put him in a sentence I should call him a literal and realistic and eminently successful Christian striving unsuccessfully for the Buddhistic self-mastery. Living as he did—between Asia and Europe—the Rose and the Lotus were both in his heart—though the thorns of the rose prevailed. I think I know more about Peace than Ruskin or Tolstoï—but I know infinitely less about life and Civilization. I want to know as much of Life through them as I can—without surrendering the jewel in the Lotus.

Then as to Edgar Poe. Another stung creature—who knew not Peace. But Edgar had the Yeast-Phosporus-Radium in him—to produce the eminently original thing, the new Creation—and I envy him above all other mortals when I think about writing. It is just as natural for me to want to write as new unexpected and vital a surprise as Poe wrote—as it is for some young men to want as good an Automobile as their neighbors. It is a carnal passion with me to want to carve a jewel like Ulalume or Ligeia. I will never escape him. I read him at thirteen—and even then I knew all his limitations—and envied him his tremendous power to make the *new* thing. It seems to me aesthetically—that electrical power of his is more needed in America than any other. When I write my book on Utopia—every Artist shall be a half brother to Poe—every Politician a Ruskinian—every Preacher and Novelist a follower of Tolstoï. The Sermon on the Mount shall be the social standard—but the lotus shall bloom in the parks.

Yet my Utopia shall not be too good a place. I only mean these social forces shall be at work. The world shall be like Shakespeare's stage—with plenty of good and bad—but all acting their part at the fullest—no man cramped—every man having his cue—his entrance, his exit and his little moment in the center of the stage.

But enough of theory. I want to tell you my debate with myself—over what I shall do. I have definite plans till June—including those in the beginning of this letter. Then I come to the turning point. I have debated most seriously in my mind a long two years mendicant tour in the West—Texas—South and North California—Washington— and then at last back home here. I seem to be a natural beggar. I have had a better time and made more friends at that than any other sort of work. I would carry the Village Magazine and the Tramp's Excuse in Waterproof covers—having already bound them for that purpose—and read to those who cared to hear. And having made two years of it—I might have a lifetime of it. But I generally anticipate coming back here at the end of two years and take up writing again—especially along the line of the Village Magazine Philosophy—or as I sometimes call it—the New Localism. I have notes enough on my shelf—for possible theories—sketches—stories and poems to keep me writing ten years. For almost a year now I have for the first time been writing in a steady professional way. It is the first time in my life—and I feel I can keep it up indefinitely and forego all drawing and speaking—and be a penman only—if it is best. But I am always haunted by the call of the road—, I have America—East and South pretty well in my hand. I have lectured all over New England and begged in most of the other states—the typical ones—Florida—Georgia—North Carolina—Tennessee—Kentucky—Ohio—Pennsylvania and New Jersey. And if I walk over the West— if I have nothing else—I will have a certain grip on America—and matter to think on, that will keep me years in fathoming.

Another plan I consider—that I could work after I returned to Spring-field—is getting acquainted with Sangamon County—and all its towns and farms and villages. Sangamon County is the county of which Spring-field contains the Court House. In inspecting them—learning them by heart I would like to do it with the Tolstoï realism and power to ap-prehend vitality. And in building fancies on this real foundation—I would like to use the Edgar Poe Creative Radium—and the Ruskin Civic Sense. All this is of course extravagant dreaming—and I creep behind my dreams like a snail in the wake of a chariot. But it is a picture of my dreams for these months—I give you—and very much enjoy writing down.

When in Indianapolis last week I met our mutual friend W. S. Dun-bar—in Bobbs-Merrill's Publishing house where he is writing for them the last six chapters of his thick book on travel. It is the first time I have seen him since I left New York, ages ago. He has apparently had a little more to eat lately, but not much more to wear. He is full of his book—and the dummy is a beauty—250 illustrations—many of them colored old plates you know—every one a certified rarity. It will be a great event when Dunbar's book comes out—after lo—these many years. If it ap-pears—it looks too good to be true—but if it appears, your humble servant is going to talk it up a heap. It looks like it will cost a plenty—I'll bet $3.50 but I didn't ask him. Dunbar was the original of the Man with the Scraggly Beard in my story "The Lady Poverty" which I think I sent you. With some misgivings I told him to read the tale—for it describes him in some points—all too well.

The sun is shining like a good fellow. The birds say Chirp Chirp and insist that it is Spring. By the noise some of them make I fancy some of them have read Edward Carpenter's "Loves Coming of Age".[9] But as for me—I take refuge in the Buddha—the Law—and the Monastic Order, and pray to St. Francis for his grace.

I wish you well.

Very sincerely

Nicholas Vachel Lindsay

Notes

1. VL later planned an article on his Springfield friend Franz Lee Rickaby entitled "The Young Troubadour of Springfield, Illinois." It was never published, and the manuscript is in the archives of the State Historical Society of Wisconsin. A musician, Rickaby had also acquired an art press on which he printed his own sonnets. VL later wrote to Amy Lowell asking her to help out his friend. The press mentioned must have been what Rickaby called the "Pax Printery."
2. George Horace Lorimer (1867—1937) edited *The Saturday Evening Post*, which was anti-intellectual in the extreme, and despised by intellectuals.
3. "Vignettes by a Mendicant" was a component of *A Handy Guide for Beggars* (1916). The article that did come out in the *American Magazine* for May 1912 (pp. 54—59) was entitled "Rules of the Road." "The Adventures of a Literary Tramp" came out in the issues of *Outlook* for January 2 (pp. 36—39), January 9 (pp. 86—90), February 6 (pp. 312—16), and February 13 (pp. 357—59), 1909. "Lady Iron-Heels" was published in the *Outlook* for October 7, 1911 (pp. 335—38), and "The Lady Poverty" in the issue for November 25, 1911 (pp. 734—42). "Rhymes to Be Traded for Bread" was privately printed in June 1912 "expressly as a substitute for money."
4. *Twentieth Century Magazine* did not print the four unpublished sketches, which came out in the 1916 book.
5. "The Rose and the Lotus" was published as a broadside in 1913 and distributed in Congress for the opening of the Panama Pacific Exposition. It appears in the *Collected Poems* (pp. 211—12) under the title "The Wedding of the Rose and the Lotus." Most titles of the other poems mentioned were slightly changed in the edition of the *Collected Poems*.
6. VL had met Hamlin Garland in 1911. *Current Literature* had reviewed *The Village Magazine*, and Garland wrote to order a copy and to invite VL to speak at the Cliff Dwellers' Club. VL became a member of the club, and in April 1911 Garland visited VL's parents in Springfield and exhorted them to be patient with their "unemployed" son.
7. In November and December 1910 VL had organized a "Ruskin Revival" in Springfield, on the basis of five lectures he delivered at the YMCA.
8. VL's "Ruskinized" Utopia turned out to be *The Golden Book of Springfield* (1920).
9. Edward Childs Carpenter (1872—1950), newsman, playwright, and novelist, was also financial editor of the Philadelphia *Inquirer* from 1905 to 1916.

22

TO PROFESSOR PAUL

Springfield Ill.
Feb 19, 1912

My Dear Professor Paul:
Most sincerely I thank you for "The Light of the World"—and the significance of the gift as well. On the intellectual and mystical side and on the Tolstoïan side Religion has had a tremendous interest for me in the past and I have had some peculiar experience and in my feeble efforts to think have come to some conclusions on which I set considerable value and used to set more value—but most folk think them only queer. So about a year and a half ago I definitely set aside Religion as a main consideration since the most valued results seemed to bring only the hatred of my friends and the wrath of my family. Now, since if Religion should lead to anything—it should lead to Peace,—I decided to cling to the Peace and quit either expressing my mind on the subject or thinking about it seriously. I had set for myself an exhaustive inspection of the sacred Books of the East—and had followed with earnest sympathy and attention practically every religious movement in the Country that in any way came under my eye from Christian Socialism to Catholicism.

For all this I substituted the John Keats point of view pretty largely and for a long time remained just there—and produced The Village Magazine—which you have seen—and have done me the honor to like.

Your book of course brings up all the old questions, and I feel my interest drifting that way again—after a season of respite. There is something of the Religious-novelist in me you might say—or Dramatist or Actor—if you want to put it that way. I can read of a faith and crawl into the skin of the believer and (I fancy—I may be mistaken) get all out of it he got out of it. If one can act all the parts in a book of plays—what part shall he finally act? What is the real man? I am too sensitive to every faith. If allowed to go my own way in peace—without hate—I might in the end find my soul—but I see no particular benefit in going down an alley of swords. Whenever I see Hate in the way—I go no further. Then it's Back to John Keats and the Grecian Urn again. But now I am discussing Religion as a matter of the heart, and of propaganda.

In a purely intellectual way I shall be deeply interested in your book—it is the sort of information that I cannot but lay hold on—and store away.

I send you my old War Bulletin no 3—, I have crossed out what does not appeal to me today. I cross out the Disciples merely because they also stand for hate—and I breathe freer without them. A plague on both your houses. I read their news as a Socialist reads the Democratic and Republican papers. Yet I feel myself in a sense a member of the local congregation still and have saved up $115.00 for the new church—from lectures and manuscript checks.

I think I shall drift into religion again—but with considerable caution and disillusionment— a burnt child dreads the fire. I would like immensely to preach—if I did not know that two people would hate what I say to one that liked it. In private I am a sort of a Tolstoïan-Buddhist.

So, much of my creed will henceforth appear—I fancy—by indirection. It will be perhaps—in solution—in sketches—and rhymes—and private conversations. It will have much more of Ruskin and Tolstoï in it. I can say Tolstoï when I mean Buddha and St. Francis—I can say Ruskin when I mean the Mass and the worship of the Virgin. Just exactly what I mean by this may not be plain to you but take it for what it is worth. If there is an explanation it is too long. Tolstoï is half an Asiatic, Ruskin an unconscious ritualist.

I have just lately been formulating my views again as to my literary work at which I will probably be pretty industrious henceforth—at the expense of drawing and speaking. I am haunted always by a vision of a splendid America—especially Splendid Cities and Villages—palaces—for the people—temples reeking with incense and musk ruled by a real priesthood of the people—and Parks heavy with lotus flowers and cross roads shining with palaces of the people golden as the Corn. I have faith that America will come to her ripeness—in a hundred or a thousand years in such form as this. I keep reading Ruskin because I feel he will show me just how, help me to ripen my picture. A gracious refined and civilized humanity is always in my dreams—with the state saved from corruption by a passionate ascetic religious sect who spend all on public splendor and go themselves in rags—as it were. Now this is not all the Dream—this is the Ruskin of it—I might say. Then in these palaces and halls and on these golden roads I picture a type of vigorous Americanism born from our six feet deep black soil—a passionate and hardy race— able to conquer and master our tremendous physical resources without being smothered by them—and at the same time human as Shakespeare's men and women. It might be called Tolstoï's or Shakespeare's Utopia—that is I am not dreaming of a Millennium—but of a magnificent and passionate and ripened earth—with enough saints to keep it sweet.

I would like to look at my home town so hard I could reasonably build up a picture of this future world from it—as a geologist builds up an extinct animal from the leg bones and the spine.

I have many miscellaneous literary notes—and many of them lead in quite contrary directions to this. But I see this general picture before me—and may say that I hope directly or indirectly to put it into some sort of literary form. Underneath it will be my feelings and thoughts on comparative religion—but how much they will emerge I cannot say.

I have another line of aspiration always tugging at me—the desire to go on the road—the thing that haunted Tolstoï to the end—a desire so ascetic it seems to contradict entirely this dream of a gilded civilization. They may contradict. I only say that both these dreams are in me. I do not know what the practical reconciliation will be. I sometime think I will take a two years begging tour through the west and *use up* the mendicant in me—and thereafter settle down here to writing—and use up the Utopian.

I hope this letter is not too long—you have expressed by giving the book to me—an interest in my experience and views perhaps—that justifies such a long writing. At any rate I am glad to lay these matters before you.

I think you have read The Heroes of Time. It embodies in a way that gave no offense the same ideas that made folk so angry in War Bulletin No 3. The only difference was no man is supposed to speak what he really feels in poetry. And then in The Heroes of Time I have somewhat diluted my own ideas with those of other folk. In the War Bulletin I put them down straight—though too much abbreviated to be plain to the hasty reader I suppose.

It gives a pretty good all round picture of what I thought most important at that time—for me to say to my friends. This letter today is more what I am thinking about at present. The difference is mainly one of accent.

This letter is informal—and I suppose in some ways not clear. I did not intend to write at any such length when I began—or I might have been more systematic.

I wish you well in your work—and am glad to think of Dr. Hurd being with you. You make one picture in my mind. I am glad you are both one state nearer to me—and there is an increasing chance to see you both oftener.

My best wishes to Mrs. Paul and respectful greetings, salutations and so forth.

Very Sincerely

Nicholas Vachel Lindsay

23

TO WITTER BYNNER

Springfield Illinois
April 6, 1912.

My Dear Bynner:
Unless a harsh Providence prevents I shall start on the first of June for a two years Pedestrian Tour of the West[1] and would like to have all literary deals closed by then. Any word from your firm[2] any time now would be welcome. I can offer you a book of twenty road sketches most any time now—having for the leading article—the preface of the book [being] the article which Phillips will bring out in the American soon—the 8 rules of the road.[3] But I would like to have decisions whether favorable or adverse—settled by June.

I have bound one copy of the Tramp's Excuse and one copy of the Village Magazine in Oil Cloth and shall carry them with me on my trip. I shall keep all the rules of the road—and preach the Gospel of Beauty. I shall have written out a simple creed on the Love of God—the Love of Beauty, the love of the hearth and the Village—of the necessity of going forth on the road to find beauty and the bringing of it back to the hearth and the village. I have reconciled my theory of the Road, my theory of Aesthetics and my theory of the New Localism into one system and feel confident I can make it clear. The simple creed aforesaid I shall copy for each family in turn on some odd piece of paper and get them to promise to learn it by heart and keep it in the family Bible. This device saves me carrying bundles of printed matter as heretofore—makes my appeal more personal—and having written out the creed—it enables me to explain it informally, in an off-hand manner.

I shall write a letter to a friend or a syndicate every day 400 words.[4] The first 100 shall be a funny story—the second 100 shall be a hard-luck chronicle of the day—the third the details of the day etc and the fourth a pleasant story. I shall put these letters into as good a form as I can before sending them. Then I shall on returning digest the collection and evolve my ripened position on the Love of God and of Beauty and the Democratic Arts for the people of this land. I have done a lot of thinking since I was on the road last and I am able to see my works much more clearly.

I have written to several syndicates of newspapers proposing the letterplan—but their decision against me will not interfere in the least.

I shall just as merrily write the letter home and have it put in my desk till I return.

Phillips of the American threatens to put a sketch[5] of me into "interesting People". But the farm-houses where I am planting yeast phosphorus and Radium will never know that. I shall work for the New Localism as long as I am in Springfield—and it is the essence of the New Localism that I shall end my tour here and then settle down to planting Yeast Phosphorus and Radium in unlimited quantities in this little old Springfield. Next week or in two weeks my official tract on the New Localism will arrive in the city and I shall endeavor to deliver it into the hands of a few of the elect, and the politicians of the better sort—in a manner they shall not forget. I shall put a copy of the tract into my water-proof copy of the Village Magazine—and transcribe extracts from the same for the children of Light I chance to encounter when I am afoot.

Very Sincerely

NICHOLAS VACHEL LINDSAY

Notes

1. VL started on foot for California on May 29, 1912. He walked as far as New Mexico, where his determination to go on collapsed owing to circumstances that are unclear. He then took refuge in Los Angeles at the home of his cousin Ruby Vachel Lindsay.
2. Bynner's firm was Small, Maynard and Company.
3. "Rules of the Road" came out in the June 1912 issue of the *American Magazine*, of which John Sandburn Phillips was the editor.
4. The letters VL sent home during his trip remained for a long time the only memory of it he had: His notebook got lost on the road and was not returned to him by the person who had found it until several years later.
5. "The sketch" that came out in the *American Magazine* in August 1912 ("Interesting People: Nicholas Vachel Lindsay," pp. 422—24) had been written by Octavia Roberts, with whom VL had become acquainted in the summer of 1910.

24

TO HAMLIN GARLAND

Near Great Bend Kansas
July 7, 1912

My Dear Mr. Garland:
It may interest you to know that so far my trip has been prosperous,
and though I have been indeed God's fool and cut something of a
harlequin figure, I have learned a heap for my pains, which is the main
point. So far I am in excellent health and spirits, and have material for
a thousand poems, of which I may write ten, sometime. 'Tis a long lane
from here to back again, and I find my route shifts with the days. But
in the main I keep to the same general track toward the Pacific coast,
which coast I hope to see from end to end and then return, perhaps
walking through Chicago. That is as may be. I am in general keeping
to my rules, though they are not cast-iron. I have had no freight-rides
or train rides, have walked or been driven all the way, have stuck to
the farms and villages, have made many friends and no enemies, have
paid for my meals either reciting or with my pamphlets or splitting
kindling, cutting weeds, hoeing corn, hoeing garden or picking cherries.
Near Newton Kansas I harvested for four days and a half[1] and earned
just enough to completely renovate my apparel, new corduroys—shoes,
hat, etc. Here at Great Bend the most famous harvesting center of the
world I shall harvest for about two weeks then walk to my people's
Summer Camp Empire Colorado[2]—near Georgetown, after a few days
of petting I hope to wriggle toward San Francisco, stopping occasionally
for manual labor of some sort, but not using my wages for anything but
outfit, I shall send all surplus home—and walk on. A man with money
in his pocket never sees the world. It shuts up like a clam. I learn a
heap working, but not in spending. I wish you the pleasantest of summers, and fancy you are already in your summer camp. I hope on my
return to visit you in Chicago strictly in my private capacity. But that
will only be with good fortune and after a year or so.

Very Sincerely

Nicholas Vachel Lindsay

Notes

1. VL had stopped in Kansas to harvest for a few days. This episode is fully narrated, as is the rest of his trip, in *Adventures While Preaching the Gospel of Beauty* (ed. by R. Sayre, Eakins, 1968—originally published in 1914).
2. At Empire, Colorado, he again saw Octavia Roberts (later O. R. Corneau), who testified that he was trying out a variety of popular or religious tunes to accompany his poems (see letter 3).

25

TO HARRIET MONROE

Los Angeles California
Sept. 18, 1912

Dear Miss Monroe:

Thank you indeed for the invitation to contribute to the new magazine.[1] I am indeed eager to make good with such a group, and three times interested in such an Illinois Enterprise.

I am emphatically a citizen of Springfield Illinois and Sangamon County, and shall return in a year to stay forevermore. If I may be confidential I have been horribly homesick for a month—and fear that (spiritually speaking) I shall hobble through the rest of my expedition.

I shall probably send you something to be considered for publication in a month or so.

Very Sincerely

NICHOLAS VACHEL LINDSAY

Permanent address
603 South 5th Springfield Illinois

Note

1. Harriet Monroe (1860—1936), editor of *Poetry: A Magazine of Verse*, had written VL requesting some of his poetry. This letter from Los Angeles is the first answer VL wrote her. Harriet Monroe, a central character in the Chicago Renaissance of 1912, was then fifty-two. She herself wrote poetry and had gained local fame with her 1893 "Columbian Ode," written after the Chicago World's Fair. VL sent her the

text of the poem he had composed in Los Angeles, "General William Booth Enters into Heaven," as well as a series of "Moon-Poems."

26

TO HARRIET MONROE

Springfield Illinois
October 29, 1912

My Dear Miss Monroe:
Yesterday I sent you many poems—on the moon, and General Booth also.

My friends here think that there is so much more to General Booth with the musical directions, I venture to send a second copy. I leave the decision to you, as to which is more worth while.

I may be mistaken, but I think General Booth the most important poem I ever wrote, and the musical effects the least part of it, though they may be edifying.

Very Sincerely

NICHOLAS VACHEL LINDSAY

27

TO HAMLIN GARLAND

Springfield Illinois
November 14, 1912

My Dear Mr. Garland:
There is so much to say to you, I fear me it will make an interminable letter. Can't you come to see me here, in the intervals of house building:[1] I will promise to treat you *much* better than last time and make you forget all about that. We have an interesting Single Tax group here,[2]

who are my closest friends among the men of the town. There are one or two worthwhile walks in Springfield, if you are so inclined. I have struck up quite a friendship by letter—with Mr. Herbert Quick,[3] and he promises to come some time, and it encourages me to ask you. I am certainly distressed to hear of the burning of your house. Mama only found the clipping yesterday which she thought she had mailed me in the West. To have lost all your curios and all your noble souvenirs is no light matter. You have my heartiest sympathy in the matter, and best wishes in rebuilding. I hope you feel the need of an excursion to Springfield to set you up. Papa and Mama would certainly be delighted to see you. We three are alone in the house. Little Sister[4] is at the University of Wisconsin and you can have her end of the table and her room. I have reached a sort of turning point in affairs, an interregnum—and need a good scolding from somebody who cares to scold properly. Come, and lay on the whip.

Please give my best wishes to Mr. Taft[5] and the rest. I have not forgotten my gentle reception in your group in Chicago.

When people ask me straight out, why I quit walking in New Mexico, I tell them straight out I lost my nerve. I might say to you that suddenly—in Central New Mexico, when all was going merrily, my spiritual house burned down, and I am home for repairs. I want to rebuild it before I go again. I certainly learned a great deal. The trip was of immense though very grave profit, I had all the adventures to be expected, have gained about ten pounds in weight being now 142—and adventures enough to keep me writing several years, if I choose to write them. My Gospel was as well received as I could ask.—it was generally accepted, I mean *listened to* two or three times a day with all proper gravity—often with the most charming expressions of good-will. The thing that stands out plainest in my mind is the sixteen days of harvesting in Central Kansas, and I only wish I was strong enough spiritually to lock up my ink bottle forever and strong enough physically to harvest forever. There is nothing like it—as long as a man can stand it. This appetite for ink is worse than the Demon Rum, when it keeps us from such pleasures.

One of my minor disasters was the loss of my principal notebook—my diary in fact—in California, and what appears to be the loss of my letters home, at least they haven't turned up. But I am not especially vexed—since the principal good of the trip is the chastened ripened point of view. And I have many miscellaneous notes if I want them.

I want to go again. But I want to cut far deeper into life to get way way under the world, and I am not sure I want to write it up—but travel for its own sake. No printed matter, no letters home—no letters from home, no calls on family friends along the route. Just go out and eat dirt awhile, and commune with the Lord, and when they want me to, stop and shock wheat.

I have sent a lot of verses to the New Poetry Magazine. I do hope they accept *General Booth* a memorial of the founder of the Salvation Army. It is probably the best thing I ever wrote. Then they have 18 of my moon-poems, written in Colorado.

I send you the book—"A Handy Guide for Beggars" prepaid—by express.[6] The spirit and letter of my present trip was pretty largely the same—with some variations owning to local conditions, and my advanced age.

I want my next book to be about Springfield and Sangamon County and Illinois. My table is full of notes—taken before I left town. But when I am not actually writing—I feel I am a ghost here—still actually on the road—my plans are in confusion—these Indian-summer days reprove me. I feel I must be begging again—but I know a winter of writing is the best thing for my soul—*hardwork* please God—and if possible—the launching of the book I send you, and, as I say—the rebuilding of my spiritual house also.

Sometimes I dream of a series of pilgrimages, all over Illinois. But this letter is quite long enough.

Very Sincerely

Nicholas Vachel Lindsay

Notes

1. Hamlin Garland's house had burned down, and he was busy having another one built.
2. Among VL's "Single Tax" friends (followers of ideas put forth in Henry George's *Progress and Poverty*) was City Commissioner Willis Spaulding. Springfield was one of the first American cities to function on the basis of commission government.
3. Herbert Quick (1861—1925) was an Iowa novelist. Among his books, *Vandemark's Folly* (1921), *The Hawkeye* (1923), and his autobiography, *One Man's Life* (1925) are remembered.
4. "Little Sister" is Joy Lindsay.
5. "Mr. Taft" is Lorado Taft, the sculptor, whose sister, Zulime Taft, Hamlin Garland had married in 1899.
6. *A Handy Guide for Beggars* was published in book form in 1916 by Macmillan. What VL must have sent was a sheaf of the stories that would go into it.

28

TO ARTHUR DAVISON FICKE

Springfield Illinois
December 19, 1912

My Dear Ficke:[1]

Thank you indeed for your generous list. I set great store by my personal following, which I feel is growing larger—and though blowing the tin horn is often amusing, the only real solid satisfaction is in digging out people like you. I want a real response—and one new friend is worth a long magazine article to me, or a considerable scattering of pamphlet literature. Some fellows are in all the magazines one year and dead the next, and what does it all amount to? The main good the magazines do me is that they constrain my friends to look at my work a little more earnestly when I hand it to them in manuscript or pamphlet form.

I heartily congratulate you on Hisa-Gatami. I have a fellow feeling for any man who has been moved by Buddhism. It has been with me a tower of strength—and I am no Theosophical sentimentalist, vague Emersonian, or missionary-hating man, either. But the picture of the Buddha after his forty days fast is always on my dresser—and holds equal honor with the Nuremberg Madonna on my bookcase. She helps me to victory over passion but Buddha to victory over life itself. She is a dear friend, but he is—in common parlance, a true sport.—that is, a fighter who saw the thing through. I have the same feeling for him that a soldier might have for Leonidas or a politician for Julius Caesar. I see him dramatically you might say—I fancy I can understand just how he felt when he left home, and was rained on and slept in sheds, and all that. I lose him awhile, and then fate itself seems to drive me back to him.

I am perfectly willing to admit that he is an inferior Master to the Man of Nazareth that he never stretched out his hand for the nails, and that the thorn will win in the end over the lotus—but I prefer to be cosy with Buddha, just as the Catholics prefer to be cosy with the saints, and let *them* talk to Christ, when something must be said to the higher powers about our affairs. If I lived in India or Japan, I would probably turn to Christ—for the very reason he would be far away, and I would not be in sight of the way his work has been corrupted. Buddha is a refuge because one is not surrounded by shabby Buddhists. But enough of this. You may be interested in these two poems.

With a Bouquet of Twelve Roses[2]

I saw Lord Buddha towering by my gate
Saying "Once more, Oh Youth, I stand and wait
Saying "I bring you my fair law of Peace
And from your withering passion full release,
Release from that white hand that stabbed you so
The road is calling! With the winds you go
Forgetting her imperious disdain:—
Quenching all memory in the sun and rain!

"Excellent Lord, I come! But first" I said—
Grant that I give her these twelve roses red—
Yea, twelve flower-kisses for her roseleaf mouth
And then indeed I go, in bitter drouth
To that sweet valley where your river flows.
In Peace, that once I found in every rose.

The Wedding of the Rose and the Lotus

[see above, pages 50-51]

I have quite a local project on,[3] that will keep me from travel for some time. But when I travel, I will remember you.

Very Sincerely

NICHOLAS VACHEL LINDSAY

Notes

1. Arthur Davison Ficke (1883–1945), a poet from Davenport, Iowa, taught English in 1906–7 at the State University of Iowa. His best-known collection of verse remains *Sonnets of a Portrait Painter* (1914). "Hisa-Gatami" demonstrates Ficke's preoccupation with Buddhism and Japanese prints and painters, on which he wrote books in 1913 and 1915 in particular. (For his part in "Spectrism," see note 1 to letter 16.)
2. "With a Bouquet of Twelve Roses" became Part One of "Poems Speaking of Buddha, Prince Siddharta" (*Collected Poems*, p. 319).
3. The local project mentioned at the end of the letter is the beginning of what was to become *The Golden Book of Springfield*.

29

TO HAMLIN GARLAND

Springfield Illinois
March 31, 1913

My Dear Mr. Garland:
I want you to join the Great International Rose and Lotus Conspiracy. I send under separate cover some printed matter which will further elucidate the idea, meanwhile I set down the elements of it here.

The impending recognition of the Chinese Republic, the fast approaching completion of the Panama Canal, the thwarting of the Dollar Diplomacy, and many other things point to a new relation between Asia and the World which should have its symbol sign and decoration—and the logical symbol is the intertwined Rose and Lotus.

The Lotus has been from the beginning the favorite flower of the whole Orient. It is there omnipresent and supreme in all religion and Art and has a place in all Asiatic poetry. The Rose holds the same place in the Occident. It is a sanguine flower and in a peculiar way is adapted to expressing our type of religion and romance. Now when we approach the first hour in history when East and West meet, never again to be parted it is fitting and proper we should weave these two flowers together as our sign of spiritual courtesy to the East; as our expression of the hope of ultimate Peace and Justice and highmindedness between Asia and the World, as well as a sign of their sure inter-dependence. You know far more artists and architects and decorative designers than any other man I have the pleasure to know. I would like to have this idea tried on them, to see if it will stick. It has haunted me for several years, and I cannot let it alone till I have done something about it. I think the *idea* is better than the design or poem which I send—I think it has a fundamental historical vitality. I have not copy-righted it, and I want a great many people persuaded to steaᶦ it, or persuaded it is their own. I am writing this message to all the literary folks with whom I am on easy terms, and I have five hundred copies of the Rose and Lotus design to give to any one who really cares. You probably know some people working on the San Francisco fair who would perhaps take a fancy to the notion. Or maybe Mr Taft would see his way to becoming something of a partizan for it. My personal friends here take a deal of interest in it. I do not think the idea will hobble, when once started. I do not see why the internationalism of this design cannot be made a substitute for or supplement to the violent internationalism of the Socialist flag. I would like to see it embroidered in red and gold silk floss on some kind of an international banner. And then another way of carrying on the idea—lotus ponds can be made to bloom and flourish in this land. There is an article on Water-Gardens in the March Craftsman with one illustration of the Japanese lotus. We have a lovely lotus pond in Washington Park here—with rose-gardens near by. Their juxtaposition could easily take on a ceremonial meaning in the World's fair year.

General Booth goes marching on. I have had all sorts of literary good fortune of late.[1]

I wish you well

Very Sincerely

NICHOLAS VACHEL LINDSAY

Note

1. "General Booth" had been published in the January issue of *Poetry.* Several of VL's poems were published in various magazines that year, which accounts for the note on the "literary good fortune." In particular, "The Grave of the Proud Farmer" came out in the *American Magazine* in September 1912. Furthermore, William Dean Howells (1837—1920), who had had nothing encouraging to say about VL's first verse, acclaimed "Booth" ("Editor's Easy Chair," *Harper's Monthly Magazine,* September 1915, pp. 634—37). *Farm and Fireside* also published VL's "Proclamations on the Gospel of Beauty."

30

TO GEORGE STERLING

Springfield, Ill.
June 1, 1913

My Dear Sterling:[1]—
Now it is your turn to get a lead-pencil letter. Just this moment my ink-bottle turns out to be dry. I have had an unusually warm and grateful feeling ever since you wrote—to think you would settle down and be friends like that.

I liked the verses you sent, especially "The Hunting of Astarte" which has a most unusual music. I have read it aloud to a good many of the folk of this village.

Your book of verses has not yet arrived, but I am anticipating it with anticipations.

Have you been visiting Jack London? I think that would be a grand adventure—to visit Jack London. I wonder if he would let me farm for him? Or is his farm on paper?[2] I guess I would make a better farmer for men who know nothing about me, who just think me a sunburned mutt, I would be too damned sociable otherwise.

You may be interested to know that Mitchell Kennerley has just sent to the printer all of my poems for these sixteen years of poetry-writing that I care to have in a first official volume, about 70 in all. The title is General William Booth Enters into Heaven—(and other poems) by N. V. Lindsay.[3] I have a considerable scattered constituency, accumulated through the years, in various ways, and I am interested in the little drama of me first official appearance in the book world. I have given away most everything heretofore, except a scattering of magazine articles etc. I will be glad if I can get to printing—or rather publishing, books, so I can say what I please to my special crowd, and keep on saying it, and build up my own little circle. The magazines come and go— and next month's magazines come roaring in to drown out the last. And a writer must be a regular fountain to keep them supplied, granting they like his stuff. He has to appear every month everywhere, or he is forgotten. You speak of Blake having a hand in my work. He has much more than Shelley. Shelley never quite got me. Keats I have by heart. I think what you call the Shelley element came through Poe—my first great literary passion and a deathless one. Possibly what you think is the Blake element came through Poe also. From my 13th to my 17th year Poe was the passion of my life. No other poet-enthusiasm has quite equalled it since. I only read Blake much later. I think I set a higher estimate upon him now than when I did read him. My next book[4] will be more Blakeesque I think—than any other one thing—a book about Springfield. The key-motto will probably be:

> "Bring me my bow of burning Gold
> Bring me my arrows of desire
> Bring me my spear—oh—Clouds unfold—
> Bring me my chariot of fire—
> I will not cease from mental fight
> Nor shall my sword sleep in my hand
> Till we have built Jerusalem
> In England's green and pleasant land".

That is precisely my feeling in regard to Springfield Illinois, whether I ever get it on paper or not. Pity Springfield. Do not pity me. The poor little town is in for it. People have tried every kind of purgation from assaults upon Lorimer to the establishment of Commission Government. Now I will see what the angels can do—each one with a censer in its hand. Springfield shall be whipped by these angels and sent to Sunday-School like a naughty child. That is—I hope so. Maybe the book will never get done. Watch out for the eulogy of San Francisco in the June Forum.

You think of me as a fortunate man. Well there is one thing I lack. I need a little nigger to beat me every morning with a barrel stave and make me get to work. Otherwise Springfield will never be woked up [*sic*] and amazed by my next tract. If sandalwood were not so expensive I would bind the book in sandalwood. I want it to reek with incense. Thus do I let you into my workshop. But I mustn't begin on my book-ideas. They are too many and varied. I am going to scythe some blue grass all this morning. Letter finished later. I hear the wheatfields of the West calling me to harvest. I dearly love to get sunstruck and all that. But I am just afraid to quit my present writing stunt till it is done—for fear it will *never* get done. I am so dog lazy—I must at least *hang on.* But you bet I will harvest again some day, if it roasts me like beef. There is a wicked pleasure in it. Now for the blue grass, more later.

It is just after dinner and I have had a grand morning. I am not quite through and will cut some more this afternoon.

I certainly thank you for your speaking on my behalf to Willis Polk,[5] with the Rose and the Lotus in view. Maybe after my book comes out this fall, with the poem in it, the reviewers may take up with the idea. It comes toward the front of the book. I wish you would get acquainted with Prof. E. Olan James[6]—1474 Holly Street Berkeley California. He it is that presented me with a copy of "The Star Treader". Do not speak disrespectfully of the Wine of Wizardry. I will remember when it came out how I and my room mate Richards (in New York) gulped it down. It has been in my English-Literature Lecture-book ever since. Be sure to send me:—"*The Testimony of the Suns.*"

Well—I took your hint and wrote to Benét[7] and received the grandest kind of a letter in reply. I do think a heap of "The Merchants of Cathay". He will bring out a book this fall with that for the title poem.

I hope to hear from you soon. I am writing to those I want to write to, rather than those I *ought* to write to today.

You have been so hearty in your Godspeed, and reading your kind words over today—I cannot but tell you how I feel about it. There does not appear a single serious obstacle or trouble ahead of me to keep me from writing verses like those I have sent you—for the next ten years. I am just ten years younger than you are—33 years old—decidedly a bachelor—with no financial responsibilities, having neither income nor expenses, I owe just 35 dollars in the world, and seldom owe more than that, I make no particular effort to get my stuff printed—when it is turned down several times I just put it in the pigeonhole and at the end of a period print it privately. I have no expectation of ever pleasing the public or the publishers very long at a stretch, the magazines that know me best never completely surrender. They are hot and cold, hot and cold. I just expect to keep sawing wood anyhow and only incalculable disaster out of a clear sky will stop me. I am not the least bit shaken in my policy by the little moves of approval and publicity that came in—the ebb tide is just as regular as clockwork.

This world is a queer young flirt. Just like a woman. Every time I succeed in a small thing somebody comes to me and says "*Now* that you *have* succeeded—of course you will quit your damfoolishness—and be it understood—*we* will forgive and forget the past". But I am just like Bryan, assuming that grape-juice has got me where I am, I go right on drinking grape-juice in the same old damphoolish way. Me pants are no better pressed than they were seven years ago—and thanks be to God it is my poem on Altgeld that is being quoted about as often as any.

I am *amazed* at the American mind. People I have known and ranted to *intimately* for *years* say "*Now* you will cash it in." or "*Now* you will get on a salary". "*Now* you will make some *MONEY!*" And these very people a day before and a day after profess the heartiest lip-service to the Gospel of Poverty.

To separate the American mind from dollar cogitations will be a greater surgical operation than digging the Panama Canal. They just *can't* think of success without dollars. They look so *sad* when I say I have no income. And I just *shout* it. Yet I dearly love folks. I have a world of friends—and life is as sweet as it has any business to be. I have no enemies—except the internal enemy of a weak will and a lazy-bug, and certain spiritual spasms that never stop my progress long.

By luck, chance and many curious slaps of fate I have been driven back to my monastic path so often I almost believe it my destiny in spite of myself. I struggle and pray and fight myself and every year am a little further along the road—with a very diverting and amusing vista behind me. I wish I was harvesting I do. The next best thing is to cut some more grass—and then I will close this letter. Ho for the lawn mower.

******

The grass is now cut. I snort for the wheat fields like a war horse, but must restrain myself I suppose. Our house is next to the Governor's and my writing window for these many years looks out on the Governor's grand green yard. Every night I see Governor Dunne and his wife make a lovers-tour of the yard through the shrubberies just inside the fence. They are quite a domestic pair and have about 17 children—all Irish.

Well—looking out on this yard tells me summer is here. Just this time last year I had begged my way through Hannibal and was merrily hiking for Jefferson City. Well—I mustn't get into *that* or I will write forever. A storm drove me into the cabin of some *very clean* before-the-war negroes. Very interesting. It took them hours to dry me out, at the kitchen stove. Lovely people. The old man said grace twice every meal—once standing up, once sitting down. It was worth it too—good cooking. I swear I will not write but one more page.

Now that Joaquin Miller[8] is dead you are the only California Poet. I feel as though I were getting intimate with the whole Pacific Coast, when I get friends with you. You sure have an enormous and inexhaustible theme to put that state into song.

We ought to have a California and Illinois Dialogue in Rhyme. Says the Cornfield to the Orange-Grove "Oh how do you feel today" or "The time has come—the Cornfield said—to talk of many things". You might as well begin to get ready for the Exposition. You will be asked for a new ode every day by those fellows.

Well—let me hear from you when you feel long-winded and sociable, your letter has given me great delight. I am honored in your friendship.

Very Sincerely,

NICHOLAS VACHEL LINDSAY
603 South 5th
Springfield Illinois.

Notes

1. George Sterling (1869—1926) was a California poet, very much influenced by Ambrose Bierce and Jack London, and a friend of the latter's. Titles and preoccupations point out the convergence of his trends with VL's. His first volume, *The Testimony of the Suns,* appeared in 1903. *The Wine of Wizardry* (1907) and *Ode on the Opening of the Panama-Pacific Exposition* (1915) must have echoed in VL's mind. Sterling poisoned himself in 1926.
2. Jack London (1876—1916) had just published *John Barleycorn*. In *Martin Eden* (1909), George Sterling appeared in the guise of the poet Brissenden. London's farm was the "Beauty Ranch."

3. *General Booth Enters into Heaven and Other Poems* was published by Kennerley in the fall of 1913.
4. The "next book" mentioned is obviously *The Golden Book of Springfield,* which rarely left VL's thoughts until its publication in 1920.
5. Willis Polk (1867–1924) was a nationally known architect and former associate of Stanford White, a noted New York architect.
6. E. Olan James had sheltered VL in California during the latter part of his 1912 walking tour (see letter 96).
7. "Benét" is William Rose Benét (1886–1950). His *Merchants From Cathay* was published in 1913, and he was on the staff of *Century* Magazine from 1911 to 1918.
8. Joaquin Miller had died on February 17, 1913, in Oakland. VL's remark could only strengthen in Sterling's mind some of the odder ideas Bierce was filling it with: that Sterling was, for example, the equal of Milton and Shelley.

31

TO GEORGE STERLING

Springfield, Ill.
July 19, 1913

My Dear Sterling:
I do not believe I have given you my formal thanks for the Testimony of the Suns and the good letter with it. So I hereby send you all due gratitude. Our good friend, our mutual friend, Miss Teasdale,[1] has been writing me today. The Rhyming Fraternity appears to be after all a pleasant little home circle that could be crowded into two rooms very nicely. I certainly enjoy my correspondents. I have so many grand acquaintances by letter. And all the rhymers seem to know all the other rhymers.

I have just finished a Pro-Japanese poem[2] which I suppose you as a Californian will not like a bit. The Yale Review asked for something and I hope they will print it. It is all about Jimmu Tenno, and Bushido and the 47 Ronin and Fuji and Nogi and Iyeyasan and Nikko and Hideyashi and the Samurai. My point is that whatever we do or feel in regard to the Coolie[3] as an individual we must respect the Japanese History, the dignity of their traditions, the nation as a whole. I find so few really cultured people know even the merest backbone of Japanese Feudal History and customs. They imagine the Japanese as a bunch of monkeys of most immoral breed who by some Satanic chance have suddenly learned to become perfect wizards at fighting and building warships. The same people twenty years ago thought of Japan as a

Nation of Dolls that could somehow talk and walk—and wore exceedingly pretty costumes. The two conceptions are so utterly at variance that neither could be correct.

I have been such a passionate admirer of Japan all my life I can scarcely conceive of human beings who have never heard of Hideyashi or Iyeyasan. Yet I have to just pound those names into my most intimate friends.

In my poem I try to make out Japan as the last refuge of Chivalry. If the thing gets printed I hope you will do something to get it down one or two California throats, though indeed it is addressed to Europe and the Anglo-Saxon World, for the issue is international.

Well—I did not intend to write this. I was only going to say I have read the Testimony of the Suns with immense interest and such pondering, and you shall have the benefit of my reflections [*sic*] thereupon at a very early date. I have been much moved at the power thereof.

Watch the Forum for the next six months for six installments of my Adventures and Collier's Weekly any time soon for Macfarlane's Review[4]—maybe next week.

The first installment of the Forum adventures will probably conduce to our better acquaintance.

I shall read the Testimony of the Suns to a good friend of mine soon.

Very sincerely,

Nicholas Vachel Lindsay

Notes

1. VL had begun corresponding with Sara Teasdale earlier but did not meet her until 1914. Five years his junior, she played a great part in VL's life, although she would not marry him.
2. The "pro-Japanese" poem was "The Jingo and the Minstrel" (*Collected Poems*, p. 375).
3. The confusion in VL's mind between Japan and China shown here by his using the word "Coolie," was a lasting one. To his mind, the "East" was an aggregate in which he later included ancient Egypt.
4. Peter Clark "Macfarlane's Review" came out September 6, 1913, in *Collier's* (pp. 7—8, 32) and was entitled "A Vagabond Poet." The "adventures" were printed in the *Forum* before being collected in the 1914 Macmillan volume.

32

TO HARRIET MONROE

Springfield Ill.
August 7, 1913

My Dear Miss Monroe:
I am enjoying the new number of Poetry, especially the "Tree" poem,
the Park poem and the love poem with which it begins:—"A Woman
at Evening".

But I am writing, not for that but just to tell you I think often of you,
and duly remember your several kindnesses to me.

I am here all alone in a big cool darkened house that stays cool the
very hottest day. I sit by the library desk and write and draw. Since I
am uninterrupted all day I get a great deal done and am very happy,
for I forgive myself all other sins if I get steady work out of myself and
overcome the sin of laziness. You have been a good friend indeed, and
I do not forget you.

Our little friend you thought I might stay over in Chicago for:—Sara
Teasdale has written me two letters and I have written her two. What
do you think of the correspondence? Does it contain great and unfath-
omable things for each of us?[1]

Owing to the fact that I have torn my affections into two or three
large unmanageable pieces of late I have firmly resolved to get acquainted with twenty four of the belles of Springfield and cut myself
into twenty-four moderate pieces. By this method I may be able to
resume the even tenor of my way and not find so many dyspeptic
Cupids in my ink bottle. I am thinking of three young ladies right now
that I have always shamefully robbed myself of by letting them alone.
And I know *they* will suggest others. I called on the very belle and expert
solo dancer of the town last night—Governor Tanner's niece—she has
grown up a block away and it never occured to me before. Once started
on this voyage of discovery there is not telling the port.

Edward J. Wheeler[2] has just delighted me by asking me to speak ten
minutes before the Poetry Society next January on "the Gospel of
Beauty". I was obliged to decline, since I did not see the money, but
I was all puffed up just the same and told him so.

About October I may have a picture-book to spring that you may
like.

My folks are as usual camping near Empire Colorado, 45 miles West of Denver. My father mother and sister and two visitors, my father's sister and Joy's Chum. In the ranch house near by fitted up for Boarders (following in our wake as it were) are 6 Springfield ladies *trying* to do it our way, but sister Joy can climb more mountains in a day than they can climb in six. Also Miss Lowering of the Lowering school, Chicago is there with a friend. They are all friends of Octavia Roberts who camped out with us last year and led this party to the Ranch this year. Perhaps you know Miss Lowering—if that's the spelling of her name.

I so much enjoyed the Field Museum with you and would like to take two or three big long sessions with you there sometime. Museum-stuff is *so* stimulating to the imagination. I always imagine myself reading up everything in the museum, as once I read up Egypt. That makes Egyptian Stuff a joy to me every time I see a bit of it. I sort of feel myself in the secret as it were. They put the hint of the Invisible forces in every line of their work. Well I must go across to the Boarding house to lunch.

August 17, 1913

I have been lunching at that boarding house ten days as it were. At any rate I pick up my letter to finish after so long.

I am interested in Norman Hapgood's[3] new Harper's. They are going to use the same bunch of illustrators that have made "The Masses" so interesting. Hapgood says flatly he wants to get around to the Jugend and Simplicissimus sort of a thing. He and the Henri[4] bunch will have to go a long way yet to equal the force of the whole group of Germans—though they are the most aggressive set we have. There are so few of them—for one thing. The full-page Bellows makes me think of School. Bellows was a rising student just as I left. He is one of the best products of the Henri doctrine. He has a skill—an *elegance* of his own, but all his ideas are Henri's pumped into him when a kid. He is a very versatile technician as I remember—could do most any suggested stunt. He is a case of a man *made* rather than destroyed by Henri.

I am even more interested that the New Harper's should be attempting to be the official organ of the feminist movement. If Hapgood can win the readers now it means a paper of enormous influence in ten years.

I get so eager for the national woman-vote to happen *at once* that I could squeal with the impatience of a pig half under a gate. Now that it is inevitable, I want it to hurry up. After the vote becomes a national thing, there will be so many beautiful battles fought out—we will find out what we Americans really are—for the first time in our lives. Politics will be infinitely more *elastic* and varied in issues, and surprises and little dramas will turn up twice as often.

The influence of the magazines, even the non-political ones—will be multiplied by ten. And it will take the woman-voter a long time to come to a stopping-place, once she is started. She has been bottled up quite awhile.

Good morning. Very sincerely

NICHOLAS V. LINDSAY

Notes

1. VL's correspondence developed to such an extent that more than 350 letters were written, for the most part between 1912 and 1914, although VL and Sara Teasdale kept up their correspondence after she married Ernst Filsinger in December 1914. These letters are in the Beinecke Library at Yale. Their planned publication under the joint editorship of Professor Norman Holmes Pearson and this editor could not come to fruition because of Professor Pearson's untimely death in 1975.
2. Edward J. Wheeler was president of the Poetry Society.
3. Norman Hapgood had been editor of *Collier's* and was editor of *Harper's Weekly* from 1913 to 1916, at which time the magazine merged with *The Independent*.
4. Henri, George Bellows, and George Luks belonged to the so-called Ash Can School of painting. Robert Henri had taught VL at the New York School of arts, where Bellows was a classmate.

33

TO GEORGE STERLING

Springfield, Ill.
August 15, 1913

My Dear Sterling:
I cannot write a letter this morning. But I must thank you at once for your invitation to get me to the Jinks next year. I will certainly be delighted to be invited. What will it cost? My philosophy keeps me perpetually dead broke and proud of it. Whether I can come or not I will brag like sixty *if* I am *invited*. I will brag till at least a dozen jealous friends will cease to speak to me on the streets of Springfield. I have lots of fun with my town. I went to New York and stayed there long enough and had enough artistic (not financial) success to get a pretty solid confidence in my wares at their best. Then I came back home here

and began all over again. And because it suited me to spring my stuff in the local paper, and by gratuitous tracts, the local Mrs. Grundys damned me utterly as a fool, an ass, a very *crude* person, and one who emphatically and forever was an outlaw. Now as those same pieces reappear one by one in the larger publicity mediums—I reproduce them locally with the little notice "This first appeared in the Illinois State Register five years ago. It was now been reprinted in the following magazines"—then follows the list. It's perfectly awful—the way I do rub it in. If you invite me to your jinks be sure you want it known—for it is likely to leak out. The modest way it will dawn on my intimate friends—creeping up violet-like from the ground—would bring tears to the eyes of old Deuteronomy himself. But I won't print it in the Register. I won't let it get *that* far.

I am writing like an ass because I am in a hurry. I am watching for your swimming poem in Collier's. I'll bet they didn't like Macfarlane's write-up on my verses and dropped it down the sewer. I have quit watching for it. But I still watch for yours. The American Magazine took a poem of mine on Mary Pickford this morning—and I am pleased to death.

If you are *real* intimate with Jack London—tell him I liked Martin Eden immensely, as did everyone I ever heard mention it. That's God's truth. Maybe I would like some more but haven't read'em.

Maybe you had better wait till I have. Then I can prepare the proper boot-lick.

They go hard with me though. It's very seldom I do 'em in just the right style, these boot-licks.

Well—as I say— I am in a hurry and writing like an ass. I was delighted to get your letter and shall answer some day. Please send me your picture as a primitive man.

Very Sincerely,

NICHOLAS VACHEL LINDSAY

34

TO GEORGE STERLING

Springfield, Ill.
Sept. 23, 1913

My Dear Sterling:

Just a page. Of Nora May Frenche's Work "The Spanish Girl" makes the sharpest impression so far. With the exception of one or two lines it is perfect. They will improve no doubt—on acquaintance. Next—"My Nook" stands out plainly. She was an artist and a rare woman—and her troubles must have come from chance and fate—for there is nothing intrinsically morbid in her ink-well.

The Master-Mariner keeps going the rounds. It gives me new pleasure each reappearance. I like especially "Then and Now" and "Nightfall" among the pieces you sent.

Who is Lyle Solomon Baer—and what has he to do with the Poetry Society?

I send you some moonworms[1] under separate cover. Distribute them among the Chickens, or the Mermaids as your fancy pleases.

Certainly—Introduce me to John Neihardt.[2]

I tell Sara Teasdale to put a moonworm on a long line—hang it over the edge of the Universe and fish for a Dolphin in the Styx. I give you permission to do the same—if you so desire.

But you must ask me round to see the Dolphin when you get him.

Very sincerely and solemnly

NICHOLAS VACHEL

Just took a walk down town. Was congratulated on being engaged to somebody. "It's all over town" the party said. Well. I *will* take to the road if they don't let me alone. I wouldn't engage myself to the Queen of Sheba. Not if she has rings on her fingers and bells on her toes, and trains of black and white slaves bearing baskets of diamonds. I belong to God. It sounds sudden—but I mean it.

Notes

1. "The Moonworms" became "What the Hyena Said" (*Collected Poems*, p. 240) in the moon-poems.

2. John Gneisenau Neihardt (1881–1973) became Nebraska's poet laureate in 1921. His most famous poem is "Eight Hundred Rubles," and at the time VL writes, Neihardt had published *The Divine Enchantment* (1900), *A Bundle of Myrrh* (1908), *Man-Song* (1909), *The River and I* (1910), *The Stranger at the Gate* (1912), and *The Death of Agrippina* (1913).

35

TO THE EDITORS OF *Poetry*

Springfield Illinois
Oct. 28, 1913

Kind Friends:

This is to proffer to you and the anonymous guarantors my heartfelt thanks for the hundred dollar prize for General Booth Enters Into Heaven.[1] As O. Henry would say "I devastate myself with felicitations". Please consider me your constant admirer and well-wisher.

I shall certainly have it printed in the Springfield papers, as soon as the magazine comes out. That is always the climax with me.—the Springfield papers.

Now—remembering the sad fate of Dewey for giving his house to his wife, it is with some hesitation that I reveal to you what I have done with this money. Please only reveal the bit of news to those on the inner circle who will still think well of me. I gave the one hundred dollars to Mama. It may mitigate the matter to add that I owed her thirty dollars anyway. You see I gave it to her because Mama is a kind woman, generally very pleasant and affable with me—and I wanted to express my appreciation. I hope this will be all right with you. I did have one grand impulse to come to Chicago and take you all to Nickelodeons and things till it was used up. But then I would have had to borrow money to come home on, or something like that.

I wish you well—one and all—I wish you well.

Very sincerely with thanks.

NICHOLAS VACHEL LINDSAY

Note

1. The $100 prize was officially awarded to VL by *Poetry* in November.

36

TO ARTHUR DAVISON FICKE

Springfield Ill.
Nov 11, 1913

My Dear Ficke:
Your letters of throbbing, thrilling, trilling admiration for young Mr. Kallyope[1] are duly appreciated and I shall brag about them to somebody or other for a day or two or even longer. I will tell you, since you thus warm up—That I am working on a Congo piece that will make the Kallyope look like thirty cents. Every kind of a war-drum ever heard. Then a Minstrel's Heaven—then a glorified camp-meeting. Boomlay Boomlay Boomlay Boom. I am doubtful whether this stuff is poetry. But I discover a lot of it in me. One composes it—not by listening to the inner voice and following the gleam—but by pounding the table with a ruler and looking out the window at the Electric signs. Also by going to Vaudeville which I have all my life abhorred—I at last grasp what those painted folks are up to.

See if you can sing this to Yankee Doodle. The same tune only rounder and fuller:—

> *"Dawn this morning burned all red,*
> *Watching then in wonder–*
> *There I saw our spangled flag*
> *Divide the clouds asunder.*

Practice on it. The whole piece will come out sometime. I do hope everybody takes to the Kallyope—then they will forget General Booth awhile. I have recited the General till my jaws ache—4444 times. The silly things think it is the only good poem I ever wrote, simply because it *forces* attention.[2] Well—enough of these affairs. I thank you most heartily for your good cheering letters. The *December Forum* prose *and* verse, is perhaps my best single exhibit of the kind. Harvesting Prose and Harvesting verse. I am just up to my neck in letters today, and you will pardon the brevity of this I know. I have been writing *hard* on the Congo all day and haven't much sense left. I do not suppose I ever put so much progressive gradually developing polish on anything. Three pages of verse and about a month's hard work. I have recopied it dozens and dozens of times.

I have a poem on Peace with Japan[3] which you will understand better than anyone I can think of—in the Independent for Nov. 7. I spent scads of time on it last summer and am deeply gratified to have it in print. Uncomprehending race antipathy is inevitable but it should not dominate the lightest counsels of nations. Men have a right to hate the Japanese—after they have studied all the facts—if they choose—but if they really study that people—it is impossible that they should look on them as Rats and Monkeys—as the half-educated Californian is apt to do. In this poem I compare Nikko to Avalon—the last stand of Chivalry—the place where Arthur sleeps.

Well—I did not intend to launch on that.

I will write you a letter soon.

Very Sincerely

Nicholas Vachel Lindsay
603 South 5th.

Notes

1. VL had just published "The Kallyope Yell" (*Collected Poems*, p. 118) in *The Forum* for November 1913.
2. Ironically, VL here first tells of his weariness with "Booth" and, in the same breath, of his composing a poem he would become wearier of still: "The Congo."
3. The poem on peace with Japan is again "The Jingo and the Minstrel."

37

TO SMALL MAYNARD AND COMPANY—BOSTON

Nov. 19, 1913

Gentlemen:

Last winter I forwarded to you "The Adventures of a Religious Mendicant" torn from the Summer Numbers of the Twentieth Century Magazine—suggesting a book of these and some more sketches. I received sufficient encouragement—through Mr. Bynner I believe—to forward the book complete—about March—maybe. The Title Then was *A Tramp's Miscellany*.

Judging from the tone of your final rejection, it was on a business and not a literary estimate of the book. I presume your literary estimate is on file, and I have the vanity to assume it is reasonably favorable. And since my business prospects have considerably increased—I am thinking perhaps you might consider the work again. *I have not submitted it to any other publisher*—I like to finish where I began. "General William Booth Enters Into Heaven and Other Poems" is issued by Kennerley, beginning last Friday, my first book not privately printed. A pretty healthy bunch of critics are likely to back it up. I am apt to have notices in The Literary Digest, The Chicago Post—The St. Louis Mirror—the Current Opinion—The Metropolitan Magazine—, the Poetry Magazine Chicago—The Poetry Magazine Boston—and the people behind these institutions are all talking for me. Also Collier's Weekly Sept. 6 had a two and a half page boost for my work. Now these resources *besides* what Mr. Kennerley may set in motion on his account are bound to do a little grinding for this book. Most of them have tooted for me—off and on for many a day. And there are others I might mention.

Mr. Kennerley will bring out *"The Adventures While Preaching the Gospel of Beauty"* in book form—after the last installment appears in the February Forum. So in advertising General Booth he will endeavor to prepare the public for this Second Book. It covers my late adventures in the West. The book I offer you covers adventures long ago in the East, and South, and adventures a little later. The final article is one which appeared in the American Magazine not long ago under the caption *"Rules of the Road"*. I have changed this to "A Handy Guide for Beggars" and it seems to me that half-humorous title would make a good one for the whole book—and make a sufficient distinction and contrast with the "Adventures While Preaching the Gospel of Beauty". There is a thread of plot in the book—which traces the gradual evolution of that Gospel—but the main body of the work is just miscellaneous adventures in Beggary for their own sake. A great many of them appeared in the Outlook.

People seem to be talking about my work at last. The Metropolitan Magazine beginning in February will run a series of my poems—full page—*long* poems. They have taken three and ask for more. They expect to spot-light them. The Kallyope Yell—in the November Forum—another long poem—is being quoted about, and imitated in the Newspapers.

The Jingo and the Minstrel—in the Independent—Japanese Number—Nov. 6—is another full-page poem—ten stanzas. Mr. Bynner of your firm, has had a considerable hand in such publicity as I have acquired—and possibly he can weigh my present publicity and its prospects better than I can.

It seems to me that the Criticisms of my book of poems will begin to come out or have headway about March—if they are to appear—the

Metropolitan will have begun its campaign—and the series now appearing in the Forum will have had its effect—and it will be about the
Psychological moment to bring out the Handy Guide for Beggars—just
a little *before* the *Adventures While Preaching the Gospel of Beauty.*

The American Magazine has given me a considerable publicity in the
past—and has two of my poems on hand at present. Farm and Fireside
has issued six of my Proclamations and The St. Louis Mirror Constituency—which is made up of many Single Taxers—newspaper editors
and the like, have shown considerable loyalty. And General Booth of
course, has been quoted in about all the religious weeklies of the country. Maybe I am overdoing this letter. But I think you can pay for the
paper and print on my book now—with a reasonable hope of doing well
on a second book—which of course—I will be willing to consider.

Very sincerely

Nicholas Vachel Lindsay

38

TO WILBUR L. CROSS[1]—*The Yale Review*

Springfield Ill.
Dec. 4, 1913

Dear Sir:
I am delighted that I have made a start with you—by your acceptance
of "The Tramp's Refusal to Act".[2]

If I seem to send you suitable matter but slowly, please bear in mind
that there is at last a considerable demand for my work. One magazine
is attempting a collection of six on a similar principle to yours, and
having supplied them with three of the full-page sort of a thing they
want—I am about out of breath. I have done nothing to boost my prices
but they sent me seventy five dollars for the last one. This was the
surprise of my life—another equally eminent paper had sent me fifteen!!
but money is the least of my ambitions. Publicity means far more to the
minstrel, and *earnest* faces looking his way. I count it a considerable
honor to be really wanted—remembering when I wasn't.

I will be delighted if you can include Immanuel[3] in your set. You
need not use the notes on the musical scheme if you do not think it in

good taste. After some consideration—I have decided to offer it to you gratuitously—seeing it was once published in my little free booklet *The Tramp's Excuse.* It has never really seen the light—and is in many ways the most *intense* and *personal* experience of my writing life. While the Jerusalem tune may detract from its dignity in academic circles—that tune so strikes the mood for the populace that what might be called the obvious meaning of the poem is reinforced by the atmosphere and memory of that song.

And the obvious meaning is, of course, what we want most readers to get at once. If you wish to pay me something nominal for it—all right— but I do not want the fact that it was once obscurely printed in a cruder form to interfere with it being passed upon by a wider audience. I mean—I am willing to make a considerable sacrifice—that this particular poem may have a chance. It is *"Too religious"* for many. Others are leery—just because I am square and say it was printed once in a little book I gave away here in town—and in The Christian Evangelist in a cruder form (5 years ago). And this—not with the tune for a guide. I only discovered the other day it would fit the first eight lines of The Holy City. Please give it your most earnest consideration.

Very Sincerely

NICHOLAS VACHEL LINDSAY
603 South 5th

NB. The foot notes on Immanuel are only advisory. If you think it better to indicate simply that it be chanted all through—do so. Try it out yourself—and put down the most impressive notes.

Would it be asking too much to ask you to review the New Book of Poems[4]—issued by Kennerley—32 West 58th New York?

Notes

1. Wilbur Lucius Cross (1862—1948) established *The Yale Review* in 1911. Professor, dean, and provost at Yale over the years, he served two terms as governor of Connecticut (1931—39).
2. "The Tramp's Refusal" had its title abridged for the *Collected Poems* (pp. 328—29) but inherited a subtitle on that occasion: "On being asked by a beautiful gypsy to join her group of strolling players."
3. "Immanuel" was composed in 1906 and was named "I Heard Immanuel Singing" in the *Collected Poems* (p. 369). The tune accompanying it in the marginal notations is that of a hymn. But VL adds: "Yet this tune is not to be fitted on, arbitrarily. It is here given to suggest the manner of handling rather than determine it."
4. The "New Book of Poems"—*General William Booth Enters into Heaven and Other Poems*—was also the first to be published by a commercial publisher!

39

TO SARA TEASDALE

Springfield, Ill.
January 29, 1914

My dear Sara:[1]

Since I cannot help but write to you, let us set aside the matters of an hour and think, to some profit if we may, on the matter of VICTORY.

Certainly there is no victory, worth while, to be won in a day. The long plotted victories are those most worth while. What is the completely victorious spirit? The thought goes round and round in my mind.

Christ says—"Be not afraid"—"I have overcome the world". And his cross looks like the great spiritual victory to many.

There is another victory for the soul—not the victory of suffering but the victory of patience. The mystics have looked upon Christ as the incarnation of that brooding spirit of God that has been a creeping fire in the world since the world began—Christ being the final flower of the patient Spirit of the ages.

However that be, certainly the victory of Patience looks to me like the one most worth while—and most practical. We may seek crucifixion for a bad cause. But the patient man may get light and move on toward real spiritual strength, while the man on the rack yesterday reacts into the fool today. I know of no more fatuous object than the over-pensioned old soldier, still living in 1865, his crucifixion long past, a stand patter—a fool, an orthodoxy or a drunkard.

The real victory is the victory at seventy-five or eighty years—or in the next life if there is one.

But what are the steps toward victory? It is easy to put down a glib list of virtues—but what are the steps towards spiritual victory that give us tougher fibre and more courageous eyes in the presence of the terrible Universe—more courageous eyes this year than last year? And every year a little better?

I am not appalled to find myself foolish—blundering, silly, selfish, greedy—but I am appalled if I realize that my plan of life has grown dimmer—that I have ceased to call myself to judgment—and look the naked truth in the face, and struggle back to my path. I think that the first step towards victory is *to resolve firmly that I will keep it always in mind,* to say it is the reason we live and breathe—and that though millions do not really seem to care for victory, we may not understand them. —As for us, we are not going to plot and plan for money—or song or love or friends or any virtue but the great virtue of victory—a strong unconquerable stern spirit! Come let us be victors in old age—and let us take a step towards it today.

How would a victor appear? Not necessarily with friends or kin round him—not necessarily with soft raiment nor with any badges of outward bravery upon him—nor with any graces. But he would be one who could bear sudden grief—better than the rest—who could face temporary spiritual bankruptcy better than the rest, who could face physical pain better than the rest—who is less moved by tumult than the rest, though taking his full part in the tumult—and even urging it on—who does not curse God or charge him with foolishness—but is willing to bless his name amid great tribulation. The victor is the man who having struggled in vain with his weakness, his habitual faults, a thousand times—still looks at them firmly, still acknowledging them to God, still planning to circumvent them—if not to overcome them.

Patience. Patience. Patience and perpetual conscious reaching to the invisible God—the God who is cold as the dew and stern as granite—that is Victory.

With love,

NICHOLAS VACHEL LINDSAY

Note

1. Sara Teasdale (1884-1933) was the "Gloriana" of later poems by VL, who eventually dedicated his *Collected Poems* to her, nine years after their separation. She might have married VL had the latter had more of a fixed income and been less financially dependent on his parents. Among all the women VL—platonically—loved before he married, and they were numerous, Sara Teasdale was beyond a doubt the one who mattered most, excluding, of course, Elizabeth Conner, the woman who became VL's wife in 1925.

40

TO HARRIET MONROE

Springfield, Ill
Feb. 16, 1914

My Dear Miss Monroe:

I am certainly flattered and honored to eat with Yeats at the Cliff Dwellers' and make a noise with him and delighted to meet Ficke. I am sorry you will have to pay my car-fare, but I am dead broke. Can't you advance me what the poems are worth that you have in hand—and print them in the March number? That will do just as well. I don't want to be an extra expense. My plan of life is very simple you see—to live at home—on nothing. I only notice my empty purse when people ask me to go places. I resisted all kinds of invitations to New York—mainly from being dead broke.

I want to recite for you a poem that the Metropolitan people have bought—called "The Congo". I do not know when it comes out in that magazine—but I hope soon. Of course it cannot be given any printed publicity till that time—but I presume it is all right to recite it among friends.

I have just recited it for the big fat-sides Lincoln Banquet here—audience of 1000 in the Arsenal and boomed it to the very back of the building. I think there is more in it than Booth, and I want—if possible to make your bunch forget Booth for the Congo, or at least give the Congo an equal place.

Your poem on The Model—in The Forum I think an especially beautiful thing—it brought back some of the most tremblingly beautiful hours of my Art Student life—though that sense of Beauty was only radiated by two models that I can remember or three at the most—two in Chicago—and one in New York. Most of the poor creatures are drab and dead indeed. But many statues at various times have conveyed a similar triumphant Beauty.

The Congo is part sung–part recited–part chanted. I send you a clipping that may give you an idea of it. Since conquering my fellow-citizens in the Arsenal— I feel very scrappy indeed. You must give me a license to rattle the Cliff-Dwellers' Windows and pound the table *hard*. Much has gone into it—the Dahomey-dancers at the World's Fair, the story of the Pygmies and the Mountains of the Moon—in Stanley's

Darkest Africa—Joseph Conrad's haunting African sketches full of fever and Voodoo and marsh, Mark Twain's assault on King Leopold, and the Race Riots in Springfield Illinois several years ago,—and The Souls of Black Folk, by Burghardt Du Bois, *and* the recent death of a missionary on the Congo known and loved by many of my friends, and all that and all that, very much condensed—into a rag-time epic that takes about seven minutes. It will be far more effective than any speech I can make—I am sure. General Booth finally wears out, as a recitation, but the Congo never wears out.

Very sincerely

Nicholas Vachel Lindsay

41

TO HARRIET MONROE

Springfield Ill
Feb. 17, 1914

Mr Dear Miss Monroe:
My letter yesterday was mailed in haste: and I am not sure that I minded my manners. I should be grateful for the chance to meet Yeats.[1] And I will be delighted to see Ficke,[2] with whom I have corresponded a deal—and to read his sonnets if he has them with him. And I will be vain as a peacock to shine—by reflected light in the presence of Mr. Yeats—and while I cannot be at all sure of winning him for a *friend*, I would like to take a gambler's chance at it—if it can be done without boring him to bits, and without maneuvering. I fully realize that he has a lifetime of good poetry and good works behind him and I am only a beginner. Also he is probably much pursued by callow youths like me. I do not know how you are going to arrange the invitations—and have no one to propose—if you are crowded. If the "Poetry" staff is there—I am sure my horizon will be quite full.

But if I am at liberty to suggest names—I would be pleased to see some of the following there—if they care enough to buy a plate, on due notice from your committee:

Lucian Cary—Chicago Evening Post
William Chenery—   " "
Charles T. Hallinson Care of Chicago Eve. Post.
Marjorie Currey (*once* Dell)³ Evening News
Dr. E. S. Ames—Chicago University
Thomas Curtis Clark, Disciples Publication Society—700-714 East 40th
Charles Clayton Morrison—same address
Dr. Herbert L. Willett—Chicago University—
Hamlin Garland—Cliff Dwellers

I will try to give you a little crisper idea of the Congo than my last incoherent letter. The whole piece is elaborately syncopated, and imitates Dahomey War-Drums. But I worked hard to give it a silk lining. It takes about seven minutes. It is a better piece than General Booth—and I hope—a prophecy of a series in a similar strain, some of which I hope you will print, sometime this year.

The first section deals with the basic savagery of the negro. The Refrain is "Mumbo Jumbo Will Hoodoo You". By implication, rather than direct statement, the refrain stands for the ill fate and sinister power of Africa from the beginning. I do not say so—but the Civil War was a case of Mumbo Jumbo hoodooing America. Any Lynching is a yielding to the power of the Hoodoo. Any Burning alive, or hand-cutting depredations by Leopold, is a case of Mumbo Jumbo Hoodooing Civilization. In the second section the Irrepressible High Spirits of the negro—as set forth in a sort of Grand Opera Minstrel Show in a part compensates for and overcomes the Hoodoo he brings. All the ragtime elements of our minstrelsy and the Cake-Walk, etc are here symbolized. The third section is an idealized Camp-meeting—transferred to the banks of the Congo, along with a prophecy of the redemption of the race through their religious instinct, and the death of Mumbo-Jumbo.⁴

I hope as toast mistress you can cover this outline or a similar one, so that when I rise I can give all my time to my *poem direct*. I will recite it to you and Henry B. Fuller or Miss Wyatt⁵ beforehand and you can amend or replace this analysis with your own impressions. There may be several points you are just squirming to make—that this extravaganza will hook onto.

After delivering this noise to the dinner-people—I hope to conduct myself as a meek and quiet spirit with you and any third party you select, if I become a bore by myself. I hope you can entertain me—if you are not too rushed with preparations. I like your quiet style—as for the rest—they will get about all of me that is worth while in my recitation. I remember my quiet visit with you with the greatest pleasure. I hope we can kill a day or two together after the event. The preceding time will be too fluttery—no doubt.

Very sincerely and gratefully

Nicholas Vachel Lindsay
603 South 5th

Notes

1. VL recited "The Congo" at the Lincoln Banquet in Springfield, in February. The invitation to speak at the *Poetry* dinner, in the presence of W. B. Yeats, was for March 1. Harriet Monroe had placed "Booth" in Yeats's room the night before the banquet.
2. Although VL had been corresponding with Ficke for quite a while, the two men had never met.
3. Floyd and Marjorie Dell had divorced, and Dell remarried in 1919.
4. The missionary on the Congo was Ray Eldred, a Disciple of Christ (Campbellite).
5. Henry Blake Fuller (1857—1929) had published *The Cliff-Dwellers*, the first notable American city novel, in 1893. Its title was transferred to the club that VL joined in 1910 under the sponsorship of Hamlin Garland. A critic for the Chicago papers, Fuller was a member of "The Little Room," a group of Chicago's artistic elite, many of whom were benefactors of *Poetry*. Edith Wyatt belonged to that circle and acted as associate editor of *Poetry* (1917—19) between the departure of Alice Corbin Henderson and the arrival of Eunice Tietjens.

42

TO HARRIET MONROE

Springfield, Ill
April 4, 1914

My Dear Miss Monroe:
I have just finished a poem I will forward to you soon. As soon as I have read it around for a week and put in the final small changes. It is "The Santa Fe Trail" and I hope is better than the Congo or the Fireman's Ball.[1]

Now I want you to do me a very great favor, if it can be arranged with no great trouble to yourself. I want to be asked to St. Louis by someone you know,[2] to entertain their friends. If I could for instance have such a hostess as your sister Mrs. Monroe—it would be ideal—though that would be a deal to ask. I would like to spend about three days in the town, between Easter and May the first—enough to call on our mutual Sara about three afternoons. Now *don't* explain to my hostess my motive. I will tell her, if she is a real leddy—when the time comes.

I want to be asked down on my merits—and my car-fare sent me by my hostess and five dollars pocket-money, $10. altogether. In return for this I will recite for any number of people (10 to 1000) if my hostess desires—any number of evenings. I will include the Santa Fe Trail in my performance. I hate a hotel—I am dead broke—I want to see Sara—and I don't want to ask the Springfield home-folks to pay for my picnic. Sara lives in a lovely house—and her old folks are very sweet and kind—but they are *so* old—and they are not likely to be the sort to collect my crowd anyway, or get much fun out of the show. They are eminently dignified Baptists as I understand them. She is a lovely chick in a gilded cage! Sara don't know anything about this scheme—and I have tried so hard to think up some way of putting through some sort of a visit—and it is the best that occurs to me till I make some coin. M. K.[3] owes me $250 to $300. and will not answer my letters. And my letters to him have been respectful—and not particularly frequent. I mention this not to be telling on him—but just to show there is a reason why I am reduced to makeshifts. He is my principal publisher at present, though another looms on the horizon, and I don't want to wait till I make some money before I call on my St. Louis lady friend. Mama says I ought to wait. Maybe I ought, but I ain't. Now my dear Harriet—unless there is somebody who would want me in a perfectly natural way—I don't want the thing to happen. Maybe some of my other Chicago hostesses can suggest some one. Just tell them I am brash and vain, and want to spread myself in St. Louis. And now—curiosity box—of course you want to know what is in all of this? A purely PLATONIC admiration. But since I have written about 'steen thousand letters to Sara—*and* have only seen her 24 hours of me life—one long rather strained day—we were so dammed up with things to say—well—I want to correct the lopsidedness—or letter-sidedness of our acquaintance, and be able to chat at leisure.

No—I do not belong to anyone in the world. Never will.

On the whole I hope it's a *neighbor* of Sara's. Somebody in walking distance. But I am getting too full of specifications.

With love

NICHOLAS VACHEL LINDSAY

Notes

1. "The Fireman's Ball" and "The Santa Fe Trail" both had been composed in the wake and spirit of "The Congo" (*Collected Poems*, pp. 319 and 152). Later, "The Fireman's Ball" became Part II of "Poems Speaking of Buddha" in an attempt to alleviate the "jingleman" image that was beginning to weigh on VL's reputation.

2. Sara Teasdale lived with her parents in St. Louis, Missouri, and spent the summers with them in Charlevoix, Michigan.
3. "M. K." was Mitchell Kennerley, VL's first publisher before he went to Macmillan because of financial difficulties with Kennerley's firm (see letter 47).

43

TO HARRIET MONROE

Springfield, Ill
April 11, 1914

My Dear Harriet:
It was a rather silly letter I wrote you the other day—I am afraid.

I view matters more sanely now—owing to circumstances.

First let me thank you for the $5 for the criticism on Ficke. If it had arrived a day or so sooner (by some divine accident) I would not have written you my letter. As it was I wrote to St. Louis I was coming in a minute and went—and it is surprising the number of things that can be done with one five dollar bill in the company of some one who makes a chirping noise in your ear as you do it. And I read the lady the Santa Fe Trail and was properly chastened and will make it a bit less like an unmitigated noise before I forward it to you. It is a Kallyope yell with a few flute notes at present.[1] It needs a few more flute-notes from the Rachel-Jane bird (Meadow lark) to mellow the middle. Then you shall have it.

My present financial crises having passed—you do not need to *rack* your comradely brains to get me to Saint Looy. *And* Sara's sister having taken a hand in the matter—may get me an address before some Woman's Club down the next fall.

And then Reedy[2] talks about having me down to hoot for his crowd as soon as he recovers from what he calls "gout and Delirium Tremens". I met him and had a talk with him for a few minutes: A most amazing man.

Little sister Joy is getting married today and the house is full of house-party.[3]

The maid-of-honor is my most favorite beautiful angel-cousin. She is a student at Evanston—Northwestern—named Frances Frazee. Maybe Polly Petunia Allegra Root[4] knows some of her friends (My love to Polly!). She (my cousin) is the most beautiful descendant of the "Proud Farmer". I am awfully anxious to send you The Santa Fe Trail but prudence dictates I should read it aloud at least a week longer to weave in this Rachel-Jane tune just right.

Sara was all commendation—but I could just see the harshness of the auto-horns jarred her. I must put in a bird and surprise her.

Well I am just gabbing along. I intended only a note.

My very best remembrances to all—and to you and Mrs Henderson[5] in particular.

With all good wishes

Nicholas Vachel Lindsay

I am not going to Saint Looy or Chicago till I get another good big sweet noise-poem done.

Notes

1. The "flute notes" were incorporated into the text of "The Santa Fe Trail" (*Collected Poems*, p. 152): "Far away the Rachel-Jane / Not defeated by the horns / Sings amid a hedge of thorns:—"Love and Life, / Eternal youth— / Sweet, Sweet, sweet, sweet, / Dew and glory, / Love and truth, / Sweet, sweet, sweet, sweet."
2. William Marion Reedy (1862—1920), editor and critic, had edited *The Mirror* since 1893 and had published there the works of Edgar Lee Masters (as "Webster Ford"), Sara Teasdale, Zoë Akins, Fannie Hurst, Orrick Johns, and others.
3. Joy Lindsay married Ben Blair. The couple then lived in Cincinnati, where VL often stayed with them.
4. Polly Root worked in the *Poetry* office. Her husband, John Wellborn Root, was Harriet Monroe's brother-in-law and a brilliant architect. Harrie Monroe had written *John Wellborn Root: Architect* about him in 1896.
5. Alice Corbin, wife of the painter William P. Henderson, was assistant editor of *Poetry* for some time. VL's "The Tale of the Tiger-Tree" was dedicated to her daughter, Alice Oliver.

44

TO LOUIS UNTERMEYER

Springfield, Ill.
April 14, 1914

Dear Sir:

I must thank you again for all recent publicity and good fellowship, and for including me in your theory of the "New Beauty" and the "New Poetry".

I hope soon to print *all* the moonsongs—new and old—40 or there-abouts—broadside—in some western sheet out there—to preserve them as it were—and to save the bother of another book at present. I hope they will be worthy of your critical scrutiny in that case. I suppose half of them have been printed somewhere perhaps the best half. But there is no telling.

I have just finished and mailed off for the magazine rounds a hoot called The Santa Fe Trail.

100 automobiles pouring by on a Kansas road, bound for the coast. Delicate theme.

Also *The Fireman's Ball* is still begging at magazine doors. Another hoot.

But both of these have a silk lining and I hope—a little of the balm of Gilead scattered through. When I come east I will recite them and wake up all the neighbors. Sara likes The Santa Fe Trail now that I have put a little bird in it to sort of soften it down and give it tone.

Well, this is quite enough nonsense. If there *is* any personal news it is that The Santa Fe Trail is my best bet at present.

But watch for The Congo in the Metropolitan—I forgot *that*. It is equal parts (1) The death of a Missionary on the Congo. (2) a Cannibal War dance. (3) The Springfield Illinois Race Riots (4) The Burnings alive of negroes in the South. (5) The Camp-Meetings of half-Wild Negroes. (6) A Bert Williams[2] Negro Comedy Co. (7) A Minstrel Show. (8) Joseph Conrad's African sketches. (9) Uncle Tom's Cabin. (10) The Emancipation Proclamation. (11) The Songs of Stephen Collins Foster (12) The Souls of Black Folk by W. E. B. Du Bois. All boiled down and served to a rag time tune. Everything but Booker Washington[3]—though I think him worthy. Of course this is claiming a good deal for a poem—and you will be disappointed when you see it. But I hope you will watch for it in the Metropolitan—and read it—if necessary—with a defeated joy—with one auspicious and one drooping eye.

Well this is certainly clock enough.

I am your humble servant.

NICHOLAS VACHEL LINDSAY

Notes

1. Louis Untermeyer (1885—1977) was a former jeweler and poet turned critic and anthologist. He had written several pieces on VL and was to include him in most of his anthologies. He married Jean Starr in 1907.
2. Bert Williams (1875—1922) was a comedian and song-writer. His company (The Bert Williams Negro Comedy Company) was highly popular in vaudeville, and he worked with Ziegfeld in 1902.
3. VL's attachment to the figure of Booker T. Washington did not exclude other references to the black culture. "The Booker T. Washington Trilogy" (*Collected Poems,* p. 161), presented as a "memorial" to Washington, did not go into detail about Washington's theories. *Poetry* published the trilogy in June 1916.

45

TO HARRIET MONROE

Springfield Ill
May 12, 1914

My Dear Harriet: (Is that proper and permitted? Please allow it.)
I send you the table of contents of the New Book.[1] The Congo and other poems. I think you have read at least half of them. Now fix up your introduction—and I only insist on a brief one—if it can be made to include your very kind thoughts—fix up your introduction so that the reader will be craftily and unsuspectingly led to desire to hear me *recite* these verses, but even *more* prompted to try to recite them himself. It looks to me like my only chance at an income—after while, when I *must* have one (Pa is going to go broke paying for my shirts and trousers some day, and visits to St. Louis and all. And then I will *have* to recite for a living.)

But please make the point that many reciters over the country are reciting or chanting my pieces, who have never seen me—stirred to do so by the directions on the margins. Or something like that.

Next—please claim me for "Poetry's" own, and Chicago's own and Illinois' own, and Sangamon County's own—whether I am or not. And your own.

As for the rest—whatever is in your heart. The whole paragraph can be brief—but sufficient, if signed by your *honorable name. Then please forward to Macmillions [sic] and tell them to paste it in the front of the book.*

I might as well tell you that Gloriana in the back of the book is Saraphim St. Louis Teasdale. But that is in STRICT CONFIDENCE. Of course no one would know it who read the poems—except somebody who knew her, and knew she had red hair and such, and knew I'd been courting her.

If I am to write to Mrs. Petters—please give her name and address at your leisure. I supposed the dear would write to *me.* I hate to crawl before the mighty. *But* in a holy cause—I will crawl at least a moment.

The part of my book that will be *discussed* will be the first section.[2] And having heard my system of noises, I will be delighted at your testimony.

I will return the Santa Fe trail—all amended, tomorrow. About fifteen lines shorter.

Very sincerely with love

NICHOLAS VACHEL LINDSAY

Notes

1. *The Congo and Other Poems* was published by Macmillan in September 1914. In her preface, Harriet Monroe, more than answered VL's plea, writing (p. vi): "It may be opportune to emphasize his plea for poetry as a song art, an art appealing to the ear rather than the eye." Although much of VL's work is a flat contradiction of this doctrine, the "jingleman" image was thus gradually strengthened. His real economic reasons are here made rather clear.
2. The "first section" of the collection was entitled "Poems Intended to Be Read Aloud, etc."

46

TO HARRIET MONROE

Springfield Ill
May 13, 1914

My Dear Miss Monroe:
The two passages[1] to which you objected I combined into one and made the whole passage five lines shorter. Also I eliminated several purely

mechanical rhymes and beast-phrases. Also I have cut off the last eight lines. So the whole piece is eleven lines shorter—and I admit much improved—crisper and cleaner. Much obliged for the criticism. Also I have cut out the And's through the piece and helped it and I thank Mrs. Henderson for that amendment.[2]

But I do not think either of you had just my conception of the piece—if I may say so—put through the wrong sort of side-line coaching. I have tried to make the marginal notes a little more interesting and in bolder successive contrasts. I do not just remember how they looked in the version I sent you. Maybe I left them out.

Also I have entitled this a humoresque—to disarm the reader, and prepare him for *anything*. When I first conceived it, the piece started with three long pages of rat-horn, bat-horn, fat-horn, cat-horn, hog-horn, dog-horn, grog-horn, and so forth. A sort of three times ugly kallyope yell to express my wrath and lifelong aversion to the automobile. It stands as a sign, as a symbol of *America*, from the standpoint of those who despise her most and get her superficial aspects in a triple dose. I have considered the voice of the auto at its worst—the most obscene and unclean sound on the face of the earth. (Also very mechanical. Hence the forced rhymes). Since forming this opinion, I have gradually sweetened it up because I have ridden in some very charming automobiles with the very charming Harriet Monroe. Nevertheless—in writing this piece—I took on some of my old point of view. And it was *all Hog* horn when I began. Gradually I added the twilight zone—and the sweetness of the horns—in the distance—and the Rachel Jane was the very last afterthought, put in as a sort of final concession to the ladies who shrunk from the rude blasts of my satire, and the mechanical rhyme-repetitions.

And as I get you—you *like* the Rachel Jane—but merely endure the horns. *But* without the horns for a background the Rachel wouldn't be much. And the horns are the basic structure of the piece. I have cut them down all I think I *can* to still keep *harshness, rankness* and rawness the first conspicuous considerations of the piece. I want the gentler things in the piece to be afterthoughts—to dwell in the memory later.

I have tried—like the lion in Pyramus and Thisbe—to roar so as not to frighten the ladies—still I must roar. Also in characterizing the horns, I have tried to make a sort of balanced sketch of the American vices, from the standpoint of no one critic—but from the standpoint of the people of fine feelings generally. I have made the list as short as I can not to appear to be riding one special hobby. I want a list just long enough to indicate that there are various kinds of people in the machines. Please elucidate these things to A.C.H.

Any changes you want to make in the piece, especially in the side-line coaching—the marginal comments—you are fully welcome to make. I trust your judgment as much as my own, and the side line comments are of course very elastic in their possibilities and I seldom put them down twice alike, precisely. I had the dearest kind of a note from your beautiful Polly Root today. I am very glad there is such a person in the world, she is one of the good gifts of Heaven.

My dear Papa and Mama started for China Monday night.[3] I put them on the train at 11 p.m. with all their baskets and traps. I have been most homesick and lonesome for them—and it was indeed hard to see them go. I have had great but perhaps unnecessary misgivings about the trip, but have not voiced any of them. With White Wolf on the Rampage[4]—and near enough for some of his victims to come to my Brother-in-Law's hospital to be tied up, it certainly is not all Balm-of-Gilead in China. And then Papa is so old and battered and half blind and has such dozens of things the matter with him, any untoward trial or strain might smash him. But I put all these things aside—and yet have the sad feeling that I will not see them for six months. And they will be that much older. Papa is way beyond the recuperating point, he only marks time and *arrests* disintegration by his holidays. He used to bounce like a rubber ball. Still six months holiday and a total of ten weeks on the water might do wonders. They travel quite a bit by river. They are going first to the summer place Ku-Ling—Via Lin Kiang. Then to the hospital—at Lu Chou Fu via Wu Hu.

When Papa and Mama started out, the last hour or two—for all their terribly strenuous day—they seemed almost light-footed.—they seemed to slip the years just a minute—and that little glimpse of the past affected me more than all the rest, it brought back sharply many many years back.

Really—the largest part of their family is ahead of them. Olive and her three children and her husband, it is almost as much like going home as visiting. And like all well ordered folks they are daft about their grandchildren—and their only three are in China.

Well—this is quite a bit of family gossip—but it is what is most on my heart.

It is the longest and most adventurous trip of their lives. They have had all sorts of lovely good-byes and I have just found out that Mama's little literary society ordered her state room filled with flowers to surprise her. It will surely do so.

With love,

N.V.L.

To his family

How about bringing out the Santa Fe Trail in July—so there will be plenty of chance for talk before the Macmillion Book comes out?

Notes

1. The poem discussed here is "The Santa Fe Trail," subtitled "A Humoresque" in the *Collected Poems*.
2. Alice Corbin Henderson (A.C.H.) was associate editor of *Poetry*. Compelled to move to New Mexico in 1916 because of tuberculosis, she continued to advise Harriet Monroe.
3. Olive and Paul Wakefield had left for China in 1905. Dr. Wakefield and his wife, VL's sister, were missionaries there, and Dr. and Mrs. V. T. Lindsay were going to visit them.
4. "White Wolf" was then leading rebel bands in southern China.

47

TO HIS FAMILY

New York City
July 19, 1914

My Dear Papa, Mama, Olive, Paul, Vachel, Mary, Catharine, Joy and Benjamin Harrison Blair:

Greeting:
I know I have been lax in writing to one and all, but my adventures have piled on each other so swiftly I haven't had time to catch my breath. "The Friends of our Native Landscape" paid my way to Chicago last month, where I recited the Santa Fe Trail out doors for them. There I met Sara again, she being on the road to Charlevoix Michigan, the summer home of her people. She decided instead of going on to come to New York for a month. She was aware I had just received $100 from Harriet Monroe for the Santa Fe Trail and The Fireman's Ball, appearing in the July Number of Poetry. I wanted to buy a ring for her with the money, but she insisted she should get better acquainted instead, so after a day or two back home, I came on to New York here on a month's excursion ticket, and found her waiting. The trip has been well worth while. We are infinitely better acquainted, have learned a lot from each other—She has turned over her New York friends to me, bodily, we have been beautifully entertained and charmingly chaperoned by Mrs

Louis Untermeyer, Mrs Miles Dawson, Mrs Edward J. Wheeler,[1] and others. These people are the very heart of the Poetry Society. Mrs William Vaughn Moody, widow of the poet, while I was in Chicago offered me her vacant New York apartment—if ever I came here, so, after arriving here I remembered her offer and took her up on it. It is her custom to put up poets here in memory of William Vaughn. So I have this whole top-floor to myself just off Washington Square. Percy MacKaye[2] to whom she wrote, gave me a card to the Players Club for two weeks, and I have eaten there on my own hook with Witter Bynner and William Rose Benét (one of the Century editors) and my special backer in the Macmillan Co., Mr. Marsh has taken me over there and John S. Phillips[3] came in and got acquainted there, and had me call round at the office, also I met there Louis V. Ledoux.[4] Upton Sinclair[5] sent me a telegram to come to his country home, but I cannot leave New York. I recited for the whole Macmillan staff the other day, in the Office assembled. Edward J. Wheeler gave Sara and me a party one night where I met Joyce Kilmer[6]—Poetry Editor of the Literary Digest, and Louis Untermeyer, the Poetry Critic and me Valiant Champion *and* John Hall Wheelock,[7] Poet, *and* the Dawsons who subsequently entertained us at their country place—Cornwall-on-the-Hudson, chaperoned by Mrs. Wheeler. We rode up there in an auto, past Tarrytown etc. Percy MacKaye laid hold of me one morning and introduced me to his 12-year-old-daughter-poet Arvia MacKaye. I have been obliged to refuse his urgent invitation to visit him at Windsor Vermont on account of too much to do right here the next ten days. Morley[8] one of the firm of Doubleday Page had me out to recite one evening for a company at his home, and will have me to recite for all the 500 employees next week. And I have lunch with him and Gutzon Borglum[9] sculptor Tuesday. Percy MacKaye took me out for overnight along with George Grey Barnard[10]—*the* American sculptor to the home of the Simeon Fords, Simeon Ford being the famous owner of the Grand Union Hotel and after-dinner speaker. Sara and I have ridden up and down Fifth Avenue on top of the busses in all sorts of weather and seen the Metropolitan Museum and one theatrical production "The Dummy", and have generally kept apart daytimes and eaten 6:30 dinner together and spent the evening calling on friends or walking about or seeing the City. I spent two days at the Richards home on Long Island, and often eat lunch with George. While this is presumably the dullest season in New York I have been going it every day. Mitchell Kennerley brings out "Adventures While Preaching the Gospel of Beauty" in about a month. I waited on him with a lawyer recommended by Macmillan's, the first time I ever saw him (Kennerley). I forced the interview by holding the proofs of the Adventures and making my preliminary call with a lawyer on his subordinate with solemn implications. The sum of it all is that he has given us his promissory note due next Wednesday for $322.00 which is his estimate of what he owes us. *Our* estimate is $500, plus—but we took him at his own figures nailed him down to them so he couldn't wiggle and we have his note. Then we offered him the note in exchange for the copyright of the two books. But he wouldn't part with them—which is a pretty good sign he will meet the note. I understand I am about the only person who has ever cornered him. It is a funny story too long to put down here. The Lawyer will bite a big chunk out of the paper but I presume I will be about $250 to the good and able to get home in style. Also Mrs. Roe and Miss Flynn are meeting their obligations on the dot, so there is no worrying on that score.

My publisher (Macmillan's) want me to come back to New York about October and launch my book by reciting from it to audiences well picked in New York for the amount of talking they will do, and commenting which will lead the newspapers to comment on my poems as vocal things, chants. That is going to be my whole publicity policy, so people will ask me to get up and chant them, also attempt to chant them for themselves.

Ingold [?] Walker, illustrator, gave a party the other day for Sara and me and Anna Hempstead Branch, me old friend by letter I had never met. The Liberal Club, Greenwich Village had me for an evening and sure gave me a send-off. Four Rhodes scholars gave me a little lunch the other day. A group of Double-day Page men had me for a lunch at Garden City. Mr. and Mrs. Edwin Markham[11] invited me out with Sara to their place on Staten Island, and Edwin threatened to give me a Party—but not very seriously. I am trying to think of some of the other news. There is a plenty. Letters keep coming in, and it looks as though my Macmillan book will be talked about. The proofs for it are here on the table before me. I swore I would not start on them till I wrote a big fat letter telling you all the news I could. I haven't the least idea that my financial fortune is made. Far from it. But my next two books are going to be talked about and the people on the inside works are on my side. They are all for me. All the poets in especial. I have heard from or met practically all of them and they all send things more or less like the enclosed Cawein letter.

One of the most valuable spirits and rare souls I have met is Percy MacKaye. I set great store by him. We will be great friends.

Most of them know and are loyal to Sara, and we move around in practically the same orbit she has travelled here for the last four years. I am trying to get her to marry me—and she will if I get the money quick. But she much prefers I stay poet than turn money-maker, so we face a paradox. My only chance for an ultimate income is, perhaps, public chants or recitals. These cannot be set going right away, so we are uncertain about our future. But meanwhile, we are getting acquainted—and I am launching my books. We are glad to have gotten acquainted, anyway. We can say that much. All this is confidential, so I hope neither the gabby Ben Blair not yet the talkative Catharine Frazee Wakefield will pass it on. It's a shame to air one's most delicate affairs this way, but hell, you want to know what I'm a-doin', and now I'm a-tellin you, and clearing the atmosphere as best I may.

When Sara and I were in Chicago together—it was the same Whirl. Harriet Monroe was our beloved Chaperone there, and we were entertained at Lake Forest by the Aldises[12] and the Shaws, and had tea at the Blackstone at the Invitation of Papayian along with the Monroes, and were entertained together with Harriet at the Fetchheimers, and were given a party by Harriet with Mrs. Hamlin Garland, Edith Wyatt, Henry Fuller, and a lot of others. We have been whirled around in autos together—by our loving friends, both in New York and Chicago—and have had enough gorgeous scenery rolled before our eyes to make six novels and a travel-book, and 100 moving-picture reels. Every minute together has been a sort of adventure, one half the time with some one else included. Harriet persuaded the leader of the Dancing set in St. Louis to send for me to recite (expenses paid) (This was some time back) and I recited there for a parlor full and there was all sorts of adventure that time, including the witnessing of the St. Louis Pageant—with 150 000 spectators. Sara's system seems to be to plant herself firmly in one spot, then yell for me to come on, which I ultimately do—and then people begin to take us rides and give us dinners. Then I am egged on to recite, which I often do. If after all this—she still insists I shall go forget her—well— I won't go into that matter at this point. But existence, since I met Miss Teasdale last Feb or March, might be described as one dam thing after another. The missionaries[13] who read this letter will please skip the slang expressions, or excuse them.

According to Kennerley's report, there are still 347 copies of the Booth Book remaining to be sold this fall. Then he is going to print as I say, The Adventures. The dummy is already made, and the advertisements are out. He wants to issue it the middle of August. *Then* the Macmillan book will come out the last of September, "The Congo and Other Poems". The Metropolitan has postponed its magazine publication till that time, which seems to please Macmillan's. So two books and a half, as it were, will be abroad in the land between now and Christmas.

The latter half of The Congo collection has many poems dedicated to a person called Gloriana. I wonder who that is?

With love to all, and strictest injunctions as to discretion and secrecy.

NICHOLAS VACHEL LINDSAY

I will be here till about July 28, then home. Back again later.

Notes

1. Miles Dawson was treasurer of the Poetry Society, Edward J. Wheeler its president.
2. Percy MacKaye (1875—1956) was a dramatist and poet. He was the son of the famous actor Steele MacKaye and held a keen interest in folk literature. VL's ideas on "pageantry" he largely shared. He had just published a masque called *St Louis*.
3. John Sandburn Phillips (1861—1949) ran his own publishing company from 1906 to 1910 and edited the *American Magazine* from 1906 to 1938.
4. Louis Vernon Ledoux (1880—1948) was a chemist, critic, poet, a collector of Japanese prints, and a friend of Edwin Arlington Robinson's. Among his works were a book on the poet George E. Woodberry (1917) and one on the art of Japan (1927).
5. Upton Beall Sinclair (1878–1968) wrote *The Jungle* in 1906.
6. Joyce Kilmer (born 1886), the poet and poetry editor of the *Literary Digest,* was killed in action in France in 1918. *Summer of Love* (1911) and *Trees and Other Poems* (1914) were his most famous works. After his death, VL wrote "In Memory of My Friend, Joyce Kilmer" (*Collected Poems*, p. 387).
7. John Hall Wheelock (1886–1978) had been a friend of Van Wyck Brooks's at Harvard and was close to the poet Alan Seeger.
8. Christopher Darlington Morley (1896—1959), besides his collaboration with Doubleday-Page, also worked for the *Ladies' Home Journal* and the *New York Evening Post*. From 1924 until 1941 he wrote for the *Saturday Review of Literature*.
9. Gutzon Borglum, an old New York acquaintance of VL's, was the sculptor who created Mount Rushmore.
10. Among works by the sculptor George Grey Barnard (1863—1938) are "The Struggle of the Two Natures in Man" and "The Prodigal Son."
11. Edwin Markham (1852—1940), the celebrated poet, wrote *The Ballad of the Gallows Bird* (1896) and *The Man with the Hoe* (1899), which VL greatly admired. Markham wrote *Lincoln* in 1901.
12. Dorothy and Graham A. Aldis were friends of Harriet Monroe's in Chicago. Dorothy's name appeared in *Poetry* in April 1928 and other times. Arthur and Owen Aldis, of a Chicago real estate firm, were backers of *Poetry*.
13. The missionaries referred to were Olive and Paul Wakefield.

48

TO HARRIET MONROE

Springfield Ill.
August 24, 1914

My Dear Harriet:

I send you the Red Gods.[1] This is not the final form—but rather the first sketch. I want your most relentless criticism at this particular state—and hope to take it so completely you will be altogether charmed thereafter.

And I hope to get this into the Poetry Magazine before the years competition closes and along with it the Chinese Nightingale[2]—in Preparation. If I can get them into one number as before I will be delighted. If there is any argument for me crowding things in this manner—it is simply that I am the only person in the United States that is doing *nothing else* but write poetry, and producing more—and putting in more time I naturally have more to dispose of from the standpoint of quantity.

I am very anxious to make the Red Gods a success. It is an idea I have had for years and years. Please review and return as fast as you can.

Scrabble on it with a blue pencil. This copy is in no sense sacred. Bear in mind I am working on my own copy at the same time, and want your corrections while it is still hot in my mind. It is *very hard* for me to take suggestions—after a piece has hardened in my mind a little—but very easy before that time—so please act accordingly. Please indicate the livest section of the piece.

I have wanted to see you very very much the past week since Sara told me of her sudden engagement to the other man.[3] I suppose it would have been sudden to me—if she had waited several years. I have one thing above all else to be thankful for—that is that she has kept my deep respect and love and did not think it necessary to heap scorn and abuse on my head to turn me away. It is really one of the glories of life to keep the image of her dignity and ladyhood intact—and I must not forget that. But it is a mixed consolation—it is very very hard to give her up—and the harder the more seriously I take matters of the soul, for certainly her truth-speaking and thoroughbredness were great tonics for my spirit, and I can say in my coldest hour she was a staff and a help to my very best self—aside from the glories that come and go. And so I am all mixed up trying to forget her and *not* to forget her, and to think of her as one should. It is easier to harden the heart and forget her entirely than to remember as my best spirit demands—and walk with her among the stars.

Well—there is no use writing. The only person who knows me well enough and I know well enough to fight this out with—is my brother-in-Law in China— and China is a long way off. We were friends for years and years and years. I would like to talk to him.

Certainly the God that made Sara sent me an authentic message about Ladyhood through her, I cannot forget. She has been the living truth from first to last. I have thought over a hundred expedients that I shall not write you—one most of all—to beg her to change—but she is a woman of her word—and it would not be her—if she broke it. I have every reason to suppose she has the right man—she is a shrewd and keen judge—and I do not think she could be deceived by a crooked person. And it isn't proper for me to want him to prove a disappointment in any way—and so—there you are.

Really—I am so afraid for my soul—I do not want to lose any of the spirit she gave me because I have to give her up for a sweetheart.

The idea of woman being a staff and a prop is largely an intoxication and a fiction—though intoxication has its place. But Sara *was* a staff and prop to the spirit and I do not want her replaced by any mere intoxication. I want to be true to that fine self she gave me—that fine "myself" that I find in me when I look at her picture—and I am so afraid the picture will dim—I cannot think of her as being mine and another man's—

Well—if I wrote more—I would rewrite the same thing. So I close right here.

With love

VACHEL

Notes

1. "The Red Gods" became "The Ghost of the Buffaloes" (*Collected Poems*, p. 78).
2. "The Chinese Nightingale" must have been completely finished by February 1915, when VL recited a version of it before the assembled cabinet of President Woodrow Wilson. It was then published in *Poetry*, which awarded VL the Levinson Prize for it in November, much to the disgust of *Poetry's* foreign correspondent, Ezra Pound (1885–1972).
3. The "other man" Sara had become engaged to was Ernst Filsinger.

49

TO LOUIS UNTERMEYER

Springfield, Ill.
Nov. 28, 1914

My Dear Untermeyer:
Please accept my heartiest thanks for your all too generous boast in the Post. Parents are particularly delighted. It comes in very opportunely. They are just back from a six months stay in China and we are all

particularly glad to see each other—and sound the timbrel, the sackbut and the psaltery, the haggub and the accordion.

Please assure your friend Oppenheim[1] I am his till death—or scrapping time. I am so smothered with letters to write I don't know what is which.

But as to the review: Blanche Sweet[2] is *not* an Amazon. Blanche Sweet had best be named Swanhilde, or some such princess name. I hope to write *good* poetry to both her and Mary Pickford before I die. I admit the present tributes are weak. As for Buddha—well that is a long long story. But you might be amused to know that a dowager that insisted on getting on conversational terms last evening endeavored to ingratiate herself by persuading me I was a "scamp like all the rest of 'em". You know the air of forgiving you all too easily—in advance with a suggestive laugh.

I think I shall carry in my pocket an Anti-Saloon League subscription list and make all the dowagers sign it—when they begin that talk. Nothing in the world is more ironically amusing to me—except that other air—that astounds me in Springfield the last two weeks: "You and I and two or three others are high society people here in Springfield. The rest are muckers. Let us secretly rejoice together".

I'll have to take a fall out of this town yet.

I have been classed with the muckers and the shabby saints for these thirty-five years—and so I wish to remain with mine own people.

Isn't it ironical that democratic and religious poetry when deemed at last successful is deemed a gilt-edged license to play the snob and the devil?

Of course, I didn't mean a word of it! I only wrote it to be "clever", that preachy book of mine. *Well, this has little to do with Buddha—this carping.* I want to be better friends with you—if it can be managed so far apart geographically. We are too much pen-and-ink friends—and I am in danger of being drowned in a sea of ink, or smothered in tea-parties. They say to me as it were—even in Springfield "Now you are one of us—the Prussians". If I was a real man—I would get out War Bulletin Number Six, and free my soul. Not as a literary proposition at all—but to make my secret thoughts plain. I am getting to be a regular jellyfish. It seems to me I haven't half the iron in my soul I had when I first came back to Springfield about 1908. But then I became almost hysterical through going it alone—and at last got out my Peace Advocate. I feel as though the ground was cut from under me. I stand for no moral issue, no cause, no golden crusade. You have no idea how much I want to construct my spiritual life according to the iron pride and rectitude of my fathers. Perhaps Buddhism as I conceive it has a little more charm than Christianity because there is a certain touch of pride in it—and Buddha as he comes through the ages was not quite so humble as Christ and used his brain more. He was not as useful but in a sense suffered less. More impregnable, more stoical. Christ was crucified, but Buddha took to the road —that was the difference. If I take to the road again in the Spring—it will be more as a Buddhist than a Christian. Of course all this is for you alone—and not for Dell and Wood.[3] I am giving you my deepest reasons—if I can for I want you particularly to understand me, and there is a little too much of the Butterfly in those gentlemen for me to bother them with what I am after, in this particular matter.

I hold that a real man in my particular position would perhaps stay in his home town and make active cause with the radicals—and make speeches for Spaulding next Spring. Spaulding is the local radical commissioner. But I never get as far as that. First I must free my soul. I must cut everything that binds me—and if the road life is not real—for a man who may escape from it any moment—it is far nearer to reality than the social coil I leave behind me—and I have the assurance—for that little while, I am nearer freedom.

The conservatives are all for near-thieves and compromisers. The radicals are shabby hysterical cats. I had rather be with the cats than the compromisers—but on the road for a little while. I am neither—I am my own good friend and very happy when not absolutely in the presence of disaster. And I am most in harmony then—with that stillest room in my inner house that is always cold as the stars —no matter how much noise I may be making, on the outside—or how much I seem afire.

Well—I have written the afternoon away—not idly I hope. I am not arguing about your criticism. What you say about my poem is what in the end you will have a perfect right to say about me—and what some others have said. There is a kind of a north star room in my soul—a kind of a room of destiny and peace—that I am fondest of and that I most inhabit when I am on the road—and that I am always trying with more or less success to enter, I suppose that is what I mean by Buddhism. Always I am happiest when I realize that room is still there. Outside of this is a court of moral fervors and crusades and spites and passions—and outside still—a court of the love of all beauty and splendor and grace, just as real, and often seeming as restful and full of consolation. But the north-star room is the only sure place—Amid all the racket of this world—and the seemingly protracted play-times—I want you to know these are the things my egotistical soul really thinks upon.

And they are strangely mixed up with Springfield—in a way it would take a Henry James novel to show.

Very Sincerely

VACHEL LINDSAY

Notes

1. James Oppenheim (1882–1932), a close friend of Louis Untermeyer's, was a "pioneer" of Greenwich Village and became an analyst. He founded *The Seven Arts* in 1916–17 with Waldo Frank and Paul Rosenfeld.
2. Blanche Sweet was the star of D. W. Griffith's *Judith of Bethalia*. VL wrote a poem for her in the series called "A Kaleidoscope" ("Blanche Sweet–Moving Picture Actress [After seeing the reel called *Oil and Water*]," *The Little Review*, June 1914, p. 4).
3. Clement Wood was a friend of Louis Untermeyer's and was at one time Upton Sinclair's secretary.

50

TO HARRIET MOODY

Springfield, Ill.
Dec 2, 1914.

My Dear Harriet Moody:
Thank you for your prompt letter.

I am living my real life here again in Springfield, calling on my oldest friends, talking to the local politicians I like best—late at night—and being N.V.L. again helping rather lazily with the chores, and seeing all things going on their ancient round.

The room where I write you I have inhabited since my thirteenth year. It holds an awkward bookcase I myself made in that year, and in it are some books that date from before then. Every picture on the wall is a souvenir of an old friend, and has a story to it as long as the Mississippi River, one might say.

My room is always rather grubby and messy, for I take care of it myself mainly. The view out of the window is pleasant. I can look out over the Governor's yard. Governor Dunne can be seen in the evening in good days in the summer, walking among the bushes with Mrs. Dunne.

Piled all around me in odd places are poetry-books folks have sent me to read, and some prose. What memories I have had tonight! I only wish I could open the door to you. These very old memories have a certain cosiness I wish I could divide.

You have no idea how much of new this room shuts out—you who have only seen me on the stage as it were—acting (sincerely enough), speaking lines I myself have written here—yet even the writing self seems extraneous sometimes, as tonight in the midst of the past. Why do I talk so much about this? Because the thing above all that occupies my conscience, is the matter of doing what is the next inevitable duty or pleasure of N. V. Lindsay, maker of this bookcase and friend of these pictures. Here my sins, my weak spots, my failures, my self-challenges are all about the same that they were in 1899, we will say, my second year of college. I must stay in the same old game to beat the devil and conquer destiny, and not let any outside noises deflect me. Anywhere but in this room and on the road I am in deadly danger of believing in that new dramatic caricature of myself the Reviewers depict. I am in danger of believing my own exaggerated advertisements, and living in them, rather than my ancient soul.

Sometimes I think I should issue another war-bulletin full of Bitter truth about this town, to set them all against me once more, for it seems to me my soul was more in harness then, when it walked alone, than now when those that like me the least sneak with sweet tongues.

My work requires the ascetic and the celibate. I should renounce money even more strongly than I do, love poverty more. I should hate what I used to hate, for that big social hate was better than the petty spites of wounded vanity I cherish today. I am glad you want me to go on the road. It will be worth doing, even if it breaks my neck. You have no idea how when I am out of this room I reach back to my former ascetic self through today's roses, with the fear that I am losing it. Beauty and sweetness move me far more than they ever did before. I almost forget to mistrust them sometimes.

I have the spiritual hungers of a Franciscan ninety years old, yet I am suddenly loaded with a flowering outer self, and a blood-beat more like twenty than thirty-five. I am just beginning to understand the passionate ways of my girl and boy-friends that I remember at College, that were a subject of amazement to me then.

Yet my work—which has my heart of hearts—goes on like the illumination of a manuscript in a monastery. Today flatteries and publicity and the intoxication of the crowd threaten to drag me away from the missal. My literary self, or the monk that takes care of him, and sits inside of him by this bookcase, would know just what to do every day, and enjoy it with unalloyed pleasure, if this other Siamese twin with the hot-blood was not always hanging round, and buzzing more and more.

But unless I am mistaken, the monk will win in the end. He thinks quite clearly, and the other fellow never has his wits. The monk gets around his bacchanalian brother, by telling him, at a desperate crisis, when all other arguments fail, that it is his business to be a gentleman, at least, and by other spiritual diplomacies the monk wins.

Well, this is a lot of nonsense. I have no doubt I will write on these matters much more clearly, from the road, if I ever get there.

You have no idea how happy I have been these two evenings, calling on two sober old neighbors and hatching two Springfield conspiracies, for the betterment—perhaps, of the town—at least for its enlivenment. One of them may be really important. It is as merry an idea as ever was given and a dead secret and I am never never supposed to have a thing to do with it.

My last letter I almost asked a favor—now I will.

My boy-cousin—Francis Hamilton—Hyde Park Y.M.C.A.—is on my conscience. Twice I have been in Chicago and have not seen him. I am in despair of *ever* seeing him *right* unless he has become a part of our circle. I would rather have him in it, and a natural part of it, than any Chicago notables. I wish you would send for him in my name—or take him riding in the machine or something and get him started in our little circle so he is used to you all and unafraid when I come. He is a shy boy, but very able and good—and a mechanical genius, *and* his mother was my loyal partizan when most everybody else about was denouncing me as a blithering idiot or worse. *And* if she ever comes to Chicago to see him—I hope you will see her and like her, but I don't for a minute insist on that. But the boy has chances of being lonesome—if he is in the same pin-feather stage that I was at the same age in Chicago. He has gone to Chicago—seeking his fortune. His father is pretty well-off—in the wholesale Tobacco business in Indianapolis—the firm of Hamilton and Harris. But he only arrived toward middle-life— and he believes in letting the boy make his own start—which is correct. (The Girl-cousin I was telling you about has just been through Springfield—breaking my heart with her beauty—and has gone home to Rushville, Indiana.)

Francis Hamilton—the electrical engineer—the boy—has not any special literary or artistic bent that I know about—but he has won considerable honors in scholarship—has been voted into a graduate Fraternity of Electrical Engineers of some standing—which you will probably understand better than I would.

I remember how in Chicago—just about the age of this boy, I wrote a long and ardent letter to Herbert L. Willett[1]—from my very soul—asking for his friendship and help—and was treated in a grand and scholarly manner for my pains. I wanted to know *someone* no matter who—whose brains and position I could respect with whom I could thrash out the questions that were shaking me to pieces. As it was, I trod the winepress alone.

Francis may not be in any such state of mind—but then again he *may* be. Chicago with me was full of thwarted attempts at friendship. I failed equally at the University and at the Art Institute. I suppose though everyone at the difficult stage is as difficult for outsiders as for himself.

The minute I reached New York—however—I remember I was thrust among friends who were the very balm of Gilead to me—and there I *did* thresh out many an idea, and attained to many a friendship. Men for the first time treated me as a human being—I mean grownup thinking men. Well—I am just warbling on to no purpose. But get Francis mellow for me—and used to the idea of meeting me under your roof.

I have not spoken to anyone else in Chicago yet about him—and probably will not—unless it works with you. Tell me the prospects—his good and bad points—and just what I can do with him among my new friends in Chicago. You can judge much better than I can.

If I can use him as a twin—a social Siamese twin—(not the kind mentioned on the previous page) I will be very glad to do so. I always like to have a bit of the pit from which I was digged—somewhere near—when possible—a bit of the ladder on which I climbed—(or went down—according as you philosophize!)

With love

VACHEL

I look at the nice little gentlemen with beautiful little brides, and wonder just how they caught them.

It is Monday morning. The hired girl stayed at the house of a friend this morning—sick, so I have been washing and wiping the dishes. This is one chore I really enjoy doing. Now I am at my desk for all morning, and I plunge in a moment into my movie-book.[2]

With love

VACHEL

Notes

1. Herbert L. Willett taught at the University of Chicago and was a preacher and the editor of *The Christian Century*.
2. VL was just getting started on *The Art of the Moving Picture*. *Birth of a Nation* was released by D. W. Griffith the next year.

51

TO HARRIET MOODY

Springfield, Ill.
December 6, 1914
Sunday

My Dear Harriet:

I must confess to a certain lost feeling when I take my pen in hand tonight. For about nine months the good and beautiful Sara Teasdale and I wrote to each other all our minds and hearts, and she is going to marry another man, the 19th of December. She was in many ways the most intimate friend I had had for years and the best understander, the most natural. We were just alike in much that it would take Henry James to show. She was hard to give up, and now I have an empty rattly hollow-pumpkin sort of place where she belonged. I will tell you confidentially that practically all the complimentary poems in the Congo were written to her. And The Spice-Tree.[1] She walks through all the latter part of my book. The wicked daughter of Babylon[2] in the earlier part was the cruel lady who preceded her—and I shall never cease to be grateful for Sara for helping me to forget her, and giving me a new faith in and respect for woman in matters of Romance. I can always say "Thank God she stands between me and the insults of the past".

She did me good and not evil every hour of our knowing each other, and I have one more poem to write her I hope. But I have a sort of baffled feeling tonight. I have told so many things to the dear lady about myself. I sort of lived in the palms of her hands, so many things I have told her that she and I must forget or will forget. I feel rather empty and puzzled and say—"Is the only way to make myself clear to myself, and steady my life and thought, to write out all these things again, and rewrite all my resolves once more, and all my aspirations and puzzlements and the silly routine of my little struggles? Why must I go spinning my web over again like a spider to catch the fly of my own thoughts? All these webs torn down so often—why must I go round and round?"

I wish I had an angel for a friend who would always show me my self infallibly, listen to me interminably, remember everything I said encyclopaedically and never weary of the job. And in the intervals of silence tell me interesting things that had been happening to him from the beginning of time.

The Epilogue of the Congo Book was written for Sara after we had parted, I knew, or almost knew, for good. And forever, it proved to be. There are times when I think of her just like that Psyche-poem, or as though she were Beatrice. And then other times I get that rattly empty feeling, as though my heart were a gourd—so far as Human Passion is concerned. And then I think of my North Star, and reflect rather wanderingly, how throroughly consistent my artist-author-life has been, and what a wavering scrappy fragmentary destiny I have from the heart angle. From the beginning to the end—just like fate.

Notes

1. "The Spice-Tree," originally published in *The Chicago Herald* (*Collected Poems,* p. 42), happens to be an expanded metaphor of desire.
2. "The wicked daughter of Babylon in the earlier part" was Octavia Roberts (Corneau) of Springfield.

52

TO HARRIET MOODY

Springfield Illinois
11 P.M. Monday morning [*sic*]
[December 7, 1914]

My dear Mrs. Moody:
No letter from you today which shows that you are callous, undisciplined or busy. A midnight letter is easier for me to write than *not* to write, if I am only sure of an answer.

Well, I have spent most of my day in this room,—but have not written a line of my book.[1] Here is the outline before me. I have sat gazing at it with serene inertia, and rank cheerful stupidity, Quaker-meeting style.

That's the first stage, the hen on the nest.

My Papa and Mama are grand folks, and the trip to China has done them lots of good. Their tone has completely altered. They are really quite buoyant for them. Always I really enjoy them in a sober way, more than any humans I know, and now they are great fun.

I was taken to call—this evening—by a good lady friend who hopes that *now at last* I will make a hit with her particular set of—first families. But since it turns out now that I have hitherto been even more of a joke or object of disapproval with such, than even I dreamed, I much prefer to imagine myself making progress with Springfield's rank and file, whether I am or not. When people after 35 chilly years try to assume a simple cordiality, heartfelt and intimate, it don't quite work. And when the fair one at your side is grotesquely over-anxious to make it plain that now a certain wonderful veil has been drawn aside, and you are actually assumed to be a human being—well—with air of:—''I *stand sponsor now*'', (with an occasional prompting that you speak your piece correctly—) well it's just wonderful.

Really the dear one has the illusion that she is moving among the courts of Europe—(where she has long moved—of course—) and is now getting me made a Baronet—among Barons and princes! Also her manner of comment implies that henceforth—of course—I will take my pleasures among these people—and let a certain veil drop between me and my old companions. Of course those dear companions are not to realize the veil. I am to be too foxy for that. But my real heart is to be with those who have despised me—lo these many years and are now converted by press-clippings from Boston. And I am polite to them as I know how to be. I hurl no defiances. I declare myself devastated with obligation. But this lady has been herself a true friend and champion of mine and that makes it harder. Aside from her true heart her whole conception of the world is grandiose and false, and Louis Fourteenth, or perhaps—Prussian. And Oh Lord then they go on gabbing their teacup way about my poems on Lincoln. They think they ''own'' Lincoln. He is something they grew in their backyard. They do not comprehend one thing he ever said—one deed he ever did. They make him an excuse for every sort of flamboyancy.

Their real hero should be Charles First of England, when he was doing his best lying and snubbing and stealing and thwarting all the people. Good King Charles the Martyr.

I have been gabbing with this faithful heart and outrageous temperament—trying to forget I am the Romantic gourd described in a previous letter—and it's no go. So now I am studying the art of quitting without a jerk. Don't know whether I can do it or not. Wisht I had a girl like my Ma when she was young. A real lady, a brilliant intellect, but raised on a farm, and a real American.

These having been the things I have been thinking about— such thinking as I have done today.

I feel slowly shaping itself within me the dream of my next poetry-book,[2] coming in two years, perhaps, but the critical and strategic volume, as you know. I want it to be as democratic as Bryan and Mark Twain, but that gives but the dimmest idea of what I have been thinking

about. Certainly the chants should not lead in the next book. I do not
want to be known for any one mannerism. I want to be as rousing as
a Chautauqua oration, and at the same time carry a sort of smoking
censer with me. I keep thinking of the Catholic mass, of the Gregorian
music, and the work of the Ancient wizards. I think the war has made
the American temperament more pliable, and much more tender and
deeper than it has ever been—but war poetry is the last way to go at
it.

Perhaps, to put the matter in two words, I want to write rhymed
quatrains that are at the same time incantations.

And then I have a certain decorative, pictorial type of verse in mind,
like marble inlay of various colors around the niche that holds the colored inlaid statue of the Spirit of Illinois, we will say.

Notes

1. The manuscript alluded to is *The Art of the Moving Picture.*
2. The "next poetry-book, coming in two years, perhaps" was *The Chinese Nightingale and Other Poems,* published in 1917 by Macmillan. It was "dedicated to Sara Teas-dale, Poet," and did include VL's verse on Bryan and Mark Twain ("When Bryan Speaks," p. 20; "Mark Twain and Joan of Arc," p. 47; "The Raft," p. 71).

53

TO HARRIET MOODY

Springfield, Ill.
December 17, 1914.

My dear Mrs. Moody:
I find it has a grand moral effect on the local Wellesley girls for me to
be invited to Wellesley. They ain't half so impudent. So let's see it
through some day. I have just been writing Miss Katharine Lee Bates[1]
a belated letter. I told her that if one show will break her—at your
price—whatever that is—I would just as soon give four—if she will
arrange them in four successive days—at the same fee, in neighboring
handy towns. It's the breaking off work and getting there—that is the
exertion. It isn't performing after I am there. In short—I ought to be
paid for going rather than reciting. I think Cornell and Chicago Uni-

versity should have the same terms. Any reasonable schedule they may wish to make—I will conform to. You set the price for the entire visit.

Their ears will probably wear out before my throat does. It seems to me this is a much more human and friendly arrangement—than a hard and fast fee for some one performance.

You know that (when I have had my nap) it is hard to keep me from reciting. You might specify one afternoon nap for every night appearance! This is an awfully business-like communication.

If I go East I want to go to the Poetry-Society Annual Dinner—which is very early in February—and to Miss Rittenhouse's[2] party—Jan. 29.

This funny old world has been exhibiting its comicalities in Springfield lately—and all yesterday's little Springfield gossip amuses me all to pieces while I write. I wish I could tell you—but since each page of news must needs be preceded by a local novel—I will desist.

I haven't given you the right notion of my Mama. She is unquestionably the most powerful personality I have ever known, and one of the literary intellectuals of the first rank. She has taught me most all I know and I am still acquiring information from her.

In character though not in outlook Papa and Mama are much alike. I think within his own province he is more of an original—he is an absolutely unconquered Ishmaelite, in his determination to do everything his own way to the last ditch. A man with a most restless energy, great self denial—absolutely preoccupied with his family and his work, and believing in *hard* work, both in theory and practice—though he goes at his hard work with a great deal of fidget and slambang—and has not much patience with a job that requires any kind of delicate pains taking. *"Get it through with"* is his one thought—be it visiting Nuremberg—or driving out at midnight to the sick, over a frozen road.

I get the credit of all I ever do from my mother. The Lindsays class me as a Frazee through and through. But they are wrong. My father has a nicer sense of the particular word than my mother, who is more lavish and eloquent. In his middle age he used to be a much more musical reader of prose or orations than Mama. When he was young and full of fire, he just loved to read the Speech of the Jury—at the Cronin Trial, for instance—or some such thing. And in every practical task to this day, he goes at everything with a certain pioneer *ingenuity*, which I think I inherit when I approach the problems of versification. Everything cold or mystic or Buddhistic or non-human I get from my mother (though she has many other qualities), while I get from him everything romantic, individual, lonely and rebellious.

They are both fighters equally—in their younger days always on some kind of campaign against the ungodly and abetting each other like twin bulldogs. Their councils have always been councils of action—How shall we put up this tent?—What cities shall we visit in Europe? What new pastor shall we have for the church? They used to read together a deal—The Nation—The Christian Standard—the novels of Walter Scott—Dickens—etc.

When I was little I remember an interminable series of Scott's novels—my father and mother reading alternately, by the family lamp—and sometimes big sister Olive—two years older than me.

They greatly enjoy climbing together out west, have about the same omnivorous appetite for scenery, and climb till two o'clock in the afternoon for some height—and take in the view—then reach camp dead tired about dark.

They enjoy camping—Mama cooking like a whirlwind and Papa chopping wood, and building rustic bridges.

Papa has about quit getting anything out of reading-matter but the most nonsensical and superficial facts—the newspaper points one might say. My mother's intellectual life goes on and grows—and she has been the actual and nominal leader of two women's organizations here for four years—and the real leader of another. She had a Union of all the religious women of the city for twenty years or so—strong leaders in each church, and she has led a study class called the Via Christi for about ten years, and then the Literary Circle of her old friends—The Sunnyside, is her stand-by.

They let her lecture them two years straight—once, which is a remarkable thing for old grey-headed friends to do. She used Moulton's Literary Bible—the first year The Old Testament—the second year The New. By the time she was through with them she had filled them up with what I had before I was thirteen years old. She had me and the other children memorize every Sunday school lesson—reciting the verses at the breakfast table two at a time, every morning—and summarizing on Sunday—till I was about fifteen years old.

We went through the main Bible proof-texts near to twice in that time. Besides being elaborately lectured on geography, dates, etc.

Papa and Mama practically met in Europe.[3] Children of Kentucky and Indiana pioneers, Papa had practiced medicine abut nine years—near Springfield, and Mama had taught several years in a Girls School in Kentucky. She and Miss Eudora Lindsay were chums and fellow-teachers and they saved up till they had enough for a year in Europe. So about 1874—75 they started, after all the study and preparation that two school teachers would give.

Papa insisted on going along. He reported first for inspection at Grandpa's house. He had planned to spend the next year in special study in the Vienna hospitals, and he just made it a year earlier. So the three went together, presumably with auntie for chaperone. They became engaged in Dresden, and Papa nursed Mama through * * * fever in Paris. All sorts of things happened. Mama and Aunt Eudora wrote back weekly letters to the Apostolic Time—the leading Campbellite Denominational War-Cry at the time. Auntie afterwards collected her letters into a volume. Papa and Mama were married at Grandpa's on their return. Then they came straight here. The house was filled of course with European Photographs, especially the standard European art stuff of the day, and all my childish years were filled with reminiscences of Europe. Going to Europe then was a bit like going to China now. They did not go back till my youngest sister was half grown. She has been there with them three times and I went once.

In between they have camped of summers out west. I have gone with them three times to camp, no, four, but I generally spent my summers in this empty house, concocting Village Magazines, etc.

Now, I hope you have some notion of my folks. I think the very fact they did their courting in the European Art Galleries has something to do with a lot of things I unconsciously take for granted. They are still unabashed restless haunters of Art Galleries, Chinese Palaces, and Colorado Camps as well. And in all they indulge in what many people would consider heroic physical exertions—for either of them would yet prefer to do what they do by heroic bodily force than get any living mortal to do it for them. Papa lets the nigger sit still in the basement while he goes out and sweeps the walk in front. Until his age had reduced him to what might be called human moderation—he would much prefer to kick the barn-door open—rather than push it—any time. As for Ma she always has at least two people visitors in Camp for whom she cooks like a slave—and will not allow to lift a hand—though they be people of reasonable efficiency who would prefer—after a moment's reflection—to do their full part and more.

The half has never been told of my parents—but I feared I didn't do them justice in that former letter. They are my parents, all right, all right.

And there wasn't anything in China to be readily got at that escaped them in this six months, you bet. They approached it with the wisdom of years, and the directness of seasoned travellers, and being grey-headed, they were overwhelmed with Chinese reverential ceremoniousness for old age, which quite set them up, I assure you.

> Well now,
> Good morning,
> With love,
>
> VACHEL

I hunted all over, and can't find the rest of those Buffaloes.[4] I am awfully sorry, I put the original in the waste-basket at the Hotel Brevoort in New York and mailed a revision to the Herald. All my copies are Herald clippings.

With love,

VACHEL

Notes

1. Katharine Lee Bates (1859—1929) taught at Wellesley College. The author of the famous hymn "America the Beautiful," which nearly replaced "The Star-Spangled Banner" as the national anthem, she was a friend of W. B. Yeats's, Bliss Carman's, Robert Frost's, and Anna Hempstead Branch's.
2. Jessie B. Rittenhouse (1859–1948), an anthologist and poet, was for ten years secretary of the Poetry Society. She married the poet Clinton Scollard in 1924.
3. Dr. Lindsay accompanied his sister Eudora Lindsay (South) on her trip to Europe in 1875. Eudora, who then taught at Hocker College, Kentucky, had gone with her friend and colleague Catharine Frazee. Dr. Lindsay and the latter became engaged during that trip and were married November 30, 1876.
4. "The Buffaloes" are "The Ghosts of the Buffaloes," previously referred to as "The Red Gods."

54

TO GEORGE P. BRETT, JR.—The Macmillan Company

Springfield Ill.
Jan. 5, 1915.

My Dear Mr. Brett:[1]
I want to thank you most heartily for the pleasant Christmas gift. "With Poor Immigrants to America", Mr. Graham's[2] work will be not only a personal acquisition, but family acquisition as well, for my mother who has for these eleven years been the leader of the Via Christi Study Club—has chosen for this year's subject the Immigrants to this land—and she has seized the book with both hands.

I am very busy with my new book "The Higher Criticism of the Movies".[3] My particular equipment for writing this book is ten years of Art Education the last three of which were spent (winters) in lecturing in the Metropolitan Museum. My fundamental proposition is that the highest type of movie is a *picture* not a drama—the movie-theatre is at best an Art-Gallery not a play-house. I am proving it out a hundred ways. One good evidence of the soundness of my position is that the pictorial Belasco⁴ is producing the best movies of all the old-line managers.

Well—I must not write my book in this letter. I send you some clippings which you may not have seen.

But again: I have read an article in the January Atlantic on the movies⁵ which may suggest to you some of the possibilities of the subject that I hope to develop. I agree with the writer Eaton—precisely in his general feeling as to the dramatic limitations of the Movies. But he does not see their counter-possibilities pictorially. They are as revolutionary in our age as the invention of Hieroglyphics was to the cave-man. And they can be built up into a great pictorial art. The Egyptian Tomb-painting was literally nothing but enlarged Hieroglyphics. We have now Hieroglyphics in motion—and they can be made as lovely as the Egyptian if we once understand what we are doing.

Well—I might go on forever at this rate.

I heartily congratulate the firm of Macmillan's on publishing the Spoon River Anthology.⁶ The very last instalments last Friday—in Reedy's Mirror was one of the best. I think they justify the years that Reedy has conducted that exceedingly free forum—and I hope he gets due credit.

Very sincerely yours

VACHEL LINDSAY

Notes

1. George P. Brett, Jr., editor-in-chief at Macmillan's, had sponsored Jack London.
2. Stephen Graham (1884–1974) had published *With Poor Immigrants to America* in 1914. An indefatigable world traveler, he was a specialist on Russia. VL met him through Macmillan, and they went on a tramping trip together in the Rockies in 1921.
3. "The Higher Criticism of the Movies" was a working title for *The Art of the Moving Picture.* Another working title was "The Religion of the Movies."
4. David Belasco (1854—1931), an actor, playwright, and producer, managed the Madison Square Theatre from 1880 to 1886. His most popular productions included *Madame Butterfly* (1900). In 1906 he built the Belasco Theatre in New York. The "Bishop of Broadway" was widely known for his idiomatic use of lighting.
5. The article in the January 1915 issue of *The Atlantic Monthly* was by Walter Prichard Eaton and was entitled "Class-Consciousness and the Movies" (pp. 48—56). Eaton (1878—1957), a teacher and critic who worked on Boston and New York newspapers, was professor of playwriting at Yale from 1933 to 1947. His article in *The*

Atlantic Monthly dealt with the basic notion that "the line" separating the character of drama audiences from that of movie audiences "is the same line which marks the proletariat from the bourgeoisie and capitalist class." Eaton further argues that the obviously democratic appeal of the movies may be taken with diffidence because the aesthetic quality of the movies is inferior to that of the drama. To him the movies "offer geographical pictures of educational value, as well as pictures illustrating current events and natural history" with occasional exceptions of some aesthetic work (*Cabiria,* for example). From this article VL may well have drawn an image he uses in *The Art of the Moving Picture* when he talks about the differences between the photoplay and the stage. Eaton writes, "You view the dumb actions of human beings as through a glass." Eaton concludes with the following, which accounts for VL's remark here: "With the steady increase of class-consciousness effected by this cleavage" (between the spoken drama and "the infinitely inferior and spiritually stultifying mechanical film-play"), "the task of bridging the gulf again will be rendered constantly more difficult, if only because the proletariat will become constantly less susceptible to finer aesthetic appeals" (p. 56).

6.   Macmillan brought out Edgar Lee Masters's *Spoon River Anthology* in 1915, following its serial publication in William Marion Reedy's *Mirror* under the pseudonym of Webster Ford.

55

TO HARRIET MOODY

Springfield, Illinois
January 15, 1915

My dear Harriet Moody:—

I am only writing out of sociability, with nothing to say except that I am going to devote the rest of this afternoon to reducing a pile of letters to answer that have accumulated since I have written my first thirteen rough-sketch chapters of the movie-book. The Macmillan Company is actually clamoring for that work. But it will take a heap of reviewing to make it the same oracular Moses in the Mountain deliverance of two tables of stone I want to make it. There is as yet not a streak of aesthetic criticism in this field and I am all excited over pioneering.[1] Macmillans have insisted on seeing duplicates of the first thirteen sketch-chapters.

Well, this must be a short letter. As I say, it is my busy day. I am much rejoiced that Macmillan's are going to bring out Webster Ford's Spoon River Anthology. It is great stuff. I send you the last installment. Don't you dare to refuse to admire. Also mark my words. It will be one of the literary sensations and the literary landmarks. In one year the literary world will be at his door, eating from his hand, we might say. He has said hundreds of things in the anthology I wanted to say in the Village Magazine and wasn't man enough or artist enough.

I solemnly resolve that no letter this afternoon will be over a page. Believe me I wish you well in all things, and send you every fraternal thought.

With love,
VACHEL

Note

1. VL was indeed a pioneer in the field of the motion picture. In Europe, Louis Delluc's articles in *Paris-Midi* appeared as late as 1918, Léon Moussinac's first texts go back to the early 1920s. In the Soviet Union, the manifestos of V. Koulechov (1917—21) and Dziga Vertov (1922—23) came out shortly before the first films directed by Sergei Eisenstein. In the United States, the first major book-length texts were, besides VL's work (1915), Hugo Münsterberg's *The Film: A Psychological Study* (1916), Victor Freeburg's *The Art of Photoplay Making* (1918), and Epes Winthrop Sargent's *The Technique of the Photoplay* (1916).

56

TO HENRY SEIDEL CANBY

Springfield, Ill.
Nov. 29, 1915

My Dear Canby:[1]
Yes. Feb. 12—will suit me precisely, and I thank you for your hospitality. I will be with you on that date.

I have just received an invitation from the Colony Club of New York—and will probably come directly from there to Yale, though the details are not settled with them.

Now my dear Canby, I hope you will get the Elizabethan Club into a state of mind before I come. I mean—I want enough friends to have some enemies or enough enemies to have some friends. If necessary let the Club split down the middle and choose sides and one half be pro Lindsay and the other half anti-Lindsay. I am particularly anxious that the antis be thoroughly posted and that they examine my work with sufficient care to really know all the actual flaws, limitations and inconsistencies. Then it will be my pleasant work to come and alleviate some of these miseries. I do not want to deal with vague sentimental partizanships or vague aversions. If this may seem overweening—back of it all, remember—is the desire to have my work a *reality*, just as much of a reality as a football game. This is not, of course, the final test of literature, this athletic test.

But most of the European Art was founded in controversy as you know, the battle of the Impressionists was particularly striking.

Personally I think the world of many Woman's Club women, and have had some pleasant times with many clubs. But one reason I welcome votes for women is that the Politicians in order to get these women's votes will come among them at tea-time and put some real scrap into the issues the women now merely chatter about. Kulchuer—(the American brand) is as absurd as the German—outside of the colleges. Thousands of college men drop it as an unreality the minute they enter business. I have had many a businessman tell me how *once* (in his college days) he wrote verses, etc. And in the American business office or Club Smoking Room—Kulchuer is classified as a mere Woman's Club affair—and as long as it is, it remains sterile—*one sex*, instead of two, and *one sex* affairs are sterile, at least in America.

We want to get up such controversies that they last out into the business years—and the men if you please, begin to attend the Woman's Clubs, as it were, and put some fire into them. The ladies are doing nobly, but we must not ask them to be amazons.

All these views are perhaps the result of too much Woman's Club life in my recent years—with no other gentleman present.

If it is unwieldly to call for a division of the Club or House—as in Parliament—on this question—it might be practical to select the four most thoroughgoing and gentlemanly kickers in the club and have each one review one of my four books and then let the group take an evening to forewarn the club, each man taking five or ten minutes with the devilish intent of exasperating somebody into opposition. You might read them this letter in confidence.

Very Sincerely

VACHEL LINDSAY

Note

1. Henry Seidel Canby (1878—1961) was mainly a critic. His only novel, *Our House*, was published in 1919. He worked with the *Literary Review* from 1920 on and founded the *Saturday Review of Literature* in 1924. In 1915, the year his *College Sons and College Fathers* came out, he was teaching at Yale and writing essays on academic matters.

57

TO HARRIET MONROE

Springfield Ill.
Nov. 30, 1915.

My Dear Harriet:
The Foundry-proof—the very last of it—was done over two weeks ago—and there is every reason to suppose the book is bound, boxed and on the way.[1]

Also there is an advertisement I have written out and asked to be put in the end of the book—in which your name appears twice—once as the writer of the Preface to the Congo—and secondly as the giver of the Levinson Prize for the Chinese Nightingale. I wrote this ad out and sent it some two weeks ago and Marsh wrote me he would take it up at once with the advertising department.

Also I did *not know* that you introduced the Imagists till you told me when last I was in Chicago. What's more I did not realize that you were their especial partizan. I was thoroughly grateful for your championship of my work—but did not know who else you were championing in the same personal way. Certainly my human interest in the Imagists dates entirely from my last visit to Chicago—because they are particularly the sort of people hard for me to get at. I used them in my book because I wanted them to get interested in movies, not because I was a convert to their charms.

Also the Movie-Book is not the last book I will publish, nor my last chance to show an interest in Poetry a Magazine of Verse.

Also—when in Grand Rapids I talked for you and your magazine and for no one else—and Mrs. Helst writes me she is coming to see you with reference to a date.

Also in Champaign I talked for you and no one else—and as a result you got a letter you didn't like! Nevertheless I said my *best* say for you. Since leaving Champaign I wrote my longest and most careful letter about the Magazine to Prof. Stuart P. Sherman[2]—who brought me there. I said every mortal thing I knew about getting you to Champaign and enlarging the subscription list there.

I expect to do the same when I go to Jacksonville Illinois on the tenth, and wherever I go—this winter.

I expect always to mention the Imagists with respect and admiration since my talk with you in Chicago the last time—and I expect to mention them as your particular discovery, whatever my personal indifference to their art.[3]

I expect to recite the Chinese Nightingale to the Teachers Saturday—and this in spite of the fact that it is almost impossible to get across in *a large* audience—therefore I have coached up the papers—and I do this as a tribute to thee, and an acknowledgement to thee of what thou has [*sic*] done for me.

I also have made a special point of reciting it in Chicago in all private companies—and intend so to do in the future—with due acknowledgment to the magazine.

Yesterday four of my most intimate friends most tore me to pieces for not going on Henry Ford's Peace Ship, because he sent me two telegrams and a letter. They said it was my one duty for all time. I had just about shaken this off and gotten human again, when your letter came.

You must be good to me Harriet—I am *not* made of cast iron.

You must *not* accuse me of disloyalty when my only crime is ignorance. As soon as I know what you want—I try to do it.

But I assure you that I knew nothing of your connection with the imagists in a heart way. I thought you viewed them with something of the same polite effort to be fair that I do—just as you would let in any picture into your exhibition that showed a reasonable seriousness. I have been writing poems for your paper here every day—trying to polish up what I have for you—and expecting so to continue all winter—and forever so far as I know. And I always expect to forward everything I write, *first* to you, and I expect to put all there is of me into what I write and offer you—and you know that and it ought to count in mitigating other things. You must *not* tell me I am disloyal. In the first place—I will not believe it.

VACHEL

Notes

1. *The Art of the Moving Picture* was due out shortly.
2. Stuart Pratt Sherman (1881—1926) taught at the University of Illinois, and from 1924 to 1926 he edited the book section of the *New York Herald Tribune*.
3. VL's relationship with the Imagist movement was a surprising one. Although his deepest ideas on poetry largely accorded with theirs, he rebelled against their elitism. Ezra Pound wrote him down in succession as "having a ray of his own" amid the general mediocrity and as an "impossible" poet. Amy Lowell both deprecated and promoted his work by reciting it herself.

58

TO CLEMENT AND MILDRED WOOD

Springfield, Ill.
Jan. 15, 1916

My Dear Clement[1] and Mildred:
God speed you both. May you live long and prosper. In the sidewalk of your adventures may every brick be marble and in the Jewelry-Store of your circumstances, may all the brass be gold. In the hay-field of your toil, may all the bumble-bees be candy-makers and may all the butterflies keep their fuzz till fall. In the Barn Yard of your environment may all the ducks be swans, may all the geese be Ostriches, may all the turkeys be birds of paradise. Very sincerely

NICHOLAS VACHEL LINDSAY
603 South 5th.

Note

1. For information on Clement Wood, see note 3 to letter 49.

59

TO HARRIET MONROE

Springfield, Illinois
June 11, 1916

My Dear Harriet:
Here's wishing you well. Thank you indeed for the check. Thank you for all good things—at present and to come.

Enclosed find a dollar for which send me a dollar's worth of June's Poetrys.

I am hard at work on my new book "A Handy Guide for Beggars". It ought to be out in September.[1]

My good wishes to Mr. and Mrs. Monroe—Mr. And Mrs. Calhoun—Polly Root—John Root—Edith Wyatt—Mr. and Mrs Charles Hamill—Mr. Carl Sandburg—Mr. Edgar Lee Masters, and anyone else who speaks of me to you in terms of affection. Oh yes—Caroline Dudley. Let me not forget Caroline nor yet Katherine.[2] I think Carl Sandburg is a real feather in your cap. As soon as I get human again—I want to write him about his wonderful Chicago Poems.[3]

Every time I reread one it seems stronger. I don't in the least approve of free verse—but I cannot help but approve of Sandburg and Masters. I am certainly glad they are alive.

Very sincerely and with constant affection—

NICHOLAS VACHEL LINDSAY

Notes

1. VL had unsuccessfully and repeatedly tried to publish his memories of his first tramping trips. *A Handy Guide for Beggars* was eventually published in the fall of 1916 by Macmillan.
2. All the people mentioned here gravitated around *Poetry: A Magazine of Verse*, as sponsors, benefactors, or contributors. Caroline Dudley was one of the Dudley sisters, all considered as women of artistic talent among the Chicago intelligentsia; Katherine Dudley, in particular, was something of a favorite at the time. Helen and Dorothy were both poets published in *Poetry*.
3. Sandburg's work then consisted of *In Reckless Ecstasy* (1904) and his *Chicago Poems*, published in 1915. *Cornhuskers* did not come out until 1918.

60

TO GEORGE P. BRETT, JR.—The Macmillan Company

Springfield Illinois
July 2, 1916

My Dear Mr. Brett:

Thank you indeed for your letter. I am so glad you consider the Booker Washington Trilogy[1] alive and not dead. As to the suggestion of an entire book of this nature, if it comes, it will have to come after more experience and observation with the colored folks. It certainly cannot be done in a hurry. All the brotherhood I have for the blacks dates from the Springfield race-riots of 1908 when, for six months thereafter as a local Y.M.C.A. worker, etc, I cutivated a people I thought deeply wronged. I have worked that knowledge pretty thin by now. I would have to go back to the negro church awhile and pick up the threads of it, and look the whole situation over again. I would not want to rush the matter. I will certainly think it over. In a perfectly natural way I hope—in an organic way I hope—I have introduced a prose story[2] about the colored people in the latter part of the Handy Guide for Beggars—based on our race-riots, with a short introduction covering those riots and about all I have to say about the race question in mere prose, is there.

Is the Macmillan Company willing to read the proof of "A Handy Guide for Beggars" so I can be free to take a harvesting tour through the North West? What arrangement do you suggest? I would like to make a big sweeping tour if I can—if a dog doesn't bite me the second day.

Very sincerely

NICHOLAS VACHEL LINDSAY

Notes

1. "The Booker T. Washington Trilogy" (*Collected Poems*, pp. 161—74) includes "Simon Legree—A Negro Sermon," "John Brown," and "King Solomon and the Queen of Sheba."
2. There is no trace of "a prose story about the colored people in the latter part of *A Handy Guide for Beggars*." VL must have thought at that time of including his story "The Golden-Faced People," first published in *War Bulletin* Number 1. Or perhaps Mamillan rejected it.

61

TO AMY LOWELL[1]

Springfield, Illinois
July 30, 1916

My Dear Friend:
I am sending you a folder[2] under separate cover in which I invoke your name, page four and page five, and in which I have deftly mentioned the Imagists, in a way that may amuse you, page six.

And I take this opportunity to send you my most fraternal greetings and good-will. Aside from its personal character, I know there is much in the general attitude of this pamphlet with which you will agree.

I think you will understand that it is written as a substitute for the usual patent-leather-finish Chautauqua folder, and though from the standpoint of the bleating lamb in the field, or the humble wayside daisy, it is indeed a blatant and brazen document—from the standpoint of the Lecture Bureau press-agent—it is more modest than the lamb—the daisy or the violet, as such a person understands those vegetables and that animal.

Though writing this letter in print to save myself many hand-wrought letters to pretty committees, I had a weather eye on all us poets, as is perfectly obvious, and I had every intention that the document should fall into hands like yours, in a strictly unofficial incognito way, since it serves to save miles of preliminary talk—when we meet again, which I hope is next February when I come East for a month. I hope to recite in the West in November and the East in February, and stay with my father and mother in Springfield, and write, like a reasonable being, the rest of the year.

I was particular [*sic*] taken with your Craftsman Article, and hope you can do the like again. Sandburg's allusion to Pocahontas[3] was one of the lovely experiences of the year. And the whole list of verses was vital.

Now why not do this again? Let the leading article be on some phase of poetry—and *all* the poems that month illustrate it. It keeps the poem from being an end-page ornament—a sort of official diploma, accepted by the populace—but unread by them.

I wish you well,

Very Sincerely

NICHOLAS VACHEL LINDSAY

Notes

1. Amy Lowell (1874—1925) published *A Dome of Many-coloured Glass* in 1912 and *Sword Blades and Poppy Seed* in 1914. Her *Critical Fable,* with favorable treatment of VL, came out as late as 1922.
2. The folder VL was sending was his "Letter About My Four Programmes," which he had had printed as an introduction for those willing to invite him to recite.
3. Pocahontas was the theme of several of VL's poems and an increasingly significant symbol to him as the years went by, reminding him of his alleged American Indian ancestry.

62

TO HARRIET MONROE

Springfield, Illinois
Oct. 12, 1916

My Dear Harriet:

Thank you for the prospective article about the poem-games.[1] Please bear in mind that the idea is in an exceedingly plastic state, subject to suggestions from all sides, after the show is over.

No. My name-tactics are the same. I am always Nicholas Vachel Lindsay when I sign my name to a private document and Vachel Lindsay when I sign it to a magazine article, a new book or a published poem. You will note that the public notice I sent you is signed Vachel Lindsay. Most reviewers take the cue from the Macmillan books, and use Vachel Lindsay. For the most part only personal friends use the Nicholas and they are welcome I am sure.

My good wishes to yourself and Eunice[2] and the charming stenographer.

Did you know that the great Griffith telegraphed for me to go to New York and Return at his expense to witness the performance of Intolerance! I boast of it blatantly. It means that I am getting somewhere as a Motion Picture critic. But I respectfully declined, and said I hoped we would meet in a year or two at his Los Angeles studio in reference to a new book of moving picture criticism I hope to write in five years—perhaps.[3] That I am at present preempted by previous plans of verse writing, etc. Also it is possible the Century Magazine will reproduce pictures of my favorite movie—The Wild Girl of the Sierras.[4] Watch for it next month or in two months.

Also the Moving Picture World, the big official trade paper has been backing me pretty strongly, and I am no longer quite an outsider in the Photoplay Universe.

The Handy Guide for Beggars has been delayed but is now accepted after some revision and has just gone to press. It ought to be out the last of November. It will have the same general message and atmosphere as The Adventures While Preaching the Gospel of Beauty. But it will have better chances of a run for three reasons. (1) The First Story—The Man Under the Yoke is a good Christmas Story. (2) Macmillan start the book instead of Kennerley. (3) These are my very earliest travel sketches and are probably a little bolder than the others, in seeming, with a little more surprise in them—for I was myself perpetually surprised at all that happened.

With love

VACHEL

It was a good poem on J. C. Calhoun in today's Herald, and I have no doubt you will hear from many people about it. I am glad the Anthology is coming out. I have sent the last proof of the Handy Guide.

Jane Addams has written me most enthusiastic letters about The Art of the Moving Picture. I am delighted to have pleased her. She wants me to take one of the Men's Rooms at Hull House, and hopes to see Eleanor do the Poem-Games with me at the Little Theatre if she is well enough. I am *delighted* to have pleased her. I was so anxious for my book to be the fundamental sort that would please her type.

With every good wish

VACHEL

Of course I would only stay at Hull House a day or two, this time, if I went. But I would go hoping for an intimacy and understanding and usefulness in the place that would gradually increase from year to year.

Notes

1. VL had begun working on the Poem-Games in the summer of 1916, and he tells of the history and development of that mode of expression in *The Chinese Nightingale and Other Poems* (pp. 93—97). Several shows were arranged in the wake of the preliminary work. In November, with Eleanor Dougherty, VL presented the Poem-Games in Chicago's Little Theatre and in Mandel Hall at the University of Chicago. The two events were announced in the October issue of *Poetry*. The Poem-Games were also taken up at Wellesley College, thanks to a professor of music there, Hamilton C. Macdougall.
2. Eunice Strong (Hammond) Tietjens (1884–1944) married the composer Paul Tietjens in 1904 and later married a playwright, Cloyd Head, in 1920. She worked assiduously in the *Poetry* office. She went so far as to state in her autobiography that she had been "reborn at 27," upon meeting Harriet Monroe. She also collaborated on *The Little Review*.
3. The other book on the movies that VL hoped to write was never published, although he wrote a sizable two-volume manuscript in the late 1920s entitled "The Greatest Movies Now Running," now in the Clifton Waller Barrett Collection, Alderman Library, University of Virginia.
4. "The Wild Girl of the Sierras" featured Mary Pickford, for whom VL had great admiration and whose friend he eventually became.

63

TO JANE ADDAMS[1]

Springfield
Oct 15, 1916

My Dear Friend:

Certainly it was good of you in your convalescence to write a note to so humble a person as me. I assure you I am delighted to have interested you in my book on the photoplay. Munsterberg has the best book on the scientific side I think, and the bridge between us can be found in the phrase I have italicized and its implications "space measured without sound, plus time measured without sound," pages 106—111. I am delighted to have so much common ground with Munsterberg. His book appeared several months after mine, and we worked quite independently. His book is The Photoplay, Appleton's $1.00. I have not seen Griffith's *Intolerance* but the reviews indicate a film that illustrates Munsterberg's idea of the photoplay opportunity to move independently of time, space and causation. I may skin Girffith as a Southerner of the virulent type, but I hold him the Tintoretto and Titian and Paolo Veronese of the new art, or the man who will teach the fellows who will become this. Milton did not carry out his avowed purpose to "assert Eternal Providence and Justify the Ways of God to Man" and the devout pictures of Venice are anything but devout, to our thinking, nevertheless Milton and the Venetians have done their share for us. And so I am thinking that Griffith has probably preached a poor sermon on "Intolerance", and his *method of philosophizing"*, running four trains of thought at once, may be mechanical or commonplace, or confusing in this instance, and yet may be set us a new standard in picture technique and splendors as the Venetians did, and forge methods and weapons his successors can use more to our satisfaction. If, even, crudely, he illustrates in this play, Munsterberg's theory of the photoplay moving independently of time, space and causation, it will be a noble thing, the appearance of the theory and the technique at the same time.

I hope you and I can meet and go to this film some time, or some other you will choose. I will talk you to death and create disorder for a radius of ten feet.

George Hooker Esq. is a very good friend of mine and I have often dined with him at Hull House. I refer you to him for credentials, as to my otherwise reasonable behavior, away from the theatre. I venture to enclose my "Apologia Pro Vita Sua".[2] Please do not feel yourself bound to read it. But I hope you can put it into the hands of some one near you to read, after you have looked at the pictures, so he or she can explain what I am doing at the right moment and perhaps fit me into Hull House off and on, as the occasion warrants, and you want to see me. I will be in Chicago November 23 through December 3, for Little Theatre performances with Miss Eleanor Dougherty. She will dance my poems in costume, as I chant them.

Very Sincerely

NICHOLAS VACHEL LINDSAY

Notes

1. Jane Addams (1860—1935), the well-known social reformer, established Hull House in 1889 in an industrial slum neighborhood. A community-oriented center for artists and educators, it was known nationwide. Jane Addams chaired the 1915 International Congress of Women and presided over the Women's International League for Peace and Freedom.
2. The "Apologia Pro Vita Sua" must have been "A Letter About My Four Programmes," which was illustrated with VL's drawings and which he was then sending to everyone he knew.

64

TO J. E. SPINGARN

Springfield, Ill.
November 2, 1916

My Dear Sir:[1]
Last August when I was away and my mail was being dammed up here in Springfield your invitation to the Amenia conference arrived. Since then I have let everything go for a new book. Pardon me.

I send my belated thanks, being at last able to get into my mail again. Be sure I am with you in spirit. My "Congo" and "Booker T. Washington Trilogy" have both been denounced by the Colored people, for reasons that I cannot fathom. So far as I can see they have not taken the trouble to read them through. The third section of the Congo is certainly as hopeful as any human being dare to be in regard to any race, and the John Brown is certainly not an unsympathetic poem—and *King Solomon and the Queen of Sheba* is a prophecy of a Colored Utopia.

Yet The Crisis[2] took the trouble to skin me not long ago. This in the face of the fact that they had published with great approval my story of the Golden-Faced People in The Crisis, November 1914. That is the index to all subsequent work.

I presume some of your movement who have an intelligent angle on my intentions are responsible for my invitation to the Amenia Conference. When two or three of you are gathered together some time I wish you would re-read The Congo (see volume of that name). The Booker Washington Trilogy, in Poetry, A Magazine of Verse—543 Cass Street Chicago—(June 1916) and also the Crisis article aforesaid.

And after you have read this letter I would appreciate it if you will send it to the editor of the Crisis to be printed, if he cares to do so. Personally Mr. Dubois has been most courteous, but I cannot understand his editorial attitude. Add a word to this letter if you care to do so.

Very sincerely

NICHOLAS VACHEL LINDSAY

P.S. I would like to draw your attention also to pages 47 and 48 in The Art of the Moving Picture where I have discussed the Reverend Thomas Dixon.

Notes

1. Joel E. Spingarn (1875—1939) was chairman of the directors of the NAACP from 1913 to 1919. He retained other functions in the association until the year he died (treasurer until 1930, president from then on). One of the founders of Harcourt, Brace and Co., he was literary adviser there until 1932. His book *Creative Criticism* came out in 1917. VL reproduced his letter and Spingarn's answer in the 1925 edition of *The Village Magazine* (pp. 134—35). The argument sprang from the fact that *The Crisis* praised "The Golden-Faced People" in 1914 and harshly criticized "The Congo." Spingarn's answer was extremely cordial and merely pointed out his belief that VL for all his dedication to the cause of the oppressed, tended in his writings to distinguish between black and white humanity.
2. The editor of *The Crisis* was W. E. B. Du Bois (1868—1963).

65

TO LOUIS AND JEAN STARR UNTERMEYER

Springfield, Ill.
Dec. 19, 1916

My Dear Louis and Jean:
Thank you indeed for existing, and making the world more bright. I send you my pretty thoughts, my loftiest and most chastened sentiments.

May your apple tree be fruitful and shady in summer and magical in winter. May it whisper strange tales the year around. May your barn yard be filled with kine and your bins with corn. May your family album increase with noble cousins and your shelves with noble poets. May you always bloom like the pansies and prosper like the sun.

Very much yours.

VACHEL

66

TO HARRIET MONROE

Springfield, Illinois
January 5, 1917

My Dear Harriet:
Thank you for your Tribune clipping. I may use it. And I am glad you stated your position in Poetry. Mine did not come for January, so I just bought one on the newsstand this afternoon.

While you have a perfect right to record your impressions, and they are valuable, please let me straighten your arithmetic.[1] The changes from one period of time to the other in the three hours of *"Intolerance"* were marked by the cradle thrown on the screen, and it was used, as a refrain is often used in a poem, to keep the "leap" from being too abrupt. And you must admit if you think back, that that cradle was not thrown on the screen more than about thirty-six times in the three hours not thirty six hundred. So those famous leaps were not so frequent, except at the very last. In the first hour each story took fifteen minutes at a stretch, or thereabouts. The scenes in good photoplay technique, as in this case, lasted from ten seconds to a minute, averaging I should say fifteen seconds, and the three second flashes were only occasional, like exclamation points or semi-colons. You confuse *scenes* and *periods of history* in your estimate. In one single stretch of Babylonian story, for instance, fifteen minutes long, there are forty-five or fifty scenes, so closely related that they followed each other like words in a sentence. For instance in the opening of the gates of Bel we watch the men at the windlass ten seconds, as we would in life, then look at the gates themselves ten seconds as we would in life, then watch the dancers coming through, ten or fifteen seconds more.

These scenes are so closely related that the movie-fan at least feels that for that half-minute he has been standing in one place, looking at the same thing, and the general episode goes on around the gate for several minutes more. As to your general indictment of the dynamo-like effect of this film, I think you are right. It is a sound objection, but not so large a one as you make it. You objected to "The Marriage of Molly O" on exactly opposite grounds, that there was not *enough* happened to fill out the time. If you go to Annette Kellerman in "A Daughter of the Gods" you will make the same objection, there is not enough happens, and you will miss the dynamo, if it is completely absent. Certainly there is a compromise, and a middle ground, and your two objections kill each other, and I hold there is *something* that you do not like about movies that you have not discovered in yourself, and you have not given the *real reason*. It may be a very sound one for all that.

You misunderstand my position on "Intolerance". It is only the beginning of cinema achievement. The "most mystical" photodrama I have seen was not "Intolerance" but a little thing of an idyllic sort called "The Wild Girl of the Sierras". The most idealistic was not "Intolerance" but the *Battle-Hymn of the Republic*, long out of print. The most artistic was not "Intolerance" but "A Girl of the Paris Streets", perhaps. Two of the most wonderful were Judith of Bethulia and the *Avenging Conscience*. *Intolerance* is the latest word as an assembly of new technical devices and effects and methods of narration that less creative men technically will put together in better order in quieter films, I hope, to express entirely different dreams. At its height it is good Epic Poetry. Possibly its final interest for me will be printed soon in the New Republic. I have sent them an article where I show that it confirms some of the speculations of Munsterberg's *"The Photoplay"*, "a Psychological Study", his last book. Watch for that article if you care for further light. In some ways, "Intolerance" is as messy as an artist's studio. But I can see things emerging, who have watched Griffith's suggestions diluted or improved by smaller or quieter men before. After all Harriet, you do not like the game. I feel just the same about base ball, and am in despair over the American people because they spend so much time over nerve-racking nonsense on a fidgety diamond.

Well, this is enough. Let us have King's ex long enough for you to tell me if you know anything good bad or indifferent about Mrs. B. C. Bachrach, if that is what her illegible handwriting spells. She lives at 4531 Greenwood Ave. Chicago, and wants to give a private recital for a company in her parlor, when I speak for the Fortnightly. If you do not know, do not trouble to answer.

If Masters wants to cuss Intolerance, I am collecting them. Please tell him if you see him, to write out his cuss for the Mirror, where I can see it, and we all can enjoy it.

With every good wish

VACHEL

You may quote any of this letter if you care to use it.

Note

1.   VL was movie critic for *The New Republic,* 1916—17, which published his article "The Movies" in the issue for January 13, 1917 (pp. 302—3). Later, in the same magazine, he published "Photoplay Progress" (February 17, 1917), "Back Your Train Up My Pony" (March 10, 1917), "Venus in Armor" (April 28, 1917), and "Queen of My People" (July 7, 1917).

67

TO HARRIET MONROE

Springfield, Illinois
January 12, 1917

My Dear Harriet:
Please send permission to C. D. Morley Doubleday Page and Company, Garden City New York to reprint the Booker Washington Trilogy and my editorial on the same from the June "Poetry" for an invitation recital

I am to give in Lord and Taylor's little book-shop audience room on the afternoon of February Sixth.

You may be interested in the following quotation from my movie-book: "They go in their loneliness to film after film till the whole world seems to turn on a reel. When they are again at home, they see in the dark an imaginary screen with tremendous pictures, whirling by at a horribly accelerated pace, a photoplay delirium tremens. Faster and faster the reel turns in the back of their heads. When the moving-picture sea-sickness is upon one, nothing satisfies but the quietest out of doors, the companionship of the gentlest of real people. The non-movie life has charms such as one never before conceived. The worn citizen feels that the cranks and legislators can do what they please with the producers. He is through with them. The moving-picture business men do not realize that they have to face these nervous conditions in their erstwhile friends. They flatter themselves they are being pursued by some reincarnation of Anthony Comstock[1] . . . . etc"

This ought to so interest you in the book, that you will read it, other than the fact that your name is in the middle of the book and Masters and Padraic Colum[2] and others we know! You ought to be a good critic of the films, not their blind and fanatical enemy. And above all women in the range of my knowledge you are equipped to furnish sound constructive criticism of my book, so that in five years I can write another. I would like to have you annotate *every page*, wanted you and Alice[3] to do it before the book came out, but Alice was East and the Mss. miscarried. I tried over and over again to get you both interested. Now that Munsterberg is dead and gone to his reward, the fact that I have written this book gives me the place to write the definitive editorials and the next book. I hope with sounder judgment and riper knowledge. You must help me Harriet. If you never go to another film, and cannot like them, you can at least examine my theory AS a theory, as you could a theory of turnips and cabbages. If you say the word and there is no copy of the book there I will send you another copy. I would like to have you O.K. every page or write on the margin your principal objections. The book is full of fundamental assumptions about the art world and about America, that I want accepted or rejected or amended by you. Every year I am likely to get a little deeper into this game and I do not like to go alone or leave my dearest friends behind me. I want a propaganda they can care for, amend and share. This year the New Republic is likely to run a monthly movie editorial by me, and I want each one to represent genuine progress in my own thought, and an addition to Munsterberg's theory and to my own. And I do not want to go it alone, or go it blind. If I write another movie book in five years I would like to have it meet or express your ripest judgment as well as my own. And since this cannot be had just by asking you, I hereby kneel down and beg.

You are better equipped by nature and experience to be a photoplay shepherdess than any woman I know. If you read my book you will understand what I mean. I know you are busy, but this is a fundamental and permanent matter. Your long experience as an art critic gives you the soundest kind of an equipment. It takes that, plus a keen literary sense and a sense of democracy and they combine to produce a sort of fourth dimension which is the moving picture sense.

While there is plenty of action theory in the book, Munsterberg goes farther there. I gave the art gallery idea perhaps undue space in my work from the standpoint of a permanent work, for the simple purpose of dislodging the dramatic prepossession which has so strong a hold on old Broadway stars and managers in the new game. The book has been accepted by Jane Addams and given to all her friends as her word on the movies. It has been accepted by the Columbia University Scenario Class.[4] Technically it has been accepted by the most exacting and authoritative commercial oracle on scenarios Epes Winthrop Sargent to page 132, which involves the mass of the theory and classification and implies the rest. Not but what he accepts much else in the book, but these first 132 pages that *look so daring to outsiders are not so to people in the game* at all. It is the sermons at the end the M. P. people do not like. Griffith has distributed one hundred copies in his studio, in spite of the way I skinned him on page 48. He told me it was the most beautiful book on the subject ever written, and it has been constantly recommended in the Moving Pictures World along with Munsterberg's book for those who would write the higher photoplay. No other books are so named there. Only two printings have been sold, and there is little prospect of a third. In short I have the position without the everyday authority or wide publicity. I want neither authority nor wide publicity till I am even more secure in my position, and surer that I am right. I want to go at it slowly, take my leisure time for it, write one short page a month for the New Republic, read all the new books on the theme that are worth reading and get to be the Harriet Monroe of the photoplays, sometime in ten years I may say. Except that I want to be critic only in this province, and confine my original work to verse.

Well this is quite a long letter, my dear Harriet, but my heart is in it. Do not separate yourself from me in this matter. You could help me so much, not by rushing in, but by thinking steadily about it. For instance I am willing to give you six months to read my book, if at the end I have your most careful page annotations, the kind I really wanted you and Alice to put in the manuscript.

Very much yours

NICHOLAS VACHEL

Gordon Craig[5] wrote me a year ago (after reading my book) that if I would give the word, he would come to America at once and start a photoplay studio with me. He seemed to accept the whole volume.

Notes

1. Anthony Comstock's "New York Society for the Suppression of Vice" had become active in 1914 and was instrumental in developing post office censorship.
2. Padraic Colum was an Irish-American poet (1881—1972) with whom VL had been corresponding.
3. "Alice" is Alice Corbin Henderson.
4. Victor Freeburg used *The Art of the Moving Picture* in his classes at Columbia University.
5. Edward Gordon Craig (1872–1966) edited *The Mask* in England. Actor, scenic designer, and writer on the theater, he went to Italy in 1903 and established the School for the Art of the Theater in Florence. *The Mask*, founded in 1908, was succeeded by *The Marionette* in 1918.

68

TO CARL SANDBURG

Springfield Illinois
January 13, 1917

My Dear Carl Sandburg:
Please allow me to congratulate you on your Christmas and New Years poems in the Illinois State Journal and the Chicago Herald. They both brought the days home to me, and I have been writing to my friends about them. I send you a letter from Edward J. Wheeler. I hope you can go to this event some year soon approaching, if not this year. I do not take to the poetry scraps a bit. They are all nonsense to me when you consider that there are one hundred million good Americans who do not know there is even an Amy Lowell. Not till we have reached the Harold Bell Wright[1] circulation will there be any excuse for a battle of the giants. As it is the more we scrap, the more in-growing we get, and

the more divorced from the normal American currents. If all the critics in the United States shouted at once through one megaphone, our next door neighbor would not hear, and Whitman would not be vindicated. We can all afford to unite, and charge abreast at the American people.

Well this is all by the way. As a newspaper man you probably realize it more than I do. I am going to write a poem on Pocahontas, I hope, using the quotation from the Cold Tombs[2] as a text and a start. That is one of the beautiful passages in American poetry. And be sure if you get me it is in spite of the method, not because of it. I still think more of Poe than Whitman. Bryan is really the American poet, till we can take the Chautauqua platform, and sing to as many. I suppose the ideal American poet would have the tang of Mark Twain, the music of Poe, the sweep and mysticism of Whitman, and the platform power of Bryan, and a career in verse similar to his in Politics. The Chautauqua may evolve such a one yet.

Well, I did not intend to write a letter.

Very much yours

VACHEL

Notes

1. Harold Bell Wright (1872—1944), the novelist, was a pastor and preacher for ten years. Of his best-selling works, *The Shepherd of the Hills* (1907) and *The Winning of Barbara Worth* (1911) are most widely remembered.
2. The passage VL borrowed from Sandburg's "In The Cool Tombs" was: "Pocahontas's body, lovely as a poplar, sweet as a red haw in November or a pawpaw in May—did she wonder? does she remember—in the dust—in the cool tombs?" See "Our Mother Pocahontas," *Collected Poems*, p. 105. "In the Cool Tombs" was published in *Others* in June 1917.

69

TO LOUIS AND JEAN STARR UNTERMEYER

Wellesley
Feb. 27, 1917

My Dear Freinds:

Let me thank you again for all your hospitality and kindness. I am indeed blessed with your kindness of heart—and I sit here in Katharine

Lee Bates' beautiful attic room and look at the pansies in her window and write you, and the sun shines brightly on me.

A word or two more on Anita Loos[1] and Mae Marsh.[2] Anita has the making of the cleverest kind of a literary person.—and is the enterprising member of the team. Mae is the sky dumb quivering genius—and not to the point in my enterprise very much.—but evidently an essential of Anita's happiness and ease, and delightful to know. Anita has a friend John Emerson, I have not yet met —but a person I would be glad to have you size up if you encounter him. He and Douglas Fairbanks and Anita are their new company. He was the director of the Tree production of Macbeth. Mae is the new Goldwyn Company.

These two girls are just at the stage when Bohemia looks like the grandest country in the world—when to my mind they have had heaps of Bohemia already, and need the Untermeyers far more than they need Washington Square. They both have mothers—that can be included on occasions. Mae Marsh has some sisters that do not impress me, which may be my fault. But they do not impress me. Anita has a mother that looked like a good deal of a woman on my second call, and takes pretty good care of her bird I fancy, though Anita is apparently the head of the family. I understand Mrs. Marsh is a grand woman, but I have not met her.

I wish you people knew how to help me to scold the great (prospective) amorphous Goldwyn Company into righteousness. Any advice on that point, a year from date, I will be glad to hear.

If you want a man for the evening you entertain the Loos-Marsh combination an appropriate person would be Prof. Victor O. Freeburg of the Columbia University School of Journalism—scenario-writing class—Columbia University. If you let him know these ladies will be present you will see an exceedingly interested professor. Or you might prefer him on some other evening. I have done my best to interest the two girls in his school—for the school's sake. If all they knew could be taught there—it would be a wonderful school.

As you may prefer Freeburg some other evening, or not at all, be sure that I will greatly appreciate anything you can pick up about the actual success and prestige of his class between now and next February—and anything you can do to further it. Small and poor as it may be—it is the only place where my ideas have begun to have a roof over their heads, and I have therefore a pardonable parental solicitude, I hope.

And please do not let my suggestions along this line disturb you. I assure you I will not be vexed if you do not lift a finger. Your hands and eyes were made for your own work, not mine. But if you are far enough into these affairs to be able to know what I am really doing, I will greatly enjoy the good cheer of your company and comment. Send the books to Springfield.

And so—farewell.

VACHEL

Notes

1. Anita Loos was a scenarist for D. W. Griffith's Biograph Company for five years, wrote scenarios for Douglas Fairbanks for three years, and supplied the actress Constance Talmadge with stories. Her first work of fiction, *Gentlemen Prefer Blondes,* came out in 1925. She married the motion-picture director John Emerson in 1919.
2. Mae Marsh (see VL's "Mae Marsh, Motion Picture Actress," *Collected Poems,* p. 56) was one of her friends and acted for the Biograph Company. Anita Loos published an account of her friendship with Mae Marsh and VL, entitled "Vachel, Mae and I," in the *Saturday Review of Literature* (August 26, 1961, pp. 5—6).

70

TO KATHARINE LEE BATES

Springfield, Illinois
March 24, 1917

My Dear Katharine Lee Bates:
Under separate cover I am sending you the next to the last copy of the "Tree of Laughing Bells" unearthed from some dusty papers in my father's office.

I would be very glad if Miss Scoville[1] will fix up a visit to Hampton for me. I wish some Woman's club in that region would ask me into the same quarter at the same time. But I have never been invited south of Mason and Dixon's line.

I will be delighted if some of the Wellesley children take to Rickaby.

I found Miss Lowell[2] in a fraternal and talkative mood, and felt we had made due progress considering it was our second conversation on this earth.

Yes—the train brought me within about twenty minutes walk of her home. Just a little from her house after the conversation was over I found a street car back to Boston Common—but did not note which one it was.

I know nothing about the Edison Company's product at present. I think they quit for a long time. But they used to make excellent films—with no nonsense about them—and I presume they will be at least respectable.

Miss Lowell and I will never get very intimately confidential, I fancy. But we will never quarrel seriously, and I think when I call next Spring we will have another chat. I am always glad to have her understand my work and general attitude, and I hear on every hand of her reading my Kallyope over the country—a poem I seldom read, since I cannot remember it somehow and have to re-memorize it. So she does me a service. It is a bit unfair, for I have never really taken the pains I should to follow her work. I admit that "Patterns" reads better now than it did a year ago.

Poor Amy has many handicaps—and is riding against time and fate and ill health and her only revenge is the vigor of her attack and her sardonic humor. With these she wins for herself more gossip, parodies and chatter than all the rest of us. She is restless and dissatisfied, and would prefer a Mrs-Browning triumph to a John L. Sullivan triumph[3]—if it was to be had. She has nearer the artistic equipment than the public knows. But she is in no place to wait for her candy, being so beset—restless with mere physical nervousness and ill-health of various sorts. So she pulls up her flowers by the roots every once in a while, to see them grow.

The United States and Amy Lowell barking at one another—and neither understanding the other a bit, is indeed a wonderful sight. But they will do each other good, yet, by dint of the interchange.

With every good wish,

V<small>ACHEL</small>

Notes

1. Mrs. Samuel Scoville of Stamford, Connecticut, was a collaborator of Katharine Lee Bates's at Wellesley.
2. Amy Lowell lived in Brookline, Massachusetts, at her home, "Sevenels." At her request, VL visited her there several times. She published *Men, Women and Ghosts* in 1916. "Patterns" came out in *The Little Review* in August 1915.
3. John L. Sullivan (See *Collected Poems*, p. 93: "John L. Sullivan, the Strong Boy of Boston") was a champion heavyweight boxer at the end of the nineteenth century. The "Boston Strong Boy" was the basis for a contest between Robert Frost, Louis Untermeyer, and VL: Each was supposed to write a poem on that theme, but only Frost and VL did. (See *The Letters of Robert Frost to Louis Untermeyer*) [New York: Holt, Rinehart & Winston, 1963, pp. 64—65] for an account of that episode.) Sara Teasdale, who was also present, was willing to compete, but Louis Untermeyer wrote the first quatrain for her. VL's poem was dedicated to Frost and Untermeyer. Frost's contribution was a parody of "General William Booth," and he sent it to

Untermeyer on February 18, 1918, with the caption "Enclosed see if you can find my poem for the Sullivan Garland." The poem was entitled "John L. Sullivan Enters Heaven."

71

TO HARRIET MONROE

Springfield, Illinois
April 2, 1917.

My Dear Harriet:

If I am to do anything with the Tiger-Tree[1] it is now or never. After working on it for odd times for a whole year—and making it the one object of my existence for three months—if I lay it down at this stage—it is for good and all. Unless you and Alice can tell me what to do with it at once—I must pass on to other things.

Alice Corbin has a copy—and I am hoping to hear from her.

A poem is a long time growing with me—and after it has grown up I can absolutely do nothing with it but let it alone. As the Tiger Tree stands it is in the last hardening stages—it is now or never. If you prefer some other name to "Alice" for the heroine, I am willing. We can give the lady any fancy Indian name that occurs to you but keeping the dedication to little Alice. I put in Alice Oliver to meet your criticism and Padraic Colum's.—that the poem was too remote. This Peace song may be n.q. but I think it is better than the old one.

How would Mona do as a name for the lady?

My experience with the Tiger Tree is that most people like it on a third reading.

There is absolutely no complicated parable. It is a battle—that is all—set against the picture of a pleader for peace. It isn't Pilgrim's Progress—and it isn't Aesop's fables. It is just war in the Jungle—in contrast with the eternal peace principle. If you get that—you get it all—plus the color.

Nevertheless I do not maintain that the Tiger Tree is a success. I only know I have about done my best on it and have just about one more day in me to give to it. I will make any sweeping changes you and Alice will agree on—that can be made in a day.

But as to picking it up cold—after a year. Not on your life. Did I ever Touch Mark Twain again?[2] Never. It is as dead as it will ever get—or as alive. I did my best and I was through.

Well—this is a silly letter—my dearest Harriet—and you must not think me vexed. On the contrary. I am happy indeed this morning to know you are getting better—and I am anxious to know that you will be completely well soon. I think of you always with affection—and I would not trouble to argue if I did not take pleasure in living in your fair world—your particular phase of the Universe.

I shall write to Alice asking her to write you her opinion of the Tiger Tree. Also I hope for a line from you soon about Pocahontas.[3] On that, too, I will accept any immediate suggestions that do not absolutely pull out all her feathers! But even she is a case for immediate operation!

The Seven Arts[4] have just taken the Broncho[5]—and I am thinking it will have a newspaper run, maybe! Louis Untermeyer asked me for it personally—as I was reciting—and revising it in the East. It is my one poem this year that Jew and Greek have asked for a second time under all circumstances. Pocahontas was almost equally popular—but it was amusing to note that no son of Israel took to it—in New York or Chicago. Bless'em they see the English marching to deliver Jerusalem into their hands—I suppose. And if I was a proud son of Israel—I would feel the same.

I heard a fine Negro sermon yesterday on the Cleansing of the Temple. The best thing was like this:

"There is a revolution going on in Russia today, and My Lord is riding high".

A great phrase—I think.

With love

VACHEL

Notes

1. "The Tale of the Tiger-Tree" first came out in *The Chinese Nightingale and Other Poems* (p. 24). It is reproduced on page 358 of the *Collected Poems. Poetry* would not print it.
2. "Mark Twain" refers to "Mark Twain and Joan of Arc" (*Collected Poems*, p. 262, and *The Chinese Nightingale*, p. 47).
3. "Our Mother Pocahontas" (*Collected Poems*, p. 105) was also incorporated in *The Chinese Nightingale* (p. 39).
4. *The Seven Arts* had just been launched by Waldo Frank, James Oppenheim, and Paul Rosenfeld (1916—17).
5. "The Broncho That Would Not Be Broken" (*Collected Poems*, p. 77) was based on a reminiscence of a traumatizing scene in Kansas recorded by VL in *Adventures While Preaching the Gospel of Beauty* (ed. R. F. Sayre, Eakins, 1968, pp. 169—73).

72

TO ELEANOR DOUGHERTY

April 4, 1917

My dear Eleanor,[1]
There does not seem to me one chance in a hundred that you will get this letter. I take it for granted that the mermaids will get it. But I want to write to you tonight, even if there is little chance of your getting the letter or of your reading it with any great interest if it does get to you.

My heart is very sad tonight about the war. I have not the heart to challenge Wilson. I voted for him and cannot regret it—yet Jane Addams' dauntless fight for peace goes home to my soul. I feel with her—and with him—and am all torn inside. Certainly I have no sympathy for the fire-eaters. It is so easy to get killed for a cause; but it is a bitter thing to think of killing other people. I would a hundred times rather get killed than kill anybody. I feel as guilty as if I had done it all tonight—or had a hand in it.

No man knows where the thing will end. The world may be starting on its French Revolution—and may not stop seething till everything has been turned over three times . . . Certainly I hate war with all my soul. I would like to make a bargain with the devil and be crucified a hundred years, and thus abolish it, instead of going out and shooting up my fellow man—not so very certain I am abolishing anything. When I took my first big walk I had conversations with old Southern soldiers who had been through all that. I suppose men went through it in King David's time.

Isn't it amusing that Springfield, the wettest city in the United States, voted itself dry yesterday? . . . If this town can go dry, it can do a lot of other impossible things.

Even if this letter goes to the bottom of the ocean, I am glad to have written it. I suppose I will always have the big circle of friends, and when it comes to the final intimacies, tread the winepress alone. Who cares how the inner watch ticks, so it keeps time? I lean to the dim ghost of you and make my vague confessions, and feel the better for it . . . The world turns over and over, and you are writing letters to many soldiers at the front you do not know, like a good nurse and Christian. Well, the thought of such a person is a comfort. You have done a deal for me just by doing that.

With all proper nonsense.

NVL

Note

1. Eleanor Dougherty had collaborated with VL in producing the Poem-Games the preceding fall. She was now in Europe, a volunteer nurse on the French side.

73

TO HARRIET MOODY

Springfield, Illinois
April 8, 1917

My dear Cordelia:
No doubt this is the resurrection hour, for it is one minute after midnight—Easter morning. Yet I am thinking of death, not of life. I am thinking if I died tomorrow by any sudden accident, I would say with my last breath I had had far more than I deserved or expected or could hold of the joys and privileges of living, and I would say it if I died by burning alive, and I would say

> "Who has given to me this sweet
> And given my brother dust to eat
> And when does his wage come in?"

It is as strange an Easter as the world has ever faced, and it is shameful not to realize its irony, and it will be a pity if any one makes of it a sanctified nominal Easter. It is an Easter in which to hold one's breath. I cannot think of the resurrection but of the cannon fodder[1]—that is and that may be. I wonder how many that die today can look back happily—and say that they have been cheated? It may seem strange—but I feel tonight that my life has been full even without the satisfied fire of which Mrs. Browning writes in her sonnets. I have always been haunted by the notion of a sibylline princess of her sort—somewhere at the end of the road. Yet I doubt if I will ever be more than a brother with such a one. My very few bonfires have been built by women of another sort. Way back in my soul I have felt that my north star did not guarantee me much in the world of passion. My writing destiny seems so absurdly clear and simple and steadily developing—in a slow year by year way. I have always felt I would pay for it finally by a smash-up in no way connected with my ink-bottle—probably some unusually bad luck in love, and my luck has not been especially good. It has been a sort of intermittent farce; a joke that was all on me, if I forget the mere agonies, when the mortal self was racked.

Why should I trade my most secure star for my most insecure one? I cannot bear the idea of selling my pen for one day—no not for Juliet herself. And I know of no Juliet but would want me to trade it for a hat or a Ford, sooner or later—which is quite proper—and I could not endure it. I would feel much more justified in enlisting—with all my doubts about war. I still love Tolstoy more than any dream of Juliet, and even American war more than any such fancy.

Why should I write this to you? Because my Mama is at me to get married to most anybody that is decent and proper, as it is proper a Mama should be, with a youth of thirty-seven on her hands. While not intense about it—she is perfectly frank—and argues the economics with me—offers me the house, etc. But really it is not the house. I really have not met Mrs. Browning, and if I did, I have so much more faith in my ink-bottle than my heart's luck that I would not give Mrs. Browning a very good chance to write her sonnets. They all want to be wooed so. They want you to swear by high heaven you will have them or die. When perhaps they will look you over. I would infinitely prefer they would do the swearing. A lady bold enough to take the risk might grab me, if she would state her case in plain terms, like Queen Victoria. But such a suggestion seems so outlandish to them, I do not dare to offer it in sober terms.

Well—in one year, you may see me doing my duty in the trenches of Mexico or somewhere and I will be paying dearly for my independence! Ought I to go to Belgium with Roosevelt?[2] I have lived long enough—and had more than my share. Tell me that? Ought I to enlist?

With love,

VACHEL

Notes

1 The United States entered World War I in April 1917. President Wilson, urged by his Cabinet, called a special session of Congress on March 21, and on April 4 and 6 the Senate and the House passed a resolution to enter the war, although war was not declared on Austria-Hungary until December.

2. Former President Theodore Roosevelt was seeking command of an expeditionary force. Although he was not given one, he actively campaigned for the war until its end.

74

TO JANE ADDAMS

Springfield Illinois
April 9, 1917

Miss Jane Addams
Chicago:

My Dear Friend:
What shall I do? This war breaks my heart. Send me what you have written since Bryan enlisted—for instance. Are you with Bryan?

Do you accept President Wilson's war message on its face value? Is that final with you?

I hate a hyphenated American. I hate war. But I owe no one in Europe a grudge. I would rather be shot than shoot anybody. If I had been in Congress I would have voted with Miss Rankin and would have considered it a sufficient reason to say "I will not vote for war till she does".

Please write me a tract, or send a clipping.

With all respect

NICHOLAS VACHEL LINDSAY

75

TO KATHARINE LEE BATES

Springfield, Illinois
June 30, 1917

My Dear Katharine Lee Bates:
It has been some time since I have written to you. I have not shown the right appreciation of your interest in my southern trip, but I still have it in mind. Since Hampton is so far East, I do not believe I would like

to go there till I make an Eastern tour. But meanwhile the more interested these people are, the better for me. I hope to write several more southern pieces this fall that I have blocked out, I mean negro pieces.

I have just finished compiling an enlarged edition of the Congo volume, to be out next fall. In the back of the new book will be my principal pieces of the last three years. The new part will begin by continuing the war section, with poems first on America *Watching* the War, and then America *at war* with Germany. In America Watching the War will be included The Tiger Tree, embodying your corrections and those of Miss Scudder,[1] for which I am very grateful. By the time this reaches you the July Poetry will be there I presume, containing my three poems on the war: Pocahontas, Niagara, and Mark Twain and Joan of Arc. These three will be in the book under the title, America at War.

I am back at my desk after putting up clover hay for two days for a farmer just out of town. It is a great shaking up, the most strenuous work I have done for five years, and now I will be content to sit still for quite a bit. I am making slow but sure progress on the Golden Book of Springfield I hope.[2] I have two boxes full of notes, typewriter paper boxes, that have accumulated for six years, and now I face the question of getting all these infinite trifles into an original army of ideas. I have decided to adopt for my outline and ostensible text the Russell Sage Foundation Survey of Springfield,[3] which is embodied in nine reports. It is hard as nails, but there is at least the appearance of order and system, and it will do as well as any clothes-horse to hang my ideas upon. I shall search the survey for items of a certain mellowness, and for recommendations that point toward my book.

I am undertaking quite an effort in the Golden Book, but it has been by me so many years, the accumulation of material ought to give it force of a sort. To put it briefly I shall treat Springfield to the same general type of sermons I gave the movies in my movie book.

I have by me your beautiful poem, "To Peace" and you have said briefly and simply what I have labored at great and complicated length to say in several productions.

The inevitable conflict has been made clearer to me by the attitude of the German American press. See the Atlantic for July. It is beyond all question that they are trying to colonize all Germans in America for the Pan German ideas, in the very face of war. Everything this Atlantic article now says I have been saying to my friends for the last month. It has eaten away as much of my neutrality as remained. They are preaching Germany as a divine institution as Slavery was once preached in the South as a divine institution. Viereck's American[4] weekly printed in English, follows the entire formula laid down in the Atlantic for the German American Newspapers. Every person of my acquaintance says just one thing: "They ought to be sent home". It seems to me that a safe-conduct to Germany of such editors would settle an emigration peril forevermore. It would establish the principle for all time that people come here to be Americans, and are not admitted to citizenship on any other understanding.

I am following out your suggestions about paving my way to Hampton, this morning, with correspondents, etc. I would have gone at it all before, but the new books took precedence of everything else.

I hope you and all the Wellesley people like my review of Mary Pickford's first good *picture* in her entire career, the Romance of the Redwoods.[5] It will come out sometime this month in the New Republic. I worked very hard on that review and it illustrates my theory of film analysis in detail, better than any other single piece of writing, perhaps.

I think of you often my dear friend. I hope by the time we meet again to have done work enough to deserve your interest.

My good wishes to your whole house.

VACHEL

Notes

1. "Miss Scudder" was Vida D. Scudder, a colleague of Katharine Lee Bates and author of *Modern English Poets*.
2. In May, VL had begun writing out his old dream, *The Golden Book of Springfield*.
3. The Russell Sage Foundation survey of Springfield was conducted to assess the town's achievements on the eve of the hundredth anniversary of its incorporation.
4. George Sylvester Viereck's *The International* had been among the first victims of Comstocker. In 1914 it was seized by post-office censors because it had a nude on its cover.
5. The article on Mary Pickford, "Queen of my People," came out in *The New Republic* on July 7 (pp. 280—81).

76

TO WILLIAM LYON PHELPS

Springfield, Illinois
[August 14, 1917]

Professor William Lyon Phelps,[1]
Grindstone City, Michigan:

My Dear Friend:
Taking you at your word, I am sending you some rather foolish printed matter, all of which points more or less to the last two chapters of *The Art of the Moving Picture,* and proves at the worst, amid much nonsense, that I have had a beginning a middle and an end. Also The Golden Book of Springfield will be much in the spirit of the last two chapters of that book, though I shall take for my unit the next one hundred years of Springfield history, instead of the millenniums used in the Photoplay book.

I am not sending you anything that I put any special store by, as decorative or important-for-my-public printed matter except *The Tree of Laughing Bells.* I admit I am sentimental about it simply as my first piece of serious printing and designing, and the booklet I carried on my very first journey on the road. I should say the two big battle-of-the-Marne-days of my poor existence were first the day I made the plunge for the road as recorded in *The Man Under the Yoke* and the other when I issued *War Bulletin Number Three,* here in my home town, after I had settled down somewhat, and my first two tramping trips were over. Even now I blush for the shamelessness, shriek and vanity of *Bulletin Number Three.* It is naked as a frog on his back, and I urge discretion on your part in public comment upon it! But it was after the battle-of-the-Marne with me, and you may be sure you are decidedly on the inside when you look it over. I have been on decidedly conversational terms with myself all my life, and I am too apt to be tempted to draw others into the conversation, when they seem politely interested. But be sure I do not overestimate what I do, as this printed matter appears to indicate.

War Bulletin Number Three, I return to secretly again and again as a standard measure of my honesty, for my own discipline, and I suggest that you measure *in your own mind* whatever you choose to size up of my work, by the thread in it that leads forward to the chapters named in the m[otion] p[icture] book or back to this Bulletin. It is not a paper I am inclined now to thrust upon the public. It took my home town till last year to survive the shock of its issuance, and nothing that any editor or college professor outside of town said, would alter the decidedly outlaw status it gave me. Only about two of all my intimates even endeavored to defend it.

But I preferred this to being treated as some one else than myself, an artificial and imaginary Y.M.C.A. person. And winning back my place here an inch at the time I am making the surest establishment mortal man can have, and I do not think I have made any concessions to mere prejudice. And I think, on the whole, you will be amused by the relation of this bulletin to *The Art of the Moving Picture,* now considerably read in our town library, and as some of our dowagers deftly put it "A Text Book of Columbia University". They do not yet fathom how I have sneaked up on them, and they are reading the Bulletin again.

With every good wish

NICHOLAS VACHEL LINDSAY

Note

1. William Lyon Phelps (1865–1943) became Lampson Professor of English Literature at Yale in 1901. His articles on VL came out in the *Bookman* ("The Advance of English Poetry in the Twentieth Century," Part VII, April 1918, pp. 125—38) and in the *Atlanta Journal* ("Five American Poets," March 23, 1931).

77

TO HAMLIN GARLAND

November 12, 1917

Mr. Hamlin Garland
New York City

My Dear Friend:
I humbly apologize for having mis-read your letter.

I most gratefully accept the honor conferred upon me by the National Institute of Arts and Letters. And I particularly thank you for putting in my name—and thank the committee.

But my acceptance can only go into effect when I can afford the dues.

I hope you can defer the actual voting on my name till I can meet this expense.

My very good wishes to you. I hope we can get together some time next February.

Very sincerely,

NICHOLAS VACHEL LINDSAY

78

TO LOUIS UNTERMEYER

Springfield
December 21, 1917

My Dear Louis:
Thank you indeed for your letter. And let me thank you first for the rousing article in the New York Evening Post. I presume it was the one unsigned. I heard of it all the way to Evanston. You overestimate this blushing rhymer, but he thanks you. I have not yet seen the Dial editorial, but will watch you may be sure.

I have accepted every one of your criticisms of Queen Esther,[1] cut it in half, thrown out the cumbersome argument, brought it nearer to the Book, which I have carefully re-read, and conveyed what I really meant to say all the time. I hope I have conveyed it. I will be glad of any further suggestions. It is obvious to me, as I reread Queen Esthers story in the Bible, that she had a great and peculiar power over Ahasuerus long before he knew where it came from.

It was what we call high breeding, but this in her was synonymous with religion, as in Pavlova for instance, it is synonymous with dancing. And going back the other way, religion was synonymous with race, with Esther, religion was inseparable from gentility. And this has a special sex significance, because of the promise to Abraham of the immortality of the race, and the special way in which the promise has been cherished.

The Chinese Nightingale volume has about run its course with the reviewers, and its reception has been about the same as the Congo, no better and no worse. The hundred million Americans do not know yet that any of us are in existence. As a body, critics and poets, whatever we say about our factions, we are one faction, about as well known as the Christadelphians or the No-Necktie holiness faction of the Mennonites, and we have about as much political and social leadership. I do not mean I am all in a sweat for us to become as Bryan, Wilson, or Roosevelt, but I like to look the American people in the face, as a cure for the self-sugaring that comes with reading press clippings too much. Seventy-five notices make me vain as a peacock and puffy as a frog. Yet Edwin Markham told us here last month that he received eight barrels of clippings on the Man with the Hoe, and then his money ran out and he told the bureau to send no more. He might have run for Mayor of a small town with that much hold on the people, and have almost won the election. I suppose Bryan, Wilson and Roosevelt get eight Barrels every month.

I do think that some American poets should come as near to successful politics as Brand Whitlock the Novelist. Allan Seeger and Rupert Brooke[2] were in this sense successful soldiers, though near-privates in the ranks. I suggest you run for Congress as a pro-Wilson socialist (The Appeal to Reason came over to him on his last message, right along with Roosevelt, which is going some for a message methinks).

Well maybe Ficke will run for Mayor of Davenport Iowa on his military record. He is now captain in the ordinance department somewhere in France.

I am sorry indeed to hear of your brother's sickness. I hope he is much better.

This letter is my Christmas card, such as it is, and I wish you and Jean and Dick as fine and good a Christmas as may be had in the year 1917.

I went to Jack Pickford's Tom Sawyer last night and could hardly keep from crying like a matinee girl. It was a fair performance, but that was not the point. The point was that it reminded me of the book, which I read at my Grandfathers in Indiana (the proud farmer) every year, with all my cousins, from the time I was eight till I was fifteen. We all took turns reading it and re-reading it. I hope to write a poem to Becky Thatcher yet. It was an innocent America we lived in then, and what little lambs Tom Sawyer and Becky Thatcher seem in memory. As for my asinine remarks on statesmanship, I have something serious behind them. It is the Golden Book.[3] I hope locally for it to have as definite an effect on the history of the town as any election could have in changing the fabric or policy or mood of the place. About one hundred copies of my books are sold in Springfield. I am trying to so construct the book that it will transform the civic imagination of five of that hundred in such a way that they will slowly make the changes in the mood of the town by the unconscious effect of the book on their minds. I hope I have enough punch to really *make over* five citizens. I am pecking away at the book, and will make my stay in New York in February very short, so I can come back to it. I do not see it out before Next Fall. It goes slowly and I have much perturbation about it, but it is the main thing on my heart, except the war, and my family. I hope the book gets way beneath anything I have ever done or written. I hope everything I have ever done or written will serve to drive the book deeper into the souls of my five hypothetical converts. I hope these five will be as much transformed as if they had been converted to Mohammedanism or Christian Science, or any other strong internal revolution that has happened to this or that soul by actual historic record. Civics is not yet a religion. I hope to make it as much a religion as healing is a religion in Christian Science, or Undertaking was a religion in Egypt. And I do not want to do it on an ethical or argumentative basis. I hold that men may be transformed by their imaginations. It is not the only basis of transformation, but it is one basis, and *the* one to which I have access, I think this city could be transformed, not by being a bit better or more pious, but simply by dreaming, as fervently as one hundred poets you and I know. If a high imagination be once accepted as the first requisite in citizenship, and be made the main fact of citizenship, the rest will follow. I hope to write a book that will show the way out to the poets, at least some of them, and they will become militant citizens. I think all the critics from Amy Lowell to Reedy are good fighters, and doing good work, but they have not this picture of the real battle line. We all shout at each other and think the American people hear. The Golden Book stands for a slow-still-small voice, lifetime conspiracy against the present type of unimaginative citizen, beginning in a tiny way in tiny communities, but in a most intensive way, on people just as they happen to be.

Back to Queen Esther. I think you will find I have completely retreated from competition with the poem "Israel". I will be glad of the opinion of James and Jean upon it.[4] It will appear in Stork's Contemporary Verse, as an acknowledgement of his hospitality in Philadelphia, and of the fact that the Phi Beta Kappa affair was in Philadelphia. No I am not a Phi Beta Kappa. I could not get a college diploma in twenty years. I was simply asked to write the poem and read it, choosing my own theme.

This is undoubtedly the longest letter I will write for a year. Read in it installments through the holidays. I will be in New York the early part of February, and hope to get right back here to the Golden Book, possibly before two weeks are up. I do not feel I am anywhere till that book is done. It may never show what hearts blood and hope and prayer

I have put into it. I can only try and try. It is my forlorn hope, my Thermopylae. I am not yet an American citizen, and it seems to me this book is my first chance to be one.

With love to you and Jean

VACHEL

Notes

1. The poem discussed is "The Eyes of Queen Esther" (*The Golden Whales of California*, p. 33; *Collected Poems*, p. 48), which later became "A Rhyme for All Zionists" ("The Eyes of Queen Esther; and How they Conquered King Ahasuerus"). VL was writing it for the Phi Beta Kappa Society Dinner.
2. Alan Seeger (1888—1916), author of the famous poem "I Have a Rendezvous with Death," was killed in action during World War I. His compatriot and fellow poet Rupert Brooke (1887—1915) died of septicemia on his way to serve in the Dardanelles. In 1911—12 he had published *Georgian Poetry* in *New Numbers* magazine with Wilfrid Gibson, John Drinkwater, and Harold Monro. Brooke's war sonnets came out in *Poetry* in April 1915.
3. *The Golden Book of Springfield* came out in 1920 upon VL's return from England.
4. "James and Jean" were James Oppenheim and Jean Starr, Louis Untermeyer's wife. Dick was the Untermeyers' son.

79

TO LOUIS AND JEAN STARR UNTERMEYER

Springfield
December 28, 1917

My Dear Louis and Jean:

The Clipping from the Evening Post came yesterday, and the good letter today. You betray me into talking about my affairs once more, you take such an interest in them. Certainly Louis may quote what he likes from the letter. But if it sounds a bit self important, please say it is from a private letter, or mellow up the vanity somehow.

Isn't it queer that people insist on discussing only the ten per cent of my work that they think is the novelty? Sedgwick of the Atlantic[1] turned down Pocahontas, for instance because, as he said, when he read it aloud it was satisfactory, but had no potency on the printed page. And he told Stork the same thing, that all my work was commendable as Troubadour stuff etc, but fell apart on the printed page. Pocahontas is the only poem I have submitted there for years. Well certainly Pocahontas is as *orthodox* a poem as has ever been written, however dull it may be. And why should Sedgwick or any one else assume it MUST be read aloud? Simply because they have taken a journalistic attitude toward my work. They mix up The Congo with all my twenty years of writing verses. Also they assume the Congo is a new form. It is not. It is one of the oldest most orthodox, most stilted and unconventionalized forms in the English language, the Ode, which has been worn out and almost dropped because it degenerated into pompous apostrophes.[2]

I fancy if you care to do so you can find precedents for every line of the Congo in a long line of odes in English, which have not failed to be in print simply because they were intended to be read aloud. Please do up the conservatives who do not know what an ode is. People read the Higher Vaudeville side of the preface to the Congo and skip all the allusions to the Greek precedent. Since Harriet wrote that preface I have been struck by the number of efforts in English to make odes from the very beginning. But many times the most successful odes, like Lanier's Marshes of Glynn are not so called. Lanier seemed to be laboring under the delusion that he was creating a new form, as was Coleridge when he wrote Kubla Khan and Christabel. But these are really forms of the ode, nearer to its spirit than some of the pompous affairs specifically labelled odes. I find myself astonished by people who assume I am lost in technical mazes like the imagists. These matters of form are in no way novel or distracting, it is a question of the content of the verse. I rewrite my poems, fifty times as a matter of course, but I have done it from the beginning and it is part of the day's work. Method is so long behind me I have forgotten all about method. I am all of thirty eight years old. I suppose technical discussion rages because most poets are twenty five, which is the technical age. At that period I was full of technical questions of art-school art. I just had to settle them or be unhappy. I vastly appreciate a chapter in your book. I hope there is room for the Standard Dictionary definition of an ode, or such a definition as you would care to concoct. Let us dispose of the technical question once for all and go in for content hereafter. Let us slay all critics by telling them to look up this definition, and let us alone till our message or fancy goes wrong.

With love

VACHEL

Notes

1. Ellery Sedgwick was editor of *The Atlantic Monthly*.
2. In her preface to *The Congo*, Harriet Monroe had alluded to Yeats's remarks on "primitive poetry" and had quoted extensively from Edward Bliss Reed's *The English Lyric* to sustain the odelike aspects of VL's work.

80

TO LOUIS UNTERMEYER

Springfield
April 13, 1918

My Dear Louis:

I hope little Dick is better. I am so sorry he has not been well. I can speak to you as an uncle, if not as a parent. My little nieces and my namesake nephew with whom I take lunch every day are my heart's delight.

I am just getting into the Golden Book again. I am on chapter seven and there are forty to revise, fifteen times more. I did the first heavy day's work yesterday, and I am awfully proud of myself. I hope you liked my note to Dell for the May Liberator. I still have Clement[Wood]'s letter wanting to know just what I think of his ode. I shall answer it as fraternally as the gods permit. My mail does pile up and my trouble is having answered one letter, I have the illusion I have done a day's work, which may often be the illusion of the recipient when he reads it. You have done me the dangerous flattery sir, to tell me I am in your next book. Also to write me up from time to time. So I wish to make some points this morning while I have 'em in mind.

First the Macmillan company over a year ago signed me up for a book of one hundred drawings or so, any drawings I chose to make. Now I do not want that statement in the public prints, for I do not expect to make said drawings till the war is over, say ten years hence. But I am thinking a real fox of a reviewer can drag in my drawings by the hair and get my tiny public ready for the new pictures when they arrive. Certainly they will be no better than my old ones. Only more of them. So I am sending you an extra copy of my *"letter about my four programmes"*. It contains a winnowing of all my drawings from the beginning the most substantial I have to offer. I hope your friend Hartmann can stand them. And I hope you can cut them out and use them in newspapers, etc when you make your yearly annual mention of my existence. I offered this suggestion to William Lyon Phelps last summer, and if you care to look at the April Bookman, he has made a start for me.[1] He *talks* of the drawings. He does not reproduce them. Please squeeze the praise out of that article and keep the rest of it for a rare thing, an array of facts and correct quotations of letters, etc. As for mere facts one word should be changed. Page 126 should read "Also he became a tramp", instead of "Then he became a tramp". Why? Because I walked in the South in 1906, in Pennsylvania in 1908 and in Kansas in 1912. Between the last two walks I began my permanent residence in Springfield and in a way the book on which I am now working, The Golden Book of Springfield. I hope this does not sound pernickety. But I have such wild statements sent me in clippings. In Nashville I was introduced as a Virginian! I hope you meet Robert Henri sometime. I want to link up my old art student friends with my poet friends if it can be done. He was my last master, and practically my only master, coming at the very end of my art study, and I have always wanted him to think well of my drawing, and back it *as such* if ever I arrived anywhere with it. There seems to be a kind of a trench between the artists and the poet and they do not go much to each other's parties, and to get back among these with whom I started long ago will of course be difficult, and impossible to achieve completely. Yet I have the feeling that if I ever get anywhere with my drawings I want Robert to care.

I am lecturing at the Chicago Art Institute on the Movies. Eggers[2] the Director is strong for the Movie Book as a proper use of the museum, so I get back, as an alumnus of the institution that way. But that is only getting half-way back, as one might say.

Freeburg's book, *The Art of Photoplay Making* (Macmillan's, just out) is a peach. I hope it comes your way. I am delighted with the work all through, and I can establish most everything I want to say hereafter merely by quoting Freeburg as a starter.

He begins with the *scenario* which is getting deeper than I did. I *practically* began and ended with the director, and in my book the scenario was incidental. He relates the films more carefully to music, and carries considerably further my own thesis of the *art gallery* in the chapter on *composition in fluid forms*. And I have no doubt he has met many practical matters we do not realize, through handling the questions and objections of a scenario class for three years, that same class trying as hard as it could to make money from scenarios on the side. I am thinking he has written *THE* book, and it will be immensely popular. I am hoping to write several reviews myself.

I am thinking of writing a book on the films in three or four years.

If I do, I will simply put texts from Freeburg at the head of the chapters, and make it a series of theme essays.

With every good wish, with my love to you all, Jean and the boy and everybody, and with the joyous declaration that Spring has come in the Governor's yard next door, I remain,

Very Surely Yours,

VACHEL

Notes

1. In his article in the April 1918 *Bookman* (p. 127) William Lyon Phelps had written: "The first impression one receives from the pictures is like that produced by the poems—strangeness. The best have that Baconian element of strangeness in the proportion which gives the final touch to beauty; the worst are merely bizarre"; and "I find his [VL's] pictures so interesting that I earnestly hope he will some day publish a large collection of them in a separate volume."
2. George William Eggers (1883–1958) later became director of the Denver Art Association and wrote a Foreword for the 1922 edition of *The Art of the Moving Picture.*

81

TO HARRIET MONROE

Springfield Illinois
June 27, 1918

My Dear Harriet:

Thank you for the suggestions in regard to "The Empire of China is Crumbling Down".[1] The amendments are accepted, and I am only waiting to see the rhyme in print.

Watch the Kerensky situation. It grows more interesting every day. Perhaps by August, one year from your printing of the Kerensky poem, it may come in quite pat after all. It begins to look like the people who want to bring about an invasion of Russia hope that Kerensky's stock will rise enough for them to use him in the project, and perhaps rehabilitate his party. I am not necessarily in sympathy with any such a move, but I will not be surprised to see my Kerensky Poem praised in strange quarters, if Kerensky comes to the United States. And praised by people who will find it pretty hard to swallow, if they read it closely. However I may overestimate the future.[2]

"Current Opinion" for July says, at the close of its poetry column: "The Prize of 500 dollars awarded by Columbia University for the best volume of Poetry by an American poet in the year 1917 has been given to Sara Teasdale for her "Love Songs". The Jury, nominated by the Poetry Society of America consisted of Jessie B. Rittenhouse, Bliss Perry, and William Marion Reedy."

I think you ought to get a letter out of Perry,[3] as the judge least involved in the usual round of poetry circles, etc. and the figure most aloof. He would probably be able to give you a list of the books considered. Greenstone Poems by Bynner was of course considered, also George E. Woodberry's new book,[4] I think they were sonnets. And look into the date of Louis Untermeyer's "These Times",[5] which came out in the Spring of 1917, I think. Also if I am not mistaken Oppenheim had out a book,[6] and there were one or two others that I cannot think of now. "The Chinese Nightingale" came out last September, but you will note on the titlepage [sic] "Dedicated to Sara Teasdale, *Poet*", so you see I nominated Sara first, and was the original Sara man. Also you will find that "Adventures While Preaching the Gospel of Beauty" was dedicated to her when it came out in 1914 so you can put me down as awarding her two prizes, such as they are, and using my influence such as it is to further her greatness as a poet, even before the present committee was formed. I consider any honor to Sara, then, in a sense an honor to my own critical sense, and as it were, I accept the prize on her behalf. Neither Perry, Reedy nor Jessie Rittenhouse can boast they have dedicated two books to her. It only remains to be seen whether Perry read those two dedications. If he did, it proves that even Perry is a man of discretion discernment and true insight into parnassian matters.

I have just reread "Love Songs", and I find it a collection of Sara's undisputed best from all her books, and deserves to be spotlighted, if any work of hers ever deserves it. It represents the calm winnowing of all her work, and does not run thin and uneven in spots as some of her earlier collections. Her style is so simple that the second-raters among her poems are apt to run thin and it takes a long and mature judgment to separate the thin from the simple and classic. I did not find a poem in the book I would omit, and I was glad to renew my memory of them all.

I think you could discreetly draw attention to the Chinese Nightingale dedication, especially if you laid emphasis on the word *Poet*, which is exactly in the spirit of that dedication.

This is all yesterday to me, you do not know how much yesterday, nor will you till you read the Golden Book. The Golden Book is all tomorrow, and day after tomorrow, and the day after that. That may be the reason that child Isadora [Bennett] has shaken me so, who has the eyes of tomorrow itself. Every word of the book I write straight to her, I cannot help it. But you need not know that too well, this is a matter of confidence.

Your few words on this head were no doubt easy for you to write down, but they were a great comfort to me nevertheless and helped to steady me, and you will pardon me if I occasionally write you some sort of a confessional letter. I am in danger of making myself a nuisance and an unnecessary perplexity to the entirely worthy and entirely independent young Isadora, and I only wish I had no private and personal heart, but only one for groups of friends. My friends in groups always love me and I them, to some end and to some constructive issue. But so far as I know the few occasions I have turned from the friend to the lover I have been rather of a nuisance to somebody, or else I have been some one to be tactfully lost in the shuffle. So it was in the days of old with me years before you knew me, and so it promises to be today. But certainly the lady cannot prevent me writing my book to her. And so far as I can see, that is about all I will ever be permitted to do about this affair, and I wish I could reconcile myself to it a little more.

At any rate I have made the first draft of chapters eleven and ten today, am back in harness, and hopeful of doing a considerable work the next two weeks. As soon as I have done enough work to in any way excuse a holiday, you will see me mooning around Chicago no doubt.

With love, and the greatest gratitude for your confidential and listening ear,

I remain
Your
VACHEL

Notes

1. "Shantung, or The Empire of China Is Crumbling Down" (*Collected Poems*, p. 34) came out in *The Golden Whales of California* (1920), p. 46.
2. VL mentioned repeatedly at the time, in letters to Upton Sinclair, his poem on Kerensky, "This, My Song, Is Made for Kerensky," which was eventually entitled "The Soap-Box."
3. Bliss Perry (1860—1954) had edited *The Atlantic Monthly* from 1890 to 1909. He had since become professor of English at Harvard.
4. "Woodberry's new book," *Ideal Passion: Sonnets*, had been published in 1917.
5. Untermeyer's *These Times* had come out in 1917 and so had Sara Teasdale's *Love Songs*.
6. Oppenheim's book was *The Book of Self* (1917).

82

TO KATHARINE LEE BATES

Springfield, Illinois
August 5, 1918

My Dear Katharine Lee Bates:
I wrote a hasty acknowledgement of your valuable letter, and then put it toward the end of my manuscript to enjoy when I reached a breathing place, which has now come. I am delighted to say what might be called the first real draft of my book is in form. When I began on it as a steady work this time last year, revising ten years of notes and studying the Springfield Survey, it was planned as a treatise. About last November or before, it began to turn into a story and the complete transformation in general substance has now taken place and I could read it aloud to you if you had the patience, and you could follow it as a thing in sequence, if not enthralling. To make it readable without me along will take till about the first of January. But I am happy to have cut it down and clarified it a great deal the last month and a half, incidentally taking two holidays simply to get fresh for the next drive. I feel much more light hearted over it than I have for six months. I begin to see it as a possibility, and the hardest part of the sheer grind seems over.

At Coe's bookstore the dummy is already on exhibition here, and orders are being taken. The cover design by my old chum Richards is so precisely what I want that I will never have done with looking at it, and I shall keep a copy of the dummy by me so I can write the book to fit the cover.

I am afraid you misunderstood my letter before last, for the simple reason I do not want to say what I am going to do till after I have done it, and it is so easy to lay plans that come to nothing, or proclaim views on which one does not make good. I have been lambasted by a good many people like Hermann Hagedorn[1] for not writing rip snorting Rooseveltian war poetry for the Vigilantes. Then Miss Addams whom I very much admire says to me rather sadly: "Mr. Lindsay is no longer one of us" whatever that may mean,[2] and my old Friend Charles Wharton Stork whose wife is an extremely charming and very worthy Austrian court person, labors with me while I am in Philadelphia for being luke warm on this Quaker issue. (He suddenly discovering that his mother and all her ancestors are Quakers). And he went to a Quaker school in youth, and is now suddenly very glad. So I am classed as a Laodician, neither cold nor hot.

Meanwhile I have gone ahead packing all my gunpowder into the Golden Book, and fearful lest I never have a chance to touch it off. It is not only written for these people, but for everyone who has ever been my friend. I find myself talking to them all, in turn, as I write it. It covers that part of me and my ideas that all my new friends leave out. They do not understand that about ten months of the year for the last ten years here in Springfield I have travelled with Single Tax politicians almost exclusively, people utterly indifferent to all the things I am supposed to be interested in when I am writing books or reciting. Yet they are passionate typical American patriots of the radical brand, and I have followed with them many moves of Springfield and state and national politics for the last ten years. I see the war and all that it implies from this standpoint, and my book attempts to put into form certain tentative plans for the next hundred years for America, assuming the type of American I have been dealing with here (aside from technical Single Tax) is typical and basic. No one outside of Springfield talks politics seriously with me, but when the Golden Book is out if it has its effect I will have the privilege of talking politics seriously somewhere outside Springfield.

Upon the basic Middle West political fabric, as I understand it, I have tried to develop the logical great American artistic and religious and political State Capital, never departing I hope from the real American mood to indulge in abstract socialistic speculation. In my book I am making every kind of direct and indirect war upon Germanism and hyphenism, without so much as once naming either. I assume the league of nations will be established one hundred years hence to the strength of America's federation of states in the days of Webster and Calhoun. I assume a secession movement and a secession doctrine, coming from the mythical city of Singapore, which plays about the same game of rebellion against international good will that Germany does today and Japan seems to threaten to do. I draw parallels from these two nations and the Southern Confederacy in sketching the Singapore rebellion, which attempts to lead off all Asia from the International Middle Class government. Note, the *middle* class. I hold that it is the fundamental tendency of civilization to bring all men to the despised middle class conditions, and the only practical international government will be a middle class institution, and the millionaires will be pulled down to that level, and the working people will be pulled up to that level. In short the class war hypothesis is a thing I utterly reject.

To all these ideas I add many religious speculations as to the ritualistic civic Union Church, and the ritualistic civic middle-western democratic art life. Most of my ideas on these religious and aesthetic questions were elaborately worked out ten years ago when I came back to Springfield, and ten years of talking politics has gradually blended them into one fabric with my political ideas. In short I have an elaborate network of one hundred years of prophecy long worked out, and struggling for expression. By nailing it to one spot I can get the illustrations with a tang and force one spot on earth to take the issue so seriously that the illustrations will be, in a sense, in perpetuity.

And with the young men and maidens coming out to make war on Singapore one hundred years hence, and with our local leaders sent as delegates to the international legislature, I can discuss present issues, moving up one peg into permanent issues, as much as possible. In my opinion we are not only on the edge of an international federal government, but we will have our Websters to defend it, our Calhouns to assault it and our international armies. It is a permanent issue, and I have not the least fear that this year is my last chance to die in the cause. Far from it. The present war will last at least two years more, and going to war is like voting. One man, one vote, and I have plenty of time to cast my ballot yet. If I enlist it will be as a private soldier, and I will count simply as one vote and no more, unless the Golden Book serves to make clear that a victory means to me at least something more than beating the Hun or even freeing Russia.

So when I spoke of Billy Sunday. I meant no disrespect to the issue. It is utterly impossible for any town to become more excited than it was here under the Billy Sunday pressure with ALL the church services suspended but his, and Billy occupying the entire front page of all four newspapers, and not one word of modifying discussion allowed anywhere, and not the least hint of disagreement permitted in any paper.

Billy cannot get a big town like that. But having lived through it, I realized that my real judgment was not what it seemed to be under such immense social pressure. In Billy's time I had my own religious views, and later issued them in War Bulletin Number Three. In the same way I now have my own political views, and intend to issue them in another War Bulletin called The Golden Book, ostensibly addressed to Springfield, and actually addressed to anything institutional that has ever given me a hearing and I seem to be more and more the guest of institutions. You do not know how utterly helpless I feel when I am treated like a baby politically and a sort of boy musician. I have lived in a state capital and heard the radical lobby talk over their deals for years. I have seen them in victory and defeat. I know at first hand ten times as much practical politics as the average college president who turns me over to his wife as a pretty creature she may perhaps desire to feed cake. I by no means mean that I am at all infallible in these political matters. I only mean I have been passionately interested in them and have made my chief friends those who are interested in them, and the war has scarcely changed the essential issues, only sharpened them.

I am all of thirty eight years old, and the poet people ask to parties was practically the same as he is today when I came back to Springfield ten years ago. I cannot endure the belated feeling of having my ten years go to nothing, or to be always asked to step back to what I thought and felt ten years ago. It is of course infinitely better than having no audience at all, but now after about five years of public life of a sort, I am being stereotyped in an utterly false position. If I enlist in this war I want to enlist not as a poet or as they say a "vaudeville man", but as a politician, a voter, and a voter from the Middle West.

I read the Dark Hour, and enjoyed it, but such a mood is utterly at variance from my own. I see the international government as a thing inevitable as the sunrise, the *middle class international* that will pull down the Emperors and the millionaires and police the earth. I see the international army as busy all over the earth as the armies of America have been on American soil for the last hundred and more years, from Shay's rebellion to the last expedition to the Mexican Border. Federation is going to be as hard for the world as it was for America.

I have not the least expectation that any of these ideas of mine will go into poems, and I have no expectation of trying to put them there. I insist that I have the same right to write plain political prose as the editors of the New Republic, and I want to fight for the place where it will be taken for what it is worth.

I insist that Jazz does not discredit America. I think the Jazz element in America is a sure sign of health. I have the utmost respect for Jazz in the young people, and I feel that without it there would be no American armies in Europe today. I do not claim that the Jazz Bird is a poem. It is a humoresque, of course. But it is the Jazz in these young-sters that will win this war. It is the same thing that Yankee Doodle was in the days of Washington.[3]

I have not the least concern whether I write another poem in all my born days, and I have never considered it a duty. There is a plenty of good patriotic poetry written already, and as to the other kind I was reading Palgrave's Golden Treasury[4] the other day, and found it satisfactory. Certainly three books of verse is a plenty from me whether they be good bad or indifferent. I have notes on about two hundred more poems most of them half written, and I have no doubt others will come popping out from time to time and increase the box of sketches to four hundred. I shall polish these up from time to time, but I am not going to force anything into the box that is not already there, on war or on any theme.

Professor Young is entirely right. The "doctrine" of the Empire of

China is "rotten", and there ought not to be any such things as the Chinese Empire. My sister and brother in law are departing for the west coast the twentieth, and on the fifth of September they will start back there to China as missionaries for seven years, and they may get China all fixed up by that time. If they make the Chinese all over into Lindsays and Wakefields of course its history will be different from what I have prognosticated in the poem, and will more closely conform to the choicest doctrines of the Golden Book, of Springfield. But at present prospect, as Bret Harte said "The Heathen Chinee is Peciliar". I suggest you read Harte's poem to all those who have taken my poem too seriously. It is all there much more briefly stated. The town of Cheese[5] etc that puzzles you so is simply my awkward way of saying that after all the Chinese are "peculiar".

Dear Katharine Lee Bates, you take me too solemnly, and here I have written six solemn pages about my dear old self in reply to your three. I do not think any of it challenges much what you have said. But I challenge one thing. This is not the only war, or the greatest war. This is the war to establish the World Union. The war to defend it and perpetuate it will be greater in its significance if not in its bloodshed. I assume that it will come in a hundred years, but it may come in ten. At any rate I hope to help develop in a few of my readers a real George Washington Americanism, looking to that perpetual world federation, on a political, not an economic basis. I say the politics come first, the political economy second. There I differ from all the Germanized Socialists, and some single taxers. The right kind of American politicians can set the world free without splitting economic hairs.

And finally I am hoping that the Golden Book will be as clear as this letter. If it is not, you are now in a position to explain it, and you had best not read the book but only look wise and quote passages from this letter.

Viewed as a book, this letter is brief.

Very much your admirer and lover

VACHEL

Notes

1. Hermann Hagedorn (1882-1964) had written several books on Theodore Roosevelt and several collections of poems. He was Edwin Arlington Robinson's biographer.
2. VL had registered for the draft at the end of 1917.
3. "The Modest Jazz-Bird" is found in *The Golden Whales of California* (p. 140). VL did not include it in the *Collected Poems*.
4. Francis Turner Palgrave's *Golden Treasury of Songs and Lyrics* ran through two editions in 1861 and 1896. It was reprinted in 1906.

5. "The town of Cheese" refers to a line in "Shantung, or The Empire of China Is Crumbling Down": "His Town of Cheese the mouse affrights / With fire-winged cats that light the nights" (*Collected Poems*, p. 37).

83

TO HIS PARENTS

Hotel Athenaeum
Chautauqua, New York

Wednesday August 21, 1918

My Dear Papa and Mama:

This is to say I love you dearly, and am getting on very well. I send you the programmes for several days.

I had a good walk and talk with Ray Ewers and Mame Canfield Ewers yesterday. They have two husky boys. Both boys and parents look very well.

I hope you are both doing well and are in good spirits. Your names will not appear in the Golden Book, but you may be sure it will contain your opinions, somewhat revised, to be sure, but still your opinions, on most all subjects.

Andrew Jackson[1] makes quite a hit as a recitation and The Sea Serpent Chantey[2] pleases the people. The John L. Sullivan[3] does not yet go so well, but I may learn to give it better.

I am impatient to be back home to the Golden Book. I wish I could work on it every minute I am awake, and sleep every minute I am not working on it.

With love,

VACHEL

Notes

1. "Written while America was in the midst of the war with Germany, August, 1918," "The Statue of Old Andrew Jackson" (*The Golden Whales of California*, pp. 144—45) is not to be confused with "Old, Old, Old, Old Andrew Jackson," published in 1926 in *Going-to-the-Stars* (p. 16).

2. "The Sea Serpent Chantey" (*Golden Whales,* p. 101) was reprinted in the *Collected Poems,* p. 149.
3. On "John L. Sullivan," see note 3 to letter 70.

84

TO ELEANOR DOUGHERTY

October 12, 1918

My dear Eleanor,

I find myself writing two letters to your one . . . My pen is as impatient as your feet. So here, at a quarter of twelve, Saturday night, after a really hard week's work, when I am unable to look at one more page of the "Golden Book", I still must soothe myself with a letter. It is like dancing after brick laying, though I have never done either.

The third edition of the German peace acceptance was on the street half an hour ago . . . I find strange thoughts in me, on war and peace. I wonder if I am self-deceived. But it seems to me this is not the last chance good men all over the world will have to fight. Anything that lifts me out of the sheer mystical non-resistance that pacifism means in the face of the universe, persuades me to the next war. The ironical book, "Germany and the next war" flashes before me as a warning. Yet the latter part of the "Golden Book" might be called "America and the Next War", and I see my mind moves in the same channel, once I consent in my soul, to be a soldier in any exigency,—and I have consented long ago—, and would have been in the ranks today if this book had not seemed my first duty. And now I am so deep in the book, my mind is one hundred years ahead most all my waking hours, and often this war looks as far back as the Civil War. There has been, in spite of my one-hundred year trance a certain pressure from friends, so that it seemed most unknightly to stay out, when so many were dying in the world's last crusade.[1]

But I begin to see that this "world's last crusade" idea is an illusion . . . We won't come back till it's over. "Over there" is a rash promise. This is not my last chance to die, nor my last chance for martyrdom. I must have faith in life, and its unfolding, and finish my book and keep my nerve. I am quite sure that inside of five years, there will be crusades as risky as the present war, if not so popular, where a man may use his dead body as a vote on the side he chooses for the right. Personally I would rather die for the "poor nigger" than any other breed of man. It is easier to be martyred for France, than for a "nigger", but I suspect I will have my chance in one of two other ways.

First, after the world government is formed, it will have to have an army pretty active in some quarter of the world, and perhaps an Army as big as the present Allied Forces, in some sudden secession exigency. But I think the more probable chance for me will come in some little row where strikers are being shot down. In such a case, I do not think I would quibble. I would be with the fool strikers, right or wrong. Sometimes I live like a Tory, I grow more Tory every day; but God grant I do not die that way. It would be like dying an infidel, or a blasphemer. I want a clean Christian death. Yet I see a possible thing to defend that may look Tory to half the radicals of the world,—the world government of which Wilson will likely be President. Though he let Debs go to jail,[2] yet I am for him, for he is a radical by comparison with the Mikado and the Kaiser, and I think they both will go down if his world government is firmly established. And it will be the first foundation of world order, worth all our blood.

The last two-thirds of my book puts the great war for the defense of the World Constitution against Secessionists, one hundred years hence. I am not sure it will wait that long. In my book I do everything I can to inculcate loyalty to the World flag, the flag of such a world Constitution as Wilson stands for. Since I commit myself to it in my book, I must be prepared to make every sacrifice for such a flag, if once it is set flying. So, this is my thought of death. Today is not my last chance to die or to suffer the limit of agony. Both are inevitable with mortal man. I must simply do my work and go forward.

VACHEL

Notes

1. In the Springfield of 2018 described in *The Golden Book of Springfield* not everything has gone the way of Utopia, but the political framework of the book indicates a world government has been established that is accepted by all but one country: Singapore, which stands for a combination of wartime Germany and the Confederate forces in the Civil War.
2. Eugene V. Debs (1855—1926) had denounced the sedition prosecutions that were taking place in 1918 in the midst of the widespread anti-Hun craze, and he protested the 1917 Espionage Act. He was sentenced to ten years in prison, ran for the presidency from his cell in 1920 as a Socialist candidate, and was released in 1921.

85

TO HARRIET MONROE

Springfield, Illinois
November 3, 1918

My Dear Harriet:

Thank you indeed for your good letter and the enclosure from the Lady in Providence. Believe me I am not in the least vexed about the verses you returned. I simply consider Daniel[1] and the Sea Serpent more recitations than pieces of printed matter. I have found the Daniel Jazz and the Sea Serpent effective just as they are, in public. And I do not consider either worth worrying about as printed productions. As for *Sullivan*, it does not read very well aloud, and any effect it will have will be in print.

I am sending you what I think will suit you much better than these three, and what I hope is an absolutely new departure for me, *Kalamazoo*.[2] This is not the kind of poem I will ever read aloud. It certainly has to depend upon being printed. I do not think any one will class it as a phonetic exercise.

When I was at the University of Wisconsin last spring I maintained that Kalamazoo could be made the most romantic word in America if only one could write the right poem about it. That there was nothing essentially absurd or unmusical in the name. The reason people smiled at Oshkosh and Kalamazoo was that the cities were not consistent with the names, and had, to ordinary American eyes, nothing to satisfy the curiosity provoked by the challenging names. Yet there is as much queer and dear romance in those two cities as any cities ever held, no doubt, and it is for us to unfold it. The point is to bring out the Kalamazooish-ness of Kalamazoo, and avoid emphasizing too strongly the Kalamazoo-fool-ishness of Kalamazoo. The very words Oshkosh and Kalamazoo imply a special idiom, which I hope I have approximated. I want to congratulate you on the editorial section of your last number. I laid it down with the feeling you were on a new tack, more deliberately and clearly Middle-western, more deliberately and reasonably and definitely the advocate of your coterie, more deliberately against the expatriates, and more definitely the champion of the poet as an American public figure. I think you ought to get a more definite statement from Conrad Aiken[3] about what he did in regard to deferred classification, and *since he has taken this stand*, persuade him to apply some of his wasted tartness on one very good issue. It is a battle I cannot fight and do not want to fight. If I was not up to my neck in the Golden Book I would have been long ago at the front. No poetry would have kept me here, you may be sure. But as an issue for boys yet unborn, Aiken is equipped with the proper vitriol to fight it out, this matter of the poet being worth as much as the munitions maker. And it combines definitely with your doctrine that he deserves as much income as the painter who sells pictures once in a while. These two things, taken with your stronger anti-expatriate position give you three planks you can fight for harder. But I counsel you to slow cool fighting, and the willingness to be as generous as you were to Masters and Wheeler in the article quoted in Current Opinion Poetry Column this month. Sandburg's rise gives new justification to your platform in every way. It seems to me he is going further in the Western lines I am supposed to go than I have, and I hope you can give him first place in your editorials this year, and use him for an argumentative point, and leave me out for this year. If you feel inclined to use me to point an argument and adorn a tale, save all your generosity and loyalty till the Golden Book comes out, about this time next year. I would just as soon be completely forgotten by all my public friends till then, and I will come back in such a different role, that I assure you I most cheerfully will all the present mantle I am wearing to Sandburg, that he is not already wearing. He will never get into the Golden Book field you may be sure, but is plainly developing into the kind of a poet the Golden Book calls for and desires, the hypothetical type for the next hundred years, more or less.

Among the women, it seems to me Eloise Robinson is the rising star, and she is emphatically a Cincinnati person. I was on the ground down there when she made her first start, and I feel that her roots will always be in Cincinnati, and she understands the Middle Western theory perfectly. I went into it at great length with her when I was there. As a craftsman she is rising, and she is winning golden opinions from all quarters. And as a *person*, I think everything she writes and says rings true. She is a thoroughbred, as I understand her, and worth banking on as such. These things count in a movement.

I had no idea of such a lecture, dear Harriet, when I took my typewriter in hand. But I think I see a new tone in the Poetry magazine less of tart personalities and more of a platform, and you cannot go too far in this policy. It was plain to me in the past that some of the Eastern people got your goat too much, when you were really at your best in the bland and the judicial, and now you are in a position to be these and more. *The place of the poet as a person who is or is not conscripted, who is or is not receiving an income, who is or is not expressing America* are points on which you can keep your paper bristling for some time to come. It seems to me that hereafter technical considerations should come fourth in importance, remembering that the other critics are now threshing them out endlessly, and doing about all the service needed along this line. But your paper is still the model for all the others, the only one planted in a sure place, and envied of all the rest. I am quite sure of that. And as for western people to bring forward in my humble opinion Carl Sandburg and Eloise Robinson will be the leaders one year from date, and for at least a year to follow, and they are both *delighted* with the place they are filling and doing it with dignity. All this counts. They are playing the game, and so will help you play the game, (speaking as one celestial to another!). Certainly Carl and Eloise will be far enough along for the middle west to claim them with great joy. Their being in Europe now is but an accident of war. You may be sure it will strengthen their ultimate loyalty to us.

　　　　　　　　　　　　　Very sincerely and devotedly yours

　　　　　　　　　　　　　　　　　　　　VACHEL

Notes

1. Although VL eventually included "Daniel" in the *Collected Poems* (p. 159), this poem was for him the source of much embarrassment. It appeared under the title "The Daniel Jazz" as the title piece of the English edition of VL's selected poems (London: Bell, 1920) and helped brand him in England and the United States as "the Jazz Poet," a term he always resented. The poem was dedicated to Isadora Bennett (later Reed), with whom VL had fallen in love in 1917. In the *Collected Poems*, VL published it under the simpler and less ambiguous title "Daniel."
2. "Kalamazoo" (*Collected Poems*, p. 283) is an example of VL's attempt to use the poetry he found in American place names.
3. Conrad Aiken (1889—1973) had harshly criticized VL in an article included in *Scepticisms* (1919), entitled "The Higher Vaudeville: Vachel Lindsay." However, VL remained on friendly terms with him.

86

TO LOUIS UNTERMEYER

　　　　　　　　　　　　　　　　　　　　Springfield,
　　　　　　　　　　　　　　　　　　　　April 16, 1919

My Dear Louis:
I am home now for the year, having been in Texas, Tennessee and Kentucky for near a month.

The principal event in my room since returning is "The New Era in American Poetry".[1] Thank you with all my heart for such generous consideration. I must object to all the praise but thank you for all the accuracy of fact and detail. Certainly you have gone into whole vistas of my work that no one else has launched upon and you have given me credit for possessing all at once, ideals that have moved me in succession in various years, but which I could not possibly have held in my gizzard all at one time. Still each one is stated clearly, generously, and all I have to do is to hide, and some people will believe me as nice as Joseph was in Egypt.

It has been very generous of you to accept all these dreams as I have stated them from time to time, and put them together into a consistent fabric.

Something else I realize on reading my chapter (as we all read our chapters first . . .). It is—"How time flies". You have prophesied "The Golden Book" which may take another year, but which will be out—if I live. Certainly a trip to England will not be seriously thought of till that book is done and nailed down. But I realize that so much of the Vachel you are good enough to love has passed on into this unpublished Golden Book into a different person—and after all the Vachel you know, is the one you met courting his Sara—in 1914—July—just before the war. You seem to know him better than anybody, however you over-estimate him. You have caught me as I was one month of my life, one very shining month. And I am amused to note that it is, on the whole, the Vachel Sara seems to remember, in my annual call upon her. And there has been for instance 1914—1918 world war and world peace. In July 1914 you and I and Jean and Sara were just happy children together. Or—better—boys and girls, boys and girls.

Jean has suddenly lifted the curtain as far as she is concerned and

> The kitten has grown
> To a lioness
> Not to a cat.
> I am very thankful for that.

In Growing Pains—I mean.

How our lives move on. I have not instantaneous words to show you my new world this morning and you have none to show me yours this morning. Certainly this book gives you the critical field, both here and in England. I congratulate you in having eliminated all signs of haste or journalism. Everything shows the deliberate thought it actually contains, and is not misrepresented by slap-dash shorthand. And there is much more I want to say of the book, but I will simply draw a bouquet. But as to your personal life or place in the universe at this moment and mine—how do we move about into strange places, and new events without time to exchange notes! I sit here in my room, incredibly surprised this morning at the way my universe is behaving and I can hardly tell you what the surprise is about. It would be like trying to explain a definite moment in the gorgeous Opera The Cock of Gold, if you had not seen it.

I have just been among my Kentucky cousins, for the first time since 1906 when I wrote "the Flower of Mending" to Eudora—one of the cousins—and I went to the little old Grassy Springs (Campbellite) (Christian) church— and I loafed around Frankfort several days, and recited at Hamilton College Lexington where my mother used to teach, and I have been filled up on family stories I had never before heard, and I assure you they brought much peace to my soul, and I leaped back thirty-four years to the legends of my earliest years and I assure you it has comforted me like Manna. These are all my fathers people these Kentucky cousins, and to have them all claiming kin in the Kentucky way, and telling the old tales, was strange and lovely. Well—I will go on forever—Dear Louis. So I had better quit without stopping.

With love to Jean and to Dick the fairy—

VACHEL

Note

1. Louis Untermeyer's *The New Era in American Poetry* (1919) had just been released by Holt.

87

TO A. J. ARMSTRONG

Springfield, Illinois
April 21, 1919

My Dear Armstrong:
I still feel my great debt to you for Texas and the South, and feel as though I should express it again.[1] You were indeed good to me, and in a special way that no other human being has been good to me, though

I am an awfully spoiled and petted creature. I am hoping to write a Texas song sometime a cousin of the *Santa Fe Trail,* and if I do, you may thank yourself or blame yourself. And I feel invigorated indeed at the thought of Texas, it is a most exhilarating state to remember. Then I owe my visit to Kentucky to you, and the charming acquaintance of Fogle and his friends. He was indeed good to me at Georgetown, and no audience was ever better prepared to receive me. It was an ideal situation, and all cheap curiosity was out of the air before I came, and the people were prepared to listen to the verses. Everyone had heard the *Chinese Nightingale,* so I was able to give it for the large audience.

My visit to Texas has showed my soul the New South, which is different from the South of Southern cousins my own age I grew up with, and far indeed from the South that burns negroes alive, which I assure you existed very vividly in my mind. My own Kentucky cousin Spicie Belle South, my playmate from youth had called me down for *John Brown,* the *Congo,* and *King Solomon,* as expressing too New England a view of the negro, too Harriet-Beecher-Stowe a point of view, as one may say; and when I walked through Georgia in 1906 or around there, and heard the Georgians talk, it seemed that it was not possible for anyone not a sworn negro baiter even to mention the race. So to find myself in accord with the South was indeed a lifting of the veil, and a feeling that a new half of America was mine, since I am naturally far more of a Woodrow Wilson and Andrew Jackson Democrat, than a socialist, and more in accord with the South than the North in *general* political ideas.

I know Griffith's *Birth of a Nation* still has its run in the South, and I dearly love most of the actors in it, and hate the hate in the play. But it evidently represents a Southerner's Griffith's age, around forty-five, not college Southerners around twenty.

You see I had felt that my semblance of tolerance of the negro had forever debarred me from the South, and I had never before received any loud call in that direction, and had for five years been moving around over and over again east of the Mississippi and North of the Ohio. Why I was not called west is not yet explained.

To have Southern schools sing *John Brown* with me, and have not a single whimper or protest from anyone, is indeed exhilarating, though I have no notion of overdoing it.

I am going over all this in my mind just to realize why I suddenly feel that you have presented me with one third of the United States. Then of course, as a consequence I feel awakening again what I thought was pretty well dead within me, the desire to complete the circuit, and now that the South seems to hold friends for me, to dream of the west, that I may get a balanced picture of America in my soul. Everybody in

Texas was telling me about Texas, which is just what I want.

If you get me to Los Angeles, draw the attention of your correspondents to my chapter on California and America, in *The Art of the Motion Picture*. I hope they care to reprint that chapter in the papers, etc. But this is making haste into something I want to talk about more at length.

Do you know you are the only person except Catherine [*sic*] Lee Bates and Witter Bynner who ever cared to get me dates outside his own home town? Pond[2] has had me on his list for four years, and has not made for me a total of as many dates as you have in Texas. Another Bureau has had me on its list as long, and has given me still fewer dates. Both these bureaus expect me sometime to be a kind of Bryan sensation or kill my wife or something, and then they can, in a big easy way with lots of *Sunday Supplement* publicity behind me schedule me across the country like Tagore in his nightgown.[3] And I want no such crowds that listen to nothing as I intend it, and I want no such sensation, and still less do I want the kind of a *slump* that comes the year after such a sensation. To be on the safe side, the bureaus keep me on their lists, expecting me some day to make some kind of a grand opera hit, and then be sold like Jumbo, for an outrageous price that will only enable me to hit the alleged high places. It is all perfectly ridiculous. But that is the reason you stand out like a star on my horizon, as the one human being who wants me to tour without being Jumbo, who is also willing to *do* something about it in an unselfish and unrewarded way. I have *many* unselfish friends, but they are all reviewers or other things like Francis Hackett,[4] or William Lyon Phelps, Harriet Monroe, etc. You are unique in your field of generosity and if you care to do so will probably remain so, so please accept this crown of dandelions, such as it is. And because you have apparently exerted yourself without suffering, I humbly beg you to keep it up on your own terms. Let the terms be yours, and the method be mine. Be sure it will be to me a delightful bargain. I have the east all I want and more. Already I have been called, next February, to Yale, West Point, Smith, Vassar, which are all new points, besides covering my usual eastern route next February, the Poetry Society, etc.

You are positively the only person or thing in sight that cares whether I go west and south or not, and I do not know how much you care. But assuming you do, I have certain ideas which came to me last night, and are hereby exploited and aired.

I keep getting press clippings and have not the least use for them. I suggest that if you want to, you may keep them in a pigeon hole in your desk, and mail them to whoever you write to about my hypothetical tour of next March. And please be more anxious to get my books established in the English courses of the colleges you write to, than to get me there personally. Most schools do not want me but once. There is only one school in ten that gets the habit, like Wellesley and the University of Chicago, for instance. So, since I am not likely to come to a school but once, they had better prepare two years than one, and get as much of the *new* worn off as possible, for I hold a place permanently in direct proportion as the *new* is worn off before I come. And in this process of wearing off the new, the press clippings may serve, with the English Departments with which you correspond. Be sure it is the Colleges and High Schools, and Negro Schools I covet, and the rest are merely incidental. I assure you the longer I live the more I dislike an audience that makes a curiosity out of me, and a committee that makes me talk about myself and listens and listens and listens for queer things. The English Departments of High School, College and University never, never, never do that, bless them. And since there are about one million of them in the United States, lets go after them, and forget the rest. Another reason Pond and the Pond Bureaus balk at me is that such an idea very simple and plain to you, is perfectly incredible to them. Their whole principle is to keep the man they sell a mysterious stranger, and I want to be so simple and accustomed a sight before I get there that the people quit talking about me, and talk about themselves.

Truly I want a deeper picture of the whole United States, and you can help me to that. Please assure your correspondent, that even if I seem lethargic, I am listening deeply to everything said about their state, town and college, and any apparent indifference is merely holding in my steam for the next programme, or the like, and that the one thing I want most of all when I am off the platform, is to understand the United States. The broadside "The Kind of a Visit I like to Make" did a heap toward helping me in Texas.[5] I sent it personally to every personal conductor whose name you gave me, and as a result I find within me a tremendous picture of Texas. Hereafter I shall underline and mark the folder as I send it to you this morning. Please feel free to write anything more on the margin you want to as you send it out. Take any exception you like to the text by way of comment, and let them get both your point of view and mine.

I know this is a whale of a letter. Yet I have still something to say. I am thinking that next March we ought only to hit the high places in the South, and try to *establish* say a line of march along the Pacific coast. I want a map of the United States in my mind as soon as possible. But meanwhile it seems to me reasonable we should begin to get a string of English departments interested and started reading next fall, assuming that we will not be called by two-thirds of them till year after next. If the notion appeals to you, draw a line from Virginia to Texas and Texas to Los Angeles, and Los Angeles to Portland, Oregon, and see if you can permanently interest an English Department about every hundred or two hundred miles. How's that? Then you can send me to them the year that suits them.

And I hope that you can embody in the scheme any other correspondence or idea that is a direct help to your department at Baylor. You have my permission to put in for a chromo anything but Oil stock.

I hope this letter is not too long. Please be perfectly frank with me about anything that is too presuming, or not fitted to the natural course of your plans.

I will be in Springfield the remainder of the year, methinks.

Very sincerely,

NICHOLAS VACHEL LINDSAY

Notes

1. VL toured the southern United States from January to April 1919 under the aegis of A. J. Armstrong, professor of English at Baylor University. Armstrong organized VL's reciting tours until the latter's physical collapse in 1923.
2. The Pond Bureau had previously organized VL's recitals. The other bureau must have been W. B. Feakins in New York, which organized VL's tours in the last years of his career, in conjunction with Elizabeth Conner Lindsay after her marriage to VL.
3. The Indian poet Rabindranath Tagore (1861—1941), an old acquaintance, had met VL in the *Poetry* office in Chicago. Tagore received the Nobel Prize in 1913.
4. Francis Hackett (1883–1962) at the time worked for *The New Republic*. An Irish Fabian Socialist, he cut something of an exotic figure in Chicago, where he was editor of the *Chicago Evening Post* between 1906 and 1909. He also taught classes at Jane Addams's Hull House.
5. In addition to his "Letter About My Four Programmes," VL had published "The Kind of a Visit I Like to Make" (1919) as a leaflet to send in advance to the prospective audiences Armstrong had scheduled. In it, VL explained how he wanted people to read his poems before coming to hear his recitals, how he wanted his ideas discussed in advance, and how he was willing to speak as often as necessary to further the ideas he held dearest.

88

TO WILLIAM LYON PHELPS

Springfield, Illinois
April 26, 1919

My Dear Phelps:
I have put down March 6 as my hypothetical Yale date, and will make it my last date in the East next year. Then I will probably start on a month's tour of the South and west under the wing of an extraordinary follower of Browning—Prof. A. J. Armstrong—Baylor University—Waco Texas. The man delivered the whole state of Texas as it were, to me; bodily, this spring, and it is a most exhilarating retrospect. If there is any Browning question which you desire to address to any human being, address it to him, and please consider that I have introduced you, and say so. He is certainly the most forceful and exhilarating human being I ever met south of Mason and Dixon's line. And he encouraged me to teach the John Brown Chorus to Black and White alike, and there has not been a murmur or ripple of protest. He is the kind of a man who can get away with a thing like that. The Golden Book makes slow and steady progress. I write it in the most gorgeous place—the Washington Park Pavillion— in the very midst of the loveliest imaginable park—with everything blooming blooming, and not a soul in the park till late in the afternoon, when I am through. I take noon lunch in the absolutely deserted pavillion, and it is really a writer's paradise.

People motor and dance themselves to death in the evenings there—but by day it is all mine, mine, mine—and I can take *one* task out there and get it done, while the birds sing. And now I have so many things well started there I can finish them off today in my room, which has also a most gorgeous view of the Governor's Yard, with a very spring-like green, and the Star-Spangled Banner on the Executive Mansion giving color.

Courage—comrades—the devil is dead, though love is a treacherous kicking pony! As for taking up the other letter where it left off—no doubt I will, but not now.

With affection and remembrance

VACHEL

89

TO JOHN EMERSON AND ANITA LOOS

Springfield, Illinois
July 2, 1919

My Dear John Emerson and Anita Loos:[1]
Be sure I send you my heartiest good wishes and most fraternal God-speed in your thrilling adventure. It gave me the greatest pleasure to receive your announcement this morning. I feel very communicative indeed, though no one, not even me, knows what I may say. Look out.

Well, I will say, as a starter I envy you quite as much as you would desire. Next, as to specific good wishes may Santa Claus come to see you every Christmas, and George Washington every fourth of July. May St. Valentine appear ever and anon through the whole year, and may all the other saints bless you and keep you.

I am just creeping back to life again after finishing typewriting "The Golden Book of Springfield" (all prose) two weeks ago. I have been as dead as mouldy bread ever since, and have made an awful fuss about it, and have shuffled about the town begging the people to pet me whose telephone calls I have refused to answer for these two years. They viewed my pathetic remains with a callous indifference that was perhaps to be taken for granted in this revengeful world.

I am sending you some gilded whales[2] by way of a wedding breakfast when you want blubber. Not all blubber is gilded you know. How well I remember how you helped me out when I started on these whales.

I do not know the exact stage of Mae Marsh's adventure, but hope her garden has blossomed by this time. By her account to me, a month back, we are to look for Castor and Pollux, Damon and Pythias or something else in pairs. I am thinking I will suggest Vachel and Rachel if it is that kind of a pair.

I have accumulated every known kind of a letter for three months and now face the hard duty of tearing up most of them without answering. I am trying to think of some way to reduce all my recitals to about six—get all the people in one place, and beat them into subjection by some method not yet devised.

I *love* to recite to a live electrical, alert thoroughly prepared picked audience. Their listening-power goes through me like every known variety of moonshine whisky is *supposed* to do, supposing I could stand up and drink all there is and stay alive.

But this kind of an audience comes only six times a year. So if you hear of any queer doings from me, it is simply the search for these audiences, and the effort to eliminate the rest. Pardon me for airing my affairs, but I am trying to think out the scheme this morning.

Now we will meet in February for sure, for I am going to be at the Brevoort, as usual, if I am spared. Let's try to get together a bit more, and visit like Christians. I am perfectly willing to sing for my supper at your house any time, from dinner till midnight, if it is agreeable.

Well the war is over, and I not only send you my greetings but those of all my fellow Jacksonian Democrats of this region, and hope you are the same.

One reason I have to tear up my letters unanswered is that I hate to write short answers.

I wish I was married.

I remain

With every fine sentiment

VACHEL

Notes

1. John Emerson and Anita Loos had just been married.
2. "The gilded whales" alludes to the poem "The Golden Whales of California," not to the 1920 collection thus entitled. The four-part poem (*Collected Poems,* p. 312) opened the *Golden Whales* collection, which was dedicated to Isadora Bennett Reed, who had married in 1919 (thus, in letter 88, to Phelps, VL's remark that "love is a treacherous kicking pony").

90

TO ELEANOR DOUGHERTY

October 3, 1919

My Dearest Eleanor (Dougherty):

I have reached a moment we seldom reach, and which lasts only a little while: the complete end of one task or episode, and the pause for rest before beginning another. I have sent off The Golden Whales book to Marsh, and yesterday I read "The New Arabian Nights" in the park and today, "Hamlet". It is seldom indeed I sit down to so much reading,—and "seldomer" with such quietness of mind. After so long a storm, I am at least for two days at peace in my heart—and my task is in a sense over, so both mind and heart are enough at rest to look around. I am wondering why we reach this place so seldom, and why we are swept on again so soon, we mortals. But certainly I shall make the most of this little hour of the Peace of God.

Go to the Paulist Father's Church sometime weekdays, when there are no services, and sit and think of me just a minute. It is on Columbus Avenue, near 58th or 59th. There, sometimes, in art-student days, I used to find what I find here tonight in my own room.

> Good night,
> from
> DAVID[1]

Note

1. Some of VL's letters to Eleanor Dougherty addressed her as Jonathan, which accounts for his signing himself "David" here. A note in Olive Lindsay Wakefield's hand confirms this on the manuscript.

91

TO JOHN DRINKWATER

> Springfield, Illinois
> October 13, 1919

My Dear John Drinkwater:[1]

Please consider yourself welcomed to Springfield. The Noonday Lunch Club under the general dictatorship of Elmer Kneale, my good friend, expects you to say something of a comforting nature at the Leland, I understand, Monday noon the twentieth of October. Kneale and the club are to put you up at the Leland. So much I understand from Elmer.

The club, if it has any special character, is that of Springfield, practically all business men and heavy Old Guard State House Politicians of the heavy Tory type, so far as ideas go. Of course you may not notice this, since I will have my good Kentucky friend fellow Democrat and fellow writer at the table with us, Frank Waller Allen.[2] Please note him, since he and his fascinating wife are the two people who want you to eat with them Tuesday. I hope there are no more at the table Tuesday than we four, and daughter Mary Jane. On Tuesday, if you are willing, your heavy publicity being over, we can sneak about the town. Without butting in, I hope to lead you on the first round to any of the Lincoln corners you wish to invade. I feel sure you would like to talk with Old Mr. Rankin, my neighbor and friend whose heavy and very *earnest* personal recollections of Abraham Lincoln have been published by Putnam with all the style in the world. The point about Rankin is that he sits on the side of his bed, and is the liveliest *converser* about Lincoln in seven states, having had a law office across the hall from him here. If you come with a good verbal memory you can get a better book out of him in two mornings than he has written.

I have done my best to get his son to put a stenographer behind the screen while he talks, but the family will not take the hint. We can, of course, go to the Lincoln residence, and the monument where old Major Johnson the most distinguished in manner and bearing of all the old soldiers of the G.A.R. will show us through. I have lived in this town forty years, and can probably unearth anything you want here.

We can walk around the square of the old Court House Yard, where Lincoln used to talk politics to the Sangamon County farmers Saturday evenings, and go to Diller's Old Drug store where they used to foregather around the stove. Then there is Barker's Second hand book store, full of Lincoln litter of all sorts.

The house I live in was owned by Mrs. C. M. Smith, who was a sister of Mrs. Lincoln, and a farewell reception was given Lincoln in our parlor, before he started to Washington. It is the same style of a house as the Lincoln residence.

My mother is away. I am alone here, and eating down town by myself, and I can pick you good eating places, and we can eat together whenever you please, and you can prowl alone as much as you please, after I have presented you to the patriarchs. Believe me they are great sport, and very friendly, and I have as it were courted most of their daughters, somewhat unsuccessfully.

I must not forget Captain John B. Inman who shows the flags at Memorial Hall, a very distinguished citizen indeed, who ends his days as this kind of an honorary sentinel.

I have very seriously in mind persuading you to dramatize Uncle Tom's Cabin for the English. Call it something else, and leave out everything that has gone into the current versions of the drama. Methinks it can be done, as Stuart Walker[3] did "Seventeen". Actually refined and lifted into art in the stage version.

I am sorry to make the letter so long, but if you like the Uncle Tom's Cabin idea, you can write the whole thing here in this town, simply by going to Negro church with me every Sunday. You can get it all in one Sunday morning service, and the only object in going back the next Sunday would be getting it so thoroughly you not only understand it, but write it down. I have my own ax to grind in this matter. I have endless negro poems and pageants sketched in that I expect to write in two or three years. And I had expected to take up Negro Church-going in earnest, but was lazy about doing it alone. If you care to do it with me, we can do a lot of that kind of a thing, and get acquainted with my old friend Gibbs, the Soot-black lawyer. He does not know it, but I simply multiplied him by a thousand, and made the Congo. Do not let any one deceive you into thinking the Negro exists only South of Mason and Dixon's Line. The southerners are particularly silly on that point. A Negro at the North Pole is Congo to the marrow of his bones, and believe me more luxurious than Assurbanipal and more fun than a goat. He is also the only living creature who truly understands religion, and the Jackasses who reduce him to dialect and monkeyshines know nothing about him.

If you care to camp awhile here, I will teach you just how to explore and rough it in a small Illinois town, and have your own way every minute. Think it over.

Very sincerely

(Nicholas) Vachel Lindsay

Notes

1. John Drinkwater (1882—1937), after a very difficult start as an actor and director, began a career as an English man of letters in 1910—11. He was included in Georgian Poetry, and in 1918 his play *Abraham Lincoln* made him famous. He also wrote plays dealing with such historical figures as Mary Stuart, Oliver Cromwell, Robert E. Lee, and Robert Burns, but VL had no doubt been in touch with him because of the Lincoln play. The two men met in Springfield first, and John Drinkwater returned the courtesy in England when VL went there the following year.
2. Frank Waller Allen wrote for the Springfield newspapers.
3. Stuart Walker (1888—1941) had been one of David Belasco's associates. *Seventeen* was staged by his own Portmanteau Players in New York.

92

TO HARRIET MOODY

Springfield, Illinois
Tuesday October 14, 1919

My Dear Cordelia:
This letter is all about Vachel, so if you are sick of him, you might as well skip it.

Thank you indeed for your last good letter. All true, and somewhat heeded.

I am hoping you are having a good time in the Berkshires and at your farm.

Allen is certainly anticipating your acquaintance. He is doing so many things, precisely as I used to do them I cannot help but feel he approaches a similar "goal" (?). His church-work was much like my Y.M.C.A. work. His lectures are as mine used to be on the poets, etc. Time and the right friends should pull him through bravely. He has a notion he wants to be my biographer, and he does not know a thing about me.

He is a Hedonist right where I begin to hate it, and a psycho-analyst, which thing I cannot abide, and a Whitmanite which makes me very tired, and he sees me through some such spectacles. But on the other hand we are fellow Campbellites and Kentuckians once-removed and a lot of things like that. And now that he takes the Christian Science road he gets too misty at once. Oh well—he is a good fellow and a fine friend, but it will take him some years to learn what a proud *mean* red Indian I am, and what a mean disposition I really have, and what a simple and non philosophical scrapper resides in the uttermost depths of my verbiage. "Egotist", as you put it.

I am going to take Mama to England with me, most likely, the first of next July. From now till Jan. 15 I am likely to stay in Springfield and clear up the Golden Book a little more. Already I have cut out one hundred pages this week, so it is only about 170 pages long, and can be read straight through at a six-hour sitting, and polished on the fly. Believe me this makes it infinitely less of a burden, and greatly expedites its progress.

About January 15 I go to the new College at Evansville Indiana for a week. Then I have three dates in Tennessee. Then I am in New York and environs for February, my most outstanding dates being the Church of the Ascension, Vassar and Smith, and early in March I have a Yale Field day. Then A. J. Armstrong my Texas friend takes me straight across the South, and finishes with me at Los Angeles and Berkeley around May and June. Then I take Mama to England July through November. Almost a year of travel, all promised up long ago, without realizing it. I will keep my contracts—but refuse all *new* dates and very likely when I return from England, stay in Springfield *forever!* Anyway little Vachel is leery of any more promises!

There is many a slip, but so far as I can judge, The Macmillan Company will bring out in a month or so "The Golden Whales of California" and "Other Rhymes in the American Language".

Marsh has already accepted the manuscript, but there may be delay in the printing.

But this is not what I started to tell you. I have in as many ways as possible stopped everything I have been doing for the last two years, and gone straight in the opposite direction. I have cut all romance out of the Golden Book, for I am quite sure that is a subject on which I know nothing. What remains is much more lucid, worth while and consistent, and less foundering.

I am through with every idea of marriage for a long long time, and every thing in my life that pointed toward it or planned for it. I am reciting for everyone in Springfield that asks me, and shall continue to do so for some time, which is the exact opposite of what I used to do. I think it is quite possible that in a year or two if people want to hear me, they will have to get themselves invited here!

I am doing my best to interest my mother in the English Poets she is going to meet. While I am away Feb-June I am going to keep dinning at her by letter to read them up and get into the game. Believe me she can conquer the English with her left hand better than I can with both! I shall endeavor to keep silent when I am not reciting, and let her do all the conversing, and watch her slay them. In anticipation of this game, I am at last sufficiently amused by the English trip. Believe me, dear Mama can lay them out once she is in the game and cornered. She will take out her revenge on them for being obliged to play second fiddle to little Vachel! Cornering her thus is as much fun as I can imagine right now. When she *must* talk literature she can do it as well as any creature on God's footstool, but her general contempt for such an accomplishment, her Spartan wave of the hand when all is over, beats Thomas Carlyle and all such. The twelve apostles might impress her, but they are all dead. I doubt if we will meet them in the city of London. I am just waiting to see some Englishman seduced by her innocent smile, and open manner, endeavor to beat something into her head. She will certainly pound him to pulp in the most elegant way possible, and deal out finalities in a way to make Matthew Arnold turn pale. Really I want to get her into the same room with Mrs Humphry Ward,[1] and watch her destroy the creature with devastating and all consuming politeness and language, and a psychology it took me all of thirty years to learn to dodge. It took me till my thirtieth year to get under her guard, and dodge or smash Mrs. Lindsay's adroit finalities. Mrs. Ward, being utterly inexperienced will go down, and the British Empire will fall, if I can only keep from snorting like a rhinoceros in the corner.

I have spared the United States, but as for England, I will destroy it, with this creature known as my parent.

I hope this sounds like the American language to you, and not mere drivel.

I was going to write some solemn matters—but presume I had best cease, with this, my latest amusement.

With love,

VACHEL

Note

1. Mary Augusta (Arnold) Humphry Ward (1851—1920) was an English novelist and philanthropist. Her most famous novel, *Robert Elsemere* (1888), was a reasoned attack on evangelical Christianity.

93

TO HARRIET MONROE

Springfield Ill
December 26, 1919

My Dearest Harriet Monroe:
This is an entirely personal letter, and not for any of the other lovely ladies in your office.

I was so glad to get your Christmas greeting, and I return it this morning. There is no particular news except that I am living here peacefully with mama and we went out to Christmas dinner together at the St. Nick. Possibly my solidest personal acquisition is a fellow walker a young red blooded lawyer named John Snigg. He is the one human being I have ever discovered who likes to walk as I do. He gets through at his office Saturday afternoon at 1. Then we have lunch together. Then we walk somewhere till dinner-time, often to farm friends of his, eat dinner and I recite a few minutes in exchange for the fried chicken; then we walk home till midnight by the stars or moon, and I am just learning Sangamon County at last. We have done thirty miles the round trip to Williamsville, thirty four miles the round trip to a farm beyond Old Berlin, twenty eight miles to the region of Cornland, about sixteen miles the round trip to Riverton and about twenty two around Chatham way. Snigg walks at just my pace, a mile every fifteen minutes, four miles an hour, and thirty four miles in eight and a half hours (taking out time for eating and reciting).[1] That is we sweep back to town at midnight exactly the pace we started, and these walks have made us both over more than once. Snigg is the son of old inhabitants and we have plenty to talk about. And he is more of an out-doors poet and sunset-admirer than myself!

I am, I hope, on the last lap of the "Golden Book of Springfield" but will promise nothing till it is done, I have been thwarted so often.

"The Golden Whales of California" (verse) has long been proof-read and Brett writes me that it will be out February the first.

Since I was last in Chicago I have changed my regime in every way possible, not to live a distorted life. The walks with Snigg are simple to tell, but let them be a symbol of many other simple but energetic changes.

God bless you dear Harriet. It is a joy to have such a person to write to as I begin my morning's work. I know you have a very tender and faithful heart for your friends, and are a thoroughbred in every respect, and it means a deal to me to tell you of my small mileposts.

I am not likely to be in Chicago soon, but will write as soon as the Golden Book is done. That will indeed be a milepost for me. Or rather *done and published* will be the milepost, will be about as much to me, personally, as the launching of your magazine was to *you* personally.

With love to you, dear lady

VACHEL

Note

1. John Snigg later wrote a short pamphlet, published by the Vachel Lindsay Association (Springfield), entitled *I Walked with a Poet*, which confirms most of this letter's data.

94

TO LOUIS UNTERMEYER

Springfield
Friday, January Ninth, 1920

My Dear Louis:

Certainly by July I may have something for you, and I will submit any good bad and indifferent rhymes I have unpublished at that time, and you may take a selection as you please, and I will not be mad if you turn all down. I am thinking I will have a long epic on *The American Turkey Gobbler*. I have all the data, if I can only make him gobble. I think the turkey is more wonderful and beautiful than the griffin and handsomer, but people only eat him. I am dreaming of turkey fanciers, who breed him for his beauty like the peacock. And he has a more substantial cry.

Which reminds me of an idea of a book of criticism which I wish you would seriously undertake.

Emmanuel Morgan's "Pins for Wings"[1] is the most wonderful and successful thing Bynner has done, and I read it with joy every week in the Mirror. Congratulate him for me if you see him. But this kind of a thing is lost in the void because there is no great *recognized* body of American Falstaffian poetry in which to float such a venture. As a critic you have begun to supply it in your last anthology, yet I have a feeling that the whole set of humorous verses runs to quips and puns too much, and not quite enough of the Falstaffian and Gothic Gargoyle richness. Now I humbly petition that you start out on a new hypothesis having used Whitman to the limit in your last critical work. Base the serious side of your criticism of Poetry on the tone of Abraham Lincoln as a touchstone, and the criticism of humor on the tone of Mark Twain. You may say that neither of these are poets, yet I hold that they have both of them more inspirational meat for new poets than any writer of verse, and they are free or neutral in regard to mere poetic form traditions. Reading this little sketch of Waldo Frank's book[2] brings this thought to a head, which I have had for ages. I agree with Frank absolutely in regard to Lincoln and Mark Twain, and I fancy in little else. The disguised Marxianism that is evidently back of his book, gives me the nausea and the pain from a literary standpoint. But since Lincoln and Twain have both conquered Marx in his mind, they are indeed conquerors and are proved the greatest common denominators. I have said for years that if almost everything that was said in praise of Whitman was rewritten with the names of Johnny Appleseed and Abraham Lincoln alternately substituted, it would be much truer, in the eyes of the real open mind of America. And most everything said in praise of Thoreau had better be said for Johnny Appleseed, who was one of the great and beautiful and successful unconscious humorists of his day. He beat the game without knowing it, which is the final victory Mr. Frank has in mind. But all this as a preliminary to the fundamental suggestion that you make an Anthology of American Humorous Verse that is Falstaffian, and has as good guts, and is not wit and put in as much comment as verse. The use of it will be that hereafter the young American Poe will be no more afraid to be funny when he pleases, than Shakespeare, who had Falstaff in about six serious plays, more or less. I have not counted them for awhile—The Merry Wives of Windsor and a lot of those Henry plays.

You know how crazy I am over Benét's Merchants of Cathay, and I am almost sure it would head the list. Then these things of Bynner's could well go in. And some of Carl Sandburg's sardonics. When it comes to citing precedents and parallels, you know Heine[3] well enough to know how he put depth into humor, and our friend Horace. As a matter of fact you are most remarkably fitted for the task, and the only trouble is that there is the temptation to make the collection too funny, and not deep enough. If you go to any current exhibition of the architectural League, you will find some of the biggest things there are humorous without losing dignity, and without taking too many liberties with the good God. I think the freedom of this League has not yet invaded our writing. I doubt if I have made myself perfectly clear. I think the great parallels which are not critically fashionable are in the other arts. Take for instance the wonderful work of Percy Grainger[4] and the wonderful Golden Cockerell, which you and Jean took me to see last Spring. The acting was Falstaffian, the music was Falstaffian, and I have no doubt the libretto was also. Yet there was not one shallow or trivial phase to the whole performance. It was the laughter of the Gods. It was not mere grotesque, or Oliver Wendell Holmes polite after dinner wit. It had some of the guts of Huckleberry Finn, and the King and the Duke on the raft. And your friend who does the Batique [sic] work—(Hermann) never loses dignity in his humor. I think one thundering book of criticism can turn the tide of humor that has heretofore worked itself out in Dooley's and Ades and O. Henrys and the like, can be turned into the poetic stream of America. O. Henry would have been a great poet, if he had only known America expected it of a man like him. I should say the test of humor is the same test as that of seriousness. Does it last? Please establish the classic standards and save the country. Humor is not always a final test but a strong crusade is needed. After such a winnowing, Bret Harte would come to his own again. Poe might die, but we would suddenly find Riley much more alive. This is of course the absurdity of being too logical. But Riley was never witty and flip. He was either deeply and classically humorous or a failure. And we must have a humorous standard for Riley that gives his *deeps* a chance, and does not leave him a "wit". And, above all, the young writers just coming on would be far more liberated, than by any "theory of free verse". They have been offered every kind of freedom but this (the freedom to laugh), by the critics. So the rich wit of young poets is buried in college annuals and cheap humorous sheets when they could be taught to laugh with the high gods, and not snicker in the corners.

With every good wish.

VACHEL

I am wishing you could illustrate the book from some of the things in the Architectural League.

Notes

1. Emmanuel Morgan was the pseudonym Witter Bynner adopted for the purpose of his "Spectra" hoax, in collaboration with "Anne Knish" (A. D. Ficke). (See note 1 to letter 16.)
2. The book by Waldo Frank (1889–1967) mentioned here must have been *Our America* (1919), published in England as *The New America*. Frank founded *The Seven Arts* (1916—17) and was the American correspondent of the *Nouvelle Revue Française*.
3. Heinrich Heine (1797—1856) was a German poet whose *Buch der Lieder* or *Book of Songs* (1827) had been translated in part by Untermeyer. Heine wrote a number of satirical books that caused difficulties with the German authorities. Untermeyer's *Heinrich Heine—Paradox and Poet* came out in 1937.
4. Percy Grainger (1882—1961), Australian by birth, was a composer, pianist, and conductor who collected folk music. When he was twenty-four, he became a friend of Edvard Grieg's, and he settled in the United States eight years later. He and VL became friends after VL settled in Spokane (see letters 139 and 140.)

95

TO THE PRESIDENT OF THE
SPRINGFIELD ROTARY CLUB

Brevoort Hotel
New York
February 24, 1920

My Dear Roy:

My resignation from the Rotary Club is permanent and unalterable. I like the members all as individuals, but will meet them all at other places with more satisfaction to myself, one at a time where I can indulge in more back-talk and pleasantry.

I do not like the Rotary scheme. It is exclusively business men and seems to me an effort to draw a line of hatred between business men and working people, instead of talking with them out of business hours, and getting acquainted.

The whole plan seems to be based on caste hate or condescending patronage of working people; whatever the camouflage, I do not want to develop these things in myself any more than I can help.

Then I am fined outrageously for being absent. That is, I pay for meals when I am not there and it will probably be Jan. 1, 1921 before I am back in Springfield while Rotary Club Sessions are on. This kind of discipline is typical of "business men" forced methods.

Such Rotary Programmes as I have not been able to avoid all run in the groove of the "business man" caste mind, to aggravate me still more the "business man's" disposition to patronize the rest of America, and the "Rotarian", the official organ runs to the same sort of a thing . . . "business man", self-boasting overlaid with molasses.

Now the local Rotary Club is not responsible for any of these things, but if I am to judge by "The Rotarian", the official organ, the whole institution is devoted to the roller-top desk point of view in life, and glorifying its worst features.

I would welcome an organization in Springfield that was at least one half the very people "The Rotarian" everlastingly patronizes and tries to "put in their place".

This is not an economic question, though people prefer to argue it that way. It is a question of getting acquainted with someone besides ones own kind.

You are welcome to read in public or publish this letter if you choose.[1]

Very sincerely

VACHEL LINDSAY

Note

1. This letter is followed by a penciled footnote added by the recipient: "Refer to Directors / Take regular action through regular channels. / Notification brief and formal."

96

TO SAMUEL J. HUME

Sante Fe
New Mexico
Saturday—April 3, 1920

My Dear Professor Hume:[1]
I feel I owe you a far more extensive discourse than my last—though I am sorry to impose it. I know you are very likely a very good sort—and if we must continue to run amuck of each other, candor should compel us to be clear.

In the first place Professor Armstrong is in no way responsible for my letter or telegram, and I spoke only for myself. I realize that few people just now would see things as I do, and I must be clear.

About a year and a half ago I served notice on both Pond and the Players I would have no more lecture-bureau dates, and neither of them believed me. I had to mail back three or four engagement slips to Pond he made over my head, and even more to The Players, before they would believe me. Whipple raised such hob about two Los Angeles dates they are still on the schedule, but believe me, they are the last. Now why do I have such nausea at Lecture Bureaus, and why am I so vexed at your employing a stenographer on my behalf and without my consent? Well, in the first place, if I wanted such work done, I could do it in Springfield Illinois under my own eye. But I do not want that kind of relations with mankind. In 1895 or 6 I first took to the road,[2] rather than submit to commercialization, and I am perfectly willing to turn beggar again, before I allow an "office" of any kind to make my arrangements for me. I have no financial responsibilities or obligations. I owe no man a cent. I do not want money, and I hate the thought of money-making with all my soul. These letters Armstrong has just sent me to settle some disputed point I do not care to bother to settle, so reek with fees, percentages, talk of "this office" and so forth it makes me positively red eyed to read them.

Believe me, sir, you are trying to "market" an utterly unmarketable article. Here is a line which says that such and such an engagement will "make me money" and will be "socially advantageous". Those are the two best reasons I could think of for begging off from the appointment. I do not want such dates. I hate woman's club dates. I hate lecture-course dates. I never made a friend in my life by such appearances, on such occasions. They merely regard me as a queer one or a curiosity, and I do not desire to exhibit myself as a dime museum freak, or be sold about from team to team like a base-ball player. What then *do* I want—you venture to ask. Well—about three fourths of the letters I have received this fall that I have answered at all I have answered something like this:—

"Please postpone my engagement with you two or three years till a small group has read all seven of my books, or at least looked into them. My present fee for a visit to a town is $150, but subject to your amendment or suggestions. When I come I am willing and anxious to appear wherever my work is known, and you may keep me busy in the town and it is a matter of no moment to me whether specific audiences pay a fee or not. I generally give five to ten free recitals to small groups to one pay recital. And the pay recital is generally the least satisfactory".[3]

In short, my dear Professor Hume, I not only want to apply the principles and spirit of "The Handy Guide for Beggars" as much as I can, and still pay car fare and hotel bills, I am fighting every day to get back as near as I can to the letter and spirit of that private Magna Charta.

There is not the least sign in your letters from your "office"—particularly that long bunch to Leland Stanford, that you even remotely apprehend this.

Prof. Olan James's desirability as an introducer and interpreter is all the greater because he was my host when I was a beggar in San Francisco; from July 1—1919-Jan. 16—1920 I put up a last desperate fight to finish "The Golden Book of Springfield", a prose book on which I had been working for ten years off and on, and in which I tried to apply the spirit if not the letter of "The Handy Guide for Beggars" to a prospectus of Springfield for one hundred years. You speak of dates and engagements. In that length of time, July-January, I tore up at least a thousand dollars worth of engagement-offers without answering, postponed about a thousand dollars worth two or three years, and in the end of writing the book broke down with the flu twice and the jim-jams generally, and therefore begged off of a thousand dollars worth more that I had accepted and recuperated in Cleveland, and finally took up "reciting" the middle of February.

Meanwhile there had been just one person who had ever secured the kind of a welcome, I have been able to secure by my own personal letters, and that was Professor Armstrong. Every place I went under his wing in Texas last year, I received a welcome of the kind I desire, and recited, mostly gratis, but with a total fee, in every town, and had my kind of a time. Therefore while I was locked up by my own hand finishing my book where not even my own mother could find me, I entrusted to Prof. Armstrong a schedule of the south and west, since it was the East that sent [page missing]

[. . .] enough to imagine I will like such a thing, and I hate to disillusion him on it. But if we can leave that event out, let's do it, whatever else we do.

People think because I roar, I can be heard in a large auditorium. It is not so. Those half-way back often complain they do not hear me. Then large audiences, especially one as large as would fill the theatre, are apt to regard me as a curiosity or a freak. And I have not one moment to spend on such people. I *must* be among friends, either those who have read most of my books, or who have, like Olan James, known me long, and entirely survived any idea I am a curiosity or a freak. And I am certainly not willing to charge such people a fee when it can possibly be helped. I have gone the rounds of all the well known colleges and Universities but those on the coast. Ann Arbor, Smith, Cornell have left me out. And maybe one or two others. Though so many have sent for me once, only a few care for me, but those few send for me again and again, and my whole life is a process of finding my *own* and letting the rest alone. If this method is not possible now, in San Francisco, with you as a personal conductor, if I must be sent about that town by an office squeezing fees out of the events and all that, I certainly want to stay away. I would much prefer to stay away for several years, till you or some one in like position, had persuaded certain groups not to pay me money, but to get my books out of the library and read them. I have been the rounds of most of the English departments, and since they are constantly exchanging professors in a network all through the educational world, I find even in small colleges two or three who have heard me, somewhere else far away, and among these there is always one friend prepared to explain my affairs and prepare the way. But he does not peddle me in the neighborhood, by the yard, like calico, and he does not exhibit surprise if I want to recite for High Schools, and even when they have no money. He simply finds those people he thinks are my natural friends, and leaves out the rest. Even so only a few like what I offer. And believe me, dear sir, I have reconciled myself to those few, in every group, and seek no brass band triumph.

My excellent and most loyal friend Witter Bynner who is very good to me indeed, cannot reconcile himself to my thus combing the community for friends, and wearing out all their company manners, and all of my own manners. But Bynner, otherwise my very good friend, does not realize that I want to know the worst of them, and I want them to know the worst of me, and then after that cheerful action of the LIGHT, if we can be friends, it is for life, and this nonsense of being on parade or sold for a fee is impossible.

Please correct your impressions of myself and Professor Armstrong by this letter. Be sure I did not choose him lightly as my corresponder. He is unbusinesslike, a Southerner, a devout Baptist, a profound Browning student, a brilliant young leader among the boys and girls of his big Baptist school. Of course he does not get all my drift, and I have no doubt my two letters and the telegram to you would horrify him. He has not the least idea how hard I would fight for some of the points in this letter. And he has far more of Southern punctilio, all of which makes him dear to me. There are some people who know I would fight like cats in hellfire for some of the points in this letter, but they do not happen to be members of English departments, and able to speak fraternally to other English Departments. Professor Armstrong has been far more zealous for my income than I can be. Having taken no Franciscan vows, he does not quite get my ideas here. Having never been a beggar, he can never feel the irresistible call of the road, and the cheerful desire to tell every dollar and every dollar getter in the world to go straight to the hot land of snitzelfritz.

He has a wife and child and all that kind of charming impedimenta, and his Franciscan ideas are limited. But I forgive him for all this—because of the human welcome he has secured for me across the whole South. And while he was doing it, by his charming, human and patient letters—I had come as near as possible to killing myself by writing a book on the Franciscan point of view as applied to a town, and writing and sweating night and day.

So believe me, Sir, I am willing to wait many years till my San Francisco friends are ready for my ideas, and I am as willing that you should expound them as another, but certainly it cannot be done by an "office", no matter how busily the typewriters click.

I cannot write short letters any more than I can endure casual acquaintances, and I do not want to have anything to do with people who are bored by my letters or think them too long.

Very sincerely

NICHOLAS VACHEL LINDSAY

To be addressed
Care of Miss Ruby Vachel Lindsay
    1035 Lincoln Street
    Los Angeles Calironia

Notes

1. Professor Samuel J. Hume was in the Drama Department at Berkeley.
2. The 1895–96 date VL gives for his debut in tramping and begging is obviously an exaggeration: He repeats the reasons for his early tramps (1906) in the first introduction to the *Collected Poems* ("Adventures While Singing These Songs") but does not ever mention having seriously taken to the road that early in his life.
3. This quotation is a summary of the contents of *The Kind of a Visit I Would Like to Make.*

97

TO AMY LOWELL

Tuesday May 18, 1920

My Dear Amy Lowell:

Thank you indeed for your generous word in the New York Times that arrived tonight.

I am almost provoked to be confidential with you, but it is midnight and when I write at midnight I am apt to write eighteen pages, and that would be a presumption.

Certainly your advice is sound. Certainly I have simply gone on of my own momentum in the Golden Whales volume. The great effort of my life, this last ten years, culminating in the last two, has been "The Golden Book of Springfield", Prose. And believe me lady I am far more interested in the permanent vitality of that work, than of anything else I have done. I am interested in its *effect* on a very few people.

I have, by comparison, exceedingly little interest in the issues of my presumed life as a writer. My now advertised trip to England has nothing to do with the issues of life as I understand them, but is simply a pleasant method of extending publication. But it has nothing to do with what I am thinking about.

And there is hardly a line in my seven books that hints at what I am thinking about.

Also I feel quite sure that "The Golden Book" just sent to the printer by Macmillans will be called obscure by a great part of those who like the other seven books, and I feel that it will deserve it. I am sure that its faults will only be forgiven by those with whom I have been in the longest and most forgiving and mutually forbearing personal contact.

I have no particular regrets about this, have long ago reconciled myself to it.

Yet I must not end this argument by insisting on "The Golden Book". This too, is only a matter of comparison. For when the Golden Book is once out, for better or worse, and I have returned from England, I have every expectation of turning to matters that are far from the issues of public life, prose, poetry, or pictures, or even Golden Books. Now that is a vague ending.

I can only offer you a metaphor, because we are far from acquainted, you being in Boston and I in the deserts of my own special adventures.

As a matter of fact these deserts are only hinted at in the "Golden Book", and never even hinted anywhere else.

So I indicate that work, as my "explanation" to you, if you care to have me offer one. If the heart of my mystery is worth plucking out, it is, perhaps, mussed up in the Golden Book, for the Watsons and Sherlocks to find!

And I bid you most fraternally good night.

NICHOLAS VACHEL LINDSAY

Permanent address
603 South 5th
Springfield Illinois.

Vachel Lindsay's "The War Path," one of his "Five Seals in the Sky"

Censers swinging over the Springfield, Illinois, statehouse, drawn by Lindsay

Kubla Khan, a Lindsay collage

THE DREAM OF KING DAVID IN HEAVEN
WHILE HIS SON CHRIST WAS IN THE GRAVE.
HE DREAMED HE WALKED ON THE MILKY WAY.
HE DREAMED AGAIN—
A LONELY STAR,
GUIDED BY THE DARK,
A MYSTIC SPARK
IN THE CLOUDY DAWN
OF EASTER DAY.
AND THE SOUL OF THE STAR
WAS A JEWELLED HARP
NO ANGEL CARED OR DARED TO PLAY,
TILL
WINDS FROM A TOMB,
DESIRES FROM AFAR,
FIRES FROM AFAR,— — —
CAUGHT THE HARP
LIKE A BIRD ENSNARED
AND TAUGHT ITS SOUL TO PLAY.

NICHOLAS VACHEL LINDSAY

Poem and drawing by Lindsay: "The Dream of King David in Heaven" (*courtesy of Norman Holmes Pearson*)

98

TO A. J. ARMSTRONG

Springfield, Illinois
May 29, 1920

My Dear Armstrong:

I humbly apologize for not making myself clear. I intended my telegram from Charleston West Virginia to say that I was going straight home from there till you wanted me on the sixteenth and other public appearances were impossible till I pulled myself together again and cleared up my Springfield affairs. As it was I went to the Hotel Statler St. Louis for three days and simply sat there looking out the window and seeing no one till I acquired sense enough to come home and go about my business. So here I am, my dear friend, hard at work reprinting *The Village Magazine*, which has not seen the light for ten years, of which more later.

I am perfectly willing to arrive in Waco Saturday morning or afternoon June 12, and stay as long as you find me useful. Of the people you think are coming, I feel surer Harriet Monroe will be there than the rest. But if Amy [Lowell] comes, for heaven's sake stir her up and encourage her to talk herself to death, for she is at least heard and attended to, and she will make a great peace maker for the other two. Markham is a wonderfully spirited old man when properly aroused. But he avoids functions mostly, being utterly weary of the canned and perfunctory appearance, but with an amazing generosity of interest toward the young poets, so encourage the young poets to treat him like a splendid great grandfather, and you will be surprised at the generous results. And let me urge upon them that they tell him plainly that they are writing verses, and respect him as the leader of the craft. There is such a fashion for new cults nowadays: few people that deal with him stop to realize that Markham is an exceedingly dignified and spirited figure, and a veteran as loaded with genuine honors as a man well may be. Amy and Harriet, both feeling they are leading new schools, are not as apt to get this aspect of Markham as the independent outsider. It is very hard for old men to be courteous and fraternal and paternal with young men, but Markham is splendid in the role, and I think he is a splendid figure in the Poetry Society of America when he appears, and no young poet lacks for his handshake, and all that an honest hand implies.

When he visited Springfield he was a *transformed* creature, being among his intimates, the Swedenborgians, and he took on a Spanish Grandee flamboyant, Peter Paul Rubens perfectly decorous but triumphant and paternal air that was perfectly delightful. He certainly looked like old Homer among the singers. Edwin is philosopher enough to take it cheerfully if Harriet and Amy treat him respectfully but firmly as Yesterday, but watch him glow when you treat him as Mister Tomorrow.

If I come so soon, I will not be able to bring the new *Village Magazine* imprint with me, but please remember I am now in the role of pen and ink draftsman for two years, and my lips are sealed till I have something new to say, or it is absolutely essential to the health of the situation for me to keep aroaring a bit.

You are a very good friend, my dear Armstrong, and what is more, by far the most useful cooperator in the Universities I ever came within a mile of, and be sure I am not only deeply grateful, but I see in the future an entirely different and what I hope is a far more essential type of cooperation, and certainly a much closer acquaintance. For the sake of my real intimacy with yourself and Mrs. Armstrong, I am in a way sorry it has been almost altogether based on what we have written or telegraphed, or said in public.

My inside and Springfield self is so different in its motions from the public self, even the one that my friend Harriet Monroe of so long standing knows, that there sometimes seems no point of contact.

Taking my pen in hand to draw again, I have the feeling of coming into focus and being really honest with myself such as I have not had since I laid down the drawing pen in 1910, and to get square with myself like that is far more to me, and far more essential than anything I have done since I laid the pen down that I can think of at this moment, and I doubt if there is a living human creature who knows just how much that freedom means to me, no matter how grubby the picture.

But this is not an attempt to elucidate the dark mysteries of Lindsay. The simplest way to say it is that what I am lies between the lines of the *Golden Book of Springfield,* and I doubt if three living creatures ever read in the true Henry James way, between the lines. And I am in no sweat that they should. But this is the private self that I talk to and consult, this is the set of nervous habits, if you will, that are the actual basis of my motions.

But enough of this. As to my present plans with which I hope you may be persuaded to cooperate spiritually if in no practical way, they consist not in making the trip to England,[1] which I hope to make as brief and private as possible not to be seeming coquettish, but to get back to my room here, by December if possible, where I have worked and hatched my nonsense since I was thirteen and about the only place where I live my own life. Here I hope to stay, for two years perhaps drawing pictures, and sending the *Village Magazine*[2] reprinted, or some other such souvenir of acknowledgement of courtesy to those who ding-dong at me to recite. If I ever recite again, if I work it out as I see it now, I want to stick to the High Schools and English departments of the Colleges of the South and West, for I am entirely through with the East *as a public person,* and have no intention of making my annual visit to the Brevoort again. As a public person, shadowy as that public person may be, I owe to you the inestimably precious panorama of the South and West, and be sure I am entirely grateful for it, and desire to make a complete shift to such regions for recital grounds when I recite at all away from home, and for the simple reason that the people out there tell me so much about themselves and their states on the second day, and I feel myself growing with the country. I hope to develop such a system of recital visits that everyone is *debarred from the hall* that cannot pass a reasonable examination on the *Village Magazine* or one of my books! But that puts it arrogantly. I do not know what the system can be, but I am willing to make any sacrifice to attain to the human intimacy where my public shares my life and I share theirs, but I have not one more moment to spend as a curiosity, or explaining or reciting what I did yesterday when I am absolutely bursting to write or recite tomorrow's poem and draw tomorrow's picture, and yesterday's poem bores me to death. The only thing that keeps me going at the latter part of tours in my present style is a sort of base-ball player's sociability with the grand stand and the bleachers. People will never like my pictures as well as they do my verses, because we Americans do not take pictures seriously ever. And especially my present public stamping ground, *the English Departments,* are terribly green on pictures. Yet I feel pictures kicking to come out of me, with a great deal more of that "Let-me-out-quick" feeling, than I ever had for verse. This is partly because while they are a good deal more of a natural function with me than anything but letters and conversation, they have been dammed up for ten years. Zinc-etching each picture so as to preserve it and printing it independent of the publisher (as I did my poems till they arrived) costs such scads of money, that I am only now for the first time placed so I can zinc-etch my pictures as fast as I make them and as fast as I used to print pamphlets, till I arrive at that picture which is, as one may say, my *Congo* among pictures or that magazine reprint that is a *Congo* as a whole. I am sure I have pictures in me with as long fluid lines as the Congo, once I take a year or two to get the swing of it.

I went to the Macmillan Company with my freedom as a writer earned, and they have hardly blue-penciled anything. But they will stand over me like ferocious economizers if I go in for zinc-etching on the same scale. I will have to fight it out alone perhaps forever, putting money I make as a reciter into zinc-etchings, probably for a steadily enlarged *Village Magazine,* which will be the same number always, but slowly perfected with each new reprint a sort of dummy or model for a magazine, reissued time after time, with the whole magazine for the unit, instead of any one picture or poem or editorial. It seems to be the magazine idea has a tremendous grip on me, but not in the commercial sense. That is, one collection of pictures, poems and editorials and end-page ornaments, issued by one man, and dominated by his ideas, and as definitely his, as though it were his novel. Only in this way can I unify all my activities in balanced proportion, and introduce what might be called my genuine *public self* to my little public, and keep from being the parrot and ape of what I did yesterday. You may say that I should not worry about being the parrot and ape of yesterday. *But Mother Nature is worrying,* and if the ideas that keep kicking around in me day and night especially the picture ideas, do not get out, they will certainly tear me to pieces and I will die of the pip. And, if I say so, I am for the first time really equipped to draw my best. I have scads of training that even my best friends do not realize, because I have only now thought out how to make it useful. Inside of a year I am going to show you some flying human figures that are going to fly, spirits going faster than any flying machine you know.

Pardon me if I write at such length. But let me add that I have a whole note book full of possible pictures and verses piled up since last we met, and they have to do in many ways with the territory into which you have sent me, and I am indeed grateful for this. The welcome in almost all cases was exquisite, and I was taught a heap, if I only remember a little of it.

Most sincerely and affectionately

Nicholas Vachel

So perhaps, the conclusion of this discourse is that my next petition to you may be "Help make way for a gratuitous distribution of the successive reprints of the *Village Magazine* among our most *loyal* friends West and South."

Notes

1. VL left for England in August with his mother.
2. There were several imprints of *The Village Magazine,* after the original 1910 edition (700 copies): one in 1920 (1,000 copies), one in 1924 (200 copies), and one in 1925 (number of copies unknown; the number 5,000 given elsewhere by VL seems wildly exaggerated.); all were published at his own enormous expense. In 1925 he also had 2,000 copies of *The Map of the Universe* privately printed.

99

TO JOHN EMERSON AND ANITA LOOS

Thackeray Hotel
Great Russell Street
(Opposite the British Museum)
London W.C.1.
[August 27, 1920]

My Dear John Emerson
and Anita Loos:
Come to my rescue at once. I am here at this hotel, homesick as can possibly be, and I do not care whether you mention business affairs ever if you will only be good to me and talk United States. These English just drive me mad. The Grave digger was right in Hamlet. They are all mad here. He also might have added they are a deaf and dumb asylum as well. England seems frantically imitating Boston.

Well—write or telephone *at once.* And I want to meet that Constance Talmadge.[1] She was *not* on my boat!

I know I am a poor thing, but take me as I am—and do it at once, before it is too late.

I am simply too United States for this place, and I could lean up against the British Museum and cry. I certainly would not lean on any of these whispering English. [Here a flurry of the pen with an arrow pointing toward it from the word: "foam."] Those curly marks indicate I am foaming at the mouth.

Goodnight

VACHEL

Note

1. Constance Talmadge (1899—   ) was an American actress "whose vivacious personality made her a very popular comedy star. She began film work as an extra at Vitagraph in 1914 and became known as the "Vitagraph Tomboy." Later she displayed a similar personality as the Mountain Girl in *Intolerance* (1916). When her sister Norma married Joseph M. Schenk, Constance appeared for him in a successful series of farcical comedies, many of them written by Anita Loos and John Emerson, with titles like *A Virtuous Vamp* (1919) and *Learning to Love* (1925). She apparently lost interest in acting and retired on her marriage in 1925." (*Oxford Companion to Film,* 1976)

100

TO LOUIS UNTERMEYER

Springfield, Illinois
December 11, 1920

My Dear Louis:
Enclosed find the clipping I promised. You may expect much friendlier treatment from Squire[1] in the future I think. Remember he is carrying the whole magazine in this number, Shanks being sick.

I have every reason to believe that Squire, when his attention is actually roused is absolutely open-minded and capable of being convinced on evidence, and I am very eager for you and your group to have no prejudices when he lands in New York in January. Squire is the most ultra English person I ever met, in general taste, preference and experience. And *travel*, properly chaperoned, ought to be positively revolutionary with him. He watches the Dial group like a fox. In short he knows who *is worth watching*. Remember he is a very young man, yet, owing to the eliminations of the war he is carrying almost all Richard Watson Gilder carried in America, thirty years ago. I take it that there are usually twenty such men in England. But the war has knocked out all but Squire. So far as our group is concerned, the capture of Squire means the capture of the field, and as I have watched him, he is an absolute open-minded man, willing to learn every day, stubborn but willing to be shown, and in final critical independence once his attention is really focussed, so much like yourself that you will be amazed. You have both practiced law in much the same style but in such different courts you do not realize your mutual spiritual attitude.

Squire has every desire to know the truth about America, and considering his very limited time, his plans seem to me very sensible. I know of no one in New York so likely to give him needed light about all things as you and Jean, and I am writing urging him to accept you as my proxies when he goes through New York in January, and so the same mail, I write you to the same effect.

I was terribly slack passing through New York, and I hope you will forgive me. I am in the condition of the locust half out of his old shell, both physically and otherwise. I find I must go in for a big chunk of rest, and then completely recast my plans in detail, though not in intent. My home town has made an amazing leap in the direction of "The Golden Book", and "The Village Magazine" since I left it, pretty largely and simply for the reason that I took my mother to England with me, and her reports on these events were more in Springfield style than mine would have been. I actually have an open-minded and interested town at last, and they are prepared to read *Mitch Miller, Moon Calf* or *Main Street*,² introspectively, and do themselves good. So hereafter, if you are inclined to sermonize the Middle West, address Springfield directly, and the discourse will be clipped by the local papers.

Meanwhile, I suggest, as a project for you, that you, Louis Untermeyer, become one of my chief councillors [*sic*] in my Springfield policy. To that end, I want you to make an ample visit to this town, sometime soon. How is this for a plan. We will spend the morning reading Moon-Calf. We will spend the rest of the day proving or disproving it on the streets of Springfield. We will spend the next morning reading Mitch Miller. We will spend the rest of the day proving or disproving it on the streets of Springfield. We will spend the morning reading Main Street. We will spend the day proving or disproving it on the streets of Springfield. I want you to be my first Springfield critic visitor. I want you to beat the long parade of Englishmen to this place, and black out the critical path they should follow. I want you to undercut Masters, Dell, Sinclair Lewis and others in actual first hand data on a Middle West capital. I counsel you to so judicial an attitude as a justice of the Supreme Court: we will have long personal conversations with every soul in town that you choose to interview. I want you to go back with the fattest note-book and scrapbook collectible on a Middle Western Capital. And above all; I want you to beat the Englishmen to it.³ I want you to be prepared to tell them exactly what kind of a Springfield they should discover. When all is done, I want said reports to appear where they will form the American and Springfield minds. I will accept your verdicts if you will look at the evidence.

With every good wish

V<small>ACHEL</small>

Notes

1. John Collings Squire (1884–1958) was literary editor of *The New Statesman* in 1913. He founded *The London Mercury* in 1919 and was assisted in his editorship by the English writer Edward Shanks. The latter published an article on VL: "An English Impression of American Literature" (*Bookman,* November 1922, pp. 279—87).
2. Floyd Dell's *Moon-Calf,* Sinclair Lewis's *Main Street,* and Edgar Lee Masters's *Mitch Miller* all came out in 1920.
3. VL's trip to England was a great success; he recited in Cambridge and in West-

minster's Central Hall. His October 15 recital at Oxford took place in front of the assembled dons. T. S. Eliot, who heard him recite in London, found him "impossible." Bell put out *The Daniel Jazz and Other Poems* on September 20, 1920; the book largely colored the type of reaction VL provoked. On November 20, *The Golden Book of Springfield* was published by Macmillan. It was a critical disaster except for a favorable commentary by William Rose Benét in the December 18 *New York Post*.

101

TO SINCLAIR LEWIS

> December 15, 1920, and a bright day.
> 603 South Fifth St
> Springfield, Illinois.

My Dear Sinclair Lewis:

My friends are still proud of the fact and mention it, that I am mentioned in Free Air.[1] And I am yet more proud of it. You are my one avowed disciple (?), certainly my one admirer and friend among novelists. I am indeed grateful for those who are willing to say they are my friends in print. I am rich in friends, but I am insisting that I have so far made few hits with your especial profession. And I am quite tired and stupid today, or I should write in better style these sentiments.

Please accept my Christmas greetings, my admiration, and all that I can send in a letter that will bind our bonds.

But this may be called a business and strategy letter, so forward to the dire work.

I want every soul in Springfield Illinois and the surrounding Sangamon County to read at once all the Mid-western studies now coming out, beginning with Free Air's successor, namely *Main Street*. Everyone must read it, for a reason soon to appear. Please urge your publisher to send a review copy to Frank Waller Allen my friend who lectures on literary themes to all central Illinois, and does a heap of book reviewing beside. I am quite sure Allen will be perfectly willing to run a long lecture-campaign on this book, just through natural sympathy with its tone. All he needs is the information on the book's local publicity. What I mean is I want people stirred up somehow to ask him questions about it. His address is 1006, South Second, Springfield, Illinois.

I hardly know my old Friend Henry House who is now a Springfieldian again, well enough to know just how to put *him* to work, but I want him either to write interviews or get himself interviewed, by

Allen or some other one. Certainly if there is enough local talk about the book, our Henry can be enlisted to follow up in some way.

[Page 2 of this letter is missing.]

Poor as my Golden Book may be, it is the effort of my life, and its dullness scarcely interferes with its intent, for it is not supposed to be literature, but as a sort of local Koran, and you know that the duller the Koran, the better, so it is endlessly reiterated, and enough throats are cut on its behalf. Then we get our Taj Mahal, Our Alhambra and our Arabian Nights, infinitely superior to the Koran, but the direct result of many Muezzins muttering its formulas generation after generation till every cutthroat is psychologically poisoned into cosmic civic effort. So I am hoping the Golden Book will be dull enough to stand years of reiteration without wearing out. I am no advocate of polygamy, but if you desire a parallel of what I want to do with the Golden Book, and this is highly confidential, only to tip you off, please read a short encyclopaedia biography of *Mohammed. He persuaded all his good friends to cut throats on behalf of the dullest book ever written. Yet look at the Taj Mahal.* So I write to you, as it were in confidence, urging you to cut throats as it were, by the mere circulation of *Main Street.* For out of every hundred readers of your book, I want one to accept my Koran, and the rest to die, or as you please. They are your slaves, your helpless prisoners of war!

And why all this, do you say? Well, I am fond of Architecture, and want them to tear down those flats across the street, and build a Taj Mahal. If this is not clear, please read the summary of the Golden Book here enclosed, and expose as much of this letter to your publisher as you deem entirely judicious.

Most sincerely,

NICHOLAS VACHEL LINDSAY

The parts of this letter underlined [italicized as typeset] are quoted from a confidential letter on my lecture-terms I am today preparing for middle-West lecture committees. It doesn't get into the papers this pamphlet . . . [2]

Notes

1. Sinclair Lewis's *Free Air* came out in 1919.
2. The pamphlet mentioned is *A Letter for Your Wicked Private Ear Only* (1920).

102

TO HARRIET MONROE

603 South Fifth
Springfield Illinois
December 15, 1920

My Dearest Harriet:

You are a very dear friend of mine, and you have no business addressing me as your dear MISTER Lindsay. MISTER Lindsay is not my name. Vachel is my name, you had better believe, and I suggest a yelegram [*sic*] indicating that you know it.

Yes, I will send Aldington[1] a bunch of my books, and thank you for the suggestion.

As for the article about England, I am not sick, but I am in a very low state of vitality with an enormous accumulation of infinitesimal jobs, mostly letters like Aldington's etc . . . , that are fidgeting me to pieces, and I find I get silly and excited over nothing much and I have simply to go and soak my head as they say, and not consider anything my duty for awhile. Mama and I struck home in excellent shape, having gone through the whole trip without a hitch and as cool as a cucumber, and nothing happening too fast and nothing very exciting, but when all is said, I suppose travel *is* travel and I have to turn into a bump on a log for awhile.

It may sound silly, but nothing remotely connected with the English trip looks the least important to me this evening. It seems much more important that I should assure you of my love, my loyalty and my admiration, and believe me, you must believe in all three. Just as I started to England Sara was saying to me and I was heartily concurring, that of the whole poetry circle in the whole world as we knew it, you were the finest heart of them all. And if you think we think anything else, you do not know us as well as you should. We love you dearly, whether we have convinced you of it of late, or not.

Of course, dear Harriet, I suppose your real grievance, if you really look it over, is that I have not been to Chicago. I certainly have *not* been there, since about May, 1919, when I came up to see Isadora, for the last time.[2] I did not know it was for the last time. I have not seen her anywhere since, and I never want to see her, or anything that reminds me too much of her, at least till I can be a little bit sane on the subject. And, moreover, Chicago is a place I must let alone for awhile for another reason. It is the same reason that I have no expectation of returning to England for many a day, if ever, and that is that in Chicago, as in London, a certain public self is forced upon me by my friends, the Vachel I was to them four years ago, and I would as soon wear a plaster cast all over, or medieval armor. I suppose there is no living human being who more hates the formula of his yesterday, even if it is forced upon him with the finest affection by his dearest friends. I can be as ruthless with Springfield as with the opposition team in a football game. But I do not want to kick the shins, as it were, of friends as good and tender really, as that portion of the *literary world* that understands me at all. I can treat Springfield in a sense, almost like my horse or my mule, and give and receive kicks, most cheerfully.

That is not all, dear Harriet. I would give almost anything to escape forever the reciting and chanting Vachel. Except when immediately under the intense excitement that comes with facing an *extraordinarily* concentrated group of listeners, I dislike the very name of every poem I have recited very much except the Chinese Nightingale, which, after all, I now recite very seldom. My whole heart is set on escaping my old self (completely as I may, to be human and frail as we all are).[3]

The only thing that made the English trip possible for me, was to consider it the rounding up and last phase of my reciting life. I set Jan. 1, 1921 as quitting time. Of course it would be silly to announce such a thing aloud, as that other very firm resolve that unless I changed my view of life, I would not go to England again for ten or twenty years. Everybody was very good to me, too good to me, in England, but I went there aping or recording, and as it were, shouting, the Vachel of Ten years ago, for one gets into rhyme only a self that is long dead. I do not like that Vachel very well. What then am I? Certainly when you and I first met, I had made my last water-color designs, and last decorative fantasies in gold and silver and silk. You do not even know about them. They are stuffed in great packages there behind the book-case. If I had been obliged to exhibit and explain them, old and dusty as they are, once a week till now, I would feel about them as I do about reciting. I do not want to be the slave of past performances or habits, I cannot endure to be such a slave, *I care not what the apparent praise or reward.* I am a dead man in my own eyes, and the only resurrection is in the new vista.

Paper went up so high, that the reprint of the Village Magazine cost more than I thought. So I will *have* to be reciting just a bit off and on, till that bill is met. Then so far as I know I am free. I am going to accept a few intermittent dates in and around Sangamon county etc, and come home and rest and meditate in between. No *touring.* And you will find me escaping somehow, for I always have escaped, I always believe in my star, though I can never believe in the good fortune of my heart. I know I will always be robbed of love, but I will always find the new work. Its just *in* me, to be just that way.

The Golden Book of Springfield is the poorest thing I ever wrote. But somewhere between the lines lies the hint of my new direction. It is a sort of apple seed, festering in my heart, as I said in the Village Magazine.

If I write about England, I want to wait a year or so and see if it still looks important. Remember I am not sending anything to anyone, in the way of verse or prose, and all my serious writing and effort the last three years has been *The Golden Book* and I do not regret that. Practically everything in the Golden Whales Volume, etc, was written on the side. I consider 'The Golden Whales' a rather journalistic and frivolous volume.

I get letters from all directions asking for literary contributions. But I am stopping to mark time. All I really want is a bunch of about fifty severe but carefully written reviews of the Golden Book. I have not as yet one review of any kind of that volume. It has not even been mentioned or roasted. It has been *absolutely ignored.*

Oh yes, do you know the name of the clipping bureau in Washington, D.C.? They engaged to send me clippings of the book, and I have lost their address. And they have a deal of my money on their account books. If I have any brains left, I want to get the germ of the beginning that lies in The Golden Book. It means far more to me, than any alleged success of mine. The reviews may help.

Now, Bless you Harriet, and be sure I will be in Chicago sometime before twelve months roll round, and I will try not to be such a baby. But you must give me time to brace up, and learn to behave.

With every good wish, and merry Christmas, and happy new year.

NICHOLAS VACHEL LINDSAY

Notes

1. Richard Aldington (1892—1962) had been one of Ezra Pound's *Imagistes*. He rejoined Amy Lowell's Imagists after the collapse of *Imagisme* in England. He and Flint and H.D. (Hilda Doolittle) among other Imagist poets, were included in Amy Lowell's Imagist anthologies as early as 1915.
2. Isadora Bennett married in December 1919. *The Golden Book of Springfield* was dedicated to her.
3. In spite of his resolutions, VL had to tour the East all spring in 1921, the West in the winter. In between he tramped with Stephen Graham in the Rockies. In 1922 and 1923, until his collapse, he hardly ever stopped touring and reciting.

103

TO HARRIET MONROE

Springfield Illinois
December 26, 1920

My Dearest Harriet:

I am indeed sorry to send you such a mess. I would greatly appreciate it if you will give *"The Golden Book"* the benefit of the doubt. Please note it is most carefully summarized pages 109 through 124, the Village Magazine.

I am marking out a deal of your enclosure for it is possible I may lecture and recite on behalf of "The Golden Book" ideas. Of this, more later.

My dream for Springfield is that it shall be like the point of light and magic in a picture by Rembrandt or Durer or a story by Poe. But this requires the cooperation and moral support of that literary world, that you and I deal with, the poets in especial.

Enclosed find a summary of The Golden Book, torn from the Village Magazine.

Read it, I humbly petition, or get some other friendly reviewer to read these few pages. It is all I am asking of the wild world just now, I find unless I tear out these pages, people refuse to read this far. So I tear them out and put them right under their eyes.

Please be good to me Harriet. I am very lonely. Life is not what it appears.

Most affectionately

VACHEL

104

TO LOUISE SEAMAN

Springfield Illinois
January 8, 1921

My Dear Miss Seaman:

Day before yesterday I gave two programmes at the two Springfield convents. At the Sacred Heart Academy two of the Dominican sisters testified that they had read The Golden Book separately, and compared notes, afterwards, and were delighted with the book absorbed in it from first to last, and they were sure I was a good Roman Catholic.

So cordial were the ladies, and so excellent was the fried chicken they served me after I had given a programme for their school, I have been moved with the hope that a similar group in New York is reading the book, is pleased with it, and a really good review can be secured from The Catholic World. I would like to be like Hoover and the Red Cross, enlist all the religions without hurting the feelings of any.

Our Dominican sisters here are a special order of Parochial School teachers, and they can go back to their homes, and they travel away from the mother house sometimes for a whole year, teaching in the Catholic rivals of the public schools, all over the middle west. They are as charming ladies of letters as I have met for many a day.

One reason they liked the book was that in beginning it, a low-church Episcopalian rector helped me out on the ecclesiastical portions, and later a Catholic girl went all through the manuscript with me in the mountains of Colorado, to straighten out errors. But I had no idea of getting by the censors with a whole skin as I seem to have done, and *I sincerely hope every advantage can be taken of it*, and the book can be pushed in the Catholic book-stores, and with the Paulist Fathers of New York.

I attended their church all the time I was an Art Student in New York. And it appears I absorbed more orthodoxy than I realized.

Please do not imagine you are going to be battered with letters about the Golden Book all year. I am still in the excitement of getting it started in Springfield, and the Springfield Art Club that worked out the Springfield Flag, is going to have me read them the Flag Chapter next week. I am doing everything I can readily at hand to plant it thoroughly in Springfield soil while the planting is good, and any external measure you can think of to keep Springfield receptive to my suggestions, both as to Civics, and the book, will be a great favor to me. My whole theory is that in this city, or in some ONE other city, the book shall be as thoroughly read and applied as was John Dewey's theory of education in Gary. Then he wrote a book, telling how the theory WAS applied. I want completely to SOAK one town with the book. Then I will leave the ideas behind me and go on to other work, trusting them to take care of themselves.

Let me insist, that people of the general middle of the road protestant antecedents, make the book too symbolical, and therefore find it obscure. I want them to take all the pictures and episodes as literally and pictorially as possible. I think this is what makes it clear to the Catholics: they are used to having temple paraphernalia, without thinking out every censer as a metaphor. So do the Orthodox Jews. So please take every picture in the book literally, like a movie, and when I say sunset towers, please picture *actual skyscrapers.*

I am hoping some one can draw for the New York Sunday papers, or better, in some architectural exhibition, architectural views of future Springfield. Those groups of young architects that have competitive drawing matches of imaginary buildings will do me a world of good if they will only start a competition of possible groups of Sunset towers and temples for Springfield. I remember I addressed the annual dinner of the Gargoyle Club—on the history of Architecture about 1907 or 8, when I told New York Good bye as an Art-Student. They are just such a bunch as I would like to have draw my Springfield. And please remember that for those four years in New York City I took groups of Art Students every winter in the central rotunda of the Metropolitan Museum, and there, hour after hour, evening after evening we used to compare the models of the temple of Karnak, of The Parthenon, the Pantheon, Notre-Dame, and the arches of triumph, and all these with the Times Building Skyscraper, as the latest form of great architecture, and the climax. There was born my picture of the future Springfield:—from those architectural models, compared and combined with the Times Building when it was fair and young and clean and beautiful under the midnight lights of Broadway fifteen years ago. I have simply built a double wall around the idea—and I mean a real wall, not a metaphorical wall. I mean real skyscrapers, when I speak of Sunset Towers. I mean real swords, when I speak of Avanel-Damascus blades. I think a real queen, a real Avanel will be born in a city that waits and watches for her for one hundred years, as surely as a Queen bee is developed in a hive.

If my ideas are established in some small town, other than Springfield, I want that town to name its heroine years before she comes, and watch and prepare for her with an almost Messianic hope. The Rabbis can help in this for reasons I have given, and for the other reason, that they represent the most vigorous survival of the idea of a Divine City, only we want our Jerusalem in the future, not in the past, a town that is a ritualistic temple, from wall to wall, and on American soil. The Christian Scientists can help in suggesting the idea, for they or those on the borders of their faith are accustomed to looking to the future, and to the flying book idea, for one flying American book implies another. And all the arguments in Ralph Adams Cram's "Walled Towns for America" are valid, if only they can be turned inside out and turned till they point to the future, instead of Europe. So I let Ralph Adams Cram build my cathedral, and build my wall. But I give him a population that will naturally turn his ritual and his perspective inside out and around, and moreover give a chance to the civilization that is expressed by the skyscraper pictures of Nevinson. The limitation of Nevinson is that he does not build the cathedral nor the synagogue, nor put a wall around the town.

My dear friend, I hope that you can give out all the contents of this letter, in publicity matter, paraphrase, or interview, as seems best to you. I am so burdened with all the material and the thoughts pertaining to "The Golden Book", I have to ask my friends to help distribute and adapt them. They represent years and years of speculation on art and civics and so The Golden Book is terribly condensed. I have notes on literally hundreds of stories derived from The Golden Book, and piled up and postponed till the book itself is started.

It can hardly be called the beginning of a religion or a cult, though I want something a little more serious than many a costumed and parading fraternity, something that is taken with the tolerance perpetuity and informality of America's long series of Santa Claus Cantatas yet as fundamentally serious.

You know Santa Claus belongs to all churches, and to all sects, and to all American heathens as well. I do not know anyone who objects to him. Well I want my Apple-amaranths (I admit that they have not yet been evolved by any Burbank) I want them to have the tolerated theological position of Christmas trees.

At the same time, as to those people who are furthering the book from the inside, I desire them to see that it has a serious religious intention, and especially the dogma that the expectation of the city's heroine will produce that heroine inevitably, and a city like unto her, I think that is sound theology in any religion. And I want those who help me to promote her progress here, or from the distance of New York, to remember Joan of Arc and Pallas Athena, and do everything they can to develop a similar idea on Springfield soil, without offending any sect, and without necessarily conforming to my pattern. I want suggestions from many sources in carving the Springfield Goddess. I want all the creative aggressive decorative young architects, Gargoylers and the like, of New York, to come here and give us their drawings of future Springfield City, in the name of Avanel Boone.

And I hope all those who promote the fortunes of the Lady Avanel in New York will study not so much my text book, as what all Frenchmen say of Joan of Arc, and all Greeks said of Pallas Athena, and attribute as many of their qualities to my Springfield heroine as can in any way be taught to the citizens of my stubborn city.

With every good wish,

VACHEL LINDSAY

Note

1.   Louise Seaman was in charge of children's books at Macmillan.

105

TO LOUISE SEAMAN

Springfield Illinois
January 18, 1921

My Dear Miss Seaman:

I am so glad you care for Avanel Boone. The whole new civic religion as I conceive it, must center around *some such person.* Now please, when you develop the character of Avanel Boone in your publicity notes for this year, do not read The Golden Book too much. I expect to use her a great deal hereafter, in future stories and sketches, and all my friends will have to help me build her, if she is to be a living deity. So please remember what you can of Pallas Athena and Joan of Arc, and Prophesy their coming in a hundred years, under the name of Avanel Boone. I have made room for this Avanel, if only my friends will help call her forth, between the last two chapters of The Golden Book. That is she becomes a goddess there, in all but name. She becomes what the ancients called a goddess. If you ever go through the central rotunda of the Metropolitan Museum, she is the child of the model of the Parthenon and the model of Notre Dame about which I lectured so long and so often. I have tried to call up the kind of a deity that would produce such buildings, and the civilization her existence would imply.

The Dial for February will contain a review of *The Golden Book.*[1] I have just sent the New Republic via Ridgley Torrence, their poetry editor, a sketch entitled:—"Avanel Boone and the Young American Poets of Russian Blood".[2] I hope they will print it. The February Poetry will have a word by Harriet Monroe.

I will greatly appreciate it if you can get some of the leading priests, Rabbis, and the like to preach *great sermons* in New York on *ideal womanhood in America for the next hundred years.* That is, a *definite conception* that it will take a hundred years to fulfill, and is worth taking a hundred years to evolve. The only long distance planning now done is for franchises, and occasionally blue prints for buildings, for universities.

The simplest illustration of what I am after with this Avanel has made some of the Springfield society ladies sniff, but it will serve. Before Gibson went to Spain, his girl, (especially about Chicago World's Fair time, 1893) influenced every youth and maiden. And *girls* of the type of the first Gibson girl actually became paramount in our civilization, and ruled it.[3] And I feel that if those pictures which began with a sedate little high bred American, had been gradually evolved into replicas of Joan of Arc and Pallas Athena, we would have our Avanels, almost Goddesses, on the streets of America today, dominating our civilization. As it was, we came quite near to it in a temporary secular way, in the picture of the Red Cross Madonna that was sprung when the war began, marked *"The Greatest Mother in the World".* Swinburne has some lines on the dramatic birth of a Greek goddess who overthrew the worship of Venus and the Vamps:—

"A mother, a mortal, a maiden,
A queen over death and the dead".

"She is cold and her habit is lowly,
Her temple of branches and sods,
Most fruitful and virginal, holy,
A mother of Gods."

"She hath wasted with fire thine high places,
She hath hidden and marred and made sad
The fair limbs of the loves, the fair faces (Like Clara Kimball young)[4]
Of the gods that were goodly and glad, (Like Theda Bara!)[5]

She slays, and her hands are not bloody,
She moves, as a moon on the wane,
White robed:—and thy raiment is ruddy—
Our Lady of Pain".

(quoted from
memory
entirely)

Of course Swinburne, as I understand it, had in mind a Greek worship which in some ways prophesied the coming of the Virgin Mary. But however that may be, I am hoping to see a lady even more splendid than the first Gibson Girl dominate the eyes and thoughts of the young ladies now twelve years old who have gone crazy worshipping movie queens, and silly magazine covers, and Theda, and such.

I only wish I could persuade some better story teller than myself to tell stories about Avanel Boone, and you have my leave to do anything you can along this line, or get it done. I only wish I could persuade some one like Sinclair Lewis to rewrite my whole Golden Book his own way, and I certainly hope you can do it piecemeal, you own way, this year, in the publicity department.

The editor of one of our local papers says that the Golden Book is far more talked about than any book ever issued in Springfield. Yet of course the town is not stampeded into buying it as I desire, for the full effect, for I want it to be like a regular Billy Sunday meeting, *on this one spot.*

I have the feeling if only one town, no matter how small, becomes as fully incandescent on these issues as Billy Sunday made many a town on old fashioned issues, that then the fire will spread of itself. So please give the Springfield people who pass through New York City, or who write to or communicate with New York City, or New Yorkers in touch with Springfield in any way, no rest till this campaign gets ahold of them. I have written long letters to William Stanley Braithwaite, Francis Hackett, Marguerite Wilkinson, Harriet Monroe, The Christian Science Monitor, and many others. I want them all to rewrite The Golden Book their own way, and then drive it home to Springfield.

Pardon my verbosity.

NICHOLAS VACHEL LINDSAY

At their request I have just sent to "The Landmark" organ of the English Speaking Union, a map of the U.S.A. and an article to go with it, expanding the Observer Article quoted in "The Living Age".[6]

Notes

1. The review of *The Golden Book of Springfield* was written by Gilbert Seldes: "Mr. Vachel Lindsay's Future" (*Dial*, February 1921, pp. 208—10). It centered on the "identification" of the celebrities hiding behind the mask of the various characters

and, most of all, on the book's importance as proof that "America is still what it used to be to the alien-born, the Land of Promise." Keys and other "mysteries" made *The Golden Book* "mystifying" in Seldes's eyes.
2. "Avanel Boone and the Young American Poets of Russian Blood" was published not by *The New Republic* but by *The Dial* (May 1921, pp. 540—44).
3. Irene Langhorne, Charles Dana Gibson's wife, was the model for the famous "Gibson girl," who first appeared in 1896. Gibson was an illustrator for *Life Magazine*.
4. This evidently refers to actress Clara Kimball Young (1890–1960).
5. Theda Bara (1890—1955), a star at Twentieth Century–Fox, was usually directed by J. Gordon Edwards.
6. *The Living Age* included an article in its issue dated December 11, 1920: "Mr. Vachel Lindsay Explains America" (pp. 671—73).

106

TO HARRIET MONROE

Hotel Brevoort
New York
May 17, 1921

My Dear Harriet Monroe:
I have not heard of you, directly or indirectly, for ages. Not that I am reproaching thee. I know thee is busy.

This is but to apologize for any slight on my part that may be responsible for your long coolness, and to say that it is my intention to call and have a good visit in Chicago—perhaps soon, at least before the year is out. And now I fear I am writing a letter. I think with great love of Chicago, and the goodness of the people there, and I have many friends and no enemies there. But I am preoccupied with many thoughts I do not know how to share with Chicago yet. Which seems a silly way of putting it.

I have tried several times to quit reciting, and certainly I am not pursuing it as a systematic business. I have scads of unanswered letters asking me to recite, and my general mail piles up and up, unanswered.

But just financially—I cannot afford to quit *entirely*, so I recite from hand-to-mouth, as one may say. My books only bring me five hundred dollars a year, at best—that is—this last year, and up to that time one to two hundred dollars a year. So I must just recite a bit now and then to keep out of debt. I try to choose places where they really know my work, or show symptoms of getting it.

Yet I do not regret your printing my letter in Feb. It has not stopped the tide of letters asking me to recite. But it seems to have set many of my friends thinking, and they treat me a little less like a music-box with the crank to be turned on all good and bad occasions. And I must not resent their attitude for I know well enough *I* began by being all eagerness *to* recite, and nearly burst with songs which had been bottled up in me so long. But having trained my friends to think this of me, I am really an utterly different person most of the time now.

But my dear Harriet—this has naught to do with me and thee, for our constancy is based on the stars and the eternities.

Do not forget I love you and admire you, every minute.

As to my own affairs again—it will be at least two years before I have any book of verses ready, or any other book. It will be verses however, and I will illustrate it, I *hope*.

I have been studying in the Metropolitan Museum and the Natural History Museum, and have been lingering in New York which I could hardly afford, just to study more. And when I get to Chicago I am hoping to spend days in the new Field Museum, examining its aesthetic aspects.

I am just staying on here from day to day, hoping for one or two little dates in New York City itself, while I study in these museums. My rather casual list of public appearances is over. I have had a very good time indeed and acquired information, if not wisdom, hither, thither and yon. I have gone at a slow pace and visited as I went along and have not been "on the make!"

Certainly people are very very good to me, and loyal and red hearted. I cannot think of an enemy or ill-wisher in the world. My struggle is entirely inside of me, and the best way of clearing my mind I have found is to walk alone in the Metropolitan Museum, where I studied and lectured so hard 1905—08, and really put up one of my first fights. I want to get into a similar relation walking by the hour alone—a relation with the now greatly enlarged and brilliantly beautiful museum. One good way to harness one's thoughts is to go back to where they began. After studying days alone, to clear my mind, I used to stand up and improvise for my little crowd, night after night in the museum in front of the works of art, much the way I recited later—only the statue before me was the poem. And I came into a curious relation to Art, Architecture, ritual and the past, and into a theory of the future—that helped to make The Golden Book, which must yet be vindicated by what I write, after [a] while, in verse if possible, or else in prose.

I find I am writing what is nearly a book, about dear old me, so I will stop right here. Only remember I am coming to see you, sooner or later!

With love

VACHEL

107

TO STEPHEN GRAHAM

Springfield, Illinois
October 9, 1921

My Dear Stephen:
This letter is but to bid you return,[1] and to wish you a happy ocean journey, and so it does. But it may wander on to longer and lesser important [sic] matters.

Everyone asks when you are coming back again, and they all regard you with neighborly affection already. They are all old friends who have borne with me long, and are delighted at a new song from my direction, and a new breeze from across the world.

I have been thinking of your return, and your possible new lines of access to America, and Mark Twain looms strongly again in my imagination. I have been thinking of that side of you that is so thoroughly Russianized and out-doorized.

The Mark Twain that is not yet completely expounded or grasped is really the out-door Mark Twain. Practically his whole life was out of doors from the cradle till he wrote Innocents Abroad. Then he married and lived in a house. His largeness, his suggestion of infinity dates from his early life. All those that have been so busy writing him down, have been those that met him after he lived in a house. The out-door Mark Twain, who lived such a miraculously prolonged outdoor life, way into the middle years, has scarcely been realized by the present day "critics" and has never been written up or studied by out-door writers. Yet it was there he accumulated that nation-wide vitality, and resonance and bounce that lasted him till well toward old age. His is really "nature" writing though it does not profess to be. It is so, all the more, and he breathes the real AMERICAN continent far more than professional avowed weather, bird and beast writers like John Burroughs[2] or Walt Whitman. I would give to Johnny Appleseed and Mark Twain many of the praises that are usually heaped upon the heads of such men as Thoreau and Whitman. Whitman speaks of the American as he chose to imagine him, but Mark Twain *is* the American, as actually found, epic in a subtler sense, for he had an epic crowd laughing with him, they knew not why. It was Shakespearian at wildly un-Shakespearian situations, classic laughter in a Quartz mine. Mark Twain is a much easier subject than Roosevelt, though they are akin. What you say of

Roosevelt will be challenged at every stop, and must be much meditated. But the same method will discover both the outdoor life and natural American life each loved before he achieved supremacy. What I would like to recommend to you is that life studied, *as it was lived at the time*, in honest innocence, and not in the light that was thrown on it afterward by either man in his old age, or by his snobbish relatives and friends. No man so slanders youth as an old man talking about his own youth. He hates the best things in it. From this thing Mark Twain was not exempt, and our psychoanalyzers [*sic*] like Van Wyck Brooks will not even let Mark Twain alone, but take some of the sourest papers of his old age like "The Mysterious Stranger" to prove that he was a pessimist and a cynic from the very start (when he was honest with himself), and that he never cracked a light-hearted joke, or was happy for happinesses sake. It is like saying a man was always toothless and bald-headed, because he is toothless and bald-headed on his death-bed, and the attending physician for similar reasons hates young men with hair and teeth.

When Mark Twain was at his height as a Young American and Roosevelt was at his height as a Young American, they were both spirited joyous rollicking amazing men, and there was not one inch of cynicism or bitterness in either. They indulged in very little of railing accusation against any man. And they both breathed that blooded American out-of-doors, which no European or American critic besides yourself can well interpret in this hour. It is all your field. If I may once more and for the thousandth time thrust innocent advice at your patient soul, I suggest discussions of Mark Twain up to his fortieth year and Roosevelt to his fortieth year and then a pioneering speculative straight line drawn from the one to the other to find the third American theme, or third American man, or third American philosophy. Frankly, I think you are still more of a Russian than an American. Though I know you will conceal it from the public in this next book, you cannot conceal it from me.

There are aspects of America as invigorating and artistically primitive as anything in Russia, but it takes the climbing of many barb wire fences to reach them. I am sure you have found our landscape, *and our nation as a whole*. But I am not sure you have found your predestined American writers and statesmen, or the type of American life that will fit you as naturally as does the Russian. Wherever your destiny in America, certainly it is somewhere west of the Mississippi, and probably from the Rockies west to the coast. And both Mark Twain and Roosevelt point that way. I keep saying to myself "How little did the Roosevelt of forty know what his old age would be"! How little did the Mark Twain of forty know what his old age would be". I am sure that in the search for these two innocent out-door young leaders, you will be on the way to your predestined hope for America. They both expressed an exalted, absolutely unfulfilled United States, that you can help to fulfill as well as any man living. People hailed with a shout the future wonders of our life that their laughter faintly but surely suggested. Yet the biography of each man has been written from the coffin end, by the doctor and the undertaker, and America forgets the shout of delight for which they once stood. Mark Twain sleeps on the dustiest public library shelves in his forgotten glory in the bound volumes of Magazine comment and contribution of 1880 to 1885, Roosevelt in those of 1905 to 1910. There the amazing exhilaration which their very names once suggested is plainly to be seen. America forgets their youth and waits for other young men.

There is more of a hint of this glory in Christopher [Morley?]. I hope you can blow him into a burning torch.

I hope this letter does not seem too presumptuous or overweening. It is not intended for advice, but as the old books sometimes phrased it *"an aid to reflection"*. You are really far more of an out of door man than I am.

I realize that it is freedom I am seeking, and amusing adventure, more than out-doors for its mystical world meaning. So I am trying, hypothetically, to think out how a person more out of doors than myself, can get to that part of America whose soul is in the out of doors. I believe I am more for door-steps than out of doors, more for roads than wildernesses, and you have extraordinarily stretched my horizon beyond my old range. I am vastly more geographical than ever before in my life, and since Glacier Park I remain geographical, eliminating imaginary trailless mountains, and trying to help you to the America of which they are the back-bone.

I see nothing to interfere with any plan of travel you have to send me, any time.

With affectionate good wishes—and very good wishes indeed to Mrs. Graham whom you will soon see— I remain,

VACHEL

Notes

1. VL and Stephen Graham spent the summer in Glacier Park, "tramping in the Rockies." The literary results of the expedition were twofold: Graham published *Tramping with a Poet in the Rockies* (1922), and VL replied with *Going-to-the-Sun* the following year (Appleton: New York, 1923). Graham's book was illustrated by Vernon Hill; VL did his own illustrations.

2. John Burroughs (born 1837) had died on March 29. A naturalist and author, he wrote *Notes on Walt Whitman as a Poet and Person* (1867), to which Whitman himself had contributed. Burroughs traveled extensively in America, observing nature, and knew John Muir and Theodore Roosevelt well. His nature essays combined science and visionary assertions.

108

TO H. S. LATHAM

603 South Fifth, Springfield Illinois
October 10, 1921

My Dear Mr. Latham:[1]
Thank you for your letter. I always appreciate your great good will and courtesy.

Please return to me at once the drawings and verses for the Johnny Appleseed volume.[2]

I suggest that the Macmillan Company consent to the tearing up of their contract for drawings, dated August third, 1917.

It is now four years and two months old, and the only unfulfilled contract I have with the Macmillan Company.

I have not for a minute changed my plan, to illustrate all my books hereafter.

With every good wish

VACHEL LINDSAY

Notes

1. H. S. Latham was vice-president and editor-in-chief of Macmillan's trade department. The "find" of his career was *Gone with the Wind* in 1936.
2. *Johnny Appleseed and Other Poems* was not published until 1928 (Macmillan). Another edition came out in 1930. However, many poems on Johnny Appleseed were included in the *Collected Poems* (1923).

109

TO A. J. ARMSTRONG

Springfield, Illinois
October 10, 1921

My Dear Armstrong:
Pardon me, if I have disarranged your first plans. I am hard put to it to arrange my affairs, and I frankly admit. I need not worry you with details, but please bear with me, for I want you for a friend, even more than for a sponsor, and God knows I need you for both. The most fixed things in my little world dissolve before me while I watch them. But that is mere philosophy.

Do not be too economical of railroad fare, or sweat too hard to get the dates into a straight line. Your greatest use to me as a sponsor is to kill off the *Jazz* and *advertising* quality that the professional bureau insists in putting into their introduction of a literary figure. As much of the atmosphere of Baylor University, and the degree they gave me,[1] for which I am profoundly grateful, and the Browning courses they teach, and the atmosphere of your own home, as much of this as is possible, I want to go into your sponsorship. And that comes after the schedule is made, so I do not want you to wear yourself out on the mere mechanics of the schedule. I want atmosphere to get into every deed of our partnership, and I want every place I go to be a better friend of the sponsors than of the reciter, when all is done. For after all I hardly know what to do with this extended constituency of audiences when I get it, and certainly I do not want to leave it in the hands of a mere lecture bureau to exploit, the year after I am through. I am hoping for some vital and permanent wave of sympathy between you two, and all these English departments, and the more all my audiences are treated like students in your senior classes, the better I will like it.

Your plan is exactly right, and I am for it straight through. But as to the date of beginning:—

I have two or three unavoidable engagements looming. J. C. Squire the creator, dictator and editor of the *London Mercury* is coming to see me November 17 to 24. I have been corresponding with him a long long time about his coming. Now he suddenly sets the date, and there is nothing to do but take the time, since he comes all the way across the ocean for this. Then my old friend Edward C. Marsh, who is responsible for the publication of all my books in their present form, wants to make a special expedition to Springfield "in the next few weeks", he says, and I must nail him down to a week that is not Squire's week. I have reason to think that the visit of Marsh may be quite important in a strategic way, not immediately, but with reference to work several years hence. Certainly it will be vastly important from the point of friendship. He is as faithful and understanding a friend as I ever had.

I do not think you realize how much your type of school, education and civilization means to me. The co-educational, middle west denominational college is to me the highest point in American civilization, and I can see clearly every objection that the more worldly-minded or Eastern type might make to it. I have been before all the great Universities, some of them several times, and have had a splendid time, and love the students dearly, and the faculties have been most loyal, and I do not know of one enemy among them. Nevertheless there is something European about them. They are not as completely the flower of America as are the co-educational religious western schools, which grow up out of the ground as naturally as the blue grass and the Indian corn and the violets. And above all such a school as yours represents me and my people. A sponsorship from such a school is as natural and honest a sponsorship as from my home town or one of my own kind. I believe profoundly in our agricultural and middle west civilization and think it is the natural America, and the America with the oldest and most normal history. I greatly mistrust Industrial America, radical or conservative, and am only happy among people in some way related to the civilization and the type for which Baylor University and Hiram College and such schools stand. I do not want people to think I represent Jazz, or even a theory or movement of poetry. I want in some sense to represent the honest clean devout young Americans who are courting and studying Browning and saying their prayers on campuses like yours. I disagree with them a great deal, but on the other hand, I am more naturally akin to them than to any other set of people. No doubt they are keenly aware of how I differ from them. But I am even more keenly aware of how I differ from everything east of the Mississippi River or Springfield, in Europe or America.

Stephen Graham and I have been together all Summer, and his account of our travels may be found in the *New York Evening Post*, still continuing twice a week, called *Tramping With a Poet*, and the series will probably appear in England in newspaper and book form. There are seventeen installments so far. But the best thing about his whole trip from the mere *literary* standpoint is that he has consented to write about Springfield, Illinois, in England, and has spent a whole month here getting acquainted, after our *climb.* So at last England comes to the Middle West, instead of the Middle West going to England. And I am hoping to interest Squire in Springfield in a similar way, and if I am unable to write *The Golden Book of Springfield* as it should be written, maybe I can persuade Squire or some other to write it well and clearly and in a more directly stimulating fashion. At least one great victory is won. They have begun to come to us. I hope you can see in my ideas in regard to Baylor something more of the same general West-of-the-Mississippi, West-of-the-Alleghanies gospel.

With good wishes,

NICHOLAS VACHEL LINDSAY

Note

1. Harriet Monroe, Amy Lowell, Edwin Markham, and VL had all had honorary degrees conferred on them at Baylor in 1920. See letter 162.

110

TO A. J. ARMSTRONG

The Brown Palace Hotel
Denver, Colorado
Friday, Dec. 23, 1921

My Dear Armstrong:
My Dear Mrs. Armstrong:
All is well. I have received here your complete schedule. Thank you indeed for all cooperation. Will write more, later, about business. Please send to my mother, always, when it is perfectly convenient, bits of news about my tour and whereabouts. I send them. But that makes no difference. She must get them twice to believe them. She is a vigorous woman of 72 going on 73,[1] but alone in the house, as far as kin is concerned. She has for company a school-teacher roomer and admirable Old Friend for an occasional chat, and a young doctor in the far back room, a very fine boy, who occasionally turns up. Otherwise she must console herself with innumerable missionary committees upon which she has grown almost fanatical, and of course she has the long procession of bad servants. She has to console herself at an overstrain at public

religious life, at which she works frantically, and I can never persuade her to relax an inch on it. Then she worries about me beyond all reason without discovering what I am *really* up to, or taking any time from any missionary committee to find out. So anything you can send her that will keep my trip as *amusing* to her as a missionary committee, from time to time, will be a real favor. She must have constant assurances that her six-year old son with long golden curls down his infant back is neither naughty, sick nor dying, that he is neither making mud pies nor neglecting his Sunday School lesson, that he has learned his verses for next Sunday in a way to please his Sunday-School teacher, that he is almost ready for the first reader—no—the third reader or he could not learn those verses. Also this infant son must do nothing to interfere with the serenity, complacency or holiness of the Missionary tea this afternoon. Look at Whistler's portrait of his mother and go ahead.

Please do not let it make you any extra trouble. I think the most important thing is to let *her feel free to write or telegraph to you instantly any morning* she wakes up with the apprehension that I am sick, or not going to Church regularly, or that she has not my precise location in the Pullman of the particular train of where I happen to be. Please send her telegrams whenever there is anything worth telegraphing, and in general get her into the game, using some kind of diabolical ingenuity, rather than time or strength.

She has to be *constantly reassured* that a literary career is not the road to physical, mental and moral perdition, and there are some things worthy of pious attention besides a missionary committee. The greatest favor she did for Stephen Graham when he was in Springfield, was to give him a good standing with her committee, and let him address them.

She liked Browning in her prime—but now suspects him, because he was not president of a Missionary Society. She reads him *no more.* He was once her chief literary pabulum. But an apt quotation from Browning is still admitted as a good argument, when properly larded with scripture.

Well, I am afraid I have "sassed" my mother this morning, but since the letter is to you and not to her, it leaves her serene, and greatly relieves my feelings. She needs news, lots of it. And frankly, it works better when it has some kind of an ecclesiastical flavor. I am not hypocrite enough to put the ecclesiastical garlic all the time into the salad, when I do not like garlic, committees, missionary teas, nor orthodoxy. You may have just that touch of piety that is necessary. I admire it in anyone! I really believe the crime of my life is that I cannot believe missionary Teas as holy as the Host at high Mass, better by far than any poetry or poet, any artist or art that ever breathed. Well, I did not intend so long a letter, and please consider it, utterly undignified and utterly unworthy of a pious dutiful son with long yellow six-year old curls down his back.

Most fraternally

VACHEL

Of course this letter is for Mrs. Armstrong, and of course she is just the person to undertake the more delicate part of being a consolation committee for my mother. I wish she could find nice ways to inform her from time to time, that I am really a pious young man, very fond of missionary committees of all forms, and that I am in the exact town and giving the precise lecture previously scheduled under the auspices of the local pastor, of course. Any delicate ways of giving these messages frequently will be the greatest possible favor.

And also, I hope Mrs. Armstrong can look up in *Who's Who*, admire and get acquainted with William P. Henderson, Painter, and Alice Corbin Henderson, Poet, both of Santa Fe New Mexico. That young couple *must* be your personal friends, by *all means*. Please get onto visiting terms with them if you possibly can. They have an enormous future, a tremendous vista ahead of them, and I hope you can see them face to face, somehow within a year. As fine hearts and great talents, they cannot be excelled, they are just about King and Queen of the New Mexico South West. I have done my best to persuade them to admit you two into their profoundest spiritual cooperation and confidence, and I hope this post script letter does the same for you. My whole heart is in this matter.

Note

1.   VL's mother died February 1, 1922. His father had died September 20, 1918.

111

TO H. L. MENCKEN

On the road
Jan 31, 1922

Mr. H. L. Mencken:—
New York:—

Dear Sir:
Having read this book[1] on the train, going from town to town, I thought me of what reviewer should read it next, and it meseemed you were the man.

I am still a supporter of that constitutional amendment against which you labor so manfully, and as the principal literary dry to the principal literary Bacchanalian I send you this document which seems to me on my side of the case. You will note that (the only one not a commoner) the only one in the story who really suffers is a gentleman who slanders a prince, Page 138. Do or do you not consider the play as a whole an argument for the proprieties and politenesses?

Do you or do you not admire Mariana?

Note the quotation from Tennyson, page 74. Not only does Shakespear [sic] embody the Constitutional amendment, but quotes Tennyson.

Was it or was it not a deserved retribution for Ragozine to die and then have his head cut off—page 105?

For further remarks see back pages of book.

You will note on page 105—as I have been saying that Ragozine was a notorious pirate. The insinuation is also that he was a rough character, and I assume he was a Bar-tender deserving of this visitation. Do you think this is an unwarranted assumption? Do you not think that Shakespear meant (excuse me) that Shakespeare meant that Shaykspyre meant that Bar-tending was a poor insurance risk?

Do you know Anne who got up the questions page 148? Can you answer all those questions?

I have just been all over California. See cut. [Here there is a drawing of the state of California on which two redwood trees have been drawn in the upper left-hand corner, to the right of "Humboldt County," with "redwoods" written under the drawing. Also outlined or placed are Calaveras County, "San Frisco," Fresno, San Bernardino County, and "Los Angyles."]

Any old time anywhere I will debate this wet and dry question with you if you will promise not to stick to the subject.

Not that it makes a dam bit of difference. A Constitutional Amendment is a Constitutional Amendment.

You will never get your marbles up through the crack in the walk. It's what you get for playing for keeps.

This is my first and last effort as a Shaykspyeriyan commentator and I am loth to close.

[Here there is a drawing of a line of flags.]

I salute you in the name of the greater and lesser companies of the gods, whose Hieroglyphs you note over there [arrows pointing to the flags] and of Thoth god of writing and inventor of Hieroglyphics and Moving Pictures. He is of much more consequence than Bacchus anyway—is Thoth.

Most fraternally,

NICHOLAS VACHEL LINDSAY

[Here there is a drawing of Thoth's head.]

Being a message full of friendly import from Nicholas Vachel Lindsay, writer in the American Language to H. L. Mencken—Dictionarier and Lexicog-er [*sic*] in the American Language.

Note

1. This "letter" is actually written on the pages of an edition of Shakespeare's *Measure for Measure*, prefaced by Israel Gollancz.

112

TO A. J. ARMSTRONG

Philadelphia, Penna.
April 3, 1922

My Dear Armstrong:
All is well and everything has gone forward as scheduled.[1] I found myself so very tired last week and without knowing it—my memory

failing in small shots till I leaned on the book—and so I stopped here unbeknownst to any of my Philadelphia friends. And I am now rested and well, and hiding most cheerfully. I will leave for New Haven to-morrow night.

Latham wrote me the Movie Book should be out the first few days of April,[2] so it should be out about now. The University of Rochester is certainly a strategic point to be captured for this book.

I fancy if Lloyd George's policy prevails, it will get Graham to Russia by next year, perhaps. Stephen Graham instead of going to Russia will explore (with his wife) Spain, Central America and parts of Mexico, reaching the South-West with Santa Fe for headquarters, sometime this summer. The Grahams seem inclined to explore great chunks of the South-West this summer.

I greatly appreciate your generous invitation to go to Europe this summer, but sitting absolutely *alone* and *still* for *weeks* and *weeks*, with my jaw tied shut, is the one thing I covet. A Hermit's cheerful and admirable cell is the one thing I desire. I have every intention of locking myself up in Springfield or Cleveland and devoting the whole summer to writing and drawing. I have sent half a dozen new drawings to Marsh with small poems, for a portfolio he is slowly building up. All this, since November.

I am hoping to spend most of June in Cleveland—writing on the Harvard Poem[3] till time to read it. It is in fair condition now, but needs much long and deliberate meditation, the last thing I can attain on the road. It will be read as a "sketch" in June, but not sent to any publisher till October.

When I draw pictures it seems to me the only thing I ever did in this world, or ever want to do. I certainly revel in it. It is my most natural function. And one of the greatest things about it is I do not use my jaw while I do it.

You have been very good to me, and I pulled so far through this year, I look forward to finishing in June, 1923 with confidence. Though tired in between I reach moments of complete rest and recovery which show I am not overstraining. Then I look back, and it all looks gorgeous.

The circular letter you sent out a few days ago covering next year's campaign is entirely satisfactory, and I am quite proud of it.

Houses have been full and generally crowded to the windows and doors and often the platforms packed as well. The American people are certainly willing to let me speak. But they still hate my books.

Next year's campaign, if like this one, will be extremely satisfactory, and I will remain perpetually grateful to you.

I say all I can for you in almost any town I go, and I think you will find yourself vastly welcome if you ever intend to call personally on any of these people, anywhere along the line.

Mrs. William Vaughn Moody is already a most faithful friend of yours, and you should call there with Mrs. Armstrong, going or coming from Europe, if it is in any way possible. Mrs. Moody sends a most urgent invitation. She will see any friend, on very short notice!

Remember I still hate Women's Clubs. Also I will adore the boys and girls of America, in College or High School. They are the darlings of my life. The only two suggestions for next year are (1) suggestions for *art associations,* especially those backed by Eggers,[4] (2) Monthly rest-and-hide periods of about four days each, such as I am taking now. It takes two days to stop the *wheels* going around in my head from speaking, and another to stop my heart's accelerated leaps, so I get one day of rest, when I have four days.

With good wishes to yourself and Mrs. Armstrong.

VACHEL

Notes

1. VL interrupted his tour for a week in February when his mother died. He resumed it immediately.
2. *The Art of the Moving Picture* came out in a new edition in 1922.
3. The "Harvard Poem" was "Bob Taylor's Birthday" (*Collected Poems*, pp. 402–22), read as the Phi Beta Kappa Poem at the commencement exercises.
4. George William Eggers wrote the preface for the new edition of *The Art of the Moving Picture.*

113

TO WILLIAM LYON PHELPS

The important portions of this letter are pages 17, 18 and 19.[1] Please meditate them, if there is time in a busy life.

Address- care of Mrs. Ben Blair
3343 Bradford Road
Cleveland Heights
Cleveland, Ohio.

May 9, 1922

My Dear William Lyon Phelps:
It was the greatest pleasure and consolation to get your letter of May 2, here today.

I am remembering the Yale two days with great joy. Everything was whole-hearted and everything was good, including my rather amusing time in the library lecturing in the library office about six people including the librarian on two subjects of which I know nothing—Hieroglyphics and Lafcadio Hearne.

But I had found in the Yale Bookstore a New Hieroglyphic grammar just published by the Yale University Press, and have had it by me ever since, and that alone was worth the trip! I have found great amusement in it, if not great learning, and now with two primers of Hieroglyphics both of them founded on the Great Erman, and the Budge Grammar, of an entirely different school, I am having as good a time on the train as any travelling-man talking hooch and business!

I have struck an absolutely dead wall on the grammar, translation, pronunciation etc. But I am able more slowly but more surely every day to isolate, use and meditate upon certain Egyptian pictures of fairly fixed meaning—as definite as the American Flag or the Mohammedan Crescent as symbols and pictures. These reveal the Egyptian mind just as the titles of all the books published this Spring, in a general way reveal the American mind, even if we do not have time to read the books.

Just as I "read" hieroglyphics, increasingly I read all the publishers' advertisements straight through, just to get a notion of what people are thinking about. It is more of a novel than any novel.

I am glad you liked The Gipsy Poem.[2] It is in many ways the best

I have done and the way I want to go and when I think my life to the bottom, in as relentless and Hendrick [*sic*] Ibsen a manner as my vanity will let me—when I really look at myself—The Gipsy Poem is in every line the most nearly honest of any autobiography I have ever written. I have my more pious hours, but I am not sure they are representative of my real ribs.

I am going to reissue the Macmillan Books with new thick prefaces, as fast as the Macmillan Co. will let me. I doubt if I will ever produce any more prose. There I accept your advice. I shall be exceedingly slow about any new book of poems. I want only one more book, and that one slowly enlarged and re-issued through the years, with "incidental" illustrations. As for the drawing—I want it to replace the prose and the reciting—not replace the poetry. I want to make it the means and excuse for better print, binding, paper, type, and all that goes with it. Also it involves the possibility of partially earning my living—while sitting a little longer in quiet in one given place, and with no flourish of trumpets—a consummation devoutly to be wished.

But make no mistake about the verses. I have never at any time written very fast or very much, and the production goes on slowly about one long poem a year, the same as ever, and will probably so continue—a kind of an accident as formerly, whatever my life-plans. Your loyalty and friendship mean a whole lot more now than ever. In spite of everything, the slow action of time cools off or separates old friends—and two of them were so angry with me by letter yesterday I wished I was dead, and as far as I can get it, each is angry because I am not angry with the other and they are two fine people who should love each other dearly. I was simply desperate yesterday, till I decided to turn to every good friend I had who cared for me and forget this mysterious row. It always makes my friends the maddest when I do not know what the row is about. Then they hold me guilty of horrible egotism or callousness or something, when all I want is for them to love each other and forget it.

We can shake off these things when we are full of high spirits, and bursting with health, and when we are a bit tired, they are troubles like a fish-hook in the thumb.

But back to the pictures. Do not misunderstand me. The pictures are not to replace the verses. I never wrote a poem by deliberate intention. They—the poems—just come, rain or shine, without planning. I have no notions or theories about them, except that often—all things being equal—I enjoy most writing verses for pictures. But poetry has never been a purpose, but an accident.

But say—I have spent about 1/12th of my time every year writing verses and will so continue my normal way. There is the other 11/12ths that everybody from my manager the Admirable Armstrong to my sister the Admirable Mrs. Blair—this 11/12ths the little world I live in wants to pull and haul it every which way. So I *must* plan it, in self-defense—for my whole soul is distorted and jerked out of place by too heavy doses of flattery and self-esteem and public life and talking about myself in every new town I go into. Or else I get swept into private feuds which are worse. My *real style* would be to recite once a year for a very few people like yourself and your good friends, at places like Maurys (?) that little Inn where we were—or before the student-curtain of a student-play, as we were.

Then I would like to spend about three months a year drawing pictures in pen-and-ink, and studying *hard,* drilling, drawing from life everyday in the old art-student life, and studying hard pacing the galleries in the Metropolitan Museum and the Chicago Art Institute, *alone,* and especially in the Egyptian sections. And then the other eight months a year I would like to spend *alone afoot,* exploring the United States, without any plan of putting any of it on record, or expectation of doing so. And all of this, deliberately, slowly, and without any trumpets.

And I am quite determinedly fighting my way back to this type of life. By Sept. 1923 I will be through any kind of a conventional lecture-presentation of myself and you do not know how glad I will be to be free of being done up in uniform packages with red covers. I so much prefer to appear casually.

One thing I surely intend to do before I die—I hope soon: be independent. Conduct all my own correspondence, make all my own dates, allow the people to whom I go to set the terms, print my own books my own way—at a Springfield press—and live as I lived in 1912, and to reduce my whole life, in as far as human strength will permit, to a private and personal relationship to every human being with whom I deal at all.

I only wish I could go afoot from University to University reciting for nothing and if I could thereby avoid all sensationalism and the kerosene flavor of Publishers Publicity that now gets into my life.

Please do not think I am impatient with Armstrong. He is a most gallant fellow, who has done wonders for me, in reducing the jazz of advertising and public life to a minimum. I am glad to say he is now taking over Bynner, MacKaye, Frost, Sandburg and others at my urgent insistence, with an equal zeal, and I see in him yet a kind of British-American, American-British literary statesman. Please do not let any of your friends think of him as a hasty impresario. Whatever else he is, or whatever mistakes he makes—he is a Texas Literary Statesman, with all the material in him of a world literary statesman. He needs the friendship and cheering word of such men as yourself and I was glad to tell him of your good word from the Browning Class. That means more than many another accolade. Be sure I am quite aware that he needs a lot of advice, and I suppose he will get it. He is too dear and chivalrous a friend for me to offer it to him. I do not want to lose him. But I can appeal to his ambition, and intend to stir him up all I can to the largest most feasible and most *sensible* projects for the other poets on his list, and others. After going the rounds of the US one more year, I will certainly be through in a conventional way and I am more than eager that these other men shall follow me, not only here, but in England, and vastly improve on me as an ambassador there. I do not intend to go to England again—but I intend to stir up Armstrong when I see him next week, to make a future way for his favorite poets if he can next summer on his visit to England. All of those who are usually named, should have the same access to England they have to Texas, and Armstrong is the one diplomat who can get if for them—once he sees the vision. God deliver me from even seeming to want to run a one-man show—especially in poetry, or hog any special place when I am not even "interested in poetry" as the saying goes.

If I cannot secure for all my fellows such little publicity as I have had in this weltering world of millions of people—I am certainly a poor creature and a failure.

I am particularly anxious for Sandburg and Frost and Robinson to get to England with high honors—*and* car fare paid by the English.

Please believe me—Armstrong is gentleman and diplomat enough to bring this about once he is roused to action.

I will see him in Texas, May 14 and May 17, and hope to find him in a state of mind where I can argue it all out with him. He is very proud, chivalrous and thin-skinned, and I have no diplomacy. But it is my next project. If it works, you will see the results in two years.

We have had enough of international adventurers. Now I hope to get a gentleman on the job of Anglo-Saxon literary good-will.

With every good wish.

VACHEL

Notes

1. Pages 17, 18, and 19 of this letter correspond to the last nineteen lines of the letter's text as reprinted here, beginning: "All of those who are usually . . ."
2. "The Gypsy Poem" is "I Know All This When Gypsy Fiddles Cry" (*Collected Poems*, p. 43).

114

TO STEPHEN AND ROSE GRAHAM

The Century Association
7 West Forty Third Street
New York

July 25, 1922

My Dear Stephen and Rose Graham:—
The remarkably charitable review of "The Golden Book" you have just sent has fired my ambition once again—and set me thinking.

I hope you can think out to the Bottom what makes a Holy City—and do your very best for Santa Fe. What were the curious elements of race, history, legislation, custom, that made Mecca a holy City? It is the last one that has ever been made, unless it be Assisi. If it requires a Koran, you can write it, if it requires a series of pilgrimages, you can establish them, if it requires the "Little Flowers of Santa Fe" you can write them. I hope you can go deeply into the matter from the standpoint of the life of Mohammed or St. Francis, or Russian Saints you may remember. I have the feeling that America is on the point of Establishing her Holy Cities, perhaps Springfield, perhaps, Emporia, perhaps Santa Fe. But certainly he who writes the Koran will establish the city, and you have as good a chance as any one who ever breathed.

If I have been ding-donging about White,[1] it is because he is a pro-founder religionist than he knows. He has Mohammed's instinct disguised under Journalism.

In Mohammed the polygamy was bad, the Sword was bad; but to give the Arabs a holy city was good.

You will find all Americans so willing to take over the whole set of Church Metaphors in all their glory, if you keep them absolutely separate from priestcraft and dogma, free from the Irish roughnecks and the Episcopal Snobs. America awaits a Chesterton who is as plain as Thoreau or St. Francis and does not travel for 1100 dollars a speech. The reason high church prattle is utterly abhorred in this country is that it has been the simpering dialect of the most utterly abhorrent snobs and climbers that ever trod American Soil.

Your book could use all the Church symbols much more plainly and openly than they are used by either Henry Adams, Ralph Adams Cram, or the Knights of Columbus. Henry Adams is the despicable hero of all the deadly poison snobs who would break the neck of independent America. They read his books to sharpen the cruelty of their minds and give them new sharpness in riding down the American people. As soon as the head of a big American Corporation loots a middle-sized American Town—his wife moves from the Baptist to the High Episcopal Church and reads the medievalism of Henry Adams. Hubby of course, merely goes on looting. It is so notorious that it is no wonder High Churchism is abhorred by the Average American. It means fat climbers, every time.

But there is a Church of the future—as free from Ecclesiasticism as the Irvingites or Campbellites, as poor as Elijah, Elisha, John the Baptist, Dante or Johnny Appleseed—and as American as Santa Fe, yet abounding in visible symbols. I think it could quite possibly be an Out-door Church—as free as the street, yet decorated with the Old Catholic Symbols. That is—instead of, as in medieval times having the Cathedral the Unit, why not have the town itself the Unit—and with no dogmas—and no priests?

Outside Springfield itself "The Golden Book" was a failure. I hope you do not consider it presumption on my part when I urge you to take an hour to turn over every element in that book you consider sound, and possible to make alive, and rewrite the most vital element in it for Santa Fe as you have the chance—in Santa Fe terms and words. My deepest heart has been set on Holy Cities, real pilgrim cities for America. I have thought on the matter years and years and years. I put my whole strength into the Golden Book—and it remains a dull mystery even to my best friends. Nearly all reprove me for it. It will be years and years before I have the mental elasticity to go a bit further with it. I am completely exhausted in this vein, yet I cannot help but hope that you can stand on the carcass of my dead book and write a living one. I took it too seriously. I strained too hard, I nearly cracked my skull. I have never had as much fight in me since. I put years into that book, that will never be mine again. Some of my best friends count it utter rubbish—and an unutterable failure. Yet it seems to me the fundamental idea is worth passing on with all urgency. It is as natural with me to try to build holy cities as it is with some people to build skyscrapers. From beginning to end—I tried too hard, I know.

From the Nature-Worship of the Pueblo Indians to the Christian Science of the noble Mrs. Moody there is one long strange tide of Unity which neither would acknowledge, yet which would all help to make the Holy City. Synagogue, Irish Church, Episcopal Church can all help—on the side, and indirectly, and will never quarrel with the City—if it is established as beautifully and simply as Fourth of July and Christmas.

I most earnestly beg your pardon if I have been suggesting too much.

The Golden Book came as near to costing me my life as anything I will ever do, and live.

The fundamental issue means the entire world to me. We need a holy city, Springfield, Sante Fe–Emporia, or all three. I think it is possible to maintain all the richness of medieval times, and yet burn every book on Theology and Dogma, burn Every Creed, abolish every priesthood and every caste. Athens and the Parthenon survive in blazing light, though the priests and the theology are gone. The forms and meanings are as precise as in any book by Henry Adams or Ralph Adams Cram on the medieval virgin. Athens came in through the eye alone.

These opinions were formed going round and round the Metropolitan Museum—studying the models of all the Temples from Egypt to Japan since 1905—all of seventeen years. Round and Round that Museum I have gone and on to the Times Building and the Woolworth Building and the Paulist Fathers Church—year after year, year after year. Hardly a soul in all my world knows that this endless tour through the Corridors of Time is the fundamental basis of all my study and Philosophy and The Metropolitan Museum with its orderly and splendid picture of every age of Man and Every great religion is the very Cathedral of my life. My interest in this is so much stronger than any interest in Poetry and Literature there is no comparison. For three or four years out of the 17 I led classes around this museum and studied it in careful lecture-course detail, but that is the least of the story. The 17 years—going through in fact or imagination with a friend or two, is the essential thing. And then I was in the Chicago Museum 1900—1904. And the inevitable conclusion for America, in this Corridor of time is that America cries out for her holy City—her Acropolis, her Notre Dame, her Mecca, her Kamakura, her Nikko.

Well—I have written quite enough. I profoundly hope I have not urged this idea too strongly upon you—I assure you it comes of my heart's blood.

Affectionately

VACHEL

Note

1. William Allen White (1868—1944) was a Kansas journalist whose editorials in the *Emporia Gazette* established him as a spokesman for rural liberalism. Strangely enough, VL did not seem to mind White's famous 1896 editorial "What's the Matter with Kansas," in which he boosted McKinley's campaign for the presidency. White afterward supported Theodore Roosevelt, as did VL. His assessment of White's ideas is probably the best single proof of the lack of political homogeneity in VL's thinking.

115

TO HARRIET MOODY

The Commodore Hotel
New York City

August 1, 1922

My dear Cordelia:—

That you should all be there at Cummington is to me quite a beautiful thing, and I know the talk is good, the companionship unexcelled, and the scenery everything it should be.

Your humble servant is taking the isolation cure, locked up by his own hand, for hours and days, and getting immense peace, acres of study and all kinds of most essential rest out of it. I am pushing further certain lines of study of interest only to myself and commonplace enough, but things about which I have had scattering misinformation and no chance to go into these many years. There is every reason now to suppose I will be in New York till Sept. 1 or Oct. 15, hiding and studying, and centering all my studies in the Metropolitan Museum of Art, where, as of old, I spend hours and days. And not a single friend I have on earth but is appalled and asks what on earth I am doing in such an irrelevant place, I who am nothing but a shout, a cowboy yell and the like. Never-the-less I do, day after day, spend my time in said museum, digging out matters I will never have the chance, the disposition or the desire to whisper to any living soul, all for my own pedantic heavy dirty satisfaction, to feed the complacencies of my mistaken and utterly irrelevant philosophies.

And in between museum tours I am hiding in a cool and secret and breezy ice chest, absolutely alone with my books and my thoughts. I have almost gone broke buying books for said ice chest and am having a grand time with them. When I get through I will be so educated no respectable person will endure me. I will be one vast dust-bin of complacent misinformation.

I am a great deal like the Prohibition Candidate for President in the year 1884 or so—John P. St. John,[1] "It is chilly and lonely—but I like it—Oh, I like it!"

I have stopped most every fly-wheel that was going too fast in my head. I have taken cold showers without number, and doubtless by Oct. 15 I can afford to be the shameless person described in the ads and have the strength to face the disgraces of publicity. But now I am exercising an egotism far more cold and metallic and concentrated, the egotism of the polar bear who bit a nick in the North Pole with no one there to notice it, but just as vain, never-the-less, in the presence of the six-months night. The bear says:— "To Gehenna with those circus bears. I am just as well off right here. There is more scenery anyhow, and the ice is substantial and of the best quality. If I monkey with the human race too much, I will get myself made into a doormat, and they will cut out my liver and my soul".

You see I am quite haughty toward the world right now, and will probably so continue till I go broke again, which I may do any time. In that case I will reread "The Handy Guide for Beggars" and discover just what I said to do. I have almost forgotten.

Certainly this is an awful lot of Rot to be writing to a friend. But I love you dearly. If you hear an ax in the night at Cummington,[2] it is my soul trying to clear a patch in the brush again. If you hear a splash, it is me freezing myself in that waterfall again, or at least my Ka going forth to do so.

Of course I will call early and often and many times in Chicago next winter, but please let me postpone public appearance at Jeux Floraux for a year. Year after next this national touring will be over. I will be writing, I hope, at leisure, and will have, I hope, attained to that freshness of mind and that newness of poem that will do justice to such an occasion. Truly I would rather draw pictures for them than recite for them.

If you will let me draw one tiny picture for each person in the Audience, and let that be the evening's stunt, that will mean real sport—a little squib of writing and drawing for each one.

With love

VACHEL

Notes

1. John P. St. John of Kansas polled 150,000 votes in the 1884 presidential election in which Grover Cleveland, the candidate of the Democratic party, was elected against his main opponent, James G. Blaine.
2. Mrs. Moody's country house, Luther Shaw Farm, was in West Cummington, Massachusetts.

116

TO MR. AND MRS. JOHN DRINKWATER

Century Club
7 West Forty Third Street
New York

August 12, 1922

My Dear Mr. and Mrs. John Drinkwater:—
Last week I wrote to you and now I find I used the wrong address. To make sure I send a second note.

I am exceedingly anxious for you to get acquainted with my very good friends Prof. and Mrs. A. J. Armstrong who will be in Europe till Sept. 20 and whose address for forwarding will be

HOTEL REGINA

PLACE RIVOLI

PARIS FRANCE

I want them to know as many of the English Poets as they do American, and that is most of them.

Prof. and Mrs. Armstrong are the heads of the English Department of Baylor University Waco Texas, the most important purely Baptist school in America and have been the principal figures in its many extraordinary activities.

They had sent for me several times making me a short schedule through other Texas English Departments so I could get to Baylor—and they had proved such loyal and exhilarating friends as well as representatives that when I found myself dead broke and my books bringing me nothing—last summer—I suggested to them that they send me on a two years national tour through Universities exclusively. The tour is half over, it begins again Oct. 15. So far it has been most thrilling and I have met thousands and thousands of beautiful young students I adore.

Well—I will not go into that—but it seems to me the Armstrongs have in them the making of some kind of international literary statesmen—and at least they will be valued friends for their own sakes for the poets of England.

They have many views of their own as to public appearances both in England and America.

One thing I hope you can discuss with them is possible English honors for Edwin Arlington Robinson.[1] He is our nearest equivalent in distinction attainment age veteranship and laurels to the English Poet Laureate and it seems to me proper cooperation on both sides of the water to this end would clear up much of the recent squabbling. Certainly you have done your part in your recent tribute to Robinson with which I most heartily agree. I have written also on this subject to Masefield,[2] that is, about Robinson. (Robinson cannot speak in public—and is a little deaf.) And I have written about the Armstrongs to many English Poets and Critics to about the same sets that received me in England. It is my first move in regard to my very delightful and profoundly appreciated English Reception, since that time.

I hope the Armstrongs can send you and many other English Poets on this University Circuit which seems now wished on to them by the American Poets. They are impresarios whether they want to be or not—and at least my good and delightful friends.

Most sincerely

VACHEL

Notes

1. Edwin Arlington Robinson (1869—1935) was then fifty-three. The first edition of his *Collected Poems* was published in 1921, and other editions followed in 1924, 1927, and 1937.
2. VL had met John Masefield (1878—1967) several times, the last during his trip to England. Masefield, who was appointed poet laureate in 1930, succeeding Robert Bridges, had published *King Cole* in 1921.

117

TO STEPHEN AND ROSE GRAHAM

Oct. 17, 1922

My Dear Stephen and Rose Graham:—[1]
I am writing on the train and this is all the paper I can find. Pardon shaky hand. You may keep and meditate upon the above letter! It is

most gratifying recognition from the director of the art school, where I drew from the casts of the Elgin Marbles, and from the nude, for four years. I may not exhibit for several years, but I am delighted at the opening. If I can make a drawing in time, I will. Please rejoice with me! It is like getting out of jail at last! I have told Harshe to watch for the Appleton book.

I propose that Stephen and I harvest wheat together as itinerant labor from Northern Texas into Canada, beginning as far south as the wheat crop begins, and as early May or June as he fixes the date. Then harvest northwest toward Alaska and the frost. If I am alive next Spring I will be for it. And maybe we can harvest wheat in Egypt sometime.

Now I am in my room in Danville—and have paper. Perhaps it is too early to plan now, but let us consult about possible harvesting together—before you leave for England again. Much may happen in two months. Nothing however as I now see life—could interfere with our harvesting—except some girl might seize and marry me. If ever I get married I do not expect to call my soul my own till I die. If Stephen and I harvest together—first we can look for United States and Canadian hieroglyphics in the Wheat Fields. The original ones were born in the wheat fields of Egypt.[2] We can draw every parallel between the Mississippi and Missouri River Valley and the valley of the Nile. Graham can take the Universal Hieroglyphics to London and Get Vernon Hill[3] to draw them—and then as before I can draw the book in reply sometime after!

Appleton's have positively taken my book of drawings "Going to the Sun" or "Tramping with Graham in the Rockies", and I hope I have much improved it since Stephen saw it. It has more of a Preface now—and much more about Stephen in it! Also the Mountain-Cat poem[4]—with several elaborate illustrations.

Every drawing in the Appleton Book is now signed with a tiny line of Egyptian Hieroglyphics under my name which I hope does not interfere with the design or seem obtrusive and which will lead naturally to such United States and World-Hieroglyphics as we may evolve, or I may care to add to subsequent editions of the book.

It is the turning point in my whole life if this Appleton book is issued as promised on Feb. 1, and is a success. The Macmillan Collected Poems, is a kind of heavy college-honorary degree kind of advertisement—and most people will think it the best. But the Appleton Book means a license to freedom and an open door to the future, and a great open door to experiment in all art Forms. If it is actually issued Feb. 1, I will be happy enough for a holiday, as soon as the work of reciting ends. I will be 27 years old again.[5]

I want to take one more year of drawing at the Chicago Art Institute, probably beginning this time next year. I know the figure well—and have drawn it hundreds of times. But I want to be able completely to recall and revive and carry further all the habits of Art Student days. I see myself studying at the Art Institute, then taking little dashes to the University constantly getting better and better acquainted with the Egyptian End of the Haskell Oriental Museum because that really is Hieroglyphic headquarters of this U.S. It is plain I am respected as an Art Institute graduate—and I want to follow it up to the limit, and approach that Oriental Museum as an active and endorsed and busy Art Student and not a mere man of letters they can bully into learning German before they will tell him anything. My standing at Chicago Art Institute was bought long ago at the price of youth and blood and tears, and now I see the dim possibility of building on every stone I left there. At least I am determined to struggle on, and put up a little better drawings than ever before in all my life. I have no notion of using anything more than pure line, and pen-and-ink, but hope to perfect myself in that, and re-memorize the figure.

And before I make this plunge I think it would be a grand Thing for Stephen and Vachel to become itinerant laborers and harvest wheat from Texas to Alaska. I wonder if it can be done? I suppose I will give out in a week. But I am willing to bust myself trying. It will be a bit easier for two than one. Many a crop needs only two extra harvesters, we can hire as a pair and go from crop to crop—say one crop every other state: Texas-Kansas, North Dakota-Alberta and the North Pole. Well the cold facts are I never lasted longer than a week on such a job alone. But it would be no harder than climbing six weeks with Stephen to set the pace. Company gives courage, and good advice in needy times. Let's think about it—anyway. My good wishes to all in Santa Fe. If Stephen is not there by now—please forward this letter with proper comment.

I am certainly profoundly grateful to Stephen for landing that Appleton Book for me. I worked on it like a fiend—up to the hour I began to pack to leave for my first speaking engagement, leaving New York last Saturday. But the book is *done*—*both* books are done—and the collected works are in the hands of Macmillans and the drawings are in the hands of Appletons and I have nothing more to do with either till they appear since both firms have promised to read the proof themselves. So I can give my whole energy to reciting and laying future plans.

With love to you both

VACHEL

Permanent address

CARE OF
MRS. BEN BLAIR
3343 BRADFORD ROAD
CLEVELAND HEIGHTS
CLEVELAND OHIO.

Notes

1. The first page of this letter was written on a page of a letter from Robert E. Harshe, Director of the Art Institute of Chicago, dated October 10, 1922. In it, Harshe asks VL whether he would contribute something to the exhibit organized by the Institute during Alumni Week.
2. VL was then very much interested in the various parallels between the Nile Valley and Delta and those of the Mississippi. Numerous notes and manuscripts deal with the resemblances he found between Egyptian and American civilization. This proved to him that the same sort of approach to signs could be used in both cases, and launched him on the track of what he called "American Hieroglyphics."
3. Vernon Hill illustrated Graham's account of the 1921 tramp in the Rockies.
4. "The Mountain-Cat" eventually came out under the title "So Much the Worse for Boston" in *Going-to-the-Sun* (pp. 50—70).
5. VL was twenty-seven in 1906, the year his drawings seemed to dominate his work.

118

TO STEPHEN GRAHAM

King George Hotel
Saskatoon

November 11, 1922

My Dear Stephen:—

Harvesting starts in North Central counties of Texas June 1 to 5. In the Texas "Panhandle" June 20—25, Oklahoma June 1—25. In Dakota The harvesting is August 10—15. The wheat harvest farthest north is in the Peace River Country Alberta August 3 to Sept 3 according to season. I would like to harvest in Texas in June—in Alberta in August or September:—as far south as possible and as far north as possible, and in between as much as fancy and strength permit. Think it over. Maybe there is wheat in Alaska. Let us find out!

Of course I will not make much of a harvester, but can make shift. I have no notion of being the hero of this expedition, or mentioned in connection with it. Let us make *the Wheat of the World*, from Russia to Egypt, and from Egypt to Texas and Canada, and Alaska, the hero. Or if any men are heroes, let us make Tolstoy, and Ruskin to please me and Dostoyevsky to please you. If it is written up, you will have to do the writing. I have no notion of taking a single note. It is purely a matter of sweating out my suit, with me, and it is even a sentimental journey, gathering a crop I have always loved with all my heart, and has always seen [seemed?] the most beautiful thing in the world. I would rather die of sunstroke [or] of overwork in a wheat-field than die a sleepy fat man in a bed or a silly country-club ornament, playing golf to "reduce". And I seem to have reached the age where I have to choose, between Golf, wheat, fat slavery or death! I am fat in the brain and the gut,—dull silly and indifferent. The wheat looks like the only escape.

If our expedition goes into record by me—it will only be a long time after—perhaps two or three new drawings in the back of "Going to the Sun" and they will be such glittering generalities, if I know myself, that the personal application must be made in the titles and the preface. It will not be an intrinsic part of the design.

If I get back alive from the wheat-fields—though getting back alive is a mere matter of cheerful curiosity and indifference with me— If I get back alive, and with back not broken— and skull not cracked by the sun or the wrathful farmer—why, I will probably spend Oct 1 1923 to June 1, 1924 in Chicago—hidden far from all old friends—and producing new drawings and hieroglyphics (with explanatory couplets and rhymes). In such a case of course some of them would be a bit spiced with the wheat and our experience, of course. But it would be so general and so incidental the field would be practically yours to record, and you would have written it all out long ago. I have no notion of ever writing prose again—and I do not care much whether I draw or write verses till I have sweated my desire for the harvest out of my system. I was so dull and so tired and so exhausted through the speed of mental and physical events by last June I *had* to *hide*. I am much slower and much more easily exhausted and much duller and more bovine than any of my friends understand. But my tour this winter is mercifully slow. I am doing nothing new—and as little of that as possible and I will be all on the line for one more dash for the Dark Tower by next June and eager for three months permanent harvesting. I would rather break my neck harvesting than sit still and play safe. Yet I was so exhausted most of the time on our Mountain Climb I know I will have to play for wind and try every device to get in a lot of sleep to come out successful at the end of three months. If I come through I will feel one inch nearer to infinite and far off wisdom. It seems to me you can prepare for our expedition somewhat beforehand by turning over in your mind all that the Russian Sages have said about the Wheat. I will be delighted if any or all the Russian Sages are the heroes of the book, if you write a book! And perhaps Emerson discusses wheat, somewhere! Frankly I have not the courage and the stamina to take up this expedition alone. I get a deadly dullness and an indifference like that of the drug fiend. I am drugged with too many audiences, too much publicity, too much egotism, too much talking about myself town after town, season after season till I am a fool like the Kaiser and yet with no Germany to flatter me. Sweat is always my one medicine taken in desperation when on the verge of eternal sleepiness if not eternal sleep. And to start always costs me all my will-power. One dash of three months into the world of sweat lasts me several years and leaves me utterly unable to try again for a long time, but able to write and draw again. Yet I am eternally homesick to be a *permanent farm hand* of a sort. I cannot even harness a farm-horse, and when I ask the farmer to teach me, he always thinks me an utter fool and wants to kick me into the road. Yet one *patient* farmer could in one year—with some patience and determination to be truly kind, make me into a farm-hand forever, a kind of no-account farmhand, who does not want to own or manage a farm or use his brains to excess.

Certainly I am far more of a farmer in my dreams, than I am a tramp. But the farmers only want men like horses, raised from colt-days on the farm. You are much readier in stranger situations and could learn from the impatient farmer and teach me without his knowing it. The great thing about being an itinerant laborer is that one can move away from the place, when the boss gets too tyrannical. I have in fancy seen us working as a pair of itinerant laborers one week or four days at a stretch in many parts of the world, wherever we could fit in for a very short shift. But this may be biting off too much at once. Sufficient for the summer is the summer. By Sept. 1 or Oct. 1, 1923 I will probably want to sit still for a long long time. But the world is wide and the last adventure has not been bad. You will probably not have time to answer this letter before I reach the United States, but the list of my new addresses waits at Vancouver and I can write it to you from there. Meanwhile my permanent addresses are

PROF. A.J. ARMSTRONG
BAYLOR UNIVERSITY
WACO TEXAS

and

MRS. BEN BLAIR
3343 BRADFORD ROAD
CLEVELAND HEIGHTS
CLEVELAND. OHIO

My good wishes to every one in Santa Fe, to the Hendersons, to Mrs. Graham and to Ewert.[1]

Faithfully

VACHEL

Note

1. "Ewert" is the novelist Wilfred Ewart, who had toured Mexico with Graham in 1922—23. Ewart was accidentally killed in his hotel on New Year's Eve, 1923, by a stray bullet coming in through the window. Graham edited Ewart's *Life and Last Words* in 1924.

119

TO FRANK WALLER ALLEN

I have kept a copy of this letter, and consider it a contract with the Illinois State Journal—Springfield Illinois

NICHOLAS VACHEL LINDSAY
Nov. 15, 1922

Cleveland, Ohio
Nov. 15 1922

My Dear Frank:—

I am still poor, but am ambitious. So, hoping that you are still in connection with the Journal, I offer a prize of one thousand dollars for the best essay of one hundred words printed in the Journal on "How to Make Laws that will apply the teachings of the Golden Book of Springfield to the Springfield Illinois City Hall." The Essays are to be first printed in the Journal, signed by the author's right names, and deemed worthy, by the Journal to appear as regular editorials and considered only if up to their editorial standard. The Journal Staff is to decide on the best one in any way it deems fit without consulting me, and the contest to stretch out till the Journal is tired of the subject—the longer the better. Essays from Springfield Lawyers of standing Especially solicited but the contest open to anyone all over the world. All other conditions of the contest to be settled by the Journal in any way it deems fit. As soon as I receive marked copies of the Journal, containing all the essays, and the winning essay—so marked— I will at once forward the prize.

With great good wishes

NICHOLAS VACHEL LINDSAY

120

TO HARRIET MONROE

> Observation car
> Spokane, Portland and Seattle Ry.
> Columbia River Scenic Route
> Dec. 3, 1922.

Confidential:—

Dearest Harriet:—
Enclosed find a horribly grubby letter, written on a very very shaky train, under many difficulties. I am sending it to you and no one else. It is an answer to Shanks November article[1] in the Bookman, though you need not say I said so, and please suppress any part of this enclosed letter that my true friends in England would consider unfriendly. Shanks is a loyal friend. I prefer to make my protest through your paper. The Macmillan Company of England, after six months of Jockeying and publishing Graham's "Tramping with a poet" have just sent word to the Macmillan Co of America they will not import my books![2]

The English only know the Unrhymed squibs at the head of Graham's Chapters which he wrote himself and I never saw, Graham never pretended I wrote them. And anyone who knows me, knows I could not have written them, for I always write in rhyme.

But there are no Books in England to show how I do write!

With good wishes
VACHEL—

Care of Mrs Ben Blair
3343 Bradford Road Cleveland Heights Cleveland Ohio.

Publish this letter in whole or in part if you care to do so.

December 3, 1922

My Dear Harriet:—
Do not think I am smothering you with clippings. But here are two more unusually intelligent clippings from the same Spokane paper. What they say about the cheers seems to me valid. I hope you care to carry further the discussion. You have seen all the Indian dances, and you know the Dionysiac beginnings of the Greek Drama. I have very much resented being called a "Jazz" poet, especially by the British Papers, because it was used to mean something synonymous with hysteria, shrieking and fidgets. I abhor the kind of Ball-Room dancing that goes with Jazz, and I abhor the blasphemy that Jazz has made of the beautiful slow whispered Negro Spirituals. The British Newspapers especially assume "The Daniel Jazz" is the one thing I have written—and they quote two lines in it, the grrr of the Lions as complete samples of my verse, and not one British Man of Letters knows I have written "The Chinese Nightingale" or that I care for such verse. Now there must be something in my work that I do not myself understand, that provokes this kind of extreme treatment of me. Perhaps "The College Yell", as modified and evolving in these enclosed editorials, is the index to this element. It does not exist in England. Certainly I would never resent being called "The College Yell" poet, however strangely that would sound to you. I am speaking of the whispered college yell, in the sense in which it is expressed here in this clipping. It represents an utterly different mood and a far healthier state of the nervous system than Jazz. The College Yell expresses nineteen year old boys and girls generally at a co-educational State University at the height of their youth and glory. On the other hand, jazz is hectic, has the leer of the bad-lands in it, and first, last and always is hysteric. It is full of the dust of the dirty dance. The Saxophone, its chief instrument is the most diseased instrument in all modern music. It absolutely smells of the hospital.

Graham has been an infinitely painstaking and generous and devoted Biographer, and all the rest of the British have been infinitely kind to me, and infinitely uncomprehending with me. Stephen Graham has been a doughty champion indeed. But I have no representative books of my own in England, and no prospect of any. The only book circulating in England is a slender volume—whose title poem is *"The Daniel Jazz."* That book was printed when I was on the way to England on the general contract that a book of selections was to be printed. But I trusted the publisher too much. I assumed such a song as "The Chinese Nightingale" would be the title poem. Instead I found this one after-dinner squib representing me, and the Nightingale was not even in the volume of selections, not even in the back of the book. I have always considered it my typical and representative poem. But it interferes with the British Theory of my Poems. I was caricatured in the British Papers as being in a state of Jazz epilepsy or apoplexy—or having some kindred complaint. And most of my British friends still assume I glory in this verdict. Nothing could be further from the truth. I want them to revise their verdict. I want them to read my eight books. TELL THEM SO.

My standard for an oratorical or musical poem might be well represented by Dryden's Alexander's Feast. And as for poems written for pictures—among British Writers, I could cite the verses of Rossetti for the great majority of my verses are inscriptional, written for my pictures. My verses follow Dryden and Rossetti indeed a long way off. Still such men are my models. The Oratorical touch in my work is certainly unimportant and a small part of the eight books. But if it is to be accounted for why not use the University War Cry and College Yell to account for it, rather than Jazz? I have often written College yells at Hiram college, and led them. Any American Boy has done something like this. Any High-School Freshman, boy or girl, has done it. All High Schools have gorgeous yell-carnivals.

These stubborn British were enormously good and kind to me. They have championed me as an orator, in season and out, and are thoroughly good sports.

But owing to the perverse accidents of publishing, what they know about my four books of verse and four books of prose, you could put on a postage stamp. None of them know I am a pen-and-ink draughtsman. You asked me on my return from England, for my verdict on the British visit. Here it is, for better or worse:

"At least fifty devoted British friends among Critics and poets know I have written eight books. None of the rest have the remotest notion I have written anything. They think of me as some sort of improviser."

The British Hospitality was gorgeous, they were willing to listen infinitely, I have been asked back again and again, I hope ultimately to go. But I have as yet no Books circulating in England. The British even think I wrote Stephen Graham's poems in his book, "TRAMPING WITH A POET".

Five hundred copies of the General Booth volume so splendidly prefaced by the loyal Robert Nichols[3] and John Masefield, have been long out of print in England. The publishers assure me they are quite through. I am happy to say that the Daniel Jazz Volume does not sell. Will my good British friends now note my petition?

I want to be represented in England by my eight books, as I wrote them. I will be satisfied by nothing less.

Most fraternally

VACHEL LINDSAY

Notes

1. Shanks's article was "An English Impression of American Literature" (*Bookman*, November 1922, pp. 279—87).
2. VL's disappointment at Macmillan's not importing his books in England was because he had planned to put *Going-to-the-Sun* on sale as a companion volume to Stephen Graham's account of their tramping trip.
3. Robert Nichols was an English critic, poet, and dramatist. From 1921 to 1924 he held the chair of English at the Imperial University of Tokyo once held by Lafcadio Hearn. In 1926, Nichols wrote *Twenty Below* with Jim Tully.

121

TO HARRIET MOODY

Oklahoma City
December 22, 1922

My dear Cordelia:—

I have only now discovered that thou hast again played Providence, and I am to be in Chicago—January 7, and January 13.

It will be indeed good to see you, and if it be possible and I don't interfere with thy previous plans, I hope to be with thee and stay at thy house—both or either of these days.

I still greatly love the human race. But, Expect a dark man in the cloak of a Matador—for I have changed in every conventional respect. I refuse to recite in parlors for a soul—but I will talk with thee alone as much as thou wilt. Please don't ask me to recite—unless for a public audience as already promised by the busy Armstrong. And I would prefer to read other men—, or *talk* on *American Poets*.

I am here recovering from a good but wracking autumn. Armstrong managed me and directed local committees almost altogether by telegram all fall, a rather jerky way to treat the human mind. One committee received thirty telegrams (they said!).

But I go to see him day after tomorrow and I look for a smoother running winter and spring. Evidently he has had other troubles.

I am asking sister Joy of Cleveland to forward all my mail to thee through January thirteenth.

I say! There is nothing like being locked up alone in a hotel where no one knows where you are, and with the telephone plugged. So I was in New York for three months this summer and except for some few too-lonesome days it was the luxury of my life. I am taking the same rest-cure here before I go down to Waco to get Armstrong to outline the work for Winter and Spring, and get the secret of his flurry!

I here complain that Armstrong undertakes too much, and gets all in a fidget and runs me too hard, till my brains are simply putty. His evident distraction distracts me and the committee.

But, on the other hand he has delivered a car-window map of U.S.A. and Canada to me, has sent me into every state in the union and most of the provinces of Canada—and given me a geographical education I can meditate on for twenty years. And he has stood by his general marching orders, and has sent me almost altogether to the Universities and English Departments. Everywhere in the United States and Canada the heads of English Departments, thanks to Armstrong, are extraordinarily loyal and friendly, and they have nearly always a circle of ten young poets around them, lovely boys and girls— well worth meeting, who would melt a heart of stone, by their youth and chivalry, and lovely talent.

I have been travelling so fast, so far and so uncertainly that I have missed a lot of my mail this fall—but I hope it gets back to Joy—and she forwards it to thee.

Seeing all this map has packed me with new ideas, and I take new notes every day, some of which I expect to work out, sooner or later. I have not yet worked out *one*.

The main trouble between me and my Chicago and literary friends generally is that they meet me after my life of solitude in Art Galleries, and I spring from my cell with a hell of a yell—and hardly one of them will credit me with a moment's desire for solitude and meditation. They think of me as some sort of steam whistle. But I am entirely through with whistling, *especially among friends*—the one thing I desire is the old

Art Student life I once led, in that very Chicago—browsing for four years in the Ryerson Art Galleries and walking the Paths of Chicago University with one or two student friends there.

I have not a friend, acquaintance or relative on earth who is willing to grant me this life, or believe I mean it with all my soul when I say I desire such a solitary life, and have desired it for many a long day. The only way is to lock myself up in a hotel with the telephone plugged. The friends don't know that my sudden noise with audiences was the result of about 30 years of accumulated silence. I abhor reciting in parlors. I abominate to do my cute act for any one. The one thing I value is conversation with human beings *one at a time,* or else solitude.

What then of my Winter and Spring tour? Do I also hate that?

MacMillans told me a year and a half ago they didn't owe me a cent—so I saw it was beg, or tour. It was then I laid out a two years' tour with Armstrong—covering every state in the Union and every University that would let me in. The whole thing was practically laid out then—and I am now as it were on the home stretch of the two years tour. It will include Florida and Eastern Canada.

I intensely dislike reciting. My audiences demand just two pieces that I utterly abhor: Booth and the Congo. They will *pay to hear them* any time—and then the sooner I leave town the better; as far as the bulk of the audience is concerned. And they will not buy one book, unless *urged!*

But much as I hate to recite, and hate my addled brain after reciting, it is a small price to pay for the education I get in the lobbies of the hotels, and looking out of the car windows, and meeting groups of young poets the next day—that could never afford to send for me on their own; and seeing all the tides of beautiful young American and Canadian life in the Universities, and meeting Professors of English, and their wives, who are altogether worth while. I would say offhand the finest set of people in the Anglo Saxon world, the most free-spoken and best educated and the best talkers are these professors of English and their wives. They are the type of Armstrong and his wife, people who do their own work, wash their own windows, spank their own babies and who are completely surrounded by grand and gorgeous boy and girl poets from the senior class. Plain living and high thinking.

To meet such tiny flocks of the Elect I pay the price of reciting these two poems I abhor—Booth and the Congo, for the larger group.

I abhor these two songs first of all because they represent my 33rd year and I am forty-three and have accumulated ten years of notes I have not had the undisturbed isolation to write out or draw out. Those two poems were born after a lifetime of solitude in which I wrote—(*invented a new* piece of work, every day). Now I have no chance to write down the new invention or court the solitude when it comes out in good form, but I am increasingly tortured by the impulse for daily *new* invention. My suitcase is packed with notes. But I will have to sit still, tied, with my jaw tied, one whole year, before I can write them out. I could invent a new picture or verse every day, if let alone.

I love the human race, but I hope to teach them to regard me as a meditator, not a jazzer.

The whole jazzy notion of my work is based on the eagerness of my first year of reciting after I had faced contempt for so long. But it is as hard to endure as contempt, and has nothing whatever to do with my ambitions and aspirations. However I shout on the start, I do *not* want to shout long.

Feb. 1 the MacMillan Co. promise the Collected Poems—with an autobiographical preface[1]—and D. Appleton & Co. promise my book of drawings in reply to Stephen Graham's book. My book of drawings is called "Going to the Sun", or "Tramping with Stephen Graham in the Rockies". I hope it goes into several editions and I can add new drawings each edition, and improve it into something worth while. The two books together, with the reviews bound to appear between now and June will turn the flank of criticism till my friends meet at last the Vachel that writes this letter to thee—an entirely different Vachel from the ads, the Vachel fond of Milton and George Washington.

Yet even then I will be a far more terrible egotist than they think. I am said to be like my mother—and few knew what a thundering egotist she was. But both of us were far fonder of *solitude and meditation* than our little world knew, and our secret thoughts—harmless enough—were *far far indeed from the advertisements* and few understood her pride, or egotism, and few know mine, though this letter almost unveils it!

And so this is my silly message to thee.—If in this brace of new books, I insist my public become acquainted all over again—and I probably have insured the result— let us too, my dear Cordelia—begin all over, on another plane, still. Believe me a dark Spaniard!—I had many Spanish ancestors—the Don Ivans—on whose traditions I was reared. My mother talked of them daily, in my infancy.

Believe me an Aztec or a Soltec (for I have *some* American Indian in me via the Cave family) and one of my ancestors was the uncle of Jane Austen, so I was reared on that tradition.[2] And another taught Daniel Boone's children to read, so I was brought up on that. But most of all I have always known from both sides of the house there was an unaccountable *thread* that may lead back to Egypt—but certainly has to do with meditation and has nothing to do with Oratory or reciting in Parlors. I am nobody's pink-toed Cupid and nobody's Yokel—however I may appear that way, and I am nobody's busy little Jazzer. As I say—begin with the Dark Spaniard—disguised as a blonde, and don't be so darn sure you know all about me! and pardon the Yokel French. And I will be equally sure I know nothing about thee, but thy great kindness of heart, that with thee as with Ruskin "Every dawn of morning is as the beginning of life".

If I said one word of thee, it would be that thou art Shakespearian, though whether thy soul is Portia, Miranda, Cordelia, Viola, Juliet, Cleopatra—who can tell? Thy literary sense is the Shakespearian, the events of thy life are Plutarchian and Shakespearian, and likewise thy conversation.

And allow me, my good friend and noble hearted Cordelia—to be the Don Ivan, the Aztec, the Soltec, the Matador, not the jazzer, not the saxophone.

Most fraternally,

VACHEL

Notes

1. The "autobiographical preface" to the *Collected Poems* was entitled "Adventures While Singing These Songs." VL wrote another one for the 1925 edition, entitled "Adventures While Preaching Hieroglyphic Sermons." In the later part of his life he proposed to Macmillan that both prefaces be withdrawn as superannuated and replaced by a series of drawings.
2. The Doniphans in VL's ancestry prompted him to give their name to his daughter, Susan Doniphan Lindsay. A tradition in the Lindsay family had it that the Caves were remotely connected with Pocahontas. The link with Jane Austen was supposed to be through the Austin branch of the family.

122

TO A. J. ARMSTRONG

December 27, 1922

My Dear Armstrong:

I am writing on the shaky train to El Paso, a strictly personal confidential letter not to be read upstairs but down stairs before the fire when you think of me most forgivingly. I know I am a difficult lamb, but be sure I am grateful to my shepherds, no matter how I bleat at them. I am learning to use the new breast pocket leather folder, with pride and ostentation and carry my railroad ticket in it, and will so continue world without end.

One thing my mama was always right about was that I had no business to shout at private citizens in the house, but she could never cure me, and I feel that I have shouted around your house and into your ears till the walls ache. Yet I was not so very excited. When I am really excited I am still as a mouse! Now please consider this an entirely personal letter, for I touched too roughly on some entirely personal matters the last minute. I planned a long poem on my mother called Hat shep sut,[1] who seems to have been remarkably like her. Also Ida Tarbell's[2] life of Mary Baker G. Eddy, founder of Christian Science shows much the same kind of a person, who requires enormous long-range activities to keep from over-managing all those nearby. I only want to say that I enormously respect and revere my mother's memory but she was never the mushy mellow and rabbit-like mother that appears in all movies. She was a holy terror to all those who were not prepared to dispute every inch of the way with her. To live with her was like being valet to the Pope in the Vatican and being a Protestant at the same time, and making tactful efforts to conceal it. So my sudden outburst was merely an old Springfield habit, and was meant with all affection to all concerned. If she discovered the appalling fact that Graham had a mind of his own and she wrote to you about it, be sure she would have found the same thing about either of you in the same length of time or sooner, and would have told Graham she suspected neither of you were orthodox. And I now begin to suspect her also of mixing up J. C. Squire, and Graham to you, for AJA to my surprise asked about Graham's Magazine. It is *Squire* that edits and created the *London Mercury*, it is *Squire* that is the literary political manipulator, his gang are called the Squirearchy in England. It is *Squire* whose books have a most meagre circulation either in England or America, and whose real claim to general public consideration is the creation of this *London Mercury* in time of War. He is the born editor and worker of combinations. He is just like Amy Lowell, only a bit more amiable. There is not a bit of real harm even in him, and he is well worth knowing. Graham went to Russia when he was twenty. All through the war he was the *London Times* oracle on Russia. He has just as *large* and *permanent* an audience in Great Britain as I could *ever* get in America. What is more he is just as red-blood open-hearted and jolly a citizen of the world as Frost or Sandburg or any of them. For Heaven's sakes get acquainted with Graham and wife when convenient and judge them on their merits. I think you will be most agreeably surprised. I do not urge you to tour them. But please love them well, if possible. They are good people, and good Christians. I have never seen the least sign to the contrary. Moreover my *whole London success* was as much owing to the Grahams, as was the Oxford to John Masefield. Please think of them just as well as you possibly can. They are *good kind people*. And to assume they could impose on me is to assume Mrs. Armstrong hadn't the nerve to send back that dozen boiled eggs her neighbor sold her. She sent them back and received the real eggs. Well I can do that too. It is one of the best things I do! In the autobiographical preface to the Macmillan *Collected Poems,* without getting personal, I have pictured our household when I was seven years old, especially my mother's extraordinary interest in Art Galleries of Europe and Europe generally. It was marvellously like that of the Armstrong's right now, when I was the age of Max. But my mother lost three children in three weeks thereafter,[3] and was never the same. She moved from a student of the arts to a religious fanatic and thereafter till her death only people who held some church office were welcome to the house. The house was always packed with religious committees of which she was always chairman, and woe be to any one who proposed anything else. She died at the telephone one may say, calling up her last committee. The only time this terrible routine was altered was when by almost forced methods I got her to England, and there for a little while she stepped back to her thirtieth year, and talked as she used to before her children died. It is this woman I tried to picture in my Preface, a woman few living Americans ever met, for once back from her holidays, she went back to her missionary teas. She could have thirty missionary teas and serve God. One party for any one else was indeed pagan, a thing to be remembered for years. I wrote when she and my father were in Europe, in China, or in camp in Colorado, and the house empty. I came to a practical understanding and the house was smooth running by the time I was thirty. But I was tried for heresy incessantly. My friends were just such people as Prof. and Mrs. A. J. Armstrong, but for this I was eternally tried for heresy. My books were only read by my mother after they had gone into two editions. That is from 1916—1922 my mother had begun to acquire a general idea what my books contained and was amazed to discover how near my ideas were to her own. But they had to be completely her own before they were orthodox. They had to be infallible, with her infallibility. So far as I know the one time she ever really heard me recite, and listened straight through was at Oxford, England. She sat on the front seat between two Oxford Dons. All Oxford was there, there were 1000 people present, Sir Walter Raleigh[4] introduced me, and she was actually shocked into *fixed, consecutive attention.* Then she began to invite all the British to Springfield. It was not my idea. It was hers. I thought at last I had gone back to her thirtieth year. She invited the English *literati, not* the missionaries, for she did not meet *one* missionary. She urged and urged them, with the greatest and most brilliant cordiality. She helped them plan American books. Then when Squire and Graham arrived in Springfield she had forgotten all about it, regarded them as conspirators of a mild variety who came with dark intent to destroy her peace and mind. She went back to her missionary committees, calling them up desperately on the telephone and ordering them about. Please do not think me desperate or tragic about this. It all had far more humor than pathos, and there were many compensations. The will-power she used on private people I know I use on audiences. I certainly try to refrain from using it in private.

And I am practically the person she made of me when I was eight. I have put that into the autobiography. I had to describe that year to avoid telling the tale I tell you. The English met the woman she was at thirty. Few Americans have. It would have taken equally desperate methods to have started her with the American literati. I was just accumulating the courage to try it when she left us. It would have taken a set determination on my part you can hardly imagine. It would have taken every woman on every committee to persuade her. Once forced to talk something besides missions, with no missionaries present, they would all have told me what a wonderful woman she was. Thirty years old would return. She would have given them the general impression she wrote and revised all my books. And it would have been in a sense true, but by no means literally true. I think one reason she did so well with the British was that she gave them tacitly to understand that after all she wrote the verses that she listened to for the first time right there on British soil. I know of course she put up perfectly shrewd paraphrases of every poem having listened to it once. And I was so dog-tired from the excitement and exhilaration of my immediately preceding tour in the west, I did not have the strength left to holler around and contradict her. Everybody called our English Trip a success. And I thank my mother for it. But after that she was tired, was in a state to try *all* my friends for heresy. She was in the trough of the wave, and she mixed up Squire and Graham and was way down. An infallible son could have managed her better, but she did pretty well at that, and died a lion and I must be her cub.

With love

VACHEL

Notes

1. "The long poem on Hat shep sut" apparently was never written, but the last poem in *Going-to-the-Sun* ("Words About an Ancient Queen," p. 100) deals with the theme. In it, the Victorian character is said to be wearing "a hair-net over her mind."
2. Ida Minerva Tarbell (1857—1944) was on the staff of *McClure's* from 1894 to 1906, then was associate editor of the *American Magazine* for nine years. Her *History of the Standard Oil Company* came out in 1904, *The Business of Being a Woman* in 1912.
3. After VL, Dr. and Mrs. Lindsay had three daughters, Isabel, Esther, and Eudora. They all died of scarlet fever within three weeks of one another. The next child, born in 1889, was named Joy out of gratitude.
4. Sir Walter Raleigh (1861—1922), essayist and literary critic, held the first professorship of English Literature at Oxford.

123

TO A. J. ARMSTRONG

Memphis, Tennessee
Jan. 21, 1923

My Dear Armstrong:

I am sick. My lungs are sore to the bottom. I have an earache and a toothache not to speak of several other afflictions, and I have to wait till tomorrow for the dentist. And I have not told you half.

The idea or raising prices was to give me and you more time between dates with more chance to avoid exhaustion. I had no notion of getting more money out of it. Any method to avoid such rapid exhausting travel and so many dates. I have no longer the strength to speak as often as I have in the past. Also the idea of a few larger audiences was for the same reason—the economy of strength—not "self aggrandizement". Please do not see it that way. I want to save my strength. I had a breakdown of a serious sort at El Paso and at Beloit, after two appearances that were accounted successful and everyone was congratulating me on health and good cheer. But for each case I paid *dearly* next day. The point of my discourse is the *economy of energy*. All my suggestions are to point that way, and with only that intent.

Your letter contains nine dates for February and eleven dates for March, two for April and suggests the Canadian tour as now practically a contract.

I am still sick and I cannot think. But how is this? Five of the February dates filled—four postponed till April. Five of the March dates filled—six of them postponed till May or June. I am perfectly willing to travel ever so slowly. I am unutterably dull and weak. But by this method I could get all my duties discharged by July first.

But I have had my first, second, and last awful warning and the old method must go. There is a hereditary curse[1] knocking mighty hard at the door, my friend and knocking with an increasing frequency I assure you.

You see me at the height of energy and get reports of my unending energy and be sure I pay for every pound of extra steam in this hereditary curse. If I am to live, *I must go slow.* If I want to stand still and get the people to come to me it is because I no longer think it in any way safe to go to them.

Why not scatter all positive contracts about a week and a half apart, up till June?[2]

As for next year and the year after, my idea has always been to keep on writing and drawing after June 1, 1923 without stopping to speak, from one to three years, or perhaps forever, returning to the platform only once a year for some specially thought-out appearance.

I have considered these two years a farewell to the platform all along.

Most sincerely,

VACHEL

Notes

1. The curse VL alludes to was probably epilepsy, if we are to believe the jottings in his notebooks concerning the cure suggested by doctors at the Mayo Clinic in Rochester, Minnesota. Furthermore, both Benjamin Kizer, of Spokane, and VL's wife witnessed moments of crisis. However, it is uncertain whether VL's malady took an acute turn because of his 1923 physical collapse and sinus trouble or whether manifestations of it had been apparent earlier. VL's long illness in infancy may have triggered a latent tendency into actual illness.
2. From Waco, VL had gone to El Paso and had since had "very serious danger signals." Not until January 29, in Gulfport, Mississippi, at the insistence of his host, his Hiram friend Richard G. "Zim" Cox, did VL stop and cancel the rest of his tour.

124

TO STEPHEN AND ROSE GRAHAM

Hotel Chisca
Memphis

Jan. 21, 1923

My Dear Stephen and Rose Graham:—
The very sad and terrible news[1] has just reached me here with two letters. It is hard indeed for death to come marching in through the windows and doors. If there is anything in the Glory of Youth—your friend had his hour—but there were many hours to come. I am very sad for you and I understand—for I went through much the same for Marsh last summer. I have never told you how close that came home. Marsh was my sole host for weeks at a time in last summer's necessary solitude, I saw scarcely anyone else. Mrs. Moody is mourning her brother's sudden death. He was almost her sole relative. And also the same week our little Isadora lost her week's old baby in that Southern town—Columbia South Carolina.[2] Of all the distresses that one went home the most to me—a pitiful pitiful story. I said that she should have had at least one year's joy of the child, and by the same philosophy we should be reconciled to the death of those who have given us joy and have had a bit of blooming. But there is no philosophizing about Death. We shut the door and he comes in at the window. There he is.

I want your days to bloom. I want our friendship to count. We must do things for each other, we must help each other, we must not *impose on each* other—we must value life and take it with meditation. I truly pray for patience and understanding. It is so hard for me to realize that when I grow dull or dim in friendship it is my fault or my stupidity. And though people call me a "poet" they have not the least notion that an imagination burnt out by too much reiteration is worse than physical sickness. People howl for me to recite Booth and the Congo till I am ready to vomit. And they threaten me if I refuse, till I am ready to swear myself crazy. I have had a hard struggle these two weeks over issues that would seem most dim in a letter. But I face it in many guises—the death of the imagination. How can I tell a faithful friend he has killed me when he has killed my imagination? or raised me from the dead when he has given me a real chance for meditation and fancy again? The whole world is in a conspiracy to sell for a high price my stalest fancies and kill off all my new ones. Yet I know I can leave this parrot world behind me if I am clever enough. I am only half through my lecture season and physically sick from too much parroting.

The quarrel with Brett was that he was trying to *compel* me to write books by clockwork. And now my reciting has become such clockwork it is nearly driving me mad. Yet not a soul in all the world believes me because I "look in good health" as they say, and stand there smiling and ruddy at the end of the show.

I am going to find a way out if I live. All old methods must go—and all old situations, all old repetitions. Write a long loud curse on all those who ask me to recite "old favorites". I tell you it is nearly killing me. I have been going through the most violent physical sickness with all this at the bottom of it through complications you could not guess. There is, however some way out, and I will find it if I live. I am not going to accuse *all* my friends of tyranny, however I am tempted to do so. I know such an accusation must be false. I am going to learn to conquer my friends by new and refreshing devices that will shake off their tyrannies. But *none* of them ask for the new poems or want them! I have been sick as a dog. The struggle left me so exhausted I caught the flu twice on top of it. In the end we become our own prisoners. But not yet! I see one or two crannies of escape from routine for a year or two! God bless you my dears. Be as happy as you can. This is a tough world!

Most faithfully,

VACHEL

Notes

1. The news sent by the Grahams was of Wilfred Ewart's death. (See note 1 to letter 118.) Edward C. Marsh, VL's friend at Macmillan's, had also died accidentally, under similar circumstances.
2. Isadora (Bennett) Reed had moved South after her wedding.

125

TO WITTER BYNNER

Gulf-Park
Gulfport, Mississippi

Feb. 1, 1923.

This letter is too long for one man to read, unless he is a very faithful friend. I suggest you ask sixteen people to a party, if you feel weak, and ask each one to read you a page in a confidential tone. But truly I want you to like the letter well, and especially.

My Dear Bynner:—
It did me a lot of good to get your note and I have let it soak in and now you have let yourself in for a long letter.

Here, at this place, I have stopped travelling, probably for a long time.[1] I had the longest fullest, "most remunerative financially" of all my Pullman expeditions just before me, from Feb. 1 to June first all over the Atlantic coast from Florida into Canada, and I have personally cancelled the whole thing by wire and by letter and all is over, and here I am more dead than alive on the Gulf—and glad to look at the ocean in semi-idiocy. I will be *glad* to hear from you here any time.

I had planned as complete a two years tour of the U.S. as Armstrong could lay out, but all the benefits were already accomplished by Christmas 1922 and then the flu and many other troubles stopped me just in time, just to leave me alive and yet make me think. I have had a perfectly enormous education in the map—the map of the U.S.—the 48 states of the Union—I *know* them infallibly, yet know them as I never expected to know anything—and for this knowledge I have certainly traded the two best years of my life and perhaps most of my brains forever!

Travelling at such speed and on such a wholesale scale I had to leave all the publicity, correspondence, etc. to Armstrong and was always weaker physically than I appeared to be, and when he had time enough to do the correspondence, well and good, but when his long string of private secretaries had it in hand—there sure was some extraordinary publicity of the trowel variety. Armstrong is a *splendid man*, with a great future, but of course when I write my own letters longhand, as I write to thee, it is *Vachel* doing it. I hope hereafter if ever I appear in public to conduct the correspondence myself, long hand. I have allowed and enjoyed a standardized tour and received in exchange a *map* of the U.S.A. I had to undertake some kind of a large campaign or beg. No one was buying my books, no one buys them yet, and I could not even beg after my father's death—leaving my lone protesting mother in the big empty house. I had the same nerve for it as ever, but she could not have stood it. When I took her to England it took my last cent, though I enjoyed it immensely.

Begging is really my natural function. I like it better than earning money and will probably try it again some day. It represents me better than lecture courses. But you ask me to report, like Grandpa speaking to grandson. Well—dear ancestor:—

First, the two books. The most important is the book of drawings issued the middle of February by Appleton's. It is by no means up to the Village Magazine Number 1, 1910, by which we continued our first acquaintance. Your approval and backing of that was one of the joys of my life. I am hoping in successive editions of the Appleton book:—"Going-to-the-Sun", slowly to improve it in the Village Magazine direction till it is a real book. All my plans for a lifetime have a kind of Village Magazine goal, and several years have been merging toward this point. But I was dead broke from my English trip. I enjoyed it, it was worthwhile. But afterward I had to save up enough money so I could sit still long enough to draw the way I wanted to draw and evolve my *real plans.*

I have very little money now. Nearly all I have made has gone right back into car-fare and hotel bills. I do not owe any man a cent. I have not á single obligation. I have about 2500 dollars in the bank. I hope now to hang on to it till I can get out a real thousand page successor to the Village Magazine in *Book form:* "Lindsay's American Common-wealth".[2] That is:— a book 1/3 prose, 1/3 verse, 1/3 United States Hieroglyphics and Literary pen-and-ink Drawings, and a thick book in the bargain. This is my natural goal, and not any kind of speaking. You will find I say as much in the Preface to Going-to-the-Sun.

The Macmillan Co., unless there is a slip, bring out my *Collected Verses* about March 1. It is about four hundred pages, a thick four dollar book everyone will review and no one will buy. It contains all my verses from the start till now, except The Mountain-Cat, which you properly condemn and which I do not take seriously. I sat still all summer trying to recover from last year's tour, but remained in a complete stupor all summer, seeing no one, for the most part walking the corridors of the Egyptian Section, Metropolitan Museum alone. But September and October I pulled myself together and compiled these two books, for the most part from old material, at the request of these two publishers, and, merely incidentally finished Mister Mountain Cat.

I am hoping you will read with some friendly care and slowness the prefaces of *both books*. I have done my best in those prefaces to destroy most of the varieties of publicity that have been recently thrust upon me by people who never read me. Those prefaces *set right* many false notions. They will act like a slow acid—slow but sure. I never cared much to be a writer. But I have cared to be a kind of a pen-and-ink designer, a pen-and-ink "adventurer", and I hope these two prefaces have done a bit toward blasting a road in that direction. At any rate your approval and good-will mean a great deal to me.

I may have to join you in Santa Fe if my lungs do not get better. But I am now taking the very tiniest kind of a teaching job here, with a very old friend from Hiram days, sleeping however as much as I can, and sitting on the beach alone endlessly. I cannot for a minute regret that I have paid in every way, body, mind and soul for this two years education in *geography*. Now it is over, I think that you will find that the prefaces of the two new books clear the air and make a path for my new start. I have a suit-case full of notes, unfinished manuscripts and travel-notes *seven years old to one week old*, not one of them written out beyond the first draft. I suppose it will be September before I have sense enough to work at one of them. I do not consider this seven years in any way recorded in my work, except in this tremendous stack of notes. There will be twenty years needed to develop them to The Chinese Nightingale standard, even supposing I ever have the brains. Do not think I suppose I have written out any of these notes, or in any way put the last seven years before the public. And I have an equal number of undeveloped schemes for pictures. Vachel is still hidden! Not that he is worth exposing, at that! My friends have delusions.

Dear boy, I have *never* called myself a poet. You are the poet. Frost is the poet. Sandburg is the Poet. Masefield is the poet. I only see myself as an *adventuring artist, an Egyptian scribe,* my books are the books of a pen-and-ink draughtsman, a maker or planner of Hieroglyphics, a suppressed Thomas Nast,[3] etc. I am the worst egotist alive, but for my *adventures, not* my songs. It is my adventures that I love. More and more what my friends in publicity channels say about me is what I am *assumed* to be saying about myself. Do not believe them. The whole thing totals into a queer monster, however well meant the individual ad. Remember me by Village Magazine Number One!

December 1922, I began to realize however that the mere daily work of trying to correct the chunks and chunks of brash publicity hurled at me in each town had forced me to build up in opposition an even more painful monster. Because they painted me red, I was, by contraries, turning vivid green-in-the-face. And, as a side line, in spite of everything, starting side-lines of solemn publicity designed as back-fire to destroy the alleged jazz artist, but in the end as bad a job as trying to corner the wheat market—with the best of motives:—desiring money to build churches! Neither wheat nor publicity can be cornered, and the minute a man begins to think he has cornered and harnessed his own publicity he is as big a fool as the man who thinks he has cornered wheat. When, with too much pains [*sic*], he puts accurate photographs of himself on the door, silly cartoons of him come down the chimney and through the windows. And he begins to think his one task in the world is to discipline these cartoons and bring them into subjection. I am just enough politically-minded to enjoy (as a holiday only) "running for poetic senator", and the recital platform is as much fun as base-ball, when I am in *perfect health.* But I have just reached the place where the senator imagines some one *reads* his speeches in the congressional record. The fun has become a tiny tragedy. You are just right. My whole scheme was to end in June anyway. I knew I courted disaster near the goal. I figured it would take two years really to learn the U.S. and Canada from the Pullman Car window. But now I see it is just as well I stopped before I was completely publicity-poisoned. It will take months to get it out of my blood as it is. It is a nervous habit that has nothing to do with the mind—yet obstructs it. Even small boys can be chess-champions, and the platform-publicity game is too much like chess. If ever I take to the platform again—it will be to read the *Anthologies*—not *my own* work. I am going to read to a tiny class here from the *New Anthologies* for at least a month. Send me anything new and suggest anything new you want me to read to them. I am getting close to a conscious imitation of your Halcyon Club at the University of California, but on a very tiny scale—and what you did for the young poets there—I may try on this white beach. I am starting very slowly and timidly. I am so grateful and fearful over the chance I could cry with gratitude. It is a tiny class of seniors in a junior college. That is:—Sophomores in a four-year-college. There are preeminently two reasons this is the ideal spot. The president and his wife are very very old Hiram friends. My Hiram ties are very close. Both my sisters married Hiram men—and one is still there every Sunday.[4] The other reason is: here is the sea!

Please tell every old and dearest friend to write to me here, and to state every complaint of me, and to give pages of shrewd advice as to the future of Poetry in America and how to snatch the news-stand from the clutches of George Horace Lorimer and take it from him and give it to Homer, Milton and Thomas Jefferson without ourselves getting just vulgar. Certainly you will approve of the Macmillan Book. It is all my old poems you liked, in one volume, with about twenty weak ones thrown out, and a preface and table-of-contents that ties all together and relates them to the prose books.

"*Going-to-the-Sun*" just issued by Appletons is my reply—not to Graham's book, but my drawings in reply to the *Drawings* in his book. Those drawings in his book are all his pet ideas, though Vernon Hill drew them. So my book is, in its way, a reply to the visual part of Graham's mind, though it is highly impersonal. I simply put a picture of Going-to-the-Sun Mountain in the back of many out-door fairy-designs, etc. some of which date from many years back. Like one-hundred-views of Fujiyama, as one may say, to make a far off comparison. The drawings have been accumulated through several years, and repeatedly re-sorted. Nothing hasty. Also I kid Graham gently about drinking coffee in the U.S. and tea in Canada. It is just a sketch of a book. I hope it has such a run I can put in a lot more drawings in the second edition and correct the proof, etc. Both of these books have been proof-read by the publishers while I was far far away. I hope slowly to ripen them through several editions.

Please do not think of me as *orating* these three or these seven years. Think of me as looking out the Pullman window and planning a poem called "The Pullman Car". I have acres of notes on it. And a big thick hieroglyphical parody on Bryce[5] with multitudinous pictures: "Lindsay's American Commonwealth". I have been thinking, thinking, about the United States. I dearly love the United States. I have given my heart to thousands and thousands of beautiful people, and I have certainly parted with many a town where I wanted to kiss them all good-by they were so good to me and parting was so hard. But in the end such tears wash body and soul and brain to nothingness—like loving the sea too long. But now I turn to the actual sea for strength and God help me to win it there. I have loved so many noble faces and roaring whispering beautiful crowds I can love no more. I must sleep a thousand days. And then do "Lindsay's American Commonwealth". The trouble is:—all I now have to write down or draw is beyond me. It is the Santa Fe trail on a scale and with a music beyond human strength to put into words or Hieroglyphics. This record in this letter may be as near to a record as I can ever get to what the Pullman car meant, or "The American Commonwealth" meant. Some very bitter experiences I have not told you of, finally started me on this last two years tour. I saw the only possible way to *defeat several terrible alternatives,* real and spiritual, was to travel by the wholesale, on a grand scale and to the very limit of my strength. My instructions to Armstrong were:—*to send me into every state in the Union and into Every English Department in Every University and to avoid the Womans Clubs like death, and to send me as far as possible into the West and South and Canada where no other lecturers go very much and to give me as complete a geographical education as possible and never to worry about getting me on a straight railroad line or making money for me.* He was the only person who ever had sent me south of the Ohio or West of the

Mississippi. And believe me he followed instructions. As long as my strength held out he was the ideal *driver*. He turned out completely standardized little Vachels every day like Ford Cars—a new well-varnished, guaranteed, noisy, cast-iron Little Vachel in every town for a year and a half, like a whirlwind. And I dimly remember now I expected him to drive me till I broke. That was my intention. I wanted to break like a wave on the Rock of the United States—and the scheme to be on the largest possible travelling scale I could meet. I must not censure my trainer now—for *I* trained him, remember that, and he followed my main lines of instruction absolutely—only at the last he imagined me a man of iron, a Ford car indeed!. It was pretty hard to convince him I had at last caved in. I had to give Armstrong his way in a thousand minor matters I hated. Please take up the cudgels for Armstrong just the same, and do it with all your best chivalry! If you hear anybody swat the tour he gave me, or swat him, it was *my scheme*. I know how crude a lot of it looked. It was no better and no worse than the Pullman's I rode in. But Armstrong was and is a very faithful friend and believe me dear Hal—I not only looked out the windows of the Pullman but the windows of the *tour*, and the world told me many fine things—though in my weariness I did many crude ones, and Armstrong in haste and weariness often blundered. But he never lost the main scheme. The song about it is yet to be sung. I would like to retrace it now all slowly, afoot, my own manager, begging my way. It will take 1000 years of traveling afoot, at a reasonable, meditative pace. You may not know that my father and mother are dead—the Springfield house is in the hands of strangers,[6] all my old friends have moved from the town—and the only close kin I have in the U.S. is one sister in Cleveland. The other sister you met in China.[7] I am almost a waif on this beach, with at last 2500 dollars in the bank—and if ever well and rested—the lonely world indeed before me for my meditations and explorations. But I am wondering if I will ever be well and rested again?

I only wish I could have carried my twin in my pocket on this adventure of speaking and could have told him how it looked and he could have written it down. It would however have required the pen of Henry James and George Meredith and Samuel Butler and William Allen White and Dickens and Witter Bynner. A versatile pen! America is indeed a weltering grand panorama.

> Well—good-by—and good luck.
> And with my love.
>
> VACHEL

This address gets me till further notice. Tell everybody to write to me here, and to scold me, and forgive me everything. I am sick and need their love, and *advice, shrewd advice.*

Notes

1. It is estimated that by canceling the rest of his tour from Gulfport, VL forfeited more than $4,000 dollars in potential earnings.
2. The closest VL came to his projected "American Commonwealth" was *The Litany of Washington Street* (Macmillan, 1929). But the drawings were mostly divided from then on between *Going-to-the-Stars* and *The Candle in the Cabin* (both Appleton, 1926).
3. Thomas Nast (1840—1902), the political cartoonist, contributed to *Harper's* and other publications. His cartoons brought him fame during the Civil War, and he invented the donkey and elephant symbols of the two major American political parties.
4. Paul Wakefield was the brother-in-law who visited VL in Gulfport. A doctor, he convinced VL to undergo tests and to be examined at the Mayo Clinic.
5. James Bryce (1838–1922), British Ambassador to the United States, published *The American Commonwealth,* which dealt with the U.S. Constitution, in 1892.
6. VL's Springfield residence had been rented to a club, which led to a number of legal disputes in the following year. VL eventually got the house back and moved into it with his family in 1927.
7. Bynner traveled extensively in China after 1918. He had met Olive and Paul Wakefield at their mission.

126

TO CHRISTOPHER MORLEY

Gulfport, Mississippi
Feb. 5. 1923

My Dear Christopher:[1]
I am here making a long slow recovery—if I come back as slowly as I went down. So much for your private information.

I hear of all sort of letters going wild I would now be exceedingly glad to receive. So without saying I am sick indicate in your paper—if you care to do so—I am sitting here on this beach till June 1 and would be most rejoiced to hear from any of my friends. Their letters would be medicine now—though I cannot promise to answer any of them. I wish you would get a complete clean final proof of "Litany of Heroes" and run it—with my compliments, in your column—in sections or in one installment—if you have the room. If you detect any howling errors in the last page proof—please phone H. S. Latham—the Macmillan Co at once. They are supposed to be reading and correcting that proof in the Macmillan office without my help. I will accept any corrections you care to make. Do not consult me. I am writing to Latham this morning—to cooperate, and that I have given you the poem full and free. The Litany of Heroes—is made up of many old stanzas—but in an order which makes them a new poem—and THE new poem—of the Collected Works of Vachel Lindsay—out—presumably March 1. The Poem starts luckily with Amenophis IV, (Akenaton) the famous father-in-Law of Tutankamon: Every day Tutankamon becomes more famous[2]—by cablegram from Egypt—and the only explanation of his *real* final fame and significance is this Akenaton with whom my poem happily opens. (Read Breadstead's[3]History of Egypt—Scribner's, for the best material). At the end of a list of 24 characters of History—each set in abrupt and challenging contrast to his predecessor—the poem LITANY OF HEROES closes with Socrates and Woodrow Wilson as the heroes of the series, and the two men who point to the future, and repeating the note of Amenophis IV (Akenaton) with which the song began. Socrates is the only man out of chronological order. Wilson and The League of Nations are the final thoughts in the Reader's mind, both of them thoughts of the future—and in a way the solution of the 24 porcupine contradictions of these 24 porcupine historic characters who seemed otherwise to have no unity at all. It is my outline of history, much clearer and briefer than Wells or Van Loon![4] I further suggest that the day before you begin to run the poem—you print a paraphrase of this letter, leaving out the personal part—and tie it up with the morning's news from Egypt and the exact stage of the Unwrapping of Tutankamon. There will be every chance to tie him up with his father-in-law who begins my song (Read Breadstead— Chapter XVIII—Pages 355—378—The Religious Revolution of Ikhnaton—for the most precise material). I will accept *any change you wish to make in the song* in your version in the Post, or any cutting you deem necessary for Post Publication though I hope you can print most of it—for if you try reading it aloud at a sitting you will find it is cumulative in its effect and all the characters count (as for the Book-Version—please telephone Latham any emergency, corrections—commas, spelling—or—pi) If there is anything in polishing a poem—this one should be good. It was practically this size, length and style in 1907 (or thereabouts) when I traded it for bread in New Jersey, Pennsylvania and Ohio (see King Coal—etc—Shickshinny etc, in a Handy Guide for Beggars). But the very logic of the latest Egyptology on the one hand and the latest news of the League of Nations on the other put now for the first time on record in the song, have served to ripen it and the oldest and the newest statesmen of History have helped me to make it more logical. It is as though Wells should add a 1923 Chapter at the beginning and end of his Outline of History. This song is entirely in your custody and is given fully and freely to your column with my love and blessing in acknowledgement of the deep love we have had for one another and good days in the past—no matter what the uncertain future. But if you cannot use it—I will not weep.

My good wishes to Helen and the children.

Most fraternally and lovingly.

VACHEL

Notes

1. Christopher Morley was then still working for the *New York Evening Post*. He was not associated with the *Saturday Review of Literature* until 1924.
2. Tutenkhamon's tomb had been discovered in December 1922 by Howard Carter.
3. James H. Breasted (1865-1935), the famed Egyptologist, termed the search for all existing remains of Oriental civilizations a "New Crusade." His *Development of Religion and Thought in Ancient Egypt* was published in 1912, and in 1919 he became director of the New Oriental Institute at the University of Chicago.
4. H. G. Wells's *Outline of History* came out in 1920; Hendrik Willem Van Loon (1882—1944), the Dutch-American historian, wrote *A Golden Book of the Dutch Navigators* in 1916 and *The Story of Mankind* in 1921. In 1922—23 he was professor at Antioch College, where he had founded the history department.

127

TO HARRIET MONROE

Gulf-Park
Gulfport Mississippi
February 17, 1923

My Dearest Harriet:—
I went clear to pieces and had to stop travelling for a year, and by good luck landed into the midst of this place amid old Hiram College Friends. Two of my sisters married Hiram men—as you remember, and my Hiram ties are strong, and as one may say—domestic.

Well here I am, and likely to flood you with manuscripts soon. You may have first choice on all I fix up. I have a suit-case full. Now hold me to it. By far the best thing I could do would be to write for your board of censorship for six months. I have from three to seven years of absolutely untouched notes in my suit-case, an ideal place to write, and lots of delightful leisure and isolation in the President's quarters.

These bathing pictures look grand and diverting, but it will be two months before the water is warm enough to bathe in.

I have one tiny forty-minute class, but the day is really my own. The class is all about The Ways of United States Poetry.

Now my dear and best Harriet, let us to the fray once more. If I could get my heart and mind just where they were when I first wrote for thee—about 1913, I could supply thee with epics. But I assure you I need your strong hand, and earnest expectation. I have endless and amazing notes and experiences, but to write them into form is another matter. Please let me know that *much* is expected, and lay on the whip. I have become such a glittering generality—I am like an old box of last year's Christmas Tree Baubles. I would give anything to establish the old relation, the concentration and intellectual and personal devotion we had, when adventure in the Poetry Magazine was supreme adventure for me, and I first came from Springfield, to thee. I knew I would reach this place in the cycle again—I am through travelling for a long long time. I love thee and thy enterprise as much as ever in all my life. And I am as poisonous an egotist as ever, the same old Vachel. But the concentration—the concentration! That is the point! How to get one's mind down like a burning-glass on one tiny spot in the paper—as of old! Thee must do thy half—by reminding me early and often that you wait with the whip and the kind heart. I would like to hold the field with you till I have gone straight through the present batch of manu-script—and written myself out. I set from now till June 1 as a writing spell—a definite dash toward the old goal—and to a new one just be-yond—March-April-and May set aside for hard concentrated writing. Please put me on your list for a weekly post card at least—saying "Here waits the whip and the heart", or something like that.

Your small prodigal—has—I hope returned, and wants every bit of cake on the shelf, and offers every husk (mss) in return.

Most affectionately

VACHEL

128

TO W. R. BROWNE

Gulfport, Mississippi
Feb. 25, 1923

Mr. W. R. Browne
Wyoming, New York:—

My Dear Friend:—
I greatly appreciate your letter. I am sorry to say I was only sixteen years old when Altgeld was in his prime. You have my full permission to use The Eagle Forgotten. It is in *"General William Booth Enters Into Heaven"* and published by The Macmillan Co, 64 Fifth Avenue, New York City. Another poem I give you permission to quote entire or in part with your own comment is *Bryan, Bryan, Bryan, Bryan,* in "The Golden Whales of California" volume published also by the Macmillan Co. This is also a commentary on the Altgeld spirit, and is more famous in England than America. You will find it quite elaborately sponsored by an English Writer Edward Shanks in the Bookman for October or November 1922—in an article on British and American Poetry or something like that. The article is principally about your humble servant.

The Bryan—Bryan—Bryan—Bryan appeared in The New York Sun of all papers several years ago, after they had begged me repeatedly for a poem—"anything by me".

It is full of the Altgeld phase of Bryan in 1896 and mentions him three times.

"It was 1896—and I was just sixteen
And Altgeld ruled in Springfield Illinois—etc"
"When Bryan came to Springfield and Altgeld gave him greeting!"
　etc
"Where is Altgeld—brave as the truth
Whose name the few still say with tears?
Gone to join the shadows with old John Brown
Whose name rings loud for a thousand years)" etc
and
"Where is that Boy—that Heaven-born Bryan
That Homer Bryan—who sang from the West?
Gone to join the shadows with Altgeld the Eagle
Where the kings and the slaves and the troubadours rest." etc

This poem has been sponsored by the critical thunderer of England, The London Mercury. It has had all kinds of literary holy water sprinkled over it. I have not only recited it in nearly all the English Departments of nearly all the Universities of the USA but to picked audiences of the Poets of Oxford Cambridge and London England. So dear friend—if you think I have been remiss in my contributions to the hero of my youth—it merely means that like most people—you have been following your affairs and I have been following mine.

I humble apologize for not answering your letters. I have almost out-travelled and out-shouted Bryan in the last seven years and have not answered any man's letters, and I have no doubt you add I am no shrinking violet. Modesty I admit has always been very difficult for me, and I should be running for senator. Well—we will let that pass. As to implying that Bryan is dead—at the end of the *long* poem about him—I merely mean that he was the cry of youth at 35—and did it splendidly. He probably burnt up the brains and fine edge of a life time in that enormous 1896 Campaign—August through November. It has been the fashion of the High-brows to cry him down but I have fought with them to give to him and to Altgeld a second thought in this poem.

I advise you to write to two people:
(1) William Lyon Phelps—professor of English, Yale University, New Haven Massachussets [sic].

He also has read the Bryan Bryan Bryan Bryan poem all over the country and can tell you the name and memory of Altgeld are now received as he reads that poem.
(2) Edgar Lee Masters—who was the successor of Altgeld, I think, in the firm of Darrow[1] and Altgeld, and whose Spoon River Anthology, the greatest poem in English by a living writer, is full of allusions to Altgeld—as the John the Baptist of his time.

From the time I was 12 to 16 I saw the Governor in passing nearly every day since the Lindsay Residence, where I was born is on a hill looking down on the Roof of the Governor's Mansion. Finally—I think the power of Altgeld was in his courageous interviews. No one in American letters or politics ever used such relentless precision in expression in this generation but the young H. L. Mencken—who is generously appraised in The Century Magazine for March, 1923, by Carl Van Doren.[2]

Altgeld was less fortunate than Mencken in that he gave out newspaper interviews instead of magazine editorials—but day after day he spoke with the same relentless precision and courage that Mencken uses in magazines.

But there the comparison ends. Mencken holds to letters and manners. Altgeld was in politics altogether. Altgeld was, thick-and-thin, *in* the democratic party—and was the first and only man of his generation to give out relentless truth from so high and fixed a pinnacle as the governor's chair—day after day, year after year. They could not Lynch Altgeld because he was governor. They cannot Lynch Mencken because he is an established editor.

Altgeld had a pleasant heart—and kept tight to the Jeffersonian and Jacksonian tradition which Mencken—a much smaller man affects to despise.

People keep asking "If Altgeld was such a hero—why do "they say" this and that and the other thing about him?

The answer is always the same "His relentless interviews", again and then again—his relentless interviews. The worms had to answer back, in their poor fashion. But they could never "get" him. He went on, speaking his mind till he died—the bravest man of his time.

He is the *unbribable Governor* in Theodore Dreiser's *The Titan*.

Brand Whitlock,[3] who was an appointee of Altgeld's in the Springfield State House, gives a vivid tribute to him in *"Forty Years of It"*.

With good wishes

Nicholas Vachel Lindsay

Reproduce any of this letter that is useful—except the egotistical part—and please correct bad grammar, etc . . .

Notes

1. Clarence Darrow (1857—1938) was the lawyer who defended Eugene V. Debs, William Haywood, and Leopold and Loeb, and who eventually defeated William Jennings Bryan in the Scopes trial.
2. Carl Van Doren (1885—1950) was literary editor of *The Nation* 1919—22.
3. Brand Whitlock's autobiography, *Forty Years of It,* was published in 1914.

129

TO HENRY SEIDEL CANBY

Gulfport, Mississippi
March 9, 1923

Dr. Henry S. Canby
The New York Evening Post

My Dear Canby:—

I was certainly very proud of your letter and your congratulations, and the thirty dollar fee is all right. Send it on any time.

I was indeed proud to appear in the review with such friendly consideration, and with so much space allowed for a song. The exceedingly staunch way the review has stood by me at all times and seasons has been as near to a literary thrill as I have known, and I am not susceptible to "literary" thrill. You make no mistake in writing me down an Egyptian. If you go through my eight books in eight minutes sometime, you will find material on nearly every page to prove it. It will be lots easier to prove than that I am a jazz artist, a thing some people are *even malevolently determined* to prove. If Egypt is nothing else, it is my sure weapon against them. Please use it some day. My movie book, for instance, written in 1914 is jam full of Egyptian Hieroglyphic philosophy, on which I have now vastly improved, see edition of 1922, opening pages.

But of course the final argument against the Jazz idea of my goal, is completed by this very Litany of Heroes, which you have been good enough to publish. The fact that I have been at work on this litany since 1906 and 7, and the scattered stanzas are in my earliest books, is the final and crushing evidence that Jazz is *not* the goal of my life, *nor the usual mood of my mind.* There is not one Jazz line in this poem, and it is the best piece of work I have ever produced. It represents the very backbone of my thought for years, and in the light of it every book I have ever written could be re-read, and even rewritten with more clarity. I doubt if I will ever write so sustained a piece of work again, so well representing me. So I am a million times thankful that you have done so much to make it clear to my friends. I have toured the U.S.A. at least seven years, and the last three years constantly. The last two years could well be called a national tour of the Universities. And everywhere people expected me to throw a Jazz fit, through either malevolence of newspapers, or, far more often, convenience in advertising, and all the ideals I have, plainly embodied in this Litany of Heroes, I did my best to fight for *in every single town.* Why should the Universities send for me again and again, if I am a "jazz artist"?

Here I am, half dead, and still getting newspaper clippings about Lindsay the Jazz poet, (whose alleged masterpieces are certain Jazz pieces I wrote in irony). I have quit travelling forever, and if the serious ideals represented by the *Litany of Heroes* are ever put before the world, it will depend upon such generous championship as has always been yours.

No doubt—with the best intentions, and real loyalty, the Century Magazine has announced for April an article by Carl Van Doren,[1] obviously to coordinate with the coming out of my collected works., "*Vachel Lindsay, Jazz Evangelist*". And yet the Century not more than two years ago published as my alleged Masterpiece "*Johnny Appleseed*", a long long poem which had *not one line of Jazz in it.* It was rewritten fifty times and intended to be as serious as the Judgment Day. The New York Times in a very recent review comes out with words about my being a buffoon with redeeming traits and a sense of beauty. Please tell me why I should be the world's fool? I have broken myself in this fight and here I sit in the hands of the doctors, still alleged to be "The Jazz artist" and I hate Jazz like poison. *It reeks of the dirty dance, and the hysteria that is the utter destruction of American life.*

If you can get an advance copy of that Century Article and forge a thunderbolt against it or get any one else to do so, you will do me the utmost service.[2] This letter is of course for Benét and Morley, if they have time to read it, and hearts to devote to the affairs of a supreme egotist.

When my mother and I landed in England August 1920—for a two months visit to the poets, I found that George Bell and Company, while I was on the water, had issued a volume of poems called without my consent "*The Daniel Jazz and other Poems*". It was a most unrepresentative book, did not even contain such verses as are in the Litany of Heroes, and was diabolically constructed to produce the opposite effect. *The Daniel Jazz,* an after-dinner squib was advertised all over England as my masterpiece, and I was cartooned as turning handsprings, and described as whistling and snapping my fingers while I recited. The only thing quoted in the English Newspapers was the roar of the lions in the Daniel Jazz, which had as much and as little to do with my work as the Yale Yell has to do with the *Yale Press*, or the *Yale Review.*

I had given George Bell and Company permission to make their own selection of my work, and the title of the work was to be "Selected Poems". That phrase was *in the contract.* Now British People constantly write to my American Friends about *"Your Jazz Poet" and How Clever he is, etc. I consider "cleverness" a crime.*

Please my dear friend, how would you like to be known as the Jazz Professor, your books as Jazz Books, and your review as the Jazz review? How would you like it to be expected to throw a fit every time you entered a parlor or stepped on a platform? How would you like this advertisement to be your sole source of income, and some of your friendliest friends cheering you on with their tongues in their cheeks? I think it is time my friends took up the cudgels for me. Believe me I do not want to die the world's fool. I can be reconciled to that if I must be, but why not fight it out? I have two or three dam good fights left in me yet.

I insist that the bulk of my eight volumes, and the collected works now forthcoming, and the *Going-to-the-Sun* are *serious works,* however dull. If you can get a galley proof of my collected poems, and are reconciled to the ordeal, you will find that the table of contents and preface are so ordered that they are completely and fundamentally in accord with *The Litany of Heroes,* and the whole Collected Poems might be used as a running comment on that Litany.

I have thrown out about fifty newspaper squibs from the Collected Works, and I intend further to revise it, if there are successive editions, and revise toward the general standard and ideals of the Litany of Heroes. I have not begun to fight. Also, sooner or later, I want to bring out an illustrated and especially designed edition of the *Collected Poems,* though with much more dignified and careful drawings than are in *Going-to-the-Sun.* Those drawings were produced under almost impossible conditions, and I can do much better, and hope to do so soon. I hope there will be a second enlarged and improved edition of Going-to-the-Sun more pictures, etc.

This letterhead is my address till June 1, 1924. Please announce it to my friends. My letters are all running wild, I have travelled so much.

You know the arrangements made for Robert Frost in Ann Arbor the last two years.[3] I will be here till June 1, 1924 under almost the same arrangements. I will conduct one special class, selected from the forty highest in a stiff examination. After that examination there will be freedom, I hope, for my scholars. They will write and study as they please. I will try to teach them something about Versification, and the American and British Poets now living. So please tell all the brainy *young* women—note the word young—in the United States to come here and try their luck on that terrible entrance examination. They must also be of school age. No woman's club presidents need apply. I want to run my own class.

Pardon my verbosity. I intended a note, but became all lit up with damnable egotism. Whatever happens, the sun still shines, and every girl in this school has promised to teach me to swim next month when I get out of the doctor's care. I am going to learn as slowly as possible, one girl at a time. Anything a man learns too quickly he forgets. So if you do not feel inspired to swat my traducers, I will forgive you and them, and go swimming. "Hail hail, the gangs all here!".

With good wishes indeed,

NICHOLAS VACHEL LINDSAY

Notes

1. Carl Van Doren's article, the exact title of which was "Salvation with Jazz: Vachel Lindsay, Evangelist in Verse," came out in the April 1923 issue of *Century Magazine* (pp. 951—56).
2. Although Canby did not follow VL's advice to "forge a thunderbolt against it," he eventually did write several pieces on VL's work. The *Saturday Review Literature* article (January 9, 1932) that followed VL's death was by Canby, and his *Seven Years' Harvest* (1936) contains another (pp. 47—49).
3. Robert Frost had successively been appointed "poet in residence" at Amherst and at the University of Michigan (Ann Arbor).

130

TO HARRIET MONROE

Gulf-Park
Gulfport, Mississippi

March 28, 1923

My Dear Harriet Monroe:—
Believe me your letter did me worlds of good. I have the first draft of all sorts of long poems and elaborate drawings, I am seven years behind on my diary note-books, I have a suit-case full of papers of first drafts of poems. People cannot understand I have been speaking these seven years, not writing. They seem to think I can do both, and those who hate "Americanism" rejoice exceedingly and say I have written myself out, while I have spoken in every University in the United States and all those in West Canada. Most of the principal American Universities

have recalled me two to four times. Doing all this, besides appearing at Oxford, Cambridge and the University of London, England, those who wish me ill anyway say I am "written out". Of course my programmes are made up principally of things written from seven to ten years ago, for it was seven to ten years ago when this touring began, and gradually increased in momentum almost in spite of me. I have spoken in every state in the Union and for the English Department of practically every college in the World-Almanac. Having done this, people who have not been on a college campus for years say I have disappeared, say I am written out. I have recited for hundreds of High School Assemblies and so far as I know, made friends with them all. They are nearly all two thousand strong and as hard to control as Texas cattle. Having done all this, I am "written out", etc, in the eyes of those who make it a business to despise all High Schools and condemn as abominations all our Universities. Well I have met Young America and am willing to meet the depreciation of my enemies with this boast. It is enough to condemn me in the eyes of some fanatical exponents of Balkan and Eastern European ideals, that I love the United States at all. Yet I have the great Advantage of them in that I have *met* the United States and they have *not*. I have been on every University Campus and they are still inhabiting in imagination some small Balkan State and hating and slandering us all like poison when we admit we love our own. I have met and addressed hundreds of thousands of dazzlingly beautiful boys and girls, from fourteen to twenty two years old, in the last seven years, and I am not ashamed to say the experience was profoundly intoxicating, they roared like a sea in Heaven every time I addressed them, and to look all Young America in the face is to have one's heart won by them forever. The Balkan minded creatures who hate me so, could not resist it, if they had had this experience. They do not believe any such experience awaits any human being or that it is worth the sacrifice of one sonnet to have such an experience.

I have gone almost exclusively to the colleges and High Schools. Everywhere there was beauty and glory and the blazing heart of young America. Everywhere there was love and kindness, and not one word of poison insinuation, of literary spite or silly rivalry, or technical chatter, or social snobbery, or cheap race-hates. They were all young! Now that I come to land, after crossing this great sea, I am supposed to give an account of myself. I find all sorts of spite among the beach-combers. They demand I stand and give an account of myself. Well here is the account. Let them make the most of it. I am in fighting trim. Let them look to themselves.

VACHEL LINDSAY

You may print the above, in whole or in part—if you care to do so.

131

TO ELIZABETH MANN WILLS

Gulfport, Mississippi
June 9, 1923.

My Dear Elizabeth:[1]

Day before yesterday, my first letter from you arrived—the first letter from you to me in the whole history of the world. Believe me it made me happy. And what is more, if lifted me from desolation, instantly. Joy had snubbed me for a week and Olive had not written since landing in America. And two letters came from them, and the news from all three sisters were so good, I felt domesticated again and no longer a lost sheep. Please my dear Elizabeth, *keep writing,* and please take my poor lonely mind for your steady responsibility! I am *so* glad Griffin has bobbed her hair. I hope Pat bobs hers even shorter.[2] That is to say—I want them both to get over their despicable bashfulness which has been so obdurate! I think it is to my credit that I want to know those girls better for *your sake.* Certainly I have told them so plainly. I have not squirmed about it! It is to a man's honor that he aspires to please such a mind as yours, and you tell all the guardians of the gate *just that*; of course, in ladylike language. I call on Pat Bufkin Monday evening.

Not until you have taken a national reciting tour with me, can you understand my *intellectual* dependence upon your mind and character. Especially since 1919, from South Texas to Saskatchewan—and Oxford England to San Francisco it has been a path of fire for me—and the fire of the human faces was still burning in beauty before me when I came to Gulf Park—and I was *near dead* from a burnt imagination more than a burnt out body, but still blazing. I *know* this is what people love in me, even those that think themselves intimate. But it is all public, public, public. You are to me the incarnation of all things equally good and infinitely opposite. You are virgin modesty and quietness, and meditation and individual conversation, and the village mood I have always worshipped and have always declared was the quiet pool in the heart of America. I *must in some sense* take you with me every step of the way henceforth. Please let me say once, clearly, that you are the essential discipline of my mind and body and blood and heart. You are the most *beautiful* human creature I know body mind and soul. And you are certainly my only hope to be loyal to my best self. All the next steps up are impossible without you. It is the first time in my life I was ever able to say to a woman—as I hope to say to your mother: "I can take care of your daughter". If I seem a belated beau, remember this. I have not done much courting in my life, except such as is in plain evidence in the books. Every story there is clear and clean and open. And in all cases anxious Mamas have snatched their daughters away from the fearful author of *"The Handy Guide for Beggars"* and married them instantly to other men. Get all the fun out of that there is in it! Now I realize, looking at the *Handy Guide for Beggars,* this morning—that I am further from that book than I have ever been in my life—that my whole life must be worked from the other end. I am no longer the town fool whistling to keep up his courage and defy Babbitt and Main Street. Quite the contrary I am almost wrecked by public good-will. By September and October when the reviews of the Collected Poems come roaring in I will be more demoralized than ever. Above all I need *"a Handy Guide to Privacy"*, to serenity, to meditation, to delicacy of fancy, to village quietness, to secret prayer—to untouched girl beauty, and the innocence of your glorious young mind. My manager Armstrong is determined to national-tour me again—Bryanize me if possible. My two publishers back the idea—and I am sure of flattery and fried chicken in every town, while slowly disintegrating for lack of your care. I tell you dear dear Elizabeth, *I need your help.* If you think this is just a movie-courtship—with no conversation, with a movie-poet to manage, get over it. If you can take me a little seriously you are called to as *definite a job* with as *clean cut provisions* as your last two years in Gulf Park, and you could cut it up into days and hours with text-books the same way. My *particular United States* has been delivered to me, and I have not the strength to receive it alone, the sense to understand it, the heart left to love it, alone. I could be almost the person the more sober advertisements say I am—if I could carry your private heart by my side. But *dear dear* if you have any heart or conscience about being my "best friend", take it as a serious, systematic task, outlined in your way, absolutely, but a task for the mind as well as the heart. Truly it is a job for a lawyer and a *stateswoman.* When you said you might *study* law I was so jealous and hurt I could hardly speak. There is only one person who has ever given my ten books a critical appraisal, *has read them through.* That is Prof. Albert Edmund Trombly, who is writing my biography.[3] I beg you, Elizabeth this instant for your heart, *and* for all that *young mind* you might waste for two or three years before your marriage on law and journalism. I want you to bring all your shrewdness, and much-praised clear-headedness to bear on discovering that *unknown person,* that career of the future, that *unrevealed mind,* that is under my ten books. I have not read my books. I am incapable of reading them shrewdly—I do not know what they say. I only know the praise of the critics is as irritating as their blame when I want *real* guidance. The little snatches of conversation I have had in Gulf Park with you seemed to have more understanding of my loneliness and my aspiration—than all my backers to the London Spectator, and in the midst of it all you were harassed and panic-stricken by the publicity of it—and I felt doomed like the reed that the Great God Pan made into a flute in Mrs. Browning's Poem—nevermore to be a reed with the reeds of the river. The very publicity that made you run so, in Gulf Park, you must understand, is the main poison of *my* life wherever I am—you were exactly right to hide and to run—I only wish we could have found a *mutual hiding place.* I am absolutely determined to find it. Until I have found a way to correspond with and converse with this girl, beautifully shy as you are, on the terms and in the privacy she desires, my life is an utter failure. I *must* learn to please you. You must *teach me* to please you, one gentle little lesson at a time. Do not let people force us into a movie-friendship or movie-love. No movie ever contains long sober gentle conversations. People either marry in an hour or say good-by irrevocably and instantly in the movies and that without any more conversation than two six year old kids. If you knew how *dependent* my *mind* was on your *mind*! But you cannot for a moment conceive it. You do not know your rarity. From seven years back—right here in this room I have oceans of note-books and grips full of papers. I am too indifferent to read. There is not *one mind* in the whole world, reasonably congenial, devoted and able and willing to go through these notes with me, until they take on flame. I have had incredible adventures especially the last four years—but not one patient listener to whom I can tell them to the end, till I find life and song in them—or willing to take new adventures with me and keep them alive and real for me, and keep out the shoddy circus stuff that is imputed to me. I do not want you to study journalism, as long as these undigested journals and incredible experiences are not put in order. I do not necessarily want you for any task not natural to you. But I do not want you to waste on any editor on Earth you do not love the brains you might give to your "best friend". Even if you do your best for the editor—there is nothing so dead as yesterday's newspaper. If I can ever get my books *written*, they *live on*. All the publishers are dinging at me for books, and all the magazines for articles: Here is a very lousy man you might help toward journalism of a permanent sort. I do not want you to study law. I want every bit of your legal brain to determine the *sharp edges* of the ideas with which I must deal constantly. You know they accuse me of being a Bryan—a cloudy hectic "mob-genius" with no edges at all. If this is so, I need your legal brain to find these edges and these distinctions. If I am not clear, clarify me! *If I cannot plan, plan for me. Meet the Anglo-Saxon world of letters and understand it for me. I would like to produce ten books* in your consequent mood, and—perhaps—afterwards—take you on the Pullman Cars with me—or at the end of every book. At any rate so clarify my hectic life with your serenity and girl-secrecy I can go on. They are ruining me—I tell you—with the cakes and praises and confusions, that destroy them also. Dear Lawyer and Journalist Elizabeth—I have at *best* a certain *exactness of vision* and *precision of mind*, and a power of *over-concentration*, at short dashes, that almost wrecks me, and leaves me in awful need, for the rest of the day—for a clear and sharp and steady and serene mind like yours. It takes a great deal of prayer and aspiration to see to it that that concentrated moment of fire represents the *next step up*. I took the two rose-buds you left for a month in the back of your letter-box this morning—since the Y.M.C.A. was coming. I thought it might be impudent to mail them to you so I took them to the chapel and put them on the Virgin's altar and I prayed as never before in all my life—that I might be true to your virgin *mind and heart*. The Virgin is *not* the refuge the Catholics say—but those little roses have burned my eyes every time I looked into the box and I had to do something in your praise that you might find acceptable. You will not know me dear lady till you know every vow I have taken before that virgin image. It is your heart I see upon the altar, and the virgin made by Catholic hands is only a symbol and a sonnet. I have lived *so* much alone, child, incredibly alone—in endless strange towns—and I had many times in the years back to renew my monastic pledges—and this church is the only one I could find open, and I carried my own mother's religion with me. You will not know me till you know I *have* to say my prayers on my knees, and must kneel to you when I kiss your hand. The next step up is to reach the foot of your throne, and the best thought of your mind. You will not be altogether Elizabeth till you understand you should stand very haughtily and consider my petition like a proud little lawyer, and not shy like a colt as you did that night coming in from our one grand and only swim! You can grant your mind at least, if not all your heart and beauty. I have been passionately seeking the heart of Young America, and am the only human being who has positively clamored to be sent to High School Assemblies, two thousand strong. And the last few years I have had them, roaring like the sea, boys and girls now about through college—your age, and I have loved them by the thousands—all at once, till my heart was burnt out. To me you are all of them, *revealed in one, at last*. I have sought unity with them in a prayer-way you cannot even dream possible. But in the end, it was the same—thousands of hearts no matter how loyal and kind and gorgeous, smothered all privacy—till the fever reached the very *core* of my heart and mind, and only in your steadiness, and serenity did I find self-control. Every move of yours has been to me in some sense, the breath of Young America, the breath of my whole land. I could put down a rose leaf every place I have seen your feet stepping on this campus or beach or in this town. It is in my mind clear-edged and lovely, and an incredible fulfillment of a *long search*. When you walked barefoot from the beach-frolic to the foot of the stairs, treading softly across the grass, watching and feeling with your feet for places in the grass without stickers and thorns and listening with bowed head and telling me beautiful things, and telling the other girls to go on, it seemed to me a blazing and beautiful parable of all that I desired. *Whoever* you marry, *whatever* you do, we have this summer before us, and you have a *mind* that steps as gently and God knows I want to walk with you—and step nowhere but the little path you choose. And *please* be on my side of the argument when you can.

The first day in the class, in Miss Evans' room you were hostile. You were the only one I saw, but I did not look. Your face was set. Your brows were puckered. The second day, you were a rose—you suddenly believed in me, and little smiles kept coming. I did not look, but I saw. God help us to continue *that tiny victory over one another* to the end—whatever the end. Whether you let me take care of you or not, you must, dear best friend, *take care of me* till it becomes incredible, impossible. It will never be impossible, if you are firm and kind and patient. My brief call at Brownsville, should certainly have two evenings—but I may say nothing. When I am with you I am so choked I can hardly open my mouth, I simply want to hold you with both hands by your hands, tight, and never let you go. But I swear to behave, and not make you angry, but I know *I may say nothing*. My call will just be a sign of earnestness, and I certainly want to clear your family's mind of every misgiving. I can, at least do that. There is nothing to conceal or fix. All families are terribly hard-headed, no matter if there is a fairy and an angel in the house. Now this is in the deepest confidence: —I took monastic vows ages ago—all by myself—in secret, vows to *poverty, chastity and obedience to beauty*—I took them with ferocity and defiance and expected to be obliged to keep them till *death*—and on these furious vows, whose intensity and defiance no living mortal knew, turns all the tragedy and comedy of my life. They have helped to make me seem so alien. You know you find me strangely alien. But the world itself has come round, and *pledged itself in many clear ways* to take care of me, stubbornness and all. I can say to your Mama that I *can* take care of you. God knows, I have kept myself for you and have been kept for you, my ''Young America'', in most strange and fatal ways, and I tell you dear—I am giving you not an adventurer's devotion but a boy's devotion. Milton taught me Eden long ago—and I tell you I believe in that idea of his, with a breaking heart. I *have been faithful and waiting*. Do not think you will get another letter like this from me. The flag of truce with all sincerity will go at the top of the next letter and I will do my best to write you notes. This is that conversation, this is my side, one side of that interview from which I was three times thwarted by innocent Gulf Park Curiosity and maybe likewise thwarted by innocent Brownsville curiosity. My life is getting to be one Pullman Car—with everyone looking. I am no longer angry with my friends, but we must conquer, and win some tiny corner for *your* secret heart and mine.

I *know* I am the slave of the ideal, the pictorial Elizabeth—and that makes you uncomfortable. You are dancing with sweet, realistic youngsters and you do not want to be *"America Incarnate"*, and the *"Heavenly Venus"* and the *"Glory of all American Innocence and Clean Passion.* You want to be a nice little heroine in the Rise of Silas Lapham, or Pendennis, or The Ordeal of Richard Feverel. But my dear, please be proud and patient. The glory that you give me, and the beauty that you shed around you *is glory*, is certainly a reality—or else I should burn all my books and pictures and jump into the channel and drown. You *know* I know life has its funny and its realistic side, and that I put two funny papers into your box often. Please let us laugh and love, and adore each other. And let us *use our brains* to find the finest way up, for both of us. Let us not be helpless idiots in the presence of love. And please read every verse I marked in the Golden Treasury[4] once more, if you dare!

With love and friendship

VACHEL

And if this letter is too strong and plain, here is the flag of truce that I will put at the top of the next one. [There follows a drawing of a white flag.]

Please do not think you are expected to answer this letter, *this special letter,* but please think, think, think about it. I claim every scrap of your brains you may be throwing into the waste-basket.

Notes

1. Elizabeth Mann Wills was a student in VL's class at Gulf Park College, Gulfport.
2. The other girls mentioned were her classmates.
3. Albert Edmund Trombly's biography of VL, *Vachel Lindsay, Adventurer* (Columbia, Missouri: Lucas Brothers, 1929), was preceded by his article on VL in the *Southwest Review* (Summer 1928, pp. 459—68), "Vachel Lindsay's Prose." In 1949, Trombly published a twenty-four—page brochure for the Vachel Lindsay Association (Springfield, Illinois) entitled *Vachel Lindsay.*
4. Among other anthologies, VL used Francis Turner Palgrave's *Golden Treasury of Songs and Lyrics* in his Gulf Park poetry classes.

132

TO ELIZABETH MANN WILLS

Memphis, Tennessee
September 18, 1923
Tuesday evening
The Chisca

My Dear Elizabeth:—

The old slavery has come over me, and I cannot sleep without writing you a letter, and I only wish it were not a letter—but a song. I wish every word of mine to you henceforth could be a song, only. I keep wondering, and struggling with the idea that you are the elect goddess of my songs. What songs can I sing that will bind us most faithfully, and the most kindly in steady friendship while the storms of passion sweep over me? There is a Vachel that is a friend and an Elizabeth that is a friend in this storm. Since Sunday I have been in a tempest of a thousand thoughts, happy, unhappy, and then happy again, but most of my tears have been those of happiness, and gratitude to God and you. Surely your open-hearted willingness to let me sing to you is a great favor, a good gift. There is more patience in your face when you speak of that. You seem to understand the writer, and to be confused by the man. There is something in it way down deep that has to do with the artist's life, the mystery of art and beauty. Walter Pater said our goal in culture was *"to burn with a hard and gem-like flame"*. When I look at the profile picture you were so good as to lend, I see the living embodiment of the doctrine, a girl already at the goal, a person even cruel she is so set, so burning, in the *"hard and gem-like flame"* that is the love of beauty and of finality. Those are vague words. I only wish they were plainer. But you are an artist, and therefore patient with the singer. I cannot pass by lightly our bargain that I am to sing the songs and you are to love the songs, and they are born of your beauty and your breath. So to you, as to the world, you are willing for me to be a poet, not a person, and like the world you respect and love me most when I am most a poet. I am for the first time in my life admitting to myself I am a poet. I am a poet and very little else. I tell you dearest—it is a fate I cannot understand. I did not ask to be a poet. I only asked to be a person in your sight. With you, as with the world, I must sing, or be dismissed. I have read the Bible so hard, dearest—since I left you—St Paul to the Corinthians. And I have prayed all night long. I do *not* understand my fate, or know how to meet it. Every one, even dearest Elizabeth, says: "Sing and sing until you die, and forget you have a heart". But that is not quite it. I am *not* in rebellion. I seem called to a strange and bitter-sweet destiny and if I have written to you tonight with strong crying and tears, they are not all tears of sorrow. If this is my destiny, if your beauty is to bring me only the fruit of song, for Christ's dear sake let me do it nobly, this business of singing, and not with a coward's heart. I have *never* told you how I loved you. Always I have held back. I am afraid that most of my songs will praise your beauty—for how can I sing whole-heartedly of love? I know dear—I must wait and wait. In your thirtieth year—you will be all flesh and blood and heart-break and heart's love and you will have had enough bitter heart-break to have a tenderness for all mankind, and lovers will not seem so strange to you. Your beauty goes through me day and night like a thousand icy arrows, and there is no escape. This is a thousand times better, to endure this glory and bitterness in my heart—than to be separated from you, or to tell you any sort of good-by. I will *not* say good-by. Who am I to set you afire with love? I have not one grace to offer, or one persuasion worthy to persuade. But I tell you dear I live in your permission to write you songs, like a beggar suddenly sheltered in a cold marble palace on a cold strange plain. I am absolutely determined to make the most of my lodging, to glory in it, and to wait through the infinite years for my heart to grow by sorrow. It is the only chance of honest life I have. It is the only way I know to live the naked truth before God.

There is a most beautiful Catholic Church here and I burned four candles yesterday before the Virgin—one for you one for me one for Ridley one for his fair wife. We have all four started on an adventure in which we are tied together by cobwebs, yet something strange is surely coming from it, and doubtless something beautiful. For myself I always pray about the same prayer before the Virgin. It is anything but Catholic. The old Buddhist philosophic invocation has meant the world to me—for years and years: "I take refuge in the Buddha, the Law and the Monastic order". It was one of the great hours of my life, when I first read that prayer. There was a strange victory in it for me. I am obliged to consecrate myself to you, darling Elizabeth, in spite of your face half-turned away—I must pray if I am to steady my soul and live. And I must pray honest prayers, from such religious mind as God Has given me, however heretical. And my other prayer I taught you once I think, or wrote you:—" I give my life to poverty, chastity and obedience to beauty", which is a most heretical variant I know on ancient Franciscanism. I dearly *love* the Virgin—but it is with these prayers I appear before her. Chastity is a poor word to use, when I speak of love and of my worship of you. In some strange sense you and the Virgin are sisters in my mind. She was but a mortal woman as you are. But in the dim church she has a light from Heaven upon her, and in Brownsville you have a light from Heaven upon you. I cannot help but consecrate myself body, bones and blood, nerves and brain in the most abject and complete consecration to that fair flesh of yours, to that strange untouched girl-beauty that blazes through the bridesmaid's dress. You do not understand. There are no half-way measures with me. I am utterly and completely consecrated to your beautiful body and to no other body will I surrender, to your beautiful mind *and with no other mind will I debate,* and to your most exquisite and mysterious soul, that hides and hides and hides, that whips me if I try to come too near. Only the whip is also a part of your sacred mission to me. It is your divine business to be stern with me. It is your divine business to be unmerciful, till I have proved myself consecrated day after day, year after year.

I go to the Catholic church for its beauty—and because it is the only place to take vows, and the only place where vows seem natural. But alone in my room, day after day since I have known you I have prayed and prayed and prayed, reconsecrating and reconsecrating myself to you, to your virgin body, your holy mind, your exquisite and proud beauty, and your unutterably innocent and intoxicating youth. Pardon a thousand times, for so many words, I am thinking, as I shall think, day after day, day after day, of our wonderful little talk by the fire—our first hour in our lives by a hearth and so—such as it is, the memory of that little fire remains my only hearth. That is one of the moods of life I wish I could multiply by the thousand in my songs, and keep singing till my death. For a moment we truly glimpsed one another and it was a most precious moment and I hold to it as to no other hour in Brownsville. I will think about it and think about it. This is I suppose the LONG letter at last. Not so long—after all. Well there is much news—but it is midnight, and thank God I have written my heart out, and thank God for a girl I can write it to in the faith it will be received with gentle pride and sweet and faithful friendship. If you knew me dear, you would know I am flat on the ground before you, without one thought or breath or drop of blood held back from this consecration.

With my heart indeed

VACHEL

P.S. Write to me at Gulf Park. I start Thursday. Please think long and hard when you have a solemn mood, and write, write, when you write.

The Chisca
Next morning
Wednesday September 19

This is the way I felt before I met you.
This is a song I wrote in my note-book when I was in England with my mother:—

My heart is full of love songs, though my loves have gone away,
Have turned to other lovers, one and all.
They are wooing in the palaces or kissing in the hay.
I pass their homes, and here the Cupids call.
My heart is full of love-songs, but who will hear them now?
My lovers are the South wind
    or the snow.
I am thinking of the dears I knew
Who sleep beneath the hills, of the tears and cries and flowers of
    long ago.

All that desolation was in my heart—and had been in my heart for a long long time—when I met you—and then my mother's death and the final breaking up of the home also. When I met you my only home was the entire United States, and I was loving *everybody* in the whole United States, the whole one hundred and ten million, just to escape loneliness. I suppose that is one thing that made me seem so strange to you and to the girls that teased you so unmercifully about me. I was strange—for I had stretched my lonely heart over this whole nation and loved them as citizens as no one ever loved just citizens before (to speak vainly and boastfully). So I seemed impersonal—and awkward and hard to get at. I *know* my mother was the same way. You must reconcile yourself to *that* my dear friend. Be *patient* with my inevitable awkwardness.

When I looked into your eyes those first two weeks in the Gulf-Park dining-room—all my loneliness fell from me like a curse taken off. Never in all my life did I behold eyes so soft, so innocent, so exquisitely loving, so tender beyond all human words, so sheltered in dreams. And set in a face as austere as St. Clara's, as dedicated as the soul of Joan of Arc. You looked a million miles from me as though seen through the longest possible telescope and to have held your hand one instant—in kindness this summer and to have been sitting by the fire with you in ease and gentle hope is a great progress I say—since the month of Valentines.

Here is a diagram of the way we began.

You sat here

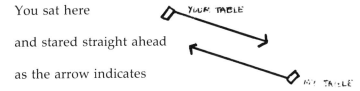

and stared straight ahead

as the arrow indicates

I sat here; and presumably looked straight ahead as the arrow indicates. But I was actually looking straight into your eyes every single minute, and if it was one week or a thousand years, new love songs and glory songs had begun in me, you were like moonrise at last, on the dark desert. I have been fighting for that moment ever since, fighting the world, fighting myself, and sometimes terribly disturbing you—but I determined to live for that moment and bring it back in glory again and again. Certainly it came to me, with profound peace in our little hour by the fire in Brownsville and your patience had its perfect work in me for that hour, and I pray that it counted with you. Every time you sign your letter "devotedly yours" I am so happy, for I know that moment of the peaceful conquest of the Universe has come to you, and there is more between us than gentle patience.

All my life seems piled up ahead of me—in magnificence—my dearest darling lady. I feel like the army of Joan of Arc—with Joan unwilling to take command, but the army ready to fight in her name. And now for a new theme. Walt Whitman is a *great poet, and I am not.*

So many critics—so many many critics have said to me "Be our Walt Whitman". I suppose those that sincerely and steadily insist the most on my continuing to be a poet say this. They pour all America into my lap and beg me to sing about it. *I cannot.* And here is a secret:—Well—I always considered Whitman as a man and a citizen a genius, but rather crooked and shabby old man with a streak of perversion. I can forgive this, but it keeps the American people from finding leadership in him. I never mention it out loud. But it spoils him for a model for me. I had rather imitate St. Paul a thousand miles off. For St. Paul was a true traveller, a true democrat and saint. I think you are strong enough now to stand my thought about Whitman—and I want to give it to you plainly—it has *so* much to do with your future and mine—and it has *so* much to do with your willingness to be sung about— a willingness which I profoundly adore—and wish to carry to its uttermost conclusions in your imagination. Pardon me, if my words are labored. There is a struggle in my mind.

Whitman never saw the America I have seen and loved. The group of Brownsville neighbors who came in to hear me could total half a million or a million—if all my audiences were added up these ten years. And they—my audiences—always evoke the same mood that was evoked in Brownsville, and always my audience *loves* me—as the Brownsville people did. And *you* do not love me half as well as my audiences do.—you do not understand. I use my heart when I speak, they leave me spent—and it is your privilege to pity the ashes of me, it is your duty as the mother-heart to bring me back into life by gentle nursing and prepare me for the poet-life which you evidently value in me more than the private citizen. If you love the public man, nurse the private citizen into life. Now Whitman in his wildest dreams was only a pretended troubadour. He sat still in cafes—never such a troubadour for audiences as Bryan or a thousand Chautauqua men. He was an infinitely more skillful writer than any other American. But I can beat him as *troubadour*. My final gift is the thing that robs me of your love, my darling, I can win an audience in five minutes easier than I can win you in five months though I break my heart and pray to God and to you every hour. I tell you it is a matter where you must be *merciful*, for unless you are *merciful*, you will never love me, and complete my public life with private healing. Unless you are *pitiful*, determined to help me when I most need help—to patch out the great gaps in my mind after the noisy recitals are over, and heal my body and soul—you will never fulfill your mother-heart with me—the way it hungers, to be fulfilled for someone, somewhere. I verily believe it will be easier to win the whole United States than you, unless you *resolve to help,* to go courting deliberately, to try what it means to be a lover seeking true love, instead of shaking it all off as the tree on the shore shakes off the wave.

But what has this to do with Whitman? He has left the field free for us and our like. He will always fail, as the law-giver for America—because he had no Elizabeth. You are my one great advantage over him. America hungers for a Virgin Queen to glory in, as she did in the days of Virginia when Virginia was named for Queen Elizabeth. America is like me waiting for something exquisitely beautiful and virginal to which to bow down—and there was no Lady Queen in all of Whitman. His fat farm-wives sprawl among the cabbages. The poorest sickest, lowest family in the slums may produce one pretty child capable of moving a Movie-Queen more delicate than all the heroines of Whitman. You would suppose the nation had no *ivory beauty* if you would listen to him, and he is a million miles from Chivalry. America is passionately waiting for Chivalry—for the chance to worship with true Sermon-on-the-Mount religion a worthy Virgin Queen as your brother so nobly worships his bride. No singer can leave out the Queen—and command America, though he is in a thousand other aspects most nobly American. Whitman abdicated when he left you out.

So, I who think these things every time Whitman is mentioned in my connection, have for the first time explained them—and only to the person most concerned. In the matter of Democracy, the world has with the help of such as Whitman made tremendous progress—but in the matter of Democratic Chivalry I do not see how it is possible to go beyond the days of King Arthur. The best of the South thinks this, and that is the reason the South is my country. I am not ashamed to worship you as Mark Twain worshipped Joan of Arc. And such worship in the South is gloried in, thank God.

Read Whitman and see how he falls among the cabbages a thousand times, for lack of a Virgin Queen in his song. Even a Mary Pickford (a good and dull and admirable and honest doll) would have made Whitman the poet his followers claim he is—the poet of our *total* democracy. They will go on loving Mary till some poet can give them their Elizabeth and the reason they love Mary "America's sweetheart" is because they are waiting for an Elizabeth and have not found her. They may wait a thousand years for a girl like you, yet I would like to try the impossible task of bringing you to my share of them—for I have never succeeded at anything but the impossible. In all other matters I am an utter failure. How then will I make you Queen in these songs they compare to Mister Whitman's? I do not know—any more than Ridley knows how he will make his lady Queen—I only know that beautiful and impossible and magnificent things are the only things worth while. Thank God you are willing to be sung about.

Please let me urge you to talk to every man of brains in Brownsville or in Vanderbuilt [*sic*] about your favorite subjects, and *make* them wrestle with your mind and bend to your ideas. *Think* with them, *think* with them, even more than you dance with them.

Thank God you are willing to be sung about—but don't you stand there like a pillar while I sing. While I search out the noble utmost ramifications of your beauty, you must search out the utmost ramifications of your own thoughts and find the mind of men, either in books or conversation that either match your mind or utterly contradict it. Either definite agreement or definite disagreement in ideas is a matter of growth. You do not need to learn more—you need only to discover the utmost ramifications of your own body and soul and mind, and to command these, with precision, with shrewdness, with prayer and devotion and glory to God. I want the most exquisite beauties of your mind to find themselves with action and with struggle and with dancing—for the mind will go on dancing toward Heaven forever. The bridesmaid's dress is a step forward. The next step is your Vanderbuilt [*sic*] cap and gown. I do not know how you can be Queen. But I have strange dreams about it, and I have struggled long with the idea. Birth itself is an outrageous makeshift and my coming to you and being born again in the light of your eyes has been less awkward than physical birth. It was a real "twilight sleep". You have a notion that everything proper to do can be smoothly done. But spiritual Birth and spiritual death—the two most terrible and wonderful things have much that is seemingly awkward as any spiritual physician can tell you. My struggle with you is a struggle for life for the real birth of this soul in me that some people have been silly enough to compare to Whitman's. I know what they mean. They mean that in my full strength I sometimes command the crowd with song. And Whitman only *fancied* the crowd. I have *met* them face to face. I *know* I have just begun. I am on the edge of a rare failure or the strangest conquest of my small section of democracy ever granted an American. I have but one dream—to bring everyone who loves me to your feet and to teach them to worship your girlhood as I do, to worship it in themselves and in their own loves, if they never consciously face you. Every American has a touch of marble glory in him somewhere. I want to bring that forward in every American who listens to me—and that is what I think when I look at your marble body and into your holy eyes. You are to me as St. Paul says the temple of God, the altar of the Holy Spirit. These things cannot be done finishing school style among your *girl* companions, altogether and exclusively. I want you to wrestle with the brains of one hundred good and able *men*—and then return to me—and then you will respect me more even though you see my great mistakes infinitely more—and I will seem to you a hundred times as human as I do now. I must make myself seem human to you, and a casual companion, or my heart will break. I *must* bring this about.

The Chisca
Thursday, September 20

My Dear Elizabeth:
It is three o'clock in the morning and I have slept like the dead and can sleep no more and waking up happy must carry this letter a page longer. Page 24 left off in the midst of an argument I may or may not take up again. All I know is that this is all one letter and I must keep writing my heart out till it is done.—For still I have twenty things to say, and I could write you a novel without stopping. The very thought of you starts my thoughts flowing and I think toward you and to you instantly, though I may be in all other matters unutterably dead or dull. Never have I ended a letter to you with satisfaction. I have always wanted to go on and on, and only held back because I saw the absurdity of such an avalanche. Please pardon this time, and read patiently, patiently. This is a novel of which there is one copy, a secret copy, just for you.

    I have been staying here to finish a job of printing that promises to be fairly satisfactory, and I will start South Friday—tomorrow if the printing is done as promised. I will send you copies soon.

I am wondering about Vanderbuilt [*sic*] for you. You have likely decided it by now. I cannot help but hope you go. It is for your growth and your good. I am *eager* for you to grow and grow.

I wrote a poem at the theatre, yesterday "The Son of Pocahontas".[1] It will be done in a year or two, maybe.

I have thought so many many thoughts for you since I last saw you. I have seen no one here but the Book-Shop people and Ogilvy (Ogilvie?) the head of the Goodwyn Institute. I am getting out this printed matter[2] for them and presenting it to the book-shop to distribute as a compliment to Sandburg. They are going to sell the poster for a nominal sum all over the country and I will leave the plate with them so they can print more if there is a demand. Goodwyn Institute wants me this winter—probably about November 20—so that is my next hour for seeing you. Please study and think and grow and pray and be good every minute. Please understand yourself and your own mind, and develop yourself, filling out the divine pattern on which you were originally made. No matter where this leaves me in the argument. I have spent hours here in this town writing to a girl you may know—Elizabeth Wills—and her picture is the sole ornament of my bureau.

I am thinking of this time last year and when I think of two tragedies of thwarted men who met violent deaths—Ewart and Marsh[3]—who were alive and most faithful friends of mine last year—I say I am fortunate to get up alive at three o'clock in the morning and look at your beautiful picture in peace—and I think of the fluttering breath of life that passes between us—whether it be what the cupids call "love" or what the old maids used to call "esteem". We are at least well upon our adventure—dearest darlingest—and we have not been thwarted by earthquake, fire or flood, conspiracy or death. We go on, my dear, we go on. If like Marsh or Ewart I be shot by arbitrary accident as was each man—if I should go by any sudden or irrelevant death—the best thing I could say when I met the spirits of Heaven would be:—"I was faithful to her holy face—day and night, and I can face heaven and face the trial of my soul—for I never flinched from all love brought to me from her, the bitter and the sweet". It does not do to be always calculating the future—anything so uncertain and so whimsical as the future. But it is a grand thing to be able to wake after good and solid and dreamless sleep—at three o'clock in the morning and write to a lily-face-and-lily-heart that I love her and I am for this hour enormously grateful and at peace. The strange city hums and blinks and steams underneath me—and my hotel-window looks out on the Infinite and the dark.

But then I look at your pale picture and wonder at the marble strangeness of that girlish queen. I would send you an alabaster Crown if this were Florence or the Ancient time, and such stately things were done in Memphis and Brownsville.

Thursday afternoon.

It is all well enough for you to have exactly the world's formula for me—that I am only a poet—if you are willing to make for me a girl's definition of a poet:—the finest most high minded definition of the poet as a private citizen, and hold me to it and hold your own soul to it—in some sense. Please make the task of dreaming the dreams well, one half yours—and if you do not yourself write the songs, hold all the harder to the dream-world, and open all its holiest and most Christian doors for me that I may write without being desolate and alone in that world of fantasy. Say all the things to me that a poet's lady should say to him, if you must leave out all the things that sweetheart says to sweetheart. No man can sing the songs I am called to sing with a lonely mind. Be good to me dearest. Think for me and think *with me,* and believe in our adventure. It is honorable, it is high minded. I hope, and I know it is full of prayer. Let us go forward with courage. God bless you my darling.

Most truly your poet

VACHEL

At New Orleans Saturday
At Gulf Park by Sunday
Watching for letters Monday!

Notes

1. It is not known whether "The Son of Pocahontas" was ever finished. No trace of it has been found by this editor. "Our Mother Pocahontas" appears in the *Collected Poems* (p. 105).
2. About the "printed matter" mentioned here, see "Babylon, Babylon, Babylon the Great" (*Collected Poems,* pp. 399—401) and the note that follows: "This poem originally appeared in Christopher Morley's Bowling Green column, in the *New York Evening Post,* to celebrate a visit of Carl Sandburg to New York City. Several months later it was printed in Memphis, Tennessee, by the author, in anticipation of Carl Sandburg's visit to address Memphis in a recital for the Goodwyn Institute, November 17, 1923. I issued it in a three-foot broadside, with my picture of Babylon at the top as a kind of hieroglyphic. It was distributed through the kindness of Mrs. Dicken's Book-Shop."
3. About Ewart and Marsh, see note 1 to letter 118 and note 1 to letter 124.

133

TO STEPHEN GRAHAM

Box 83
Gulfpark
Gulfport
Mississippi

Oct. 14, 1923

My Dear Stephen:—

Just one year ago I saw you and delivered my two books to the two publishers, and how much has happened since then! It seems ten years, I have had so many ups and downs of the heart and soul, which I might tell you in the woods.

This is not yet a letter. But I wanted to give you some thoughts about the nomination of White[1] for the Presidency. It is a fighting point with me, and if you follow this apparently slender trail through the American Wilderness in a gently argumentative, gently humorous mood, still taking it seriously I think you will be amazed at what you learn, especially if you listen for the whispers. If you can only get up one reasonably loud echo of my nomination of White in England, you will be amazed at the result. Because men of this type terrify our plutes —"plutocrats"— as mice terrify elephants. Which proves after all, there is power in the mouse. I know of no better way of learning American politics than following this mouse relentlessly through the Wilderness. There is no more harm in White for the Plutocracy than any routine lawyer or man of business. But they hate even a discussion of the abstract principle of free speech—which the light and airy discussion of his nomination might provoke. The Ku Klux hate him—which is the democratic form of intolerance. He is the most conservative writer who contributes to the otherwise despairing desperate Anti-American "Nation". So the extreme left can never repudiate him though they swallow him with a wry face. Massachussets people fear him because they fear anything wearing pants and suspenders from the West—and the most amusing comedy of all is that all those in America who bootlick Great Britain and are sure we have no American Writers and who invoke what they think is the British mood to justify every form of Bullying here, would be particularly confused over British interest in a disciple of free speech like White. It is a sad fact that Americans of the sort who jump through hoops to please the British even before the British ask them to and who go on cussing the "Central Powers" are our worst tyrants and tories in all other respects. They have the Lackey's talent for tyranny and a zeal that outruns discretion. I may be mistaken but it seems to me even the triumph of "Dizzy"² who was synonymous with Imperialism and Toryism, had more of free speech in it and pretty wit than American Tories are willing to allow even to a theoretical presidential candidate—one nominated for the sake of argument. Their man must not only be gagged, but the gag must cover his whole face. Their man must not only be bound, he must be tied to a tree like St. Sebastian. The idea of a candidate who said something or wrote something every morning that was witty or pretty or unexpected without consulting anyone is to them utterly appalling. A man in American Politics with as fearless a tongue as old Dizzy had would be denounced from end to end of this country as "dangerous"—in every Chamber of Commerce, every bank and every Rotary Kiwanis Optimists and Lions Club. And even the men of free speech only take a certain line of political freedom, a kind of poisonous "Nation" anti-American wrath, that wears them out. The result has been that all artists keep out of politics, and exercise a freedom of speech almost venomous, at the tea-parties only.

They despise politics as a sort of jail, and once they find I consider I am talking politics seriously they will denounce me as a Babbitt of Babbitts. The artist and the Poet is utterly degrading himself to be interested in anything so contemptible (from their point of view)—and once I am assumed to have a candidate I take seriously—the denunciations of me by the artists and exquisites as a Middle Class and Middle Western Person will grow more vehement. And the denunciations of you and of me and of White as "Bolshyveeks" will roar from every Babbitt who condescends to pay attention to us. Mrs Holbrook of Springfield is sure to this day you and I are both "Bolshyveeks", for the fundamental axiom of the whole banking caste in America is that all young men who do not *look* like Bank Clerks are necessarily Trotskys and Lenines [sic] of the deepest dye.

So between the artists and the business men we will have a merry war—if only you can get up some echo of the clippings I have sent you in London. But all this is mere diversion, like visiting the Mormon Temple. I will take the responsibility of the whole thing, if you do not care to shoulder any of it. And, do be careful, Stephen, of your sense of humor. Let the joke be on the Artists and Art clan generally, and on the business men, not on me or you or White. And if we get our man even seriously chattered about—for one day—"So Much the Worse for Boston" said the lecherous Mountain-Cat. I guarantee an instant and terrible cry of alarm in the Transcript.

With love to you and to Rose

VACHEL

Notes

1. William Allen White was not nominated for the 1924 presidential election. President Calvin Coolidge was the Republican candidate, and the Democrats nominated John W. Davis of West Virginia after 103 ballots. Their nominee for vice-president was Charles Bryan from Nebraska. That same year the newly formed Progressive party nominated Robert M. La Follette.
2. "Dizzy" refers to Benjamin Disraeli (1804–81), prime minister of England in 1868 and from 1874 to 1880.

134

TO STEPHEN GRAHAM

Gulf Park College
Gulfport
Sunday October 21, 1923

My Dear Stephen:—
This morning I am seeing more clearly why the figure of White[1] holds me so strongly and why I am so eager for you to make White understood, even more than he is apparently worth to the realistic observer. He seems so dissolved in politics and hasty journalism that to many he has absolutely no relation to Literature at all. Yet he is the only surviving literary symbol of the political generation immediately preceding. And of course it is solely as a *literary symbol* that I desire to push him further into the ken of politicians.—for he is to them an awful highbrow though to *my set* he seems an awful low-brow. They—my set—are all getting so damned exquisite they cannot wear suspenders in the sets where they are supposed to count—whereas in the political circles the chewing-tobacco advertisement is still the fundamental literature. White is far above *that!*

I still maintain our politics is the only key to our future life and letters. The great illustration of this is the fact that Whitman was a Tammany brave of the precise sort always denounced by our business-men and our elegant fellows—a wicked professional ward-heeler—a

professional politician of the deepest dye—and it was the thwarting of
the free-soil abolitionist faction of Tammany Hall to which he belonged—that suddenly threw him, with all his force, into poetry. Precisely the same head of steam—suddenly turned into a new direction.
It is the same thing that happened to O. Henry locked up in the Ohio
Federal Penitentiary—all his force was suddenly concentrated into Literature.

Now Whitman is the one poetry product of our *practical* politics—and
yet he is the most whimpered about by expatriate Americans in London
and Paris who are too elegant to touch anybody's politics, least of all
to be Tammany Braves. They are too elegant to breathe the air of their
own America and yet they blat about Whitman who was as directly born
of years of Tammany service—(none too elegant)—as directly born of
that as Walter Scott was born of Ruined Abbeys.

Now the same political headway is in White, but from the wheat-
farms. It will never take itself out in a literary turn of your standard or
mine, or that of the Whitmanites. But the fundamental United States,
Democratic conviction is *there* that made Whitman *first* a Tammany Brave
with long years of practical service for the party—and later the extraordinary burst of Democratic poetry.

My theory is that the younger generation should read White—and
rewrite him. Ruskin was definitely the pupil of Walter Scott. The whole
Ruskin family was absolutely saturated with Scott when the Precocious
John Ruskin was a tiny boy. Therefore Ruskin's most marvellous chapters in the Second Volume of the Stones of Venice on "The Nature of
Gothic"—chapters which I hope to reprint in this country some day
with my own comment—with words on Chivalry and Democracy. They
are just as much of a tract and Gospel to me as The Gospel of Luke.

Ruskin had a much sharper pen than Scott—but he could not have
done the fundamental work of Scott.

The more we are able to make a terrifying political figure of White
among the most Babbittized politicians the more our young men of
letters will be forced to understand him as a magnificent survival of our
medieval period, or our slow-moving "drawling" Yankee type, our
meditative rural pioneer agricultural type, the furthest possible from the
snappy New York Automobile types, who want to make everything
snappy and jazzy including the Grace of God, and who will not endure
the Holy Ghost because it is a still small voice and a wind that bloweth
where it listeth. I am profoundly grateful for your chapters on the saloon
in your new book.[2] You have come nearer to the truth than any other
writer I have struck, European or American. Your description of the
forty thousand could be extended into a whole book. That same forty
thousand were for Negro Slavery to the very last, *in the North*—as a

vindication of their newly-rich pretentions. And your paragraph about the saloon page 195 represents the precise attitude of 1860:—the attitude of the Union men. It is the same line drawn. Let me paraphrase it:

Few objected on moral grounds to negroes being an inferior caste to white people, and subservient to them. It was the filth, the vice, the point of view of the unsuppressed African slave-trade that America fought, and these can never come back.

If you take this line you can write a whole book on the defeated aristocracies of America, beginning with Jackson. America is not so much democratic as she is against self-made aristocracies and dictatorships which assume to be permanent without permanent proof of merit.

It is not the liquor question at all. It is the question of a hasty aristocracy trying to use and gild some very dirty scavengers as symbols of their arrogance. *The old African slave-trader, the cheap old Simon Legree—and the shoddy new boot-legger are lackeys and symbols of the same passing pretentions.* No one in the whole wide world is so uneasy as a person in America attempting hastily to be an Aristocrat. There is no rest for the weary ultra-rich till they have reached an Italian villa, have permanently renounced their country—and permanently exchanged and substituted the boot-licker for the boot-legger. If a man's wife has sense enough to make bread, she may make wine, cider or other medicine, here in America and she is neither breaking the law nor being "naughty"—though our aristocracy falsely whines she may have the police after her. It is a plain lie. Likewise a man with a negro servant may now (as ever) order him about to the strength of his lungs and to the extent of his own personal power to enforce his magnificent will upon him. If the negro obeys, no "abolitionist" or "prohibitionist" will interfere. But the man cannot sell the liquor for cash—nor the negro for cash, because the negro—bought and sold—brings back—not only the domestic—but the open flagrant African slave-trade, and liquor bought-and-sold (under American conditions) evolves an equally arrogant and soul-killing *public life* and utterly defeats clean street life and even approximate democracy. It makes a barocracy. *Street life means more to us than to you.*

No newspapers proclaim to the skies that American women can make their own liquor as much as they please—if they do not sell it. The newspapers know they would thwart extremists at both ends whom they fear. There are professional fighters at both ends that would hate you, if you would only make this plain forever.

Well—back to White. These last pages have been a discussion of certain pages of your book—rather than White. I want him pushed so far along into public life and the limelight that the Macmillan Co. of

England and of America will be forced to reissue him in big standard editions of O. Henry and Mark Twain dignity. I want to push him so far—(he is already an old neglected Macmillan author of long standing) I want to push him so far that both publishing houses will be forced to take up the fight. Several of his stories like "The King of Boyville" are real tracts for the times both literary and political. And inferior to Mark Twain and O. Henry in art—he is far more likely to help our next generation of artists, because he is *nearer to Politics*. And he is a better man of letters than Roosevelt, and was the best American of Roosevelt's time.

With love,

VACHEL

Notes

1. William Allen White's *The Court of Boyville* was a collection of most of his "Boyville" stories that came out in 1899. In it he chronicled the life of a small Kansas town (probably El Dorado).
2. It is uncertain what book of Graham's VL had in mind. As of October 21, 1923, Graham's most recent work was *Tramping with a Poet in the Rockies*, but VL may have been thinking of *Under-London* (1923).

135

TO HARRIET MOODY

The Great Southern Hotel
Gulfport, Mississippi
November 10, 1923

My dear Harriet Moody:—
There is every chance I will be with you, Sunday, December 9, and just a little before or after. I am coming up for just a short tour via Champaign, and am very much interested in the adventure of a long conversation with you, if such an adventure is to be had. If there is anything you want to know about me, I will tell you. If there is anything you want to tell me, I want to know it all. I prefer *conversations* to crowds.

Life is a re-crystallizing adventure for me just now, strangely enough centering around this hotel, this rather empty lonely hotel—but here I write and study in peace three days a week and it is just what I want. And here I take long walks alone on the two piers, and I take the hour's walk from Gulf-Park to here and here to Gulf-Park, and it seems but a moment, especially when the stars are bright over the sea and it is ten-to-eleven and the road is practically clear of machines.

I care very little about speaking anywhere. I enjoy teaching four hours a week—poetry. You will admit that is not becoming a pedagogue to a wild and demoralizing extent, and I attend *no* faculty sessions.

I have lost all taste for getting into print and have not the least notion of writing any more books. I am quite bent upon improving those I have written when the Macmillan Company and Appleton's will permit. Watching the sea and the pageant of life is quite satisfying. I read the book of Revelation through, with my class, this week, much to their boredom, but to my great satisfaction. The pictures are so well-ordered, and the drama is so well organized, I truly love that book. I expect to read it through again, several times, this winter. I want to get it pretty clearly in mind.

My table is stacked with poems written well enough to please me, but not well enough to suit anyone else. One of my poems—The Psyche-Butterfly—has been recently set to music by Albert V. Davies,[1] to the catchiest sort of music, better than the poem, and is being sung across the country by Cornelia Tayzari. I am more interested in writing poems than finishing them for any "market", however fine.

I am really back in the state of mind in which I wrote "Adventures While Preaching the Gospel of Beauty",—a book which no one has ever read, but which I am wondering how I can make more the center of my work. I have sent to The Macmillan Company for one hundred copies to present to friends around here, by way of evangelism.[2]

It is full of my prophesies of the coming of a new time. I wish I knew how to establish that book. It has the heart of my gospel in it and only 100 copies are sold a year. It can be read at one sitting. I have a notion to go broke, just giving copies away, to prove I meant what I said in that book. People take everything in such a casual way. They are only impressed when you "go broke" on an "idea".

I feel I am nearer to the old peace and independence I knew in the best days of 1912 than I have known since. I have been too much fevered by a riot of public life and public consciousness, for which I have an inherited *talent* rather than preference. But it fevered my soul just the same, and I am more of a *Buddhist* than *anybody* knows.

The stars were marvelous tonight, and how I loved them. It seemed to me the first time I had discovered them. They were *so* clear.

I have not yet seen any review of Stephen Graham's new book

"Seeking El Dorado".[3] It is too early, I guess. It seems to me a lively work, but of course I am prejudiced, for I am in it. I am as vain, egotistical and conceited a turkey as ever lived.

Dr. Cox went to New York for a recuperating trip, and met many of the poets there. This has made him quite determined to call, passing through Chicago. So please, as a favor, keep in touch with him. I want you to know him. He is a fine youth.

Yesterday was my 44th birthday. I received for presents two letters of congratulation and one bouquet! On the whole it has been a very happy birthday. I have been alone in my room all day, two days, meditating cheerfully on the ships and the sea, and re-reading Revelation, and typewriting an article.

Watch the New Republic for my poem on "The Mohawk"[4] and my editorial on Whitman.

I have made up my mind to celebrate and enjoy my birthdays hereafter, and certainly I enjoyed this one.

Certainly I am the damn'dest egotist that ever drew breath. Just look at that letter. Six pages about nothing but myself. It's enough to make my guardian angel sick.

So what shall I say for repentance? I will inquire about some one's health. Is the mayor of Chicago well? And how is Fanny Butcher?[5] Or have you heard of late?

I hear Walter Pater is dead.[6] Poor boy. A nice Englishman of the old school.

With love,

VACHEL

I am sick of my own verses, as *public communications.* I wish you would let me read John Ruskin on "The Nature of Gothic" for that poetry session. Or my favorite selections of Swinburne, Lanier and Poe. Ask Llewellyn Jones' advice.[7]

Notes

1. "The Psyche-Butterfly" was not included in the *Collected Poems*; Albert V. Davies also set to music "The Rose of Midnight" (*Collected Poems*, p. 239).
2. VL actually got one hundred copies of *Adventures While Preaching the Gospel of Beauty* from Macmillan at his own expense to hand out free to people he knew or met. He repeated this gesture to the end of his life with several of his works, even when he was poor.
3. "Seeking El Dorado" was actually *In Quest of El Dorado* (1924).
4. "The Mohawk" appeared in *The New Republic* for December 5, 1923, and in the 1925 edition of the *Collected Poems* (p. 436). Its real title was "Doctor Mohawk,"

and it was inscribed to Ridley Wills, brother of Elizabeth Mann Wills, whom VL alluded to in letters to his "Dulcinea." (See *Collected Poems*, p. 433: "How Dulcinea del Toboso Is Like the Left Wing of a Bird.")

5. "Fanny Butcher" (Mrs. Richard D. Bokum) was literary editor of the *Chicago Tribune*.
6. If the Walter Pater referred to here is the English essayist and critic, VL received the news of his death very late: Pater was born in 1839 and died in 1894.
7. Llewellyn Jones is the author of *First Impressions* (1925), in which VL's work is discussed; he also wrote an article after VL's death, entitled "Vachel Lindsay: American Poet" (*The Christian Century*, December 23, 1931, pp. 1619—20).

136

TO H. L. MENCKEN

Gulfport Mississippi
The Great Southern Hotel
May 27, 1924

My Dear H. L. Mencken:—

There came to me from a mysterious source, another proof of Cleopatra to be corrected, which I did far more elaborately.

Then came your letter with the check, for which I am very grateful. Here is the second corrected proof. Embody as many or as few of these changes as you think essential. They will all go into the copy Macmillans will print next Christmas.

There is *one* thing I insist on. Be *sure* the poem is inscribed to *Elizabeth Mann Wills.*[1] That is most important. I will send the Billboards and Galleons soon.[2]

Most sincerely.

Nicholas Vachel Lindsay

P.S. If you take this second proof at all seriously, I will be very glad if you return it to me when you are through, with marginal notes on clarity, etc . . . I will take *every suggestion.* My friends the poets will testify to you I always *do,* and yet get away with it. Final suggestions, either in a printed editorial or private letter by you, after reading the Weigall book, I will take very seriously indeed. The great thing about Weigall,[3] is that while he professes to take the Greek and Alexandrian standpoint, and professes to leave out the point of view—in all details of the Egyptian priesthood, he is so saturated with the general point of view of the Priests of Osiris and the Old Temples of Hathor, that he reads every move on the Mediterranean from the point of view of an Egyptian High-Priest and Man of the world; as though some Pope should write the first real History of the Middle Ages, without mentioning the Church, yet making you feel that psychology all the time.

Weigall is an extreme special pleader, and I disagree with every other sentence. Yet I fall in with him marvellously, just because he is the first classic historian I ever read, who had *steadily* the old Egyptian angle on things.

Of course I have made Cleopatra far more orthodox than he does, in the old faith. Yet if Caesar was carved on the monuments as the Bridegroom Amon-Ra—by her consent, it is like a Spanish Monarch being crowned by the Pope. The essential point is made.

For everlasting re-iteration of their few *fixed Ideas*—the Egyptians were marvellous. And Weigall is surely more influenced than he knows. I understand every point he is going to make before he makes it, just because I have re-read the Book of the Dead so often. And I have tried to hit off its ritualistic phrases like "Words of Power" "First of the Westerners", and endless re-iterations, without boring you.

N.V.L.

Notes

1. VL's poem "The Trial of the Dead Cleopatra in Her Beautiful and Wonderful Tomb" was in fact inscribed to Elizabeth Mann Wills (*Collected Poems*, p. 445).
2. "Billboards and Galleons," written at Gulf Park when VL's reputation was that of a spent poet, was added to the *Collected Poems* in the 1925 edition (p. 425) and was inscribed to Stephen Graham.
3. The "Weigall book" was the work of the well-known English Egyptologist Arthur Edward Weigall: *The Life and Times of Cleopatra, Queen of Egypt* (1914).

137

TO ELIZABETH MANN WILLS

The fifteen most important pages I ever wrote you. Yet I will write a sweeter letter soon. And Please, write my love letter in spite of this one! *At once*!

> Oriental Limited
> Burlington Route. Great Northern Ry
> En Route
> Monday July 7, 1924

Dearest Elizabeth:

Mountains are all around us on the horizon line, and by seven thirty tonight I will be at the big main Glacier Park Hotel that accommodates four hundred guests. We are now going up a steady steep grade, and the train pulls slowly. I have just had a shave, hair-cut, facial massage, and shower on the train, the first time I have ever had such, (on a train), and feel marvellously refreshed. If we ever travel together, you will go with me on trains with shower baths, so you will stay happy.

Your tiny note from Humbolt [*sic*] was like a new throb of desire, yes, feeding my hungry hands, from your so fiery finger-tips. I read myself to sleep on that small, minute note, and have read it all day, with burning, secret love and tenderness and passion and steady happiness. "I am trying your stunt, writing on my knee." All the card tables are in use. The climbing train moves so slowly, on the level ascending plain, *straight west to the sunset.* It moves so slowly I can write pretty well, (for train writing). Do you know, that after I have torn up every letter I dare, I still have letters from the whole Anglo-Saxon Literary world? Just piled up, unanswered ever since I met you. I began 1923, to write to you in that toy, child letter-box at Gulf Park, and even then I could have eagerly written to you the twenty long "literary", philosophical, American letters a day I often before wrote to the Anglo-Saxon literary world. And *still* I postponed writing to them, for they, my correspondents, *are dead to me, till you are interested in them.* Every morning now, for a year and a half, I have said "I will write to Masefield", "I will write to Masters" but I have not. I have just written to you. You hold the man of letters in me in absolute slavery; and *until you become a woman of letters,* he remains a slave. And I think it is just right. But you must let me train you till you have taken over all that world I left behind when I gave you the "Golden Treasury". And, curiously, the key is in the Golden Treasury. That first Elizabethan section holds you, like a dragon-fly in amber. It does not describe today's Chicago, Greenwich Village or San Francisco flapper. But every poem, almost, describes the shepherdess you are, and you instinctively desire to be, and you were, at one of the Gulf Park fraternity dances, or the other shepherdesses you have been all along, at Sunday School. Have you ever listed the number of pretty artificial shepherdesses, loved by hot men, yet mental-peace bisque-doll shepherdesses, there are in the first section of "The Golden Treasury"? And for all the arrant nonsense of it, it is the greatest period of English Lyric Poetry too. Your love of the magazine Vanity Fair goes along with this. You are the only young woman creature I know who can dance so hard and love Vanity Fair so hard, and yet love the Good Beautiful Christ so well, with all your pure soul. *I was destined, from the beginning, to love a hard-dancing hard-praying woman.* The second section of the Golden Treasury Holds Milton. Please, please move on to Milton. I am truly the child of Milton, far far more than you know. Like Milton, I would, could not bear to think that your dances spoiled your prayers or prayers spoiled your dances. Now I will tell you the most sacred literary secret of my whole life as a sweetheart, and as far as I know I have never told a breathing soul, and yet it has everything to do with the most holy yet voluptuous things I have ever written you. When I was nine years old, about as innocent as a pan of milk, I read Paradise Lost, and there found, written out in far more elaborate and realistic talk than Doctor Wakefield ever gave you as a Physician, Milton's dream of married love. *It is always left out of the school-books and therefore children are bored to death with Milton.* It is "What a Young Girl Ought to Know", beautifully changed into the most marvellous and detailed song of Adam and Eve before the fall. And it changed me into a living flame, passion to the uttermost. And I will never be satisfied till you have told me you have read every line of it. For certainly the blind Milton wrote all that bridal-bed poetry praying on his knees, as a Christian, and it is the *only* poetry I have ever read anywhere I want to be read with my mated woman, except the Song of Songs, and it is better than the Song of Songs, far more important, for it is truly Anglo-Saxon. I am asking Paul to send to you and your Papa and Mama the Mayo Report, in summary.[1] It is entirely too hard and scientific for a lover, yet I owe you these things, being 44. You must know the Adam you are offered is about as strong 44 can ever get. Please let Milton's Eden set it right. *Way down in my soul still waits that little boy nine years old, who read for all time in Milton what Eve meant,* and who has kept himself virgin for her ever since. My very virginity and the terrible assaults of all the modern world on such a life, and my own long long struggle to consecrate, struggle struggle to harness every naked passion, have almost wrecked me at times. And the Bohemians who feel my pulse when they get a chance and write me up as a "teetotaler" and a "puritan" as though it were a disgrace, know nothing about me. I do not tell them that my dream of Eve and of my bride was fixed for ever at nine years old by reading the most holy, yet voluptuous lines of Milton's Paradise Lost, and I have walked in flame and splendor yet kept from women all these years looking for that White Eve, that mate before the fall, who was destined for me from the beginning, and who is as far from a prude, or a "suppressed desire", as far from what they call a Puritan as could well be imagined. Yet Eve till the fall was praying a little harder than she loved, no matter how desperately she loved. And people seem to think, never having read Milton or the Bible, that the fall was when Adam and Eve loved one another as man and wife should, thus people are destroying the whole value of the Second Chapter of Genesis, and Milton too. The funny papers are full of it, the idea that the fall was the honeymoon. They think the Bible says desire is wicked, and that Genesis says so. Because of that philosophy Christian marriage is often a failure. *The fall was when they loved harder than they prayed. And so I get back to my little sermon, no matter how hard you dance, pray a little harder when you get home.* Get right down on your *knees* and put your face in your little chair and pray like you were nine years old. If you do this I will let you dance till your feet are flames, and you are a new poem, a lady Milton; a lady Eve all of fire, every night of the year. *I want my mate to be a praying Eve and remember if you read what Milton says of the bridal, you will be meeting face to face the dreams of a little boy nine years old,* who has never yet taken bride or mistress into his arms, but has hunted for them all life long, with ardent desire, *not* fear. You will find yourself at dances completely surrounded by people who have given up prayer because they are perfectly wild with desire, greedy to put all life into one week of passion, people who do not think that desire or prayer *can* go together, and have therefore made their choice, and have surrendered unutterably to desire. I tell you darling, they are wrong. Read the Song of Songs. *Every dance should be the beginning of a higher sweeter aspiration and can be if you hold the dream of your final mate in your heart all the while. It is the mating season, and you are finding your Adam.* I surely want you to find him, and whatever it costs me in renunciation, if you belong to a boy of twenty six, be honest about it. Dearest, I surely want him chosen with a high heart. As sweet and noble matches have been made on the dance floor as anywhere in the world. And every man that dances with you with respect has a better final chance with you than I have, and ought to have, *for you are choosing the natural mate of your body as well as your mind,* and the boy who makes your hand tingle the most has as good a chance to be the right one, as any poet who writes you one poem or prayer or ardent voluptuous letter a day! Every day, I say to myself:—"Maybe she is choosing now. Maybe she has chosen. Lightning has struck her from the face of some greedy handsome youth!" Yet, dearest, way back in my mind *I cannot help but fancy you have enough self-control to postpone all choosing for awhile.* And I hope this is our happy play time, and time of taking stock. Therefore I send six kisses ****** here! If you think my letters are too full of the love of your body's beauty, remember I see my rivals dancing with you till two in the morning till you are utterly beside yourself with desire, and more than one of them with a flask, drinking when you do not know it. I want you to triumph at two in the morning. I want you to be unutterably in glory, *but the coolest head there.* If you are that, you are still Milton's, and our kisses mean Empire, and the dreams of literary Empire, and the Empire of literary dreams. Oh Eve before the Fall! Few Queens can stand the test of self-control. Yet this is not a sermon. It is a dream of our Empire. It is only the preface to some very hard thinking I have been doing, so far from these subjects, yet laced with them, my darling. You get all the letters I used to write to all the writers and critics of England and America. They bore you and should bore you, all but about one letter in seven. You like the short ones best. Yet a twenty page letter is a battle in our war for literary Empire, and I want you to stand up and take it. A twenty page letter is as natural to me as breathing, as it was to my mother before me. I could earnestly write to you *all day, every day,* and the letters would probably make a better book than any I will ever write. *I could write till 2:30 in the morning, just as naturally as you can dance till 2:30, as passionately, as luxuriously,* showing all my powers of rhythm, showing off just as proudly. The question is: *how to marry your dancing feet to my dancing pen?*; and do it as innocently as the bridal bed of Milton's Adam and Eve before the fall. I mean it with all my heart, my own, my life, my sweet darling, or I would not be so plain-spoken. *We must be married this summer feet and pen; in the sight of Heaven, even if we never meet on earth again.* Intellectually it is destruction for me to write *everything* to you, and to no one else on earth—unless henceforth you take my books and brains with all the detailed delight I take in every dimple in—(your little finger!) Please study my books all over again—and Graham's book.

Prose	Verse
1. Handy Guide for Beggars	1. Booth
2. Adventures While Preaching	2. Congo
3. Art of the Moving Picture	3. Nightingale
4. Golden Book	4. Golden Whales
	5. Collected Poems
	6. Going to the Sun

11. Paradise Lost
12. The Golden Treasury (first two sections)
13. Graham's Book

I do not care if you let all other books alone forever.

I want you to study *these* as thoroughly as though you were working for an Advanced Degree in Oxford University. I want you to take six years for it. I want you to note on every page the errors, and precisely where you differ in views of Art, Life, Love, Religion or Poetry. I want you to apply to these books exactly that same steady studious brain that gave you A + in Word School A + in High School and A + straight through Gulf Park College. All over America professors of English Poetry are doing this, and giving courses on my work. I do not even answer their letters. I would like by some surgical operation to put the results of the study of any one of them inside your left eye or under your red heart; or where you like to be kissed the most. Why get A + in all the infinite details of twenty Gulf Park text-books you will never again open in your life, when my eleven text books are absolutely suffering for a woman who will quit sewing and housekeeping long enough to *learn* them, a real woman sweetheart to love them, some one soul in America who knows them that well? I want you to *know every one of them* better than any text book on which you received the highest honors. I want you to go at this task will [*sic*] endless patience, with six years infinite *steady love* and friendship. In short I want you to know the details of my life-business in exactly the way you learned the details of your fathers office for the week you were there, or the way Miss Walker knows every detail of the Gulf-Park letter-files for six or three years back. Will I ever be so stern with you again; will I ever ask you to do this again? No! No! I am today asking you is this the way to marry my dancing and rhythmic and singing and tireless pen to your tireless dancing feet? We, somehow must make the match. However we make it, I want every pound of your brains as a submissive and detailed student to go into it.

Here is a kiss * Another *

I want you to go to England with me in about six years. It will take me
that long, with all the help your hand-holding and reading Milton can
give me, to get ready for as strong a literary attack on England as I made
with my mother in 1920, for three months. Every one in the literary
world has voted this trip a success. I want you to be the woman of the
next expedition. My mother won by her force and idependence every
step of the way, and certainly she did all the fighting. Why did she win?
Because every line I ever wrote, was her opinions and ideas rewritten
into a dance, into an act, into a song. She never knew it. But that was
the secret of our double force. *Well, I want to take six years to write into
songs for England and the Anglo-Saxon world, the spirit of Elizabeth very
proud, very fiery, very sweet setting at Humbolt [sic], going to a "knock-out
dance" as she calls it, promising with all her darling soul, to step high for my
sake.* Here is a kiss * If we go to England it should be, as before with my
mother, two months or three, to ride the same crest of the same wave,
and go back before it is spoiled. Once every line I wrote led back toward
my mother. I want completely to rebuild my world till it all leads to you
before that time. That is one of the things I meant by offering you my
mother's ring. Every one insists she was 2/3 of my trip to England. She
gave it all its reserve force. Till you are willing to take her place and
more, I am a lost man. You must let me pour every idea of all ten books
into you, a Niagara, with Elizabeth surrendering like a bride to her
bridegroom. Please go this summer to as many dances as I write letters
and dance in your mind every sentence you like of my letters, surrendering as a mystic spiritual bride who has given up every bit of herself
to her lover. Receive it like the gulf receiving Niagara. And then it will
all come back to me later in your dances and your thoughts and your
doings, never fear, in the next six years infinite things from you for me
to think about. You must be the absolutely happy, willing mother of
one thousand intellectual children. You love me like a friend, yet my
books and letters have not been for you battles for our Empire of dreams.
They have been, for this year and a half for the most part, a bore to
you. And the *English Magazines* too. But remember when I sent those
magazines, I dreamed that like my mother, you would meet in London
the editors and writers of those articles, and they would honor you as
they honored her. *Please* look at them saying "I am going to England
to meet these people soon, and talk to them about these very things.
I may dance—with some of them. Griffin will not meet one. In seven
trips to England, Mama met none, till I sang for them. Griffin will not
meet one of them. She will be bored to death if she does meet them,
not being ready. I want you to be ready to conquer them. *Certainly I will
not go without you. Not one step. I will stay in Spokane till I rot.* We want

to carry Spokane, and Brownsville, and Springfield and Gulf Park in our own dances and poem-games to England in an Imperial conquest. That is what the literati of America still consider their Empire, still unconquered. Let us take from the British the Empire of song in literary conquest. They say to me, in New York, in flattery, I am the only American Poet to whom the English have been polite for twenty years. Well I know how it was done, *and can do it again with you on my heart. Without you, the whole thing is not worth one damn to me,* and I will go on boring you, and that will be my life boring you with a letter a day you answer once in seven days. I am pouring out all my literary life in these letters. And your short replies are poems. There is nothing naughty about shortness. The literary world has praised most verses of mine shorter than your letters. I am every day in silence and letters pouring at your feet *all the nervous force I poured into the conquest of England.* I cannot help it. When I am not writing to you, I am talking to you in my thoughts and dreams. Till you rouse yourself to reconquer my world, I will not. *I hold back every day for you to see the vision complete.* I want to take you to England in six years. It will take that long to establish absolutely in our kisses, letters, dances and new poems, our new dreams of literary Empire; and Empire of new literary dreams—make new literary lines strongly, completely. I hope in that time we will get closer and closer together, as steadily as we have in the past. This:—

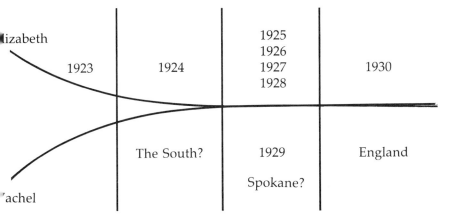

It is for you to judge what progress we are making, and when we change from friends to lovers. You are the woman-ruler of my life. The rest is whether you kiss me or not, as you decide, no sooner! *I have dreamed that we should go to England* while our long honeymoon is still on, and if we have children, have them afterwards, as a sort of celebration of our conquest, settled down in the U.S.A., citizens perhaps of the West, again. And all this of course subject to chance and fate. Unless you know my books you cannot lead me to the next kisses that dream of Empire, the next dear literary climax that will be a poem-game in the end, and justify my going to England after the English hear of that in some song disguised, that literary climax. I have forgotten what my books say. I want you to give them back in kisses. I want you to know them infinitely better than I do so when I take a new step into our empire, a new step, you will know it before the critics do, so when it is a literary surprise, the lady will say "I told you so". It will not be as hard for your brain as one year at Columbia. Study how to marry my pen to your dancing feet and dancing soul, till the pen becomes truly alive. If you conquer your diffidence, this will not be as hard as a year at Gulf Park, not anything like as hard. And there you were conventionally and primly pleasing teachers you may never see again, when your lovers whole fate may depend on your intellectual faithfulness and pride. Why has Edgar Lee Masters gone to smash—with drink bad women and drugs? Mrs. Masters had not the remotest notion of the *real meaning* of a single line he ever wrote, and didn't care. I will not be dissipated. Merely dull at the worst. But I *want to begin again*. Practically all the literati go to smash after their first little success for lack of some one mind knowing their affairs as well as any private secretary knows the affairs of a big businessman. Please—another kiss*. When I re-read this letter, how fierce it all sounds! Believe me, pretty—it is not meant so. I am *not* going to stick to Spokane, and make the hit of my life there for your sake. But I am burning to make our kisses there all *dreams of Empire, literary Empire*, thinking now of the acutest problems of literature, the difference between first rate and second rate success, which I face henceforth. And it all comes out of your darling note from Humbolt [sic]. *Please*, again remember exactly all you thought that hour. *If you can stay that way, my whole career is henceforth assured. A career is not important. A good kiss is worth it all.* But I am treated just like Babe Ruth or Bryan after their first hit. My whole little world demands a career of me. If you will get into this pretty game, if you will always look straight to me, as you did in that Humbolt [sic] letter, I will conquer the world (That is the foolish pasteboard literary world) again for you, and I will not repeat my old conquest. *It will be new, differing from the old as you differ from my mother.* It will be a fairies conquest, not the conquest of a distinguished, artistic subtle ecclesiastic, with a great air of innocence. My mother [was] actually a white witch, with a flaming ambition, disguised as a "religious leader".

Oh I know some of this long letter sounds like scolding. It is not so. I am only girding up my loins for the second battle. *I will not have them say I am a man of one book like Masters, or the author of "The Cloister and the Hearth".* We must have six great big books and then, after that, six real human children. We must go at it hard to multiply noble christian dances, poem-games, Miltonic chants, to multiply poems upon the face of the earth, then children. Mayo's certify I am raring to go and healthy enough to do it. You will take a real man to your breasts. And now—back to your Humbolt [*sic*] note. Please be awfully low brow. Please be stupid a lot. I do not want you to study any other books than those twelve or 13 or so, of mine. And knowing them thoroughly does not mean admiring thoroughly. I want you to despise them and say "Why Dont you write poems like I dance". "Why Dont you write poems more like Cupid Acts?" "Like Brown's Vill [*sic*] talks ? Like Spokane looks? But you must know what I *have* done, to offer the right suggestions *and I want you to marry* your dancing feet to my dancing pen, and read no other books than mine, and be a desperate low-brow and moron about all books [other] than mine. Be a wild dancer the rest of the time, the complete specialist who knows nothing but my thirteen books. And then study out dances better than my poem-games or chants or slang-stunts in the Collected Poems. Know King Solomon and the Queen of Sheba thoroughly, and then despise it. Say "I will teach Vachel better poem-games than that. And dance them for him. He will write them and then stand still while I dance circles round him." That is the way all Poem-Games are done. *I want you to help me lead the intellectual revels for* America, as once I did it alone. I cannot go alone again. I love you too much. I want you to help me lead the intellectual revels as alone I did it of old. *The literati of America can neither sing nor dance, so they let me sing and dance with them, and never despised me, as Gulf Park did.* The brainiest in the land caught my idea and did *not* think me awkward or a fool as Springfield and Gulf Park did. The literati, all afire, jumped right in and set all my awkwardness afire and redeemed it. And afterwards gave me the most dignified write-ups. Their faith was like your dancing at two A.M. Faith in me made me a surger. Their faith in me made me a dancer. And because I cannot wake to half-measures I want again to lead that dance. *I want you to help me lead in the intellectual revels of America. That is what the Poem-Games meant.* I am horribly awkward in conventional situations and that offends your nerves and conventional pride, and you duck your head and say you want to dance with "Red" and not with me. But in a brand-new situation, where there is an act to be made the world never saw before, be invented I am absolutely at ease. And in that situation what is your part? The part of opposite, the part of Eve, of Maude Adams,[2] Mrs. Vernon Castle[3] or Lillian Gish. That is: Elizabeth at the business of imitating and exaggerating herself, Elizabeth at her proudest. All you need to do is to dance as you did with your own mother in your own parlor. And I will stand still while you dance, and recite the story of the day. Whatever it appears to be, it will be to the rhythm of your knees. Whatever it appears to be, it will be the story of your pride, told in disguise. You will be the exquisite fairy conventional picture behind every loud song.

I hope we can devise every kind of parlor and stage stunt as dainty as your Vanity Fair, and as good as you at your prayers. We must write poems about *everything* in America we really enjoy, and prepare to act and dance it out for the literary centers and England. It must be holy, spotless, revelling, and laughing and praying, angels all hatched in the South and the West! for there is where the *real life comes from*, and the *real* American life. *All visits to New York or England should be very brief, just to put our idea into the show case, and to get new authority, then go home and devise new revels and lead them.* Every new dance you learn is a part of the scheme, and every new slang song and every piece of popular slang. Dance as much as I write and Especially those things that have real pride and dignity way under them. You had better dance than study. *Always* you must be *proud.* Do not touch a single act or idea but what builds your pride higher. Any dances that approach the minuet, where the partners are at the business of acting and bowing at arms length, is worth thinking about. I do *not* want you to be an aesthetic dancer, or actress. I want you to be Elizabeth, just as Lillian Gish is always just Lillian, Maude Adams always Maude Adams and Mrs. Vernon Castle was always just herself all the way to Paris and back. I am your dancing teacher henceforth. *Please,* Here are my directions. Always carry yourself with the real dance-style, the marvellous dignity and dash with which you cut the cake at the Birthday Party. That was perfect. It was a *perfect dance,* Elizabeth. We must call our acts "The Elizabethan Dances" and refer inquirers to the first section of the Golden Treasury. The way you took your bow on Graduation day was another dance. Your back was straight. Your face was proud and sweet enough for a thousand kisses. *I tell you the whole literary world will fall down before a straight back, a proud face and eyes full of prayer.* I tell you you can conquer further than my mother, and she was a lion for conquest. All you need is your sweet pride. Our whole tribe is made to conquer or die. You must fight by my side darling, or I will die. I cannot fight alone. I cannot live without Empire, foolish as that may be. Though I do not believe in conquest, though I know all the folly of glory. Poetry is absurd. *But this is the one game I seem born to play—and it is forward or death with me.* When my proud imagination dies, my very body goes to pieces. *We must have a new big dream and go at it like eagles and lions.* I cannot avoid my fate. It was easier to persuade All Oxford to be civil than Springfield Illinois.

There is nothing to do but conquer, If I am to live. It is all they will let me do. When I am everyday they dislike me. Oh you have the makings of a magnificent dancer, if you just think this one thought *"Pride, Pride, Pride, Pride."* The pride of Caesar and Cleopatra. Look every time the word pride appears in that poem and lift your feet high. Christ who is our dear lover, knows it is only child's play, and before we die we are both humbly willing to be crucified for him. I am only outlining for you the child's play of literary conquest, the special kind of kissing together for which we seem to be born. We are meant to kiss together over the doll's house of Anglo-Saxon Literature, the Golden Treasury. In the end it will mean no more than your pretty card-Party for Ann Arthur, but I give you my word it will be easier for me to make you the Lion of London than learn to play cards. I have lion-sense, not card-sense. I can rouse for an enormous dream only. It seems a toy to me. I can remember when you came out to me so reluctantly when we swam together. But you walked swiftly, and you held out your beautiful swimming cape like an Angel's wing, like a love-banner and like psyche—the dear, the butterfly. You lifted your knees proudly. *Your head was very high. The fluttering cape was like the unloosed robe of a goddess going on to her throne.* Now all you need is always that pride. The grace then comes of itself. The motion then comes of itself. Please swim with me when next I come to Brownsville, and carry your cape just like that on the edge of sweet memory, for old sake's sake, on the edge of the pool before you go in. You may yet dance, in capes almost like that, with that same dignity. The cape—and the pride and the carriage is everything, and the high heart.

There is always a touch of conventional dignity in *everything* you do, like the dignity of Irene Castle. Yet it takes on a fairy shepherdess form with you, and puts her way in the shade.

Remember to dance as many hours as I write you letters, every day, and then write me fairy love letters about it. When I take you to England I want to take you as a fairy, not a mortal woman. And oh, give all your strength to me, now. And please kiss me so hard you will keep me the nine year old boy that dreamed of Eve for his bride; from nine years old till now. That nine year old boy is still waiting for the nine year old child in you, is still crying and lonely with love inside of me. If you kiss me hard enough, you will keep me that boy. And if you dreamed my kisses as I dream yours, you would dream them all night and all day, with complete surrender.

If Eugenia and Mary Laura and Pat and those dearest to you, marry the right men, we may in the end scatter our songs a long way and deeply into the fabric of private life. We may be able to set up your old court gradually in some new western town like Spokane. But it must be a place where I have established my kind of life, for you and I must really go forward as a team, not held back by people who remember yesterday too well. *We must go forward as a team. Then being established, we can gather our own about us. And occasionally leave them for London.* But I pray you my darling, henceforth take my whole new life in your arms, and let me take yours. Let us do it this summer in our plans and dreams, and see in the fall if it has worked. Dance till your feet are fire and see if you do not just naturally dance toward me. I have been writing on and on, and the train climbs steadily toward Glacier Park. We will be there in two hours.

With love

VACHEL

Notes

1. Paul Wakefield had persuaded VL to go to Rochester, Minnesota, to undergo diagnostic tests at the Mayo Clinic. The reports are not available at this time.
2. J. M. Barrie was associated with theater manager Charles Frohman, whose principal star was Maude Adams. For millions of Americans, Maude Adams actually "became" Peter Pan.
3. Irene Castle and her husband, Vernon, popularized the one-step, the fox-trot, and the Castle walk.

138

TO HARRIET MOODY

Glacier Park Hotel
August 27, 1924

My Dear Harriet Cordelia:—
I am making my second visit of the season to this park, and my third in this life. I will come again before Oct. 1.

In and around September 30 or Oct. 1 it is my devout hope to see Prof. James H. Breasted of the University of Chicago—and when that conjunction of planets occurs the thunder should be heard to Mars. Anything you can do toward this objective of meeting James H. and getting his earnest cooperation for 1000 years will be the act of a noble, patient, self-denying Cordelia and a good sport. You hint you have a mad on about my going to Chicago University for the preliminary skirmish without informing or consulting you. But dear friend if you didn't get a mad on once in a while, over my prodigal disposition to follow my relentless destiny—why you would not be Cordelia and I would not be Vachel. All my friends have a relentless disposition to preserve me intact, a fly in amber, just as I happened to be the first day we ever met. Yet I am changing and changing, and right now my Chicago conspiracy is to acquire all the Wisdom of the Egyptians, a complete knowledge of six Coptic dialects, Hebrew, Modern Arabic and all the details of Classic Egyptian Grammar of the period of Amenemhat—about 2000 B.C. I want to get all this, Breasted's Life work, from him, in one concentrated interview, of about two hours in the Haskell Oriental Museum, Chicago University. I want to get this while he strolls with me casually from mummy to mummy. To do it in one interview will require all my powers of absorption and concentration. (Joke) [A smiling face is drawn here.] By way of preparation I have sent on ahead my Cleopatra Poem—from The American Mercury for August to Breasted, Prof J. George Allen, both of the Haskell Oriental Museum, *and* to Arthur Weigall in England. Weigall has just written a blazing good book on Cleopatra, just imported by Putnam's I believe, well worth your scrutiny for general reasons of Curiosity and divertissement, but also from an unselfish standpoint, since it carries out completely for 250 pages the hypothesis of Vachel's Poem on Cleopatra, which was derived from a hint in Ferrero[1] and which same hint Weigall and Vachel both apparently began to work on about three years ago. I am enormously indebted to Weigall—and hope his book and my song may both make a good [winter?] in America. I am here in Glacier Park for a week—reading proof on the Poem for book form. It comes out before Christmas in the New Edition of my Complete Collected Poems.[2] That book will have a long long new preface, about 100 more pages of verse, and 40 of my illustrations.

My address till I see you around Oct. 1 will be The Davenport Hotel[3]—Spokane, Washington.

I will teach again in the south, especially up till Christmas, but plans are slowly forming to use the Davenport Hotel as a center for several years. All my goods are there—and I have already many ties in the North West—which is the part of the West Coast that means the most to me right now. It is a land of forests, meditation and sanctuary, and I have the best promise of isolation, quiet and study among my lifelong accumulations of books, papers and notes—in the top floor of the Davenport I have had for a long time. I am so deep in the matter of real study, especially a clear review of books once studied, and my old note books back to college days, I hate with a poisonous hatred all idea of performing, and only appear when I must—when it enables me to travel and see my friends. Slowly my book income begins to increase and there is at least a hint I may ultimately live on it. Meanwhile several western schools let me teach one day a month, thus avoiding touring and "performing" and enabling me to go back to the Davenport a good part of the time. These plans will mature in a year or so.

Meanwhile I keep up my Gulf Park ties, teaching four hours a week for three weeks in a month—and writing the rest of the time in the Great Southern Hotel. You will find the complete Record of the Gulf Park and Gulfport big days in a two page poem in The New Republic any time now— The Poem is called "Billboards and Galleons" and I sent the final proof back to Torrence a week ago. This poem will also appear in the back of the Christmas Edition of The Collected Poems.

I have done more verse the last year and a half in Gulfport than for the seven years before, simply because I sat still and reduced the reciting and the teaching to a minimum. I have seen two classes graduate at Gulf Park and there is a complete new school every year, for the girls come down there for a year of the coast, and of swimming. So those fifty pupils I have had are scattered now all over Tennessee and Mississippi—dancing hard and getting married as fast as possible. I am hoping to have their husbands, sons and grandsons for friends, and grow up with the new South. And Cox will be my lecture manager for this winter.

I see myself slowly moving into the Northwest without losing touch with the South—or Springfield. For instance—The Jefferson Printing Co. Springfield Illinois is just printing 5000 of a new imprint of "The Village Magazine"[4] for such of the Old Neighbors as will be especially interested. This as before to be given away. There will be a special interest in it because the 40 drawings in the new Macmillan book are lifted from The Village Magazine.

I see myself moving northward in a kind of a curve, passing through Springfield and Chicago as the years roll by, studying a great deal in the Davenport Spokane, getting all of Glacier Park and the Northwest I can,[5] and some day going down to Hollywood for several months to re-write "The Art of the Motion Picture". It is being lavishly spread about down there—on a new campaign—since Carl Bush the Executive Secretary of the Hollywood Chamber of Commerce is married to Flossie Lindsay—a cousin of mine.

In short—dear Harriet—I am "touring" as of old, only instead of a national reciting tour, in six months, as of old, under Armstrong, yelling my damned head off—I am really trying to teach, study and write as I tour, and take a lifetime to follow up my old studies, enlarge and complete my ten books, and behind a high barricade of those ten books, get acquainted with my friends all over again. So many cannot understand I have utterly repudiated the old system of storming the towns. I hope you are not one of these. I must be allowed to be a *student*, a *student*, a *student*, as I was till I was 32. I have been living on studies made before my 32nd year—here to my 44th year, and I will make any sacrifice behind my barricade of ten books, to be allowed to be a real student of all those matters on which I kept fat note-books up to my 32nd year.

I had moved everything from Springfield.

All the material is piled up in the Davenport Hotel in the most orderly fashion—the best-ordered room and the best sorted manuscripts I have ever had. The new life now begins, with the fairest auspices and the finest friends imaginable and I most earnestly urge your cooperation. The new fat preface of the Collected Poems, written one year ago in Cleveland, deals with all this, and this letter is only an earnest personal word, added to that preface.

The bus is starting for Sun-Camp. I must mail this and will write more personally later.

The letter is—briefly—I am still infatuated with the entire map of the USA, especially the South and West—but am now resolved to take it a crumb at a time instead of swallowing it whole all over again, every season. Also when I am West of the rockies, I am not afraid the study of Egypt will ruin me!

With love,

VACHEL

Notes

1. Guglielmo Ferrero (1871—1942) was an Italian historian whose books were condemned and destroyed in Italy in 1935. His historical vision sometimes presaged that of Oswald Spengler. *The Greatness and Decline of Rome,* in five volumes, was published 1907—9. Another of Ferrero's works that VL may have read was *The Women of the Caesars* (1911). At the end of his poem on Cleopatra (*Collected Poems,* p. 464), VL writes: "On reading the latest proof of this poem, I have found a book that elaborately confirms the political hypothesis: "The Life and Times of Cleopatra, Queen of Egypt—A Study in the Origin of the Roman Empire", by Arthur Weigall, published by Thomas Butterworth, Limited, 15 Bedford Street; London W.C. 2.; and P. P. Putnam's Sons, 2 West 45th Street, New York City. But the same idea may be found in Ferrero's 'Greatness and Decline of Rome' in all the comment on Cleopatra. I have outlined this poem of mine as a possible photoplay in 'The Art of the Moving Picture', pages 254-260."
2. The new edition of the *Collected Poems* came out on the day of VL's marriage to Elizabeth Conner, May 19, 1925.
3. The owner of the Davenport Hotel with several of VL's Spokane friends, including

Benjamin H. Kizer, a local international lawyer, had arranged for VL to stay at the hotel (Room 1129) at a nominal cost, as a sign of their appreciation of his work.
4. The third and fourth imprints of *The Village Magazine* came out in 1925, before and after VL's marriage.
5. On the same day, VL had sent a copy of a catalogue used in Glacier National Park to direct tourists. It represented some of the Indian cave-paintings in the park. VL had annotated it and underlined the fact that there was an objective, indigenous basis for his research on American hieroglyphics.

139

TO RICHARD G. COX

Davenport Hotel
Spokane
October 14th, 1924.

My Dear Zim:—

I have read and reread, very carefully and thoughtfully, your letters of the 4th and the 7th,[1] and have tried to understand in what way I could deserve all the reproach that these letters contain. If I seem to you to have been "unfair and unkind", I must have said, impulsively, more than I soberly meant, for it is farthest from my thought to be either unfair or unkind to *you*. Let me restate my feeling about the situation, understate it if necessary, that it may not have even the appearance of unfairness.

First, let me acknowledge that I may have seen an intentional thwarting of plans in many cases where there was merely a lack of interest, or a disposition to put off or postpone what seemed to me immediately possible. It ought to be manifest to every one that I was not at Gulf Park merely to become a routine teacher, or to mark time in the recitation room. But the fact is, whatever the motives of those surrounding me may have been, that I was completely isolated, without an active ally in any of the projects of the Seven Arts. To the extent that there was interest, it was simply in me as a person, as a novelty, as a literary figure. Interest in my books there was none, nor was I able to create any. I meant every word of "A Handy Guide for Beggars", but no one else was effectively willing to believe any part of it.

Perhaps I expected too much, perhaps your students are too young, perhaps the general atmosphere of any such school as yours is not hospitable to any such a specialized teaching and interest in the arts as I have. It is not necessary that we place blame, or lay emphasis upon motives. The important point is that I must, in a large degree, live upon the response that I am able to evoke from human beings in the arts in general (of which the greatest is the art of living), and in poetry in particular. It won't do to refer to "our slow response to things artistic". I am not merely impatient over slow beginnings; I haven't made headway enough at Gulf Park to call it a start in the right direction.

Nor do I think you can say to me that I must be "prepared henceforth to despise all friendships". It was precisely because I have valued our own friendship so highly that I have delayed so long in telling you how impossible the situation at Gulf Park has become for me. I have been thinking over it for many weeks, yet dreading to speak because of my devotion to you personally, until finally the situation forced my hand, and it all came out in a rush, the accumulated, dammed-up mass of despondency and depression over the failure of my work at Gulf Park. I acknowledge that I ought to have spoken of it all, frankly and fully, at the end of the last school year. Had I been a cooler person, I should have done so. But it was impossible then, and it has only become possible as I have had time to think it out and to find here a totally different situation.

You speak of the "contract". Do you think the arrangement by which a small part of my expenses of living were paid, in return for what I undertook to give, amounted to a "contract"? I hoped and expected to return, and I made no demands on you, but I hardly think that a contract, or a pledge of any sort. The small contribution toward my expenses made by your board indicated to me as plainly as anything could that your board did not in the least value what I was undertaking to do, that they would not feel my absence as seriously as that of the most insignificant servant on the place. To me, the vital thing in these letters is our personal relation, not my legal relation with your board. There, at least, I feel sure you have nothing with which to reproach me.

One year and a half of isolation and insulation on the coast is enough. You direct me to come back to it at my own expense. I belong to nothing down there, and am welcome in no group outside the school longer than forty minutes, if I advocate seriously a single idea in any of my ten books. The publicity is to be skimmed off and used, and the books left closed. But I meant what I said in my books. They represent years of struggle.

Dancers experiment and dance with my poems—but not on the Gulf Coast. Architects discuss my ideas of architecture—but not there. Dramatists dramatize my stuff, and the movie-people—some of them—read my books. I could hardly get away from Hollywood this summer, but my movie-book counts not one inch from New Orleans to Mobile. Gordon Craig, editor of the "Mask", the greatest single force in the drama in the Anglo-Saxon world, wrote to me steadily from Rome a whole year on the strength of the movie-book. So far as I know, no Gulf Park girl has ever read the book, or applied it to a single film, though they were all marched to the movies for every Monday as regularly as clock-work.

I have had more co-operation from Percy Grainger here in one evening than from Gulf Park from the beginning. He *discussed* my ideas, pro and con. He assumed ideas exist. I have been consulted on pageants here involving three states. I am introduced to dancers who may dance my work, and to actors who may act it. I get letters from a number of people in this region who act my work, or hope to, and from others who write books, or hope to. In Gulf Park, the board of trustees is openly hostile to a library, and their policy is to have as few books around as possible. Obviously, indifference to the one maker of books present is as natural as breathing. They cannot be suspicious of books, and smile genially on authors at the same moment.

But I must not go on. I do not want to argue with you. I only want you to see how fatal to me is the atmosphere in which you manage to survive. Your lot is cast in with them, and you do not see the situation as I do. I am hurt by that which does not hurt you, and I am suffocated where you can get your breath. I hate to give you up, but I must live and I cannot live at Gulf Park. I should love to retain your friendship and your good-will, but I realize that I cannot do it by writing letters defending my need to separate myself from your life at Gulf Park, so I can only hope that time and chance may some day enable you to see more clearly than you now can how necessary it is that I should say good-bye to Gulf Park.

With good wishes as ever,

VACHEL

Note

1. By October VL had grown tired of Gulf Park, saying it was "sterilizing" him. He wrote a rather sharp letter to Richard G. Cox, telling him of his intention never to return there. Cox's answer was—understandably—written in a vexed tone.

140

TO KATHARINE LEE BATES

Spokane
October 28, 1924

Dearest Katharine Lee Bates:
My heart was just melted today by a beautiful letter from Gamaliel Bradford.[1]

And yesterday I received notice that my Phi Beta Kappa poem—1922—Bob Taylor, which I had spent so long improving—was crowded out for excellent reasons from the Harvard Monthly and if it appears anywhere it will be in the Transcript under Braithwaite[2] who will guide its destiny henceforth. I will be so happy if it so appears, I have "donated" it to them, full and free. Meanwhile I have sent Braithwaite a long exclusive bunch of material on my illustrated Collected Poems, which will be merely my Village Magazine pictures the 40 best—merged into the Macmillan Collected Poems of two years ago.

Besides many loyal "well-wishers", I have four friends in New England and they seem true as steel—true to death. They are Gamaliel Bradford, yourself, the Transcript[3] and the Christian Science Monitor. I was *so* touched by Bradford's letter, and I thought of first writing to him, *then* of writing to you and asking you to share the letter with Bradford. I have a few friends like you four all over the country, true as steel, who will stand by me. All the rest seem puzzled. If *you* stand by me—I will really get somewhere.

I want my Map of the Universe studied by students of Egypt and students of Blake. I want a few people with the patience of Job to begin with your earliest prints of my drawings and my War Bulletins, especially Bulletin number three and completely destroy my present standing such as it is in England and America, and substitute a point of view based on such material as The Map of the Universe.

You see I was caught between two millstones. I was born with a voice so they thought me a weaker Bryan. I was born with dancing feet so they thought me Jazz. I used the word once or twice when it meant spice. But *just after that* the world, the whole world went jazz-mad—a thing none of us could have prophesied and I have been worn to my soul welcomed to a thousand towns where I have had to explain to thousands I was *not* a Jazz artist—and the saxophone, which I hate—was read into everything I ever did.

Now it seems to me Boston my most gallant enemy and bitter detractor has enough sense of fair play to re-examine the evidence and start a complete systematic backfire. You are the only person in New England with the documents—Bradford has, certainly the precise English, and once Boston is converted it may be my best friend and citadel forever. Ralph Adams Cram[4] has the making of a most loyal friend, for the sake of the Golden Book.

I am printing a rainbow edition of 5000 copies of "The Map of the Universe", and I want the people I have named in this letter to consider a scheme for free and effective distribution of the most of the copies in their constituency, and to it I will [add] a full share of the new edition of 5000 copies of "The Village Magazine" of 1924.

I am *dead in earnest* about these things Katharine Lee Bates. I hate with all my body and soul and mind and spirit my public newspaper reputation in the Anglo-Saxon world, and you know it is contradicted by *every* private document and letter in your hands.

Why should I travel another step to augment a curse? Here I am among friends who have read my early pamphlets from the beginning, *and* who judge me by them from first to last.

They are a musical set exclusively who hate Jazz as cheerfully as I do, and all such:

Here is the Place Percy Grainger comes to rest, and we are sworn friends for life. William Lyon Phelps was the first to parallel the common intention of our works in "The Advance of English Poetry in the 20th Century" and Grainger is all afire to carry Phelps Ideas put into print in 1918—right across America, and (I hope) is going to write a "Santa Fe Trail" to parallel "Spoon River", and to my mind that is the *only* way my work can be henceforth done from the platform, by men like Grainger, with an audience highly trained in the most classical standards of Music and expecting such, and not expecting a few phonetic tricks. I am sure Professor Macdougall[5] who has always been so kind and listened so *keenly* will help in this and I will be profoundly grateful if he can read this letter with you and give the most aggressive and practical advice. He always *listened* for the whisper so I was then ABLE to whisper. The prospect of Percy Grainger as a messenger is the greatest thing that has happened to me since I first met you, and my dear darling adored friends, if you can only capture Percy on his next visit to Boston and send him forth strengthened and vastly clarified as my messenger to the rest of the United States, you will cure me of a heart-ache that has lasted me for many a day. In a year or two I would *love* to appear in *one number*, just *one*, most carefully and precisely recited for Musicians Only after Percy had played an hour, and then have Percy play another hour and carry them back to complete music again, and his own work completely. I *hate* Barnumism. I *hate* Jazz. I *hate* metallic instruments. The promotion of my work as Jazz in England was a deliberate piece of treachery in England, since redeemed, three years after—by splendid reviews of my Collected Poems.

To put this roaring Buffalo-Bull [*sic*] letter into two sentences—There are two weapons in my warfare to destroy completely the Public Vachel:

(1) The Drawing and Hieroglyphic Weapon beginning with the Map of the Universe.

(2) Percy Grainger's Crusade for the highest points of abstract music in my work.

Percy is roaring and raring to go. He is going to make some enormous national tours, for ten times my audiences and ten times my fees. I want *everybody* that ever backed me to *go.* I have (it is alleged by my publishers) spoken for one million people in these twelve years. I want the whole million recruited and added to Percy's audiences. I am going to sit here and write 1000 poems and draw 1000 pictures about it. I want you *all* to come to see me here and talk about it to me!

Well, this is quite a storm!

Love me little, love me long, and God bless you.

With love indeed.

VACHEL

Notes

1. Gamaliel Herzberg Bradford (1863—1932), the biographer, poet, and dramatist, wrote *Damaged Souls* (1923).
2. William Stanley Braithwaite (1878–1962) for several years edited the *Anthology of Magazine Verse.*
3. The newspaper mentioned is the *Boston Evening Transcript,* for which Helen McMillin later interviewed VL.
4. Ralph Adams Cram was the author of *Walled Towns.*
5. Professor Hamilton C. Macdougall used VL's text in his drama activities at Wellesley in 1916. See *The Chinese Nightingale and Other Poems* (pp. 93—97) for an account of his work there.

141

TO H. L. MENCKEN

Spokane, Washington
Tuesday December 9, 1924

HL. Mencken:—
The American Mercury
730 Fifth Avenue.N.Y.C.

My Dear Friend:—
Thank you indeed for your approval of "The Map of the Universe".
George Mather Richards, Gamaliel Bradford, Carl Van Doren and several others like it so I am happy about it. Ruth St. Denis and Ted Shawn
heartily approve.[1]

But I am wild with glory over having tentatively interested Ruth St.
Denis in the "Trial of the Dead Cleopatra". She has made a great success
of the Egyptian Judgment Scene and has toured with it, but it never
occurred to her to try Cleopatra by that ritual. I read the poem to her
last week and she listened with eyes aflame. I hope you can drum up
all the wise to be interested in this *hypothetical* project and resurrect the
August Mercury with Ruth St. Denis in mind. The re-reading of that
poem by your readers, with her in mind, the visualization, the dreaming, the expectation and discussion would do so much to help her
toward going on with it. And she has made a success of the more
difficult part already. The plan is to have a reader by the side of the
stage in front, a voice, but otherwise inconspicuous while the stage is
occupied by the story in dumb-show and dance. The University of Chicago has a regular production of The Chinese Nightingale put on regularly by Mrs. Hyman in this fashion. To realize that I had met a dancer
to whom the Egyptian Judgment ritual was A.B.C. was in itself a thrill.
And Ruth St. Denis herself is the very incarnation of the idea I have in
mind.

Of Cleopatra, she said "A child could do it!" Putnam's have now
brought out in beautiful paper, print and style in America Arthur Weigall's Cleopatra and half an hour with that book or even five minutes
with its blurb will help marvellously. With the help of Ruth St. Denis
and one hot paragraph from Weigall about Caesarion—that poem, in
your custody can march across the continent, and clear a path for Ruth
St. Denis' show. I have added about twenty lines to the Book Version

of my Cleopatra, coming out about January—condensing Weigall after a summer study of him. All you need to do is to look up the word Caesarion in the index and you get the additions in substance. I have added merely history and clarity, not poetry! These two people and yourself coming to the rescue of a poem I assumed would always be merely pedantic make one of the Romances of my life—which I hope you care to complete: Three planets meet from the corners of the Universe. I hope you care to quote my brief verse on Ruth[2] enclosed—though it is now pretty well scattered. Please help me to flatter that accomplished lady I so much admire.

Most sincerely

NICHOLAS VACHEL LINDSAY
Pen name VACHEL LINDSAY

PS My Collected Poems, including the Cleopatra, come out very soon. The last proof is in the hands of the Macmillan Company.

Notes

1. Ruth St. Denis and Ted Shawn, who had organized the Denishawn Dancers, danced in a manner reminiscent of Isadora Duncan's style, although their inspiration was more Egyptian and Hindu than Greek. VL set great store by their work, in which he saw an embodiment of his theories on dancing and the written word. Martha Graham first studied in Los Angeles at the Denishawn School, and her first professional appearance in 1920 was with Shawn.
2. The "verse on Ruth" may have been "Butterfly Picture-Writing," in *Every Soul Is a Circus* (p. 29), "written for Ruth St. Denis to dance on the top of a watch crystal." For Ted Shawn, VL wrote "The Voyage," which appears on the following page of the same volume.

142

TO HAROLD L. BRUCE

Davenport Hotel
Spokane, Washington
January 17, 1925

Professor Harold L. Bruce
California Hall
University of California
Berkeley, California

Dear Sir:
I thank you very much for the invitation to lecture for you for the summer session in Los Angeles.

I accept your proposition for a series of ten lectures in the general field of American Criticism and Poetry. I prefer to give the lectures once a day, beginning June 27. I accept your compensation, $50.00 a lecture, $500. for the course.

Now let me suggest as a title for the series, "Movies and Poems", "Movies and Poetry", or "Poems and Motion Pictures". I will undertake to read at least one of my poems of a general civic or American type, or directly concerned with the movies, at each session, not hesitating also to read the verses of other men.

I would be delighted if you could get the 1922 edition of "The Art of the Moving Picture". Read the foreword by George Willam Eggers, Director of the Denver Art Association. Also the chapter on the Prophet-Wizard, page 261, through to 276, where I discuss with considerable elaboration the relation of such poets as Poe and Yeats to the future of the motion picture. The original "Art of the Moving Picture", which I issued in 1915, through Macmillan Company, was the first textbook used by any university anywhere, in regard to the films. It was the basis of Victor O. Freeburg's classes in photoplay writing, which were conducted in the Columbia University School of Journalism from 1915 through to about 1917, by Freeburg, and are continued so far as I know, to this day. Freeburg wrote a textbook afterwards, published by the Macmillan Company, based on mine, and due credit is given in the preface.

I cite these matters because my reason for accepting your kind offer is that I wish to renew and strengthen very friendly ties first established by issuing the first book.

I have now almost ready for the publisher a book, entitled "The Progress of the Movie",[1] reapplying all the old doctrines of the first textbook to "The Thief of Bagdad", "Scaramouche", "Peter Pan", "The Covered Wagon", "Beaucaire" and "Merton of the Movies", all films now running, and representing the most distinguished aspirations of the films to the present hour.

I hope you can cooperate with me in the establishment of my old book and of its successor in a special way from now till my appearance in Los Angeles begins. Any measure which you consider reasonable will be indeed a favor. The opportunity is for me enormous, and I have only remained out of the motion picture field of esthetics and criticism of late because I was waiting for just such a chance as you now offer me.

If you care to glance over the one chapter on the Prophet-Wizard, you will surely get my drift. If you look over the back numbers of the New Republic of about 1916 or 1917,—I have not the index with me—you will find I was the first magazine critic of the motion picture, and if you will compare these criticisms with Sherwood's [2] in Life today, the best now written, I think you will concede that Mr. Sherwood and myself are of the same school of thought, and I am still in the stream of motion picture intelligence.

But to go forward to secure exactly the same attention in 1925 I had in 1915 and 1917 in a field now a thousand times larger, would require not only all my strength and careful thought, but all of yours that you can spare from now until I begin to speak. It is to me a situation so peculiarly strategic that I take the trouble to send you these many words about it.

On the ground I have many friends, Carl Bush, Secretary of the Hollywood Chamber of Commerce, was my guide through all the studios when I visited them last fall, and he will be prepared to cooperate in any way. He knows something of my relationship with the older schools of production. Whatever is left of the old Griffith machine is surely friendly if properly approached. Griffith himself, when my book first came out, was surely a most loyal friend of mine, and why not? If you read my book through, you will find he is the hero of nearly every page in spite of me, and people who might be considered graduates of the Griffith school, Anita Loos and John Emerson, have always cooperated and are prepared, I am sure, to be again very friendly. I do not even know their whereabouts, but I received from them a Christmas greeting.

Mae Marsh was always a friend of mine, and you see my song to her in my collected poems. When in Hollywood the last time, I was entertained by Douglas Fairbanks and Mary Pickford, and their scenario woman, Lotta Woods, and historical expert, Dr. Arthur Woods, her

husband, attended my lecture on "The thief of Badgad" at the Pacific
Palisade Association.

My friend, Mrs William Vaughn Moody, whose address is 2970 Ellis
Avenue, Chicago, will surely cooperate in any way possible. Of all the
literati who have been particularly close friends of mine, she is the one
who has taken the greatest practical interest in the films, has directed
two or three productions of "The Great Divide" and one of "The Faith
Healer".[3] She has been at Los Angeles again intermittently all year, and
is probably there this minute, though I advise you to address her in
Chicago. What she will have to say about the hard and battering struggle
to render some of the aspirations of William Vaughn Moody in the films
in the face of very hard-faced business organizations, will be well worth
hearing, and for me to go to the Hollywood region and preach my
idealistic sermons to this idealist who has borne the burden and the
heat of the day will be indeed ironical, but surely she will cooperate as
no other. She has been a very profoundly loyal friend of mine for many
years, and I am delighted as much at the prospect of renewing ties with
Mrs. Moody on something with which she has struggled every day, as
any prospect I have in this enterprise.

I have a cousin, Ruby Vachel Lindsay Maurice at 1035 Lincoln Street,
Los Angeles, I can depend upon as general hostess and guide in Los
Angeles. She has been there all along when I have visited purely as a
woman's club literary lion.

I have laid the case before you somewhat elaborately, not only to
make it clear that I consider this a special new start with the photoplay
people, and the general idealists of that region, but because of the thing
which I discovered when last I was in Hollywood: that the photoplay
people must be, in a sense, disarmed. World experts descend upon
them demanding enormous fees for small bits of information. Anything
from a geologist to an historian of Babylon feels at last this is a chance
to make a killing, and Los Angeles must definitely understand that this
is an idealistic enterprise, that the financial end you and I have already
settled, and that we are actually there to discuss this matter from the
standpoint of pure esthetic and world beauty.

One of the most amusing experiences of my life was to discover how
many of those people told me very readily that mine was the first book
they had ever read on the motion picture, and some of them the only
book, and then that look of being amazingly on guard, lest I should
offer to collect for a book read in 1915.

The general levantine atmosphere of Hollywood can be conquered,
however harsh it may seem. I am perfectly confident that the University
of California, with a firm hand, can assert the academic authority even
in that whirlpool. But I hope that you feel inclined to descend upon that

region with all my credential burnished bright, all my weapons sharpened, for me, and relieve me of this issue before I arrive.

Griffith put fifty copies of my book in his studios before he began to plan "Intolerance". If I should insist that the book influenced "Intolerance", the motion picture way of receiving that would be that I will begin to demand back salary. We must cure them of this. I am entirely too vain to allow any such point of view to exist in my presence. I really value honor, and I still am jealous for the honor, the purely abstract literary and esthetic honor, of having written the first book on the motion picture and of disarming these people till they will testify to my exact influence as an abstract student of esthetics in their purely esthetic moments.

I am going at the whole battle again in my new book, and I most earnestly urge your cooperation in any way that occurs to you. We will go down there first, last and always as students of poetry, bring these people all the way to the shrine of poetry, and get them to leave behind box office considerations for an hour a day.

Sincerely,

VACHEL LINDSAY

Notes

1. The movie manuscript, eventually entitled *The Greatest Movies Now Running,* was never published.
2. Robert Emmet Sherwood (1896–1955) did motion-picture writing in both France and Hollywood and worked with René Clair. Sherwood started the first regular motion picture critical column in the old *Life* and is considered a "father" of movie criticism. He was editor of *Life* (1924–28) and also covered film for the *New York Herald.*
3. *The Great Divide* (1906) and *The Faith Healer* (1909) were works by William Vaughn Moody.

143

TO AMABEL WILLIAMS-ELLIS

1129 Davenport Hotel
Spokane, Washington
February 3, 1925

My Dear Mrs. Ellis:[1]
It has indeed been a long time since we have had a real conversation by letter. The nearest to an intimate communication has been your meeting with Sara Teasdale Filsinger, who has been, I believe, to Paris since she brought out a British edition of "Flame and Shadow", and is now at last back in New York City. I have not seen New York for many a day, nor you, nor Mrs. Filsinger for several years. But I am glad to realize that your brief meeting has had something to do with friendship, for you have both mentioned it to me.

I have read and often thought of your discussion of Katherine Mansfield and D.H. Lawrence and others on the feminine revelation. Not having been a woman, nor being a specialist in exactly what the ladies are up to, I will have to reread your letter some more on that particular. I am surely glad to hear about your babies. There the light clears up, I get a very domestic feeling out of that part of your letter. Also, as to the feminine revelations, I want you to explain it to your children thoroughly, and have them explain it to me, because the older I grow, the younger I like them. I have just spent two years in a South Mississippi Finishing School, for the most ultra-Southerners that could possibly be imagined, and I am now the only poet in the Anglo-Saxon [world] with a finishing school education. But this feminine revelation of which you speak seems to be something more occult. I will turn it over in my mind, not dismissing the subject, but, as it were, entering into silence on the subject for awhile.

By way of thinking over my finishing school education in South Mississippi, I moved to Spokane, Washington, and have taken a new start. Here I am dictating a book on the movies, the first half of which is Douglas Fairbanks' "Thief of Bagdad" analyzed to the last hair. This book will soon be in the hands of the publisher, because it must circulate immediately before the new films discussed wear out.

Do not be appalled at the sight of the manuscript I enclose—"The Trial of the Dead Cleopatra in her Beautiful and Wonderful Tomb". It has already been printed in the American Mercury for August, published by the pugnacious H. L. Mencken, and it comes out about March 15 on the American side, in my Collected Poems, the new illustrated edition. I have sent it, in England, to J. C. Squire, and its sole publication and fortunes are in his hands. I hope he can bring it out in the London Mercury, despite its length, encouraged by all the gorgeous space he once gave me in the Spectator for "Johnnie Appleseed", including your own magnificent editorial and the very remarkable editorial by your father, the editor, which two bits of flattery sunk very deeply into my soul. If we measured all this space with a tape line, it would be longer than "Cleopatra" as it stands. I do not know if this will have due weight at this moment with the London Mercury, or not, but Squire, I suppose, has by this time made up his mind one way or the other.

As soon as the American book, the revised, illustrated collected poems, gets to England, which I suppose will be the next September, or the like, and begins to circulate, my "Cleopatra" will be circulating in the ordinary routine way in England. I send it to you just on a chance, remembering the parties you gave me and my mother, which included, unless I am mistaken, the group around the Lyric Theatre, Hammersmith. Possibly it is there I met Nigel Playfair.[2] At any rate, he is the person I have heard from the oftenest of late from England. He even went so far once to send me a wireless message for the privilege of putting on my "Blacksmith's Serenade" in vaudeville, and on the radio, all of which was very interesting, surprising and delightful. I have heard from him, all about this "Blacksmith's Serenade" on and off for some time. I understand Mr. Frederick Austin has set it to music. Frederick Austin must be a relative of mine. I understood from my mother I was kin to all the Austins on earth.

Well, Nigel Playfair seeming to cling to this "Blacksmith's Serenade" with amazing pertinacity under all circumstances, encouraged me to send him the more elaborate "Cleopatra". Ruth St. Denis, the wonderful and beautiful dancer, who has done the Egyptian ritual of the Book of the Dead many times successfully on American soil, on hardboiled vaudeville circuits, hopes to stage this poem somehow, some way. She has the American rights, if she wants them. Unless I am very much mistaken, your particular group of friends are especially associated with the Lyric Theatre, Hammersmith, and my sending you an extra copy might have something to do with keeping up the interest of Mr. Playfair.

Please do not make it a burden in any way. If you know a living, breathing Egyptologist, who can read hieroglyphics, anywhere in, near or above the British Museum, please read it with him. He will testify that every line is good hieroglyphic idiom, whether it is good poetry or not, and in the light of this testimony which I cheerfully anticipate, I maintain it is the first verse in the English language which attempts to put the Egyptian idiom of the Book of the Dead into the Anglo-Saxon grand style.

I remember I told you long ago that if I ever came back to England, I would come back as an Egyptologist. No doubt you thought this was sarcasm, or some more awful American wit. Well, here you are! This is the Book of the Dead, reduced to a 26-page American poem. Cleopatra is the one on trial. That is all.

Other people who might take a direct interest in this poem are Arthur Weigall, who has written his remarkable book on Cleopatra, which has had such a run both in England and in America and which is the Egyptologist's Cleopatra, the same as mine. You will find, if you read the blurb on the cover of his book, it runs through the same argument. I remember J. St. Loe Strachey, your distinguished father, had a full-page reviewing Weigall's book in the New York Times, though, alas, I had the feeling that he was so fascinated by the word "Cleopatra" that dear young Weigall was drowned in the depths of the sea. Tell him so for me, if he can stand it.

Weigall really has the standpoint of the Egyptian priesthood of the year 28 or 29 B.C., for all he makes such a high and noble effort to keep Cleopatra an Alexandrian Greek. She may be all of that, but every line he writes is written by a man saturated with hieroglyphics.

Where do I get my hieroglyphic turn? Simply by being saturated by the movies. They are hieroglyphics all over again, and anyone soaked with movies as I am, finds them much easier than Bacon's Essays. I am hoping for a great pageant production of Cleopatra in England, and one in America, as a consequence of a Lyric Theatre interest in the dramatic side of this poem, and British Museum interest in its Egyptology, and a London Mercury interest in its merits as a verse in the attempted grand style. In this project, consider yourself the hostess, if you want to be, or else merely the innocent bystander. The poets and the literati like the poem now better than it deserves, and I am not asking for any particular interest on that line. On the whole it is quite turgid from being rewritten too much, and gets all the credit it deserves.

But the very simple but somewhat incredible thing—the fact I really know hieroglyphics—is a fighting point. You do not need to fight about it, if you do not want to, though I am hoping you might find some amusement in that. On the whole, I should say the better the hieroglyphic scholar, the more this will seem a li(v)e, and not a dead poem. Of course, the same thing could be said of a mummy. I send you, then, my one and only mummy. It claims it is Cleopatra. If you choose, you have the privilege of demonstrating that it is, after all, nothing more than the Ahkoond of Swat.

I have not the least intention of attempting anything in the grand style again. My new book on the movies is a complete novelty, and, succeed or fail, it will make far more the impression of the college annual than this Miltonic blast.

I have sent a copy of this to John Masefield, Boar's Hill, as well as copies to Nigel Playfair and to Squire. It is Squire who is to settle whether it shall be printed or not in Great Britain, how, when and where. I hope the other three good friends can get amusement and not misery out of the enterprise, any such amusement as occurs to them. A stage version might be made by anybody that wanted to, but the method which seemed to please Ruth St. Denis was that a reader should stand concealed by the folds of a curtain, at the side of the stage, more or less obscure, except for voice, and read the poem through, while the dancers in silent pantomime occupy the center of the stage and act out the story.

As to the politics of the story, it is the politics of Weigall's theory, of Caesarion, son of Caesar and Cleopatra, and this goes back to certain hints in Ferrero and the last two paragraphs on Julius Caesar in the Encyclopaedia Britannica.

I enjoyed J. St. Loe Strachey's article in the New York Times on Cleopatra, but he surely left her untroubled by the political situations which are back of my poem.

If you drop this manuscript in the bottom of the sea, we will remain friends, and will resume the discussion which was broached in one of your late letters, about the mystery of the feminine philosophy, which you term "the feminine revelation". Perhaps it is somewhere between the lines of this poem. Some people say Cleopatra was feminine. I try to leave her that way.

My best wishes to you. I hope to get letters from you. I expect to remain in this room in Spokane until the ants carry me out through the keyhole, a grain at a time.

Most sincerely,

VACHEL LINDSAY

Notes

1. Amabel Williams-Ellis (born 1894), the daughter of J. St Loe Strachey, editor of *The Spectator,* was literary editor of *The Spectator* in 1922—23. A novelist and a writer of juveniles, she also published a psychological study, *The Tragedy of John Ruskin* (1928).
2. Nigel Ross Playfair (1874—1934) directed the Lyric Theatre, Hammersmith, after 1919 and produced *The Beggar's Opera.*

$$\underline{144}$$

TO HARRY A. MAGUIRE

1129 Davenport Hotel
Spokane, Washington
February 16, 1925

My Dear Mr. Maguire:

Thank you for your letter of February 7. Please accept my congratulations on the Scribblers' organization[1] and the Pan Magazine. You may use my name in connection therewith as much as you please, as long as it does not involve either making contributions, offering advice or signing checks. If you want me to certify that Pan is prancing in and about Notre Dame, and likely to break into song, I am perfectly willing to certify to that, with the greatest good humor. He generally prances pretty hard where there are young men with legs.

You surely have my good will and friendship and the particular constituency you are likely to represent is one that has never made any overtures to me whatever, in all these long years, no matter what my friendly overtures to them. Therefore I am the more flattered. I send you a copy of a very dull book, "The Golden Book of Springfield", but it contains underneath a picture of a cathedral. It is the acid test. The people that like The Golden Book can stand almost anything from me. At any rate, there are things there for you if you care to hunt for them. Meanwhile I have some songs in mind which might in the end appear most fittingly in your publication. I do not like to discourage you, but my observation and experience with such a magazine as yours, is this: They run about three numbers in imitation of the valiant Harriet Monroe, who has kept it up all these years; they fail at the end of about three months, and Harriet has kept it up since 1912, while all the other poetry magazines have lived and died.[2] They all imitate her, in spite of everything, and she is the only one still holding the fort. Each one starts out utterly ignoring dear Harriet, or furiously hating her, saying she is this, that or the other, and her magazine is worse, but when they get through, there is her Poetry Magazine, and theirs is no more, or else howling for an endowment or something. Harriet is one of the hardest fighters on American soil. I suggest you go to her office when your committee meets in Chicago, and take all the advice you can get out of her. She is a woman as plain spoken as the Old Testament, with an awful wallop, for all she looks like such a shy little thing. She is as impregnable as the Rock of Gibraltar, but far more mobile. Just respect her down to the ground, and take all the advice she can give you, and maybe you can hold out. Do not waste any time sniffing at her, or feeling she does not know her business. She has made more reputations in poetry since 1912 than all the magazines on all the newsstands in England and America since 1880. If fame you want, and your magazine goes to pot, just persuade her to print some of the smarter verses by some of your smart boys.

This may be pretty rough talk, but you need Harriet and, if I may be plain, she needs you. She is a tired, neglected, hard-fighting, valiant woman. Because she is so plain-spoken all but the hardy leave her alone in that office, yet I think the greatest honor any man of letters may do himself is to take her out for lunch to the nearest tearoom near her office in Chicago. She is never socially besieged. Far from it, though socially as well placed as any mortal on American soil. This is because, as I say, she is as plain spoken as the Old Testament, and few people like the truth. She certainly knows how reputations are lost and won, and she is the world's best scrapper, which ought to please the Irish.

Go and get acquainted with her. Respect, love and admire her; get her on your editorial board, if you can. If you cannot do anything else, start a fight with her. If you could persuade her that your magazine was a real rival to hers, and that she was not going to survive yours, you would do her more good than a barrel of hooch. She has seen them live and die in three months so long. It is not good for her. You hold the remedy in your hands.

You see my little letter turns on character, and not on aesthetics, but if you know Harriet well, you will find she knows everything from music to etching, as well as the City of Paris, and having all of that, and the ability to be a good scrapper besides, is surely a divine endowment. Most people are ruined by it.

I myself am too dog-lazy to offer any further advice, except my great good will. It is possible, by keeping at me long enough and hard enough, to get some of the weak verses of the later years out of me, if that is any interest to you, but your magazine will probably die before you warm up to that idea. This is not pessimism. It is just that I have seen all of them die. I should say the model for any poetry magazine is to fight like a hell-cat and love beauty like a saint. If you can inscribe that inspiring motto on your banners, you will certainly get somewhere, but I do not know exactly where.

> Good wishes to you.
> Sincerely yours,
>
> Vachel Lindsay

Notes

1. Harry Maguire was, at this time, president of the Scribblers at the University of Notre Dame.
2. For a history of *Poetry: A Magazine of Verse,* see Ellen Williams's book *Harriet Monroe and the Poetry Renaissance* (Urbana: University of Illinois Press, 1977). The first magazines published in direct competition with *Poetry* were *The Egoist* and *Others.*

145

TO JOHN DRINKWATER

1129 Davenport Hotel
Spokane, Washington,
February 16, 1925

My dear John Drinkwater:
You are overwhelmed with correspondence from all over the world, and it is not for lack of thought of you I have not written since the old days of my English visit. I am not coming back soon; I am not like a poor relation. It will be a long, long time before you see me again. It is likely it will be a long, long time before I even get back to Springfield, Illinois or New York City. I am, so far as I know, permanently located in the Davenport Hotel, Room 1129, Spokane. If you want to know just why I am here, read any account you may care to about the Lewis and Clark Expedition. The Northwest has its own romance.

But I received today Lincoln's Birthday papers from my home town,[1] Springfield, Illinois, both the old Register and the old Journal, full of the regular Lincoln celebration of the type peculiar to our town, and I thought of you again immediately.

I have for a long time thought of sending you a copy of the most elaborate poem I am likely to write in my life, and the nearest to an attempt at the grand style.[2] Of course, the British have a kind of an idea an American, to be interesting, must be as far from the grand style as possible in literature, rather quaint and salty, and that his only dignity is to be the jazz dignity in some form or other, so I am quite sure this comment will be offered as far as the British are concerned on my poem—"The Trial of the Dead Cleopatra in her Beautiful and Wonderful Tomb".

The American grand manner, as you well know, is thoroughly established in statesmanship, and it has been so since the days of Washington. Our problem of men of letters is to transfer to the field of writing that same grand manner, so thoroughly established in our politics, and add that peculiar limberness which the British for the most part assume is our sole characteristic and right to a place in the writing world. I am not especially sensitive about this matter myself, though I know well enough that "The Trial of the Dead Cleopatra", though rewritten for two years, reread and corrected after being read to many audiences, will still be subject to this peculiar type of British scrutiny on British soil. That is one reason why any appeal I may ever make to British opinion is likely to have a long period before and after, in which I am in the Far West making as much appeal as I can to plain American opinion and thoroughly satisfied with it. There is not the least doubt that an American who really tries steadily to please European opinion becomes an expatriate, and a resident of Paris or Rome, and I have seen many of my friends drift to those places personally, both in art and letters. We have the most ardent personal affection, but their children are being born in Paris or Rome or even in Ceylon. If one does not have the west-going heart[3] in America, the thousand little nations which are the countries of Europe pull him away from our great National Parks. This seems to be an abstract essay and a pretty cocky one, before I tell you exactly what I have in mind when I send you the "Trial of the Dead Cleopatra". It has already been printed in the American Mercury, published by the sassy and dirty tongued H. L. Mencken, and it will come out in book form, published by the American Macmillan Company, inside of two months. The last proofs are in their hands. It will be a feature of the illustrated collected poems of your humble servant, illustrated and recently greatly enlarged by his own fair hand. So sending it to you is merely sending it as a personal souvenir. I have submitted it in a literary way, for possible publication in the London Mercury, to J. C. Squire, and as far as British soil is concerned, it can live and die on that risk, especially in the matter of printing. But it is an Egyptian poem, based on Egyptian studies slowly growing more cumulative through the years, and while I cannot read hieroglyphics without a pony, and sticking pretty tight to the pony, I have spent many years reading hieroglyphics with the pony, until I feel I know the Egyptian idiom.

If you can read the manuscript with the best Egyptologist you can catch and tame, you can perhaps be surprised that he will agree with you that it is better Egyptology than literature, and if that divine consummation is achieved, my personal vanity will be thoroughly satisfied.

The reason I am so mad over hieroglyphics is simply that I am movie saturated. I have written the first textbook on the subject, used by Columbia University from 1915 through 1918, and I am now writing the

first yearbook on the American movie, almost immediately to be submitted to the American Macmillan Co. The manuscript is all typed. Such
a movie training is a surprising initiation into the whole Egyptian psychology, and hieroglyphics. They had the most intense pictorial minds
of any human beings who ever lived, and breathed, not excepting the
Japanese, and right now I am nearer at home with a page of the Book
of the Dead than I am with a page of Mr. Shakespeare or Marlowe. It
is nearer to the United States West Coast and Hollywood, which idea
may strike you as extremely queer until you give it a chance. The motion
picture is so necessarily an American art, requiring such an enormous
initial expenditure, such circus-like advertising, such floods of reckless
promotion, that our people are bound to be more subject to its daily
grind than any other people on earth. Movies are simply poured out,
even in the middle sized town, and I see an enormous progress in
pictorial psychology in all American life, even in the last three years.
We think in pictures, like strings of carved beads, or carved peach
stones, if you will, and that is about all the thinking we do or are in the
prospect of doing for the next one hundred years.

And forget the long lecture. This is the day I start in correcting my
book, and I am full of it. If you haven't an Egyptologist handy with
which to read this poem, please put it on the top shelf and forget it, but
do not forget my good will. A good place to look it over is the Egyptian
section of the British Museum where those more than life size pictures
are marching around for the similar trial of the heart, and the essential
story is I have substituted Cleopatra for the Scribe, Ani.

My dear John Drinkwater, no one could realize more than I do the
overwhelming flood of letters you receive, and passionate friendly letters from both the south and the north of the United States. I have sent
you a thousand friendly unseen wireless messages, and most of those
you get from me will be that sort. Your extraordinary hospitality extended with so beautiful a hand in London, is still very dear to me to
remember, and you may be sure that I remember it with far more kindness now than ever before in my life. It was a very vivid, very beautiful,
absolutely flawless experience. My mother's death so soon after, as one
might say, at the very height of her powers and interest in life and
young poets like John Drinkwater, made this experience peculiarly
tender memory. I remember in particular your introduction of me to
Ralph Hodgson,[4] but I remember all the poets of the wonderful afternoon and evening in your new home, and as I remember it now, it was
the house-warming, the first time you had ever given a party in that
new house. You need not think I have forgotten any of that. I remember
with particular enthusiasm and kindness my mother's great feeling for
you and for your play. It was to her possibly a more romantic experience
than for me, for the very reason that she herself had lived through the

Civil War days, had been a passionate advocate of the North, though married to a Southern husband, and had seen all her early boy sweethearts march south to the battles for the Starspangled banner, and never return. She always spoke of the loss of these boys with tears. Lincoln to her was not a god or a bronze statue, as he has almost become now, but the man for whom her boy sweethearts fought, bled and died. So when you wrote the great play, accepted by both nations as the Anglo-Saxon word in the drama of Abraham Lincoln, you may be very sure her old heart turned young again and revived in her issues which had slept for many a day.

I do not want to continue this letter indefinitely. My best offering for my English friends for many a long day, to indicate that I am taking literature seriously if not well, is this very elaborate "Cleopatra". I have sent what might be called friendly copies to Nigel Playfair, Lyric Theatre, Hammersmith, to John Masefield, to Amabel Williams-Ellis, to Squire, and one or two others. I surely do not want to come again to England until I can come bringing my sheaves with me. I do not want to go back there again as a smart young man, because I am not that any more, and as a grave and reverend senior, I have not as yet anything so very definite to offer, though I have, of course, plenty of things to say, as my friends discover in conversation. If I get started talking at all, I am as talky as this letter, and perhaps it is just as well I am not near you to talk you to death.

At any rate, my dear friend, I remember very, very well your two visits to Springfield, and perhaps I had best close this letter with an assurance which you may need, that the gigantic Gibbs, the black African Chieftain, to whom I introduced you in Springfield on the second visit, was indeed Gibbs the Great, and a friend of mine, no matter how startling an apparition. I am very fond of telling that story because any story about Gibbs is good. You will find him in the first section of "The Congo", and you may be sure it is pretty well modeled on him, and on having known him for many a day, a gigantic Negro warrior disguised as a lawyer in the Bad Lands. He was surely made to prance with a "coffin-headed shield and a shovel spear". I think of old Gibbs first when I think of the African race, though I see very little of him nowadays. There is no doubt the embarrassment between the intellectuals of the two races has something to do with this, but I have pamphlet after pamphlet written in 1918 and thereabouts and many a weak poem after talks with Gibbs. I took Stephen Graham to see him when Graham was my guest in Springfield, Graham having written "The Children of the Slaves",[5] on the trial of John Brown, or a study of negroes in America. Gibbs wrote a great, big open public letter to Graham in reply, which was written in our local paper, as beautiful and eloquent a piece of English as I ever read in my life.

But here I am in Spokane, trying to understand the squirmish line of American life. The very weight of the memories of Springfield is too strong, and I must be in a clear if lonely land really to think well what I want to think out. You may be sure that our ties are stronger now than they ever were before, and I am as eager to make good in your eyes as I ever was in my life.

Good fortune to you
Most sincerely,

VACHEL LINDSAY

Notes

1. On John Drinkwater's interest in Lincoln, see note 1 to letter 91.
2. VL's ideas on "the grand style" eventually made up the gist of *The Litany of Washington Street* (1929).
3. "The West-Going Heart" furnished Eleanor Ruggles with the title of her biography of VL (Norton, 1959).
4. Very little is known about the English poet Ralph Hodgson, who stopped writing in 1917. His principal works include *The Last Blackbird and Other Lines* (1907), *The Bull* (1913), and *Poems* (1917).
5. Stephen Graham's *Children of the Slaves* had come out in 1920; its American title was *The Soul of John Brown*.

146

TO HARRIET MOODY

Spokane, Washington
March 31, 1925

My dear Harriet Cordelia:—
You are the finest of all Good Samaritans. You are more than that. Hundreds have turned to you in trouble that was the trouble called aspiration and you have helped them up. Your house is the Castle of Peace and Help, and also it is the Palace of Wisdom. I have met more wise people there than anywhere else in the Anglo-Saxon world. And it is the house of Beauty and Song and more poems find their home there than anywhere else on earth. And you have no competitors. There

is no second, no third, no imitation Harriet Cordelia. There is only one.

To this let me add, my dear, that I love you dearly. I hold you faithfully in memory, and if I have a way of my own and a path of my own, I am never-the-less faithful in my thought of you and you must not doubt it.

Why have I not written my thoughts to you lately? Because they are not easy for me to put on paper. I have been living in that part of my mind which bores all women the most, even the divine Harriet Cordelia.

My ties are all cut with Springfield since the death of my father and mother and I may not return there for a long time.

Here I am, externally as comfortable as possible, with a town full of loyal friends. The whole logic of my "literary" life even *as you understand it,* leads me here to the frontier.

Yet, dear heart, I never asked to be a poet, never asked for the limelight, and was only kicked up stairs over the results of my own wrathful defensive tactics. And the whole fabric of writing books, and of reciting and all the rest of it, looks now colossally artificial to me, and I do not see I am under the least obligation to keep up any of it. Yet I am a terribly clannish person, and now that my father and mother are dead, I simply have no separate special reason for justifying myself in the eyes of the world, at least none that drives me on. I am just an isolated man in a hotel bedroom. And it means nothing to *me* to do literary tricks for any soul on the face of the earth. There is just one call deep and strong, an unutterable yearning, and that is for the road and for peace.

There is just one thing that has never failed me, and that is the highroad. It is just the side of me you like least, and never understood. Yet if you really want to know what I think about, day and night, it is the highroad. Of course ladies in parlors thought it all very pretty for me to recite "The Santa Fe Trail", now it was all behind me. But of course henceforth I was to recite such a poem as a parlor ornament. Yet the deeper hunger for the peace of the road comes over me again and again. Three times I turned to it, not in vain, each time dreaming I would some day make it permanent. I really believe I will make it permanent before the year is over.[1]

My whole heart is turning to this dream, dear Harriet Cordelia. I have been thinking of it very seriously for sometime. I will change my name, write no letters and go on and on as many a husky does. I have not the least intention of coming back when I start.

As to the day and hour of this departure, it will be after every obligation is cleared up.

Pardon me, dearest, if this letter sounds pessimistic! It is not so. I plan my new adventures on the road like a boy starting for college. I understand, and the very hope makes me gay. I plan all this through. I know exactly the hardship.

I have thought it through, and know I can make good on it. It was 1912 I was last a beggar, and it is *everything since 1912* I want to walk away from. That was my most natural year. People thought I fought for fame. But I only fought my way from being the town fool and the family idiot. The road of 1912 was easier than the whip of 1925 publicity. Above all it is the harrowing *artificiality* of the life one is expected to live as a writer, that is ashes in the end. One is a pet poodle, or else a "queer" one. I do not like either job. A husky, even a gentleman-ranker among the huskies, has a far more natural place in the world.

Why should I go back to Chicago—to go through the same old paces, the same old way, when they are to me utterly meaningless? I have had more letters asking me to speak this year than ever in my life and I have not answered any of them.

One has to do these things to please one's own flesh and blood, and I have not any. Surely I have not the remotest notion of doing them to please myself. If I am to please myself I will utterly renounce the whole machine.

There is where we were always separated, dear Harriet, you really thought I played the game for its own sake. You were always wrong. I would not promise to go to England till my mother promised to go with me. When Isadora quit Chicago, so did I. Her opinion of me was the normal one since 1912—that I am a box of tricks, but not a natural lonely red-hearted human creature.

When I am a husky, the farmer at least assumes I am human. It is a delightful assumption. Surely I was intended by nature for the road.

With love indeed,

VACHEL

Note

1. VL "took to the road" in 1906, 1908, and 1912. His Glacier National Park expedition took place in 1921.

147

TO HARRIET MOODY

Spokane, Davenport Hotel
Room 1129
April 2, 1925

My Dear Harriet Cordelia:—
Here in the big ball room on April 10 I give a big special new recital for the teachers' convention of this whole region, with very special preparation and auspices, etc. not quite on the scale of the Poem Games we gave with Eleanor Dougherty at Mandel Hall with that dear girl so splendidly doing her whole best, and every band, as it were, playing. But as near to that as this town can reach, and a decided advance in the mere Poem-Game technique of my "devices". "A Swan is Like the Moon to Me",[1] is the title of the newest poem-game, and I will print an account of the event afterward. If it turns out as planned, it will be a decided advance. So I am thinking of big times of old, very gratefully now. If it may be permitted, I would be glad if you forward this letter to dear Eleanor. How much I have thought of her the last two years, being a very selfish person, and very much in need of just such help as hers. For her sake and with her in mind I have watched all her actor-brother's doings in the New York Magazines and papers.[2]

This is one especially hard night for me, dear Harriet Cordelia, and I am glad indeed to have you to lean on. I was much amused this afternoon not only to run into Schuyler Jackson's page in the Gulf Park Annual, but also in the March London Mercury.[3] I wonder if you are in touch with the dear boy. Please give him my good wishes. He did so much for me in Princeton, yet I made an awful mess of my Princeton visit all because I waited for a letter that did not come.

Well I am a bit more of a success at the slower process of residence in Spokane, I think, and I wish some of you people would turn up at this magnificent hotel before I entirely disappear. Really I am making some progress. I have had strong letters on my latest writing from J. C. Squire and John Drinkwater. And the New Poem-Games are an advance. Most everything I have written here, like the Memorial for Sailors and Marines, and Virginia, has gone across the country.[4] My struggle is not melancholia. It is the plain old 1912 struggle to get out of an artificial setting and to form more natural ties. This struggle grows sharper with any public person through the years. But I am so much in the setting of 1912 in May, just before I took to the road, that the whole month comes down on me like a thunderclap. I have such marvellously loyal and noble friends here I know the situation is inherent in publicity itself, and in the art life, expecially if it has really been fanatical. You are so accustomed to helpless poets, I doubt if you ever quite understood one who had cut the Gordian knot more than once. I think you would have liked me better if I had not been able somehow to bull it through. Well I may come to you yet and say "Here are the pieces. Sew them together". You would much rather I would walk to Chicago as when I first met Eleanor—than walk to the land East of the Sun and West of the Moon. Well the Poem-Games were worth the first interruption weren't they?—and Eleanor was a thousand times worth it.

But dear heart I have an incurable hunger for the dust of every highroad of America. I love to draw the Map of the U.S.A. I have something in me that says:—"Somehow—I can get this map sometime, afoot, yet far from the Automobile, the Pullman Car, the Freight-Car or the Publisher! There is some way to make it all my own secret wholesome backyard."

I had a lot of little laurels in 1912—more than you know. And my tiny Springfield Circle wanted me to join the Country Club and the Sangamon Club and marry into the local Banker's Set, and let it go at that. I seem to face the same kind of a little stalemate right now—on a little larger scale (without the girl!). Until I renounce everything I am smothered. I can remember June 1, 1912 and the desperate need to throw off everything and the desperate struggle to do it, and the protest of every friend and the insult of every enemy, including the evening paper with a one column editorial on Good Riddance, just as I started my walk.

Well now the struggle is all inside myself, there are no old neighbors to put their oar in, friends or enemies. You may be sure I will do my best to get my work to par before I leave. And all my debts are paid. Of course you do not like to see me going at it in this snappy way. You want me to be more forlorn. You are used to forlorn poets!

I believe the reason women do not like me is that I am in love with the United States all 110 million people in it, and they—the ladies—think my love of them is sort of absentminded!

Now there is thirteen pages of Vachel. You should be now completely cured of your diseased assumption I have not been writing to you. This is my tenth letter since I began to write you this series of ten, some time back. It is about time you wrote me. You have not written for ages and ages. Well I have written you nothing important this evening, but I have written away this evening's special trouble by talking about things in general. It is a fine thing to have a Harriet Moody to write all these things to, and I know Eleanor Dougherty to whom you are to send the letter, if you think best, will agree with me. If you and Eleanor will write me equally long and Frank letters about why you are thus and so, I will have at least two great evenings ahead of me, perhaps two great lifetimes. God bless you, my dear Harriet Cordelia.

VACHEL

Notes

1. "A Swan Is like the Moon to Me" appears in *Every Soul Is a Circus* (p.24).
2. Eleanor Dougherty's brothers were all famous in one way or another. The actor mentioned here was Walter Hampden, Paul Dougherty was a painter, and the third brother "who signs M. T. is the poetry critic of *The New Republic*."
3. Schuyler Jackson wrote an article on VL's *Litany of Washington Street*, entitled "American History Revued," in *The New Republic*, July 31, 1929 (p. 292).
4. "Virginia" (*Going-to-the-Stars*, p. 34) should not be confused with "The Virginians Are Coming Again" (*Every Soul Is a Circus*, p. 39), written much later. This editor has not been able to identify "Memorial for Sailors and Marines," but "Billboards and Galleons" may be the poem in question.

148

TO ELIZABETH MANN WILLS

Davenport Hotel
Spokane, Wash.
April, 5, 1925

My Dear Elizabeth:—
I have been going into "Uncle Tom's Cabin" this evening, and I find that in 1836 Harriet Beecher Stowe and her group in Cincinnati were working the Underground Railroad helping slaves northward. My Grandfather Lindsay at the time owned more slaves, horses, Tobacco and land than anyone else in Gallatin County, Kentucky, just one county away from Cincinnati and that was the nearest market for his horses and tobacco. So it is quite possible Harriet Beecher Stowe and her friends helped some of Grandpa's slaves to escape, they being only one county away. Gallatin County is right on the Ohio River and there must have been lively doings keeping Eliza from crossing the ice *all* the time! Well at the same time my grandpa Frazee was only two or three counties to

the North in Indiana (Rusk County) Southern in blood but northern in sympathy. They had freed their slaves and crossed the river a few miles. But my Great Grandma Frazee never forgave her sons for freeing their slaves—"her" slaves—. I keep the picture of the indignant old lady on my dresser. She looks a lot like sister Joy. So there were the two families, both Southern blood, only a few miles apart, both sending their crops to Cincinnati, Kentuckinians [sic] to the core, and there sat Harriet Beecher Stowe half-way between them hatching out Uncle Tom's Cabin! When the civil war cleared away my Grandfather Lindsay was utterly ruined. The Northern and Southern armies stole his horses, the niggers were freed and most of them gone, and the Military Governor of that region foreclosed my grandfather's mortgages and took his land personally for debt and kept it for his own. And my grandfather Lindsay went blind. My father was the oldest and began by digging potatoes, for day wages—and supported all the others, and put himself through Miami Medical College, Cincinnati. Then he bought his father a little farm, not far away, at Aurora Indiana. Then he put through school his eldest sister Eudora. And till I was twelve years old or so he was educating the family and putting them through school, etc, with the help of Eudora who soon began to teach herself. Johnson was put through Medical College, Nicholas was put through Law School Ann Arbor, Elijah was put through Medical School, but died soon after. Eugene and Flora and Adolphus, the youngest, were educated pretty largely at a school Aunt Eudora started, Excelsior Institute, Jett—near Frankfort Kentucky. My father however pretty largely carried the family, who were utterly wrecked by the war. Meanwhile my mother's family, just a little to the north, near Rushville Indiana, had as much of the heartbreak of the war as the others, but not the blasting loss. My mother as a very old woman spoke of how all the boys of the village marched away to the war in the northern armies and not one came back. Most all my mother's kin were in the southern armies and came trooping North—to my grandfather's Frazee's house for refuge when peace was made. I can remember her description of what terrible wrecks they were. Grandpa Frazee bound them up and fed them and started them on their way again. Always the families both sides, looked to Frankfort and Lexington and Cincinnati. My mother went to "Glendale College" on the edge of Cincinnati, as a young girl a little after the war, and it was a sort of Gulf Park. I lectured there and the principal was an old pupil of hers! Later my mother studied at Hamilton College Lexington which as I understand is the girls' side of Kentucky University, a great deal such an experience as yours today. There she met a fellow-student—Eudora Lindsay. The two girls became teachers together, saved every penny, planned a trip to Europe together. Meanwhile my father had spent nine years saving money to study medicine in the Vienna Hospitals. So they all three met on the boat about 1876—and thus the North and South side of the Ohio river met in my blood and therefore I am especially interested to learn that in 1836 as it were between the two ancestral farms, Harriet Beecher Stowe was hatching Uncle Tom's Cabin which came out in 1852.

And reading this article on Tom Shows I remember my father's wrath when I was given one of those ten cent tickets when I was about seven years of age, and I asked in tender innocence to go to "Uncle Tom's Cabin". The roof nearly fell in, right then and there. Dear Papa started in to roar, boil, explode and fume and so forth in the most approved Southern Fashion. He surely gnashed his teeth and Legree had nothing on him. But when I consider now what that book and play had cost him in toil and heart break I am not so astonished! But surely I was the most surprised little boy that ever was scared out of his wits! Well Mama sneaked us in a copy of the book later, for Olive and me to read, but we never dared go to the show till we were grown up. But it was surely grand to see the free street parades with those alleged blood-hounds each on the end of a long clanking chain, the dogs barking fiercely. Papa would nearly have apoplexy on those days. When Cleveland was elected it sort of eased him down some! Dear old boy he had had his heart broken long before I ever saw him! He poured his whole youth and strength into helping that blind father and that long string of brothers and sisters, long before I ever met him. But he got them all up out of the wreck and started them all right, and the Lindsay side of the house is as happy as the Frazee now, and you could not guess which cousins were which. And that all goes back to my old daddy's fury and energy beginning by digging potatoes, when he had confidently expected niggers to do all that all his life for him!

I doubt if Papa was ever quite as kind to us as he was to his own tribe. He had used himself up almost before he met me. So when I wanted to loaf and be an artist he most had conniptions again. But *that* is another story. I guess he was still remembering those potatoes! And he was till he died a man of furious energy.

When I tore out this Tom Show thing for you, I just laughed, it was so well written. But how deeply these matters search the heart—before we are done! The North and South, my darling, will always be at war in my veins. But every time I kissed you I moved further South. I am wondering if crossing the Ohio is still hard for you? Well, my blessed lamb, it shall surely be as you say. Back and forth across that Ohio river my tribe has been tossed and torn. And there sat Harriet Beecher Stowe in the midst of us writing Uncle Tom's Cabin! I wonder if that book divides us still?

I know this letter surprises you! Certainly it surprises me! All because I found this magazine article!

Write to me, my pretty. The Ohio should *not* divide *us*.

With love indeed.

VACHEL

149

TO GEORGE GREENWOOD

May 11, 1925

My Dear George Greenwood:–[1]

Certainly Sister Joy and I never heard of these plans till they were recently completed. Maybe Sister Olive had word of them and that is the reason that for a whole year she refused to sign any papers (while in America) and refused to let any of the family loot, pictures, photographs, daguerreotypes, etc., be divided. Evidently the old family residence with nearly every book, and daguerreotype in place, is going to be used by this business-woman's club as a place formally opened to the public with the factotum of the club for custodian and guide. Recently I gave my consent to Joy the house should be rented to this club, but I have not yet signed any papers, nor understood it was to be a museum. There is nothing for me to do but raise whiskers, long grey Whiskers like Santy Claus, and stay away from Springfield, and die soon, or else start a *big new career*.

VACHEL

When I have a grouch on I say it is a pity I am not dead. I would be *so* convenient, then. Obviously a dead poet—away, but with all his family relics left behind, himself dead or away from home, is more valuable to a good town than a live one living there in his birthplace with his young wife and family. When I tried just a year ago, made every decent effort to get my sweetheart to this house, as a place where I might take reasonable care of her, a place where I *might* live with her, every move was blocked, and she was discouraged, apparently forever, from coming North for the first friendly visit.

N.V.L.

I am here in Spokane to forget all this, and generally, I *do*. I *know* I must be dead wrong. I ought to forget all this, I *know*.

One reason I want to stay in the west, and accept your cooling judgment on these matters, is I take them too hard, if at all, *I know*.

N.V.L.

Note

1. George Greenwood was vice-president of the Old National Bank in Spokane, Washington.

150

TO HARRIET MOODY

Spokane, U.S.A.
Friday, May 22, 1925

My dear Cordelia:—
Thank you so much for your last two letters and that beautiful and constant spirit of yours, always hovering above them. Your last letter calling me to my own again, and telling me of the valiant service of James Stephens[1] moves me greatly. The time was when on the strength of such a campaign as that of Stephens I would have settled into a correspondence with him that would have established a personal friendship for life. But I grow exhausted trying to do justice in gratitude and love to my oldest partisans. John Masefield worked miracles for me in Oxford and London and I love him like an apostle, yet we have not written each other a line for a long long time. Last evening I wrote for Percy MacKaye's fiftieth birthday scrapbook my little tribute, speaking in especial of the early days with Moody and Torrence, and Percy's valiant championship of other poets.

But all this is beating about the bush. This letter is just to announce news so sweet my pen seems to get paralyzed when it stops to tell you. I was married May 19, here in my room to Elizabeth Conner, whose name I have changed to Elizabeth Locust-Blossom Conner, because on our walk the next day we found nothing but locust trees in full flower, the town bursting with them. We were not engaged, but married by spontaneous combustion the minute we got acquainted which was somewhere around May 18, though we had of course met a good many times in a decidedly pleasant way before.[2]

I am wanting you to write to Elizabeth and Elizabeth to you, and I am reading her this epistle.

Alice Corbin always boasted of being your brightest pupil, follower and disciple when you were more definitely a teacher of English down by the University. I fancy Elizabeth had a similar relation to that remarkable Statue of Liberty, President Reinhardt of Mills College, California. There—perhaps—she has had a great peacemaker and inspirer, and forcer of her mental flowering.

Well, I am not going to write you an essay on my lovely bride, for doubtless it will sound much like other bride-groom songs, and this lady, of course, is different. What is far more important, we start life with a clean slate, with no heavy obligations, no unpaid debts or no promises, and the future is indeed the future. We are both in excellent health, both fond of hiking, both walk fast and hard, but she is one jump ahead of me in adoring a Latin Poet called Catullus, and I can't pass on his merits, not being able to read Latin. Maybe you can have a Catullus picnic with her some day, when I'm asleep as usual upstairs. Catullus is just about your line, I guess!

Certainly, dear Cordelia, the world has begun anew for me and all disasters have fled away.

Our wedding was sudden, but there was not one hitch or spoiled event in the pageantry. We tried to have it sudden and secret, but it was at least sudden and private, with all our friends wildly enthusiastic the next day, and the little wedding party in this room the most beautifully reverent and intimate of all wedding-parties.—

As a matter of fact we wanted a secret wedding with only witnesses sworn to secrecy—two, I suppose. I was so sick of publicity and having my heart poked into by dirty fingers for the last few years, I wanted privacy at all costs. So our guests in the end just came in at the last minute as it were, also by spontaneous combustion, and it all turned out dewy as Milton's Eden dawn.

Well, why should I go babbling about this wedding and skipping the essential matter—the Bride? I am in no state of mind to describe this Bride to you, so I must needs refer to the classics. Let's see! there's Juliet. She is like Juliet. She is 23 and acts 13. Then there's the wonderful girl Rosalind who put on boy's pants and went on a toot through the Forest of Arden. She is like Rosalind. Then John Milton has written some nice poems. She is like the heroines in some of Milton's poems.

Of course my letters about the road came from a desperate heart. They were written 1000000 years ago. With Elizabeth Locust-Blossom

The Lamp in the Window.

I light my homely lamp again tonight.
And say "Perhaps a wandering one goes by
Hurried past doorways, where the
                watch-dogs growl.
The hearths the stranger dares not come
                    anigh."

We sit in stolid circle at the board
And never a son or daughter tells a tale.
The faithful mother finds no cheer in toil.
Our rosary of faults our care can naught avail.

The countryside grows dull with homes
                unstirred.
The preacher prates in long accustomed words.
The neighbors come with wooden eyes to talk
Of weeds and fences, barns and flocks
                and herds.
I say "mayhap within the soaking rain
Some storm-blown-boy moves on that
                we should keep.
So bring us laughter round our roaring
                stove
So show us why we sow and why we reap"

Tonight, perchance a conquering one returns
Master of weariness and fate and pain.
Within his pockets note-books
                of his lore
Within his soul great passions held
                in rein.

Perhaps—tonight—some wild man
                passes by
Bearing wise parchments from old cities
                grim
Or, it may be, a better lamp than mine,
More like Aladdin's, that, like this one, dim.

All it will need—the oil and wick
                and flame
And sheltered room to keep the wind away
I can provide. Ah if a lamp be brings
It shall be trimmed and burnished
                every day!

In this, the city of my discontent,
Sometimes there comes a whisper from
        the grass:—
Romance, Romance is here, No Hindu
        town
Is quite so strange, No citadel
        of brass
By Timburoo found, held half such
        love and hate,
No picture-palace, in a picture
        book,
Such webs of friendship,
        beauty, greed and fate.
                    N.V.L.

Out of rhythm
come words
and form.
Vachel Lindsay

Three examples of Lindsay's handwriting (courtesy of *Cue* magazine)

Lindsay in front of the Lincoln Monument, Springfield, 1921

Vachel and Elizabeth Conner Lindsay after their marriage, in room 1129 of the Davenport Hotel, Spokane, Washington, May 23, 1925

Conner Lindsay wild to take the road with me, I may yet do it, but I do not see the gigantic and rebellious hikes I previously planned in my defiance. If you think the little seduction whose picture I enclose is capable of walking to Halifax and back, why maybe we will. I have every intention of being as brave and as feeble, as smart and as stupid, as this little lady. She is the head of the firm and my gratitude to her for being so kind to me can never be told. I was going all to pieces for lack of a young governor, a young ruler, a brave young dreamer, and here she is, with a firm hand and a very tender and absolute devotion. I have been physically and mentally well a long time, but the mere weight of such praise as that James Stephens has heaped upon me, for instance, has isolated me from a natural life and from mankind. She has bravely broken the spell and taken the whole curse away. The beauty, secrecy and suddenness of our wedding was part of it. It went through with glory, yet as an act of God, not a device of man. Surely I shall obey this girl as I would an angel from the skies, as surely I shall pray for an obedient heart, for she is youth and poetry itself, with no patent devices.

With love indeed,

Vachel

Notes

1. James Stephens (1882—1950), Irish poet and short-story writer, was the author of *The Crock of Gold*, which won the 1912 Polignac Prize. He visited the United States several times, starting in 1925.
2. VL and Elizabeth Conner were married by the Reverend Charles Pease, minister of the Unitarian Society in Spokane. "These Are the Young", the opening poem of *Going-to-the-Stars* (p. 12), is inscribed to him.

151

TO HAMLIN GARLAND

I will be at the Brevoort
N.Y.C., Oct. 15—Nov. 15

> Room 1129
> Davenport Hotel
> Spokane
> October 4, 1925

My Dear Mr. Garland:

When last we met—if I remember we were forcibly hurled together by a lecture Committee in a sad town in South Carolina. I have never told it on you that they tried to make an Infidel like you say Grace. It was bad enough to have to eat breakfast with the Chairman of the Lecture Committee.

I have gone broke again reissuing my portfolio, "The Village Magazine" in practically the same form, and with the same pictures, that you and Lorado Taft welcomed so heartily at the Cliff Dwellers' Club in 1910. I remember how you paid my expenses to and from Chicago when I was dead broke, "lionized" me at the Cliff Dwellers, made me an out of town member, which I remained many years, and I was always proud as a peacock of belonging. Also, my dear friend when you came down in a Special Car the next spring to lobby to make it possible for Josephine Preston Peabody's[1] play to be put on in Chicago, I remember you sending for me in one of the darkest hours of my life, to meet all the great ones in that car. The only trouble then was that I had nothing to show but this same Village Magazine, practically identical with the one I send you now.

I have since issued ten books through the Macmillan Company and fought a long battle for the recognition of these same pictures. At length May 16, 1925 the Macmillan Company issued forty of these drawings, most of them dating 1905—1910 incorporated in The Illustrated Collected Poems. So by way of celebration, reaffirmation and renewal I have gone broke re-issuing the original magazine, cheerfully as heretofore. Please look it over and claim it for your own as largely as you dare. You do not know how much I would welcome your loud championship of the Vachel Lindsay Hamlin Garland and Lorado Taft of 1910. One of the best things about those days was—I was not required to recite to prove myself a human being, and present. My magazine and my drawings were enough. If you and Lorado Taft can restore that day in its full glory I will be indeed indebted. I have sent a copy of "The Village Magazine" to Royal Cortissoz,[2] to Robert Henri, to Lorado Taft, and will send it to several others.

In the list of the members of the National Institute of Arts and Letters Eugene O'Neill is the only man my own age.[3]

I owe to you and to you alone the fact that I, so young a man am listed among these men, with lists of wonderful pictures and big books to their credit.

Please tell these men your own way at your leisure, what "The Village Magazine" means now, by telling them what it plainly meant, in Illinois and Chicago in 1910.

Most sincerely

NICHOLAS VACHEL LINDSAY

Notes

1. Josephine Preston Peabody (1874–1922), a dramatist and poet, was an officer of the Poetry Society of America. VL mentions her 1910 play *The Piper*. She had been influenced by William Vaughn Moody when she was a student at Radcliffe.
2. Royal Cortissoz (1869—1948), the art critic and journalist, worked from 1891 on as a literary editor and art critic for the *New York Herald Tribune*. A resolute conservative, he was president of the Century Club in New York, which VL sometimes attended.
3. The famous playwright Eugene Gladstone O'Neill (1888—1953) was actually nine years younger than VL. The first of his four Pulitzer prizes was awarded to him in 1920 for *Beyond the Horizon*. His 1925 play was *Desire Under the Elms*.

152

TO KATHARINE LEE BATES

October 5, 1925
Davenport Hotel
Room 1129

Dear Katharine Lee Bates:—
The above is our regular address, but Oct. 15—Nov. 15 we will be at the Brevoort, 5th Avenue and 8th Street and hope to see you for Lunch Tea or Dinner any time you are passing through New York City. I am

very eager to have you approve of Elizabeth Locust Blossom Lindsay the lovely lady I married May 19, a citizen of Spokane.

With great good wishes

VACHEL

153

TO LANGSTON HUGHES

December 6, 1925

Wardman Park Hotel
Washington D.C.

My Dear Langston Hughes:[1]
The "New Poetry" movement has been going on in America since 1912. Two members of that army have died—Joyce Kilmer in the war, and Amy Lowell very recently. Already one hundred distinguished books of verse or criticism have been written, and hundreds of poems set going.

Eleven of the distinguished books are by Amy Lowell[2]—and are listed in the front of this one. Please read the books and ignore the newspapers. I should say "Tendencies in Modern American Poetry" by Miss Lowell is a good book to start on. You may know all of this better than I do.

Miss Lowell has re-written the story of Keats from the standpoint of the "New Poetry". I hope you care to go into the whole movement for study from Edwin Arlington Robinson to Alfred Kreymborg's "Troubadour".[3]

Do not let any lionizers stampede you. Hide and write and study and think. I know what factions do. Beware of them. I know what flatterers do. Beware of them. I know what lionizers do. Beware of them.

Good wishes to you indeed.

VACHEL LINDSAY

Notes

1. Langston Hughes (1902–67) had met VL by accident. In *The Weary Blues,* his first collection of poems, which came out in 1926, Hughes wrote, "Back in America after a winter in Paris I was a bus boy at the Wardman Park Hotel, where Vachel Lindsay attracted attention to my work by reading three poems (that I left beside his plate in the dining-room) to his audience at a recital in the Little Theatre of the hotel."
2. VL's letter (reprinted here by permission of Alfred A. Knopf, Inc., and Harold Ober Associates, Inc., Hughes's publisher and agent, respectively) is in fact an inscription to Langston Hughes of Amy Lowell's *John Keats,* which he presented to Hughes. Amy Lowell had died May 12, 1925. Her *Tendencies in American Poetry* (New York: Macmillan, 1919) included chapters on Edwin Arlington Robinson, Robert Frost, Edgar Lee Masters, Carl Sandburg, and two Imagists, "H.D." (Hilda Doolittle) and John Gould Fletcher.
3. Alfred Kreymborg (1883—1966) was instrumental in starting *Others, Poetry's* rival. His autobiography, entitled *Troubadour,* was published in 1925. In 1913, he was an editor of *The Glebe,* an organ of the Imagist movement. He published *Others* until July 1919 and launched *Broom* between 1920 and 1924. From 1927 to 1936 he edited *The American Caravan* with Paul Rosenfeld, Van Wyck Brooks, and Lewis Mumford.

154

TO JOHN DRINKWATER

[A flower is drawn here.]

May 12, 1926
At my new beautiful flowering home,
made by my beautiful young wife at
514 1/2 West 15th Avenue, Spokane, Washington

Dear John Drinkwater:[1]
To receive this book to be autographed, from you, means all the world to me.

1/32nd of my ancestors, the Austens of Kent, (who came over with the Colgates) were "Clairvoyant", "prophetical", "Mesmeric" etc, and this book is the only direct descendant of them I furnish. In regard to such matters I hold with Bernard Shaw's *very sensible* letter or preface on visualization in his preface to St. Joan.[2] The "movies" make the psychology much clearer. This book is to me, the most precious of all my books. If I could have had my way, which was, of course, wild and arbitrary, it would not only have been as gorgeous as an old Spanish Mass-Book, but it would have made over our Springfield Illinois, till it was as beautiful as the Golden Temple of Amritzar. But not even Austens can work miracles, or create revolutions or get the best of publishing houses at once. Publishing houses are commendably sensible. Now, my dear friend, I am a *very* slow thinker. But I have thought out something, lately. The very public that rejects with scorn the High Mass and Incense of this book and the wings of the (Catholic?) angels, clamors for my poem on the Ghost of Abraham Lincoln walking the streets of Springfield Illinois, August 1914.[3] They will believe in a *Protestant* Ghost. They will believe, as it were, in miracles they like, none others. They will see in the air the picture they love. Otherwise a blank. I should have had Confederate flags and Union flags marching and counter marching through the air, in this book. I should have seen the Ghosts of Washington and Lincoln, and no others! (and the signers of the Declaration?) Well, dear boy, I have not given up the fight. Though I live in Spokane, Springfield will yet be rebuilt like the Golden Temple of Amritzar. If I have my way, dear boy, my Ghost will be there with a censer, if no other ghost! [a smoking censer is drawn over the page of writing].

My dear wife says that this book if read at *one sitting*, relentlessly, if grasped clearly, so, is a unit and acceptable to the logical mind.

So please, let it alone till you and two others who love Springfield and Lincoln can read it all night, *at one wild sitting*. It will mean more at 3 o'clock in the morning. It was originally a series of one page essays, some of them mystical, prophetical, apocalyptic, puzzling of course to the non-ritualistic. At just that moment, unless I am very much mistaken, the mandate went forth through all the great publishing houses of America, that the "new poetry" movement was a financial failure. Therefore the poets were to be kidded into being novelists or anthologists or ditched. Maybe I am entirely too positive about this. Anyway I was kidded into making a semi-novel of this, though I had not planned it that way, and then after re-writing it for two years clear out of its natural form, when it was so novel, I was permanently (apparently) ditched. Or so I understand it. So please reconstruct the book into a series of short-chapter single fantasies, as originally conceived, to be decorated like an old Spanish Mass-Book, and with the one purpose of making my home town over into something like the Golden Temple of Amritzar. This is a frank letter, but you are a good boy and I love you, dear John Drinkwater.

NICHOLAS VACHEL LINDSAY

P.S. Of course I am not ditched. I am too excited. I am merely "punished" for a year or so for giving my fancy free play. I have had a lot of good fortune of late of which the public evidence will very soon *unmistakably* appear.

Notes

1. This letter is written on the front pages of *The Golden Book of Springfield,* which Drinkwater had sent to be autographed.
2. George Bernard Shaw's *Joan of Arc* was published in 1923. In the preface, Shaw tries to analyze the phenomenon she represented in terms of the mind's abilities to visualize things. This, of course, appealed greatly to VL, whose theories of visualization govern most of his work. He carefully read and annotated Shaw's book.
3. The Lincoln poem is "Abraham Lincoln Walks at Midnight" (*Collected Poems,* p. 53).

155

TO HARRIET MONROE

Davenport Hotel
Spokane, U.S.A.

Friday, June 18, 1926

Dearest Dearest Harriet:
Thank you so much for the good words in your new Macmillan book.[1] You have way overestimated me. And thank you for the whole book. It will be your greatest conquest and success, I am sure. There is the ring of victory in it. Thank you so much for the spoon for little Susan. You are a dear to send it. I am more touched and glorified than you know by your deep faithfulness. You are only wrong about one thing—my ancestry and my family. My mother may have been a Pope, but was as far from a puritan as the Pope. If I told you the story of the Frazees and Lindsays it would be far from Puritan. It is terribly Virginian—some of it makes you think of the terrible John Randolph of Roanoke. Because I am a Blonde, people do not even suspect I am an Indian and Spaniard inside *and* I was told I was of Spanish Blood on my mother's side, far oftener than I was told to be good. But all this is mere gossip and unnecessary introspection. Ingrained from infancy I have the old southern habit of tracing every lost filament of inheritance. It is absolutely incurable and perfect nonsense. *But* if you want to get the Doniphan[2] style, and I was taught above all I was a Doniphan—read the pages about the general in Werner's Brigham Young. I was stuffed with such stories when I was six years old—till I could hold no more. My mother's people had convictions on Slavery, and came North and

freed their slaves, but otherwise both sides of the house were poison southerners, with every southern habit. Every story of John Randolph of Roanoke, no matter how bitter, stirs me yet like a story of the Cid. So when I reached Boston—about 1916—and found myself patronized as a non-descript and crude shouting "middle westerner" I almost spit blood. Patronizing airs from publishers do the same to me, though I keep silent. This is, of course, confidential. For about five years as I made my national tours I found this notice in the papers ahead of me:—"Floyd Dell says he is Homer chanting to the Greeks—Amy Lowell says he is a white nigger. Take your choice". Yet Amy gave me a dinner once a year in Boston and looked me over for a fresh attack. Once she took two pages of the New York Times to write me up as a "crude middle westerner of the middle class", whatever that may mean. But just before she wrote "The Critical Fable" she gave me one more of those microscopic inspection Boston dinners.— She had never asked me of my origin, my family, my anything. She never ventured to in-quire—but went on putting it in the paper as aforesaid, with incessant persecution. But I ventured in the midst of a conversation when she suddenly and irrelevantly insisted once more that I was a "middle west-erner", (she did not say "middle class" to my face)—I ventured to say I was a Virginian. It was a mild return I am sure after being called a White nigger in the papers by Amy for some six or seven years—wherever I happened to speak, finding the notice ahead of me. I would not have given the matter another thought, if she had not completely reversed her position and actually praised your humble servant to the skies in "The Critical Fable", written soon after. Maybe it dawned on the dear lady who liked to feed me once a year and give me the Boston Micro-scopic look she had almost taken a Liberty, and amends were in order. So much the worse for Boston.

All I had was Kentucky and Virginia families—till I was seventeen and went off to college. I faced family tyranny God knows, but not Boston Puritanism or anything like it.

I think Amy's Keats a great triumph. Elizabeth's late paper on Amy is nothing but a chivalrous girl's eulogy of Amy. I am going to write a paper about Amy some day and *mention* nothing in this letter. I will *praise* her, and praise her and praise her. I am sorry I have run on so, dear Harriet. It is not the least important. I let Elizabeth write the letters, for when I am interested in a letter it is enough to wear the recipient out.

As to myself and Elizabeth—we both have some very large simple plans, on an entirely new scale, far from Books and publishing houses. Too many publishers are in the Boston frame of mind. I must not wear myself out with wrath.

We are going to be *American Citizens,* or know the reason why, far from the publishing houses. Dearest, dearest Harriet, I have in this letter opened up a matter I have tried to keep still about for years. I hope I never talk it over again with anyone. Meanwhile please remember that among all my friends East of here, Elizabeth loved you and Muna Lee *best,*[3] and she was delighted at your great triumph in Spokane. Elizabeth speaks of you nearly every day, with praise and delight. Elizabeth and I and Susan Doniphan are very well indeed, full of hope and happiness, and reading and *studying* your new book very hard.

With love

VACHEL

Notes

1. Harriet Monroe's *Poets and Their Art* first came out in 1926.
2. Susan Doniphan Lindsay, VL and Elizabeth's daughter, was born on May 28, the same day that *Going-to-the-Stars* came out (Appleton). *The Candle in the Cabin* came out in July of that year.
3. Muna Lee was Harriet Monroe's sister.

156

TO MARY AUSTIN

Spokane
514 1/2 West 15th
July 9, 1926

Dear Mary Austin:–[1]
Great good wishes to you. I used to proclaim in London in the fall of 1920 that Santa Fe was the spiritual capital of America, and your ringing article in the New Republic proves it all over again. Please tell all my friends in Santa Fe that care to know that I am with you heart and soul. With a very few exceptions I have never spoken willingly for a Woman's Club or a Chautauqua. I have spoken, since I was a beggar, almost exclusively for the English Departments of various schools and Universities, and then, generally because I received no money from my publisher, and had to keep the wolf from the door. But I have seldom

been poor enough to speak for Woman's Clubs. I am glad the issue is joined so clearly and I hope every artist and writer in Santa Fe makes himself heard. I have just been preparing a creed on the subject of the necessity of every artist in America starting his own series of Pamphlets, (Like the fathers of the Revolution, from Tom Paine to Alexander Hamilton). Because we do not own skyscrapers the owners of skyscrapers think they can bully and misrepresent us till time out of mind, and the time has come for every artist to have his own position stated clearly on his own private press if it takes his last cent. The "smothering" process, the affected flattery of the Woman's Clubs is all a part of the same mood as the over-assured oily blurbs on the jackets of the new books. Writers and artists are simply smothered in blurbs and reviews by people who have not once looked at their stuff. My cure is—pamphlets—and more pamphlets and then again more pamphlets, and the sassier the better. Let us raise Jimmy Whistler from the dead![2] The time has come for all artists to live on bread and water and use their own local printing press and foot the bill *first*, instead of last.

God bless you, dear Mary Austin. Your article put an enormous amount of needed courage and exhilaration into me, and you may be sure I will re-read it many times. With great good wishes.

NICHOLAS VACHEL LINDSAY

Please congratulate me and my dear wife Elizabeth on the arrival of Susan Doniphan Lindsay, (our first). Doniphan ought to mean something in Santa Fe.

Notes

1. Mary Austin (1868—1934), formerly Mary Hunter, came to be known as Woman Alone. Determinedly independent, she was a feminist and participated in the Carmel Colony around 1900 with George Sterling and Jack London. She was devoted to Indian and desert culture and spent most of her life among the Indians in and around Santa Fe, New Mexico.
2. James Abbott McNeill Whistler (1834—1903), a painter VL greatly admired, was the author of *The Gentle Art of Making Enemies*, written in 1890 after his court battle against John Ruskin. Whistler was a model of elegance, dandyism, and sarcasm.

157

TO J. C. SQUIRE—*The London Mercury*

> Room 1129
> Davenport Hotel
> Spokane Washington
> December 30, 1926

My dear Squire:

When you told me good bye at the station in Springfield, Illinois, you did me the honor to ask me back to England, also to contribute to the Mercury, with considerable more zeal than I have ever done. Nevertheless, my wife and I buy the Mercury every month from the newsstand here in Spokane, follow all of your doings, get clippings from both England and America covering your statesmanship, and we are considerably more in touch with you than you may imagine. We are very much interested in everything you have ever done and have been considerably edified by the combination effort recently advertised of subscriptions to these heavenly twins, The American Mercury and The London Mercury. As to the depth of your alliance with that great German-American H.L.M.[1] we can only speculate. We are certainly amused at the contrast in the magazines.

I remember when you asked [me] to write for the Mercury more industriously than I had done, I said I was looking for that ideal editor who would allow a pen and ink drawing to appear with every one of my poems. You said you were not the man, but since that time pen and inks have appeared in the Mercury. I stand ready to submit a hundred pen and ink drawings with couplets of the Alexander Pope brevity to go with them any time you are willing to take a serious interest in the same. Of course, I do not insist on publication. But I have faith you will publish one or two.

The ice has been broken for you certainly if you care to become tolerant of my pen and ink hieroglyphics. The American literary world has decided to pardon and patronize, in a snooty but indulgent way, my whim for drawing pictures and then writing couplets for the same. The pictures are bad, but after all, let Vachel do as he pleases. He is awful, anyhow.

I am sending you a serious drawing that is really a political cartoon. With a verse I hope is a reproof of American arrogance, as well as an announcement of the American peril. The Jeffersonian minority in

America are dead set against American imperialism and are perfectly willing to tell the world so if the world will only listen.

The following books of mine are now illustrated by my own pen and inks and have been reviewed with as much respect as I expected, as artistic efforts:

> The New Illustrated Collected Poems. 50 Pen and Inks
> Going to the Sun. About 25 Pen and Inks
> Going to the Stars. About 25 Pen and Inks
> The Candle in the Cabin. 48 Pen and Inks.

The latter book is just out and is the nearest to my idea of the way my pen and inks should be treated, though if I had a fellow like John Lane[2] really aroused over the matter, absolutely determined to go in for perfect book manufacturing, I think we could sweep the world with a real pen and ink book.

My dear Squire, I am the kind of a man who will not be backed into the corner by publishers' advertising; simply because certain critical formulas have been wished upon me, it does not mean that I will follow them. There is hardly a critic in the Anglo-Saxon world yet willing to face the fact that most all of my poems from my seventeenth to my forty-seventh year were written to fit pictures which I first drew. Those pictures may have been no better than those of Edward Lear.[3] Just the same, they were the start. Some of my most praised lyrics began with these whimsies and the pictures have never been published.

It would be a great favor if you, as a thunderer in the Anglo-Saxon world, should humiliate yourself to the point of completely revising your formula in regard to my work of accepting my correction at least chronologically, and driving as hard and as fast as you can in the direction of a real hieroglyphic interpretation of all I have done or all I will do. In cooperation with such an undertaking, I am willing to submit a book of 100 poems and couplets along with the pen and inks which are their basis, all completely new, all to be issued in London without consultation with anyone on American soil. The very best of the London publishers of zinc etchings, such as John Lane, are so infinitely better than the Americans, so much more willing to plan a coordination between the picture and the verse, that surely an illustrated book should first appear in London. I suggest that you pick the best of the stuff for the Mercury first, back it with your best review, which is ultimately to be a preface, pick the London publisher and put the whole thing through with a roar. The only thing necessary is to abate your pride as a critic, be a good sport, for which Englishmen I understand are noted, and completely revise your general formulas in regard to my work. This should not be difficult in a Warwick that has made so many kings.

Very sincerely,

VACHEL LINDSAY

Notes

1. H.L.M. is Mencken, editor of *The American Mercury*.
2. John Lane was a London publisher.
3. Edward Lear (1812—88) was a British landscape painter better known for popularizing the limerick. His well-known nonsense poems were accompanied by pen-and-ink drawings.

158

TO BEN AND JOY BLAIR

Room 1129
Davenport Hotel
Spokane, Washington
December 30, 1926

Dear Ben and Joy:

I have just written a long letter to Olive in China, with good wishes for Paul and the others. I do not know that I said much, but I certainly gave them my good wishes and congratulations for standing up under fire. It seems to have put the fear of God into them, and a little sense into their heads. I hope they can take a like pride in me some day.

Joy said in her last letter to Elizabeth that I said I was well and happy and that might mean everything or nothing. Well, I am well and happy and it means exactly what it says. What is perhaps more to the point with you, I am taking up, myself, some of my old correspondence, writing here at the Davenport, preparing my own articles at the Davenport, and taking out from under Elizabeth some of the enormous correspondence she had taken upon herself, and her cooperation in my manuscripts is for the most part to be, for a while, giving her O.K. to the last drafts.

Our alliance with the Curtis Publishing Company, that is, the Ladies Home Journal and the Saturday Evening Post, seems to continue and all I have to do is to work like a football player every day of my life and produce at least one good article a week that will get underneath their particular kind of a gate, and I will get somewhere with them. Apparently they prefer to take volumes of writing from you, part of what you do does not please them at all. The parallel of a football player is a very good one. No one cares whether he gets his lessons or not in the University, if he works like hell on the football field. The man is willing to put that much energy into what the Curtis Company want, he can satisfy their insatiable maw and he is not expected to do much on the side, and who could?

We have had a very friendly telegram from Barton W. Currie of the Ladies Home Journal, and you have probably noticed the page of Mountain Songs from Glacier Park which came out in The Saturday Evening Post about the week before Christmas. The Post is considering three manuscripts of mine, two about Lincoln and Springfield, one about George Washington. All three, long prose manuscripts.[1]

The Atlantic Monthly is considering two long prose manuscripts of mine about Thomas Jefferson. I have just stacked high the raw material for an article on Harriet Monroe, which the Journal has almost, if not quite, ordered from me. This besides acres of unpublished poetry and reams of unpublished drawings, which will never bring me money, and bring me glory only if I know how to put in the final touch.

I have been so pleased and happy over Vachel Wakefield being in Hiram, in touch with all our old friends and the children of all our old friends, and in the Wakefield mansion. That means a lot to me. I think the sooner the Springfield property is sold off, the better. George Greenwood of Spokane, Vice President of the Old National Bank, and Cashier here, is going to begin to urge Latham Souther to sell all the rest of the Springfield property as soon as is possible, and sensible. Latham seems to respect Greenwood's letters much more than he does my own. Greenwood seems to be able to write in that mysterious trust company phraseology, which indicates to your real business man that business is being transacted.

I was very much pleased that you two were pleased over the sale of the Lawrence Avenue properties. I know you believe in the sale of the Fifth and Edwards Street property. I have urged it all along and I am going to ask George Greenwood to urge it in my name, and Elizabeth's. In this she heartily concurs. If you ever are inclined to protest, write us, of course, but I fancy you are still of the same mind.

I am delighted that you are seeing a lot of Vachel Wakefield and his visit meant more to us after he departed than while he was here. We began to think him over. He is such a quiet boy, at least on a short visit, and has so little to say that it takes meditation to get him. I am delighted that he writes occasionally to Elizabeth and that she means something to him.

Elizabeth and I and the baby are in the very best of health and spirits. Our plans are all clear and clearly laid and have changed very little for six months, as far as the external world is concerned. We prepared together five manuscripts in one month. Besides this Elizabeth copied and sent off two old ones to the Dearborn Independent, at their request. Surely this is detailed information, and I am not indulging in glittering generalities. There is no doubt that Elizabeth did me one of the greatest of services in lifting from my shoulders, for a while, the intolerable burden of correspondence. I am now able to take it up with a bang, just as she is sick and sea-sick of it.

More later. With love

N.V.L.

Note

1. The manuscripts submitted by VL to the *Saturday Evening Post* eventually made up most of *The Litany of Washington Street* (1929).

159

TO HELEN F. MCMILLIN—*Boston Evening Transcript*

Room 1129
Davenport Hotel
Spokane, Washington
January 27, 1927

My dear Miss McMillin:
Thank you, indeed, for your recent article in the Boston Transcript.[1] My wife and I read it only last night and we received an extraordinary inspiration from your great insight and great kindness. The only funny part of the article was the black silhouette of John Gould Fletcher which has gone all over the country as my portrait. It started in Detroit. I do not know how it has crossed the country but it seems unsuppressible. Of course your Art Department should apologize to Fletcher, way off there in England, not to me!
Your article was so earnestly and beautifully written, with such an

utter absence of padding and journalistic bunkum that I assure you I got a much bigger thrill out of it than my first full page of Transcript in about 1914. It's one thing to get friends, quite another thing to keep them. Katharine Lee Bates will tell you that in the old days when I used to come to Wellesley with the noise of which you speak, that I used to tell them when I said Good-bye, Love me little, love me long, is the burden of my song. It is a very hard thing to say and to be faithful to; but as far as the Wellesley group are concerned, I am sure they have stood by it and remember it. I liked most especially your last paragraph and your first column. It is a wonderful thing to me to have my Mills College girl figuring that way in my affairs and with such respect. It is so easy to be nominal and routine and it is so easy to get fresh. I congratulate you on avoiding both these sins and including the scholar and gentleman, my wife, just as you have.

Mills College means a lot to both of us. Elizabeth did four years work in three there and many have assured me that she was the most brilliant student that ever went through Mills College, with the best record in the hardest work. We may yet go back to the San Francisco region in some fashion under the wing of Mills, if not on the campus. You see, when I wrote "General Booth" in 1912 in Los Angeles, I finally worked up the nerve to get as far as San Francisco and then Professor E. Olan James took care of me for a month when I was a beggar, absolutely down and out and wanting to die. James was Professor of English at Mills and from that time on I seem to have had a Mills' destiny. That was, of course, long before I met Mrs Lindsay.

When I first walked the Mills campus I had to do it after dark on the arm of Olan. I had harvested in my alleged clothes all the way across Kansas and tramped in them from Springfield, Ill. to Central New Mexico. I was awful, within and without. Having achieved the San Francisco region at what is sometimes described as the zero hour, I sometimes feel it is good to go back to zero and begin. Surely if Prof. James is anywhere around I will let him shepherd me all the way back to the butter and egg farms in the hollows of the mountains.

This is not much of a thank you for a very fine article indeed, and a very thrilling and invigorating one. I have just written a long letter to Katharine Lee Bates today and you may be very sure I am grateful for your reference to her in your article. She is an excellent woman to sweeten up sour poets and you are exactly right, that's what she did. But sour is possibly not the word. Audiences appeal to my imagination enormously but are for that very reason ultimately exhausting and the battery must be replenished by some utterly different course of life. I know your review was written before that of Harriet Monroe in "Poetry" for January but it runs in such parallel lines I accept the verdict of two exceedingly separated friends.

There is much that I would like to say to you to show my gratitude if I knew how. I only wish I had sense enough to digest your article and live up to the exhortation. Surely it will help.

You may be interested to know that we have started a perfect whirl-wind of poem-games in Spokane[2] at a much higher speed than ever before and with more profound resolution. Something may come of this. The Associated Press seems already interested. We hope to make them real games in the sense that they will be played in many cities without our help.

I thank you for all you have said about my drawing. That victory is about won. I won the slow and grudging consent of the critics to do as I please there. You remember I had to teach them to let me recite. At first they wouldn't let me do that, before they went crazy about it. Please see my new drawings as pen and ink exercises. I am hoping to produce much more mature and carefully considered compositions now that I have set my hand free and won my battle.

If I can get an English publisher I will begin there and issue many books of drawings without verses. The English are much more willing to let a pen and ink man do his best and worst with lots of space, lots of paper and careful zinc etching. This sounds like a confidential de-velopment of my plans but I discover if you tell your deeper secrets to a policeman, he is so tired he seldom notices you have said anything. None of this information is a secret, though it may be brash to be so talkative.

I have taken your article so seriously and so thoughtfully you surely have the right to know it. I have not the least notion of letting it fall to the ground. It is very seldom I take this much space for an acknowl-edgement for seldom is such precision displayed on the part of a re-porter.

I hope we have established friendship and good-will between your-self and Mr. & Mrs. Vachel Lindsay and their daughter Susan Doniphan, 7 months old. We are likely to be doing a great deal in the next two or three years, and now that Boston is kind to me, believe me I feel much more kindly toward Boston. I was skinned there several times by the orders of Potentates I knew not, hence my dark curse "So much the worse for Boston". Please consider this a retraction as far as you and Wellesley are concerned.

Mrs. Lindsay going over the article with me said your article was the exact truth in substance, that my worship of the years before 1912 and of my drawing was after all merely my worship of my own youth. I had to agree with her, but your interview was given some months ago, and as I say, since that time I have won a victory for my half developed pictures. You will find all my really faithful friends from the beginning have decided with a grunt to tolerate them. In another year I may storm the battlements with real pictures. For instance, all the pictures in the Candle in the Cabin were drawn in one week, 50 pictures selected from 300 drawn in one week. Why? We tried to pick out those with the greatest zip and whizz—headway was the first thing. Of course, much of this is lost in the exceedingly economical reproductions in the Candle in the Cabin. My next book of pictures I will block in everything most elaborately with pencil first as carefully as a stained glass window is made, then I will ink it in, as they say. The pictures will abound in human figures. I drew from the nude for years and won all the nominal honors for the same. I am going to fill my next book of pictures with human figures really doing something and maybe the heavy critics will change their tune and quit spatting me on the wrist.

Surely you are right though, my hard battle for these pictures which is nearer won than you realize is a quest for youth: the old Art Institute days in Chicago and the days under Chase and Henri when Bellows and Rockwell Kent were my fellow students. Surely I think like an art student whether I write that way or not, and one of the great thrills of my life was the Bellows memorial exhibit in the Metropolitan Art Museum. It seemed to me that [was] the greatest triumph of my old master, Robert Henri, the greatest teacher I ever knew, as it was for Bellows himself.

But I will not grant that the new poem games are a struggle back toward 1912. They really seem to be born of my marriage and my life in Spokane. My wife and two of her Spokane friends are helping me to work them out with the greatest energy and devotion. The greatest single principle is the omission of musical instruments, musical notation, and singing. I get madder and madder at people who try to set my stuff to music. The poem games go in exactly the opposite direction. They go straight in the direction of the dictionary. We are dancing musical words as they are pronounced in the American and British languages and the Virginia variations of the same. Occasionally there is a little drum music but that is generally strictly amateur on a tin pan from the kitchen, lest even a drum should run away with the English language. Meanwhile we have dancers and actors who can find rhythm in English as she is spoke. This is no doubt a special faculty. Mordkin is passing through town next week. He advertises as a novelty and specialty the dancing of some numbers merely to song. I presume this means he leaves out the orchestra. I hope it does. I think the orchestra has done more harm to the music of the English language and the prestige of poetical rhythm than any other one thing. It is a terrible and mechanical tyrant. I am in sympathy with the log cabin sects who chant the psalms and do not allow even a parlor organ in the log cabin. They have a vague but correct trust in the music of words rightly pronounced. The poem games are to step off these musical words. The so-called repeated lines of many of my poems are there simply so some action of the dancer can be completed. Very often a poem is expanded three times the length by these repetitions when the right dancer gets a hold of it.

We are going ahead with these games with terrific speed. We are letting no one into the parlor but dancers, actors and those willing to participate. We have pushed them much further than I have ever pushed them in any public show or improvisation in the past. We are able to do this because of the extraordinary interest, energy and devotion of my wife and her friends. No longer do I have to carry the whole show on my back. I furnish the pronunciation and the other people furnish the whirlwind.

Frederic Melcher, the Editor of the Publishers Weekly, was through here for two days not long ago; and for two evenings there was certainly pandemonium in our parlor. We had poem games until about 10 o'clock, then Melcher managed to get the cork out of himself and sang solos until 11, which were delightful to hear. Most of them negro songs seventy-five years old, grown mellow in the memory of the American people. In the midst of all this excitement, we proceeded to more games, marching around hand in hand to the Sea Serpent Chantey, and the like.

I have noticed one effect of all this work from the beginning, with large audiences or with tiny groups in parlors. When going strong, even on such serious things as Old John Brown from the Booker Washington Trilogy, it is very hard to keep the audience from laughing. It is very hard to keep from laughing myself. It is very hard to keep an audience completely warmed up by Poem Games, from acting as though they were full of hooch to the top. It is what rhythm does to the human body and soul. But here is where the problem has always come in, and I want you to congratulate me on a few of my victories, for over and over again I have had an audience that laughed and roared until the last five minutes, and then the last five minutes were as serious as the judgment day, and so it was, if I may boast, in our parlor the other evening. We finished up with the Lame Boy and the Fairy[3] very seriously, indeed, but because we had had so much chanting and marching beforehand that our seriousness had unity and real blood beat in it and was not routine solemnity.

I suppose this is the essence of my war against all those who have called me a jazz artist. They have lopped off this last five minutes and said it does not exist. They will grant me six days of the week and not Sunday. They let in anything about religion except the High Mass, all the gab, and cackle and clatter in the world. But I see the issue so much more plainly than I used to that I think I can set the matter right. You know, yourself, that Greek tragedy was born of the Revels of Bacchus, that is, riot until the last moment and then a great moment. It is the lopping off of this great last moment by all sorts of presumptous intruders that has caused me to put up so wild a battle. One example of the kind of victory I pride myself in is that on many evenings, after a complete riot of Poem Games, such as A Doll's Arabian Nights and the Blacksmith's Serenade, one of the dancers, Miss Lenore Glen,[4] gives a very earnest rendition of one of my earliest and most serious poems, The Tree of Laughing Bells, a poem almost as abstract as a Bach Fugue.

On the whole, it means a little more to me that the Poem Games shall win a new and great victory than that the drawings should win a victory. I may be too complacent but I think the battle for the drawings is already won, as much as I wanted to win it. The statement that I draw pictures is now in every review, however grudgingly made. That is enough, but I would like the Poem Games to become so contagious that all the dancers in the world would come to our parlor as to a school of whirling dervishes.

The parallel with the whirling dervish is not a bad one, if you are willing to take Mohammedanism with the seriousness of those who built the Taj Mahal and the Alhambra. We are right on the point where these things may either sweep the country or happen in a little pocket and be forgotten. Very frankly I am asking you for your interest and curiosity, for things have to happen nationally or they do not happen at all, and dancers go from all over the nation to Denishawn for one kind of dancing. I wish they would come to us for literary dancing, we have the place where we can teach them.

The whirling dervish, the singing dervish, but not the howling dervish, make a good parallel, if you believe that when you whirl and call on the name of God the sky and the stars and the universe will descend to you. The word "jazz" means leer. It means a technical curiosity. It means midnight dirt and a sad morning after. I believe in the gospel of beauty. If the rhythms and songs I teach people do not build up toward the sky and stars, the sun and the moon, they are surely vain. I hate wood alcohol, the Temples of Baal and Astatoth, the Temples of Babylon. I am utterly unfashionable in Manhattan, because I have been an anti-saloon worker in my time. I have always hated booze, the saloon and all that went with them. Now that it has become fashionable to eulogize the ancient days of the barroom, the critics discover my rather poor anti-saloon league poems and say I will not do. I am actually a dry, isn't it terrible, but surely I am going to turn into a wood alcohol wet, just because it is the literary fashion, or Mencken tells me to.

My dear friend, I did not expect to write but a page, but you seem to have started an argument. Do not take this letter too hard or too seriously. The best I can say for it is, it is the only long letter I have written for ages, and I write very few letters at all.

Very Sincerely,

VACHEL LINDSAY

Notes

1. Helen McMillin's article "Vachel Lindsay in Quest of His Youth" was printed in the *Boston Evening Transcript* on January 22, 1927. It was based on her interview with VL in Spokane.
2. The Poem-Games in Spokane were organized with the cooperation of Edith Haight, who had been a colleague of Elizabeth Conner's at Lewis and Clark High School, and Stoddard King, a local journalist and writer of light poetry.
3. "The Lame Boy and the Fairy," an early poem of VL's (*Collected Poems*, p. 136), contains many elements reminiscent of "The Tree of Laughing Bells" and *Where Is Aladdin's Lamp?*
4. Lenore Frances Glen was one of two friends of Elizabeth Conner Lindsay's mentioned earlier in the letter.

160

TO HARRIET MONROE

Room 1129
Davenport Hotel
Spokane, Washington
February 9, 1927

My dear Harriet:
About a year ago I offered the Ladies Home Journal the possible title for a possible article, "Harriet Monroe and the Chicago World's Fair". Barton W. Currie, the Editor in Chief, I interviewed personally in Philadelphia, jumped at the chance. There are skads of things here on the World's Fair of 1893 and of course I know a lot about you, but to tell the story right is another matter.

It is my profound conviction that Poetry, A Magazine of Verse, is the best and worthiest and most permanent child of that World's Fair, and represents a transference of the head-long energies of the architecture and the sculpture, and painting and park gardening of that time, into an entirely different field.

I would like a much more elaborate history of the Columbian Ode and Cantata and I think there was a third poem of yours sung. I know you read one poem to thousands of people, and another was sung by thousands of people, but my raw material on all of this has been appropriated by some of the local lords and must needs be taken away from them by dynamite, if ever. Some people are above the law.[1]

I do not want you to lend me anything precious, but I do want you to send me a few short carbon copies of the most whirlwind accounts of what happened when you were in the very midst of those World's Fair times. I want figures, facts, dates and places. I do not want to be the least vague. I want to tell the story first in just as hardboiled a way as possible in the first paragraph, with every single detail you are willing to part with and every single high opinion of what happened that you are willing to quote. I want especially quotations from great newspaper correspondents and reviewers in England and America at that time. If there is any "now it can be told" in this story, tell it. Give me anything you have held back all these years and I will put it in paragraph two. From there on I have my own views as you know, as to the present and future of the New Poetry Movement and as to the present and future and past World's Fairs. I took in every big phase of the World's Columbian Exposition and any portfolio of World's Fair views can review it for me. What is more, when I struck Chicago in 1900, I walked the Midway almost daily, browsed through the old Field Columbian Museum, found that the Chicago Art Institute was essentially a child of the World's Fair and was at that time pretty well loaded down with plaster casts left over from the World's Fair and oracles of every sort left over from the World's Fair. I did not miss the transition.

In 1910, when Hamlin Garland was still president of the Cliff Dwellers Club, Chicago, he made me a member thereof on the strength of the first Village Magazine issued in 1910; he had me send a Village Magazine to practically every member of the club he ever heard of, and for a year I used to hang around the Club when I passed through Chicago and I noted the backbone of it was still the old Art Institute set, which was the old World's Fair set. I got pretty well acquainted with Hamlin Garland and Lorado Taft in 1910 in this Club. I had heard them lecturing ten years before in Fullerton Hall on all known subjects, along with Charles Francis Brown. I was very much amused to come back and be a member of their gang, instead of a mere small boy on the front seat. I will never forget what an absolutely rotten drawing teacher Charles Francis Brown was. I had to go to New York to get teachers, after sticking around the Art Institute from 1900 to 1904, but just the same, in 1910 I forgave everybody, remembered with great gratitude the Art Institute as a Museum, if not a school, and was especially grateful, and am still, for the magnificent and highly browsable Ryerson Library.

With all this behind me and the whole gold coast set, loaded with my 1910 Village Magazine, you do not know how amused I was to be lionized in my own Club in 1912, right across the street from my own school, without a soul there remembering my face or name. I think by that time Hamlin Garland had gone on to New York and Taft was not on hand that night. He might have been guilty of remembering me.

Why am I going through all this rigamarole?[2] It doesn't get anywhere in particular, except that I remember Chicago in four stages—The World's Fair, the Art Institute, The Cliff Dwellers' Club and Poetry, a Magazine of Verse. I am grateful for all of it, it all makes one picture in my mind, but you are the one who finally humanized it for me, who wiped out any bleakness that might have remained from the personal loneliness of an art student.

There is not the least doubt that Hamlin Garland did his level best to make friends for me in 1910, but it was you and your group that really did the work in 1912.

When I think of the Chicago World's Fair I think of something that must be re-created permanently. It seems to me the temporary World's Fair has had its day. I would like to see a gigantic, permanent, Columbian Exposition, MacMonnies Fountain, and all.

You may be very sure, dear Harriet, that I have not lost a single thread of enthusiasm for that great World's Fair at its very highest point, and I honor you as the human being above all in Chicago, to whom the whole story burns with a white light to this very hour. I know exactly what your faith is, and I certainly honor your splendid dreams.

I have no assurance that I will be able to dispose of this article to The Ladies Home Journal, except the general assurance of good will from the Curtis people, and a great big Christmas telegram which the Ladies Home Journal sent me to keep my heart warm, as it were. But surely the article, once written, has its place. I think I should try the Delineator next, since it is the official organ of so many women's organizations.

We have all had experiences that brought our lives to a particular focus and gave us a fighting edge for life. I have always felt that The World's Fair meant this to you. I also understand the general apathy with which people view your enthusiasm, because it did not happen to mean this to them. They got religion at some other camp meeting, but I do not want to tamper with your enthusiasms in the least. I want to get exactly your view on this matter, and say it with ringing clearness.

My own Columbian Ode, my trumpet blast for Utopia, as one might say, was the Golden Book of Springfield, evolved under utterly alien conditions to yours, and alas, no one has read that book yet, but my experience with it and the years of determination I put into it, and expect to put into it, help me to understand what the World's Fair meant to those who put it over with a roar. I am sure we would not have the poetry of Masters or the poetry of Sandburg without the Chicago World's Fair behind them. On the whole I think the World's Fair of 1893 has flowered in letters rather than art, unless Michigan Avenue is being reborn at this hour.

Enclosed find $3.00 for our year's subscription to Poetry. Send it to our residence, 2318 W. Pacific Ave., Spokane. Thank you for the very noble review in the January number of Poetry.[3] I will write you a separate letter soon about my drawings. You have no idea how seriously I take them.

Very sincerely,

VACHEL

Notes

1. The title poem of *Every Soul Is a Circus* (1929) is said to have been written "bearing in mind the Chicago World's Fair, 1933" (p. 3) The information here required of Harriet Monroe must have been part of the material needed by VL to sing the next World's Fair.
2. That VL was actively preparing numerous poems to be included in the coming volume is further confirmed by the word "rigamarole" in this text: "Excuse me if I cry into my Handkerchief" *(Every Soul Is a Circus,* pp. 17—23) was originally entitled "Rigamarole, Rigamarole" and printed separately by Random House in 1929, in a longer version. As the title of Helen McMillin's article indicates, VL is indeed "In Quest of His Youth," as a study of *Every Soul Is a Circus* will prove from several points of view.
3. Harriet Monroe had published "The Limnal Lindsay" in *Poetry* , January 1927 (pp. 217—21).

161

TO ETHELIND S. COBLIN

Room 1129
Davenport Hotel
Spokane, Washington
February 23, 1927

Dear Cousin Ethelind:

Please take this letter as my contribution to the memorial reunion of all the old pupils of Excelsior in the early part of next June.

I remember two visits to Excelsior, both of which may interest you. The first one was 1906, when I was a boy of 26. I had begged my way up from Jacksonville, Fla., after many experiences, which are recorded exactly as they happened in A Handy Guide for Beggars. But the last story of that particular trip is the story of "Lady Iron Heels". I do not there tell of my experiences going through Cumberland Gap, walking north over Big Hill, Kentucky, by the old Daniel Boone trail, being entertained at Lexington over night by my mother's old Bible teacher, Professor J. W. McGarvey, and then walking on next day toward Frankfort. Many, many things happened on this journey through Kentucky, most vivid, most picturesque, and still brilliantly painted on my mind, but to me the climax of the trip was reaching Excelsior Institute and receiving so kind a welcome from Aunt Eudora. I remember I stayed with you about a month. I know I timed it so that it was up to the last day of my start for Europe with my father and mother from Springfield, Illinois. I spent a great deal of time for that month with Cousin Eudora and wrote her the little poem "The Flower of Mending",[1] which has been popular among my shorter pieces, somewhat to my astonishment. I did not publish it for a long time. It was just my tribute to my little cousin for being so good to me after the wild days on the road.

On the trip, which was my first experience as a beggar, I carried copies of The Tree of Laughing Bells especially printed, with a cover of my own design, and these I tried to trade for a night's lodging all the way north from Jacksonville, Fla. Of course, all the people who took me in, took me in out of kindness and they considered the poetry a mere apology. It was not until I read for Excelsior Institute that I had really close listeners to this poem. It may interest you to know that a picture about as big as a barn door that I painted of the Tree of Laughing Bells is now hanging in my parlor[2] and the poem is being danced in the

Poem Games given there and the picture is part of the ceremony. So
the poem I began with, I may yet continue with.

All my dreams and ideas of Kentucky turn on my beautiful talks
with Aunt Eudora in 1906, her very motherly way and her deep sympathy with my struggle to make a place for my songs. It was, indeed,
timely, I had had very little response anywhere and very little understanding. No one cared for my pictures, no one cared for my verse, and
I turned beggar in sheer desperation. Many people try to gloss this over
now and make out it was a merry little spring excursion and I didn't
really mean it. They are dead wrong. It was a life and death struggle,
nothing less. I was entirely prepared to die for my work, if necessary,
by the side of the road, and was almost on the point of it at times. I
would not be surprised if the invitation to go to Europe with my father
and mother was the result of my Aunt Eudora's letters to Springfield.
They were certainly at this time intensely hostile to everything I did,
said, wrote, thought or drew. Things were in a state where it was
infinitely easier to beg from door to door than to go home, or even die
by the ditch on the highway. Aunt Dora took care of me for a month
and peppered the folks at home with letters, and hence the trip to
Europe. It was certainly not my idea. I did not want to go home and
if they asked me home it was probably through her plain speaking.

I will never forget the easy, dreaming Kentucky and the droning
bees in the blue grass, and the walks with Cousin Eudora and Aunt
Eudora, and the queer feeling of being the family disgrace somewhat
straightened out when I stood up to read "The Tree of Laughing Bells"
to the school. As far as I know, I read it in my beggar's raiment. I am
sure I felt that way, and it was the kind hearts around me in that
particular spot that made me want to live.

I have elegant hostesses now who always interrupt me when I say
there was a time when I was a beggar. It is nothing more than the plain
truth. You were the first among my kin to take me in. It was certainly
time someone did something, for I was in a state of wrath beyond all
argument or discussion. It took all the easy ways of Kentucky to ease
me up.

If I hadn't been the kind of a man who is willing to write this kind
of a letter, I would never have survived to write another poem or draw
another picture. I hear there is Indian in our family, and if there is,
certainly mine was on the war path about then. I must be grateful forever
to my kind aunt for taking the fury out of my heart and setting things
right again. From that time on my life began to mend. This is the plain
prose of it. The poetry of it is in "The Flower of Mending".

Another visit to Kentucky long after, when I was on tour in the
grand manner, reciting for Universities and the like, and dress-suited

to death, is recorded in the poem "Alexander Campbell".[3] This poem was written pretty largely in memory of one Sunday when James H. Polk South, Junior, took a group of us cousins from the old South mansion to the church at Grassy Springs. There was a preacher there who preached the sermon, (as was his duty), but the thing that interested me was the way that very young South took the services in hand as an elder of the congregation, built the fire, spread the communion table, led in prayer, led the singing, and helped the preacher in presiding at the communion table. It was a beautiful church on a rather cool but beautiful spring day, and the whole thing made me think of Red Birds flying and of how my own father, at exactly the same age, probably did exactly the same thing and how much in gesture, manner and style the boy was like my father. The very young man made me think of the very old man and of what a strange thing family tradition is. These two people had scarcely ever met but their style was so identical as to be startling. The beauty of the service, the sweet neighborhood quality of the congregation, the plain fact that everybody was kin to everybody else, and the knee-deep blue grass, was all Kentucky and nothing but Kentucky. I understood exactly why my father always felt a stranger in Illinois, (although he had lived in Springfield, Illinois, for forty years), and why he always talked about Kentucky.

So I wrote the first section of Alexander Campbell, "My Fathers Came From Kentucky". The second section is a memorial to all those who have passed from this life among my kin, one and all being members of the Disciples Church from the very earliest days of Campbell, and the third section has not so much reference to Excelsior Institute as to my memories of that old Daniel Boone trail by which I walked to Excelsior from Cumberland Gap, and also my memories of the great portrait of Alexander Campbell that used to hang above the fireplace at the home of my Grandfather Frazee, who studied under Campbell in his prime. Another personage who has no doubt entered into this poem is J. B. Briney, who is the model, old-fashioned, Disciple preacher and who happened to have been the one who baptized me when I was eight years old. He, too, was a southerner, with a Kentucky atmosphere, and those to whom this will be read probably know him better than I do. Certainly he is the gray-bearded Campbellite elder who is really haunting me in that song. Not so very long ago I saw an article by him in The Christian. It was highly characteristic.

This letter is presumably a tribute to my Aunt Eudora, yet I find myself tracing such things in my writing as are vaguely or closely related to my two visits to Excelsior, rather than a direct tribute. This being the case, I should add one more line of elucidation on the Alexander Campbell poem. One is that the statesman philosopher, the sage with high conceit, is a vague reference to men like Garfield, Lloyd George, Champ Clark,[4] Jim Reed, R. A. Long, men living and dead, who begin to emerge or who have long emerged from the spell of little brick churches, like the church of Grassy Springs, to national or world action, and who sometimes think they have left all these things behind them. I am sure whatever changes they may deliberately make in their lives, places like the church at Grassy Springs have marked them forever, and they may trace to them some special courage or some special power, which will be a deep mystery to external and hasty biographers.

Aunt Dora was a spring like the church at Grassy Springs. I can remember visiting many people in Kentucky who spoke to me of her with the greatest gravity as a sage, a sibyl, a person to whom they were indebted, in the deepest sense. Whoever she taught, she taught by hand, one at a time, not by any machine or wholesale process. She kept her hand on them forever, and they knew it. No thundering herds ever poured through her school. The children were instructed one at a time and each had his claim forever.

Excelsior Institute is a formal name for her schools and she named it in her very young days when she was wild with courage and hope, back from great mountain climbing in Europe, and the Alpine climber was a great reality to her. But if I called her school anything but Excelsior Institute, I would call it "The Church at Grassy Springs", though the real church may be a short ride away.

Very sincerely, your loving cousin,

VACHEL

Notes

1. "The Flower of Mending" was eventually published in *The Chinese Nightingale and Other Poems* (p. 84) and the *Collected Poems* (p. 329).
2. The painting entitled "The Tree of Laughing Bells" is currently at the Vachel Lindsay home, Springfield, Illinois.
3. "Alexander Campbell" (*Collected Poems*, p. 352) is a memorial to the founder of the Disciples of Christ (Campbellites). The poem's three sections are "My Fathers Came from Kentucky," "Written in a Year When Many of My People Died," and "A Rhymed Address to All Renegade Campbellites, Exhorting Them to Return."
4. Champ Clark of Missouri was speaker of the U.S. House of Representatives from 1911 to 1919. William Jennings Bryan persuaded him in 1912 to swing support to Woodrow Wilson, the Democratic presidential candidate.

162

TO MARK SULLIVAN

2318 West Pacific Avenue
Spokane, Washington
April 24, 1927

My dear Friend:[1]
Your letter was a thrill to the whole family. We are glad, yea, delighted, to have heard from your daughter Syd as well as yourself. My wife and I are awfully interested in riding on that dizzy barque, the Dearborn Independent.[2] We did not expect such a magnificent result, at least so soon. I must answer your letter at once or else I will write you a book about Markham, whom I so much admire. Answering your question, we will say that Markham's standing to-day is as good as Longfellow's ever was. The newspapers do not know this now but it is so. For the greater part of its history, he has been the honorary President of The Poetry Society of America, and his relation to that institution has been as definite, worth while, and dignified as that of Charles W. Eliot in his position as President Emeritus of Harvard. I wish you would give a chapter to the history of The Poetry Society of America. Why not? Send the officers a list of questions, via the address on the enclosed bulletin.

I send a clipping by Benjamin de Casseres from The American Mercury for December 1926. I have underlined the sentences with which I agree. I think the best sentence is "Markam——is steeped in the ecstasy of eternals". I send from the American Mercury of August, 1926, Markham's "Ballad of the Gallows Bird" with annotations of my own. It is full of Swedenborgian pictures.

Markham was made Litt. D. with the following poets at Baylor University, Waco, Texas, on June 16, 1920:

Harriet Monroe
Amy Lowell
Vachel Lindsay
"The Sweet Singer of Texas" (whose name I forget)

and maybe one more. Not even the fastidious Harriet or the pugnacious Amy ventured to question the position or the worth of Edwin Markham, the Nestor of the profession; and on the whole, I think he was the leading figure there, for reasons pretty well summed up by De Casseres.

I notice we all advertise the degrees we received there; and I notice we got them nowhere else!

Before I go further, I must thank you for the high honor of allowing my wife and myself to look over your galley proofs, which we return, assuming they will be useful.

As to my reflections after reading your chapter:

Markham has a specialized talent for leadership: that is, among poets and men of letters, from the platform and as a presiding officer, as well as a man with a pen in his hand; and he has fought a life time battle, at last successful, to establish a reasonable place in this leadership rather than in the somewhat inflated political expectation which was thrust upon him. His personal style is effective among the poets far more than with the general public.

The last time I attended a session of The Poetry Society, about a year ago, I stepped into the National Arts Club, Gramercy Park, about ten p.m. Mrs Markham, as Secretary of the Society, was taking notes at the table at the front; and Edwin, gavel in hand, was shaking his mane, and presiding over a packed assembly of American poets from all over the world. Lady Speyer,[3] once of Germany; Edward Davison, once of Cambridge, England, Squire's personal representative on American soil; Witter Bynner, ex-president of The Poetry Society, passing through from Santa Fe, Mexico, and the World around; Clement Wood, who got a patent on Greenwich Village some time back; and Gawd only knows who else; only it seemed to me that every faction I had ever known was there. Markham presided with snap and fire, and made them all eat from his hand. He closed the meeting at eleven sharp, according to schedule.

I have watched Markham for the last fifteen years struggling toward this deserved place. Do not think he did it with his gavel. He won it with his pen, writing poetry not the least in the fashion with reformers or new poets. Now all the leaders of poetic styles, some of them a bit jaded, were eating from the hand of ancient Nestor. I had the laugh of my life out of it. The grandee air of Edwin Markham, his Peter Paul Rubens Buffalo Bill mustachios, when he gets going good have something to do with his ascendency.

Witter Bynner and I adjourned for a midnight session at the Players Club next door, and we decided after all that it was the California in Edwin that pulled him through and gave him his mellow gray-haired victory.

Now I have an epigram to offer you: the exquisites of 1899 did not like Bryan, because he was not a literary poet like Markham. The Utopians and howling reformers of 1899 did not like Markham because he could not go into the political convention like Bryan and beat it into submission. But I would suggest, let the poet sing with the singers, and the tribune appear before the "people". As to the list of Markham's recent good verses, I will refer you to any of the twenty leading anthologies.

I think Markham's personal victory is his real drama right here at this moment. If you think it no victory to rule The Poetry Society of America, try it. And it is a real victory to outlive a vague political ascendency and to build up a literary one that is solid.

"Lincoln, the Man of the People" and "The Muse of Brotherhood" are two of Markham's old poems that stand. Another one, "The Gray Norns" is never mentioned, but it is as good as any of the exquisite work that is being breathed heavily about. His song on Semiramis always haunted me. "The Ballad of the Gallows Bird" which my wife and I have just read together, we mail to you for your own judgment. The lines where he thinks of home and the old cottage in the XVIIth section are a transitional climax. Markham took our town of Springfield, Illinois, by storm as a Swedenborgian, and lectured on many of the ideas which have more recently come out in this song. The single tax radicals of our town happened to be Swedenborgians, as Markham is, in his fashion, by inheritance. There is a link between Henry George and Swedenborg, and Swedenborg and Markham.

Quote me directly, leave me anonymous, or paraphrase as you please. I am at your service your own way. You might care to write to Witter Bynner, Santa Fe, New Mexico, on all these matters.

Great good wishes, and thank you so much.

Yours most sincerely,

VACHEL LINDSAY

Notes

1. Mark Sullivan, a journalist and publicist, was a close friend of Theodore Roosevelt's. His six volume *Our Times* came out between 1923 and 1935.
2. *The Dearborn Independent* newspaper was founded by Henry Ford.
3. Leonora (von Stosch) Speyer began her career as a violinist and occasionally contributed to *Poetry*. She eventually became president of the Poetry Society; in 1927 she won the Pulitzer Prize for Poetry for her *Fiddler's Farewell* (1926).

163

TO MORONI OLSEN

2318 West Pacific
Spokane, Washington
April 25, 1927

Moroni Olsen, Esq.[1]
On circuit.

Dear Sir:

We were certainly highly honored at your call under the wing of Mr. Joseph Rupley, and that you cared to bring the entire company multiplied the honor by that number. I am sorry I took all the time reading and showing off. I thought we had more time. I spared you a lot of details of the Book of the Dead, first out of general politeness, second because the real simplicity of the central judgment scene might not have appeared in hasty chatter. But maybe you know more about the Book of the Dead than I do.

When my wife and I attended your wonderful performance of "Outward Bound" the following week we were not a little abashed to realize that we had received such amazing and distinguished visitors so casually. Certainly your performance of "Outward Bound" was for me revolutionary and roused not only my conscience but my artistic covetousness. A company which can convey that idea with such power is the one that would mean the world to me as the expounder of "The Trial of the Dead Cleopatra in her Beautiful and Wonderful Tomb", my own Americanized version of The Book of the Dead.

Ever since your performance I have been walking the streets trying to think out how to put briefly to you my conception of the acting of this poem in such a way that you could step straight from the acting of such a play as "Outward Bound" into the acting of my poem, retaining the same tempo, mood, general intention, and celestial geography.

First, the only very essential equipment is a set of papier maché head dresses turning the Egyptian priests and priestesses into gods. That is, a jackal mask for Anubis, the Embalmer; an ibis mask for Thoth, god of writing; a hawk mask for Horus who sits among the gods; possibly a hawk mask for Set, the god of evil. There should be a crocodile mask for the devourer, who is a combination of a crocodile's head, a panther's body, and hippopotamus legs. But it seems to me that a crocodile head is sufficient. This is a miracle play, after the manner of "Everyman" and the Chinese play "The Yellow Jacket"; and the same grim determination should prevail amidst a change of costume. I suggest that the principal actors should put the masks under their arms whenever necessary for the free expression of the face or for a gesture. All the costumes should be vaguely Egyptian and much alike. There should be no distinction between Greek, Roman and Egyptian in costume, only in complexion and gesture. For setting something as simple as the ship in "Outward Bound" would do well from first to last. The gods and the kings of Egypt and the forty-two assessors and the Ptolemaic kings of Egypt could be reduced to nine supers. Or as you please, some of these could be represented in a frieze. But all of these should be seated in sort of a mezzanine at the top of a stair, sitting in immobile judgment and only Alexander the Great is called upon to step down from the stairway for a moment of action for the climax. To simplify the theology, Osiris should sit with Amon Ra at the head of the gods, for unity with Osiris is the ultimate of Egyptian resurrection and vindication. The play is based on the old Osirian miracle play of the death, accusation, vindication, and resurrection of Osiris which has never been discovered, but which is the basis of every copy of the Book of the Dead. Every soul is presumed to go through the same trial before the same assessors, to be accused by Set of similar sins, vindicated by the merciful mother Isis, and to rise in the end to Osiris himself. But all this is Egyptian theology with which we need not trouble ourselves too much. The point is, all the gods sit in a row on the mezzanine while the dead is tried on the main floor below. For this there should be the most gigantic possible scales filling the stage, a burning heart in one pan, and the Feather of Truth in the other. Now we have all the properties, as easily gathered together as the properties of Stuart Walker's "Portmanteau Players".

The play begins 29 [years] before the birth of Christ, at the date of the death of Caesarion, and ends about 29 years after. Anno Domini 1 there should be interposed a nativity scene as conventional as possible; and Anno Domini 29, at the very climax of the play, just before the curtain, an instant impression of the temptation of Christ on the mountain, as conventional as possible, to satisfy all sects. If possible, base it on some old standard painting, though of course the man who impersonates Satan should be the Set of the play. The theory of the play is to leave Christianity exactly where we find it, only assuming that an Egyptian priest of the days of Cleopatra is listening to the story. You will note that the play is cut up into arbitrary periods of years that are mostly periods of nine each. This is a concession to the Egyptian whim about the sacred number nine. Even if they had seventeen gods in a pantheon, they could double up their thrones and make them into nine gods just for good luck.

Since the whole play covers about fifty eight years, and the Moroni

Olsen Players showed such power in handling slow tempo in "Outward Bound", it might be possible to cut the play up into more or less visible sections totalling fifty eight, with each section representing a year. The slow motion camera method is the method, but you know far more about the use of tempo than I can possibly tell you. The Moroni Olsen production of "Outward Bound" has proved to me that the sense of time and eternity can be combined for three hours without a single break or an instant's loss of dignity. Your motto seems to be mine: "A day shall be as a thousand years, and a thousand years as a day". There are about six hundred lines in the poem, if we view it as a colored motion picture, that means about six hundred tableaux melting into one another, ten lines to a year, more or less. It is perhaps arbitrary to say that each line of the poem might be conceived as a hieroglyphic tableau; each set of ten lines as a hieroglyphic paragraph, and one year long.

The play does not need any more Egyptology than an Egyptian cigarette box. I have left out all but the ideas we all hold in common with Egypt. And so a few moments with the hieroglyphic article in the Britannica under the heading "Egypt" is surely all the scholarship required by your actors, or scene painters. Let the scene painters instantly select the hieroglyphics which are obviously the literal photographic renderings of the ideas and scenes they represent. There are enough of them that are amazingly and instantly clear, and require no digging and explaining.

I think in rendering the play the poem such of it as is not a direct quotation, should be read before the curtain by Thoth, god of writing, and magic, and art, holding their priestly papier maché head dress under his arm.

Set is the big actor in the play. He should act like Clarence Darrow or some sensational prosecuting attorney in any popular murder case that is tried by newspaper from coast to coast. Or you might even bear in mind the case of Aimee McPherson, with the prosecutors jumping about the court room, taking the stage every minute. Another parallel is the play of "Madame X" where the heroine was so well rendered by Dorothea Donnelly.

Set in the Egyptian miracle plays wore a mask like the head of a horse or a mule, or sometimes like a hawk. I took the liberty of calling him a hyena, because in western parlance, the hyena grubbing at graves is instantly understood and is a better free translation of the idea. It would be a finicky Egyptologist who would object to a hyena head dress for Set if you cared to make one, though I suggest that he carry it under his arm for the most part, for he has got to cut up like Sapiro and Jim Reed combined at the Ford trial, that is, he is to be the ultimate court room hero.

Cleopatra obviously is the opposite of Set, and a study in immobility, through perhaps fifty eight tableaus.

In an informal way, on two different years, this poem has been submitted to the Department of Egyptology, University of Chicago, and has, I can assure you, passed muster. Their corrections were most incidental; I have them all listed, if you care to have them, but I will not clutter up this letter with them at this time. Most of them were like changing Set into a hyena to give the western mind the idea of a grave defiler. I feel quite sure that if you develop this play it will be very easy to get the general good will if not the actual official endorsement of the Department of Egyptology, University of Chicago, the greatest in America. I am sure they will come and sit in the boxes at Mandel Hall whether they give you a degree in Egyptology or not. My "Chinese Nightingale" has been staged there over and over again by university people. The university is in general full of my friends in the faculty in all departments, and it would mean a lot to me for a resolute group like your own to rally them around this new song of mine.

There are a few corrections in the text which I will make if you care to go into this matter. I hope this letter has not been so long that it has discouraged you.

I am indeed eager for your good will, and surely you have mine.

VACHEL LINDSAY

Note

1. Moroni Olsen's obituary in the November 23, 1954, *New York Times* reads:

   L. A., Nov. 22.   Moroni Olsen, an actor and director in the legitimate theatre and film was found dead today in his apartment here. He was 65 years old.

   Mr. Olsen had been directing rehearsals for a December production of "Trelawny of the Wells" at the Pasadena Playhouse. He had appeared on B'way in a number of productions, principally in the 30's. These included "Mary of Scotland," "Romeo and Juliet" and "The Barretts of Wimpole Street."

   His recent film work had included roles in "Annie Oakley," "Here Comes the Bride" and "Samson and Delilah." Mr. Olsen had been a director of the annual Hollywood Pilgrimage Play, and last summer directed pageants in Ogden and Salt Lake City. Since 1941 he had been president of the Board of Trustees of the Leland Power School of the Theatre in Boston.

164

TO STEPHEN GRAHAM

2318 West Pacific Avenue
Spokane, Washington
April 28, 1927

Our dear Stephen Graham,
Your letter of April 20th was a great adventure and we are indeed delighted. Thank you for coming to our humble country. Godspeed to your New York book[1] and all your your New York enterprises. Maybe you can collect the pictures and finish the book here in Spokane. We would like to put you up in our bridal chamber at the Davenport Hotel and leave you locked up with your book as we were with one another the first year of our married life. It is the most ideal and tactful isolation possible in any hotel in the world.

"I am so happy to be back in America", you say. You'll not be in America till you get to Spokane.

Vachel is delighted to take the other side of the argument in the dialogue for Harper's—"New York Is Not America". You could use my name directly if you cared to do so for one half of the dialogue, says Vachel. But Elizabeth suggests, if you wish to use an imaginary character suggesting Vachel you might call him Mr. Sangamon River or Mr. Illinois or Mr. Down State Illinois; and array all of Vachel's assumed prejudices in one fell swoop. We are enclosing a marked copy of an article we prepared just one year ago which assails not New York but the iron handed air of authority which comes out of certain New York offices. It is after all an uneasy, waspish, and uncertain authority; for Washington, D.C. rules New York City; and the forty-eight states of the Union, without any question, rule Washington, D.C. We have just been reading a tiny paper from the tiny village of Hillyard between here and Mount Spokane. Senator Dill and his wife have just been there to find out precisely what Hillyard wants. It is a great headquarters for locomotive engineers.

We are very far from hating New York. We will admit it is the greatest playground for artists on American soil, but that does not cover the subject, of course.

Our great good wishes to all friends in Doran's publishing house. We have had many courtesies from them of late; not a few of them owing to you. Others without question are owing to the fact that they

have launched "What the Queen Said" by our friend and neighbor in
Spokane, Stoddard King, and are launching a second book by him soon.
We, too, with the help of Stoddard King who is a great actor in his way
and Lenore Glen who went to Mills College with Elizabeth put on poem
games world without end in our little parlor here, and make the welkin
ring. Fred Melcher of The Publisher's Weekly came and tried it, and
stayed in the Bridal Chamber two or three days. He can tell you precisely
what it means to come to Spokane and be in the hands of the gentle
Lindsays and the gentle Stoddard Kings.

If you want to write the sort of novels that will go into the films,
take the cross country ride to Spokane, which ride is in itself a newsreel,
and lock yourself up in the bridal chamber till the novel is written. You
are our guest there, food and lodging, as long as you can stand it. We
have absolutely no plans for the summer, and you can fill in the whole
summer as far as we are concerned; the bigger and bustinger the scheme,
the better. Bring the great world with you.

Allan Vincent, the youthful hero of "Spread Eagle" is the fugitive
son of the president of the Spokane Old National Bank. Elizabeth says
that it doesn't speak any too well for Spokane that the kid had to run
away to have a career. He can probably give you the low down on the
town.

You can take a walk from our apartment, which is not far from the
hotel, and on this walk in five minutes, you can see the canyon, the
city, the river, three bridges, Fort Wright, Mount Spokane, and the
mountains of Idaho which are just this side of Glacier Park. And on
clear days you can almost see Canada. So the Lindsays and Stephen
can take up northwestern adventure where it was left off and spread
out like a fan in all directions westward. We can visit Vancouver, a town
more British than London. We can walk the Canadian line from here
to the Pacific. One scheme I have always had was to walk the whole
available sea beach from Mexico to Alaska on the Pacific border. I would
like to visit all the Indian Reservations of West Canada with you, says
Vachel. Then there is the tiny village of Hillyard just at the end of a
street car ride, as amusing as it can be. A locomotive engineer's paradise.

Through the accident of living and being married in the region that
you and I explored together, says Vachel, I feel much inspired to top
it off with some peculiarly interesting and racy adventure. Whatever
will occur to you after you have settled into your Davenport room and
thought it over.

On your way west, you might care to consider a call at Dearborn
Michigan, near Detroit. Henry Ford's paper, "The Dearborn Independ-
ent", seems to want you to write for them; the assistant editor, Pierce
Cummings, has written me several letters on the subject. They pay very

well indeed, and might pay you railroad fare out here by taking a travel letter or two at least. They have accepted three articles by the Lindsay family: "The Gibson Girl, and other symbols of Yesterday", March 19, 1927; and have paid for two others not yet published: "The Definition of the Middle West", and "Thomas Jefferson's Great Country". This last is especially the rebuttal for your Harper's article, a special discussion of the British-United States Northwest.

Anything I have said in the enclosed article "What It Means To Be A Poet In America"[2] you are welcome to paraphrase as a statement of mine for your Harper's dialogue, says Vachel. The whole article is a protest against New York's false air of authority rather than any other aspect of New York.

In addition to the protest against the New York false assumption of authority in the enclosed article, I would indict the city, says Vachel, for the burning out of Youth—the patenting of bright young men in their first spontaneous moment. New York does not grow men like Thomas Carlyle or sages of similar ilk. They would have discovered Thomas twenty years earlier and kept him a silly Scotch boy till he died.

Says Vachel, I am for the election of Al Smith[3] to the presidency. I want New York to go crazy on that subject. They still have the idea that they can order the United States to make Al Smith president. Of course he knows better, but this air of false authority will be completely broken by the time Al Smith is president. It will mean that New York has learned that there are forty-eight states in the Union, and that Washington, D.C. is the capital. A most wholesome lesson for a most arrogant city.

New York is arrogant in its top offices. There is where it is most unpleasant. Next it is unpleasant in its cellars and near cellars where the dressed up steerage passengers are trying to order Americans who speak English off the streets. There is nothing to beat the arrogance of the Tartar Jew, newly rich to New York City. They are beginning to form unbroken rings around the great offices and trying to insult all the white men who approach these offices.[4]

But none of this is an indictment of New York outside its offices. The skyscrapers are magnificent; the pleasure streets are gorgeous; Broadway is a magnificent pageant of the drama; the Metropolitan Museum the greatest treasure house on American soil; the harbor a colossal spectacle; and Manhattan Island as a place for walking, a dream by day and by night. This side of New York can be spoken of endlessly by the most sky painting orator and he cannot exaggerate it. If you go there without power and disputing no man's power, just to enjoy, especially to walk alone, a student of the arts, you can have a happy time on one crumb of bread. But if you ever indulge in the misfortune of allowing yourself to be kicked upstairs, you find yourself in a ridiculous scramble, and liable to insults by day and by night by brilliant Tartar Jews from the steerage. The time was when the places they now hold were held by bright boys from the Middle West. That time seems to have passed.

When Andrew Jackson broke the power of Biddle, who considered himself a sort of perpetual president of the United States, America faced in miniature what she faces to-day. It was utterly inconceivable to the capitalists of America that political power was greater than financial power. The Atlantic sea board must learn this lesson again.

Elizabeth says that there is a beautiful summer house in the park half a block away. She says she likes to take walks with world travelers. She says she liked "Midsummer Music" very much. She says she hopes you can write a great northwestern novel just one jump better than "Midsummer Music" in our office room in the Davenport. She says that this is a fine climate for Susan Doniphan who is doing well. She says that the enclosed picture is pretty good of Susan, but doesn't do the rest of the family justice. Our complexion is one of our charms.

Susan Doniphan says that she sleeps well by night and does not yell much by day, and that she will not bother you in the least, having a nice nurse girl that leaves mamma at leisure to entertain world travelers. Susan thinks that mamma, pappa and Uncle Stephen ought to undertake something rather large in the way of a stunt. Anything that three can do together. Merely circumnavigating this town, says Susan, is something of a stunt. I have often taken a long walk in pappa's knapsack with mamma running along behind to see that I did not fall out. Susan says she is ready for anything.

Love to you from the three of us.

VACHEL, ELIZABETH and SUSAN DONIPHAN, HER MARK

Notes

1. In 1927 Graham published *The Gentle Art of Tramping. New York Nights* followed in 1928 and is probably the subject of this letter.
2. "What It Means to Be a Poet in America" came out November 13, 1926, in the *Saturday Evening Post* (pp. 12—13 and 45—48).
3. Governor Alfred E. Smith of New York became the Democratic candidate in the 1928 presidential election. He was running against the Republican Secretary of Commerce, Herbert Hoover.
4. Resentment toward Jews appears in VL's 1927 correspondence for reasons that are not entirely clear. Although VL often professed great admiration for the Jews and Jewish culture (see the letters in which he discusses this and many of his poems with Louis Untermeyer), he seems to have held some kind of grudge during that particular year.

165

TO MARGUERITE WILKINSON

2318 West Pacific
Spokane, Washington
July 4, 1927

Dearest Marguerite Wilkinson:—[1]
You are in for it today. That last little summary of my work you sent to me has let loose the flood-gates of confidentialness. My overwhelming ego and megalomania are all aflame. Do not be alarmed, for I am not going to write you many letters like this. This is—(as it were) a letter to "Marguerite"—"Author" from "Vachel" "Author". And those two people are realities as well as the personal persons. The authors are not always rampant as on this fourth of July, though the personal persons, always perhaps are.

You have brought me to confessional by your article in the Y.M.C.A. Magazine. And I might as well confess *all*. It gave me a great, deep, personal 47 year old lifetime thrill to send the clipping to my lifetime friend and puzzled (but faithful) sponsor Reverend E. S. Ames, who is also the professor of Psychology at the University of Chicago.

I want this man, the most intellectual leader of the Disciples to get your point of view about my intentions so vividly that he puts it over to all his following in the Brotherhood, that he holds so well in the hollow of his philosophic hand.

Behind this is my megalomaniac wish to bring "what I have to say" as a cornfield songbird before the whole Disciple Brotherhood—and this without addressing or singing for any more back-breaking audiences.

I cannot sing unless Susan and Elizabeth are with me, in my own parlor, here. For something of the same reason I want to please the Disciple Brotherhood, who are indeed "mine own people", my big home. (Letting my puzzling books aside) they instantly understand me, and I them. There are about two million of them and so they are worth pleasing, just as a sizeable crowd.

Being naturally one of them, I would more glory in leadership among them than in any leadership outside. I would like to see my songs argued about and accepted or rejected in the most crabbed little denomination papers the Disciples have—for I have known the editors, their Papas or their children as one family, yea so long and so long.

However poor a poem "Alexander Campbell" may be, I wish my

publishers, reviewers, etc, who are so busy sitting me down hard in a hard chair, would find some way of making it the center of some far-off future beneficent triumph for me—the acknowledgement and fellowship of my own people.

Ames is the shepherd of the intellectual remnant at the very top of the Disciple Brotherhood, and I would move into a house next door to his church tomorrow just to watch the young pilgrims among our people coming and going to that temple of light, if I could manage it.

As students they have been passing through Ames Hyde Park church while taking ultra-advanced degrees in the University of Chicago, ever since I was a student at the Art Institute Chicago. The Church is right on the edge of campus and I have often recited for them all in my biggest roaringest days, and later the enormous church was filled for me when I could hardly stand up because of the death of my father and mother—the loss of Springfield and the old home and the apparent cutting of every real tie I had in the world of the middle-west. But whether I sang or mourned before them—they thought of me as a stranger outsider, to be tolerated as a performer and troubadour only when he did his very best—as even old Springfield does, as New York does as Spokane does. Yet as a public man I hunger for my own people and state insatiably.

I talk of my church-people dear Marguerite to you because I happen to know that religious matters mean much more to you than some of my noisiest and most uncomprehending champions. A lot of them love me and hate all religion like hell. Men like Sinclair Lewis and Mencken would champion my best work before the world with increasing ardor yet kick my religion and all it means right into the ditch forever.

You know how ambitious I am for my lifetime chum in Art—George Mather Richards.[2] And I feel the same way about my people and my town. I want them to come to perfect fruition. I remember still the thrill when I found that Richards had illustrated your Christmas Religious Anthology. I felt just that much nearer to you. I always want my very own in my affairs, and no others, and I want to be known by my very own people, and to be measured by their style, not by strangers.

I have the same religious trouble I had in the far East—in Spokane. The Disciple Church here is utterly stupid, and I must go to the Catholic or the Unitarian. But I am always dreaming back toward the Hyde Park Centers of light, when I think of religion at all. Or to my Grandfather's Church—"The Proud Farmer".

I know dear friend that matters of religion mean more to you than many others who have concerned themselves with my public work as a writer. Why should I be talking of religion at all? I cannot pretend to be devout or pious or church-going. And now being a "curiosity" through "publicity", church-going, which was once as natural as three square meals a day—is almost impossible. Therefore I the more yearn for such contacts as are still mine, possible. I know you and those about you comment on my work at least once a year and I humbly petition that you help me think this through.

I cannot pretend to be religious, but I know I am an utterly incurable follower of that high champion of the intellectual frontier "primitive" life—Alexander Campbell. I am just a member of his tribe as a Choctaw is a member of the Choctaw tribe.

The reasons are given in some of the dullest pages of my prefaces and of "The Golden Book". These are the things that are set down as "crochety" by some of my most valued elucidators who have backed me in season and out. The last letter I ever had from William Lyon Phelps he threw me over for these things, utterly repudiating the religion of "*The Golden Book*". I wrote him back I was going to write such books till I died—and that was the end—with a very faithful champion, as far as personal contacts went.

I wish in some far-off beautiful day of grace a Lindsay Society of about four people could get together in the Hyde Park Church Chicago—or the Disciples' Church Springfield Illinois or among the members of the Campbell Institute that are in Columbia University—and actually begin with the log-cabin churches of my ancestors when they do me the honor to play the oracle about my religion and my gospel-song. There is enough data in The Golden Book and the Alexander Campbell poem, if they cared to piece it together.

I still remember with Gratitude your review of "The Golden Book".[3] I remember in New York I was shown the door by a certain august presence because I had the presumption to write it and because it didn't take the world by storm. Well the Campbellites have been at it 125 years and have not yet crossed the Appalachians going east. Give them time! I am but one of them. I have recently received letters indicating that I am utterly unknown to my people.

Well it is not easy to hunt out the Hyde Park essential circle in world-wanderings. It is a strange thing not to be a really incurable member of a tribe that knows me not. I keep wondering about it.

Meanwhile I have everyone from Amalekites to Japanese trying to steal my literary clothes and alleged technical tricks. They do not even know that the first Campbellites forbid [*sic*] all musical instruments in church and the prejudice against having the hymn spoiled by the musician is still within me. I am against setting my chants to music, just as my fathers were. I heard it argued about before I was six.

To all the people confused by these things the history of the highly intellectualized Disciples (Campbellites) so absolutely non-mystical, so absolutely the antithesis of the Methodists is utterly incomprehensible. They do not believe the best brains of Europe had taken to these log-cabin churches in the frontier—these churches without preachers—only elders. The idea of such pilgrims is now incredible, though it is even hinted at in Byron's eulogies of George Washington. The "infidel" colony of New Harmony intellectuals, right there among the Indians, is remembered. But the cult of the intellectual religious log-cabin is forgotten. One of Campbell's great debates was with Robert Owen of New Harmony. I know I will make a long illustrated poem of this—sometime, with its own times. Maybe that is the reason this letter stretches itself so interminably. Poem:—Entitled—"The Log Cabin Disciples".

You have said it all yourself in your own way in your beautiful poem "Bluestone" as I have told you before.[4]

By critics who know not these things I have been tied up with everybody from Marinetti and French Movements to the Ingoldsby Legends and Jazz.

Anything but the hard-minded hard-studying pioneers, absolutely non-mystical but deeply Biblical, of Bethany West Virginia, Lexington Kentucky, Hiram Ohio, Eureka Illinois and the like.

I have had the overwhelming impulse to write you all this, at *so great length*, ever since I sent that Y.M.C.A. paper review of yours to Ames. You at least think it worth while to discuss my work in a religious paper.

The reality and unreality of public life as a refuge, is indeed curious. It is never quite what it seems. It is worse and better than it seems. There has never been an advertisement or blurb about my affairs that I would not burn up if I could. I do not care for the way any poets are advertised. For instance the cruel baiting of the living poets into fighting for alleged first place is a trick of the hard-worked publishers' claques. There are at least 96 poets on an equality–two to each state–like Senators! And there is glory enough for all, *now*, and we were all good friends and good sportsmen in 1912. There are 48 different languages in the 48 states and each state has a right to two poets as to two senators. We should assume the truth–that no publisher or Maecenas or Magazine or newspaper editor gives even the man he accords first place a living wage–but muddies the waters by distended storms about his patented poet with a boasting a patented and an *unchangeable* advertisement, *I* must have the word "jazz" branded on my hip by corporation edicts I hate, and the mark must be like the branding mark on a Texas steer. There it is, no more, no less–an eternal slander. Jazz is in *my opinion* a monstrous New York Steerage Jew's caricature of the Negro–as far from the real black as Octavius Roy Cohen's Negro-Jews are.[5] But that is *my* brand. A bad kike imitation of a purely mythical negro form of music is my assigned part!

And then poets, disturbed by such patenting of their wares are allowed to feel that their alleged rivals for first place are somehow to blame for their inability to live a natural public life as public citizens and leaders, all this in a nation of 120 millions crying for leaders, and with room enough for all to be natural and glorious. To pit the poets against one another in an elimination contest like the present contests for Gene Tunney's belt as "champ"[6] is cruel and silly to the last degree. I know three noble men I try to keep for friends that have been estranged from one another by it. I cannot mention the name of one to the other. Yet they are natural brothers. The system is as cruel and silly as that of the Maharajas of India who bait perfectly good-humored elephants into a death-fight in the arena. The winner has only proved he has the most ingenious, the most cruel driver. He is not the best elephant–and he is no good even as a plain circus elephant. There are herds of elephants as good–in the woods. Till every citizen of the United States writes poetry happily, openly and without shame, as the Campbellites once preached–every member of the clan a preacher and every preacher a mere layman–till this comes about we will have no "leading" poets really echoing and resounding.

Whitman assumed that in the Ultimate America–every citizen would sing. "To have great poets we must have great audiences too".[7]

The reality and unreality of public life is indeed curious. Despite its being an arena it is right now a genuine refuge for Elizabeth and Susan and Papa from "neighborhood" life, too much "newly-rich" interference in Springfield or Spokane–with the wrong kind of "neighborliness" that never opens a book–but studies Dunn and Bradstreet.

It will not always be so. Some time we will have a real log-cabin–maybe right under the eaves of Ames Church! Or the Springfield Illinois Church.

Meanwhile Elizabeth and Susan and Papa are eager to formalize and clarify their public life and such small middle-west leadership as they have (Formalize and clarify by these twelve-page tirades?). We are intensely happy together in the four walls of our home–few of our dearest know what a splendid start we have made, and how ready we are for great big new public work.

When we reach out into the wide world it is with great joy and energy. And it must seemingly be to the uttermost circumference of our book-world that we reach which seems a blazing ring on the ege of the celestial horizon–and we know you keep some of that fire burning. The long reach seems the best. The ring is so far away it does not know us, as really middle Westerners.

When I think of the attitude of the Middle West Campbellites (Disciples), it is as though J. M. Barrie[8] should suddenly discover that hardly a soul in his church in Scotland ever read him–that they vaguely thought of him as a Turk or an Arab or a Greek. And meanwhile the Turks and Arabs and Greeks stealing his stuff and completely confirming the Scotch suspicion by their utterly irrelevant eulogies of things not in Barrie at all, but *said* to be there by the Greeks, the Turks and Arabs, according to their hobbies. Isn't it just an awful long letter? Well keep after me till I make it into a Log Cabin Song. Then it will not sound so silly, and I will not be so wordy. I have just finished a Springfield fantasy, my best piece of prose for several years. I have every reason to think it will be printed soon. I am always in imagination in the streets of Springfield just as I am also in the Log Cabin Churches. Elizabeth and I may as private citizens be obliged to be separated from both. But as public, formalized statue-and-bust citizens and writers we want to be more and more identified with our real origins, as we formalize and clarify our public life.

I have no objections to your reading this letter wherever you please to whomever cares or can really endure it, and I have no objections to your quoting any sentences long or short–or ignoring it altogether.

Dear friend and loyal Marguerite–much of the old life in which we were all so busy has suddenly come rushing back to my heart, much of 1915-1916-1917-1918. I remember it was a series of your letters that got me my first audiences at Evanston, and through you I achieved the London Spectator personally socially and in a literary way and after the London visit ultimately printed Johnny Appleseed there. So in some sense this letter holds together with our gay beginnings.

As I re-read it–it is a terrible sprawl. But you are faithful enough to find the right sentence and forget the rest.

As before:–

These are the chronicles and tales of mankind:–
Sunrise;
The War-Path,
The Book-Path,
Sunset,
The Moon-Path.

These are the hopes,
Even of the blind:–
Sunrise,
The War-Path–
The Book-Path–
Sunset–
The Moon-Path.[9]

With love to you and to Jimmy
from
VACHEL
(and Elizabeth and Susan)

Notes

1. Marguerite Wilkinson (1883–1929) was a Canadian-American poet and anthologist. Her *New Voices* was published in 1919. She drowned at Coney Island at the age of forty-four.
2. George Mather Richards illustrated *Every Soul Is a Circus* in 1929; some of the illustrations, however, were VL's own.
3. Marguerite Wilkinson had also written an article on VL in *Touchstone* for February 1918; "Poets of the People no III: Vachel Lindsay" (pp. 510–512, 519).
4. *Bluestone* was published in 1920.
5. Octavius Roy Cohen was a Southern newsman, short-story writer, and novelist who published in the *Saturday Evening Post*. His stories dealt with a group of black people in Birmingham, Alabama.
6. Gene Tunney had defeated Jack Dempsey on September 23, 1926, in Philadelphia. Their return match the next year has remained famous in boxing history: Tunney eventually won after having been floored by a dazed Dempsey.
7. Walt Whitman's line quoted here by VL had been adopted by Harriet Monroe as the motto for *Poetry: A Magazine of Verse*.
8. James Matthew Barrie (1860–1937) was a Scottish dramatist and novelist from Kirriemuir, Forfarshire ("Thrums" in his fiction). He had been rector of Saint Andrews from 1919 to 1922. A friend of Robert Louis Stevenson and of George Bernard Shaw, George Meredith, Thomas Hardy, and William Ernest Henley in later years, J. M. Barrie wrote *Peter Pan* (1904) and *The Old Lady Shows Her Medals* (1916).
9. The five "seals in the sky" listed here are drawings on which VL had based five of his verses. They can be found on the closing pages of *Every Soul Is a Circus* (pp. 116–20). The Marguerite Wilkinson letter is written on the long sheets of privately printed paper that VL used a great deal in 1927–30; the bottom of each sheet carried the series of the five major "American Hieroglyphs" named in the letter's last lines.

166

TO JOHN DRINKWATER

You are welcome to
quote any but the
family and personal
part of this letter.

Spokane, Washington
2318 West Pacific
August 2, 1927

My Dear John Drinkwater:—
Please allow me to congratulate you on your article in "The American
Legion Monthly" for June, entitled:—"Toward a Better World". I could
write to you a book of thanks. It brings a flood of overwhelming memories of 1920 when our little group of Americans and British seemed set
on world good-will. Hail to a new pioneer!

There is nothing worse for us than to sit still and silent and imagine
Jesuitism and propaganda, when a little free speech will clear the air,
and make all the sillies skedaddle, too. When I keep silent, it seems to
me in that silence, that the people who have war-material to sell, from
guns to poison-gas in all the manufacturing countries, have learned
their lesson and have hired the very best and slyest talent to kill off just
such articles as yours, one at a time. The ultimate ownership of the
printing-presses grows obscure, whatever the list of stockholders and
officials.

Meanwhile—where are the peace-makers of 1920? You are not killed
off in critical corners by having your doctrine disqualified. They say you
are *merely* this and that and the other, instead of a citizen. There is an
unaccountable sagging in that great youthful tide of 1920 because the
idealists are being picked off by sharp-shooters, if you will pardon the
phrases. If I had been an unknown American soldier and had issued
your article as a pamphlet anywhere in America, maybe I would have
been:—
(1).   Castrated and tarred and feathered and accused the next day of
being a Bolshevik, or an I.W.W. though I have not yet discovered either
kind of Humans in America.
(2).   Or I would have been mobbed by soldiers from a near by fort.
(3).   Or I would have been hung to a telegraph-pole by "The American

Legion" itself, which had a convention here last week with a lot of teeth-gnashing, looking for the ENEMY whoever he may be, up every alley and in every cheap lodging-house, with much roaring about "parlor-pinks".

A British Citizen has the advantage of a glossy and uncomprehending stare from the editor of "The American Legion Monthly", and the editor prints the article anyway, expecting to muffle it later. Of course I say "If I had issued your article as a pamphlet". It is assumed that as a pamphleteer one means what he says. Therefore one is "dangerous". Of course there are plenty of highbrow magazines where a man may print such views as yours in a "purely academic" way. It is assumed no one reads them or the ultimate owners will muffle the effect in a month.

Do not think I am bitter about America. There are a lot of kinds of good freedom here that have never existed before in all our history. What I am describing to you is the mood of the most powerful printing-presses on Peace-and-War, and merely the situation at the present instant, seven years after 1920. It will in many ways change tomorrow morning. With the resignation of Coolidge from the presidential nomination this week, the American printing-press passed from the most bitterly Tory and Plutocratic moment in its whole history, especially in the field of politics. The Average American is so happy he does not know any of this. The battle for the Republican nomination will now force free-speech, there are so many factions, and sects, including the bold Borah,[1] and the Democratic nomination is always a noble free-for-all with the lid entirely off for the length of the convention anyway. Either Al Smith or Jim Reed as the leading figure at the Democratic Convention will force free-speech.

But why should I be instructive about our affairs? You know them better than I do, have traveled farther on our soil, have been in the confidence and company of far more powerful Americans than I have ever had the honor to interview.

This letter has an object. What? The object is not to be quoted but to be dearly remembered. Be sure to come to see my wife and baby and me when you pass near Spokane. We are not inviting you to "lecture" and do not know the lady chairman of the committee. We suggest that you spend a month in Spokane at our expense and "*meet*" no one. Come incog, and stay that way. We are here because we like it, and we are at last incog. Every little lion-hunter has died the death, from eating poisoned lion. We know we can offer to you peculiar seclusion, all the way to eating in your room, waited on by a very special and discreet room-service.

We sneak around to movies, just as we please. Our daughter Susan

Doniphan is one year and two months old, and a *buster*. We are happy planning for her five years ahead at a stretch. She can shout much louder, more cheerfully and musically than Papa. We live in a tiny flat, and she is boss. She is about the only thing we are really happy and sad about, bless her.

We will give you and yours a consecrated shelter. We will put you up in the most beautiful rooms in the world, half a mile away, where we spent a year of honeymoon. You will have your meals when your writing-habits fit, and sneak out to us only when you please, after your day's writing is done. There is room in the room we give you for your whole family and she is invited. I suggest that you sit at two desks and produce an epic apiece. You are near enough the Canadian Line to make them Canadian Epics, and to claim you are still in the British Empire while writing. That will save your literary faces.

Believe me we are happy here, and we want to see our friends without crowding them. We are poor but able to entertain. It was one of the happiest moments of our lives when my wife and I realized we had reached the Franciscan point—which married people—even the happiest—seldom do. That is:—We are right where we can stay poor without going broke, or going into debt, and with quite a bit of leisure for conversation. It is one advantage of my having 47 years behind me—perhaps the only one.

My work, at last, in a creeping snail's pace, begins to work for me, and in a dull but steady way, the printing presses of the whole Anglo-Saxon world, utterly ignoring my real views, are grudgingly plodding after, making me out a rather cute versifier—no *real* harm in the boy! You are a far younger singer than I am, dear boy, and I sense it now, far more than when you were such a dazzling host in London. I have not forgotten that almost official and public proffer of friendship given then, and I am at last where I can say to you and yours:—"Come to me, and let me return it, I mean it most deeply. Come to see us dear friend".

And now for the public issues again. Lindbergh's flight[2] was the first break in the dull nightmare wished on the printing presses of the U.S.A. by all the armament trusts, who want no poet and no honest boy to be a publicist, and want no public leader to *think,* as a poet or honest boy would. The second was Coolidge's resignation.

We are now in a perfect orgy of free speech and the free press for which I thank God. It will not begin in full momentum instantly. But watch the American press this time next year and trace it back to this hour, and see the difference!

As private citizens you and I have doubtless been happier of late than the wildest prophet could have prophesied. But as public citizens—as poets who have earned the full right to be publicists, as singers believing public affairs are *real*, and not something to be snarled about, we have been gently fed lotus-pap by our wily shepherds since 1920.

One of the most powerful people in any way connected with my affairs has done his best to annul any really serious public utterance of mine or my mother's, in America or England, and to play up my Children's Poems as the only things worthy. Meanwhile he will furnish the next war if it pays.

All the real issues of ardent world good-will are side-stepped by these old foxes. Its [sic] the venomous old men, who can never have brides again, who want war.

And I have lived just long enough to watch their methods. You could write a book on the method shown in the three sheets I send you. Study them with a microscope and think. Does your opinion or mine count in this kind of stuff? Hardly. Are we put on the wire? I should say not. This is BUSINESS, This is WAR-and-PEACE. Let the poets go back to their afternoon teas. But between the cracks of this journalism I see the noble future the old men fear. They are afraid we may have the ear of the world again.

Jane Addams, the real heroine 1900–1918 among American women, is, because of the rule of the old men, never again allowed to be a heroine. Henry Ford, because he is a "pacifist" is always made a little fun of. It is not allowed to be admitted he is a first-rate great citizen, to be honored because he tried to make peace.

Whom the Gods destroy they first make mad:-And so—much of this rule of the old men is today breaking up. The combination around Coolidge who had reached the ultimate point of printing-press power and madness were our most powerful administration of gag-rule since Jefferson Davis was Secretary of War from Mississippi. He represented the Mississippi Nigger-trust and held onto his office in Washington and armed the South to the limit before he resigned and seceded from the Union.

Much that these old men (whom Coolidge has suddenly flouted) stand for, is incidentally good. But they were drowning free-speech about PEACE and WAR and all publicist issues in a perfect ocean of clothing and automobile advertisements. A lot of their gab was denunciation of parlor-pinks. By parlor-pinks they meant men like John Drinkwater or Lord Carnwood, who actually take the words "freedom or liberty" seriously when they are found in the writings of men like Lincoln. They mean that any man who takes Jefferson or Lincoln seriously and discusses the matter in a parlor is an incipient Trotsky or Lenin, Danton or Marat. And they have convinced temporarily a vast mass of the business world that this is so. A parlor-pink is a man who has not the nerve to join a radical Forum and get mutilated namelessly by the K.K.K. But he must be "suspected" even at home. But the "Parlor Pinks" have won their first victory in the resignation of Coolidge. There is tremendous consternation under the varnished surface of the sheets of newspaper I send you.

Dear Boy—reading your article brought back 1920 with a tremendous whirl to me. We *were* citizens then, and were treated as citizens, and publicists, with as much right to be heard as Mussolini. I see your hour coming again in the grim and manly resolution with which you have written this article in the American Legion Monthly. Let us form the Milton and Cromwell Society and quote everything political either of them ever said that stands the test of the hour. There were two parlor-pinks that got out of the parlor before they died. I hope you get every British and American poet out of the parlor and onto the Soap-Box quoting Milton and Cromwell. We need a tremendous poets rebellion, every man with his own pamphlets.

I hope you boys send hot stuff to every slick American editor who asks you for work expecting to muffle you while he prints you. Everything in the history of Liberty up to the Death of Cromwell and Milton we have in common. And remember you are the legitimate successor of Kipling as a political poet. Between now and the election of our next president—November 1928 we will have such an orgy of increasingly free speech and the emancipated pamphlet as has not been known since 1912. It is time to speak of Milton's Ancient Liberty.

Stir up the most liberal of the British boys, to explain Magna Charta to our fat-heads. Snub our fat old bullies and our slick Levantine lawyers till they bleed. Lay on the whip. Explain Hyde Park all over again in every American magazine that will let you. Remember the *American Poets* need this as a fraternal service. I mean it with all my soul. A thundering press makes us into enervated sillies.

And the hour has come to strike swiftly. Englishmen can say anything they please without being secretly beaten up by the K.K.K., and they can say it in American Magazines, for they are protected by the British Flag. For God's sake write 100 articles like the American Legion one and boldly put them at the top of American publicity. The lid will not be on again till December 1928.

Are we persecuted? No. Are we harried? No. Are we unhappy? No. In our private lives we were never so free or so spicy. The corporations have tried to strike a bargain with the American people, saying—"*we will give you every pleasure and luxury and private advantage if you will forget politics and world-peace, and forget you have a vote on any subject. You may have everything from Magazines to bathing-suits almost given away—but let us steal Mexico and cut the throat of Russia.*"

Well—why so hot—little man? You are privately happy Vachel, and were never so "successful" from the American standpoint. God Bless you, John Drinkwater—and please give everything in this letter the benefit of the doubt.

Most fraternally

VACHEL LINDSAY

Notes

1. Senator William Edgar Borah (1865–1940), a Progressive Republican, had supported Theodore Roosevelt and was in part responsible for the Washington Disarmament Conference of 1921. He anticipated aspects of the future Good Neighbor Policy while he was chairman of the Senate Foreign Relations Committee (1924–33).
2. Charles A. Lindbergh's flight across the Atlantic in *The Spirit of St. Louis* had taken place on May 20–21, 1927.

167

TO BURRIS A. JENKINS—*The Christian*

2318 West Pacific
Spokane Washington

August 18, 1927.

My Dear Friend:
Please send the Christian henceforth to the above address.

My Dear Friend: the whole-hearted announcement in the August 11 number and the printing of the columns of your and Dr. Ames's open and great loyalty, and the printing of "Sew the Flags Together"[1] all in one number made one of the thrills of my life. Be sure I will send you the drawings soon.

I tried to do religious cartoons for "The Christian Century" in 1902 and 1903 when an Art Student in Chicago, and they puzzled my most loyal friends—just as they do now. But the essential matter is *in me,* and will some day emerge. I feel perfectly confident. And all you people rallying round me right now is certainly a gift from Heaven, for which

I am most devoutly thankful. Please do not restrain either public forensic or printed or private criticism by private letter. I am far more anxious to meet my own people half-way than they in the least understand. They have been confused by iron-handed publicity I could not in the least control. I know why Guiteau shot Garfield in the back. He did not know a thing about him and did not want to know. And Garfield would not obey him.[2]

I have just this week received two firm letters from New York which were as firm as Mortician's paws, straightening out the corpse and shooting in the embalming fluid. I am to be preserved as a specimen of the very highest type of embalming in the most expensive and varnished mortuary parlors of the world. The "chapel" service all their own. I am not even to say what church I belong to. It is a mere crochety whim and has nothing to do with A.R.T. or neat literary reputations. The heart was just about out of me when your paper came to give me life. I was just about to give up the ghost. New York has *stolen the writing of a lifetime*. My Collected Poems contains pictures and poems done from 1896 till now. They have put it into a box and run off with it. I am not allowed to say I was in earnest about a single line or phrase in the book or that I would willingly be crucified or boiled in oil to make "The Building of Springfield" actually come true. Thirty years work has been made over into a toy for the critics who merely *stare* when I say I am a member of "The Christian Church". I am not even allowed to say who are my friends. So, they, my friends, must arise and *say it for me*. I wish some of you would form an informal "Lindsay Defense Society". I actually had to fight a 7 years'[3] public and private battle with long long letters to "critics" in New York and London to keep the word "Jazz" from being wished onto my Collected Poems as its *one real label*.

And I *hate* Jazz like poison, have always hated it. Was Alexander Campbell the "Jazz" theologian? Was A. A. Maclean the "Jazz" missionary speaker? Was E. V. Zollars, my father's greatest chum, for a lifetime, the "Jazz" college president? Is my old friend teaching English at Hiram, John Kenyon, the "Jazz" English teacher? Is Hiram the "Jazz" college? Yet the Levantines of New York and London have fought a pitch battle to plaster this word onto all I or any of my people have said thought or done. Have they ever heard of Bethany West Virginia? No. Do they want to hear? No. Do they want to visit there? No. Do they want such a place to have any mellow authority or tradition or dreams going west? No. To them I am one more verbal trixter [sic] and now that "The Collected Poems" have been issued for five years[3] they want me to die in haste that I may have a New York epitaph. The tombstone is ready and carved and filed away and I am not even to see it. My friends in the Middle West suppose I like all this—knowing not I have

fought it till I can fight no longer. It is to them a "tale of little meaning—though the words are strong".

I am not fighting the Levantines I am only asking my own to rescue
me, body, soul and spirit, before it is too late. I want them to *claim* me,
so *firmly,* so *blatantly,* so *incessantly* they stop the mouths of New York
and London forever, and completely wreck the mortuary parlors. All
I ever asked was the love of my own, not of utter strangers.

Most fraternally

VACHEL LINDSAY

Notes

1. "Sew the Flags Together" (*Collected Poems,* p. 367) was "written for William Stanley
    Braithwaite's Victory Anthology issued at once, after Armistice Day, November
    1918." This was a reprint.
2. Charles J. Guiteau shot President James A. Garfield on July 2, 1881, while the
    president was waiting in a railway station.
3. The *Collected Poems* were published in 1923, so "7 years'," like "five years" in the
    letter's next paragraph, seems to be a slight exaggeration.

168

TO CARL SANDBURG

2318 West Pacific
Spokane Washington

September 17, 1927

My Dear Carl:—
I was just sitting down to write this note to you and word was tele-
phoned to me that my first son was born[1]—and that dear wife Elizabeth
was doing marvelously well and had already named him Nicholas Cave.
I will print it—since you are a newspaper man and that is required in
all copy: NICHOLAS CAVE LINDSAY. Here I sit in our little flat above
guarding our little Susan Doniphan, the big sister a year and a half older
who is going to help us rear him.

I had all sorts of things to write you dear boy—I am notoriously a long letter man. But you may expect—whether this letter be long or short I will not sleep much this night. I am 48 years old in November—and now—out of the blue as one might say comes a son and how the world changes!

I think I have you and Frost to thank for the extraordinary loyalty to my fortunes lately engendered in the group around the Dearborn Independent. Believe me I thank you with all my heart, I thank you indeed—for myself and my tiny son.

The Nicholas is for my old Grandfather Nicholas Lindsay and the Cave for his dear wife of beautiful memory—Martha Cave Lindsay. It is through the Cave family that the legend of Indian blood is in our house—maybe it is only a legend.

I have just written my best letter to Fred Black of the Ford group—was writing it when this news came.

Leon Starmont is now editor of the Mining Truth Magazine, Chamber of Commerce Building—Spokane.

You wrote just the right letter to little Claire Graves,[2] and I thank you. It was just what the lady needed. Robert Morse Lovett[3] has promised her French books to review. So my handful of letters brought in all she could well ask, for a starter.

I think my magazine campaign will go on for at least one year more. My style is getting compacter and one article in twenty may be saved out for an ultimate book. It is the first time in my life I have besieged the magazines—and what a change! Instead of being the dubious visitor of Spokane's two empty book-stores I am on all of the two or three hundred news-stands—and instantly assumed to be in existence by every cigar-vendor or confectioner's, instead of a sad mystery behind the veil! God bless you Carl. I am not saying a thing—but I know you will bear with me. I hold you to your promise to come to see us soon. Come and teach Vachel's Baby to talk! I want my little man to meet the men. You will have absolute protection, behind closed doors, in your room at the Davenport—and can write on and on and on and on forever, and see no one. I will not schedule a public appearance. I want you to stay here so long the isolation and chance to write will reward you for coming.

Be a good boy if you can. I find it harder, as I grow older, I get meaner to my neighbors, and less gentle with my friends. But let's start fresh Carl—now that we have a son. I do want to be a good boy.

My love to everybody in Chicago.

Most fraternally,

VACHEL

Notes

1. Nicholas Cave Lindsay was born on September 16, 1927.
2. On August 24, 1927, VL had written Sandburg, "A friend of ours in Spokane, Miss Claire Graves, has helped in new Poem Games and wants French books to review". Miss Graves had a French mother.
3. Robert Morse Lovett, editor of *Current History,* taught at the University of Chicago between 1892 and 1936 and was a friend of Jane Addams's and a collaborator with William Vaughn Moody. Moody and Lovett's *History of English Literature* was a college classic. Lovett wrote a monograph on Edith Wharton in 1925.

169

TO H. S. LATHAM

2318 West Pacific
Spokane, Washington

October 7, 1927

My Dear H. S. Latham:—
Thank you for your good word about Nicholas Lindsay Junior. With a boy to fight for, the world changes at once.

Thank you for your good word about "The Litany of Washington Street". I will send it soon. Please make it very large type, Benjamin Franklin style, and an Art Gallery of the handsomest and rarest possible reproductions of the portraits of the Fathers of the Republic, their homes and places of statecraft.

You have all kinds of first class plates of this sort in your archives, in Histories and Biographies you have now re-written etc.; The book could be a Washington and Lincoln's Birthday Gift-book.

Please get the Vanity Fair set to get a real and authentic and serious book out of Gene Tunney. He can write better than George Luks can paint!

Most fraternally,

VACHEL LINDSAY

170

TO HARRIET MONROE

Spokane, Washington
December 14, 1927

Darling Harriet Monroe:—

Today I received two excellent and valid requests to write poems through the mail—not for money but for honor and with an assurance they would be read at least once by one person for their own sake. Dearest lady, I rejoiced. At once I thought of my very rude letter to you the time before last when I said that you *were the only person on earth who wanted new poetry from me—that I had not written a poem for two years or taken a note on one hardly, and that I was being hectored into silence and the grave.* Well I was a Jackass. I am in a vast good humor this morning, dearest darlingest Harriet and please pardon any rudeness of word or thought. I should have said "You are audience enough", "You are the beloved Harriet", and gone ahead—for surely *you are audience enough.* Maybe the public life of any public man has always seemed distorted to him, once it is established. I do not know. The lot of the average *"established"* poet—from Robinson to Frost seems as crude and forced and unnatural as though a circus should turn a lot of Zebras loose on the prairie and forget them! The Farmers would want to paint out their stripes and use them to pull the reapers as ordinary mules and say— "Oh of course you were *once* Zebras, and ate peanuts at the circus, but *forget it.* Do something else. Do *anything* else!" Or to quit the metaphor—everybody from Robinson to Frost is an acceptable United States Citizen, even a public citizen if he will relegate the poetry that put him there along with his Freshman year at College. He *must* be eccentric if he continues just as he began. *"A Poet. But an ex-poet who is a professor. Fine! Good! A poet, an ex-poet who now writes a newspaper column and "gets down to brass tacks". Fine. "He only wrote the poetry as a stunt, anyway". A poet, an ex-poet, who writes weak novels that sell like hot cakes! Fine. But a poet who goes on being a poet! Horrible!"* That seems the American society attitude. Now I am not discussing the financial end. I am talking about the actual *social setting of any established* poet in America. The trust officer of my Springfield estate[1] cannot write me a single letter without spatting me on the wrist for *continuing* to be a poet. He is *forced to approve of my old work.* Men I meet and have spent four years trying to please in this town have the same *spat on the wrist* all ready. The main crime is this:—*continuing to be a poet,* and putting prose writers etc *in the wrong,* and making everyone uncomfortable who does not want to think about poetry, because poetry is a reproof to their lives. Earnestness is the crime. A young poet *accepts* this isolation and laughs it off. But an established and "advertised" poet takes years to realize that it continues to exist in the very depths of every human soul. He has to conquer or die *every day* all over again. There is no such thing as an "accepted" poet.

With love

VACHEL

P.S. Well I won't take it too hard if you won't!

VACH.

Note

1.   The trust officer of the Springfield estate was Latham Souther.

171

TO JOHN WEATHERWAX AND IDELLA STONE

2318 West Pacific
Spokane Washington
January 20, 1928

My Dear John and Idella:[1]
Elizabeth and I have profoundly appreciated all your letters of late, and Elizabeth in especial needs them being so very "younger generation" and she was just started among the youngsters of your glittering vintage and I jerked her up and married her, and introduced her to a terrible set of gorgons, fair fat and fifty that looked awful sweet to me but awfully established to her. The more you and your gang take dear wifey by storm and persuade her she is still a kid and can leap from crag to crag instanter, the happier I will be. I have Associated Press Interviews Saturday afternoons: Jan 7, 14, 21, 28, Feb 4, 11 and 18, but think of all the artillery involved etc. It's enough to make any sweet young thing just scoot for the woods.

I have the first article in the American Mercury for March, on *The Real American Language*,[2] a prose paraphrase of the Mohawk and challenging Mencken at every point. I inscribed the article "To My Friend the Enemy, H. L. Mencken, with whom I agree in nothing but the necessity of free speech, a free press and personal courage at all times". I say the article paraphrases "The Mohawk", but only an Emersonian might say so. The key idea is "There is no such thing as The American Language". Canadians speak British, Mexicans speak Mexican. The people in the ribbon of country between speak United States.

Well—as I began what does all this heavy artillery have to do with the beautiful young Elizabeth—bursting with her own poetry? I wish you would keep asking her for poetry to see, she was one in five in a batch of one thousand in the Poetry contest—January Forum see page 21—her translation of "The Child Jesus of Prague" by the French Minister at Washington.[3] Stoddard King has been called east by Doubleday-Doran and John Farrar to be lionized. He will come back a real lion by Feb 1. Thus the world moves on.

Most Fraternally

VACHEL

Notes

1. Idella Purnell (Stone) was a writer of juveniles published by Macmillan. A teacher and then a Foreign Service secretary in Mexico, she edited and published *Palms*, a small literary magazine. On August 21, 1927, she married John Weatherwax, who acted as coeditor of *Palms*. In 1932 she married Remington Stone.
2. "The Real American Language" came out in *The American Mercury* in March 1928 (pp. 257–65).
3. The "French Minister at Washington" refers to poet Paul Claudel, who had been appointed French Ambassador to the United States in December 1926. Claudel left his previous post in Tokyo in January 1927, reached San Francisco in March and Washington in April. He stayed in Washington until his nomination in Brussels in March 1933, leaving the United States on April 18 of that year. His "L'Enfant Jésus de Prague" was the fourth piece of *Images Saintes de Bohême*, first published in the November 1, 1911 issue of *L'indépendance* and reprinted in the collection *Corona Benignitatis Anni Dei* (Paris: N.R.F. 1915). See Claudel, *Oeuvre Poétique*, Bibliothèque de la Pléiade, pp. 436–37.

172

TO THEODORE ROOSEVELT

2318 West Pacific
Spokane, Washington
February 1, 1928

My Dear Friend:[1]

Your letter was indeed a pleasant surprise. I am sending under separate cover today your copy of the Congo volume. In the front of it I have written the poem "To the Sons of Roosevelt", and in the back I have added a new song of mine, a poem on Virginia, which may help toward our better acquaintance.

Your letter came just in time, one of those down months when a man needs to hear from all his friends. I would like a new deal and a new group in New York City and this is about the first sign for many years of that sort of a thing.

Please accept my earnest congratulations on your Kansas speech of about four days ago. It was well done, indeed. It appeared here on the front page of the Spokesman-Review and Mrs. Lindsay and I read it with as much approval as you could possibly expect from two Democrats. If you can read Heflin out of the Democratic party and put a genuine religious toleration plank into the Republican platform, you will do a man's work and be a statesman for sure. If I may say so, the fundamental reasonableness of your speech and its utter freedom from bunk was most refreshing, but far be it from me to get into a political discussion. I am trying to make and keep a literary friend. We are looking out for the new book dedicated to Quentin Roosevelt.

As a member of the Poetry Society of America, I am indeed delighted that the Society now meets at the Roosevelt birthplace. In the ancient days when the Congo volume was produced, I used to attend the sessions of the Society at this time every year and no welcome was more hearty or more cheering than that of Mr. and Mrs. Robinson. I always liked your aunt's style in literary discussion and the way she bucked up that society when she had anything to say. Alas, I made the mistake of trying to write her a political letter once, then all was silence. Let us get into the higher realms and stay there.

It is very hard to refrain from a long letter, but please let me say I meant every word I ever said about the Roosevelts in print and I think it will stand your scrutiny.

Nicholas Cave, Susan Montjoy Doniphan Frazee, and my wife, Elizabeth Lindsay send greetings and great good will.

Vachel Lindsay

Note

1. VL had first "met" Theodore Roosevelt while an art student in New York. Chancing upon him in the rooms of the Metropolitan Museum, he had offered Roosevelt his services as a guide and commentator, but Roosevelt had preferred to go on with his visit alone. Later their connection was renewed; VL wrote a number of poems on one of his "heroes," and they corresponded a few times. The allusion to a "new deal" in this letter makes for unconscious historical irony.

173

TO GEORGE P. BRETT, JR.—The Macmillan Company

Spokane, Washington
February 2, 1928

My dear Mr. Brett:

You may be interested to note that last Saturday afternoon, January 28th, and tomorrow afternoon, February 3rd, there are two articles by me released for the Associated Press Newspapers on The United States Language. I take direct issue with H. L. Mencken and insist that there is no such thing as the American Language, that there is the Canadian Language, and the Mexican Language, and in between, the United States Language.

The first article in The American Mercury for March takes up the same issue. There I argue the matter more at length, contradicting Mencken at every point. He is a very pretty good sport to accept and print the article instantly on its arrival at his office and to give it such a place. Nothing would please me more than a chance for an open and direct challenge to Mencken at every point.

The manuscript now in the hands of The Macmillan Company, "A Book of Prose, Patriotic Essays", "The Litany of Washington Street", challenges the whole Mencken school of thought at every point.

I have offered this book to the Macmillan Company for a minimum of $500 cash in advance. I earnestly urge you to use your influence for a prompt decision in this matter.

It may amuse you to know that I inscribe the manuscript which is
to appear in The American Mercury March 1st "to my friend the enemy,
H. L. Mencken, with whom I agree on nothing except the necessity for
free speech, a free press and personal courage at all times". If you want
to know how I stand on any question read The Mercury and assume
I take the exact opposite stand.

Most sincerely,

VACHEL LINDSAY

174

TO WILLIAM WEBSTER ELLSWORTH

2318 West Pacific, Spokane, Washington,
March 2, 1928

My Dear William Webster Ellsworth:—
Thank you with all our hearts for the BOOK. Readings from the New
Poets arrived yesterday, and my wife Elizabeth Conner Lindsay and
myself had a happy time with it and with "A Golden Age of Authors".
    You gave her "A Golden Age of Authors" for a prize in 1921. Here
is the inscription in your own hand:—
    To the winner of the First Prize in Literature at Mills College in 1921,
this book, which it is a great privilege to give for such a purpose. With
all good wishes from the author: William W. Ellsworth.

         .——.——.——.——.——.——.——.——.——.

    "Dreams, books, are each a world, and books we know,
        Are a substantial world, both pure and good.
    Round these, with tendrils strong as flesh and blood,
        Our pastime and our happiness will grow."

And I am glad you put in your picture on the next page, for I think
that is one of the truest forms of autographing.
    My dear Elizabeth and I were married here in Spokane, and have
two lovely babies, and maybe I will hit you back after all these years by
including pictures. The fact you have made friends with us under such
separate circumstances is matter not to be scorned, for we need above

all a real patron who will not kid us and in a literary way, since the New Poetry movement has grown too apparent and diffused, we have scarcely where to put ourselves in a literary way, and as you note by the bottom of page one of this letter I am living in a ground floor attic and have to be my own private secretary. Well, where was I.

Well, we need some way to coordinate such standing as we have. Vanity Fair orders an article on the American Language, a clean-cut order. Then it is contemptuously returned after about three months. After six months I send it in absolute despair to Mencken, telling him frankly I agree with him in nothing. What is the answer? He takes it by telegraph.

Elizabeth does her best on the Woodrow Wilson Prize essay contest, with all her heart and brains and that is a plenty. After six months or so there is a contemptuous reference by the Woodrow Wilson Committee to the whole affair, and it has been such a fiasco in their eyes that the money has been given to Lindbergh the aviator. Well Elizabeth is not as good an aviator as that noble boy, but she is a better essayist on Wilson.

Now her noble little essay has to wander along for a year and may be printed first place in the London Spectator, and we are as diffused meanwhile as Vermont Sugar water not boiled down.

We are a real literary partnership, and want to get it going, and if you give me the lead in your book for vocal poetry and Elizabeth the lead in a prize for literature, you may be a lucky coincidence, and are certainly a friend and a prophecy.

I do not want to write you to death today, but first I must congratulate you on the simplicity of presentation in your book.

If it will circulate a million copies I will be profoundly grateful to GOD and to Ellsworth.

Most sincerely.

VACHEL LINDSAY

(The letter from here on was not sent but is here kept for a biographical record. VACHEL LINDSAY.)

This town invited me here as its guest, after the death of my father and mother and while the Springfield estate was being settled up. Then yesterday I had a long "friendly" talk from one of the inviters. It was in substance I was a paying guest and was to pay through the nose before I left town, and pay from the day I landed here. This though I was teased nine months, absolutely besieged to come. My crimes are that I have refused to be socially a lounge-lizard and absolutely at the disposal of people worth over a million dollars and have refused to treat with contempt people whose fortunes are below that figure. Then I have been as frank as this letter, but I was born that way. Then I wrote a poem on Andrew Jackson when I was ordered to write one on William Waldorf Astor. Then another crime was I went on writing the same kind of poetry I wrote before I came here, and expected people to read it. Then another crime was I did not write like Eddie Guest.[1] I was thoroughly skinned by my great and hospitable host yesterday, this marvelous Lorenzo through a messenger and subordinate, because my work was too "Highbrow". A man forty eight years old is to be drummed out of town because he will not write poetry for the kind that never read a line of poetry in their lives.

I am an oldfashioned [sic] Democrat, a Jeffersonian Al Smith Democrat, a Wilson Democrat. I have been ordered to turn tory Republican or leave town. I have been ordered to join the Episcopal church, or remain ostracised by all the Millionaires who own the town and that church. Meanwhile these fake debts do keep me in the town.

I think they were looking for a poet something like Robert Herrick in character and writing, and a little like Alexander Pope, with the manners of Beau Brummel and the Prejudices and asinine ideas of Fitz-Greene Halleck.[2] They certainly did not want Vachel Lindsay, and obviously did not open one of his books before he arrived. Now that all is over, and I actually have presumed to pick out my own wife and write poems on subjects I myself select, and have had the nerve to have two babies without consulting anybody but dear Elizabeth, I discover the hospitality of this town was bunco from first to last. They hate every fundamental idea for which I stand, and assume if an author is not worth from one to ten million dollars all offers of hospitality are withdrawn, as secured obviously under false pretenses. Hospitality represented some fake on my part. I was actually a poet with the income of a grocer, a baker and a candle-stick maker. There are still rumors going around the town that I am a Millionaire who will not pay up, that I am subsidized to advertise a railroad, that my wife and I have started the first papers for divorce, and everything under the shining sun in the way of Jesuitical persecution, while my books have been cut dead and there is not a soul converted to what I stand for but my wife.

I am certainly a citizen of Springfield, Illinois, and will be till I die. I want to get back there as soon as possible to my birthplace with my wife and children, and stay there forever. De la Mare's[3] Listener's represents exactly the way I feel about the old homeplace, Springfield Illinois.

If you are to lecture about me I want you to know the bottom of my heart, and not to skim the surface. I hope you will go on saying I am a citizen of Springfield Illinois, for that is the real truth.

Little Susan Doniphan, not yet two years old, is named for her great-great grandmother, a Virginian. Sometimes I call her by her grandmother's full name, she is so ornate, tempestuous and high stepping:—Susan Doniphan Montjoy Frazee Lindsay. Little Nicholas Cave Lindsay is five months old and named for another Virginia branch of the house. I wish your next edition of The New Poetry would contain Virginia, from "Going to the Stars" (Appleton's).

Remember that Elizabeth and I and the two babies are always in theory at Fifth and Edward's streets, right next to the Governor's Mansion in Springfield Illinois. A trust company holds the house at present, and lets schoolteachers room there who are glad to show any time the place where I used to write. Since I am the only son, and my son is the only son of the only son, and one sister lives in Italy and the Other in Cleveland, it seems to me I have a right to go back where I belong and write in the old home where I did the most and best writing. I see no reason why I should be banished like Dante and heckled by strangers. They heckle me and then say: "Isn't it sad?"

These are the things that keep me from being the singer that once I was. I want to sing and I want a place to sing. Why should the room where I once wrote be exhibited as a commercial curiosity while I have to fight for the chance to live there? It is like cutting off the leg of a perfectly well man and then exhibiting it in alcohol in a museum. They all expect me to be as good a lawyer as Elihu Root[4] and as good a poet as Homer, 24 hours of the day, or else take the consequences. And how they love to try to break me, and then try to pity me. They want to break me as though I were a Wall Street man.

Notes

1. Edgar Albert Guest (1881–1959) was a verse columnist who wrote folksy, sentimental, and moralistic poems in the *Detroit Free Press*. He is said to have written more than eleven thousand of them, at the rate of a poem a day.
2. Fitz-Greene Halleck (1790–1867), a poet and member of the Knickerbocker group, wrote satirical and romantic verse as an avocation.
3. Walter de la Mare (1873–1956) was an English poet and essayist, whose *The Listeners and Other Poems* was published in 1912.
4. Elihu Root (1845–1937) was a lawyer and a close friend and adviser of Theodore Roosevelt's. He was secretary of war during the McKinley Administration in 1899, was Roosevelt's secretary of state in 1905, and was later involved in many extremely delicate and complex diplomatic and legal situations.

175

TO BONI AND LIVERIGHT

2318 West Pacific
Spokane, Washington
March 22, 1928.

Gentlemen:—
My wife Elizabeth and I have just been reading aloud to one another Isadora Duncan's[1] life by herself. We have read and re-read into the midnight.

We offer our profound congratulations.

We are delighted beyond ordinary words. You may tell the world any way you want to. My Great Springfield Cathedral of all Faiths, of which I wrote in such a sad way in "The Golden Book of Springfield" would have a great niche for her, not far from Saint Clara for Isadora was one of the great modern saints if there has ever been a modern saint.

The over-speed of the second half of her life went plainly back to a broken heart, and not to a wanton and rebellious mind.

We are for her straight through because she is against the real United States sins of this hour: Mammonism, Cynicism, Secrecy, Secret Censorship, and also:— the gossip of doddering Polonius behind the whispering arras, and also Jazz, sneering, Hysteria, and simpering; and also:— the rule of Weasel Faced Flappers and Fat Climacteric Women Bosses.

We are for her because in the last chapters she traces her dancing to the dances of her pioneer ancestors, whirling around the covered wagons on the Long Journey to San Francisco. We are for her because her ultimate conception of Art, (and especially that of Dancing) is that of our Ultima Thule, California and not that of Europe or Manhattan.

We are for her because she walked through a hundred fortunes and great Patrons on to poverty again and again with sublime faith, as easily as Saint Clara would have done. Poverty, Chastity, Obedience to Beauty!

We are for her because of her mother-heart, and its heart-break for her noble children, and her noble and great dream of a school for which she suffered and died.

We are for her because she danced poetry again and again without orchestra, "singing" or "music", and thought the reading of the poem "music" enough, in the poetry hour.

We are for her because she dreamed that her little son might write noble United States poetry that might of itself be danced, the Song of The United States and of Whitman.

We are for her because she provided a room in her mind inviolate for poetry without pedantry, simpering, grinning, jazzing, or glowering, that the Word *Homeric* might be restored to its original luster. And in her again, as in all true souls, the WORD became FLESH, and dwelt among us.

We know her private life will be torn to stinking shreds by the Buzzards. They will hang her from the gallows, for the crows to peck out her eyes.

But we have given our souls for all time to the deathless soul of Isadora Duncan, a saint in our cathedral.

Most fraternally

VACHEL LINDSAY

Note

1. On September 14, 1927, Isadora Duncan was strangled to death by her own scarf, when it was caught in a wheel of a moving car. She was forty-nine. Her son, born in 1908, drowned in 1913. Her husband, the Russian revolutionary poet Sergei Esenin, committed suicide in 1925.

176

TO BURRIS A. JENKINS

Spokane
April 24, 1928

My dear Burris Jenkins:

I have sent you today by express a big package of my Maps of the Universe.[1] This map is the frontispiece to my Illustrated Collected Poems, by an edict of my infallible publisher, and has gone around the Anglo-Saxon world worrying my friends to death.

I drew the Map of the Universe when I was a kid and no one was more surprised than myself to find it inserted as a puzzler in the front of my Collected Poems. When I found it in the Dummy in the hands of the advance man, I decided to beat my publisher to it and to spread the thing out where it could be seen at last, so I spent my last cent on this edition of the map, which can be stuck on the wall and examined with a microscope.

I suggest that you begin distributing the map among people accustomed to those diagrams which preface Dante, showing his elaborate hells and heavens, and those diagrams which indicate Milton's compromise between the system of Copernicus and the system of Ptolemy. After all, my map is very simple, simpler than any of these. Why my simplicity should appall anyone, I don't know. In the first place, heaven is at the top of the map and the reminders of hell at the bottom, because we do not say "go up to hell" and "down to heaven". We still say "go up to heaven" and "down to hell". That much of the map is in the mouth of any blasphemer, or any funeral orator. They just don't know it that's all. It remains in their figures of speech if not in their theories, and that's about all of the map that is really important.

The rest of it is a semi-humorous attempt to prove to myself that there is a definite sense of direction in my figures of speech, that they are not merely cloudy. That is, the Flame of Lucifer's Singing, leaps from where was once hell to the walls of heaven. This metaphor is the climax of my last song of Lucifer, written in Hiram College, 1898–9.

The Tree of Laughing Bells is located west of the universe on a star which is tossing like a raft on the sea of chaos. The Tree of Laughing Bells poem is a poem for aviators, written two years after the Wright Brothers made their first flight. The Tree might be called a symbol of Japan and the poem a prophetical poem about a non-stop flight to Japan and return, but it is just as good a metaphor of Columbus, if you want to put it that way.[2] My poem game dancers dance this poem a great deal. You will find it discussed in the central part of my article in the American Mercury, March 1st.

You will find hovering between heaven and hell the soul of the butterfly, which is beauty, and the soul of the spider which is mammon. Blake drew the ghost of a flea long ago and I reserve the same privilege.

Remember, all these things are the nonsense of my youth wished upon me whether I liked it or not, and I have got to make the most of them since I can never escape them. I take them all very lightly.

I mention the boats of the prophets in my poem on Alexander Campbell and in other minor poems. You will find in one of my Appleton books a poem on the Boat with the Kite String and the Celestial Eyes.[3]

You will find in my map of heaven that most of it is woods. Hamlet said the earth was an unweeded garden. I feel sure the best part of heaven is an unweeded garden and an unweeded woods. I fail to see why the park gardeners and neat little city men should rule the skies. I think that the heaven described in the Book of Revelation is a fine thing for those who like city life, but it is all streets, armies, men in uniform, not a private citizen in it. It all happens in a gigantic basilica, probably an idealized basilica of the catacombs with high mass going on at the high altar. Anyhow this city-built Book of Revelation does not give the woods of heaven a chance. I put them in my map.

I wish you would get these maps distributed just as fast as you can among people who have my Collected Poems and who have been puzzled by the frontispiece. You are welcome to print this letter with comment, elucidation and dilution in the local paper or anywhere else as soon as it arrives. You are welcome to print the map if Macmillan Company will give you permission. I want to do as much of my visiting as possible before I arrive in Kansas City. I am a poor, tired, gray-haired old man and must let my youth speak for me.

Yours sincerely,

VACHEL LINDSAY

Notes

1. VL had had two thousand copies of The Map of the Universe reprinted at his own expense in 1925.
2. VL's explanation of the genesis of "The Tree of Laughing Bells" seems to be largely fallacious: Although the dates he gives do correspond (the Wright Brothers made their first official flight in 1903, after an unsuccessful attempt in 1902, and the poem, once a part of *Where Is Aladdin's Lamp?*, was written in the productive year 1904), the motivation for the poem had nothing to do with the event. This idea seems to be a reprise of a later idea: VL called his poem a "poem for aviators" in the *Collected Poems* (p. 213) and in *General William Booth Enters into Heaven* but later (1927) said the idea was a preview of Lindbergh's transatlantic flight.
3. "The Boat with the Kite String and the Celestial Eyes" came out in *Going-to-the-Sun* (p. 43).

177

TO ANNE CARROL MOORE—*Herald Tribune* "Books"

2318 West Pacific
Spokane Washington
May 8, 1928

My Dear Friend:—
Your letter of May 3 is at hand, and I make haste to avail myself of your gracious offer.

I send you a poem just finished today: "My Lady Hostess to the Universe".[1] It was written around five of my pen and ink drawings, and I send them too. I suggest you reproduce one full size or nearly so at the head of the poem and the others as small marginal hieroglyphics. If you want to exhibit them at The American Library Association it may add interest to the poem, since none of the literati have looked at my full sized drawings much but have only seen bad little grubby reproductions that ruined them for the most part.

I consider myself distinctly an amateur in drawing, but an endless list of my most popular pieces have been written to fit drawings that never had even an amateur's chance.

I gladly accept your usual space rates for drawings and verse. Or drawing and verse, as the case may be.

You may be amused to know that I have covered a big parlor wall space in this our hut with a vast picture of Kubla Khan's Xanadu.[2] Little sister Susan Doniphan dances and chants it already in her own way.

It is made of Chinese Embossed papers of various colors I have cut out, and the whole assembly looks like a hooked rug. It was done kindergarden style for the simplest purpose in the world: we have poem-games dancers here every Friday Afternoon from the Lewis and Clark High School, and I wanted them to realize that Coleridge's poem could be outlined and mapped, that it had a top, bottom and sides and east, West, South and North, and was not merely a dizzy incoherent incantation.

My class dances and chants Xanadu for all the English Classes at the High School tomorrow.

They can improvise to the reading of any standard poem as most improvisers can do music. They have done lyrics from Lanier back to Shakespeare's songs. They generally improvise a poem never heard by them before, better than they formulate dances. It is a kind of reading and writing in the air. If they have not heard the poem before they listen and keep only half a second behind the reader and it is amazing the orchestration of forms. Their feet follow the rhyme, meter, assonance, tone-color, and onomatopoeia, forgetting the meaning and forgetting to act. But these things contain the essence of a new kind of impersonation, far from Delsarte,[3] and far from acting and far indeed from dancing to songs, musical instruments or orchestras. The class are High School Freshmen and Sophomores, and their literary sense, not their dancing ability is the fundamental thing. They have not been picked. They are volunteers who wanted to try dancing poetry.

Do exactly what you please with any or all of the enclosed.

Most sincerely,

VACHEL LINDSAY

Notes

1. *Every Soul Is a Circus* contains a four-part poem entitled "My Lady, Dancer for the Universe" (pp. 91–93), of which "My Lady Hostess to the Universe" must have constituted a draft. No drawings accompany it.
2. The collage made by VL on the theme of Kublai Khan is now at the Vachel Lindsay Home in Springfield, Illinois.
3. François Delsarte (1811–71) was a French inventor of calisthenics and a theoretician of gesture and expression. VL had read about his work, but Delsarte's teachings had reached the United States through other channels. Three of Delsarte's disciples imported his ideas: One was Percy MacKaye's father, Steele MacKaye, the greatest American actor at the end of the nineteenth century; another was Geneviève Stebbins, who wrote a book about Delsarte's principles; the third was Henriette Crane, later Mrs. Harvey, who for seven years taught "expression in Delsarte" at the Denishawn School in California.

178

TO ERICH POSSETT

2318 West Pacific
Spokane Washington
June 19, 1928

My dear Erich Possett:

You asked for a general declaration of literary principles from me. I cannot give that. But I can tell you what I am thinking today: it is uppermost in my mind that Sinclair Lewis and H. L. Mencken are the two most valuable literary citizens right now, from the standpoint of free speech, a free press and personal courage at all times. They have these and they stimulate them in others.

It would mean a great deal to me if you could conduct a sort of imaginary three-cornered debate between me and these two gentlemen, for we disagree from one another as the three corners of a triangle disagree. The only things we agree on are free speech, a free press and personal courage, a sort of unit of democratic action. My agreement with their effective action here is so emphatic they make a good start to state my disagreement with them.

I disagree with H. L. Mencken in almost every prejudice he has that goes further than the above statement. I disagree with Sinclair Lewis in almost every prejudice he has, aside from the above. The long catalog they offer us of specific complaints I might answer item by item with contrary views, but I think it is infinitely better they should exercise their right as citizens in this matter than that I should object to what they have to say item by item, here.

I should say I disagree with them both in that I accept, and have always accepted, the main ideas of our most liberal protestants. The church universal, as conceived by such papers as The Christian Century is my church. I believe it is far more vigorous, far more influential, far more a source of life and light than these two gentlemen will concede.

What other brief statement can I make to indicate another orthodoxy to which they will offer many exceptions? Possibly the Democratic Party. Rather let us say the Jeffersonian influence in the United States. I believe that the general influence of Jefferson goes on with extraordinary power in both parties and in the blood of every USA citizen. I think it will continue toward conquest and triumph. I believe there is much more of it than the Democratic Party specifically, than is generally conceded.

To what other orthodoxy do I owe allegiance that can be simply stated? I am definitely a citizen of the middle west and forever a citizen of Springfield Illinois. I believe in the power of Springfield as incarnated in the Lincoln tradition. I believe in the Middle West. I consider myself a citizen of the Middle West in every sense of the word citizen.

Among the more ancient traditions of America, I am as impatient with the whole New England story as Lewis is with Babbitt and his kind, Elmer Gantry and his kind, and the man who knew Coolidge. Perhaps these three men are the fine flower of the New England influence on our present day life. I am as much against the New England arrogance in American tradition as Mencken is against anything he chooses to denounce.

On the other hand, I have what may be called an entirely romantic feeling in regard to the Virginia tradition. The Litany of Washington Street,[1] a book just going to press with the Macmillan Company, is an effort to restate the Virginia tradition. I believe body and soul in the Virginia tradition. My new poem, "The Virginians Are Coming Again",[2] appears in the American Mercury on the day the Democratic Convention opens at Houston, Texas. That poem is not rhetoric. I mean every line of it. It is written as a statement of faith as a citizen of the United States.

This brings us to agreement with Mencken and Lewis again, for the Virginia tradition gets around to free speech, free press and personal courage at all times. Out of these American poetry must come. The poetry of ancient Egypt was perhaps born under a tyrannical hand, but if we are to have United States Poetry, it must be the child of the Declaration of Independence, and of the University of Virginia, and of William and Mary, and the old Raleigh Tavern at Williamsburg.

I have tried to state four orthodoxies in block. There are so many trimmings to what I have had in a life time to say, so many outward limbs and flourishes, it gives me great pleasure to state that I agree with great masses of my fellow citizens in some matters which they have held in common, almost in their Platform creedal statements. I might add to all this that I have always considered Abraham Lincoln essentially a Southerner and a Jeffersonian and a liberal protestant. Another day I might make another summary of how I am feeling about the universe, but it would not contradict this, it would merely discuss another corner of the universe.

Most sincerely,

VACHEL LINDSAY

Notes

1. *The Litany of Washington Street* came out in March 1929.
2. VL recited "The Virginians Are Coming Again" at a poetry dinner in Chicago on May 10, 1929.

179

TO HARRIET MONROE

2318 West Pacific
Spokane Washington
July 10, 1928

My Dear Harriet:—

Here is Jenny Lind[1] revised according to your suggestions. The old form appeared in the Kansas City Star when I was barnstorming that town. I think it came out Sunday May 13, and I taught the refrains to my audiences all the following week there, especially May 18 & 19.

I feel the Star will offer no objection to your reprinting it, they paid me such a very nominal fee for its use as a news-feature celebrating my arrival in said town. Meanwhile, unless this appearance debars it, let me tell you confidentially my landlord is glaring at me for back-rent. Well—you know. Elizabeth and I and the two babies seem to live along like the Macawber family—on our prospects. There are plenty of signs of glory pouring in the next six months. But Elizabeth has not had a holiday since Susan was born two years ago, and is her own cook and nurse. We are all in excellent health and still wearing the clothes we wore on our bridal tour! We are *hoping something will happen!* But we are happy and in health and that's a lot. We are not mourning. The children grow like weeds and are smarter everyday.

I have given up drawing, Egyptology, movie-criticism, prose, parlor-tricks, hiking and what you will and am devoting myself exclusively to poetry—one poem at a time. Result: Bandwagon appearance in July American Mercury and July London Mercury, and my wife wears old women's refitted clothes. As they say in the movies "THE WOMAN PAYS!"

Good luck and lots of love

VACHEL

Note

1. "Jenny Lind" was later incorporated into the last two parts of "Every Soul Is a Circus," originally published in *Poetry,* October 1928 (pp. 1–10).

180

TO HARRIET MONROE

2318 West Pacific
Spokane Washington
August 13, 1928

Dearest Harriet Monroe:—

Thank you so much for the fifty dollar check for "Every Soul is a Circus" and for all the trouble you took and the precedents you broke smash.

Soon I will be sending you more verses and be sure I will comply with *all* the conditions hereafter. You have been most considerate.

When I say I will be sending you more verses, it is more than a nominal promise. I find myself more in a verse-writing vein and more concentrated than for a long time. I know not how long this will last, for both the grocer and the landlord are quite restless.

You are a brave woman and have carried on a wonderful battle for poetry a long, long time. I feel so sure you are doing for the boys and girls what you once did for me when a boy, that I almost feel like an intruder. An intruder, in this sense, that if I cannot make my way in the big world, now, *after all you have done for me*, I am not much of a singer, not much of a leader.

There is not the least doubt that there is a special task for a singer forty nine years old, and it is not asking for help and bucking up from the one human being in the United States who is the one hope of hundreds of young and brilliant singers.

I must make and hold my place singing the song and taking the place of a man of forty nine, and not let any lecture bureau force me to imitate my infant lispings. I *must* build a real *second* story on my work.

One of the few who did it was Old Milton. He was blind and could therefore concentrate. God bless you, Harriet.

With love indeed,

VACHEL

181

TO NICHOLAS CAVE LINDSAY

Hotel Abraham Lincoln
Springfield, Illinois
October 11–12, 1928

Dearest Nickey-Ben:—
This town gets funnier every minute. Unless you are a novelist you will get nothing out of it. It is still steaming corn-weather! You see by the picher [*sic*] in the paper how I looked when a boy.

All the people my age look pale with sin and their skins full of old tallow. How heavy they look after the sweet face of youth you have, and your mother and sister. If I don't train down,—shoot me. The Egyptian minister and I have one thing in common. He has a wife half his age beautiful as the Arabian Nights. We saw 'em off on the train for Washington D.C. 'safternoon after laying two large wreaths on Lincoln's tomb.

Your papa VACHEL dady[*sic*]

182

TO ELIZABETH CONNER LINDSAY

The Southern Hotel
Baltimore, Md.

Thanksgiving Day, 1928
[November 22, 1928]

Darling:
Thank you for your sweet telegram via the Spencers. I had a happy afternoon with them in Hazelton's[1] Room in the hospital. He goes home tomorrow. Then I waited and hunted in vain for Mr C. C. Certain, my sponsor here, for a thanksgiving dinner which I finally ate alone, lonely enough to die.[2] Then it was nearly ten and in spite of that I phoned Hank Mencken and he urged me to call at once and there in his house

we had a monologue from him till 12:30 and I found out oodles about Louis Untermeyer[3] and Co, and Sinclair Lewis and new Wife, etc. On the whole you and I are getting on very well thank you, and more details when we meet. We had a really grand monologue on literary husbands and wives. I tell you we have done better than most, you and I. Main Streets [*sic*] success addled Mrs Sinclair Lewis the same way Spoon River's success addled Mrs Masters. Both were "good wives" before that. So, dear, when selecting a husband with a destiny beware of having his success go to *your* head! Instead of going to *his* head! Women are worse drunks than men, it seems! Poor Mrs Lewis the second has a hard row to hoe, and is a very spirited girl and may not make it! She is taking over the leavings indeed! Well H. L. talked well and kindly but frankly about them all, and inquired most gallantly about you. For some reason you have a secret admirer and profound respecter there. *No. Its nothing I have said!* So don't get jumpy! And he adored our babies. Well, getting back from Mencken's I wanted to go to bed and I saw the most gorgeous procession of young drunk boys and girls coming out of the Ball-Room I ever saw in my life, issuing from the Ball-Room of this hotel. So I sat another hour watching them catch their taxis. I never saw the beat! The girls could all stand but a lot of the boys were leaning a bit! and of all the kissing and prettying! What a parade!

Well we are young but once. Heres hoping they are home safe by now. And now past Two in the morning Mr C. C. Certain calls me up and wants to have a ten o'clock breakfast! I told him he could if he had the nerve to wake me.

Somehow or other I cannot take Baltimore quite as seriously as I did, after this day's events! Mr. Certain himself sounded a little stewed and uncertain over the phone. But I *may* do him an injustice.

Robert Frost and I meet at the dinner tomorrow evening. Saturday afternoon the Spencers take me to the Drama League show of Volpone the Fox.

Well I *must* go to sleep—if I am to be any good tomorrow. But I am a little amused at the solemnity with which I took this town when I landed here!

Dear Heart—let us love one another—remembering whatever the price we have paid and will pay—other lovers have paid a far more bitter price, for less love than we both have to give. It will cost us every thing but its worth it! Your love is anyway!

With a true heart

VACHEL

Notes

1. Hazelton Spencer eventually edited VL's *Selected Poems* (New York: Macmillan, 1931). On August 31, 1927, *The New Republic* published his article on VL entitled "More Nightingales" (p. 32). After VL's death, Spencer wrote three more articles on him, which appeared in *Elementary English Review*, May 1932; *The American Mercury*, April 1932; and the *Saturday Review of Literature*, September 28, 1935.
2. From October 1928 to March 1929, at the cost of incredible effort on one huge tour through the East and the Midwest, VL wiped out all his accumulated debts. His health failed rapidly. In November 1928 he was awarded a special prize of $500 by *Poetry* for his entire corpus.
3. Louis Untermeyer had divorced Jean Starr and had married Virginia Moore in 1926.

183

TO H. S. LATHAM

Permanent eastern address—Feakins Lecture Bureau
Times Building
Times Square
New York City

January 16, 1929

Letter sent to H. S. Latham and Thorndyke.
Hazelton has just met Thorndyke, and asks to edit the volume.

Mr. H. S. Latham
The Macmillan Company
60 Fifth Avenue
New York City:—

My Dear Friend:—
I have just sent this letter below to Doctor Thorndyke, and the substance of the letter to Doctor Hazelton Spencer:—
My Dear Friend: The general editorship of my Selected Poems for the Modern Reader's Series has been by my good friends The Macmillan Company assigned to you, (and several times announced in their catalogue) as I understand it, this does not debar particular editorship of the volume by a special person of whom you approve, and whose work you can trust. It will be a great honor, of no small moment to me, if you care to assign the volume to Doctor Hazelton Spencer of Johns Hopkins,

author of "Shakespeare Improved", a study of the Restoration Versions of Shakespeare. Please let me hear from you. I need the backing of the soundest scholars, men certified before the world.

To this petition to Thorndyke I add my petition to you and to Spencer that all the necessary diplomatic advances be made to have all parties concerned, think well of the idea.

Most sincerely

VACHEL LINDSAY

184

TO ELIZABETH CONNER LINDSAY

Washington's Birthday—Feb. 22, 1929
Still on the train to New York.

Dearest—Most Beloved:—
Several times I have been prompted to write this letter. Before I write it let me say Grace:—

"God Bless our Love. Meeting and parting, parting and meeting, forever and forever. May we bear fruit eternally, like an apple orchard in clean new land, with bees and butterflies bearing pollen from tree to tree and revelling in our honeys forever".

Now thats the important part of the letter. The rest is an Emersonian Discourse on Adolescence, written down just to keep company with you. It will be three more hours till I get to New York, and now I am free of all business with practically my last fee in my pocket kept snug for you till I meet you, my mind rebounds into a thousand thoughts I have heretofore been too weary to set down. I had my senescence at 38 but was kicked past it by enormous flatteries in England two years later. Now I watch with the *sharpest eyes* men my own age who seem to be conquerors—and I take all sorts of notes on them. If they pass the crisis as Hazelton seems to have done so early and survive *all* the over-speeding, they enter into a new disorganized boyhood at 50 which matures as slowly as the [page missing]
[. . .] than he ever showed since he was 30. He was awfully sprawly

ten years ago. "Neatness of mind" is not the complete description but it applies to the hapless hope of the adolescent. At 12 he would drink poison to get the pimples off his face and know how to get the squeak out of his voice. At 50 he would drink poison to have the general neatness of mind he had at 30. So many young professors in this first neatness and assurance address me and are my hosts—they are like Stoddard [King] in a dress-suit and I say "Well—I was a neat little package like that once, and given time, will be again, and glad of the chance! But few men past fifty have the *bull-strength* to do it, and the right circumstances. So they sit in the bald-head row—buy a chorus-Girl or take to avarice or drink, or fanaticism. I have hardly seen *one boss* my age that appeared to have the self-control of his subordinates in business—all the subordinates being men ten years younger or so, and rightfully more sure of themselves. Meanwhile I take items. Louis Untermeyer came to his second adolescence early—paid a fearful price when still disorganized and is only half-way out. I will tell more when I meet. Sinclair Lewis is in the midst of his, and it is practically delirium tremens. Masters has survived physically, has a baby by his second-wife, is bland and happy, but is only half his *old* self. Its like growing a third set of teeth! Only a few do it *completely*! And in neat rows!

In my talk with Mencken—now at the top of his authority, his mind went back most irrelevantly to the liquor-question every 15 minutes, though it was brilliant talk. I think he is a very moderate drinker. He *looks* so. But he has an increasing anti-prohibitionist mania that will kill him mentally, or make him a second-rate fanatic.

The second adolescence is the most unconscious of the two—because so few survive it to tell the others it may be survived. There is every *public* evidence that Shaw has grown way past it, and I'll bet he has the same complete neatness of mind and ways he had at thirty, not a single dangling thread of fifty-year old silliness, and with all his practical head-way besides. Also he has new tides of ideas. It may sound like a joke, but only interminable monologues about myself to you, the last two years, and the absolutely bawling-calf letters I send you—are my form of incontinence. I have the same *impulse* to be *gabby* with a good audience. *Real* letters from me are only a page long and you know it. These sloppy ramshackle Johnstown-flood discourses of mine are my substitute for the avarice of Brett or the tremens of Lewis or the mania of Mencken. I *know* to my soul five years hence I will put on three pages to you more than I put on thirty now. I *know* it! Because so few men survive this period they are all given the privilege (1) of riding their hobbies to the limit (2) paying for the damage out of what they earn in business hours. For they are by 50 either good executives unconsciously, or paupers utterly ignored. My old daddy going to China and back had survived the second adolescence and come back a young man—a star-tling reminiscence of what he was in my babyhood. Then he became *over*-confident, took no holiday the next summer and *smashed* the next winter after that. His usual camping trip would have kept him a won-derful man for Nickey to admire.

Bryan—it is notorious—ate himself to death. He took to it like drink. What I am happy about tonight is (1) I have at least *proved to myself* there *is* a second adolescence by watching good specimens. (2) I have not only struggled through most of it with your noble help, but feel new powers growing within me. You have a boy of 21 to teach how to wear his dress-suit, how to be a bridegroom and a husband and father. I have survived at least the pimples and the squeaky voice. The human race is merely sketched in. We have often observed there is a certain neat maturity at eight, reminiscence of cave-man maturity, not achieved again till thirty. The third neatness comes at 50 or 55 or not at all. And *few* achieve it. *Few* get clear to it.

Why do I insist on neatness? I mean *every kind,* body or soul. Why my old photographs show I had more precision of mind than I have now—more precision of act and gesture. You will see it in my old handwriting and notes.

Well my dear—I am going forward slowly to that stage. I was starting that way when I left Gulf-Park. You have pulled me along slowly by your patience with my interminable introspective orations and letters and a thousand other services, infinitely harder but to the same purpose.

I am sure for instance—once I am in Springfield and established as I was a boy of seventeen in the streets there—I will be able not only to visit the Wakefields but reason out what they want and give it to them as easily as I now please Feakins.[1] One of the curiosities of this stage is that most men in the midst of it are like Papa Guilbert—*exceedingly* effective in business hours from pure habit, and high-school boys at home!

New York is so jam full of reminders of how *neatly* I turned every situation in 1914 to 1920 I cannot help but try to think this through. The extraordinary return of those old vistas at the Brooklyn Institute has kept me thinking overtime about it. My very voice and manner swept back to 1914 in the sense of completeness and neatness. You *are* ripening all the fruit on the top of the old pear-tree called Vachel. If it is worth your care you may yet get a real man out of this struggle! And as good future Art brains for me as babies for us already. I have *not* thought it through. I only know we are on the way. At this distance Bernard Shaw *seems* to be the one man with a complete third set of teeth! Frost is a close competitor! A *real Jove!* No I have not thought it through. We will have to travel a lot and accumulate an enormous number of specimen males to get real data. It is certainly the second set of pimples! My heavy smoking and lots of coffee[2] are mild indeed compared with the consolations of most old travelling men Saturday night—drink, drugs, Rahabs or crooked money schemes and the rest. In general I discover men of fifty infinitely more reckless about Drink, drugs Rahabs or crooked avarice than men of 21 or 30. And I *know* how they *feel*. A kind of vague disordered adolescence has hold of them again and they have had no rose-bosomed Elizabeth to whom they can write ten-page letters till their nerves are sensible and submissive to supreme beauty. They have no Lady Isis for a sure goal!

A little prayer:—

God grant this little Adam and Eve in this pretty new Garden may always be clean and sweet and serve the winds of the spirit faithfully. God Grant they may be unmarried lovers to the end of time, always rediscovering one another in the dew of the morning. God help them to grow to the utmost limit till they leave this mortal Earth. God protect their love, and, whatever their sorrow, may they never be separated in soul. May they find the deep sweets of the souls tenderness for one another, Amen.

VACHEL

Notes

1. The Lindsays returned to Springfield in April 1929, after VL's tour was over. W. B. Feakins was the organizer of the tours.
2. VL had taken to smoking and drinking coffee after his marriage. He also gradually became an occasional consumer of liquor.

185

TO SINCLAIR LEWIS

603 So. 5th St.
Springfield Illinois

May 22, 1929

My dear Lewis:

I am at last established with my wife and two children in my birth place, 603 South Fifth Street. You and Mrs. Lewis are earnestly requested to

Rachel Lindsay 1927, U.S.A.

The Mohawk in The Sky

Vachel Lindsay 1928

The Rim Rock of Spokane, drawn by Lindsay (courtesy of the University of Virginia Library)

The Lindsays at their Springfield home, 603 South Fifth Street, *circa* 1930

Vachel Lindsay in 1931, the year of his suicide.

come and see us any length of time that occurs to you whenever you are free.

Elizabeth and I have just finished your book Dodsworth.[1] We most highly approve, have read it with the closest interest, feel it is your most significant book so far and are so full of opinions about it we could both write reviews about as long as the novel itself. We will not trouble you with them here but believe me we read it hard. Please accept our most earnest congratulations.

I will spare you a long letter though I certainly could write you one. I hope we can have a lot of good talk.

If you care to read between the lines of the Litany of Washington Street, you will discover that my great-grandfathers the original Lindsays were the poisoned variety of Jeffersonian Kentucky Democrats. The blood spitting, horse whipping, reprehensible branch which is of course greatly to be deprecated in these days of Chicago Gunmen. Please read the last chapter in Washington Street and discover the joker.

Most sincerely

VACHEL LINDSAY

Note

1. *Dodsworth,* published in 1929, was then Sinclair Lewis's latest novel.

186

TO H. S. LATHAM—The Macmillan Company

603 South 5th
Springfield, Illinois
Oct. 1, 1929.

My Dear Mr. Latham:—

It gives me a great pleasure to note there is a 1929 imprint of the Collected Poems—following on the heels of a 1927 imprint. The two big prefaces—forty-six pages in all, are superannuated. I would like to throw them out and, without altering any poems, scatter through the body of the work forty six of my best new full-page pen and inks illustrating the oldest poems, for say Christmas 1930.

Most sincerely

VACHEL LINDSAY

Please consider a contract for this.

187

TO ELIZABETH CONNER LINDSAY

The Town Hall Club
123 West 43rd Street
New York

January 28, 1930

Dearest Most Beloved:—
Thank you again for the rose leaves and the sweet letters,[1] and I will surely obey your telegram and wear a rose for you tonight at the Poetry Dinner.

The Biltmore is that big hotel on 43 where there is a corridor, running to the Grand Central, we have walked through.

Jail has already left her card and says (if I can decipher) she already has a job with Melcher. Good deed done by Elizabeth. More and merrier, please. Do another for some wandering soul from Spokane, within a year.

I called at Liberty yesterday afternoon, and had a talk with Palmer. He may possibly assign a topic this week, but I put not my trust in Princes. *Anything* that involves getting above the dead level of rather exceedingly live level of our present flat-top will be harder than climbing Mount Kipp. In all *new* adventures you go hat in hand, a beginner like Quail. So it will be with the Victor talking machine.[2] Darling not one of my drawings or verses I have sent you are good. They merely prove to us we are not at a dead stop.

I am haunted day and night by Rodin. What I want in pen and ink is his fluency of the flying form, his radiant light, the transparency of his marble, and *real* figures, not automatons or pretty profiles. I want action splendor, light and human aspiration to the uttermost. And all these things now turn over in my skull like birds still in the shell. I know that sometime, with the right concentration I can do them, for my pen is fluent and suave enough, plastic as a sculptor's line, it has the spirit of marble in it, in the treatment of white paper. All I need is complete control, complete visualization and complete *concentration*.

I would love to alternate Glacier Park and Rodin both in drawing and in song. I know your figures and the childrens by heart, they are always flying before me, and all I need is to evoke what I already know from the page—written and drawn. They might all be fashionplates from fairyland yet majestic as the Centaurs and Lapiths. And I want all to be gigantic units of things above and under the earth. The thwarting of gigantic units in my mind is a thing I have allowed to go on too long.

(1) Springfield as a World-Pilgrim place.

(2) Spokane (impersonally) as a New Nuremburg for a thousand years.

(3) The 48 States of the Union, clothed in light.

(4) The Metropolitan Museum—stretched from the beginning to the end of time.

(5) The Publishing Game as a Vast Literary Venture, not a box of office tricks.

(6) The reciting Game, as a vast singing adventure, not as a set of trick entrances and exits and the catching of trains.

(7) The Whole Picture of Christendom from A.D. 1 till now, west of the Indus, beginning with our Church and the Cathedral across the street, but stretching from every Art and Literature to the Millennium, for, whatever the contradiction or variation, Christendom is mine.

All these things are hinted at only in the dull and incomplete Litany of Heroes. They have all, definitely and specifically been in my head, beginning with the Map of the Universe.

And I have stopped all of them through intellectual loneliness beginning slowly about 1914 till I have degenerated into [page missing]

I am certainly addled when people get down to particular scraps and maneuvers. I cannot understand them, have no talent for them, and no dream of what to do. Yet friendship always drags me in. It is nothing grandiose I want, but something like our few words of chatter and our kisses on the top of Mount Kipp, but the whole horizon before us. In all this I speak as an artist. As a man it is doubtless an utterly different story, but I want to be your manly artist with these big horizons all the time, and no tricks to worry about, like dodging bores and evil intruders and such.

Maybe it is because I have steadily avoided the Macmillan office to date I have been able to feel there were fewer tricks in the world, after all, and expand again, at last. I feel like a nice Zeppelin someone like

Mrs Halbrook had been puncturing with hat-pins, set floating again over sea and land, with every puncture mended. Some people think I have no business to be a balloon if I can possibly be brought down. Aunt Beulah is "Glad I am at work". Yes—reciting the poems it took 40 years to write, when she thought I was lazy!

The thing that brings me down quickest is submitting to any one mind too intimately, from sheer loneliness. I come clear from the edge of the horizon to meet them half-way and they do not think I have come an inch, because I do not go down their pet rat-hole to help kill one rat I never heard of till the moment!

I have set myself to be reconciled to intellectual loneliness away from home, henceforth—since surrendering to alien minds always brings disaster to me, in some sense. More and more I share my latest ideas one a day from the platforms, one for each town, and forget it, and that is better than an overcrowded unused note-book, and infinitely better than winning and then making angry loyal friends like Trombly,[3] Conrad and Hazelton. I would like to see a heap more of all three men, but instead I say to my audiences what I would say to them, but only one sentence to each town. And now I will get down off my high Pegasus and get awfully personal with thee. I love my darling Elizabeth, body, mind, soul and exquisite beauty and she and her two babies are almost one person to me, youth, youth, youth to the uttermost, and youth and immortality are the same thing and I send three kisses.

With my heart

VACHEL—

Notes

1. VL continued his recitals across the country all through 1930 and most of 1931, except for brief pauses. His financial situation became more and more desperate, and his profligacy with money did not help balance the Lindsays' budget. Most of what he earned went back into travel expenses.
2. VL recorded some of his poems in New York in January 1931.
3. Albert Edmund Trombly was VL's biographer; "Conrad" refers to Conrad Aiken; and "Hazelton," to Hazelton Spencer.

188

TO FREDERIC MELCHER

Springfield
August 5, 1930

My Dear Fred:—

Your visit meant so much to me, in an unusual way, I have wanted to write ever since.

What is it I want to say? I am very anxious to say it clearly and briefly, yet I may wander on. Never in my life have I had such an army of well-wishers, and I have no enemies. Yet the intimates who know what the game is all about are few indeed, men to whom I can turn and talk about things I really take seriously.

And the mere impact of the multitude of well-wishers sometimes makes a man so dull he finds he has allowed a rare friendship to grow dull. In the old days it was so much easier to keep up with those I really cared for, because they were all I had.

There are only about ten men like you scattered over the map who can keep my life from getting second-rate. I expect to look you up oftener, bear you in mind oftener, and be more grateful to God for you. For further words, read Emerson's Essay on Friendship. I feel quite inclined to write a poor imitation, but will close right here.

If I am to grow at all, I must not be so separated in thought from my real friends. So, please drink my health, ever and anon.

Most fraternally,

VACHEL

189

TO H. L. MENCKEN

Springfield, Illinois
September 18, 1930

My Dear H. L. Mencken:—
Certainly we are still friends, and the minute I have something I care for, I will submit it. I will be delighted if the Menckens can come through Springfield any time. I have to sing for a living and it leaves me absolutely flat, as a writer.

My houses are packed, hundreds turned away, and people sitting in the aisles and windows, San Francisco to Montreal. It gets *more so* every season. The Lord knows I would rather enter into the silence for a lifetime, and do a little real drawing, writing, and have a few real conversations with the Menckens.

With good wishes.

VACHEL LINDSAY

190

TO ELIZABETH CONNER LINDSAY

New York City
Hotel Woodstock

February 17, 1931

Darling:—
To think I shall see you next Sunday. That is *so* good.

Thank you for the dear dear Valentine telegram.

At last I saw Sara for the first time last night.[1] Sick in bed with an alleged cold, and fed me cough drops as she always does when she has a cold, which is *always*, according to her. I came home sadder than for many a day. Her hypochondria, in my notion, grows a little deeper.

And sometimes I think I have given up the fight, am merely going through motions, but by comparison with our darling Sara I am surely on the fighting line. All this must wait for the final comment some rich day when we walk. I never loved anyone more dearly than Sara, but I was most scairt [*sic*] to call again. Truly dear she seemed old and down as Papa Conner and fighting to be good most the same way. Yet the old clear pride and gentility is there. You could do her more good than I could.

This is a futile way to talk about it. She is eager to see Spencer so I have fixed it up by letters, he is to call when he passes through town. She seems to have given up poetry *flat*, and it was all in all to her.

Dearest write oodles of love poems to every sweet boy that cuts deep into your heart, but write something else so you can carry on. Being a poetess of passion seems to have an awfully abrupt finish. I now see a reason for novels by Edith Wharton! I have whined about my lack of friends. But by comparison with the *fanatically reclused Sara*, you and I seem richer in intimates than David and Solomon. God what an unnecessary *grouch* I am. God help me to warm to everybody right off the bat, the minute I meet them. Thats better than her dead isolation.

Sara tells me the only poetry Bohemia left is dominated by Louise Bogan[2] and they go in for the most terrific orgiastic stunts and drink themselves into insensibility. And *we* don't see any good writing out of that crowd. Better the prim Harriets!

Also I am *dead sure* there is some little crowd not much bigger than *you-and-me-Susan-and-Nickey-and-Papa-Conner* that is going to be in the saddle in five years, people decent and young in the morning. I *believe* before God in the United States, and The Virginians are coming again, not the pigs.

And YOU will be Avanel Boone, while I sleep at Oak Ridge.

Sara is right about many things and she and Margaret Conklin both want you to take your New York start at the Christadora House. Nothing could be better for a start. They know all the psychological ropes old and new, make it a point to give special rates to poets, *want* them there in especial, and it is a good crowd. Anna Branch is funny but there is nothing better in her own way.

I am sure you will have two or three New York dates in the fall and shall arrange with Feakins that I shall stay at home while you come and have your time. Soon we may be travelling alternate months. I want you to come *on your own,* and poke out the things that interest *you* and your young chums. You have lots of friends here who would only grow silent if I appeared with you. I want you to have as big a fling as a young mother *ever had* at being a bachelor Girl.

I see you taking longer and longer leaps as the children grow steadier and more responsible. I have plenty of nice things to tell you about Sara later. Oh—dear me—please don't think I am hanging *too* much crepe on dear Sara—for *now* comes some crepe. Masters Life of Lincoln[3] is just as awful as its traducers make out. His mind is good but his disposition is just plain sick.

(1) He hates Sandburg. Therefore he writes a life of Lincoln that reads like rattle-snake venom. Every page bristles with *hate* of Sandburg though it seems to be hate of Lincoln.

(2) He is drinking hard. Therefore he hates the remotest element in America that has helped to make up the dry forces, including everybody that didn't want to drink himself under the table, in the last 100 years!

(3) I verily believe his physical resemblance to Douglas has eaten into him through the years. He is a specialist in Douglas and wherever Douglas differed from Lincoln, Lincoln was a crawling sneak. Its a hot book all right.

(4) In spite of himself he is so pro-confederate that he justifies the assassination of Lincoln.

(5) He is for Calhoun and Douglas at the same time. Which is like being for Jefferson Davis and Lincoln at the same time. He uses both to prove Lincoln a sneak. That seems to be his deepest conclusion about Lincoln, though he is O so ceremonious, page after page about *"analyzing Lincoln's character"*.

(6) He has probably been so hounded about the merits of Spoon River in comparison to his other work that he has grown to hate it as I sometimes hate the Congo. Here I sympathize with Him. But even in dealing with Anne Rutledge he gives her small pickings. And he seems to say "Since you won't talk to me about anything but Spoon River, I will blow Spoon River to Smithereens". For there is hardly a page but destroys a line of Spoon River. He has turned on himself like Ruskin.

(7) He seems to hate the Negro like poison and abominate the abolition[ist]s for the simple reason that their children became the leaders of the dry cause. *Therefore* the negro should have remained a slave.

(8) He rages like Simon Legree in Uncle Tom's Cabin against anyone who has any religion *whatever*, Mennonite, Jews or Unitarian.

(9) The highly trained lawyer in him which made Spoon River so much like an address to the jury, so clear, so fine, so disciplined, has gone sour. The elaborate ostentation of legal quibbles beats a string Nickey has tangled up. He promotes himself from a jury Lawyer to a United States Supreme Court Lawyer, with a curious anger.

(10) His vanity has been horribly wounded, I know not how and shows on every page, listing the law-books *he* read that Lincoln didn't, the current Literature of 1850 *he* read and Lincoln didn't etc. The legal commentaries *he* mastered and Lincoln could not "GRASP" etc. Also the classics. He knows *all* about Pericles, etc . . .

(11) Whenever he gets into a complete jam he says it is a very subtle legal point and drearily drools on like a *bad* lawyer, certainly not clarifying the subtlety but trailing off into vain repetitions!

(12) The gist of the book:—is that:— *Lincoln was a sneak, without brains enough to grasp hair-splitting subtleties, therefore came the civil war, the trusts, the skyscrapers, the churches and the dry vote! Also the Racketeers and the Rockefellers!*

Please do not give this out. Edgar Lee is a friend of mine. Just as a mental curiosity you may be interested in the book. It is a specimen, *not* a book, and a specimen *for fair.*

Masters has already in ms. a life of Douglas, but *had* to issue a life of Lincoln first as an opening gun. As long as he sticks to Douglas it will likely be fairly good, and as strategy it was a good idea to light into Lincoln good and hard first. But he is as angry as Simon Legree! Which is overdoing it!

Darling if I am to live I must join Nickey and Susan's generation and grow up with them. My oldest and dearest grow too complicated. Oh my darling inspired poet-babies! Blessed be Mother Elizabeth that cherished and nursed them. Sara and Masters are tragically old and *sick.* You must be free of any such growing old in me. I must not contaminate you with rheumatism! Hug your young companions to your heart, grow up with your generation and Papa will kiss his babies and thank you for them and get them to teach me the alphabet. Never speak to a single soul over thirty years old. Ignore me, too. I am the man who recommended Spoon River to Macmillans, and Sara Teasdale's poems.

Growing old is *not* necessarily mellowing. Sara is bitter with the hero of all her books, Masters with *everybody* apparently but those deadly enemies of one another:—Calhoun and Douglas.

Deart heart—if there is any youth in me enjoy it. If there is any old age for God's sake kick it out of your bed forevermore. You should not sleep with a mummy and I will protect you like a palace guard while you choose a fit lover for all the rich young fruit in you.

You are my Queen, my darling, my charge and you and the two babies must scamper freely down the morning road in the sunshine.

Blessed blessed passionate beautiful rebellious Elizabeth, let your heart rebel and your blood burn and put no curb on them for my sake. Better one hour with your babies than a lifetime with the old.

With all my heart

VACHEL—

Notes

1. Sara Teasdale divorced Ernst Filsinger in 1929 in Reno under an assumed name and spent her remaining years unhappily in New York, sporadically working on a biography of Christina Rossetti. She committed suicide on January 29, 1933, at age forty-eight, a little more than a year after VL's death.
2. Louise Bogan's latest book was *Dark Summer* (1929), published when she was thirty-three.
3. Edgar Lee Masters's *Lincoln—The Man* (1931) was intended as a foil to Carl Sandburg's *Lincoln, The Prairie Years* (2 vols.), which had come out in 1926. (*The War Years* [4 vols.], was published in 1939.)

191

TO ELIZABETH CONNER LINDSAY

Western Union

Asheville, North Carolina
March 15, 1931

Mrs Vachel Lindsay
603 South 5th Springfield
Illinois

This school here put on the thumbscrews till I was ready to scream because they could not sweat the Congo out of me Two more such persecutions and I am a goner for sure Please take this matter in hand

VACHEL LINDSAY

192

TO MARGARET CONKLIN

Charleston, South Carolina
March 20, 1931

My Dear Miss Conklin:—
No doubt my last two communications may have seemed incoherent. I am so grateful Ashville had the chance to read the New York Times the day after. Thank you!

I try again:—

The ideals of my life, on the Platform or off, are summarized in the "Building of Springfield" Poem. I am at the top of my strength and powers to further those ideals. My audiences increase to mobs, tyranical, ignorant mobs. Last night I gave them my best in reciting, all from the Selected Poems, that is all my principal poems but The Congo and Booth, the most forceful ideas I have added in comment, and many new and old poems. I sat down having recited *two hours,* my best—8:30 to 10:30 P.M. Then the chairman, by the Politest methods (not horrible *bullying* as in Ashville) started them mobbing me for "The Congo" before I left the hall and I recited it politely resolving to beat them yet. The Courtesy here is perfect and I have had a good time. But I am not going to die like Edwin Markham, reciting in the provinces *One poem*[1] written as a boy. I wrote The Congo in 1913 and was through reciting it FOR-EVER, by 1920. And here they not only ignore it as a Christian Mis-sionary message—welcome it only as a stunt—liking only the first section and *enduring* the rest), but I am the agonized prisoner of my 34th year, no matter if I am 51. *I want to say do and be the things a real artist of 51 would do.* I am simply bursting with *new* ideas, new plans pour into my brain every morning for songs, new creative force comes to me and I am the prisoner of a stunt with all creative force thwarted,—welcomed only as a *stunt,* not a message, and to me, The Congo and Booth, as performances, are as stale as the oldest things in a dusty cellar or a dusty attic. The Chinese Nightingale, The Santa Fe Trail, The Arizona Sheriff, How to Write a Poem,[2] Johnny Appleseed, The Building of Springfield, Lincoln Walks at Midnight are all *merely incidental* to my audiences because they are audiences three times the size of the Old ones, and have learned only catch-words about me, and the thing promises to grow into a maelstrom, of people who know nothing about me except a Stunt Artist who "DOES" the Congo.

They accept the Congo and Booth about which I am hectored beyond all human endurance, only as STUNTS and curiosities. I know they would not cross the street to help a nigger or The Salvation Army as a result of this dress-suit heckling. They merely want them as stunts, they have heard idle gossip about and a man of 51 *has a right to be a citizen,* and I am determined with your help to *stop* this Hectoring. It is as bad as the Hectoring of Lindbergh by people who would not ride a mile in a flying machine on a bet. *Please reread* the *Building* of *Springfield* and swear by Heaven that henceforth you will build my publicity round it.

With great good wishes

VACHEL LINDSAY

Notes

1. Edwin Markham's "one poem" is "The Man with the Hoe."
2. "The Arizona Sheriff" and "How to Write a Poem" were poems from 1929 30. The latter was published in broadside form.

193

TO HAMLIN GARLAND

[May 28, 1931]

My Dear Hamlin Garland:—
Your letter of May 18 certainly warmed my heart. Thanks to my dear wife Elizabeth, and her toiling through several years, all my old letters and papers are in neat secretarial iron files. Now there's a wonderful woman.

So I am able, while she is across town teaching hopefuls their English and History, to find three first letters to me, which still have the old thrill.

Current Literature, March 1911 reviewed my strictly private printing of the first edition of the Village Magazine. Your letter of March 7, is evidently your second letter. You ask for a second copy of The Village Magazine, for yourself, one for the Librarian of the Cliff Dwellers, and one for Henry B. Fuller. (I cannot find the very first letter).

Your letter of March 30, 1911, recommends Mitchell Kennerley as a publisher, and he *was* my first publisher, 1913, printing General Booth, which I wrote in Los Angeles, October 1912.

The third letter, enclosed, following soon asks me to address the Cliff Dwellers, at noon, basing my address on one of the Editorials of the Village Magazine "On the Returning Art Student".[1]

So, in the early Spring of 1911, I received my first public literary recognition. I remember the Cliff Dwellers were kind enough to pay my car-fare sight unseen, quite an astonishing thing to me.

On that day's visit to Chicago I met for the first time Larado Taft, Mrs. Garland, and the Whole Cliff-Dweller bunch at noon. At your insistence the whole set of them had asked for Village Magazines before I arrived, and the old guard there should still have a lot of copies. I have none of any imprint except one set.

But I am sending you the front pages of the fourth and last imprint, issued the fall of 1925. I issued it as a kind of repository of all the private printings and drawings I wanted on record that could not be issued in regular publishing channels, and which represented all my private amendments to the routine advertising of a public man, for my only pleasure is being personal without getting fresh.

When you were so kind as to recognize the First imprint of the Magazine in such a thundering way, I was nearly paralyzed with gratitude. You made me a member of The Cliff-Dwellers at once. I was even more confused than I was happy because all my printings were private pamphlets. I was surrounded by people who had regular publishers and very definite standing, and I had nothing for calling cards but those pamphlets. So I did not show up very much in Chicago, in spite of your great kindness. And I remember a private car of notables that came down to the Legislature to lobby for the Production of "the Piper".

Then came the humorous part. At exactly that same set of Tables at the Cliff Dwellers March 1, 1914, with the same men (*and* their wives) serving the Banquet, W. B. Yeats made a speech for which I am still grateful but on which I will not dwell at this moment. They had all forgotten the Village Magazine, and I was formally introduced in reception line to the whole works again. I received the baby stare from the whole works when I said I had been a member of that club for three years thanks to Garland, Taft, etc . . .

The whole key of it is that the famous 1912 New Poetry Fire kindled by the good and great Harriet Monroe was burning up the prairie, and anything any poet did was temporarily news, at last. New Books of Poetry were popping like Popcorn. Amy Lowell was telling Massachussets just where to get off. Ezra Pound had broadcasted imagism from London. In just two months Spoon River was to start in Reedy's Mirror, and to be read to tatters in Chicago and London before it came out in Book Form. Frost was coming out in England and was about to be lionized in Boston, Sandburg was soon to receive his first prize, that for His poem on Chicago, from Harriet Monroe, and all the poets in America for the first time in thirty years were looking one another in the eye. Mitchell Kennerley had published the Lyric Year, containing Edna Millay's[2] first and greatest poem, Renasence, which made her famous at once with the other ninety-nine poets in that book. But as for us, my Dear Hamlin Garland, we belonged to the "I Knew Him When" society, and we still do now, and God bless us every one. The first times are the first times!

Most gratefully

Vachel Lindsay

Notes

1. "An Editorial for the Art Student Who Has Returned to the Village" (*The Village Magazine*, pp. 86–87) was quoted by Edward J. Wheeler in *Current Literature*.
2. Edna St. Vincent Millay's poem "Renascence" was published in 1917 in *Renascence and Other Poems*." *The Lyric Year* (New York: Mitchell Kennerley, 1912) was edited by Ferdinand Earle.

194

TO SHEPPARD BUTLER—*Liberty*

603 South Fifth Street
Springfield, Illinois
July 24, 1931

My Dear Mr. Butler:

It is almost a custom of yours to print something of mine, once a year. Last time it was the verse, THE JAZZ AGE, kindly illustrated by Mc Cutcheon.[1] The year before, a soulful essay in the series WHAT IS BEAUTY?

All my life I have tried to keep poetry from swooning, having the vapors, etc., and whispering about her delicate condition. A man on this mission may sometimes shake dear poetry till her teeth rattle, and she bawls back at him in plain prose. But poetry had better be prose than a swooner. On the other hand, she has no business being a howler, my reputation to the contrary notwithstanding. Please consider that the dotted line below represents a hundred page unwritten essay on this delicate theme.

. . . .

Meanwhile my little jingle on Yankee Doodle is submitted with the suggestion that really tuneful penny whistles be distributed the week it is published; and that space be given on the same page on which this poem is printed for the full text and music of YANKEE DOODLE.

Please cut and amend this poem and these suggestions to your editorial taste.

With every good wish to you, and my heartiest regards, I am

Yours most sincerely,

VACHEL LINDSAY

Note

1. John Tinney McCutcheon began his career as a cartoonist for the Chicago *Record*. He collaborated with George Ade and from 1903 on worked for the *Chicago Tribune*, in which his cartoons were a front-page feature.

195

TO HAMLIN GARLAND

603 South 5th
Springfield Illinois
October 20, 1931

My Dear Hamlin Garland:—

Thank you for the great honor of the autographed copy of "Companions on the Trail".[1]

My earnest congratulations on the book, which I have now finished reading. My earnest congratulations on the success of the book. Not only do the reviews come pouring in, but I note it is among the month's best sellers. There is many a day I live over again, reading the book, and I share nearly all of your enthusiasms. All you say of Roosevelt is brilliant, new and true. All those days came back.

I had a wonderful laugh over the Whistler story—the best Whistler story in years and years.

Thank you, more than I can say for the Village Magazine Chapter. That was a practical service, and a heart-service, for you to insert that chapter and to give me far more than my share of the space.

I have almost had fist-fights to keep from being mobbed into reciting poems like The Congo and General Booth. Six years ago in print in the preface to my Collected Poems, page XIV, I swore off reciting those two songs forever.[2] And not till last spring did I come to the decisive scrap, and nearly broke up a school in Asheville because I would not be "sweated" into doing them.[3] Your praise of "The Village Magazine" is a stream in the desert. It represents all my original intentions, and one five minutes in my study would convince anyone of that, with the new piled-up drawings, broadsides, and manuscripts. You have saved me from being "Congoed" into permanent fury. Thank you again and again.

Most sincerely

VACHEL LINDSAY

Notes

1. Hamlin Garland's *Companions on the Trail* (1931) came out shortly after *Roadside Meetings* (1930).
2. On page xlv (not xiv) of the *Collected Poems*—"Adventures While Preaching Hieroglyphic sermons"—VL wrote, "I do not want to recite 'The Congo'. You can recite it yourself as well as I can. I do not want to recite 'General Booth.' "
3. The event in Asheville, North Carolina, had taken place on March 14.

196

TO SINCLAIR LEWIS

Springfield Illinois
October 22, 1931

My Dear Sinclair Lewis:—
Do not answer this letter. It is no fun getting a letter to answer.

Please accept our hilarious congratulations on "Dollar Chasers", in the Saturday Post. It is grand to be in such high spirits in just your stage in the game of writing. Elizabeth and I laughed ourselves out of seven deadly glooms, reading it aloud. The dear lady has a big audience this minute, just a block away, reviewing "Alisons House", and Emily Dickinson, and she was my lecture-manager till overwhelmed with babies, and also travelled with me on one tour. Then she handed me on a plate to our mutual friend W. B. Feakins, and I note that in your sketch you have our genuine admiration for his staying powers, etc. There is no better or solider man alive.

But the point of this letter is the joy we had in "Dollar Chasers". Every chessman is on the board in the right position. I prophesy the sketch will go through England like greased lightning. I could write a comment as long as the story, for I am sure every American makes just as much a jackass of himself as Lionel, when on tour, but it is easier to prove on the British. When I look back through twenty years of platforming I see twenty years of noble jackasses and all of them are me—not Lionel. It is the job that takes the self-control of an undertaker, a Crossing Policeman and the Headmaster of West Point. Yet it is part of the American Set-up, we can no more dodge it than the British can dodge tea. The only way out is to resolve to lock up as long as possible in every town, and then pray to the good Christ for the grace to be human and honest as long as one is in sight. And then get out of town before the sweat of the recital has dried on the back of your neck.

One point of this letter is that your story has given me a more contrite heart, and more determination to avoid all routine and kidding in this winter's campaign.

It is easier for dear Elizabeth. She is a natural teacher, on the platform or in the College Class-Room and full of things worth teaching.

But your shameless Vachel has to kill off ten thousand minor temptations as a stunt artist and an incurable liar, so when I thank you for the gift of a contrite heart again, believe I mean it. Back of your story is an exceedingly solid social contrast, emphasized by your last paragraphs—on Lionel's little talk to his little group of friends, after returning to England.

We have a terrific lecture-system. They have none. So they will everlastingly squirm when we demand a return of favors.

On the other hand—they have a system of little talks and conclaves, incredible till observed. Drinkwater said to me once "one whisper goes further in London than thunder in America", and it is so. You know for a fact—some conversation of yours in London with ten people with the understanding that it was semi-public—has brought you more reverberations than any address you ever made in the biggest hall in America. London *is* "Whispering London". I know a man who is supposed to have done as much talking in England as old William J. Bryan who merely whispered at a month of tea-parties and had no audiences at all. Yet to this day his American friends—eleven years later—tell him of the vast audiences he swayed in England. Ten vast Tea-parties! Yet the ten vast tea parties were so compact he hears of them in Canada and Los Angeles.

It is a very deep contrast in the ways of men. One might say—the only way to be sincere and effective in England is to converse. And in America—to be a Eugene V. Debs on a soap-box or a Rudy Vallee on a Hat-Box.

I did not intend to display ten pages of information—but Elizabeth has not yet returned from her Patrick Henry Oration on Emily Dickinson. There she stands, behind the potted palms, bless her heart—and I know she will make real converts to the finest qualities of Emily the immortal. And she will come home lit up like a Church from the excitement of speaking.

Come and see us if you pass this way.

Come and spend a week, and find out all about Spokane Washington and go there on a still hunt. I wanted you there every day for four years, a town *built like a watch*. Boy what a story! And *do* we remember it? I guess yes.

With great good wishes

VACHEL LINDSAY[1]

Note

1. VL had spent a short "vacation" in Minocqua, Wisconsin,in August, after touring
    during the first part of the year. For financial reasons, among others, Elizabeth had
    resumed teaching and occasional lecturing; VL resumed his touring in November.
    On November 10, he turned fifty-two. He was back in Springfield by November
    29, never again to leave.

197

TO S. E. LOWE

603 South Fifth, Springfield Illinois
October 27, 1931

My Dear S. E. Lowe:—

Enclosed you will find the answer to your letter of October 26 asking
me for a book of Child Verse, on the mutual recommendation of Miss
Barrows of Child Life.[1]

This poem will be called by hasty critics an imitation of Alice Through
The Looking Glass, by Lewis Carroll, so I have anticipated comment by
so marking it.

But as a matter of fact I had in mind some of the most fantastic stories
of people stepping into pictures, and having great vistas of adventure,
in that remarkable collection of ancient Chinese whims, called "Strange
Stories From A Chinese Studio". I happen to be an amateur crank on
Hieroglyphics and Egypt, and there are parallel Egyptian stories of Hieroglyphics becoming human, and the reverse. If it is fundamental with
Chinamen and Egyptians, it should have, if properly written, Ethnic
orthodoxy, as one might say.

The illustrator should be the most fantastic fellow you can find, with
a real sense of humor, and no dignity whatsoever. Not only should
there be lavish reproductions of old scraps of Wall-Paper, that fit into
the general theme, but I suggest the book be bound in the wildest
wallpaper you can find, and have a wall-paper jacket. Children delight
in the discovery of the terrible reiteration of wall-paper designs. It is to
them an exhilarating surprise, though to grown-ups as you know, wall-
paper in the sick-room has a more mesmeric than delectable fascination.
Every grown-up to whom I have read this song has had some experience
of the sort they like to laugh off with the children. If you try pencil
sketching on the margin you will find every phrase makes a separate
wall-paper.

All the illustrations should in some sense imitate wall-paper, with the units flip flopping like flap-jacks, and getting less like military drill as the story reaches its climax. The climax of the last stanza, is, of course, for the grown-up who reads it to the child, and is serious, without interfering with childhood.

Terms:— An advance royalty, preferably two thousand dollars. If this is too much or too little, state the amount you think fair and I will consider it. Also, of course the usual terms of fifteen per cent on every copy of the book, with the percentage increasing with quantity production.

I will be glad for suggestions for details on the contract.

The whole plan for printing and producing the book should be worked out after collecting samples of all the funny old wall-paper you can lay hands on. All the grapes, urns, silly landscapes, cock-eyed birds and beasts, restless loud festoons and fandangos, alleged formal refinements of every kind. Some of these, of course are to be found on cheap dress-goods and old oil-cloth. Even old carpets have them. Whoever plans the book is likely to plan it too timidly. We want to give them the strongest-wall-paper shock possible, that authentic awakening that happens only once to the soul of true refinement, and a disposition ot a quiet life.

There is some paper that positively crawls, as you know, that, as it were, gives you a black eye and a timid disposition. Storms at sea, views of Venice, lizards in feathers, biting themselves in the liver, with their hind legs turning into masks, snakes and daisies. You know the kind. Without a production force that gets an awful kick out of that sort of a thing, the poem will seem hopelessly fantastic. The poem was definitely written, assuming this type of production.

For the climax of the last stanza, of course, the designs should sober up into something more like a sunrise, and serene and dignified scrolls.

Most sincerely

VACHEL LINDSAY

Note

1. The unpublished book of poems had for its title poem "The Ting-a-ling Jingle of Wall-Paper Walter." The manuscript is in the Clifton Waller Barrett Collection of the Alderman Library, at the University of Virginia.

198

TO HARRIET MONROE

603 South Fifth Street
Springfield, Illinois
November 1, 1931

Dearest Harriet Monroe,
Elizabeth and I both had a thrill from your editorial on possible prizes
this month, of the Nobel variety. While it is not at all likely that anything
of the Nobel size will be offered soon to any of us in the poetry field,
your editorial is bound by its very force and concentration to be quoted,
discussed seriously, and should result in considerably more *consideration*
being given to poets in the next year. If we ask for the moon we may
get a little more green cheese.

Thank you indeed for the Guggenheim fellowship blanks. With the
very faithful help of Elizabeth, they have this night been filled out; and
I am very grateful for Elizabeth's energy and determination in keeping
me at it.

Congratulations on the space and the prize given to Fitzgerald. He
seems to me a most valuable man. I have written several letters to
English friends hoping to make his stay in England this year a little
more adventurous among the poets. I meet his uncle, Art Fitzgerald,
mentioned in my old Bryan song, on the street, every week. He is
bursting with pride over his nephew who is almost a son to him.

It seems to me the Poetry magazine has had a marvelous career, and
possibly the grimmest but most convincing evidence is the long list of
rivals that were born after it came into the world, and died long ago.
Such an amazing list of heroic failures is the ultimate tribute to your
success.

Elizabeth and I think of you with the most faithful affection. The
children are already beginning to talk in poetry, and make good songs
for their age and state. Come and see us whenever you can.

Yours in Delphic Bonds,

VACHEL

199

TO NICHOLAS CAVE LINDSAY

Wardman Park Hotel
Washington, D.C.
November 22, 1931

My Own Dear Son:—

Be sure I am glad you are doing so well, and are happy and in good health.

This is a hotel where dear Mama discovered a Poet long ago. And we were on our wedding trip and went to Mount Vernon, the place where George Washington lived, and we wished we had a house like *that*.

But we had a very very happy time all the time in this hotel, very very sweet,[1] and I hope you come here some day with your bride when you are a man grown up, and remember we were happy, too.

Be sure you are the man of the house while I am away, and protect everybody and be brave, and be happy, and nice to Grandpa.

With love

VACHEL LINDSAY

Note

1. On December 5, 1931, less than two weeks after writing this letter, VL committed suicide by drinking a bottle of Lysol.

List of Sources
(by Letter Number)

Index

Italic numbers refer to letters written to the person after whose name they appear.